WORKS ISSUED BY
THE HAKLUYT SOCIETY

Series Editors
Gloria Clifton
Joyce Lorimer

A WALK ACROSS AFRICA
J. A. GRANT'S ACCOUNT OF THE NILE EXPEDITION OF
1860–1863

THIRD SERIES
NO. 32

Figure 1.   Captain James Augustus Grant, 1863. This engraving by S. Hollyer appeared in Speke, *Journal of the Discovery of the Source of the Nile*, p. 420. The engraving was based on a photograph taken in Dingwall after Grant's return home in July 1863. He was said to be clothed as he had been in Africa. However, when S. W. Baker met him at Gondokoro earlier in 1863, he had described Grant as being in 'honourable rags'.

A WALK ACROSS AFRICA

J. A. GRANT'S ACCOUNT OF THE NILE EXPEDITION OF 1860–1863

Edited by

ROY BRIDGES

Emeritus Professor of History,
University of Aberdeen

Published by
Routledge
for
THE HAKLUYT SOCIETY
LONDON
2018

First published 2018 for the Hakluyt Society by
Routledge
2 Park Square, Milton Park, Abingdon, Oxon OX14 4RN

and by Routledge
711 Third Avenue, New York, NY 10017

Routledge is an imprint of the Taylor & Francis Group, an informa business

British Library Cataloguing-in-Publication Data
A catalogue record for this book is available from the British Library

Library of Congress Cataloging-in-Publication Data
A catalog record for this book has been requested

ISBN: 978-1-908145-16-1 (hbk)
ISBN: 978-1-351-25336-9 (ebk)

Typeset in Garamond Premier Pro
by Waveney Typesetters, Wymondham, Norfolk

Routledge website: http://www.routledge.com
Hakuyt Society website: http://www.hakluyt.com

MIX
Paper from
responsible sources
FSC
www.fsc.org
FSC™ C013985
Printed in the United Kingdom
by Henry Ling Limited

The Hakluyt Society acknowledges with gratitude the contribution made by
The National Library of Scotland and its staff
to this new edition of
Grant's *A Walk across Africa*

The Library has permitted and facilitated the use of the
James Augustus Grant manuscript journals, correspondence and other papers
as well as the 147 sketches and watercolours which are in its care.
The Library has in addition generously contributed to the costs of reproducing
the colour plates in this volume.

For Jill

CONTENTS

LIST OF MAPS AND ILLUSTRATIONS

Maps

Colour Plates

All of the plates are direct reproductions made for this edition by the National Library of Scotland [NLS] of a selection from Grant's original watercolours and sketches which he had bound together in two portfolios now preserved at the NLS as MSS. 17919 and 17920. There are also a few pictures left loose which are classified as MS. 17921. It is not clear what criteria Grant observed in allocating pictures to either of the two principal portfolios.

Between pages 290 and 291

Figures

As in the case of the colour plates, apart from the frontispiece, the pictures incorporated in the Introduction, the nine photographs taken by Grant, and the three illustrations on pages 385–7, all the figures are reproductions of Grant's watercolours or sketches contained in the three NLS files, MSS. 17919, 17920 and 17921.

PREFACE AND ACKNOWLEDGEMENTS

Well over 150 years have passed since the Royal Geographical Society of London sent an expedition to East Africa whose aim was to establish exactly where the source of the world's longest river, the Nile, was to be found. The leadership of that expedition was entrusted to John Hanning Speke. He chose as his second-in-command James Augustus Grant whose published record of the Expedition, *A Walk across Africa* (1864), is the subject of this Hakluyt Society edition.

From October 1860, the two men walked inland from the coast of East Africa to the region where the Nile was believed to have its source and then travelled on down the river to Egypt, reaching Cairo in May 1863. It will be argued that Grant's account of what was achieved is especially valuable to modern readers because it is a shorter and much more systematic analysis of the proceedings than Speke's detailed day-by-day narrative. Although Grant's text is, indeed, relatively short and not overburdened by detail, reference can be made to his manuscript daily journal from which the published text is derived. In this edition the manuscript journal has been quoted from time to time in order to amplify or explain certain episodes. The attempt has also been made to highlight Grant's scientific work for he was a trained scientist who deployed his specialist knowledge and skills to explain the environment and the people encountered during the 'long walk' of the exploration. Another key feature of Grant's activity was his determination to create a visual record of what the men saw of the people and places in the regions they were exploring. The 147 sketches and watercolours he made plus a few photographs are given considerable prominence in this volume as materials which are an integral part of the results of the Expedition and which also constitute the first ever visual record of a vast area of East Africa and the Upper Nile valley.

All this facilitates the task of placing the Nile Expedition in the context of the history of geographical exploration and the history of Britain's engagement with the extra-European world during the nineteenth century. Equally important, and much less frequently provided in most earlier accounts of the exploration of East Africa, is the African context. Grant's observations and his growing sympathetic understanding of the people he had earlier been taught to regard as 'savages' make it possible to explain something of the African realities which faced the Expedition.

Considerations such as these justify attention to Grant's work, especially because his name is not one which in the past has normally been given a prominent position in any accounts featuring the explorers of East Africa. Earlier comparative neglect arose for two main reasons. Firstly, an erroneous impression was created that Grant was no more than a second string to Speke of whom he was, it seemed, an always loyal supporter. This was an impression for which Grant himself was to a large extent responsible. Following Speke's unfortunate death in September 1864, Grant became reluctant to say anything which might seem to mar his former companion's posthumous reputation. Hence it was a dozen years after the Expedition before he began, for example, to publish his own botanical results. A second factor which has militated against proper attention being paid to Grant is that he was not actually with Speke at what was regarded as the crowning moment of the Expedition on 28 July 1862 when the source of the Nile at its exit from Lake Victoria was reached. This now hardly matters when set against all the other activities of the Expedition; in the long run, discovering the people who lived near the source of the Nile was arguably more significant than the source itself. Moreover, during the Expedition, there had been long periods when Grant was separated from Speke and was in effect working as an independent explorer. Even more important is independence in another sense. Grant was making his own record of the experiences and discoveries and this record was created by a man who was much better educated than his leader and who was able to provide a superior understanding of the significance of what they had seen and experienced.

More and more academic writers are now beginning to see the value of paying careful attention to what explorers reported and, which is also noteworthy, the manner in which they did so. This attention is a welcome change from the past when the field tended to be left to the writers of popular biographies of the explorers. Some of these efforts may be instantly dismissed but several well-written and serious biographical studies of the more famous explorers have appeared which deserve attention. Nevertheless, the main themes in such works have been what might be called the adventure story aspects of exploration with the protagonists portrayed as battling against difficult climates, wild animals, and awkward and unreasonable local people. Further interest has been created by highlighting the complications caused by disputes between the travellers themselves. Real understanding of what exploration was, why it was undertaken and its results has usually been lacking in such works and, if any attempt at all has been made to cover the African context, it has rarely been made with any knowledge.

A new edition of Grant's book provides an opportunity to attempt a more rounded and comprehensive treatment of the Expedition's context and significance. The introduction and the annotations of the text are designed to explain something of the intellectual, practical and political factors involved in the Expedition and its results while at the same time linking these factors to the reality of the Africa and the Africans encountered. It is proper to begin with the Nile itself. The actual aim of the Expedition, after all, was to reach and identify the river's source. This was a major concern of the Royal Geographical Society (henceforward RGS) which, by 1860, had become an extremely powerful and influential organization in Victorian Britain, occupying a sort of quasi-official position in its relations with the Admiralty, the Indian authorities and the Foreign Office. At any rate, all three provided support of one kind or another for the Nile Expedition believing, no doubt, that it was in the public interest to have access to maps showing the true position of the source of the Nile. The Nile was important not just for 'geographical science' but also because it 'fed' Egypt, a major region of interest for British and Indian governments. The Nile was significant, too, in a rather different context; speculation about its source had been a notable element in attempts to describe and explain the world made by classical, Byzantine, Arab and European scholars for well over two thousand years. Paradoxically, therefore, when Speke and Grant produced a map showing the 'true' source of the river, they were not only not the first to do so, but were also to become part of a long-lasting strand of cultural and intellectual history. The most important constituent of this strand was the evidence apparently provided by the second-century AD astronomer and geographer, Ptolemy of Alexandria. For this reason, the Introduction to this edition attempts a realistic analysis of the true worth of the information provided by Ptolemy about the source of the Nile. This is justified as essential background to the Expedition's inception, as an explanation of the controversies which Speke's account of the source stirred up and, not least, by the clear need to counter the misunderstandings and absurd things which have been written about the Nile source especially in relation to evidence from Ptolemy. It is suggested that a better way to understand the Nile is to consider the geological and geomorphological realities of its development.

It seems to me as the editor of this edition that the key to a proper understanding of the history of Nile exploration and controversy, especially in relation to the position of Ptolemy, was provided in 1854 by no lesser person than the founder and first Secretary of the Hakluyt Society, William Desborough Cooley. Hence the initial acknowledgement I make for help received must be posthumous thanks to Cooley. His modern successors as the very much more efficient managers of the Hakluyt Society have my warm thanks. The project has received special help from the resources of the Society's Harry and Grace Smith Fund in order to ensure that extra costs involved in the reproduction of the illustrations and maps may be met. Successive presidents and Council members have been patient and forbearing in the face of the rather extended gestation period for this Grant project. In particular, I am grateful for the support of Captain Michael Barritt, President until 2016. I wish also to acknowledge the Society's former administrator, Richard Bateman, who has given me much support and help. For most of the period during which this volume was in preparation, Dr John Smedley represented our then publishers, Ashgate, on the Council. His practical advice and guidance, especially in respect of the illustrations, have been very much appreciated. In each of the volumes published by the Hakluyt Society, the names of the Society's Series Editors receive a brief mention in the preliminary pages. There is precious little evidence beyond this of the prodigious amount of work they undertake in order to maintain the Society's standards. I have been particularly fortunate to have had the work on Grant overseen by Dr Gloria Clifton. She has combined meticulous editorial attention with enormous patience and forbearance; I am most grateful to her.

Like Desborough Cooley himself, the Hakluyt Society has sometimes had a somewhat equivocal relationship with the RGS but my own association with the latter has always been a happy and productive one. My original academic research as a postgraduate student was centred on the history of the RGS whose archives I used extensively. Although the present edition is not based on those records, I am indebted to my acquaintance with that Society's history for such understanding as I have of the background to their Nile Expedition of 1860. More directly, I am grateful for permission to reproduce some of the photographs which Grant took and which are now in the Society's care.

As the note at the beginning of this work acknowledges, the form this edition of Grant's work takes has been made possible only by the use of materials from Grant's very extensive papers which were acquired for the nation in 1979 by the National Library of Scotland. Not only has the Library helped me by affording access to these papers and giving permission to quote from and refer to them in this edition but it has also generously contributed to the project by providing new digital scans of the illustrations which appear as colour plates. The National Library is a Scottish and British asset of great value which must be safeguarded. Yet it is more than an institution: so much depends on the expertise of the officials who manage and give advice on the materials under their care. When I first began to take an interest in the resources of the NLS as far as Grant and other explorers were concerned, I received much valued help and friendship from Ian Cunningham. During the period of the particular process of preparing the present volume I have been in receipt of the interest and aid of Alison Metcalfe. I warmly thank her for her friendly support.

Grant's eminence as a botanist and plant collector naturally meant he developed a strong association with the Royal Botanic Gardens at Kew and I found it a useful and enjoyable task to visit the Gardens and consult relevant records there. Virginia Mills and Lorna Cahill in the Art and Archives section of the Library at the Gardens were helpful during my visit and later answered my questions. At the Linnean Society, Elaine Charwat also kindly answered my questions about Grant-related materials. Grant's other principal scientific interest was ornithology and I have much benefited from the advice on Grant's notices of African birds from Stanley Howe who has an astonishing ability to provide bird identifications and descriptions based on up-to-date criteria.

Marischal College and University in Aberdeen was Grant's alma mater. It became a constituent part of the University of Aberdeen which was later to award Grant an honorary degree. Aberdeen is my own university and I am pleased to acknowledge its support for my academic activity. In relation to the present project, I thank Michelle Gait in the Library and Archives who always ensures access to relevant materials and to all the Hakluyt Society volumes. In the Cartographic Section of Geographical Studies, I found Jennifer Johnston very kind and patient in dealing with my requests as she prepared four of the maps in a clear and acceptable form. Through its Development Trust and the College of Arts and Social Sciences, the University has generously provided financial support so that the extra costs involved in including so many illustrations may be more easily met. Vice-Principal Professor Margaret Ross has taken an interest and arranged for this support. I am most grateful to her. Professor Ross actively promotes the vision which shaped Marischal College in Grant's time and which I have certainly found a key characteristic – Aberdeen as an international university which at the same time has extremely important local roots.

Grant's own local roots were in Nairn and I am deeply indebted to the Nairn Literary Institute for the substantial financial contribution they made over twenty years ago through the Isobel Rae Trust so that I could have Grant's pictures photographed and begin to learn how valuable a resource they were. The Trust also contributed to the costs involved in having some of Grant's manuscript journal transcribed. Several publications resulted but it became clear that my original thought that the journal could be reproduced in its entirety for publication was unrealistic. Nevertheless, as the present work will show, it is possible to draw on the journal for important evidence. More recently, through the kindness of Mrs Hazel Macfarlane, the Institute has also contributed to current expenses in connection with the illustrations. Mrs Macfarlane herself has been very helpful over various matters involving Nairn. I thank her and Mr John Rose Miller, the author of studies of the *other* James Augustus Grant, for his advice and interest.

Winsor and Newton Ltd, which provided most of the sketching and painting materials used by Grant in the 1860s, has shown some interest in the project which I hope will continue.

I am particularly grateful to Mrs Margaret Mortimer not only for a very substantial contribution to the costs of reproducing the illustrations but also for the interest she has shown in the concept of this edition. Several other individuals have been kind enough to provide financial support including Mrs Janet Gunn, Mrs Jenny Bridges, Richard Float and Frank Bridges.

The Introduction to this volume has much benefited from advice and suggestions made by several individuals including Sarah Bridges, Dr Katharine Reibig, Professor John Bridges and Alastair Bridges. As will be apparent, I owe a great debt to my friend Dr Patrick Edwards for his translation work in connection with the treatment of Ptolemy's work in the Introduction. Naturally, however, none of these individuals is responsible for the views expressed or for any mistakes which remain.

Other friends whose work in the past or more recently I wish to acknowledge include Dr Robert Blyth, for earlier help with transcriptions; Ian Young, for very valuable help over photographic matters; and Christian Reibig, who checked some continuities in Grant's later chapters.

More recently, Barrie Fairhead of Waveney Typesetters and Mary Murphy, copy editor, have been instrumental in producing an acceptable text, while at Routledge Alaina Christensen and Michael Bourne have been efficient and helpful in ensuring that the Hakluyt Society's standards are maintained. I thank them all.

Finally, as ever, I am grateful for the love and encouragement I have received from my wife, Jill.

Roy Bridges

LIST OF ABBREVIATIONS

The usual Hakluyt Society conventions have been followed as far as abbreviations are concerned but there is one important change from these norms. In the case of MS or MSS signifying Manuscript or Manuscripts, the alternative form, MS. or MSS. has been adopted. This is the form preferred by the National Library of Scotland and has been adopted here because the materials from the NLS Grant collection are a basic component of this edition.

C.-in-C.	Commander in Chief
f.	Folio
kms	kilometres
HMSO	Her Majesty's Stationery Office
Hobson-Jobson	Henry Yule and A. C. Burnell, *Hobson-Jobson: being a glossary of Anglo-Indian colloquial words and phrases, and kindred terms; etymological, historical, geographical, and discursive,* London, 1886.
MS./MSS.	Manuscript(s) and more particularly seen in the call signs for the NLS files of Grant materials.
NLS	The National Library of Scotland, Edinburgh.
ODNB	*The Oxford Dictionary of National Biography*, on-line edition, www.oxford.dnb.com
OED	*The Shorter Oxford English Dictionary on Historical Principles*, ed. William Little, 2 vols, Oxford, 1933. *The New Shorter English Dictionary*, ed. Lesley Brown, 2 vols, Oxford, 1993, has also been consulted.
RGS	The Royal Geographical Society

A NOTE ON PREFIXES IN BANTU LANGUAGES

As the Expedition progressed, Grant showed greater and greater interest in the languages spoken by the people he was meeting. He began to realize, in particular, how important prefixes are in Bantu languages. All nouns and adjectives have a stem which is modified or made more precise by use of a prefix. Unfortunately, his understanding was by no means complete before the 'Bantu Line' was crossed in what is now northern Uganda and he encountered peoples like the Langi or Acholi whose languages worked rather differently. What he had learned probably came from members of his own group of porters most of whom were from the coast or from near Lake Malawi. For example, the coast prefix designating 'people' in the plural is 'Wa-' whereas in other areas it might be 'Ba-'. Many writers have tried to avoid such problems by using just the stem of a word but of course the speaker of a Bantu language would never naturally do this. Such complications mean there is potential for confusion and inconsistency and this is unavoidable in this edition if only because Grant's own text is as he prepared it in the light of his own understanding in 1864. It reflects his confusions while the Introduction and footnotes reflect later usages. It should be remembered that no Dictionary or Guide for Kiswahili was available until 1882 and so Grant had to understand the language and seek to represent the sounds of it he heard as best he could. In the notes to his text, where possible, his versions have been given in modern form.With these problems borne in mind, it is nevertheless useful to note the following principal prefixes in use:

M'- or Mu-   A single (one) person, e.g. a Muganda
Wa- or Ba-   People, e.g. the Banyamwezi. Grant usually used Wa- though this was 'wrong' for e.g. the Banyamwezi or the Baganda.
U- or Bu-   Place or country of, e.g. Buganda. But because Grant and Speke used the coastmen's system, Uganda was the name by which it became known. (The usage persisted, rather illogically, to designate the whole country now so called and Buganda is properly used for the original kingdom and place of the Baganda.)
Lu-   Language
Ki-   Characteristic of

In the Introduction and notes, particular groups are normally given the appropriate prefixes for, respectively, the place and the people, e.g. Unyamwezi and Banyamwezi or Bunyoro and Banyoro.

GLOSSARY OF NAMES AND TERMS

When Grant arrived in East Africa in 1860, he knew nothing of Africa, Africans or the languages they spoke. As he gradually began to learn from the porters on the Expedition and from those Africans he met, he tended to try to represent the sounds he heard using his own system of orthography as he made entries in his journal. Many of the results were to appear again in the text of his book which is reproduced here. However, particularly at the beginning of the journey, Grant remained very much under the influences of his Indian experiences and so tended to use many Hindi or Anglo-Indian terms to describe what he saw. To a certain extent, too, Grant's upbringing on the fringe of the Highlands of Scotland and his education in Aberdeen influenced his vocabulary with terms which may be unfamiliar to modern readers of English. As far as possible, terms whose meanings are not apparent are explained in footnotes but a certain number of expressions, names of people or places, or names of customs tend to recur and a few of these are recorded in the glossary which follows. The glossary also contains, it should be acknowledged, certain terms which have become recognized in academic discourse on African-related matters but will be less familiar to general readers. In the original edition of his book in 1864, Grant provided on pp. xv–xviii his own 'Explanation of Names and Terms'. This has been drawn on to a certain extent in what follows but, no doubt as a result of its being drawn up hurriedly just before publication, it is of limited value; it omits terms which ought to have been included and does include many words which were not much used in the text.

In what follows, not all Grant's sometimes idiosyncratic spellings are followed. He tended, for example, to use 'oo' where 'u' is now more generally employed. In Buganda especially, it was often difficult for Grant to distinguish between someone's real name and the name of his office; the latter generally prevailed.

Bakungu	(sing. Mkungu) The major chiefs in Buganda. Each had a function at court and ruled a particular area or 'county'.
Bana	(also, Bwana) 'Sir'/ Master.
Bantu	Peoples whose languages are related and who occupy nearly all of Africa very roughly south of 1°N latitude.
Bantu Line	The dividing line across Africa between the Bantu to the south and Nilo-Saharan/ Nilotic/ Afro Asiatic peoples to the north.
Baraka	Freed slave; commander of Zanzibar men in the Expedition, good interpreter and negotiator; a great rival to Bombay.
Bari	Nilo-Saharan people of the Nile valley south of Juba.
Batongoleh	(sing. Mutongoleh) Lesser chiefs in Buganda.
Bhanj	(also Bhangi or bangi) Indian hemp, cannabis.
Boma(h)	Palisaded camp or settlement.

Bombay	(c. 1820–85) Effective leader of the Expedition's porters and guards; an interpreter and negotiator; rivalled by Baraka.
Budja	Leader of the Baganda who took Grant from Karagwe to Buganda.
Buganda	Most important of the kingdoms in the interlacustrine region on north-west shores of Lake Victoria; reaching its full power as Speke and Grant arrived.
Burzah	A 'summerhouse' or reception house.
Caravan	A trading party consisting of human porters who carried the trade goods. Speke and Grant and other explorers copied the caravan arrangements for their expeditions.
Diabeah	(also, dahabeah, dahabeeya) A sailing boat on the Nile.
Ensete	The wild banana (plantain).
Frij	Freed slave, sailor, became Grant's chief servant and interpreter.
Florikan	(also, Floriken, Florikin) Bird of the bustard family.
Fundi	Skilled person.
Gani	An ethnic group of non-Bantu people known now as part of the Acoli (Acholi).
Ghaut	Strictly, a pass through a range of mountains but this Indian term came to mean the mountain range itself and this seems to be how Grant uses it.
Gurrah	Large cooking pot
Interlacustrine	The land region surrounded on one side by the lakes at the northern end of the Western Rift Valley, i.e. Lakes Albert, Edward and Kivu, and on the other by Lakes Kyoga and Victoria. The region might also be defined as that containing the most sophisticated kingdoms of the Bantu societies, including Karagwe, Buganda and Bunyoro.
Jambo	(also, Yambo) The normal form of greeting in Kiswahili.
Jowari	The Indian term for the grain sorghum.
Kabaka	The king of Buganda.
Kagæra	The river entering the western shore of Lake Victoria near the present Tanzania-Uganda border which Grant initially miscalled the Kitangule and which he, probably rightly, regarded as the affluent whose source may be regarded as the most distant of the Nile's ultimate sources.
Kamarasi	The Omukama, i.e. king of Bunyoro.
Kamaraviona	The term Speke and Grant used for the office of chief minister in Buganda – 'he who manages everything'. More usually known as Katikiro.
Kanga	Guinea fowl.
Katikiro	The most important chief in Buganda, mainly because he controlled access to the kabaka.
Kaze(h)	The name used by Grant for the Arabs' and coastmen's settlement established in the key chiefdom of Unyanyembe in the heart of Unyamwezi. More usually known as Tabora.
Kidi	Term used by Grant for Nilotic people, the Lango.
Kisuahili	Kiswahili: the language of the Swahili people of the coast, already in 1860 becoming a lingua franca for East Africa.

xxvii

Kitangule	Grant's name for the Kagera River.
Luta Nzigé.	(also, Lweetanzigeh) The African name for the lake which Samuel Baker was to call 'Lake Albert' in 1864 after Grant and Speke had by-passed it in 1863.
Mabruki	Servant to Speke; ally of Bombay.
Madi	Nilo-Saharan people of Nile Valley.
Manioc	Root crop, cassava.
Marikani	(also, merikani) Unbleached cotton cloth originally brought by Salem traders from Massachusetts; rolls became in effect larger units of a form of currency.
Mfumbiro	Grant thought there was one mountain to his west when in Karagwe and planted in British minds a desire to control it. In fact, the Virunga volcanoes lie north of Lake Kivu.
Mfungu	Vulture.
Mganga	Medicine man or witchcraft etc.
Mombas	The port of Mombasa.
Mukama	(also, Omukama) A king; term used in several interlacustrine kingdoms.
Murwa	Ulezi, small grain, a kind of millet.
Mutesa	Kabaka of Buganda during Grant's visit; was to die in 1884.
Mwengé	Drink made from plantains.
Nanga	Small stringed musical instrument.
Ngoni	The ethnic group originally based in South Africa including the Zulu, some groups of which invaded East Africa from the south from 1835 onwards. Known in the regions Grant reached as Watuta.
Nilo-Saharan	Linguistic classification according to some authorities for peoples living north of the Bantu Line. Includes Langi and Acoli peoples some of whom Grant met as Bari, Madi etc.
Nilotic	(also, Nilo-Hamitic) Alternative designations for some or all Nilo-Saharan peoples.
Nyanza	(also, Nyassa) Lake.
Nyanzig	Thanks and the act of giving thanks in Buganda.
Pagazi	Kiswahili term for a porter.
Pokino	Title of the chief of the key Buganda 'county' of Buddu on the kingdom's south-west approaches.
Pombé	Beer or other alcoholic drink.
Posho	Daily ration of food; pay.
Ptolemy	(c. 100–170) Geographer and astronomer of Alexandria, whose *Geography* incorporated information on the source of the Nile.
Qualæ	Partridge-type bird.
Ripon Falls	Waterfall where Nile flowed out of Lake Victoria. Named by Speke after President of the RGS in 1860, the Earl de Grey and Ripon. (Falls now submerged as result of hydro-electric scheme.)
Ruanda	Interlacustrine kingdom around Lake Kivu.
Rumanika	King of Karagwe with whom Grant developed close relations.
Seedee	Sidi. Anglo-Indian term for any African.

Sorghum	Indian millet, guinea corn. Usually, according to Grant, made into a sort of porridge or 'stirabout'.
Stirabout	Mainly Scottish term for oatmeal porridge but can also mean a commotion.
Sultan	Grant tended to use the term to designate the ruler of a petty kingdom.
Tembe	House, especially flat-roofed house.
Toorki	(also, Turki) The Egyptian and other traders from Khartoum on the Upper Nile.
Ugogo	Dry, almost semi-desert area of central Tanzania.
Ukuni	A chiefdom among the Banyamwezi north of Tabora where Grant spent several months. Properly Bukuni.
Ulezi	See murwa.
Unyamwezi	The large region of central and north-western Tanzania occupied by the Banyamwezi, speaking the same language but politically divided into a large number of autonomous chiefdoms. The men pioneered creating links to the coast for trade and many became porters.
Usui	Another chiefdom among the Banyamwezi south of Karagwe. Properly Rusubi.
Wahima	(also, Wahuma) The often originally pastoral groups becoming the ruling clans in the interlacustrine kingdoms.
Wangwana	Freed slaves, especially in Zanzibar.
Watusi	Another term applied to the Wahima.
Watuta	A group of the Ngoni plunderers.
Wazungu	White people, Europeans.
Wezee(s)	Grant's term for people of Unyamwezi. Presumably his own contraction of Wanyamwezi.

A NOTE ON MEASUREMENTS

Grant used Imperial measurements, the metric equivalents are as follows:

1 inch	2.5 centimetres		1 ounce (oz)	28.3 grams
1 foot	30.5 centimetres		1 pound (lb)	0.45 kilograms
1 yard	91.4 centimetres		1 stone	6.4 kilograms
1 mile	1.6 kilometres		1 ton	1016.0 kilograms

INTRODUCTION

1. Grant and His Contribution to the Nile Expedition of 1860–1863

Grant, His Book and This Edition
This edition consists of the text of the 1864 publication *A Walk across Africa or Domestic Scenes from My Nile Journal* by James Augustus Grant (1827–92) who was second in command of the Royal Geographical Society's Nile Expedition of 1860–63 led by John Hanning Speke. The spelling and punctuation of the original text has been retained but it is fully annotated and also supplemented by a limited number of extracts from the extremely detailed journal which Grant kept during the Expedition and which is now in the care of the National Library of Scotland (hereafter NLS). It is also supplemented by reproductions of the 147 sketches and watercolours made by Grant (also in the care of the NLS), which constitute an important element of his record of one of the key journeys in the history of European exploration. Reference is also made to Grant's very considerable contribution to biological sciences, especially botany and ornithology.

One of the aims of this edition is to demonstrate that Grant was a distinguished traveller and scientific observer whose talents and importance have been overlooked ever since his return from the Expedition in 1863. A parallel aim is to fulfil one of the stated purposes of the Hakluyt Society which is, 'To promote public understanding of the stages by which different parts of the world and their different societies have been brought into contact with one another'. This is expressed more succinctly as 'inter-cultural encounter'.[1] A much fuller discussion of what the study of such encounters might entail is found in Mary Louise Pratt's now classic work *Imperial Eyes*, in which she formulates the idea of 'contact zones'.[2] Grant's record provides an example of 'co-presence interaction' in a 'contact zone' with the actual physical location involved being East Africa and the Upper Nile in the middle of the nineteenth century.

Grant was the fifth child and fourth son of James Grant (1790–1853), the Minister from 1815 of the parish of Nairn.[3] After education at Nairn Academy and then Aberdeen Grammar School, he attended Marischal College and University, Aberdeen, for two years.[4] Then his father's friend, James Augustus Grant of Viewfield, after whom the child was named, used his earlier Indian connections to secure a commission for his young protégé in the 8th Native Infantry of the Indian Army.[5] In India from 1846, Grant became

---

[1] Hakluyt Society, *Annual Report for 2014*, p. 4; *Information and Publications for 2014–2015*, p. 3.
[2] Pratt, *Imperial Eyes*, p. 7 and *passim*. The implications of this work are discussed below, pp. 54–5.
[3] Scott, *Fasti Ecclesiae Scoticanae*, vol. VI, p. 444.
[4] Anderson, *Fasti Acadamae Mariscallanae*, p. 513; Grant, 'Memoranda', p. 5.
[5] Miller, *Viewfield: Last Years*, pp. 9, 97, 104–6, 111.

involved in various campaigns, not least the conflicts following the rebellion in 1857 which the British called the 'Indian Mutiny', when he was wounded, losing his right thumb and forefinger.[1] Earlier, in 1854, he had come to know his fellow Indian Army officer, Speke, whom he joined in some tiger hunts. This association prompted Speke in 1860 to invite Grant to join him on the Nile Expedition.[2]

Speke had been with Richard Francis Burton on an earlier venture organized by the Royal Geographical Society (hereafter RGS) which had reached Lake Tanganyika. Speke alone had branched off northwards during the journey back to the East African coast and in August 1858 reached the southern end of what he dubbed 'Lake Victoria'. Convinced that 'his' lake was the source of the Nile, Speke persuaded the RGS to send him back to East Africa to vindicate his claim. It was hoped that a Nile trader, John Petherick, would have a boat on the Upper Nile to meet the Expedition. Between 1860 and 1863 Speke and Grant made their way through what is present-day Tanzania to Tabora and then trekked northwards west of Lake Victoria to Buganda. In July 1862, Speke reached the point where the Nile does, indeed, debouch from Lake Victoria but for reasons which were to create questions and controversy, Grant was not with him at this key moment.[3] The two men went on down the Nile to Cairo and returned home for Speke to produce his long narrative of the Expedition, *Journal of the Discovery of the Source of the Nile*, which was published by Blackwood later in 1863.

As the preface to *A Walk across Africa* makes clear, Grant had not originally thought of producing any published work of his own relating to the Nile Expedition. This was perhaps in part a result of his natural modesty, in part because he had made an agreement with Speke by which he promised to 'renounce all right to publishing in collections of any sort on my own account until approval of by Capt. Speke or the RGS'.[4] The Agreement implied that Speke had the right to use any materials which Grant might produce – as indeed Speke did to a very great extent in his own book. As far as the RGS was concerned, there was considerable disapproval of Speke by the end of 1863 because he had not provided the Society with the first and definitive account of *their* Expedition. At the same time, many felt he was behaving badly towards Petherick, whom he accused of various shortcomings although the trader had met the explorers on the Upper Nile. All these reservations had emerged whilst Burton and his allies were making determined attempts to discredit Speke's claim to have reached the real source of the Nile.[5] Sir Roderick Murchison himself, the dominant figure in the RGS, wrote to Grant to say that he thought the second in command's name ought to have appeared on the title page of Speke's book.[6] Clearly, the RGS would have no objection to Grant's publishing his own book. When the decision was finally made is not altogether clear but it was probably

[1] Grant had been promoted from Ensign to Lieutenant in 1851 and became a Captain in 1859. He would become a Major in 1866 before retiring in 1869 with the Brevet rank of Lt Colonel. Grant, 'Memoranda' pp. 7, 9, 12, 15, 20, 28.

[2] This edition tells of his ensuing experiences as an explorer. Some mention will also be made of Grant's later career. However, it is not the intention to provide a full biography of Grant although his life and work, which embraced Scotland, India and Africa and included influence on private and official affairs in London, would merit one. Voluminous records, especially those at the NLS, would make one possible.

[3] The problem of the Nile source is considered in more detail below, pp. 34–47.

[4] Edinburgh, National Library of Scotland (hereafter NLS), MS. 17922, Agreement of 16 April 1860.

[5] Bridges, 'Speke and the R.G.S.', pp. 37–40.

[6] NLS, MS. 17910 f.1, Murchison to Grant, n.d. (c. April 1864).

agreed when Grant had a meeting with John Blackwood of the great Edinburgh and London publishing firm in the spring of 1864.[1] In the event, as the Preface shows, Speke himself encouraged Grant to go ahead very shortly after the Blackwood meeting. It seems likely that, as a matter of honour, Grant must have sought Speke's approval.

Thereafter, Grant worked with incredible speed and dedication so that the book was with the printers by December 1864. Two thousand copies were to be printed with a selling price of 15 shillings, to yield an expected profit of £500 of which Grant was to receive £200 and a further £100 when 1,750 copies had been sold. There were no illustrations, presumably because versions of much of Grant's work had already appeared in Speke's book and because Blackwood, already worried by the comparatively poor sales of Speke's work, feared the production costs of illustrations would make Grant's publication unprofitable.[2]

Reviews of *A Walk across Africa* were very favourable after its appearance in December. Not surprisingly, the *Nairnshire Telegraph* welcomed a work by 'our hero' while the *Glasgow Herald* commended Grant as an 'intelligent naturalist' who had provided 'great scientific and general interest'. The *Manchester Guardian* thought that Grant had compensated for Speke's omissions and poor literary style and that Speke's unfair monopoly of the credit for the Expedition was now ended. Given that Grant attempted to provide some picture of African life, it is interesting that more than one reviewer remarked as did *John Bull's*, '[African] people are not the savages we are apt to imagine them'. The *Daily Review* concluded that 'This is an account which could only have been written by a gentleman'.[3] The encomiums of 1864–5 remain justified.

That Grant was a gentleman, however, may not be sufficient justification for a new edition of *A Walk across Africa*, especially as Speke's smaller-print, 650-page account of the Expedition remains available as the principal narrative. Yet that book has some shortcomings while Grant's work has its own particular virtues. Speke's book is for the most part a day-to-day narrative portraying the Expedition as an adventure – a progress despite natural and human barriers. No fewer than 120 pages are focused directly on Speke's twenty-week stay and daily experiences in the fascinating Kingdom of Buganda. By contrast, Grant was present there for only six weeks. On the other hand, being marooned to the south in Karagwe for five months, because of his poisoned leg, did give him the opportunity to garner much valuable information on that kingdom which was then at a crucial stage of its development as the 'gatekeeper' for its more powerful neighbour to the north. There were other periods in the Expedition, too, when Grant was operating independently, for example during over three months in Ukuni (properly, Bukune). Thus Grant contributed different information from Speke. This information includes three chapters on the journey through the Sudan region and Egypt which, if no longer exploration, was highly interesting travel; Speke had ignored this phase of the Expedition in his narrative. Much more important as a distinction between the two books is the fact that Grant's much shorter work attempts to be more scientific and systematic. It will be noted that each chapter, without being tied to a rigid structure, tends to relate to a particular region whose physical characteristics, flora and fauna, and the

[1] NLS, MS. 17916, Grant, Journal, 1864–76, 21 May 1864,
[2] NLS, MS. 17932, Blackwood to Grant, 30 November 1864.
[3] These reviews and others are gathered together in NLS, MS. 17935.

characteristics of its people are dealt with in turn. This structure facilitates the task of providing modern annotations which supplement or explain Grant's observations. Moreover, since the book is based on Grant's remarkable manuscript journal, the opportunity has been taken to quote directly from that journal at certain key points. What will be even more noticeable is that this new edition is accompanied by most of Grant's original 147 illustrations. These were entirely omitted from the 1864 issue, although the explorer himself certainly regarded them as an integral part of a proper record of the Expedition. Both the journal and the illustrations are more fully discussed in what follows, as are the characteristics of Grant's approach to the natural and human features of the areas he traversed. All these considerations justify what is not just a reprint of an 1864 publication but a demonstration of Grant's real distinction and importance as an African traveller.

Grant the Efficient Second in Command

Grant's first obvious achievement is the one that has usually been accorded to him in the works, both the popular and academic, that have cause to mention him. He is seen as a loyal and self-effacing second in command to Speke, the actual discoverer of the Nile source in July 1862. Certainly, he helped to manage the 'caravan' of porters and to negotiate with African leaders during the three years of the 'long walk', as the Prime Minister, Lord Palmerston, later called it.[1] This was a walk from Bagamoyo on the East African coast opposite Zanzibar to Gondokoro on the upper waters of the Nile before boats carried the two men and their few remaining African assistants down to Cairo. As will be shown below, Grant's relationship with Speke was not without its complications but he was certainly supportive and efficient and contributed a great deal to the task of ensuring that the Expedition reached its goal and returned safely. However, it is altogether wrong to assume that this is all that needs to be said about Grant's contribution.

Grant's Manuscript Journal

A second and lesser-known feature of Grant's contribution is that he kept an extremely detailed record of all that happened and all that was seen during the Expedition. The record is in the form of a small quarto-size manuscript diary consisting of 372 pages nearly all of which contain closely-written observations in a usually miniscule hand.[2] This journal is a mine of information; even David Livingstone's remarkable records of his travels hardly match it in this respect. More than one of the few scholars who have examined the journal have considered the possibility of reproducing it in published form so that its contents could become more generally available. In practice, this would mean much concentrated work for many months simply to transcribe the journal and then an impossibly long and unreadable volume because Grant tended to produce something of a cross between notes and proper sentences punctuated somewhat randomly by dashes or full stops. Naturally, Grant used his own journal as the basis for *A Walk across Africa* and the book is a remarkably ably-produced epitome of the journal. Nevertheless, at certain points of

---

[1] See Grant's Preface, below, p. 71.

[2] The Journal is now in the care of the National Library of Scotland as NLS, MS. 17915. It covers the period in his life from 23 February 1858 to 31 December 1863. Grant kept a journal during most of his adult life. Hence there are three earlier ones dating from 1846 and two later ones taking the record almost to the time of his death also available at the NLS. See Figure 2, p. 5.

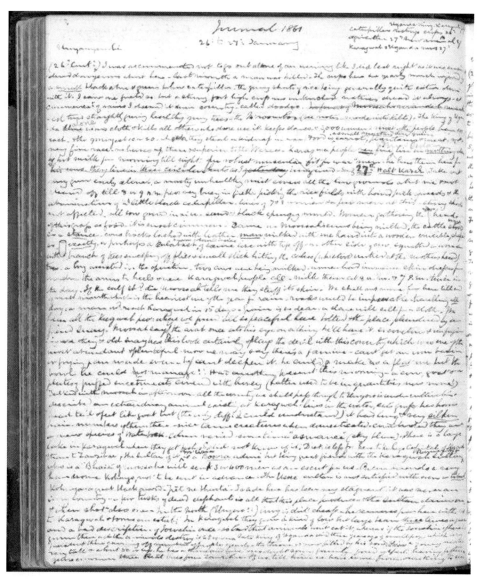

Figure 2.   A page from Grant's journal, 25–27 January 1861. Obviously fearful of running out of paper, Grant wrote in a very small hand in a style which was halfway between formal prose and notes. The record is enormously detailed and would be impossible to reproduce as a continuous coherent narrative. The original is a bound quarto-size volume of 372 pages, 320 of which are the actual day-to-day record covering the period 23 February 1858–31 December 1863. The Journal is now preserved at the National Library of Scotland as NLS, MS. 17915. Reproduced by permission of the National Library of Scotland.

particular interest, a limited number of direct extracts from the journal have been added to the version of the book which follows.

It should be noted that Grant used his journal as the basis of three of his other publications. In 1872 there appeared in the *Journal of the Royal Geographical Society* a hundred-page article recording the work of the Expedition.[1] As he explains at the outset, Grant's aim was to make up for what had been seen as Speke's remissness, ingratitude and commitment of a solecism in not himself providing anything more than twenty-five pages about the Expedition for the RGS. This the Society had regarded as 'brief and imperfect'.[2] Grant made it clear that he rejected any slurs on Speke's character but nevertheless saw a need for this new record. In practice, there is very little in the narrative of the Expedition which adds to what was in Grant's own book published eight years before[3] although the final pages provide a systematic account of the fauna encountered, with some attempt to attribute the observations to Speke.[4] Whether members of the RGS Council regarded Grant's article as compensating for Speke's discourtesy to them in 1863 seems not to be recorded.

The other publications based on Grant's journal both date from 1884–5 when British public interest in the Sudan was intense because of Gordon being beleaguered in Khartoum. A systematic account of the camel route across the Nubian Desert to avoid the great bend in the Nile appeared in the *Proceedings* of the RGS while Blackwood published his thirty-eight page account of Khartoum.[5] Neither added anything of substance to what appears in Chapters XVII and XVIII in *A Walk*.

There is some evidence which suggests that Speke's own record of the Expedition sometimes drew on Grant's Journal.[6] After all, Speke insisted that Grant renounce all right to publish on his own account and he seems to have interpreted this agreement to mean that all the records of various kinds which his second in command produced should be at his own disposal.[7]

A final comment on the journal is to note that those who wish to do so may consult the original of this remarkable record at the NLS in Edinburgh or in the form of a microfilm which was issued in 2005.[8]

Grant's Visual Record

A third major contribution by Grant to the Nile Expedition becomes obvious when one opens Speke's own published *Journal of the Discovery of the Source of the Nile.* Of the handsome provision of some seventy-five illustrations, no fewer than fifty-two are

[1] Grant, 'Summary of Observations', pp. 243–342.

[2] Bridges, 'Speke and RGS', pp. 39–40.

[3] For this reason, not more than one or two passages from the article are added to the edition which follows.

[4] Grant points out that the record of the flora (nearly all of which was his own work) had been deposited with the Royal Botanic Gardens at Kew.

[5] Grant, 'Route March'; Grant, *Khartoom*.

[6] For example, the passage in Speke's *Journal*, p. 558, describing the departure from the kingdom of Bunyoro seems remarkably close to the phrasing in Grant's journal.

[7] See NLS, MS. 17922, Agreement between Speke and Grant, 16 April 1860. As noted below, Speke's book on the Expedition depended heavily on Grant for its illustrations whilst the impressive 30-page appendix listing the plants collected was entirely the product of Grant's work.

[8] *Papers of James Augustus Grant and John Hanning Speke*, Adam Mathew Publications. The journal is contained in Reel 5 of this collection.

engravings based on Grant's sketches and watercolours. There is a paradox here. No one can regard Grant as a talented artist despite the lessons he took whilst a university student.[1] This is hardly the point. Grant was certainly not trying to produce pleasing or exotic images for the benefit of a later reading public. On the contrary, his earnest desire was to contribute to the scientific record of the Expedition with faithful depictions of what was actually being seen. Hence, not surprisingly, his original intention had been to emulate the increasing use of photography in India for official as well as popular purposes.[2] He took twenty-seven photographs in Zanzibar and on the coast of the mainland, of which nine are reproduced here.[3] Grant used the then-favoured wet collodion system but soon found that there were two great drawbacks: work in the dark tent was enervating and exhausting while carriage of the cumbersome equipment became a serious problem. When the Expedition was some little way into the interior, therefore, Grant decided to revert to his sketching block and his Winsor and Newton watercolours but his rather naive belief that he could produce images faithful to reality remained. Faithful or not, the 150 images of one kind or another which he produced during the Expedition (in addition to his botanical drawings) in most cases represent the first ever visual record of the landscapes and peoples of vast areas of East Africa and the Upper Nile Valley. For that reason alone, if none other, they deserve attention. Yet, until comparatively recently, little notice was taken of them. The handsome portfolio containing some twenty of the most impressive watercolours published by the National Library of Scotland[4] was perhaps too large and unwieldy to become widely known and used. The present writer's article of 2006 reproduced eight of the images and attempted to discuss their importance.[5] In 2009, Leila Koivunen published an excellent study of the images in nineteenth-century travel books on Africa and dealt very fully with Grant's work.[6]

Koivunen refers to the way Europeans' representations of Africa can reveal more about their ideas than about the real Africa and she stresses the need to recognize the 'interplay between, culture, power and representation'. This questions the approach adopted here which is to see Grant's work in terms of his attempt to reflect reality as he observed it.[7] Certainly, pictures may be as culturally loaded as writings but Grant's very inexpertness as a creative artist means that all he could do was to try to show things as he saw them at the time. His very lack of skill can be seen as an advantage. This judgement, however, applies to the original images. Until late in the nineteenth century, the images produced by travellers were published in the form of engravings based on the originals but actually produced by artists who were unlikely to be familiar with the original reality. For the most part, Grant's illustrative work has been known only through the engravings in Speke's book and a professional artist's engravings may well convey cultural overtones. The engraver principally employed to produce the pictures for Speke's book from Grant's

---

[1] From a noted artist, Patrick Auld. See Bridges, 'Images of Exploration', p. 63.

[2] Falconer, 'Photography in Nineteenth-Century India', pp. 269–71 and *passim*. Falconer notes that administration cadets were able to get tuition in photography from 1855.

[3] See RGS Photographs, shown in Figures 6–14, pp. 87–95.

[4] Edinburgh, 1982

[5] Bridges, 'Images of Exploration'. In 1993, the Hakluyt Society printed Bridges, 'Grant's Visual Record', with seven of the pictures reproduced in black and white.

[6] Koivunen, *Visualizing Africa*. Five of Grant's pictures are reproduced in black and white.

[7] Koivunen, *Visualizing Africa*, p. 6.

originals was J. B. Zwecker who, interestingly enough, had worked not only on other travellers' books but also on R. M. Ballantyne's adventure stories for boys. Certainly, it is possible to show that Zwecker distorted some of Grant's drawings to produce what seemed to him to be appropriate scenes and no doubt he was influenced by his own cultural assumptions (and perhaps Ballantyne's). Nevertheless, the example here from Speke's book (Figure 3)[1] may be compared with Grant's original[2] in which he made some effort to show the form of the instruments and the way the musicians held them; even if Zwecker's portrayal of Africans is not convincing, the details which Grant depicted have been reasonably well preserved.

One should not automatically assume that a published picture like the one of the musicians will be more imagination than reality. Nevertheless, if one is looking for evidence on life in East Africa in the 1860s, Grant's rather amateurish drawings are better than even the careful work of a skilled man like Zwecker.[3] One particular case of a considerably altered version of a Grant drawing raises some important issues about how we should attempt to understand and interpret illustrations based on an explorer's work. The engraving in Speke's book, which is reproduced here as Figure 4, shows Grant as a Scotsman, complete with plaid shirt, knickerbockers and a deerstalker and taking part in an African dance. It seems likely to have been a joke at Grant's expense probably arranged by Speke.[4] The original sketch did not show Grant. One might add that a frisson was added to the engraving by depicting Grant's dance partner as a bare-breasted female although the caption referred to the partner as Ukulima who was actually a male chief whom Grant described as 'a fine old fellow'.[5] Koivunen's take on the situation is that the man Ukulima is deliberately made 'devoid of masculinity' while the white male was inserted into the picture in order to juxtapose the two cultures with Grant as the personification of 'normality, civilization and culture' amid the 'uncontrolled and barbarian', scene of Africans dancing. Koivunen is heavily influenced by the remarks on this picture made by Barringer who holds that his clothing and manner make Grant seem the 'personification of British civilisation'.[6] Yet Barringer has clearly not seen the original picture by Grant; his argument is entirely unconvincing and the supposed explanation for the transformation of Ukulima into a woman nonsensical. Very probably, Speke asked the engraver to include this music-hall image of Grant as a Scotsman as a little joke which one might expect one army officer to play on another. Certainly, Grant did not walk across Africa wearing a deerstalker and the other 'Scottish' garments but a flannel shirt and unbleached drill trousers.[7] It is true that, as Koivunen points out, Speke writes that Grant 'had been dancing with Ukulima'. However, Grant himself merely says that Ukulima asked him to join in the dances held when another chief visited.[8] Grant describes in a journal entry during his long stay in Ukuni (Bukune) what must be the dance he depicted:

---

[1] Speke, *Journal*, p. 122.

[2] Reproduced as Plate 32. All the plates are in a single colour section in the centre of the volume and are not referenced by page number.

[3] Bridges, 'Images of Exploration', pp. 72–4.

[4] Bridges, 'Grant's Visual Record', pp. 20–21.

[5] Grant, *A Walk*, p. 94.

[6] Koivunen, *Visualizing Africa*, pp. 202–3; Barringer, 'Fabricating Africa', pp. 172–3.

[7] Grant, *A Walk*, Appendix A, pp. 449–50, here pp. 380–83.

[8] Speke, *Journal*, p. 138; see below, Chapter VI, p. 153.

Musicians.

Figure 3. Musicians of Buganda, June 1862. This is the version of Plate 32 as it appeared in Speke's *Journal of the Discovery of the Source of the Nile*, p. 212.

Grant dancing with Ukulima.

Figure 4.   The dance at Doondah. This is how Speke's book, *Journal of the Discovery of the Source of the Nile*, p. 138, showed the dance with Ukulima, who has been transformed into a female, with Grant as a comic-book Scot. For the reality in Grant's original depiction, see Plate 10.

Great dance this afternoon for children & men. Each man flings himself about, jumping or [?]
sham fighting, firing, mimicking in the most ridiculous way, women amongst them standing
and shaking their arms and bodies as if in spasm & shrilling when the old sultan joins in, to
his amusement, certainly. (NLS, MS. 17915, 23 June 1861)

The description makes it clear that Grant was a spectator, not a participant. Neither in his
book nor in his journal is there any justification for the depiction of him dancing as in the
woodcut engraving. Nor is there any warrant for saying that the picture is an attempt to
symbolize civilization against barbarism. This matter has been treated at some length
because some commentators can read rather too much into an explorer's reports or a book
illustrator's depiction of a scene. Of course, Grant had unconscious biases and cultural
assumptions but it is better to rely on straightforward historical evidence, where that
exists, to explain his activities.

Koivunen rightly mentions the importance of Aaron Penley (1806–70)[1] but perhaps
fails to give sufficient attention to the way his instructional booklet (published by Winsor
and Newton) encouraged a traveller like Grant, who said that it was his 'guide through
Africa', to try to depict things as they actually were. Penley in effect discouraged any
artistic licence or symbolism.[2]

Perhaps Grant was usually happier depicting objects which were still and whose features
he could take time to depict accurately. Although, as will be explained, there are problems
over determining how much botanical illustrative work he did, when he did it and the
present location of the records, Grant did show notable skills as a botanical artist. Other
illustrations were clearly intended to provide zoological information. It is less obvious but
nonetheless important to realize that many of the illustrations reproduced in this volume
showing African peoples were part of Grant's attempt to contribute to the science of
ethnology as it was understood at the time. This is especially apparent in the cases of
illustrations where he depicted agricultural practices, weapons and the like.[3] In fact, Grant
regarded all his pictures as part of his attempt to produce a proper scientific record.

One unexpected result of Grant's artistic activity was that it helped to foster good
relations with Africans he met. There was often intense interest in the images he produced
(or the family photographs he had with him). Maybe Livingstone's results with his magic
lantern were more dramatic[4] but Grant seems often to have found his images a good way
of establishing friendly relations and obtaining information. Another previously
unnoticed effect of Grant's showing his pictures was to encourage imitation. It is not often
that one can date a cultural import precisely but it would seem that certain Baganda in
1862, wishing to be able to draw visual images themselves after seeing Grant's work but
having no means of manufacturing paper, began to use instead the barkcloth which they
produced in abundance and on which they could inscribe marks.[5]

Grant the Scientist
Grant's most important achievement was to make significant contributions to Victorian
science. This is not to imply that he is a neglected original thinker nor to ignore the fact

[1] Koivunen, *Visualizing Africa*, p. 59.
[2] Penley, *System of Water-Colour Painting*. Grant's note is in a copy of the 17th edn (1858): NLS, MS. 17927.
[3] See, for example, Plates 4, 5, 37 and Figure 23, p. 99.
[4] See *Livingstone's African Journal*, ed. Schapera, vol. 1, pp. 8, 9, 126 etc.
[5] See below, Chapter X, p. 239.

that by 1860 all travellers were expected to claim to be contributing to science.[1] He was, though, a notable example among the Victorian travellers and observers who helped to accumulate the vast store of data in the field sciences which provided the basis for new understandings of the natural world and its processes. His dedication to scientific collecting makes it not altogether inappropriate to rank him, at least for the period of the Expedition, with better-known naturalists of the Amazon like Henry Walter Bates (whom he was to come to know well) and Alfred Russell Wallace.[2]

Grant was far better educated than his companion Speke. More particularly, by reason of the courses he had taken in 1841–3 at Marischal College and University,[3] he was well prepared to make valuable observations and collect specimens over a large region not hitherto the subject of any investigations in the natural sciences.

Grant was a 'private student' at Marischal College which was a normal status for young men who did not wish formally to graduate but who wanted to round off their education and perhaps acquire some practical skills before entering their professions.[4] Grant took classes in Natural Philosophy (Physics), Chemistry, Mathematics, Natural History and Botany.[5] The two latter classes were probably the most influential as far as he was concerned and also the ones taught by the most distinguished field scientist in Aberdeen at the time, Professor William MacGillivray (1796–1852). MacGillivray was a remarkable character who made long field trips and who had thought nothing of *walking* to London from Aberdeen in 1819 to examine the bird collection in the British Museum. After that London walk, MacGillivray decided that the Linnean system of classification of plants and animals had been superseded by that of Cuvier. At that time he believed in the fixity of species, as did most other scientists. By the time he taught Grant, however, he had stated in his *Manual of Botany* that 'all species have a tendency to form varieties' and may 'undergo changes from climate, cultivation and other influences'.[6] His biographer says that, had he lived to 1859, he would have accepted Darwin's theory of evolution. Although he produced significant publications in botany, MacGillivray's principal interest was ornithology and he became a long-standing friend of James Audubon, the two men sharing a concern for accurate illustrations. MacGillivray published a *History of British Birds* which, incidentally, introduced his own system of classification.[7] It is noticeable that MacGillivray's two major interests, botany and ornithology, were the two sciences which clearly most occupied Grant (together with the same desire to illustrate the plants and birds) while perhaps the Professor's walking exploits were to be emulated in the 'Walk across Africa'. Grant became a friend of MacGillivray's teaching assistant, Dr Mathews Duncan. Whilst in Aberdeen, he lodged in the house of his Mathematics teacher, Professor Cruickshank. In 1872 Grant took the trouble to have a special dedicatory page

[1] Bridges, 'Exploration and Travel outside Europe', pp. 57, 61; Kennedy, *Last Blank Spaces*, pp. 37–41.

[2] See Hemming, *Naturalists in Paradise*. For a general view, see Robinson, 'Science and Exploration' although he says little on the 19th century.

[3] Aberdeen's two universities, Marischal College (1593) and King's College (1495), were forced by Government to amalgamate in 1860 to form the University of Aberdeen.

[4] McLaren, *Aberdeen Students*, pp. 106, 109. The cost of graduating and the sitting of severe examinations, then unusual for other universities in Britain, deterred many from graduating.

[5] Grant, 'Memoranda', p. 5. As noted above, Grant also took unofficial classes in drawing and painting.

[6] MacGillivray, *Manual of Botany*, 1840, quoted in Ralph, *MacGillivray*, p. 86.

[7] This information is drawn from Ralph, *MacGillivray*, pp. 22, 55–6, 86 and *passim*. Dr Ralph also wrote the excellent account of MacGillivray in *ODNB*.

of the Linnean Society edition of his flora printed for Cruickshank which read 'in grateful remembrance of the happy years of boyhood spent under your roof where my first lesson in observing was spent and where I acquired a taste for Botany under the kindly influence of your son'.[1] Clearly, then, although Grant was destined to become a soldier, his training in natural history, especially botany, well qualified him to undertake what was to prove pioneer scientific work in Africa.[2]

As noted above, in 1872 Grant attempted to produce a systematic account of the scientific work of the Expedition ostensibly as part of his continuing campaign to restore the reputation of his late companion, Speke, although surely he must have wished to indicate something of his own scientific accomplishments.[3] This account of the walk from Tabora to Khartoum divided the territory covered into five 'regions'[4] for each of which Grant said something about the height above sea level, the climate, (rather uncertainly) the geology, the drainage, the settlements and, finally, ethnology as he understood it, that is, the character of the people, their arts and crafts and their governance. In the 1870s, however, the discipline of regional geography had not yet been developed and Grant's approach seemed to promise more than he could actually provide in explanation of the connection between physical and human development in equatorial Africa. Separately, in the last forty pages, he dealt with what were really his own principal interests, flora and fauna – shortly in the case of the former as he was planning a separate publication for the Linnean Society and at rather excessive length in the latter as he listed animals shot or noted by Speke and others. Certainly, the article appeared more systematic than the earlier *A Walk* (or Speke's book) but closer examination suggests that the body of the article was largely a retelling of the narrative of the Expedition. One of the oddities is that when covering drainage, Grant avoided saying much on the question of the source of the White Nile, no doubt because in 1872 whether Speke had really identified its main source remained a matter of controversy.

Observations on Meteorology and Climate
Grant began to keep records of what he called the 'Temperatures and Rainfalls' but these were not made every day and do not go beyond 1861, presumably because he was incapacitated with an ulcerated leg at that point and could not take observations.[5] Later on, he did make other observations whilst he was in Buganda and Bunyoro. The great Victorian scientist Francis Galton, who pioneered the science of meteorology,[6] made what

[1] The page is contained in a copy of the *Transactions of the Linnean Society,* 29, 1875, held in the Special Collections of Aberdeen University Library Lib: R f58 (6) Gra.
[2] Perhaps another example of Grant's serious interest in developing his knowledge and skills was that, while a young soldier in India, he learned to play the cornet and took lessons in the theory of music as well as gaining a qualification in 'Hindustanee', as the language was then known. Grant, 'Memoranda', p. 9.
[3] The article appears to have become the immediate reason for Grant's having been elected a Fellow of the Royal Society on 12 June 1873.
[4] Grant said that Burton's work adequately covered the area between the coast and Tabora ('Kazeh') while north of Khartoum was well known. Grant, 'Summary of Observations', pp. 244, 247. His view that Burton's works adequately covered the country between the coast and Tabora explains why he says comparatively little about it in *A Walk across Africa*. However, his pictures, notably Plates 2 and 3 and Figures 23–37, pp. 99–106, do provide something of a record.
[5] NLS, MS. 17922, ff. 4–5.
[6] Forrest, *Francis Galton,* pp. 76–82.

he could of the observations in an appendix which he provided for Speke's *Journal of the Discovery of the Source of the Nile*, entitled 'Climate of Victoria Nyanza'. The Expedition had been long enough in the vicinity of the lake for it to be possible to say something of climate, not just the weather. Hence Galton worked out the mean temperature (68°F) and the extremes (82° and 51°F), the estimated annual rainfall (49 inches) and prevailing wind directions (mainly easterly).[1] These figures showed that, although this was a region through which the equator passed, the heat was moderated because of the elevation – another factor helping to make the interlacustrine region look attractive to later Europeans. As the notes to the Preface of the main text will make clear, Galton strongly advised Grant to steer clear of what, probably rightly, he regarded as Speke's very misguided views on climate. He pointed out that, 'all you two men saw is a mere strip of land in the Equatorial Zone'.[2] Later on, when he produced the 1872 article for the RGS, Grant did attempt some remarks on climate and weather. In the first of his five designated regions, the Expedition was present for almost a full year and so Grant was able to state the highest and lowest temperatures, estimate the annual rainfall and point out which were the driest and which the wettest months. Grant's second region included Karagwe where he was laid up with illness for the best part of six months and so his remarks are more based on general observations than actual record keeping. The third region included Buganda which Grant described as having a climate which was 'decidedly relaxing'. For his next region, the Upper Nile, Grant provided information in tabular form but the only weather observations were wind direction.[3] Altogether, one concludes that Grant's contribution to meteorological studies was, for the reason Galton gave, inevitably limited. It was, nevertheless, the first ever scientific record of weather and climate over a vast tract of tropical Africa.

Flora and Fauna

Apart from their geographical discoveries which will be discussed later, Speke and Grant made their most significant contributions to science in the information which they provided on the flora and fauna of East Africa and the Upper Nile. The fauna recorded were perhaps essentially the 'bag' of the big game hunter, Speke; any scientific assessments were provided by others.[4] Grant, although also a keen enough hunter, had a greater scientific interest than his companion. He had one gazelle named after him and the name has persisted.[5] Several of his pictures include animals or animal heads.[6] His 1872 record of the fauna is much more systematic than anything Speke provided. Insects, fish and reptiles are noted but it is clear, both from the 1872 lists and the observations in his manuscript journal and his book, that Grant's principal zoological interest was ornithology. He listed no fewer than 140 bird species, some of which he identified on the journey from available books and others which were classified after his return, one of the

---

[1] Speke, *Journal*, Appendix F, p. 624.

[2] NLS, MS. 17909, Galton to Grant, 24 November 1864.

[3] Grant, 'Summary of Observations', pp. 247–8, 252–4, 263, 276–7, 296–301.

[4] Speke, *Journal*, Appendix C: 'List of Large Game Bagged by the East African Expedition', p. 619. Grant rather unconvincingly tried to show that some zoologists' interest in the game animals shot made Speke a scientific observer. See Grant 'Summary of Observations', pp. 306, 310, 312.

[5] Grant's gazelle is now accorded the scientific classification *Nanger granti*.

[6] For example, Figures 27, 30, 50, 51, 57, 80 and 87, pp. 101, 102, 145, 207, 267, 332.

francolins and a kind of guinea fowl being named after him.[1] As will become apparent from notes on the text below, modern ornithological classifications differ considerably from those current in Grant's own times. Even so, it is clear that Grant did make great efforts to provide a record which materially contributed to the accumulation of reliable data for an important branch of natural history and this included the identification of a few species hitherto unknown to science.[2] Some of Grant's depictions of birds may be seen in Plate 44 and Figure 71.[3]

Even more in evidence are new plant species. Leaving aside those he found in South America on the voyage out, Grant collected 837 plants, no fewer than 761 of them having been collected over the vast distance of his line of march from latitude 7°S to latitude 25°N. The plants were sent back to the Herbarium at Kew Gardens in two batches. The first consisted of all the plants collected up to the time of the travellers' sojourn in Tabora, 500 miles inland, and was entrusted to African porters who carried it back to the coast for onward despatch to Britain at some period at about the end of 1860. All the plants and seeds subsequently collected were carried with the Expedition and brought back to Britain in May 1863.[4] Both sets formed the basis of important collections at Kew and of several listings plus a major illustrated article in the *Transactions of the Linnean Society*.[5]

Despite the significance of Grant's botanical work, considerable uncertainties remain about how it was conducted in the field and how the information was passed into published form. A few of these uncertainties arise from Grant's modesty about his own methods and accomplishments. For example, he claims that he began collecting simply as a pleasant pastime rather than to achieve scientific results and was surprised when interest was shown by the experts at Kew. He adds that it was a last-minute decision to buy for a few shillings some drying paper in which to preserve specimens.[6] The truth was that he collected very assiduously and systematically, giving a reference number to each plant and, as noted, was keen by the time the Expedition had reached Tabora to send specimens back to Kew. Grant also took great trouble to note the local names for the plants he saw. Indeed, he pays particular tribute to the assistance he received from a very knowledgeable porter from Unyamwezi, Manua. Grant adds that the Africans he encountered were helpful over his collecting and could often be informative. Moreover, they never interfered with the specimens. There was deep interest on his part in the way plants were used for food, medicine or even magic charms. As Grant remarked, 'the natives are more intelligent

---

[1] Grant, 'Summary of Observations', pp. 315–27.

[2] The identifications of birds mentioned by Grant in the annotations to the text in this edition has been based largely on Williams, *Birds of East and Central Africa*, and Cave and Macdonald, *Birds of the Sudan*, but it is recognized that these are now rather outdated authorities. DNA sequencing has resulted in the recognition of different phylogenetic relationships from those previously assumed. Mr Stanley Howe has kindly assisted with his own very impressive and much more up-to-date ornithological knowledge, as will become apparent in many of the footnotes with the text below. To some extent, resources now online such as the Avibase Checklist of World Birds have been consulted.

[3] See p. 260.

[4] Grant, 'Summary of Observations', p. 302.

[5] Grant, 'Botany of the Speke and Grant Expedition'. The *Transactions* of the Society record that Grant read the account of his botanical work to them in December 1871 but it took until 1875 for everything to appear in print, presumably because of the time required for all the drawings to be made.

[6] Grant, 'Botany of the Speke and Grant Expedition', p. 1.

about plants than people give them credit for'.[1] All the collecting and the connected information gleaned shows that he was far from being just an amateur; Grant was in truth a serious scientific observer. The fact that he used drying paper rather than professional drying cabinets (which he had used whilst on board the ship taking him to East Africa) was simply because there were always problems over the amount of equipment which could be carried by the ever-diminishing number of porters as the march progressed.

The specimens which Grant had collected were arranged and classified at Kew. The then Director, Sir William Hooker, arranged for a classified list to be made by Dr T. Thomson.[2] He, assisted by Grant in periods of detailed consultations, must have worked incredibly quickly in order to meet Speke's desire to have his companion's botanical results included as an appendix in his *Journal of the Discovery of the Source of the Nile* which appeared in December 1863. The list occupies thirty-three closely-printed pages with Thomson's classification into families, genera and species according to the then accepted taxonomic system. The number Grant gave each plant as he collected it seems to have been recorded in this list for specimens which were deposited in the Kew Herbarium. Of these there were well over 150. Grant's own notes of the latitude and elevation of the spot where the specimen was found were added, plus, frequently, his notes on the appearance and the uses made of the plant. Local names also appear. Out of some 750 plants collected, Thomson thought that at least three-fifths, or perhaps two-thirds were known species (although some of these had not previously been found in Africa) but some eighty to a hundred of them were new to science.[3] The importance of Grant's own input to the publication of the listing can be gauged from the entries in his journal from 29 October 1863 when he went to Kew to meet the great Sir William and then to work with Thomson on the collection and the list every day until 10 November, the only break being on a Sunday for attendance at Kew Church with Sir William's equally famous son, Joseph Hooker,[4] and Thomson. On 1 December he was back at Kew to spend three days with Thomson going over the proofs of the list just before it was published. For Grant it was 'all most enjoyable' and he was impressed that everything at Kew was 'so systematically arranged'.[5]

The numbers which Grant gave to each plant he collected had been recorded on labels attached to the specimens and these numbers were also recorded in a notebook with some accompanying information. Of course there were many plants, including the trees, which were simply too big to be carried away and so Grant made some sketches in the notebooks. Clearly, Thomson had access to the labels and the notebooks when he added numbers to the 1863 list of those plants going into the Herbarium but quite what happened to these notebooks and where they are now is not clear. Among the voluminous Grant papers at the NLS, those in MSS 17936–7 are catalogued as 'Copy of the original notes and drawings from life of the plants collected by me during the

---

[1] Ibid., p. 6.

[2] Thomas Thomson (1817–78) had an adventurous botanical collecting career in India and Afghanistan before returning to Britain in 1851 to work at Kew classifying his own and other collections. *ODNB*.

[3] Speke, *Journal*, pp. 625–58. Thomson's remarks are on pp. 657–8.

[4] Sir Joseph Hooker (1817–1911) was the son of Sir William Hooker and clearly became a friend of Grant, whom he seems to have regarded as a worthy scientific correspondent.

[5] NLS, MS. 17915, Journal, 29 October–10 November, 1–3, 7 December 1863. The proofs came from the printer on 7 December.

Speke & Grant Expedition in /60/63. J. A. Grant'. What is in this file would seem to be copies of his drawings or depictions of the original plants in the Herbarium Grant made at the time when the Linnean Society publication was being arranged, presumably to help the professional botanical illustrator, Mr W. H. Fitch,[1] depict some of the plants accurately. The copies are often attractively drawn but it is impossible to say whether Grant embellished and improved his originals because the original notes and drawings made during the Expedition seem to have been lost.[2] This is despite the fact that the NLS Catalogue goes on to state that the *actual* originals of Grant's drawings are in the Library at Kew; unfortunately, that is not the case.[3]

The drawings at Kew, like those at the National Library of Scotland and despite their attribution to 1862–63, which implies they were made *during* the Expedition, clearly date either from the period in 1863 when Grant helped Thomson produce the list of plants for Speke's book or the period some ten years later when he was arranging for the publication of his flora by the Linnean Society. There are about eighty-five drawings or watercolours each manifestly originally executed on separate pieces of paper of varying size. These have been bound together to produce a bound volume.[4] A prefatory note in pencil says that these papers were found among Dr T. Thomson's effects after he died in 1878[5] and that, following correspondence with Col. Grant, it was decided they 'better be bound and lettered "copied from Col. Grant's botanical notes"'. This note in itself does not clarify the question of when Grant made these drawings and the obvious inference is that they were made in 1863, the time of Thomson's making the list for Speke's book.

Correspondence from 1863 does not settle the date question. What it does do, however, is confirm that Grant's Expedition botanical notebooks were something different and separate from this Kew volume (or the drawings at the NLS). Letters from Grant to Dr Joseph Hooker refer not only to the actual specimens of the plants collected by him and sent to Kew but also to 'my two notebooks' which he also sent to Kew on 20 July 1863 and mentioned in later letters that year.[6] The eighty-five drawings bound together in 1878 themselves often have written notes on them in Grant's hand which sometimes say 'I cannot remember' and this could be a comment of late 1863 relating to the Speke volume list preparation or of 1871 for the Linnean Society publication. On

[1] Walter Hood Fitch (1817–92) was closely associated with the Hookers, father and son, and did most of his extensive and very impressive botanical drawing for the Royal Botanic Gardens at Kew. *ODNB*.

[2] The drawings of plants and botanical notes which appear among the end pages of Grant's Journal were made when he was at Cape Town on his way to East Africa. They serve to show how devoted he was to botanical studies but have no reference to his botanical activities once the Expedition was underway. NLS, MS 17915: inverted pages at end, pp. 40–45.

[3] The drawings and their accompanying notes in NLS, MS 17936, have been examined and they show that Grant usually adds the number shown in the list in Speke's book and there are other indications that these copies were made almost ten years after the return of the Expedition to Britain, most notably these indications being Grant's references in the notes to later travellers than himself.

[4] Kew, London, Royal Botanic Gardens: Library Art and Archives, 'Notes and Sketches of African Plants, by Col. Grant'. This is (probably wrongly) dated 1862–3, and is described as one volume of manuscripts and watercolour sketches.

[5] On 9 May 1878.

[6] Kew, London, Royal Botanic Gardens, Director's Correspondence, vol. 87, docs 104–8, Grant to [Joseph Hooker], 28 June, 20 July, 4 August, 15 August, 3 October 1863. The correspondence also alluded to the idea of producing a Flora of Tropical Africa to which Grant would contribute but this idea came to nothing at the time.

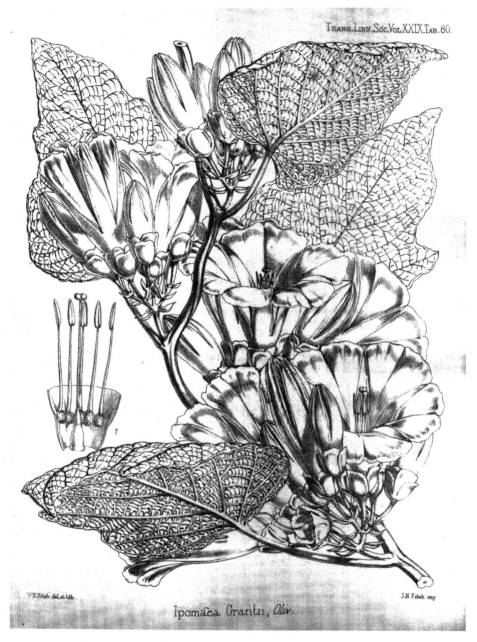

Ipomæa Grantii, *Oliv.*

Figure 5. Fitch's Drawing of *Ipomæa grantii*. One of the superb botanical drawings by W. H. Fitch for Grant's Linnean Society flora. This shows *Ipomæa grantii*, one of half a dozen or so specimens new to science Grant discovered. It is a climbing plant collected in Bunyoro in August 1862.

the pages of drawings, Grant's notes often give a number from 'Speke & Grant Expedition' which is presumably the number from the tickets which were attached to the original specimens and recorded, one supposes, in the now missing notebooks.[1] Perhaps the notebooks were for some reason not included in the sale of Grant's papers to the NLS which occurred in 1979 or were they were lost during his lifetime?[2]

That it is likely that the drawings at Kew were designed to help with the Linnean Society List may be inferred by the correspondence preserved at Kew from Grant in the years 1870 to 1875. At the end of 1870, he tells Hooker that he has been in correspondence with Dr Bentham, President of the Linnean Society, about his plants, saying that he hopes the Society will be prepared to produce an illustrated volume or volumes listing them. Dr Thomson had agreed to provide the descriptive part and the botanical artist, Mr Fitch, would execute the pictures. It would seem that four fellows had objected, presumably to the cost of Fitch's work and so Grant offered to put up the considerable sum of £500 himself. Grant adds that he has the support of Hooker.[3] By 12 December 1870, the project had been approved but it took many months before all the details were agreed including the extent and character of the drawings. Most of the delays appear to have been caused by the time it took Fitch to complete his work.[4] If that is the case, the wait was well worthwhile for the line drawings the artist produced are exquisite.

The Linnean Society publication[5] is a notable achievement. Grant provided maps of the route of the Expedition and an introduction describing his activities and the regions through which he and Speke had passed. He went on to provide fourteen pages of 'Native names for African Plants'. The species were enumerated in 155 pages by Professor Oliver.[6] Most of the entries are accompanied by notes written by Grant himself based on the information from his two notebooks compiled during the Expedition. Then follow 136 of the drawings by Fitch. Later botanists concerned with East Africa relied on Grant's list. The great naturalist as well as colonial administrator, Sir Harry Johnston, recognized the importance of Grant's pioneering work in botany for Uganda.[7] The definitive *Flora of Tropical East Africa*, which was one of the great examples of scientific endeavour during Britain's control of East Africa, and produced a hundred years after Grant's activities, continued to cite him among other collectors.[8] The compiler of a list of the grasses of Uganda in 1947 had clearly consulted both the flora in the appendix to the Speke volume and the Linnean Society work.[9] Grant deserves to be recognized as one of the more

---

[1] 'Notes and Sketches of African Plants'.

[2] Elaine Charwat, Deputy Librarian at the Linnean Society, and Lorna Cahill, Acting Archivist at the Royal Botanic Gardens, both very kindly checked the records of their institutions to see whether the two notebooks might be present; nothing could be found.

[3] Kew, London, Royal Botanic Gardens, Bentham Correspondence, vol. 87, no. 110, Grant to Hooker, 2 December 1870, Grant to Bentham, 2 December 1870.

[4] Kew, London, Royal Botanic Gardens, Bentham Correspondence, vol. 87, nos 1603, 1604, 1605, 1612, 1619, 1620, Grant to Bentham 11 and 12 December 1870, undated letter, 30 September 1871, 20 January 1872, 1 July 1875.

[5] Grant, 'Botany of the Speke and Grant Expedition'.

[6] Daniel Oliver (1830–1916) was Keeper of the Herbarium and Library at Kew from 1864 until 1890. *ODNB*.

[7] Johnston, *Uganda Protectorate*, I, p. 329.

[8] Turrill and Milne-Redhead, eds, *Flora of Tropical East Africa*, 1952–76.

[9] Eggeling, *Grasses of Uganda*, pp. 20, 23 etc.

notable scientific botanical collectors of the Victorian era. This botanical work in particular, as well as the other scientific work that has been mentioned, indicates that he was certainly much more than a traveller who happened to accompany Speke.

Ethnology

It is clear that Grant believed that he must attempt to be as scientific about African societies as he was about botany. He notes that his attention was more directed to the habits of the people than the geography of the country[1] and it is significant that his own first public utterance on the Expedition was in a talk he delivered to the Ethnological Society on 30 June 1863.[2] When he prepared his 1872 record of the scientific work of the Expedition he tried to say something in a systematic way of the African societies encountered. His attempts in both 1863 and 1872 are best understood as contributions to Ethnology.

Ethnology was a term which, according to *OED*, first appeared in 1842 and was taken to be the science of races and peoples, their relations and their distinctive characteristics. The varying definitions since 1842 of ethnology, ethnography and anthropology – cultural, physical or social – reflect deep and complicated changes in attitudes to the non-Western cultures of the world.[3] In Grant's case, he would probably have accepted the position later set out by Manchip White:

> An ethnologist was a man who journeyed to different quarters of the globe to record the material culture of a native people and to acquire museum specimens of their tools and weapons.[4]

Grant could not bring home many museum specimens but he could and did draw pictures of tools and weapons which are a further significant aspect of his artistic work. Fashions and weapons in Unyamwezi, weapons or beer brewing in Buganda and skin costumes[5] are examples among many. It is possible that the detailed drawings Grant made of a brutal execution for adultery were justified in his mind by the need to provide accurate information on social customs.[6]

To modern eyes, the information provided on African societies in the guise of ethnological data appears confused and too often affected by Grant's own cultural assumptions. Not surprisingly, too, given his background and the period in which he worked, there was a strong tendency to make judgements which attributed all perceived evils or social problems to the effects of slave trading.[7] Grant tended to exaggerate the real power of 'chiefs', whom he assumed to be despots, and, perhaps more seriously as far as reliable observation was concerned, to suppose that each people and its chief occupied

---

[1] Chapter XIV, pp. 316–17 below.

[2] The address was summarized in the *Illustrated London News,* 4 July 1863, pp. 22–3, and was later published in full as 'On the Native Tribes' by the Ethnological Society of London in 1865. Grant noted in his journal that the attendance at the meeting was a 'failure'. NLS, MS. 17915, Journal, 30 June 1863.

[3] See, for example, Kuper, *Anthropologists*, pp. 14–16, etc.

[4] White, *Anthropology*, pp. 11–12. The author goes on to explain that the ethnographer interpreted and wrote up the discoveries of the ethnologist.

[5] See Plates 5, 22, 31, 37.

[6] Plate 18 and Figures 45 and 46, pp. 142–3.

[7] Grant, 'Summary of Observations', pp. 250–51.

a defined area and to reflect this in his mapping.[1] This sort of assumption by Grant and other travellers was to influence later British colonial practice as administrators tried to introduce 'indirect rule' through 'chiefs' whose traditional powers were much more circumscribed than they imagined, especially in the political and judicial spheres.

What Grant was attempting to do for ethnology is best exemplified in one of the tables he provided for the 1872 article.[2] The headings are: name of race, presence of guns, dimensions of spears, shields (wood or leather), dimensions of bows and arrows, caste marks and teeth marks. This mish-mash of information emphasizes the unsatisfactory nature of ethnology or at least Grant's poor conception of what would be useful.

In his attempts to explain the peoples of the regions through which the Expedition passed, Grant's greatest apparent shortcoming was to fail to highlight clearly the 'Bantu Line'. In his 1872 account of the region he calls 'Uganda to Gondokoro',[3] he forgets to include a section on peoples yet this was when the Expedition crossed what is regarded as one of the most important linguistic and cultural boundaries in Africa – that between the Bantu to the south and the variously-titled 'Nilotic' or 'Nilo-Saharan' peoples to the north.[4] The address he delivered to the Ethnological Society includes the rather contradictory assertion that:

> one apparently identical race of negro overspread the entire land from the coast to Gondokoro and onwards down the Nile – that is to say if you leave out their tribal marks, their dress and their dialect ...[5]

Unless this was a rhetorical way of saying that there *were* differences, this statement is the more surprising in that Grant appeared to accept the 'Hamitic myth' which assumed that any advances in 'civilization' by the Bantu and other negroid peoples had been brought about by Hamitic people invading from the north. It had actually been first promulgated by Speke's Chapter IX and was most clearly set out later in what was once regarded as a standard work, Seligman's *Races of Africa*.[6] Grant's narrative and relevant parts of his journal show that he was certainly aware of the linguistic change as well as some differences in the appearances of accoutrements like spears as he left Bunyoro and crossed the 'Bantu Line'.[7] In fact, he notes 'an entirely new language' between Bunyoro and Gondokoro[8] and it is perhaps justifiable to assert that he did recognize the 'Bantu Line'.

Rather than the scientific observation of a linguistic boundary, most contemporary readers of Grant's work would have noted his emphasis on the importance and potential for development of Buganda. He provided an interesting observation which one does not find in Speke's work. After enthusiastically characterizing the kingdom as 'the garden of

---

[1] See Plate 1, the very attractive map which Grant drew and coloured of 'The route from Bagamoyo to Gondokoro' now in the RGS Collection and which must have been executed when the explorers met Baker in February 1863. Each differently coloured area is identified by the name of its people. The map was also reproduced in Crone, *Sources of the Nile: Explorers' Maps*, no. 5.

[2] 'Summary of Observations', p. 262.

[3] Ibid., pp. 284–95.

[4] See e.g. Middleton, *Encyclopedia of Africa*, I, pp. 156–7 and end-paper maps.

[5] Grant, 'On the Native Tribes', p. 87.

[6] Speke, *Journal*, pp. 246–60; Seligman, *Races of Africa*, pp. 12–13, 162.

[7] See below, Chapter XIII and the extract from the journal referring to a 'guttural' form of speech, p. 291.

[8] Grant, 'On the Native Tribes', p. 87.

Equatorial Africa' he notes the drawback that the king is 'cruel, despotic and harsh'. Yet, he goes on 'people feel able to take a pride in their country'.[1]

Even if Grant's ethnological observations are considerably less impressive than his botanical ones, it is worth noting that, in practice, he took the African peoples he met as he found them and generally dealt with them fairly and pragmatically. Grant was certainly capable of discerning observations which were freer from condemnation than those of many of his contemporaries. He later made it clear that he disapproved of the way Stanley was willing to embroil himself in hostilities between Arabs and the Banyamwezi.[2] Grant's own caution and good sense was just as well because for most of the Expedition he and Speke were very much at the mercy of their African hosts; it is an error, unfortunately a now not uncommon one, to regard them as proto-colonialists dominating the Africans they encountered. This was very far from being the case.

2. Prelude to the Expedition: East African Development to 1860 and the Idea of the Nile Expedition

East Africa by 1860
The inland areas of East Africa, including the Upper Nile valley, were a region which had seen successive groups of Iron Age peoples occupying what was in general a difficult environment by reason of climate, vegetation and disease. In the two thousand years up to about 1850, the principal process was one by which the negroid people classified by anthropologists as Bantu had gradually taken over most of the region roughly south of the 1°N line of latitude, although ebbs and flows of Bantu groups continued. To the north were Nilo-Saharan[3] peoples who sometimes attempted to dominate or interact in other ways with the Bantu across the so-called Bantu Line. Various kinds of political and social arrangements had developed ranging from stateless societies to sophisticated despotisms. None of these societies had developed writing and there were no true urban centres. Various forms of religious observance existed.

The situation on the coast, however, was very different. Urban centres did exist in the form of city states which should be regarded as essentially part of the maritime world of the Indian Ocean rather than of mainland East Africa. By AD 1000 these coastal communities had become Muslim. Contacts between the coast and the societies of the interior did exist; for at least two thousand years societies of the Middle East, India and China had wanted slaves, ivory and a few other more or less exotic products and these were obtained from the interior. Yet the scale of the trade was small and there is little evidence that any visiting traders went inland for any distance; certainly, no real knowledge of the interior was gained by the outside world.[4]

All this was to change after Vasco da Gama sailed round the Cape, along the East African coast and on to India. This heralded a major incursion into the Indian Ocean

---

[1] Ibid., p. 86.

[2] RGS, Correspondence Files, Grant to Rawlinson, 14 December 1871.

[3] Various other terms, such as Nilotic or Nilo-Hamitic and various sub-divisions have been in use. Basically, classifications are linguistic.

[4] See the discussion below on classical knowledge in relation to the Nile problem, pp. 38–9.

system of trade and culture by his fellow Portuguese from the beginning of the sixteenth century. Most of the coastal cities came under Portuguese control and their influence extended into the interior at least along the valley of the Zambesi River and intermittently to the Lake Malawi region. However, the essentially ecclesiastical and military Portuguese state was not supported by a sufficiently well-developed economy to maintain its dominance. In the seventeenth century, the economically more powerful Dutch challenged Portuguese ascendancy and there was also a resurgence of Arab trade and conquest led by Omanis from Muscat on the Persian Gulf. It was they who finally took over the great Portuguese citadel of Fort Jesus at Mombasa after a three-year long siege in 1698. During the eighteenth century, the Indian Ocean trading system came to be dominated by the French and the British but with the Omani Arabs as the third most powerful group in the Persian Gulf–East African coast region. Omani Arabs kept their control of the coast cities except in the south where the Portuguese maintained a somewhat precarious hold on Mozambique and the lower Zambesi valley.

As trade burgeoned, increasing numbers of slaves and quantities of ivory were demanded from East Africa and influences from the Indian Ocean began to affect the societies of the mainland interior. The situation was complicated and varied from place to place but the general pattern was that Africans in the interior responded to the lure of the coast where attractive goods like beads and cotton cloth could be obtained. The parties of elephant hunters from Unyamwezi are a prime example of groups who became also traders, selling their ivory at the coast for cloth and beads.[1]

By 1815 the British with their Royal Navy and their Indian Navy had achieved political dominance in the Indian Ocean region but troubled themselves little directly with the East African coast. Having made an alliance in 1798 with the Omani Arabs of Muscat to secure the Persian Gulf gateway to India, they were content to allow the Omanis to carry on their slaving and other trades in East Africa undisturbed. Seyyid Said, who became ruler of the Omanis in 1806, was happy with this arrangement which secured his position in the face of internal rivals like the Mazrui clan or the French or even over-enthusiastic British naval commanders like W. F. W. Owen who tried to make Mombasa a British possession in the 1820s. The snag for Seyyid Said was that the British began to put increasing pressure upon him about the existence of the flourishing slave trade. In 1847 he was obliged to accept a treaty by which he agreed not to export slaves from his East African possessions. This was not too serious a limitation since, even with the presence of Royal Navy patrols in the area, the smuggling of slaves to Arabia and India was not too difficult. More important, it was now increasingly the practice for slave labour to be used within East Africa, most notably after the cultivation of cloves on the islands of Zanzibar and Pemba was introduced from 1819. As Grant's evidence tends to show,[2] the habit of using unfree labour among interior societies had spread, although whether this was more a development of indigenous practices or of coastal influences is debatable.

Indigenous practice or external influence is a question that might be asked in respect of many other features of the history of East Africa in the earlier part of the nineteenth century. Older patterns of inter-regional trade in foodstuffs, iron tools and weapons or copper ingots tended to become subsumed in trade patterns linked to the coast. This

---

[1] See Figure 6, p. 87, for a group photographed by Grant.
[2] See, for example, Chapter V, below, pp. 128, 134.

caused certain tensions as did an accompanying development of very great importance. This was the new practice of traders from the coast going into the interior to get their slaves and ivory directly instead of waiting for Africans to bring supplies to the coast. Hence, for example, from the 1830s and 1840s, Banyamwezi elephant hunters cum ivory traders became porters in the pay of Arab traders rather than independent groups. It was the developing network of Arab trade routes (albeit principally based on indigenous ones) plus the habit of forming large 'caravans' of porters which created a sort of infrastructure of transport. This transport, by reason of trypanosomiasis and other animal diseases, had to be human. Nevertheless this infrastructure made it possible for the European explorers to penetrate East Africa. All the activity by Arab traders, such as the clove growing in Zanzibar, was made possible, in turn, by capital provided by Indians whom Seyyid Said (now increasingly spending his time in Zanzibar rather than in the Persian Gulf) attracted to East Africa. Seyyid Said also encouraged traders, especially Americans from Salem, as well as some Europeans, to come to Zanzibar for ivory, skins and gum copal as well as the cloves.[1] However, some of these foreign traders brought firearms which began to be taken into the interior with the inevitable negative results.

These changes were the cause of disputes and disorder as some Africans reacted against the coastmen or tried to exact larger presents for themselves – hongo – from the encroaching coast merchants. Many African 'chiefs', in fact, began to try to exert more powers than had been traditionally theirs and even to make claims over particular territories (so encouraging the European misconception of Africa being split up into discrete areas each inhabited by one 'tribe' ruled by one despotic chief). How far the Zanzibar Arab penetration of the mainland constituted any sort of political control is problematic. By and large, it is probably true to say that Zanzibar did have much prestige and therefore influence but that both Arab traders themselves and African leaders accepted the Sultan of Zanzibar's authority only to the extent that it suited them to do so.[2]

It was not only the influences emanating from Zanzibar and the coast that created a disorderly situation in East Africa. By the time of Grant's visit, the Upper Nile was coming under ever-increasing pressure from Nile traders based in Khartoum, as he was to observe. As he and other travellers also discovered, there were also various essentially internal and indigenous developments which affected the lives of East Africans. A consequence of the *Mfecane* or 'scattering' of peoples caused by the rise of Shaka's Zulus in South Africa in the 1820s, various groups of these Ngoni people, whom Grant knew as the Watuta, had spread north across the Zambesi after 1835 and became marauders whose ruthless military tactics were feared – and imitated. In the north, meanwhile, the pastoral Watusi or Tutsi tried to impose their control over more and more Bantu groups.

The whole tendency of all the influences which have been mentioned, to which were added problems caused by periodic famines, not to mention disease, was to produce situations of what one might called 'warlordism'. In some cases, traditional rulers, as in Buganda, took on new powers enforced by violent means while in other areas new authorities in the form of warlords might emerge to claim hegemony. It is by no means

---

[1] See Chapter II below, p. 80. Burton, *Lake Regions*, II, pp. 387–419, provides an enormously detailed account of the commerce of Zanzibar and East Africa as it was in the late 1850s.

[2] Hence, the later British policy from the 1860s to the 1880s of trying to control East Africa in some sense by dominating Zanzibar was never entirely successful. See pp. 61–3 for discussion of this issue.

surprising that Europeans, including Grant, were inclined to see East Africa as a region of considerable disorder. While they were not unaware of the complex series of developments outlined here which had produced this disorder – indeed, it is largely their evidence which enables us to identify the factors involved – they were far too prone in most of their public utterances to attribute all the evils from which East Africa suffered to the 'backwardness' of the people and/or the effects of the slave trade and to assume that it would be possible to end the latter by introducing some kind of 'legitimate trade'.[1]

By 1860, whether, and if so, to what extent, the problems of East Africa should become a matter of public policy for Britain – or in practice, the British Indian authorities – was increasingly a question for discussion. Undoubtedly, the reports of the explorers, especially those by David Livingstone, much encouraged the discussion. Clearly, however, any discussion must be informed by more thorough knowledge of the region, including maps of what was actually known of the existence of mountains, lakes and rivers. It is therefore a mistake to assume that explorers were just adventurers seeking fame and interpreting East Africa simply in terms of their own social and political prejudices. They were an absolutely vital part of the process by which, for better or worse, East Africa and its peoples became linked to the wider world – a process on which, by 1860, there was no going back.

The RGS Nile Expedition
By the 1850s, growing British and British Indian interest in East Africa had been reflected at the RGS in London. The very uncertain information available from classical sources and from Renaissance-period Portuguese reports was now being supplemented by even more confusing accounts filtering through from the Arab traders. All this was interpreted by 'armchair geographers', especially William Desborough Cooley and James MacQueen, in papers before the Society. Then it became known that two missionaries in East Africa, J. Ludwig Krapf and Johannes Rebmann, had seen snow-covered mountains and heard reports of the existence of large lakes even further into the interior than they had penetrated.[2] Clearly, reliable data about East Africa needed to be obtained. In 1856, the RGS, now in a much more prosperous condition than it had ever been since its foundation in 1830, responded to an initiative taken by Colonel W. H. Sykes, then Chairman of the Court of Directors of the East India Company, and decided to send an expedition to East Africa. The Society obtained very limited Government financial aid and chose to send Richard Francis Burton as leader, with another Indian Army officer, John Hanning Speke as second in command, to East Africa in order to 'ascertain the limits of the inland sea known to exist'. They were then to proceed northwards to 'the range of mountains marked upon our maps as containing the probable sources of the Bahr el Abiad (the White Nile), which it will be your next great object to discover'.[3] Burton and Speke travelled west from Bagomoyo to Tabora and then reached Lake Tanganyika on 13 February 1858.[4] That they were unable to find out where its outlet lay was to leave scope for much later argument. On the return journey, when they had reached Tabora, Speke made a 'flying trip' northwards and on 3 August 1858 attained the southern shore of

[1] These issues are discussed in more detail below, pp. 61–2.
[2] See Bridges, 'Introduction to the Second Edition', Krapf, *Travels*, pp. 58–64.
[3] Bridges, 'Speke and the RGS', p. 29.
[4] Burton, *Lake Regions,* II, pp. 42–3.

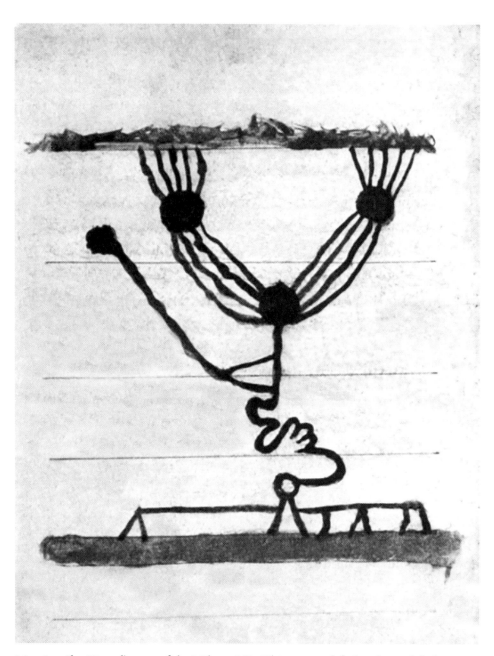

Map 1.   Ibn Hawql's map of the Nile, c. 960. This is a modified and simplified version
of the map. The original was probably based on a version of Ptolemy. North is at the
bottom of the map. The concept of the Nile which has intrigued and, arguably, grossly
misled commentators for well over a thousand years is well shown. The Nile has its origin
in an east-west chain of mountains. The sources flow into two lakes whose waters combine
in a third lake. From this lake, the river then flows north, is supplemented by a major
stream from the east (the Blue Nile from Ethiopia) and then makes its way down to Egypt
where it divides into the streams of the delta region. New drawing and photograph by
Ian Young.

Map 2.   Mercator's map of 1576 showing the sources of the Nile. In this map, Mercator, the best-known cartographer of the Renaissance, retained the basic Ptolemy-derived concept of the Nile shown in Map 1 but in a rather more sophisticated form which incorporated some up-to-date information available from the Portuguese about the Ethiopian region and the East African coast. From Mercator, *Tabulae Geographicae*. Reproduced by permission of the University of Aberdeen.

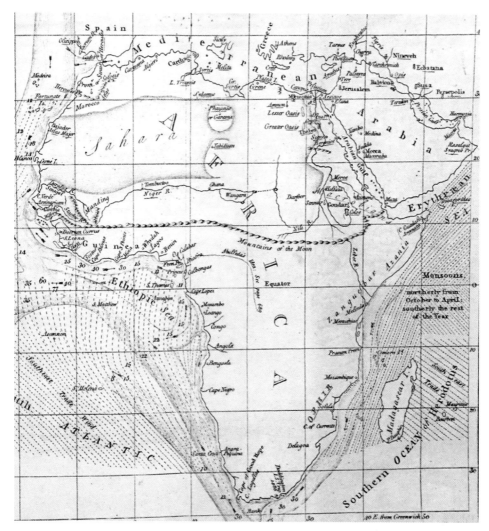

Map 3. James Rennell's map of Africa of 1799. This map, drawn by the prominent cartographer James Rennell, was intended to show the ocean currents around the continent. However, it is also instructive on the continent's interior. The 'reforms' of Delisle and d'Anville are followed so that the centre of the continent is effectively blank. Clearly, the real source of the White Nile together with the other lakes, rivers and mountains of the interior remained unknown. Yet despite this realism, the myth of the existence of the 'Mountains of the Moon' as an east–west chain of mountains (in fact, physically incompatible with the geological structure of Africa) was, even in this age of the Enlightenment, still inhibiting true understanding of Africa's geography.

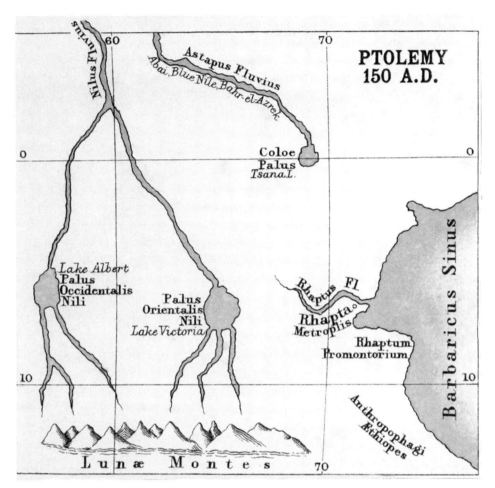

Map 4.   Sir Harry Johnston's interpretation of Ptolemy's information on the Nile. In his *Uganda Protectorate* of 1902, Johnston provided this map showing what he claimed was Ptolemy's concept of the Nile source. Note that the two lakes are designated as Albert and Victoria. Given the fact that he had lived in the region, it is difficult to know where Johnston thought the 'Lunæ Montes' could have been.

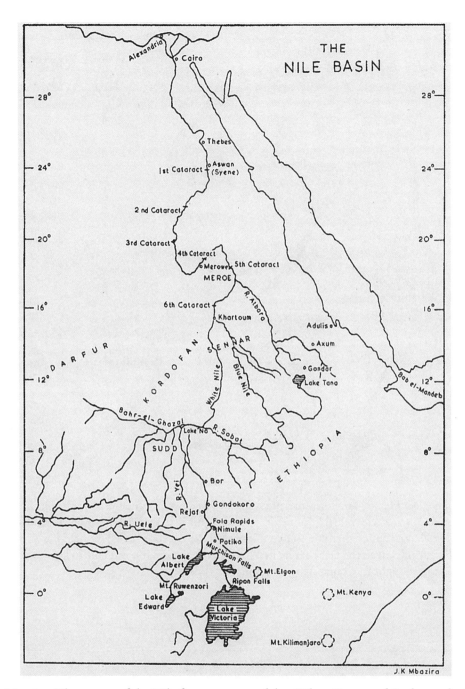

Map 5.   The course of the Nile from source to delta. When Grant and Speke reached
Gondokoro (near present-day Juba), their pioneer primary exploration came to an end
but, crucially, they had discovered the main elements of the Nile's headwaters in the
interlacustrine region including the most obvious source of the Nile where it debouches
from Lake Victoria.

30

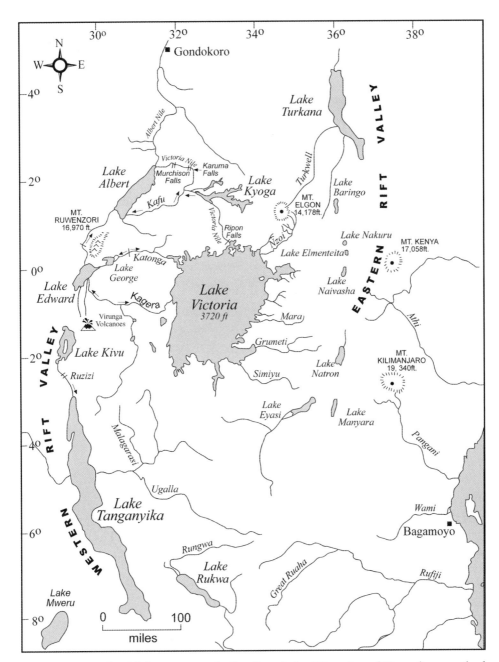

Map 6.   East Africa's lakes, rivers and rift valleys. Lakes Victoria and Kyoga lie on a tilted plateau a thousand feet or more above the floors of the rift valleys to the east and the west. Note that Lake Baringo lies in the eastern rift valley and, contrary to local reports heard by Grant, has no connection with Lake Victoria or the River Aswa as he was led to believe it might. Note also the pronounced north–south trend of the rift valleys.

31

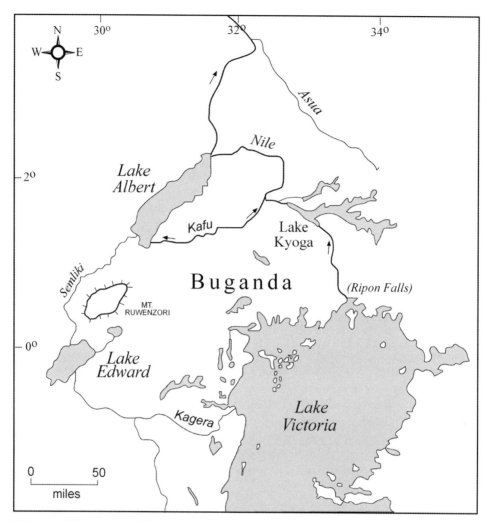

Map 7. The course of the Upper Nile from Lake Victoria to Juba. The course of the upper waters of the Nile in more detail to about 3°N near Juba is worth noting if some of the difficulties about identifying its source are to be understood. The river takes a tortuous course through Lake Kyoga and there are several abrupt bends resulting from its complicated evolution. Clearly, there was plenty of scope for argument as well as scope for continuing claims by the credulous that Ptolemy knew about the Nile's source.

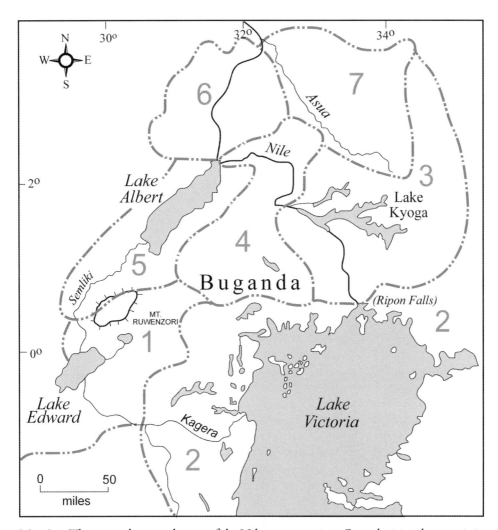

Map 8.   The seven drainage basins of the Nile source region. Complexities characteristic of the region of the Nile's source are further emphasized by this map showing how rifting and tilting have left, not one straightforward Nile basin, but no fewer than seven drainage basins. 1. Lake Edward; 2. Lake Victoria; 3. Lake Kyoga; 4. The Victoria Nile; 5. Lake Albert; 6. The Albert Nile; 7. The River Aswa. Based on a simplified version of the Hydrology Map in *Uganda Atlas*, 1962.

another lake which he dubbed 'Lake Victoria'.[1] Speke claimed that this lake must be the source of the Nile and in June 1859 the RGS was persuaded to send him back to East Africa to see if the claim could be proved.[2]

This decision much annoyed Burton who thought that his own discoveries were being overlooked and by the end of the year the breach between the two men was complete. Burton's hostility towards Speke was to affect the geographical arguments about the source of the Nile.

At the time when he was negotiating with the Society over his new expedition, Speke met a Welsh mining engineer, John Petherick, who had been working in Egypt since 1845, ostensibly to locate coal for the Khedive's benefit. Petherick found trading for ivory far up the Nile valley more profitable than the fruitless search for coal deposits. He now offered to have one of his boats and relief supplies available to 'succour' Speke at Gondokoro.[3] The RGS welcomed this idea and arranged for a public subscription for funds and persuaded the government to pay £300 per annum as a consular salary for Petherick. The Society expected Petherick to have two boats at Gondokoro by December 1861. The agreement was imprecise and the proposed date for the meeting absurdly unrealistic both for Petherick and even more for Speke. Meanwhile, Speke himself had chosen his former hunting friend, Grant, to accompany him. The RGS agreed, elected Grant to the Society and the two men left England in a Royal Navy warship in April 1860. A further complication in the developing situation was that a private traveller, Samuel Baker, who was wealthy enough to finance his own activities, had decided to attempt his own expedition up the Nile to the river's source. He set out from Egypt in April 1861.[4]

Speke and Grant knew nothing of Baker but their expectation that Petherick and his boats would be encountered on the Upper Nile was an important factor in their attempts to keep their Expedition moving towards its goal and its ability then to return home. Throughout the period from when they set off from the coast in October 1860 to their arrival at Gondokoro in February 1863, this expectation affected their behaviour. Soon there would be controversy about the arrangement with Petherick to complicate arguments about whether the Expedition had actually established the location of the source of the Nile.

3. The Nile Problem: Controversy and Credulity

> Concerning the original fountains of this river, there are manifold opinions and all of them uncertaine ... But if I recorded all the fables which our writers report concerning Nilus, I should seeme over tedious unto the Reader.[5]

The Importance of the Nile
In the first half of the nineteenth century, the information on the sources of the Nile available in geographical works like Pinkerton's or in Atlases such as that of

---

[1] Speke, *What Led to the Discovery*, pp. 305–6.
[2] Bridges, 'Speke and the RGS', pp. 29–30.
[3] Gondokoro was the effective southern limit of communication on the Nile by boats; it is situated near the modern city of Juba.
[4] Bridges, 'Speke and the RGS', pp. 32–4.
[5] Leo Africanus, *The History and Description of Africa*, III, pp. 936–7.

Tallis[1] was rather vague. The White Nile was shown as flowing north from a long east–west range of mountains referred to as the 'Mountains of the Moon' (see Map 3). As noted above, in the 1850s, more attention began to be paid to East Africa as the missionaries Krapf and Rebmann reported snow-covered mountains and lakes in the interior and armchair geographers offered their views. It was a reproach to enlightened nineteenth-century civilization not to be able to show where one of the world's major rivers had its upper course and sources. Moreover, Egypt was an area of increasing strategic and economic importance to Britain, to British India, and to France. Its viability clearly depended on the Nile and the river's annual floods, yet modern Europeans were just as unable as their classical forebears had been to explain why the river swelled seasonally with no visible cause.[2] Those classical forebears remained a very strong influence on the elite of Western Europe whose education was still classically based. Even the working-class and largely self-taught Livingstone seems to have embraced the idea current since the Renaissance that the path to knowledge was to find out first what Greece or Rome said on any matter. In the case of the Nile, the best-known answer had been provided by the Alexandrian scholar Ptolemy (c. 100–170). It was widely believed that Ptolemy had shown the Nile's waters to come from two lakes which, in turn, were fed by steams from mountains known as the 'Mountains of the Moon'. The great cartographic pioneer, Mercator, no less, had shown this answer to the problem (see Map 2). The armchair geographers of the 1840s and 1850s now enthusiastically began to consult and interpret in their own fashion the information which Ptolemy could apparently still provide. To a greater extent than had been the case since the Renaissance, Ptolemy's work was discussed by geographers in the mid-nineteenth century.

The growing obsession with the Nile and Ptolemy's evidence could have tragic consequences. Two of the tragedies directly impinged on Grant. A young German scholar, Albrecht Roscher, tried to prove his theoretical claim that Lake Malawi was one of Ptolemy's lakes.[3] He was murdered just after reaching the lake in 1858. His alleged assassins were executed in Zanzibar in Grant's presence.[4] In 1864, Grant's companion Speke, very likely because he was distracted from his usual care with firearms by anxieties over the prospect of debating the Nile question with Burton, accidentally shot himself dead on the day before the scheduled encounter.[5] Burton was clearly intending to argue that 'his' Lake Tanganyika was Ptolemy's 'western lake reservoir' of the Nile.[6] Less directly relevant to Grant's life but certainly a part of the Nile story, was a third tragedy involving David Livingstone.[7] He said he believed a rediscovery of what Ptolemy's informants had learned was necessary although what killed him in the end was a myth reported (and disbelieved) by a much earlier authority, Herodotus, that there existed fountains of the Nile on two hills; Livingstone died in the swamps of Lake Bangweulu searching for those fountains.[8]

---

[1] Pinkerton, *Modern Geography*, 1802, pp. 591, 594 and map p. 590; Martin, *Illustrated Atlas*, p. 132.

[2] Dueck, *Geography in Classical Antiquity*, p. 65.

[3] Roscher, *Ptolemaeus und die Handelsstrassen*, 1857.

[4] See Chapter II below, pp. 81–2.

[5] Speke's tragic sudden death heightened the concern and intense interest in the Nile arguments. Some suggested that Speke had committed suicide rather than face Burton. See Maitland, *Speke*, pp. 209–29.

[6] Burton, *The Nile Basin*, pp. 31–65.

[7] Although Livingstone attended Grant's wedding in 1865.

[8] See Livingstone's letters printed in Blaikie, *Personal Life of Livingstone*, 5th edn, pp. 317, 331–5. Livingstone went so far as to give modern names to the mythical fountains, as the maps in *Last Journals*, clearly show.

These tragedies – for tragedies they were – underline the seriousness of the quest for the Nile source. Whatever additional reasons there may have been for expeditions, the Nile was a real concern not just for geographical societies but for a much wider section of the British public.[1] Regrettably, added interest in the Nile question was created by the personal disputes which accompanied the geographical arguments. The most obvious dispute was that between Burton and Speke. As noted above, Burton was disappointed and angry that 'his' discovery of Lake Tanganyika was being overlooked as the new expedition was being planned. Burton began to discredit Speke's claim that Lake Victoria was the source of the Nile (although he had not initially rejected the idea) and he enlisted the aid of Ptolemy to justify his doubts. His argument amounted to saying that because the 'Mountains of the Moon', from which the White Nile took its rise, were in the position assigned to them by Ptolemy, Speke's Lake Victoria, to the south of the mountains could not be the source. These ideas were elaborated in Burton's *Zanzibar, City Island and Coast* written in 1858–9.[2]

Well before Speke and Grant set out, therefore, discussions about the Nile source very much revolved around Ptolemy and were to continue to do so for another ten years or more after the explorers had returned and Speke himself was dead. Consequently, it seems important to establish just what information Ptolemy did provide about the source of the Nile and the 'Mountains of the Moon' before going on to discuss the way the information was received and utilized by the time of Grant's Expedition. The discussion must also include some attention to the way Ptolemy has been interpreted since the middle of the nineteenth century as this has affected the context in which the 1860 Expedition has been seen by later biographers and historians.

The Nile Source Passages in Ptolemy's Text
The texts of two of Ptolemy's works have survived and the relevant one is his *Geographia*. In this work the passages which bear on the Nile source question are limited and scattered unsystematically; Ptolemy was clearly not very interested in geographical descriptions. Three different translations into English from the Greek have been consulted. Dr G. P. Edwards, formerly Head of Classics at the University of Aberdeen, was asked to produce as literal translations as possible, with results not very different from what can be found in what was for long the standard available translation made by Edward Luther Stevenson in 1932,[3] which is the second version. Thirdly, two of the passages much more recently translated by Berggren and Jones are included.[4]

Book I Chapter ix

Next, also, with regard to the voyage between Aromata and Rhapta, he [*sc.* Marinus] says that a certain Diogenes, one of those sailing to India, while he was returning for the second time, when he came near Aromata, was pushed off course by the north wind, and having the

[1] In the last of his Barsetshire novels in 1867, Anthony Trollope has the Rev. Josiah Crawley, despite being beset with a false accusation and the hostility of the terrible Mrs Proudie, unable to ignore the question of 'the sources of the Nile of which men now speak so much'. *Last Chronicle of Barset,* 2006 edn, p. 874.

[2] Burton, *Lake Regions,* II, p. 178; Burton, *Zanzibar,* I, pp. 38–40, 495, II, pp. 302, 306–7, 312. Because the manuscript of the latter book was lost, it was not actually published until 1872 when Burton took the opportunity to continue his attack on Speke in Volume II, again citing Ptolemy.

[3] Ptolemy, *Geography,* trans. Stevenson [1932], 2nd edn, 2011.

[4] *Ptolemy's Geography,* ed. Berggren and Jones.

Troglodyte land on his right, in twenty-five days he came near to the pools out of which the Nile flows – the promontory of Rhapta lies further south of these by a short distance ... [Edwards]

Marinus tells us that a certain Diogenes, one of those who were accustomed to sail to India, having been driven out of his course, and being off the coast of Aromata, was caught by the north wind and, after having sailed with Trogloditica on his right, came in twenty-five days to the lakes from which the Nile flows, to the south of which lies the promontory of Rhaptum ... [Stevenson, p. 31]

He [Marinus] says that a certain Diogenes, who was one of those who sailed to India, returning the second time, was driven back when he got to Aromata by the *Aparktias* [north] wind and had Troglodytike on his right for twenty-five days, and [he then] reached the lakes from which the Nile flows, slightly to the south of which is Cape Rhapta ... and [Diogenes] said that he sailed along Trogloditike for twenty-five days ... [Berggren and Jones, p. 68]

This is the most important of the four passages. Although there is a slight ambiguity, surely 'twenty-five days' refers to sailing time along the coast and not to land travel. It is also clear that Diogenes is not recorded as having described anything.

Book I Chapter xvii

We learn from merchants sailing from Arabia Felix ... that [passages relating to the coast] ... and the marshes also from which the Nile flows [are reported] to be not close to the sea itself but far inland. [Edwards]

The lakes from which the Nile takes its beginning are not near the sea but very far inland. [Stevenson, p. 38]

And we learn from merchants who have crossed from Arabia Felix to Aromata and Azania and Rhapta ... And the lakes from which the Nile flows are not right by the sea but quite far inland. [Berggren and Jones, pp. 79–80]

This could be taken to be evidence that some information was available at the coast about lakes in the interior, but how could it be known they were connected to the Nile?

Book IV Chapter vii

Where the Nile forms a single river from the streams flowing into it from two marshes or pools lying higher up. 60:2 north. That one of the pools which is furthest west 57 south 6. That further to the east 65 south 7. [Edwards]

Where the Nile river becomes one through the union of rivers which flow from the two lakes 60 2 Western lake 57 south 6 eastern 65 south 7. [Stevenson, p. 108]

Here is the alleged position of the lakes but the information is vague. It is also separated from the next quoted passage, to which, surely, one might have expected it to be connected, in a separate chapter. One possible explanation is that here is evidence of insertions by later hands.

Book IV Chapter viii

So around this gulf there live man-eating Ethiopians, to the west side of whom there extends the mountain of Selene [the Moon] from which the lakes of the Nile receive the snows, and the limits of the Mountain of Selene have the degrees 57 south 12, 67 south 12 30. [Edwards]

Around this bay the *Anthropophagi Aethiopians* dwell, and from these toward the west are the Mountains of the Moon from which the lakes of the Nile receive snow water; and they are located at the extreme limits of the Mountains of the Moon 57 south 1230; 67 south 1230. [Stevenson, p. 109]

Here we first learn of the 'Mountains of the Moon' which have appeared on countless maps in various guises for the last millennium or more and provoked much discussion. Nevertheless, this is the only mention of them in the Ptolemy text. Another translation of the relevant passages may be found in an appendix to the Hakluyt Society edition of the *Periplus of the Erythraean Sea*. The wording is slightly different but the essentials are the same.[1] It is now established, incidentally, that the Periplus dates from AD c. 50 and has very little information on even the coast of East Africa; it cannot possibly have been the source of Marinus of Tyre's stories about Diogenes.[2]

The Transmission of Ptolemy's Data
It has to be said immediately that no map by Ptolemy is known to exist. If one ever did exist, as one or two scholars believe is possible, it has not survived.[3] Most authorities are doubtful, pointing out that, in the pre-printing ages, it was much more difficult to copy and circulate maps than texts. Although he was considerably more 'scientific' than earlier classical geographers who saw their subject as a literary genre, Ptolemy was essentially an astronomer concerned to make lists of positions and certainly not interested in geographical descriptions of regions.[4] He would not have thought of Africa as a separate continent but an extension of his known world curving round south of the Indian Ocean. Not until 1508 did a map of Africa shown as a separate continent appear.[5] All the 'Ptolemaic maps' which we have are, in fact, later constructs of one kind or another.

Whatever Ptolemy may have known or thought he knew about the sources of the Nile, many complications arise because of the way his ideas were transmitted to later ages. During the European 'Dark Ages' and the early medieval period, Greek and Roman scholarship was preserved by great scholars of the Arab and Byzantine civilizations. Although there may have been earlier versions, an Arabic translation of Ptolemy of AD 827–8 is known,[6] and slightly later, a map by Khwarazmi showed the basic two-lakes scheme. A world map by Ibn Hawqal produced in the tenth century used Ptolemy and showed the 'Mountains of the Moon' as well as lake sources for the Nile (see Map 1).[7] The traveller and scholar al Masudi (c. 896–956) became familiar with Greek literature and his alleged map gives an idea of how ideas about the Nile source may have been passed on, for example to al-Idrisi whose world maps based on Ptolemy also clearly show all the standard features of the Nile source idea – the 'Mountains of the Moon' producing streams feeding two lakes whose waters come together in a third lake from which the Nile

---

[1] *Periplus of Erythraean Sea*, trans. and ed. Huntingford, pp. 173–4. Why Dr Huntingford chose to include his views on the 'Mountains of the Moon' is unclear. After all, the Periplus does not mention them. A 2nd-century BC Periplus has no pertinent information as it deals with the Red Sea. *Agatharchides of Cnidus*, trans. and ed. Burstein, pp. 1–12.

[2] *Periplus Maris Erythraei*, trans. and ed. Casson, pp. 6–7 and *passim*.

[3] Dilke, 'Culmination of Greek Cartography', pp. 178–80, 190.

[4] Romm, *Edges of the Earth*, pp. 3–4; Dueck, *Geography in Classical Antiquity*, pp. 76, 100–102; Buisseret, *Mapmakers' Quest*, pp. 14–19; Bunbury, *History of Ancient Geography*, p. 611.

[5] Stone, *Cartography of Africa*, pp. 9–10.

[6] Karamustafu, 'Introduction', *History of Cartography*, II, bk 1, p. 10.

[7] Tibbetts, 'Balkhi School', p. 122; Tibbetts, 'Later Cartographic Developments', pp. 138–9.

flows to Egypt. Al-Idrisi lived in Sicily until his death in c. 1165.[1] However, the main route by which Ptolemy's ideas reached Western Europe was probably via Byzantium.[2] Maximus Planudes (c. 1260–1310) and others used Ptolemy and a Latin translation initiated by Jacopo d'Angelo was made in about 1409. In 1477, a great milestone was reached when the first printed edition of the *Geographia* was published in Bologna together with maps.[3] Thereafter, as printing became more widely available, editions of Ptolemy began to proliferate and this 'discovery' of the Alexandrian astronomer's work was regarded as just as important a piece of new knowledge by Renaissance scholars as the actual voyages of discovery made by the likes of Columbus or Vasco da Gama. Even so, more and more discoveries outside Ptolemy's *oikumene*, or basic known inhabitable world, shifted the balance in the 'eternal Renaissance dialogue between ancient authority and modern experiences'.[4]

By the time of Ortelius and his 'Atlas' of 1570, the purely Ptolemaic maps were present only for historical reasons. Yet this by no means meant the end of Ptolemy's influence. The text of *Geographia* continued to be consulted and cartography continued to be influenced by his concepts. Of course, the configuration of the East African coast and some knowledge of Ethiopia had to be made to conform to the discoveries of the Portuguese navigators but Ptolemy reigned supreme for the depiction of the interior of the continent, as the example of Mercator's map of 1578 makes clear. The basic situation for long remained essentially the same, as the maps of all the great Dutch cartographers in the seventeenth century bear witness.[5]

Even the eighteenth-century cartographic revolution did not end the influence of Ptolemy. The well-known jibe in Jonathan Swift's *On Poetry, a Rhapsody* of 1733 reads:

> Geographers in Afric-maps
> with savage pictures fill their gaps
> and o'er unhabitable downs
> place elephants for want of towns.

This is usually taken to be a criticism of cartographers who concealed their ignorance with little pictures and mythical features which were shortly to be removed by more enlightened men like Delisle and d'Anville. In fact, Swift was mistaken: elephants were placed on maps of Africa together with troglodytes, cannibals and other exotic features justifiably, it was considered, because Ptolemy had said they were there. It is also a mistake to assume that the maps of Africa produced by Delisle and d'Anville brought about an elimination of all Ptolemaic material despite their new large empty spaces. D'Anville's 1749 map of Africa retained the Mountains of the Moon at the headwaters of the Nile.[6] Other maps had this fabulous range stretching over almost the whole width of the continent. Ptolemy's *Geographia* was still being quoted, not least, as noted above,[7] by the 'armchair geographers' of the 1850s.

---

[1] Ahmad, 'Cartography of al Sharif al Idrisi', pp. 156–9, 168.

[2] Dilke, 'Cartography in the Byzantine Empire', pp. 271–2.

[3] Buisseret, *Mapmakers' Quest*, p. 16.

[4] Relaño, *Shaping of Africa*, p. 1.

[5] Ibid., pp. 177–82.

[6] Relaño, *Shaping of Africa*, pp. 217–18, says that d'Anville is not really a harbinger of the 'scientific era' but remains essentially a Renaissance figure.

[7] See p. 25.

Interpretations of the Ptolemy Text: the Credulous and the Sceptical

A convenient version of what is often popularly thought to be Ptolemy's account of the Nile was provided in Sir Harry Johnston's work of 1903, *The Nile Quest*. Indeed, it appears that a good many commentators have innocently assumed that since Johnston's book is a most useful account of Nile exploration altogether, his approach to Ptolemy's evidence will be authoritative.[1] This is what he says:

> one Diogenes, who, on returning from a voyage to India in about 50 A.D., landed on the East African coast at Rhaptum ... Thence, he said, he 'travelled inland for a twenty-five day's journey, and arrived in the vicinity of the two great lakes and the snowy range of mountains whence the Nile draws its twin sources.' ... It is more probable that he merely conversed on the coast with Arab settlers and traders who told him ... that at a distance of twenty-five days' march in the interior began a series of great lakes from two of which were derived the twin sources of the White Nile; that farther to the south of the most western of these two lakes was a range of mountains of great altitude covered with snow and ice, and named for their brilliant appearance of white the Mountains of the Moon. The Nile, he was told, united its twin headstreams at a point to the north of these two great lakes, and then flowed through marshes until it joined the River of Abyssinia (the Blue Nile), and so reached the known.
>
> This story was told by Diogenes to a Syrian geographer called Marinus of Tyre ...

Johnston goes on to explain that it is only in Ptolemy that we find any record of the work of Marinus which has otherwise disappeared and he unequivocally asserts that this was real information about the Lakes Victoria and Albert and the Ruwenzori mountain massif.[2] A simple comparison of the quoted passage and the extracts from Ptolemy's text printed above makes it clear that Johnston has gone a very, very long way beyond the actual evidence in his apparent determination to make modern evidence fit the classical model.[3] A year before *The Nile Quest* appeared, Johnston had already published his version of Ptolemy's Nile information in the form of a very explicit map which showed Lakes Albert and Victoria as Ptolemy's two lakes (see Map 4).

The determination shown by Johnston to make modern discoveries fit Ptolemy's alleged information had been shared by many others from the time of Grant to that of Johnston. 'Ptolemy appears to have been the first who formed a correct idea of the whole course of the Nile' asserted Grant's fellow explorer Stanley, who was perhaps trying to show that he was worthy to join the great and the good by including a long chapter on classical knowledge of the Nile in his account of his Emin Pasha Expedition.[4] Burton, as has been shown, used Ptolemy as an intellectual weapon in his disputes with Speke. What is more surprising and worrying is that the practice of assuming Ptolemy's evidence anticipated modern discoveries of the Nile's sources has continued since the time of Johnston. Moving well into the twentieth century, one can note that John Buchan, in what must be one of the worst of his many books,[5] in 1923 repeated the basic Johnston

---

[1] Moorehead, for example, praises Johnston's book and clearly used it for his own description of Ptolemy's evidence. *White Nile*, pp. 4, 363.

[2] Johnston, *Nile Quest*, pp. 22–3.

[3] Moorehead, *White Nile*, p. 4 and his map p. 3, compounds the errors by saying that the information was incorporated on Ptolemy's 'celebrated map' and is followed in this by Jeal, *Explorers*, pp. 26, 100, who also accepts the version of Ptolemy provided by Johnston.

[4] Stanley, *In Darkest Africa*, II, pp. 290, 312.

[5] Buchan, *Last Secrets*.

version of the story. Even the eminent classical scholar, E. H. Warmington, said of the reports allegedly brought by Diogenes to Marinus of Tyre, 'However incompletely verified and inaccurately recorded ... [they] were a tolerably close approximation to the truth of the great secret',[1] while Sir Percy Sykes's *History of Exploration* of 1934 accepted the validity of the Diogenes story. More recently, in a long and detailed study which seems otherwise to be carefully researched, John Udal states that Diogenes had provided 'an astonishingly accurate description' of the Upper Nile region.[2] The very distinguished editor of the *Periplus of the Erythraean Sea,* mentioned above, Huntingford, actually justifies what he says on the 'Mountain of the Moon' (*sic*), by observing that 'Unreason may sometimes be right'.[3]

It may seem that 'unreason' afflicts not a few of those who write of the source of the Nile and Mountain, singular or plural, of the Moon. As the great Victorian scholar of ancient geography E. H. Bunbury observed in 1883, 'the blind, almost superstitious reverence with which Ptolemy was regarded in the Middle Ages has descended in some degree to our own days'.[4] Thankfully, at least one scholar, no less than the founder of the Hakluyt Society, William Desborough Cooley, had little reverence for Ptolemy and his information on the Nile source. Cooley's work on Ptolemy appeared in 1854.[5] This was just before the great RGS exploratory journeys in East Africa began. Unfortunately, the considerable reputation which Cooley had enjoyed as a geographer in the 1830s and 1840s was beginning to wane. He was too prone to denigrate and pick quarrels with practical travellers who might seem to question his 'theoretical discoveries'. He had already denied that the missionaries Rebmann and Krapf could have seen snow on the summits of Mounts Kilimanjaro and Kenya in 1848–9.[6] Cooley also picked quarrels with the RGS, who treated him nevertheless with generosity. Yet for them he was an anachronism, insisting as he did on the sort of work based on ancient sources which might have been appropriate in 1800 but was so no longer in 1850. Now the Society wanted and expected first-hand reports from travellers. Hence *Ptolemy and the Nile* did not attract the attention it probably deserved.[7]

Cooley's text is not altogether easy reading but he makes four essential points. He notes, first of all, that the information derived from Marinus of Tyre is not properly integrated with Ptolemy's text and was probably a later insertion. Secondly, the information from Diogenes cannot possibly refer to the actual Nile; it must, said Cooley, be an account of the 'Nile of Mogadishu', in other words, the river now known as the Wabe Shebele Wenz, which flows along near the coast in what is now Somalia. Thirdly, given the real nature of Diogenes' information, neither Marinus of Tyre nor Ptolemy himself can possibly have known about the area alleged to contain the source of the White Nile. In fact, suggested Cooley, the information about two lakes and so on was really based on actual, if somewhat confused, reports about the source area of the Blue Nile in Ethiopia. The fourth major

[1] Warmington, *Greek Geography*, p. xxxvi.
[2] Sykes, *History of Exploration*, pp. 39–40, 244; Udal, *The Nile in Darkness*, I, p. 495.
[3] *Periplus of the Erythraean Sea*, ed. G. W. B. Huntingford, p. 176.
[4] Bunbury, *History of Ancient Geography*, II, p. 553; but Bunbury thought Ptolemy did have some real knowledge: II, p. 615.
[5] *Claudius Ptolemy and the Nile or an Enquiry into that Geographer's Real Merits and Speculative Errors ...*
[6] Cooley, *Inner Africa Laid Open*, pp. 89–109.
[7] For Cooley's career, see Bridges, 'William Desborough Cooley'.

suggestion was that the idea of a range of 'Mountains of the Moon' was a much later insertion in the Ptolemy text.[1] These ideas remain well worth attention, although it must be added that they were accompanied by some rather less credible assertions. Cooley thought that the White Nile contributed little to the Nile floods in Egypt[2] so that the source of the Bahr el Abiad or White Nile was an overvalued problem.

After the major East African exploratory expeditions were complete, the attendant arguments continued. The distinguished geographer E. G. Ravenstein published a major article in 1891 in which he developed some of Cooley's ideas, notably favouring the suggestion that Ptolemy's data was actually about Ethiopia. Ravenstein's paper provoked an enormously elaborate riposte by Henry Schlickter 'proving' that every feature which by then had been discovered by Burton, Speke, Grant and, more lately, Stanley had been perfectly well known to Ptolemy.[3] After another half-century or more, Cooley's ideas were taken up by O. G. S. Crawford who used principally Fra Mauro's map of 1459 to show that the Ptolemaic features on the Nile sources were really in Ethiopia; Renaissance mapmakers had spread them south on their maps in order to provide some sort of coverage of a large part of the interior of the African continent. As for the 'Mountains of the Moon', this term derived from Mount Chamir, lying to the east of Lake Tana which is the source of the Blue Nile. In Arabic, 'chamir' became 'kumar' which means moon. Crawford points out that it is easier to copy than to invent and that we should therefore expect to find the origins of the Ptolemaic material in identifiable features, mostly in Ethiopia. He adds that 'the last enchantments of medieval Africa lingered on into the nineteenth century'.[4] We might now further add 'and into the twentieth and twenty-first centuries'. For, despite Cooley, Ravenstein and Crawford, credulity of the sort displayed by Johnston seems to have prevailed except in the cases of a few specialist authors such as Relano or Berggren and Jones, although even the latter pair seen to think that Diogenes had information about lakes close to the coast.[5] Whatever the current situation, Ptolemy had certainly remained, despite Cooley, a legitimate source of information in Grant's time and so remains part of the context necessary to understand his Expedition.

The Nile Problem on the Ground: Geology, Geomorphology and Hydrology
In considering the question of the Nile sources few commentators, if any. have considered the basic natural conditions of the Nile valley and, more particularly, the Nile source area. Even a simple outline map of the Nile basin shows that the world's longest river has a rather complicated course (see Map 5). The natural conditions associated with the Nile go far to explain why nineteenth-century explorers found it difficult to establish which river ran where. The consequence was that there was much uncertainty and scope for argument. Given these conditions, difficult enough for men with sextants, altimeters,

[1] Cooley, *Ptolemy and the Nile*, pp. 2, 3, 13, 26–7, 55–6, 76–85.
[2] Ibid., pp. 112–13.
[3] Ravenstein, 'Lake Region of Central Africa', pp. 302–3, 305–6, 308 and *passim*. Schlicter, 'Ptolemy's Topography of Eastern Africa'. Schlicter should clearly be included among the credulous.
[4] Crawford, 'Medieval Theories about the Nile', pp. 7, 12, 17–18, 22 and *passim*.
[5] Relaño, *Shaping of Africa*, pp. 62, 82, 182, 185, 197–8. *Ptolemy's Geography*, ed. Berggren and Jones, pp. 161–2.

Admiralty tables and so on, it is impossible to believe, incidentally, that Diogenes, if he existed, or any other very early traveller could possibly have sorted out the relief and drainage and been able to say which river was the Nile and where its source lay.

Most of the region is formed by what geologists call the Basement Complex of igneous and metamorphic rocks from 600 million to 3,000 million years old which have been folded, faulted and intruded by later volcanic rocks. These ancient rocks now form a plateau roughly 5,000 feet (1,524 metres) or more above sea level. On either side of this plateau are the Eastern and Western Rift Valleys with some associated mountains (all, notably, structurally running north–south unlike the physically impossible 'Mountains of the Moon'). The rifting is the result of tectonic activity with associated volcanic events which may have gone on over some millions of years and which continues to be in evidence right up to the present.

It is important to realize that the complications of the Nile's course arise because the whole river system is in a state which geomorphologists describe as 'immature'. In other words, the system is young in geological terms and has not had time for normal erosive forces to produce the regular profile with no waterfalls and cataracts or sudden bends from source to mouth characteristic of a mature river. The Nile is actually the world's longest river and passes through five different geological regions. It is the first of these regions, the Great Lakes Plateau or interlacustrine region of East Africa, where lie the sources of the river, which principally concerns us.

The tectonic movements already referred to as affecting the plateau region began only about 30 million years ago. The fact that these tectonic events have continued into the present era explains why some experts have argued that the modern course of the Nile developed as recently as in the Pleistocene, say, only 25,000 years ago. Whether it is over a longer or shorter period than this, the key point is that the extent and catchment areas of all the great lakes have varied considerably as a result of rifting and tilting and also climate changes. According to some authorities, for example, it is only as recently as 13,000 years ago that what we know as Lake Victoria actually became connected to the Nile river system.[1]

Detailed arguments over the precise timing of developments in the Nile's history need not concern us here. However, that geomorphological history has resulted in features which even a glance at a simple map make obvious enough. It is clear, for example, that it is the Western Rift Valley which has much affected the Nile's course in the area of Buganda and Bunyoro explored by Grant and Speke in 1862–3. The floor of its valley lies well over 1,000 feet (305 metres) below the level of the plateau and so the river is marked by a series of cataracts and falls as it flows down to the level of Lake Albert.[2] As well as producing rift valleys, tectonic activity has gradually raised the plateau and produced a tilting down towards the east so that originally westward-flowing rivers have become swamps or now flow in the opposite direction. The form of Lake Kyoga is one obvious result of tilting. There are numerous examples of river captures, as when, for example, the northward-flowing Nile was captured by a stream flowing from east to west and is thus made to flow westwards into Lake Albert (see Maps 7 and 8).

---

[1] Goudie, 'Drainage of Africa', pp. 437, 439, 441–8.

[2] Lake Victoria is reckoned to have an altitude of 3,720 ft (1,134 m) and Lake Kyoga 3,392 ft (1,034 m) but Lake Albert is only 2,018 ft (615 m) above sea level.

The most important result of tilting has been the gradual formation of the principal source of the Nile itself, Lake Victoria. It lies in a depression on the plateau land. Relatively shallow with an ill-defined fringe, it is markedly different in character from the rift valley lakes such as Tanganyika and Albert (see Map 6).

The consequences of this geological and geomorphological history may be seen in the character of the hydrology of the Nile source region. The tortuous course of the so-called Victoria Nile from Lake Victoria itself to Lake Albert, plus the fact that part of that course is through Lake Kyoga, is apparent from a map of the interlacustrine area which highlights the great river's course (see Map 7).

An added complication which needs to be taken into account is the confused nature of the drainage of the interlacustrine area. The watershed between rivers flowing into the Western Rift and others on the plateau flowing into Lake Victoria or Lake Kyoga is indeterminate, with even a few rivers which may flow either way in the same valley. The waters from the Ruwenzori Mountains reach the Nile system in most complex ways and do not actually contribute much. The watershed between drainage southwards into Lake Victoria along its northern coast and the drainage northwards into Lake Kyoga is actually very close to the coast and hence one channel to the north has been able to break back to Lake Victoria; this channel is the Nile as Speke saw it at the Ripon Falls in July 1862 (see Map 8).

As Lake Victoria gradually filled up during very recent geological history, this outlet to the north had become more possible. Also in recent geological history, the north-flowing stream was captured by the still westward-flowing waters of Lake Kyoga but which tilting had transformed into a very swampy area. Near Masindi Port and at a confluence with the Kafu River, the Nile makes an abrupt bend north, then north-east before being captured again at the Karuma Falls (which Grant rightly saw as significant) to flow westwards and down into the Western Rift Valley and Lake Albert itself. The Nile then flows out of Lake Albert northwards until its confluence with the Aswa River[1] to join the latter in flowing north-west in the fault-guided valley.

To describe the Nile's course in words in this way serves to emphasize how complicated the hydrology actually is.[2] It is no wonder that there was confusion and argument. The situation was made worse by the fact that Grant and Speke were prevented from following the course of the river from the Karuma Falls to Lake Albert (which they encouraged Samuel Baker to visit) and did not regain the Nile itself until they reached the area of the confluence with the Aswa. This left great scope for Speke's critics to say that he had not proved that the river he had seen issuing from Lake Victoria actually *was* the Nile.

It is worth adding that the complications described not only made exploration in the era of Grant and Speke difficult, but also, surely, serve to make it impossible for Ptolemy or Marinus of Tyre, or the alleged traveller Diogenes, to have had any real knowledge of the White Nile and its source. Even if, 2,000 years ago, a traveller already acquainted with Egypt and its great river had managed to walk from the East African coast to the

[1] See Chapter XIV below, pp. 318–19. The Aswa River, as Grant's 1863 map showed, was a puzzle; could it also have its source in Lake Victoria via a link through the connected Lake Baringo? But surely a lake cannot have two major outlets. The answer, of course, is that confused reports had caused the problem: Lake Baringo is in the Eastern Rift Valley and has no connection either with Lake Victoria or with the Aswa. And the Aswa is quite separate from Lake Victoria.

[2] Map 8, p. 33, showing the hydrology in the area in which the course of the Nile is situated, may help to clarify the situation.

interlacustrine region, how could he possibly have known which river in that area was the Nile? It is equally impossible to believe that any individual or expedition could successfully have negotiated a way from Egypt southwards along the entire 4,000-mile length of the Nile through the Saharan desert, then the swamps of the Sudd and then on to the complications of Lakes Albert, Kyoga and Victoria.

The conclusion of any investigation into the history of knowledge of the upper course and source of the White Nile in any form which could be assimilated by the educated world must be that it was not, indeed, until the Expedition of Grant and Speke in 1862–3 that the truth emerged. Any other view ignores historical evidence and demonstrates only a credulous determination to accept 2,000-year-old myths. If there is any credence to be given to classical, Byzantine, Arab and medieval European theories about the Nile source, it must be directed to seeing these theories as reflections of some real knowledge of the origin and course of the Blue Nile in Ethiopia.[1]

4. Grant's Geographical Work and His Views on the Nile Problem

Grant's Geographical Observations and the Creation of Maps
At the time when Speke and Grant made their journey, geography as a subject practised in Britain was in a rather unformed and uncertain condition. On the foundation of the RGS in 1830, it was said that the subject conferred 'just and distinct notions of the physical and political relations of our globe'.[2] This implied simple descriptions which it was the job of travellers and explorers to provide; there was no notion, apparently, of the need to consider the relationship between the physical and political. Intellectually, there was little advance on the picture of the subject provided by John Pinkerton's *Modern Geography* of 1802 which had some introductory material on astronomy, latitudes, longitudes and climate but nothing (unsurprisingly at this date) on geology. Almost all the work consisted of narratives based on political divisions, history and related concerns.[3]

In fact, as geology and other natural sciences developed rapidly in the early nineteenth century, it became increasingly difficult for geography to embrace these subjects and there was a clear prospect that 'physical geography' would become a quite separate subject. Because the RGS was so attuned to the needs of practical men looking after Britain's interests around the world who needed basic information and accurate maps, physical geography meant, largely, some reasonably clear pictures of the disposition of coasts, mountains, lakes and rivers accompanied by the establishment of dependable latitudes, longitudes and heights. This would enable the production of useful maps. The RGS certainly made obtaining such information its principal task and much was expected of Speke and Grant in this respect. During the 1860–63 Expedition, Speke used his sextant to good effect and produced 104 latitudes and 20 longitudes – an impressive achievement.[4] Apart from Grant's flora collecting and listing, he took weather

---

[1] In this regard, see above for the discussion on the work of Cooley, Ravenstein and Crawford, pp. 41–2.

[2] Markham, *Fifty Years' Work of the R.G.S.*, p. 19.

[3] In Pinkerton's work, Eastern Africa merited only one and a half pages out of 700. Pinkerton's approach was of the kind characteristic of another product of the 'Enlightenment' of the late 18th century, W. D. Cooley, the founder of the Hakluyt Society. See Cooley's *Physical Geography* of 1876.

[4] Speke, *Journal*, Appendix D, pp. 620–22.

observations and participated with Speke in using boiling point thermometers to calculate heights.[1] In the context of later arguments about the source of the Nile, heights were vital information since rivers do not flow uphill. In addition to the sextants, artificial horizons, rain gauges and so on, which made these observations possible, the two travellers used compasses to enable them to check the directions in which they were travelling and the bearings of distant objects seen but not visited.

All the data collected from the observations made with all these instruments enabled reasonably accurate maps to be constructed. In this work, once again, Grant's contribution seems to have been the key one. In fact, he was able to produce an attractively coloured map in February 1863 when he and Speke were still in Africa at Gondokoro.[2] It was the map which Grant there showed to Samuel Baker so encouraging him to go on to see and name Lake Albert. Its main features remained the basis of maps produced by home-based experts after the return of the Expedition, such as the map in the *Illustrated London News* and the maps ascribed to the prominent Scottish geographer and cartographer Keith Johnston in both Speke's and Grant's books.[3]

There are interesting differences between the versions of the Johnston map in the two books. For Speke (as he obviously must have insisted) the 'Mountains of the Moon' are clustered round the northern end of Lake Tanganyika in order to maintain that 'Burton's lake' could not be possibly be a source of the Nile. It is notable that Grant chose to have these mountains removed from the version in *his* book; it was a silent criticism of his companion and a sign that he did have misgivings about Speke's theories. Grant's version of the map also shows the whole course of the Nile down to Egypt, as Speke's did not.[4]

Naturally, Grant's original map, based as it was on a single traverse plus often imperfectly-understood local testimony, has many errors. The discussion on his ethnology has already noted that to designate tribal territories as if they are minor kingdoms is misleading. Even so, there is much to be learned from Grant's map. For example, the area he chooses to show as that of Buganda is a relatively narrow strip around the north-western shores of Lake Victoria. Only with the aid of British allies a generation later were the Baganda able to expand enormously the area they dominated.

Whatever we might learn today from Grant's map, what his contemporaries seized upon was, naturally, how he showed the course of the Nile. After all, the main object of the Expedition was to establish whether Speke's claim that Lake Victoria was the source could be proved.

Grant and the Nile Problem

It is difficult to be altogether sure what Grant's attitude to the problem of the Nile's source actually was. Although, as has been noted, he decided after Speke's death to dedicate his book to Speke as 'the Discoverer of the Source of the Nile' and to defend Speke's reputation,

---

[1] Ibid., Appendix E, p. 623.

[2] See Plate 1 and Map 9, p. 65. On this map, Grant shows the altitude of Lake Victoria to be 3,553 ft (1,083 m) which is less than 200 ft (61 m) below the actual height.

[3] The February 1863 map was taken over as 'his' by Speke when later presented to the RGS. But Grant's modest 'J.A. Grant fecit' remains in the bottom left-hand corner. The map is reproduced in Crone, *Sources of the Nile: Explorers' Maps*, no. 5.

[4] The maps in the two books are large folding ones; that in Speke's book in the original edition bound in at the beginning while in Grant's book a pocket at the back was preferred.

he clearly remained unwilling to be drawn deeply into the controversies even as late as his 1872 article. When he and Speke rejoined one another after Speke's visit to the Ripon Falls, the account in neither his book nor his journal exhibits any resentment or unhappiness about his not having been involved in this crowning moment for the Expedition. Yet nor does his reaction seem to show any evidence that he felt any exultation over the Expedition's having been successful. He had also seemed to be rather unhappy about the reception at the RGS just after the two men returned to Britain. In the part of his book written before he knew of Speke's death, where he described the Kagera River (which he initially incorrectly called the 'Kitangule'), and how it fed its waters into Lake Victoria, there is just a hint, perhaps, of a thought that the lake must have lots of feeders and so the outlet from it might not be so very important.[1] Perhaps, too, Grant felt with considerable justice, as one can now see, that his scientific observations and his accounts of the people encountered were just as important as identifying the actual source of the Nile.

5. Grant's Reputation and the Place of His Work and Exploration: A Survey of the Literature

The Aftermath of the Expedition
An examination of the available literature which might be expected to mention Grant and to contribute to an understanding of the man and his place in history reveals that there are major issues to be confronted on questions related to the exploration of East Africa and its significance in British overseas history and in the history of the societies of Africa itself. The context for this discussion is the aftermath of the Nile Expedition. Grant himself returned to service in the Indian Army and found himself in Africa again when he was second in command of Intelligence for the military expedition under Napier of 1867 which defeated the Emperor of Ethiopia. He was awarded the Star of India (C.S.I) and promoted to Lt Colonel, and soon afterwards retired to become active in the RGS and other African-related concerns, as well as taking an active part in the public and church life in his native Nairnshire.

Meanwhile, despite Speke's claim that the Nile question was settled, many had remained doubtful while Burton and his allies, including the veteran geographer James MacQueen, were notably hostile to the man himself. Speke did not help his cause because he had failed to provide for the RGS what the Society regarded as an adequate account of the Expedition. He also seemed to go out of his way to blacken the reputation and the career of Petherick (who had family ties to MacQueen) by accusing him of failing to use publicly-subscribed money to meet and help the Expedition.[2] Even Livingstone was led to doubt whether Lake Victoria existed as one body of water and to convince himself that he could find the ultimate source of the Nile further south; after all, Lake Albert, which Samuel Baker had reached in 1864, must have feeders. By 1870, however, geographers were becoming doubtful about Burton's claims[3] and then Keith Johnston translated for

---

[1] See Chapter IX below, p. 216.
[2] Bridges, 'Speke and the RGS', describes and explains the controversies.
[3] A. K. Johnston, *A Map of the Lake Regions of East Africa*, 1870; Wakefield, 'Routes of Native Caravans', with an appendix by Johnston, 1870.

British readers a German geographer's analysis of lake levels to prove that Livingstone could not be working on the sources of the Nile.[1] Shortly afterwards, Stanley's practical observations on his 1874–6 expedition finally vindicated Speke.[2] Speke was vindicated but by then he was long dead, having accidentally shot himself just before he was scheduled to debate the Nile issue with Burton at the British Association meeting of September 1864 in Bath.

As noted above, arguments about Ptolemy and the Nile sources might continue, but it began to become apparent that what Grant had said in his address to the Ethnological Society about the people of the Nile source region was perhaps more significant for the future. Uganda, he reported:

> one cannot mention but with enthusiasm. It is the garden of Equatorial Africa; continually watered, its tropical, perpetual luxuriance is most marvellous: there is nothing that will not grow ... while though the king is cruel, despotic and harsh, people feel able to take a pride in their country ...[3]

Clearly, the region was worth fuller scientific investigation and its relatively sophisticated people likely to be receptive of Christianity and commerce. Indeed, East Africa more generally should perhaps no longer be left to the Zanzibar or Egyptian slave traders.[4] It is important to note that the Nile source arguments and then the reports of Speke and Grant had attracted much attention not just in Britain but in various parts of Europe; the Paris Geographical Society and, in the German region, August Petermann's Geographical Institute with its increasingly influential journal, *Mittheilungen*, carried regular reports of British expeditions. A French translation of Speke's *Journal* appeared as early as 1864.[5] The friendly reception of Grant in France and award of medals to him by both the Pope and the King of Italy may be taken as signs of this wider interest. Hence the context for any discussion of the significance of Grant's work embraces not only British interests but also European-wide concerns and it includes not only geographical questions about snow-covered mountains on the Equator or the source of the Nile but also much more important issues about the future of East Africa. That future included various European initiatives with which Grant became connected and then political annexations which meant that, before the end of the century, the whole of Africa was a patchwork of European colonies. The significance, if any, of Grant's Expedition in that process of historical development is the explicit or implicit question at stake in any discussion of Grant's work.

Grant's Reputation in Older, Popular and Biographical Works

It is argued here that Grant deserves to be remembered as one of the major explorers of East Africa. It must be conceded that this has not been universally recognized. Even Ray Howgego's now indispensable work of reference on explorers does not accord him an entry in his own right.[6] A great many popular and semi-popular works have been

---

[1] E. Behm, 'Dr Livingstone's Exploration of the Upper Congo', 1873.

[2] Stanley, *Through the Dark Continent*, I, pp. 1–28 etc.

[3] Grant, 'On the Native Tribes', p. 86.

[4] This was the message conveyed in a digest of the books by Speke and Grant which appeared in 1868: Swayne, *Lake Victoria. A Narrative of Explorations in Search of the Source of the Nile.*

[5] *Les Sources du Nil*, trans. E. D. Forgues.

[6] Howgego, *Encyclopedia of Exploration 1850–1940*, pp. 866–8.

written about Burton, Speke, Livingstone, Cameron and Stanley as the travellers whose discoveries of great lakes and previously unknown rivers and whose arguments about the sources of the Nile created so much interest in Europe during the mid-nineteenth century. In such works, Grant tends to be accorded a rather secondary role. As the unremarkable companion of John Hanning Speke, he was 'the epitome of the unemotional, loyal Scot'.[1] It is worth quoting Alan Moorehead's assessment more fully:

> In Grant Speke had found an ideal companion ... He was the perfect lieutenant. He must surely be rated as the most modest and self-effacing man who ever entered the turmoil of African exploration; he never puts himself forward, he never complains, never questions any order of his leader ... Grant's devotion was entirely fixed upon Speke and it was almost doglike in its completeness.

No doubt this was intended to be a compliment but it hardly suggests that Grant will be a very interesting subject. Indeed, Moorehead goes on to quote General Gordon as dismissing Grant as 'something of a bore'. However, he then tempers his verdict by remarking:

> Yet it would be foolish to regard Grant as a colourless nonentity. He was a cool and very steady man, a soldier and sportsman well out of the ordinary ... a competent artist and a genuine amateur of botany [who] had been awarded a medal and a clasp for gallantry.[2]

In the end, then, Moorehead does try to leave a favourable impression. Yet it will be argued here that neither the faint praise for the modest man nor the more positive endorsement which follows quite gets to the truth about Grant. He believed it right to defer to one's appointed leader. Nevertheless, his regard for Speke was not always in evidence and it was certainly far from doglike devotion.

Most popular and semi-popular accounts of Grant and many other explorers of his era interpret an African exploratory expedition as a personal struggle to cope with difficult terrain, disease, wild animals and obstacles created by 'primitive' people who behaved in unpredictable and certainly unreasonable ways. Very often, the personal struggle is given added piquancy for readers when it is seen as including the need to cope with European companions.[3] One personal issue which does deserve attention is Grant's relationship with Speke which was somewhat more complex than the unquestioning loyalty mentioned by so many commentators.[4] His relationship with the porters, guards and servants of the Expedition is also worth some consideration.

---

[1] Rae and Lawson, *Dr Grigor*, p. 159. Many other works, old and new, have similar descriptions: Robert Brown, *Story of Africa and Its Explorers*, 1892–95; Harry Johnston, *Nile Quest*, 1903; Alan Moorehead, *White Nile*, 1960; or, more recently, Tim Jeal, *Explorers*, 2011, not to mention the numerous biographies of the major travellers.

[2] Moorehead, *White Nile*, pp. 50–51. Although Grant was rewarded in various ways for his gallantry and good sense in various military encounters in India, the medals Moorehead mentions appear to have been essentially campaign medals. He received the medal and clasp for Mooltan and the Battle of Goojerat (*sic*) in 1848–9 and the medal and clasp awarded to those involved in the relief of Lucknow. Grant, 'Memoranda', pp. 9, 15.

[3] The Burton v. Speke controversy over the source of the Nile and various personal matters, which is discussed above, and in which Grant inevitably became to a certain extent involved, is a prime example, as are Livingstone's rather fraught relationships.

[4] Even Speke's biographer refers to Grant as a 'staunch and unfailing supporter'. Maitland, *Speke,* p. 188.

Grant's Relationship with John Hanning Speke

This edition is certainly not designed to be a character study of an explorer of which there are already too many examples. Nevertheless, Grant's temperament and outlook did affect his relations with Speke, and with the porters and guards who made up the Expedition party. These relationships, in turn, did have a considerable bearing on his dealings with the Africans he met in the 'contact zone'. They affected, too, the manner in which *A Walk across Africa* and his other records of the Expedition were produced. Hence personal relationships do deserve some attention. A verdict like Moorehead's that he was just a loyal second in command needs extensive revision.

Even the early relationship with Speke which included a tiger-hunting expedition was not without its complications: 'of course I say nothing but the man's cheek is what I am astonished at'.[1] The problem was Speke's 'bagging' a tiger which Grant thought he had shot. If there were similar problems in the course of the Expedition, neither the text of *A Walk* nor the journal refer to them; in fact, Grant very rarely records his own inner feelings even, for example, when Speke alone visited the actual source of the Nile. Most references to Speke appear friendly: 'Old S. most kindly seeing after my comforts'.[2] And yet an impression is gained that towards the end of the Expedition, Grant was beginning to have some reservations about his companion's behaviour. The impression becomes a certainty for the period after the two men had returned to Britain until, indeed, the time of Speke's tragic death in September 1864. By that point, the relationship seems to have become somewhat cold and distant.

Two recent writers have made much of Speke's love affair with the Muganda girl, Meri, which is revealed in the uncorrected proofs of his book.[3] When the information in these proofs was first revealed by the present writer in a published article, Speke's sexual activities were considered less noteworthy than what was revealed about the way the publisher's reviser distorted the actual political situation in which Speke and Grant found themselves involved in Buganda.[4] Without any such evidence, back in 1864, James M'Queen was able to read between the lines of the actually published version of the book and guess that Speke had indulged in what he regarded as sexual improprieties.[5] The affair took place before Grant reached Buganda. Is it possible that he became aware of what had taken place and disapproved? He must have been well acquainted with liaisons between British men and Indian women and, indeed, the brother of his mentor and namesake, James Augustus Grant of Househill, apparently had children by an Indian lady.[6] As a son of the manse and, as far as one can tell, not himself in the habit of taking mistresses, it seems likely that Grant would probably have disapproved. Whatever may have been his thoughts on either Speke's sexual adventures or on the necessity of his solo march to the Nile source, there is more than a hint that he began to be unhappy about Speke's behaviour towards Petherick at Gondokoro. Mrs Petherick said that, in contrast to Speke, Grant always

[1] NLS, MS. 17914, Grant, Journal, 12 May 1852.

[2] NLS, MS. 17915, Grant, Journal, 10 January 1862.

[3] Jeal, *Explorers*, pp. 157–62; Kennedy, *Last Blank Spaces*, pp. 195–8. Speke burned all the manuscripts he had used to write his book. NLS, MS. 17910, Murchison to Grant, undated [c. February 1864].

[4] Bridges 'East African Travel Records', pp. 190–91.

[5] Burton, *Nile Basin*, pp. 105, 146–7, 179–80.

[6] Miller, *Last Years of Grant of Viewfield*, p. 204.

behaved in a gentlemanly way.[1] After the return home, Speke's continuing vendetta against Petherick incurred the disapproval of the RGS, as Sir Roderick Murchison himself was not slow to tell Grant. The Society's President was most unhappy about Speke's failure to provide a paper for the RGS before publishing his own book. He added that he thought Grant's name should have appeared on the title page of Speke's book.[2] Grant's old friend of Aberdeen and Marischal College days, John Cruickshank, wrote to him that Speke 'had not done you perfect justice in his book'.[3]

During this period, Grant's own reservations about Speke and his speeches became very noticeable and these reservations may in fact explain why Grant embarked at all on the task of producing his own account of the Expedition. Soon after their return home Murchison had organized the great RGS reception for the two men which Grant found 'uncomfortably crowded'. 'I am too nervous', he reported, and 'said very little' while Speke 'talked away'. On the following day, Speke lectured before the Prince of Wales at the Royal Institution. 'A wretched failure, I thought it' said Grant who had, however, been gratified by the Prince's interest in his drawings. On 30 June came Grant's own lecture to the Ethnological Society which seems not to have been either well-attended or very notable.[4] He soon retreated to his homeland in Northern Scotland to receive the freedom of Nairn before travelling to Newcastle for the 1863 meeting of the British Association where he lectured to a 'mass of ladies' on 31 August.[5]

As was noted in the section on Grant's botany, he spent much of the period between October and December 1863 at Kew working on the flora which appeared as an appendix to Speke's book.[6] Although he met Speke briefly on 3 November, there was little regular contact. He did not at all like *Journal of the Discovery of the Source of the Nile*. In its present form, he told his friend John Blackwood, 'many parts are slightly indecent and too slangy in expression ... and I should like to see it cut down to half its dimensions ... He sadly wants the advice of a friend ... [I] have written him regarding it.'[7] One suspects that Grant was also upset by the portrayal of himself dancing with a bare-breasted female, an issue which has been discussed above. On 14 December, Grant, together with his friends Dr and Mrs Grigor of Nairn, travelled to Paris at the start of a European tour which was to last until 13 May 1864. It seems almost certain that he chose to be absent from Britain in order to avoid what he knew would be the controversies provoked by the appearance of Speke's book. He was well received in Paris, Florence and Rome and met the Pope, Pius IX, who gave him a medal.[8] After his return, he was reluctant even to attend the RGS meeting in May 1864 at which he was to be presented with the highly prestigious Patron's Medal and 'not a wink I had slept' the

[1] See Chapter XV below, p. 328 n.2.

[2] NLS, MS. 17910, Murchison to Grant, undated [c. April 1864], and NLS, MS. 17931, 5 May 1864.

[3] NLS, MS. 17932, Cruickshank to Grant, 30 December 1864.

[4] NLS, MS. 17915, Grant, Journal, 22, 23, 30 June 1863. An account of the meeting with modified versions of some of Grant's pictures was published in the *Illustrated London News*, 4 July 1863.

[5] NLS, MS. 17915, Grant, Journal, 18 May, 25 and 31 August 1863. Grant also received the freedom of Dingwall on 28 September 1863.

[6] There are hints that Grant thought Speke's own appendix on the fauna of East Africa was somewhat inadequate.

[7] NLS, MS. 4181, Grant to Blackwood, undated [c. November 1863].

[8] Rae and Lawson, *Dr Grigor*, pp. 159–62.

night before.[1] At this period, Murchison wrote a long letter to Grant about Speke. Using very intemperate expressions, he castigated Speke's 'wild and impracticable scheme' of regenerating East Africa and deplored his visiting France and 'gallivanting with Louis Napoleon'.[2]

By this time Grant had decided that he should write his own account of the Expedition. This was agreed in March 1864 with Blackwood and with Speke's approval.[3] It was not, however, until 7 June that he began 'scribbling for the first time at my book' and the writing continued over the next few months.[4] Meanwhile, it had been arranged that Speke would debate the Nile question with Burton at the meeting of the British Association in September. Surely it is significant that Grant had decided not to be present on this occasion. Clearly, he disliked disputes and had his own doubts about Speke's ideas on various matters, including the Nile. The original title of his book was to have referred to Speke as the 'Discoverer of the Victoria Nyanza and the Source of the Nile'[5] but in the event the doubt was removed by dedicating the book to his companion as simply the 'Discoverer of the Source of the Nile'. Everything had changed when the news reached Grant on 17 September that his companion had shot himself dead. Chapter XIV is interrupted to report his reaction to the terrible news from Bath and Grant blamed himself for 'not having gone thither'. There is an intensely felt more immediate reaction in his journal where he describes arriving at the home of Speke's parents and entering the draped room where lay the coffin of 'the poor dear fellow whom I now felt I loved so much'.[6] The unconscious use of 'I *now* felt' must surely indicate that Grant had been feeling somewhat estranged from his companion.

From this point, his attitudes changed and Grant was to spend much of his subsequent life defending Speke's reputation and so earning himself the reputation of being simply the supporter and apologist for his leader. Yet it would be misleading to assume that he in any way ceased to be an important figure in his own right after September 1864. He complained when Baker was given a knighthood for his discovery of Lake Albert. This was partly because he was annoyed that the more important discovery of Lake Victoria and the source of the Nile had brought no award for Speke and only belatedly a CB for himself. Murchison found it necessary to try to mollify Grant.[7] When later, finally retired from the Indian Army, he produced the articles recording the scientific results of the Expedition, it was as much to establish his own claim to scientific and popular acclaim as to rescue Speke's reputation. He was successful in this claim in that he became a widely respected and widely consulted figure very much involved in affairs connected with Africa.[8] At the same time, his prosperity assured by a marriage in 1865[9] to Margaret Laurie (1834–1918), the great-niece of Sir Peter Laurie (1778–1861), former Lord Mayor of London, who had left her £40,000 in consols, he bought a fine house in his beloved

[1] Murchison had to exert considerable pressure on Grant to make him agree to be present. NLS, MS. 17931, Murchison to Grant, 5 May 1864; NLS, MS. 17916, Grant, Journal, 23 May 1864.

[2] NLS, MS. 17910, Murchison to Grant, undated [c. April 1864], 20 May 1864.

[3] NLS, MS. 17931, Speke to Grant, 22 March 1864.

[4] NLS, MS. 17916, Grant, Journal, 7 June, 14, 17, 20 September 1864.

[5] NLS, MS. 17934, *A Walk*, proof copy.

[6] NLS, MS. 17916, Grant, Journal, 27 September 1864.

[7] NLS, MS. 17910, Murchison to Grant, 17 August, 26 October 1866.

[8] See below on Grant's later involvement with African-connected affairs, p. 62.

[9] NLS, MS. 17932, R. P. Laurie to Mrs Grant, 4 May 1881. For Sir Peter Laurie, the great-uncle, see *ODNB*.

Nairnshire and became a leading figure in that part of the world as an elder of the Kirk and promoter of local causes. After his death, his wife sensibly opposed the idea of adding his name to the Speke memorial in Kensington Gardens.[1] The great window in Mitchell Hall in Marischal College, Aberdeen, the large gravestone in the cemetery in Nairn and a brass plaque in the crypt of St Paul's Cathedral all commemorate Grant in his own right.

Grant and his Relationship with the Expedition's Porters and Guards

As there had been troubles over the payment and treatment of the porters on his previous expedition, Speke was anxious to manage things better for the Nile Expedition by making proper agreements with the new group, although there was a continuing reliance on the way of organizing a 'caravan' developed by the Zanzibar Arab traders. He wished to continue to use Hindustani to communicate with his followers, which was a considerable constraint given the small number who could respond in that tongue. Fortunately, it included the vital men, Bombay[2] and Baraka, who effectively conducted many of the negotiations with African leaders. Grant also had only Hindustani at the beginning of the Expedition but it is clear that he began to become familiar with the main language of the porters, Swahili. Arrangements did not work out altogether smoothly: of the 176 men who set out only 18 'faithfuls' led by Bombay remained at the end. These losses were principally a result of desertions caused by factional disputes between followers of Bombay and those of Baraka as well as disputes between coast men and Banyamwezi from the interior. In all of these disputes, African leaders, not least the Kabaka of Buganda, were prone to intervene.[3]

As military men, both Speke and Grant had the instinct to try to manage the caravan as though it were a military detachment, even giving the men sword exercises.[4] Over time it became clear that negotiation and sometimes conciliation were more important than military discipline. The gradual change can be detected in Grant's record of the Expedition.[5] He becomes more and more interested in the men and their beliefs and the stories of their lives. He begins to see that they do have some stores of knowledge, for example, on plants. Some of that knowledge will find its way into his Linnean Society flora which includes a section on local names and uses. He even discovers, to his amazement, that there is appreciation of the beauty in a landscape. Grant's relationship with Frij,[6] one of those who knew Hindustani and who was supposed to be a private servant to him, was especially important. Clearly he often found the man exasperating but also someone on whom he could rely. Generally one could say that he showed good sense in his personal dealings with the members of the caravan.

Grant and Academic Travel Literature

One prominent development of the last two or three decades which has significance for those interested in a traveller like Grant has been the appearance of a large literature of

---

[1] Maitland, *Speke*, p. 227.

[2] See Figure 9, p. 90, for Grant's photograph of Bombay.

[3] The complex story of the porters on the Expedition and their relationships is fully analysed in Bridges, 'Negotiating a Way', pp. 106–14.

[4] See Chapter V below, p. 136.

[5] For his initial description of the caravan and its unruly porters, see Chapter III below, pp. 85–6.

[6] Frij is depicted in Figure 62, p. 210..

post-colonial studies which have been largely inspired by Edward Said and his concept of 'Orientalism'.[1] Travel writing for Said did not reflect actual reality but a manufactured 'reality' useful to the West in its process of controlling the Orient. The idea has been taken up in relation to other parts of the world. The influential *Imperial Eyes* by Mary Louise Pratt is focused primarily on South America but takes in Africa. For Pratt, 'the great significance of travel writing [is] as one of the ideological apparatuses of empire'. She cites an episode reported by Grant when he was joined by his African followers in admiring a view of Lake Victoria as illustrating how the explorer was exhibiting the 'monarch of all I see' syndrome: the Africans are shown as confirming the European achievement giving readers a feel-good impression of empire. Given Grant's position at the time as crippled and entirely dependent on the goodwill of local political personalities, he was far from being a dominating imperialist. Nor does his own record of the occasion suggest that he is doing anything more than learning more about his African associates and throwing off some of his earlier prejudices. The most useful of Pratt's concepts, as noted at the beginning of this Introduction, is that of 'contact zones' – which are defined in various ways including one which is probably most useful for a study like this: 'social spaces where disparate cultures, meet, clash and grapple with each other'.[2]

Pratt assumes that these zones usually involve relations of domination and subordination, as does Tim Youngs who has provided the most important post-colonial approach to the travel literature of East Africa. He emphasizes that to read a traveller's discourses as empirical evidence is to be misled; the writer must be seen in the context of the culture to which he belongs. In this way 'beliefs and perspectives which made possible the physical exercise of imperialism and colonialism' are revealed. Youngs treats Grant with considerable disfavour because of his 'higher-class disdain of trade' and because of the 'unctuous false humility' and the 'hypocritical modesty' of the preface to *A Walk* which he sees as 'arrogant self-depreciation of one who knows himself to be a position of power'. Moreover, Grant's observations on Africans are actually to be seen as reflections of his own worries about his own social position, the position of Britain and perhaps, it is implied, his sexuality when he reacts to an attractive young African woman. The exchange of presents in the latter case helps to persuade pre-capitalists to accept capitalist values.[3] The heavy criticism of Grant who was, perhaps, genuinely modest but overdid the expression of that modesty, is less important than the assumption that one cannot take any observations as representing the truth about what is reported. In the case mentioned here, it may be pointed out that the exchange of gifts was very much, and remains, an African practice. Above all, it is a mistake in analysing Grant's encounters with Africans – male or female, ugly or beautiful – to say that he wrote as someone who knows himself to be in a position of power. Quite the opposite was the case: throughout the journey Grant and Speke were at the mercy of Africans who gave them shelter and help. Travel-writing studies can provide very important insights but they too often seem to be made without adequate understanding of the historical circumstances obtaining when the subject authors were making their journeys. Nevertheless, Youngs's work is an

---

[1] Said, *Orientalism.*

[2] Pratt, *Imperial Eyes*, pp. i, 4, 38, 204–5, 208. See below, Chapter IX, pp. 213–29.

[3] Youngs, *Travellers in Africa*, pp. 2, 5, 93–4. See below for Grant's Preface and, for the young woman, Chapter VII, pp. 172–3.

important reminder that travellers like Grant were indeed conditioned by their own culture, although that does not necessarily mean that true facts cannot be extracted from their books. It is the contention in this study that Grant did see beyond his own culture with some success and that we can learn about Africa and Africans from him as well as about his preconceptions.

Grant as an Actor in African Developments and a Source of African History
Whether the assessments of the character and personal relations of Grant by earlier and popular writers such as Moorehead, or the more recent judgements of travel-writing specialists are justified or otherwise, neither class of literature provides satisfactory conclusions on the nature of his encounter with either the African environment or, even more importantly, the African peoples he met. In many earlier accounts of exploration, Africans provide only an ill-understood exotic or threatening backdrop to the exploits of the hero of the story and in later ones, they are usually portrayed as hapless victims of imperialism. Both views are insulting to the people involved. Exploration is part of a process – a process of considerable importance in history by which different peoples, in this case European and African, came into a closer involvement with one another. How this came about is a story which has to take account of the Africans and their actions, not just those of the Europeans – whether the latter are seen as enlightened bringers of civilization or wicked exploiters. Just where and with what precise effects Grant's Expedition and the other forays into East Africa fit into the process of closer involvement is a matter for argument among historians. Given the fact that the territories Grant traversed came under colonial rule for sixty years or more, the question is surely worth careful attention.

It is true that some writers who have written popular accounts of the exploration of East Africa do show an awareness of the need to address wider historical questions. Jeal is a case in point.[1] In most cases, it has to be added, however, that one notes a tendency to write still in nineteenth-century terms and to show little awareness of modern academic scholarship on either British and European overseas history or the history of Africa.[2]

If, because of their concentration on personalities, many writers may be criticized for not satisfactorily answering the wider historical questions, have academic historians provided better ways of looking at Grant and his work? One immediate response to that question is to note that in the 1960s and 1970s, as African history came into its own in African, British and American universities, very little obvious attention was paid to the explorers. Indeed, it was unfashionable to mention them as actors on the historical stage because, understandably at that time, they seemed to be too much part of the apparatus of European influence and control which was currently being dismantled in the new African states. The relevant volumes of neither the *Oxford History of East Africa*[3] nor the *Cambridge History of Africa*[4] included chapters specifically on the exploration of East

[1] Jeal, *Explorers*, Part II, *passim*; McLynn, *Hearts of Darkness*, pp. 303–38.
[2] It is tempting to apply more generally the verdict of Professor A. G. Hopkins on the account Jeal gives of Stanley – that it 'by-passed modern research' and presented a dated image. 'Explorers' Tales', p. 679.
[3] Oliver and Mathew, *History of East Africa,* 1963. Grant is mentioned once in a very short passage on the explorers, pp. 337–8.
[4] *The Cambridge History of Africa*, V, p. 42, notes that Speke and Grant stimulated Egyptian interest in the Bantu interlacustrine kingdoms but apart from bibliographical citations otherwise ignores their work and this despite there being a chapter on European interest in Africa.

Africa while Iliffe's *A Modern History of Tanganyika*[1] did not allow men like Burton, Speke and Grant to figure in the text or index. Paradoxically, however, most such studies made ample use of the explorers' published works for their evidence on African historical developments although, as noted above, some commentators would now hold that they were unwise to do even that.

The large literature on African history which developed between the 1960s and 1980s, then, did not accord much historical importance to the explorers as an influence on East African peoples and their development.

By and large, this observation remains true for a later generation of historians of East Africa although there has certainly been no hesitation in the continued use of the evidence provided by the travellers. This is particularly noticeable in the case of Speke and Grant because of the continuing tendency for historians to focus on the interlacustrine kingdoms. Buganda especially has received much attention. Wrigley produced a study of great importance which points out that Speke and Grant were the first persons to write words in and about Buganda. This primacy is seen as significant testimony in the context of elucidating historical traditions and myths. In fact, Wrigley is inclined to accept the evidence of Speke and Grant about the number of rulers (kabakas) who have actually existed in preference to some later formulations of the kingdom's history. Grant's evidence on Mutesa's brothers and on Mutesa's attitude to some traditional rituals is especially important. Wrigley agrees with the picture which Speke and Grant paint of Buganda as a place of despotism, violence and cruelty.[2] Other relatively recent publications on Buganda include two exceptionally valuable analyses by Reid and by Hanson. Reid, in particular, places much value on Grant's evidence on African practices and trades such as fishing. Yet he insists that in general he disagrees with the attitudes of such informants as Grant even while he values their evidence.[3] Hanson uses the explorers' evidence in a penetrating study of the way power was distributed in Buganda.[4] Both works, incidentally, have engravers' altered versions of Grant's drawings on their covers, as does Koponen on the covers of and among the illustrations inside his study of the economic history of pre-colonial Tanzania. Yet this latter work, surprisingly, otherwise seems to ignore the 1860 Expedition.[5] Doyle's book on the original great kingdom in the interlacustrine region, Bunyoro, refers to Grant's observations.[6] Abdul Sheriff's work is the best general account of the way Indian Ocean influences in the shape of the activities of Zanzibar and coast traders affected East Africa and also draws on Grant.[7] Another example, incidentally, of a book using a Grant-derived picture without understanding is the important collection of studies edited by Médard and Doyle on slavery in the region. Nevertheless, Grant's written evidence is seen as significant on the economy of the key region of Unyamwezi and on the existence of indigenous slavery in East Africa before the external demands from the Indian Ocean or Egypt began to affect the situation.[8]

[1] Iliffe, *Tanganyika*, 1979. Nor in this work do Speke's and Grant's published works even appear in the bibliography.

[2] Wrigley, *Kingship and State*, pp. 6–7, 9–11, 26–7, 110–11, 224. See Chapter X below, p. 236.

[3] Reid, *Political Power*, pp. 6, 7, 16, 162–3 etc.

[4] Hanson, *Landed Obligation*, pp. 66, 101 etc.

[5] Koponen, *People and Production*, pp. 258, 285.

[6] Doyle, *Crisis and Decline*, pp. 18, 30.

[7] Sheriff, *Slaves, Spices and Ivory*, pp. 64, 183–4.

[8] Médard and Doyle, eds, *Slavery in the Great Lakes Region*, pp. 76 ff., 235, etc.

Like earlier writers, these scholars place importance on the evidence of Grant and Speke; like their predecessors, too, none sees the travellers as in any way significant actors on the African historical scene in the 1860s. This is understandable: for the most part, explorers were under-funded and could not afford parties of porters and guards large enough to intervene in local conflicts. Speke and Grant were generally careful to avoid involvement in local disputes as in Unyanyembe where the Arabs were fighting certain Nyamwezi groups or in Bunyoro where the ruler wanted their help in putting down a rival claimant for his throne. Even so, one should not ignore some examples of a direct observable political or social impact, perhaps without the explorer always knowing he had had an effect. More often, there were less tangible effects which might be characterized as making peoples encountered more aware of the wider world. Such developments have been analysed and discussed in the case of Speke and Grant, especially during their stay in Buganda where the two men became deeply embroiled in the daily struggle for the favour of the kabaka which was the staff of Ganda life. They taught something, too: 'Bana I love you because you have come so far to see me and have taught me so many new things' said Kabaka Mutesa. Moreover they made the kabaka and other rulers aware of wider political realities.[1] Grant also can be shown to have had cultural effects with his sketches and painting activities.

Even if it be granted that the immediate impact on Africa and Africans of an explorer like Grant was limited or intangible, may it be assumed that he did influence fellow Europeans who became concerned with Africa? This raises the whole question of the place of an explorer like Grant in British and European overseas history.

Grant and British Overseas History
In the same period that pioneering works on specifically African history were appearing, several very important studies of European imperialism in Africa and European international relations in relation to Africa in the 1880s and 1890s were published. Few of those which covered East African developments suggested that the slightly earlier exploration was a factor to be taken into account. In their hugely influential work, *Africa and the Victorians*, Robinson and Gallagher saw little sustained popular British interest in mid-century Africa; even Livingstone was but one of the 'heroes of an hour' and the philanthropy associated with his name no more than a 'public garb' for the 'official mind'.[2] Sanderson's study of the scramble for the Upper Nile[3] does not even mention Speke and Grant, the first European visitors to the Upper Nile who had provided detailed descriptions of the region and its peoples. The two large and detailed volumes on imperialism and colonial rule in Africa edited by Gifford and Louis together manage to mention Speke and Baker in passing just once.[4] Uzoigwe's study of British imperialism in Africa at least devotes one page to what he judges to be the effects of exploration as far as Uganda was concerned and he implies that Speke and Grant created a situation for subsequent informal British influence.[5] Even Uzoigwe does not make his case in any detail

---

[1] Bridges, 'Negotiating a Way', pp. 129–30.

[2] Robinson and Gallagher, *Africa and the Victorians*, p. 24.

[3] Sanderson, *England, Europe and the Upper Nile*.

[4] Gifford and Louis, eds, *Britain and Germany in Africa*, p. 121; Gifford and Louis, eds, *France and Britain in Africa*.

[5] Uzoigwe, *Britain and the Conquest of Africa*, pp. 172, 192.

and the general unwillingness of the imperial historians of the later twentieth century to explain what influence, if any, men like Grant had on later European developments remains a fact.

Some historians who are not particularly concerned with African or imperial history have in recent years turned their attention to geographical explorers and the culture from which they came in ways that go far beyond the concerns of the popular biographers or earlier writers on exploration like Robert Brown or Sir Percy Sykes.[1]

No figure in the geographical establishment in the metropole was more important and influential than Sir Roderick Murchison. In a brilliant essay, James Secord showed how Murchison the geologist made his science 'imperialistic'. Then Robert Stafford analysed his whole career as Director of the Geological Survey and dominant personality at the RGS arguing persuasively that Murchison was capturing the world culturally for Britain through geology, geography and exploratory expeditions. Stafford believes that Grant and Murchison, as 'fellow Highlanders', had an affinity and describes the ways the latter obtained honours for the explorer as well as arranging the tumultuous popular reception for Speke and Grant in 1863.[2]

Whether Murchison was the real inspiration for Grant's later 'imperial' activities may be open to question but there is no doubt that Stafford is right to show the RGS as something more than a simple promoter of exploration for its own scientific sake. The question has been very powerfully developed by D. N. Livingstone. He claims that 'imperialistic undergirding' of the RGS and its projects existed from its earliest days in the 1830s and that Victorian geography was intimately bound up with British expansionist policy overseas; there was 'complicity in Britain's imperial ventures'.[3] One might ask for greater precision chronologically in tracing the ways in which geography was connected with 'imperialism' which, after all, underwent a good many changes during the nineteenth century. The work which most thoroughly and sensitively discusses the RGS and its intellectual position is that of Felix Driver. He sees the Society as a centre for information exchange and notes the heated debates over the actual nature of geography, especially where exploration was concerned and the difficulties over reconciling 'observation in the field' with 'reflection in the study'. In commenting on Grant, he provides an enlightening short discussion on the way a portrait of Grant and Speke depicts 'reflective and determined men, engaging their powers of reason, in the Search for the Nile'.[4]

A younger scholar, Adam Wisnicki, has produced a series of articles on explorers in East Africa which demonstrate a mastery of the post-colonial studies of metropolitan attitudes but more unusually succeeds in relating what can be learned from these studies to actual activities in the field. These embrace such practical matters as trade routes, cartography, the use of Africans' information and so on. Although Wisnicki has latterly concentrated on Livingstone and makes no particular judgements on Grant, his views on how awareness of African realities can modify our understanding of travellers' narratives are certainly apposite for this edition.[5]

---

[1] Brown, *Story of Africa and its Explorers*, 1892–4; Sykes, *History of Exploration*, 1934.

[2] Secord, 'King of Siluria'; Stafford, *Scientist of Empire*, pp. 11, 21–2, 169–72.

[3] Livingstone, *The Geographical Tradition*, pp. 166–72.

[4] Driver, *Geography Militant*, pp. 19–21.

[5] Wisnicki, 'Cartographical Quandaries'; 'Charting the Frontier'; Rewriting Agency'; 'Field Notes from the Lualaba River'.

Perhaps Wisnicki, like other writers mentioned, is too unspecific in his use of the term 'imperialism'. To a lesser extent, the same is true of Dane Kennedy who sees explorers as demonstrably bound up with the broader imperial interests of Britain. His approach means that East African explorers are put in a context which ranges over the rest of Africa and Australia and he has a great many wise and discerning comments to make on the nature of exploratory activity and the way, for example, it was affected by travellers' contacts with indigenous peoples. Yet he has no doubt that travellers engaged in the search for the source of the Nile used geography to conceal 'more ambiguous enterprise than the Victorian public ever appreciated'.[1] Kennedy emphasizes that recent studies have shifted exploration 'away from its longstanding triumphalist associations' and perhaps more importantly, points out that travel books tend to be essentially autobiographical. The result is that narrative accounts of exploration become biographies of great men.[2] In the light of this comment, one may observe that one of the virtues of Grant's book is that, as if aware of the problem, he does attempt to make his account analytic and systematic rather than purely autobiographical. Kennedy does briefly acknowledge Grant's botanical work and the importance of his Scottish background and Indian experience but, even for him, Grant remains essentially, it seems, 'a loyal lieutenant' for Speke and consequently an unflagging enemy of Burton.[3] With some justice, Kennedy points out that explorers were inclined to conceal how reliant they were on indigenous sources. Again, one might question whether this is true of Grant, as indeed Kennedy seems to do at one point. In his desire to downplay the extent to which East African explorers were really in charge of their expeditions, Kennedy greatly exaggerates the independent authority of the Sultan of Zanzibar and the extent to which the Arab traders of the interior took any notice of his authority unless it suited them to do so.[4] Indeed, he overlooks local African power in East Africa.

Stephen Rockel takes a similar stance claiming that 'a transregional multi-ethnic culture' had long facilitated trade, communications and the movements of people, commodities and ideas. He goes on to say that this infrastructure made possible European exploratory progress which 'followed well behind'.[5] While it is true that Burton and subsequent travellers organized Arab-type 'caravans' of porters and guides, Burton himself was clearly only about ten years behind Arabs who had by no means supplanted local African regional trade patterns by the time Speke and Grant reached the interlacustrine region.[6]

Despite a degree of exaggeration in setting out his thesis, Rockel is surely right to emphasize the need for an understanding of the explorers to take account of the way they interacted with African systems of trade. More generally, he points to the need to see exploratory work in the context of both African and imperial history.[7]

---

[1] Kennedy, 'The Search for the Nile', p. 4; *Last Blank Spaces*, pp. 263–4 and *passim*.

[2] Kennedy, 'Introduction', *Reinterpreting Exploration*, pp. 3–6.

[3] Kennedy, *Last Blank Spaces*, pp. 37, 51–2, 66, 81, 87.

[4] Ibid., pp. 120–24.

[5] Rockel, 'Decentring Exploration in East Africa', pp. 172–8. These ideas are more fully developed in the same author's *Carriers of Culture*, pp. 3–23 and *passim*.

[6] On these matters, see Bennett, *Arab versus European*, and Sheriff, *Slaves, Spices and Ivory*.

[7] Rockel, 'Decentring Exploration in East Africa', p. 178.

Grant and British Overseas Activities and Interests

Robert Rotberg's introduction to a collection of studies of Africa's explorers says the aim is to portray them in an African rather than European context but observes that they seem to have little or no impact on Africa; only indirectly did their influence on fellow Europeans help to make the areas explored 'accessible to evangelical, colonial and martial penetration by whites of a number of different nationalities'. Yet Rotberg doubted whether there was any causal connection between the exploration and these later activities: 'the onset of colonial rule might have come about irrespective of the explorers'. Hence explorers were 'intellectual middlemen, as precursors but not progenitors of imperialism'.[1] This verdict in effect justified the rejection of any importance for explorers in the works of writers such as Sanderson or Robinson and Gallagher.

Presumably Rotberg assumed that the imperialism to which the explorers were precursors was the imperialism of the powers who took part in the 'Scramble for Africa' in the 1880s and 1890s. Yet more recent writers, such Pratt, Kennedy and Youngs whose work has been discussed above, insist on the connection between the explorers and imperialism. Even if instead of using the term 'imperialism', one substitutes something like 'the overseas interests and attitudes of Europeans and their governments', the lack of precision remains. Just what effect did the explorers have? The very first significant historian of modern East Africa was in no doubt. Sir Reginald Coupland's chapter on exploration said that it was 'scientific and humanitarian; there was no trace in the explorers' accounts 'of what came to be called "imperialism"'. Presumably by that term he meant the territorial annexations of the 1880s and 1890s. Somewhat illogically, perhaps, he also says that economic and political results of exploration were 'slow to mature' but that it was the explorers' revelations on the slave trade which called for intervention.[2] This is begging a question and does not get us very far.

Coupland wrote at the time of the British Empire's greatest extent when even some of its critical subject peoples would not have questioned, for example, the disinterestedness of its nineteenth-century commitment to ending the slave trade. Serious historians of British expansion (if not all popular writers) are now long freed from the blinkers which tended to restrict the vision of Coupland's generation.[3]

It will help to put the work of Grant and his fellow travellers of the middle of the nineteenth century in context to refer to two rather different, yet both most impressive works. John Darwin charts what he calls the 'Rise and Fall of the British World-System 1830–1970' and his chapter on 'Victorian Origins' is particularly apposite; it would be tempting to quote it *in extenso*. The imperial system 'emerged by default not from design'; 'old networks and lobbies ... managed British overseas interests and the new ones that sprang up to promote commercial, land-seeking, emigrant, humanitarian, missionary or scientific enterprise'. The 'men on the spot' created what Darwin calls 'bridgeheads' where resources from Britain were added to local resources to make these bridgeheads grow or perhaps, in some cases, fail to do so. An infrastructure of telegraphs, steamships and railways linked these sub-empires to the metropole. All this was made possible by the dynamics of a changing mid-Victorian society and perhaps almost equally – certainly as

[1] Rotberg, 'Introduction', *Africa and its Explorers*, pp. 3, 10–11.
[2] Coupland, *Exploitation of East Africa*, Chapter VI, pp. 102–33; 102, 130, 131–2.
[3] Although there is an unfortunate tendency among several commentators to assume that the whole empire was like Kenya or Rhodesia with their gross injustices for Africans.

far as East Africa was concerned – by the largest bridgehead of all, India. Darwin is careful
to note, however, that British power and influence was not overwhelming; even the
bellicose Palmerston knew that 'British strength had its limits'. It should be emphasized,
in fact, that British governments generally were most reluctant to be drawn into overseas
commitments in the mid-nineteenth century.[1]

The detail of what was happening in Britain itself is best understood by consulting a
work by Peter Cain and Anthony Hopkins first published in 1993 and issued in a second
edition in 2002. They developed the concept of 'gentlemanly capitalism' in analysing the
emergence of British overseas power and influence. In other words, they emphasized the
importance of the City of London and the service sector connected with it; these were the
successors to aristocratic power, not the industrial bourgeoisie. Cain and Hopkins do not
reject the findings of historians of imperialism who concentrate on crises on the periphery
but these, they insist, must be linked to an understanding of what was happening in the
metropole.

The pages which Cain and Hopkins devote to East Africa in the mid-century serve
as a realistic corrective to many of the assumptions which post-colonial writers have made
about developments there, not to mention the position of Britain. Even in the late 1880s
the British government was still trying to maintain its policy of avoiding direct involvement
by putting East African concerns in the hands, not now of the Sultan of Zanzibar, but
of a new chartered company; in fact, when formal annexations came, it was a sign of the
failure of this policy and of British weakness in the face of foreign competition.[2]

The most important thing to be said about Grant in his career as an Indian Army
officer and explorer as well as in his later public life, is that he was a quintessential example
of a member of a 'service class' which was closely involved with the 'gentlemanly capitalists'
and their concerns. The 'service sector' consisted of administrators, engineers, surveyors,
soldiers and sailors who operated around the world and certainly included explorers like
Grant. These people were usually drawn from a middle class of minor gentry, teachers
and ministers of religion. The travel books and the journals they read certainly informed
them either accurately or otherwise on life in East Africa and other parts of the non-
Western world. The travellers, including Grant, had excellent relations with Lord
Palmerston and most probably assumed that his non-annexationist but forward policy
was the right one for Britain in a region like East Africa. Many connected with India also
believed in such a policy, not least Sir Bartle Frere,[3] the high official who befriended David
Livingstone, and hoped to promote commerce and Christianity in East Africa.[4]

It is significant that, after his return to service in the Indian Army following the
Expedition, Grant was to serve as an Intelligence Officer in the Abyssinian Expedition of

---

[1] Darwin, *Empire Project*, pp. 23, 24–6, 47, 52–5, 650–51.

[2] Cain and Hopkins, *British Imperialism*, pp. 3, 27, 115, 331–5, 397.

[3] Frere (1815–84) began his career in India in 1842, becoming Governor of Bombay in 1862. He befriended
Livingstone, negotiated the end of the Slave Trade in Zanzibar in 1873, became influential in the Church of
England, was a prominent member of learned societies and became President of the RGS. His career ended
when he was the unlucky Governor of Cape Colony from 1875.

[4] Cain and Hopkins, *British Imperialism*, pp. 308–9; Bridges, 'Historical Role of British Explorers', pp. 10,
12–13, 16 and *passim*. These arguments are set out with particular emphasis on the role of the RGS in Bridges,
'Europeans and East Africans in the Age of Exploration'. Although his origins were rather different, David
Livingstone came to identify himself with the 'service class'.

1867, one of the relatively few cases where there was direct British (or in this case largely Indian Army) intervention in Africa. Presumably he was chosen because of his experience of Africa. Even more significant after his final retirement was Grant's close involvement with what the present writer has termed 'unofficial imperialism' in East Africa.[1] In effect, figures connected with the RGS, four or five missionary societies, commercial interests, especially those centred on William Mackinnon, forward policy-favouring administrators from India were, to use Darwin's formulation, attempting to make a bridgehead there. Plans were certainly ambitious enough, to judge by the projects to establish a transport infrastructure in the region consisting of steamboats on the lakes, the use of elephants, a Cape to Cairo telegraph and so on.[2]

The 'unofficial empire' in East Africa may be said to have had some sort of actual existence in East Africa from about 1876 to 1894–5; by the latter date formal territorial annexations by Britain and Germany had taken place.

Four factors may be said to have made it impossible for the projects to succeed in creating a viable alternative to colonial rule as a means of promoting desired changes in African lives whilst also protecting British interests. First, difficulties arose in the case of the most prominent explorer of the 1870s and 1880s, Henry Morton Stanley. His relationship with the RGS was at best ambivalent and indeed also with Britain and its government even though he eventually became an MP. Grant himself knew not whether to welcome Stanley's confirmation that Speke was right about Lake Victoria and the Nile source or condemn his often brutal tactics. Stanley's activities became increasingly designed to further the interests of King Léopold II of Belgium and Léopold is the second factor making the survival of a British 'unofficial empire' unlikely. In September 1876, when delegates from various geographical societies, including Grant, attended Léopold's Brussels Geographical Conference, it seemed that the King's aims were philanthropic and internationalist and that they could be accommodated with the wishes of men like Grant or the commercial aims of William Mackinnon.[3] British Foreign Office officials were more sceptical and, indeed, it soon became apparent that Léopold's aims were to make a fortune from Africa, and the brutal exploitation in the Congo Free State soon began. There can be no doubt that when Léopold switched his attention to Africa, he was very much influenced by the reports of explorers, especially British ones such as Grant, Baker and Cameron, as well as Stanley (who was in Africa at the time of the Conference).

There is a powerful argument for saying that, if there was any one factor which precipitated the international rivalry which manifested itself in the Scramble, it was Léopold and his ambitions. This is a view which, by and large, is taken by Wesseling who says the Geographical Institutes played a special role in the partition of Africa.[4] Many hypotheses can be advanced on what caused the 'Scramble for Africa' but it seems clear that the international rivalry which arose in the last two decades of the nineteenth century seemed a very strong reason for grabbing territory before a rival power stepped in. In the

---

[1] Bridges, 'Towards the Prelude to the Partition of East Africa', pp. 89, 105 and *passim*.

[2] Bridges, 'RGS and African Exploration Fund'.

[3] Roeykens, *Léopold II et la Conférence*; Bridges, 'The First Conference of Experts on Africa'. 'I had a magnificent suite', reports Grant and he noted that eight different liqueurs were on offer at the opening ceremony all of which he tried, not wanting to appear to reject the King's hospitality. NLS, MS. 17916, Grant, Journal, 12 September 1876.

[4] Wesseling, *Divide and Rule*, pp. 88–9, 105, 119, 124–5.

face of power politics, schemes for a sort of philanthropic unofficial empire were not easy to sustain.

In any case, there was a third factor militating against the likelihood of success for an 'unofficial empire' in East Africa. Those involved in the various schemes were inclined to believe that Africans would react positively to their initiatives by becoming collaborators and even flock to the 'stations' the Brussels delegates planned to set up. It is certainly true that some stations were set up and missionary societies did produce converts – most notably the Church Missionary Society, which was given advice by Grant, in Buganda. In general, however, it proved to be a naive assumption that 'simple' African societies would immediately see the merits of conversion and a Christian lifestyle involving 'legitimate commerce' in their economic life.

A fourth factor which greatly complicated matters was the latent or sometimes actual hostility of Muslim influences from Zanzibar or Egypt. In the former case, Britain's anti-slave trade measures not only created an increased demand for slaves on the East African coast but also became causes of friction between missionaries' freed slave settlements and Arab slave owners. The Egyptian attempt to take over the Upper Nile region had been very much encouraged, like Léopold's activities, by the information British explorers provided about possible riches in the region. Indeed, the Khedive employed one of the explorers, the blustering and untruthful Samuel Baker, and other Europeans to establish this empire of the Nile. The general result was misery and disorder which no unofficial activities by British missionaries and explorers could ever mitigate. In addition, Egypt and the Nile were potential subjects of contention between Britain and France. The whole situation eventually required the use of considerable British military power to resolve it.[1]

Generally in East Africa, given the interests of Africans and Arabs plus increasing international competition, the chances of establishing some form of unofficial European overlordship became remote. It proved necessary to impose official rule. Yet, despite the failure of 'unofficial imperialism', its effects were important in that the ideas behind it continued to be pursued under the umbrella of official rule. In this sense, explorers like Grant did have an impact, not only on the period of what Coupland himself called the 'unofficial scramble',[2] but also on the period of the Scramble itself and subsequently. As the foregoing discussion may have indicated, to trace that influence does involve detailed historical investigation and it is over-simplistic simply to assert, as so many commentators seem to have done, that explorers were agents of imperialism without explaining what that means.

Grant in Retrospect

As far as Grant himself is concerned, it is clear that he did have some impact on the Africans he encountered and on various groups in Britain who took an interest in Africa, although discerning these impacts is not always a simple matter. Certainly, the view of some post-colonial writers that a narrative like Grant's does not really tell us anything about African societies is badly mistaken; especially in this case. Grant arranged his text to present information which, as it is hoped the annotation will help to demonstrate, does provide interesting and valuable human and scientific data. It is also a mistake to assume that Speke and Grant were in a position of power during their period in East Africa.

[1] Ibid., pp. 35–69.
[2] Coupland, *Exploitation of East Africa*, p. 319.

Sometimes, perhaps in ways they did not always themselves appreciate, Speke and Grant did have a local impact and became involved in local politics but there were also less obvious ways in which they made some intellectual impact on Africans and their understanding of the wider world. As far as the ostensible object of the Expedition is concerned, even the fact that he did not actually see the source of the Nile does not alter the significance of what Grant does tell us about the river and its course. His memorial in St Paul's justifiably refers to him as 'Grant of the Nile'. In the long view, the resolution of the Nile problem, interesting and important as that is in the progress of discovery and accurate delineation of the Earth, may be less significant than the way that the two men, and Grant in particular, for better or worse, began the process of bringing East Africans, especially those of present-day Uganda, into a political, economic, religious and cultural association with Britain.

If one attempts to fashion a final judgement on Grant and his significance, the question is not whether or not he was an 'imperialist'. That is a term which not only now has condemnatory overtones but which is also far too imprecise. It is better to see Grant as a key figure, perhaps in some ways *the* key figure, among the relatively small group of British geographers, administrators, businessmen and missionary leaders who were keen to make East Africa a focus of their efforts to bring about beneficial change in that region. Their attempts took place at a period when, as they rightly believed, the British government would be unwilling itself to take any part in their schemes. As a convenient shorthand, the efforts of this group in the 1870s and 1880s have been dubbed 'unofficial imperialism.' A. G. Hopkins has stated that: 'The imperial presence, informal and formal, was important, and now needs to be studied impartially, whatever view is taken of the morality and consequences of empire-building.'[1] The term 'informal' Hopkins uses may be taken to embrace what I have called 'unofficial imperialism'. For reasons given above, unofficial imperialism could not be successful given various developments in the later nineteenth century which affected Africa. Nevertheless, it was a period in which both African and British people learned more about each other and developed attitudes which were to persist well into the next century. On the British side, in particular, a large literature grew up, much of it the result of further travel and exploration, four or five missionary societies established interests in East Africa and some trading links were established. How far these interests actually encouraged the British government, when international rivalries finally forced it to become involved, to declare the need to defend a 'sphere of interest' is debatable. Whatever the answer to that debate, there is no doubt that the ideas and attitudes derived from the period of unofficial imperialism remained extremely important. James Augustus Grant's key position in that period both as an explorer and a later advocate of activity in East Africa makes him a person of greater significance than has generally been recognized. His main memorial now is the text which follows of *A Walk across Africa*. Many travel narratives are, in effect, more or less exciting adventure stories set in an exotic environment. In his book, Grant tried, and arguably succeeded in his attempt, to produce an account of East Africa which was systematic and informed by the science of the time, yet remained readable with plenty of incident, descriptions of new information on the environment and the flora and fauna and, most notably, a sympathetic account of the peoples encountered.

[1] Hopkins, 'Towards a Cosmopolitan History of Imperialism', p. 232.

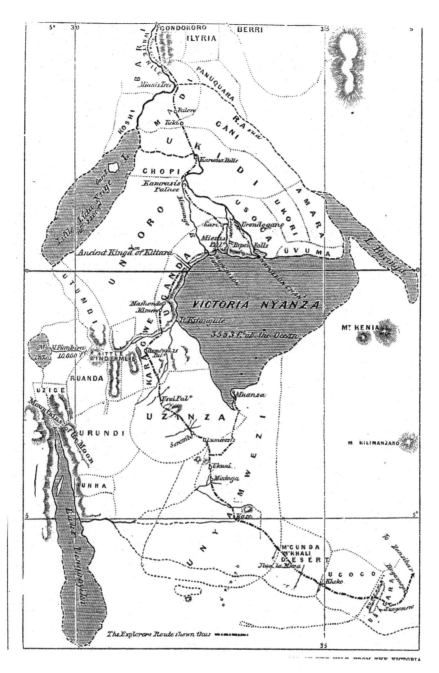

Map 9. Grant's February 1863 map showing the result of the Expedition redrawn for the *Illustrated London News*. This is a version of the original shown here in Plate 1. As reproduced in the *Illustrated London News* of 4 July 1863 shortly after the return of Grant and Speke, this gave the RGS and others in Britain an immediate idea of what the Expedition had achieved. Most notably, the map identified the source of the Nile as being in Lake Victoria. However, it also showed how Grant interpreted the general layout of lakes and rivers in East Africa and the Upper Nile whilst the Expedition was still in progress.

65

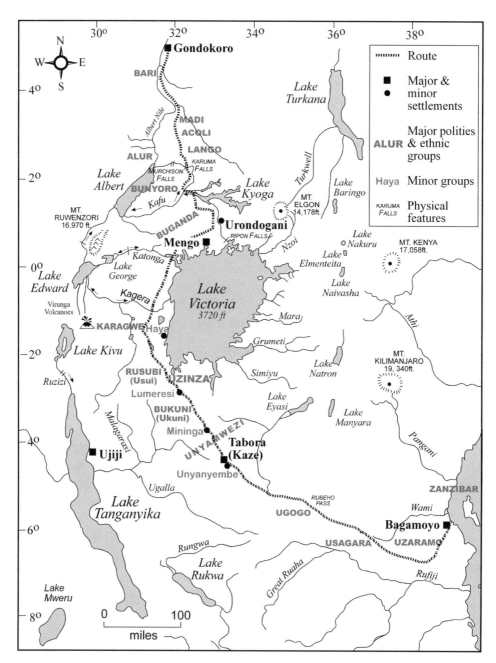

Map 10.   Route map of the Expedition from Bagomoyo to Gondokoro. This 'walk across Africa' lasted from 2 October 1860 to 15 February 1863. From the latter point, Grant and Speke were taken by boat down the Nile to Egypt; they were then no longer explorers but travellers. An attempt has been made to show the general position of major locations and ethnic groups encountered in the regions which are now Tanzania and Uganda. It is not claimed that a map at this scale can show the route with absolute precision. See also Plate 1 and Map 9 for an indication of how, in February 1863, Grant himself interpreted what had been achieved.

THE TEXT OF
A WALK ACROSS AFRICA
WITH EXTRACTS FROM THE JOURNAL

PREFACE [by J. A. Grant]

[Pages vii–ix]

IT is not without considerable anxiety and reluctance that this volume is submitted to the public. Having contributed my botanical notes, drawings, and meteorological registers to Captain Speke, I never dreamt of a separate publication. My Journal, however, was a very copious one, daily entries having been made during our expedition; and some personal friends seeing these notes, conceived that a selection from them, describing domestic scenes in Central Africa, might not be unacceptable. The geographical part of the expedition, and its brilliant result, had been fully treated by my lamented fellow-traveller; but further details as to the ordinary life and pursuits, the habits and feelings of the natives, and the products of the country, appeared likely to possess a certain degree of interest, if not of value.[1] This opinion was entertained by Captain Speke himself, who addressed to me the following request and advice on the subject:—

"79 ECCLESTON SQUARE, *1st June* 1864.

"MY DEAR GRANT,—I really wish you would write your experiences in Central Africa, from Kazé to Gondokoro. In doing so, try as much as possible to give, relatively, a corresponding valuation to each succeeding country,[2] in the order in which you passed through them—I mean, as regards the products and the capabilities of the countries, the density of their populations, and the different natures of the people, as well as the causes affecting them. Personal anecdotes, especially illustrative of the superstitious inclinations of the people, will be most interesting. But nothing can be of such permanent value to the work as a well-defined account of the rainy system and its operation upon vegetable life, showing why the first three degrees of north latitude are richer than the first three in the south,[3] and how it happens that the further one goes from the equator, the poorer the countries become from want of moisture. I maintain that all true rivers in Africa—not nullahs—which do not rise in the flanking coast ranges, can only have their fountains on the equator; but the people of this country have not learned to see it yet.[4]—Yours ever sincerely,

"J. H. SPEKE."

[1] The issues raised in this paragraph have been discussed in the Introduction, notably, the reasons for the publication of Grant's book, his journal, his science, his relationship with Speke and his interest in and relationship with the African societies he encountered. See above, pp. 2–22.

[2] Grant's mapping did attempt to delineate 'countries' but this was misleading; although territorialization of political authority was becoming more common, most East African societies, insofar as they thought of their own identity at this time, did not associate it with territorial space.

[3] On inadequate evidence, Speke was perhaps trying to show the effects of the seasonal changes brought about by the switch between the Indian Ocean's south-east and north-east monsoons.

[4] Even on the basis of evidence which was available in 1864 about Africa's rivers, this was manifestly not the case. A nullah was the Anglo-Indian term for a watercourse and usually meant a seasonal or dry one; see *Hobson-Jobson*.

I shall not attempt to comment upon the rain-system of the elevated land we traversed at the equator, but merely remark that in this region fruitful showers were constantly falling like dew.[1] The influence of these showers was, that although the flora was not so tropical as in countries which are at a far lower elevation, and though this quarter of the globe, from all accounts, receives less rain than any other portion of the equator, still the country might be termed a garden of fertility and richness.

My acquaintance with Captain Speke commenced as far back as 1847, when he was serving in India with his regiment. We were both Indian officers, of the same age, and equally fond of field sports, and our friendship continued unbroken.[2] After his return from discovering the Victoria Nyanza, he was, as is well known, commissioned by the Royal Geographical Society to prosecute his discovery, and to ascertain, if possible, the truth of his conjecture—that the Nile had its source in that gigantic lake, the Nyanza. I volunteered to accompany him; my offer was at once accepted; and it is now a melancholy satisfaction to think that not a shade of jealousy or distrust, or even ill-temper, ever came between us during our wanderings and intercourse.

The advice of my friend, as given in the above letter, coincided with my own views. The scenes and descriptions here recorded are from life—transcripts from my Journal made on the spot,[3] without any reference to books, or any attempt at embellishment. Some of the details may appear trifling—all of them are very imperfectly related; but they are at least *true*,[4] and they will help, I trust, to render my countrymen more familiar with the interior life of Africa, to which Livingstone and Speke have recently imparted fresh interest, and to which the attention of Christian philanthropists is now turned.

The plants which I had the pleasure of gathering during our expedition consisted of above seven hundred species, fully eighty of which were quite new to science. The most useful are noticed in this volume; and the whole collection has been presented to the noble Herbarium of Kew Gardens.[5]

The title chosen for my narrative was suggested by a circumstance which I may perhaps be pardoned for mentioning, as it forms one of many kind favours received from Sir

[1] It was upon the advice of Francis Galton, the most scientifically-minded member of the Council of the RGS at the time to whom Grant had shown his proposed Preface, that Speke's advice on the 'rainy system' was rejected. Galton was a pioneer in meteorology who had provided an appendix to Speke's book on Grant's weather observations. He was contemptuous of Speke's ideas which he dubbed 'crude and ignorant'. NLS, MS. 17909, Galton to Grant, 24 November 1864.

[2] As has been shown in the Introduction, this was not altogether true either in relation to the two men's earlier relationship or the situation in 1863–4. However, after Speke's death, Grant would not acknowledge that there had ever been any differences between the two of them.

[3] Again, this is not the case; as will be shown below, although Grant did occasionally quote directly from his journal, or echo its phraseology, it was, as he said, a 'very copious one' and in a semi-note form. Even a series of transcripts from it would have been unreadable. In fact, the book which follows is a very competent epitome of the journal.

[4] Grant may perhaps be forgiven for thinking that even his most immediate impressions will be objectively 'true'. Of course, first reactions by travellers will be affected by prior assumptions and current situations. Nevertheless, as I have argued in detail elsewhere, the immediate comment, where it is available, should be consulted for the purpose of obtaining basic data, as well as the more easily accessible secondary stage of a written-up journal or the third stage of a published book or article. Bridges, 'East African Travel Records', p. 190 and *passim*. It is fair to regard Grant's book as a reasonably faithful reflection of his first-stage observations even if this preface is manifestly affected by what has happened since the Expedition ended.

[5] See the section on Grant's science in the Introduction above, pp. 15–20.

Roderick I. Murchison, K.C.B.,[1] the able and zealous President of the Royal Geographical Society. Last season Sir Roderick did me the honour to introduce me to Her Majesty's first Minister, Viscount Palmerston, and on that occasion his Lordship good-humouredly remarked, "You have had a long walk, Captain Grant!" The saying was one well fitted to be remembered and to be told again; and my friendly publishers and others recommended that it should form the leading title of my book.

Dingwall, Ross-shire, *December* 1, 1864.

---

[1] As shown in the Introduction, Murchison (1792–1871) had important influences upon Speke and Grant. His standard biography is now Stafford, *Scientist of Empire.*

CHAPTER I

[Pages 1–10]

Plymouth to Zanzibar [30 April 1860–17 August 1860][1]

On the 30th of April 1860, Captain Speke and I embarked at Plymouth on board H.M.'s steam-ship Forte,[2] 51 guns, bearing the flag of Admiral the Hon. Sir Henry Keppel, K.C.B.,[3] and commanded by Captain G. W. Turnour.[4] Generally speaking, few persons care to hear details of a voyage to the Cape, although, in a frigate with 640 souls on board, a greater variety of incident as well as interest might be expected than in an ordinary sailing-vessel. Eight days passed smoothly; on the ninth day we gladly stepped on shore to enjoy the bright island of Madeira, with its scented shrubberies, which, though hotter than the temperature on board ship, were exquisitely refreshing and delightful. Here, for some days, dances, picnics, rides, walks about the picturesque ravines, and cricket-matches, formed the chief occupation. A farewell waltz was danced on board ship, and the deck was like a brilliant May-day, crowded with ladies wearing gay sashes inscribed with the name of our good ship Forte. Our next fete was on the Queen's birthday, when the poop was gracefully hung round with large silken colours, and the Admiral gave a bountiful entertainment. The crossing of the Line was duly commemorated in the old nautical style, with douche baths, and effective applications of steam-hose in the hands of joyous young middies.[5]

The lottery as to the hour of arrival at Rio de Janeiro was won by the only lady on board;[6] and on entering the magnificent bay—a most lovely sight—we were saluted by a

---

[1] Grant's chapter headings gave a summary of the content of each section and did not always give dates. They have been standardized here for the convenience of the reader, but the text itself has not been changed, apart from the additions taken from the manuscript journal, which are clearly indicated.

[2] This was a screw steam frigate of 400 horsepower. *Navy List*, 1860. Grant did not use italics for ship names and his practice has been retained for the text of the book.

[3] Sir Henry Keppel (1809–1904). This somewhat controversial naval commander, who eventually became an Admiral of the Fleet, was taking up his appointment as C.-in-C. of the Cape Station. It was possibly on this voyage that he had 'unlawful relations' with the wife of Sir George Grey, then Governor of the Cape, who did not speak to his wife again for 36 years. *ODNB*.

[4] Grant has given the wrong first initial to Captain Edward W. Turnour whose seniority dated from 1857 and who had been appointed to the *Forte* in January 1860. *Navy List*, 1861.

[5] That is, midshipmen; in effect, naval officer cadets.

[6] Grant's reticence about her identity is understandable. This lady was presumably Eliza Lucy Grey, née Spencer. Lady Grey whose (allegedly unconsummated) liaison with Keppel on this voyage led to the long estrangement from her husband (see above, n. 3). For her part, Lady Grey alleged that her husband had adulterous relations with many women, black or white. *ODNB*.

perfect storm of cannon and music from the Brazilian, French, and American men-of-war lying off the town. On landing, the mule carriages, the dingy sallow look of the people, the dazzling displays of jewellery, and the artificial flowers made from the feathers of gaily-plumaged birds, particularly struck us; and a drive to the botanical gardens to see the avenue of betel-palms, and a walk to the neighbouring woods, deepened the interest of Rio. As cholera raged in the town, several parties took steamer to the head of the bay, passing richly-foliaged islands in their course. Hence, forty miles of rail, through swamp and forest, brought us to the foot of mountains, which we ascended in omnibuses drawn by four mules, passing on the way others, handsome animals, laden with bales of goods for the interior. The drive was most interesting, every curve in the Simplon-like road unfolding fresh beauties. Treeferns, the papau,[1] and air-plants of every colour, clothed the hill-sides. At dusk we reached Petropolis, a hill sanatorium, where we remained two or three days, enjoying its many natural beauties and the fine cool air.

Embarking again at Rio, the day after we left shore our attention was arrested by the cry of "Man overboard!" The life-buoy was slipped and the cutter lowered. We saw the poor fellow struggling with the buoy, and then disappearing; but he was picked up, and the ship stood on her course again, the whole taking place in less time than I have taken in mentioning the fact. Oddly enough, the hero of the scene got a fortnight's salt-water grog for having been in some forbidden place when the accident occurred. During the night of the 22d June, the tramping, rushing to and fro, and shouting of commands on deck, told there was a storm, and sleep was impossible. Sixteen hours afterwards, the sea still raging in striking magnificence, and the ship running along at eleven knots, the cry was again heard "Man overboard!" and every one sprang to his feet. Such was the discipline that, from the time I first heard the alarm till I saw the boat lowered in charge of two of the officers, Wilkinson and Gye, only two minutes elapsed. The man is seen clinging to the buoy; in the dusk of evening he is lost sight of; the boat also disappears; the suspense is painful; "burn a blue light;"[2] the boat nears the ship; every one holds his breath, till at length the simple words, "All right, sir!" convey joy and gladness to all. The hardy English tar who had caused such excitement, actually assisted in rowing the boat back to the ship. We, of course, had our storm off the Cape—a midnight scene; and though we had four boats washed away, our mainyard sprung, and water rushing wildly through our cabins, the noble ship bore the strain most gallantly, anchoring the following day, 4th July, in Simon's Bay.

Sir George Grey,[3] the Governor of the Cape, whom the Forte was conveying to his seat of government, was a true friend to our Expedition,[4] and evinced the deepest interest in its progress. By his influence we obtained a grant of £300 from the Cape Parliament to supply us with a dozen baggage-mules. Two honourable members, who formed the minority, when the question was put, sagely remarked that "It was nothing to them *where* the source of the Nile was; every one knew it was south of the equator;"—not a bad guess!

---

[1] The pawpaw *Carica papaya*. *OED*.

[2] 'A firework producing a steady and vivid blue-coloured light, used for signals.' *OED*. Also known in the Royal Navy as a Bengal Light. Information supplied by Captain Mike Barritt.

[3] Sir George Grey (1812–98). Himself an explorer of Australia in the 1830s, Grey became Governor of the Cape and High Commissioner of South Africa in 1854 and later of New Zealand. He was always keen to promote British enterprise around the world.

[4] See Casada, 'Grey and the Speke-Grant Nile Expedition' and 'The Governor as Benefactor'.

In the Governor's body-guard, when he called for volunteers to cross Africa, there was not even this minority—not a dissentient voice was heard; all wished to go, and we selected ten—a corporal and nine privates of the Cape Mounted Rifles.[1] When paraded for our inspection, they reminded me of the Goorkas[2] of India. On the 16th July two teams of beautiful bays pulled up at the Admiral's house, Simon's Bay, where we then were, conveying these ten volunteers, who sat in the open four-wheeled vans looking very smart with their red caps, much to the envy of some Forte marines, who would have liked to go with us.

The embarking of the unmanageable mules was kindly effected by Mr Wilkinson of the Forte; and having bidden adieu to all her officers, we sailed that night for Zanzibar in H.M.'s steam-ship Brisk, 16 guns, Captain De Horsey.[3] Sir Henry Keppel and Staff, on a tour of inspection, were also on board. The first night was one of intense discomfort. We were shut up within the walls of a screen-berth 10 feet by 10, the cots bumping against each other, a rolling sea, and half-a-dozen mules kicking and neighing in their misery all night long, and directly overhead. The officers, however, were extremely kind, and their wardroom so cheerful, that we soon forgot these midnight annoyances. Every morning a man named Long, a sailor, who said "he knew how to manage mules, as his mother kept a team," would report that the mules were "all alive." This was *very* superfluous news, for we had been hearing their music overhead all night. Often at dinnertime Long would take the favourable opportunity of exercising his mules about the deck, and giving the middies a chance of a ride. At roll-call of a Sunday, some of the names of the crew sounded very oddly. For instance, three Kroomen[4] dignified themselves with the titles of "King John," "Soda-water," and "Prince of Wales;" while my servant answered to the name of "April." He was a jet-black man, and one of the "Tots" (Hottentots),[5] whose first essay as valet much amused us. I had never had pillow-slips on board, and he, thinking that I ought to possess them, found one for me the first night in the shape of my empty clothes-bag— a feat most creditable to his ingenuity and sense of cleanliness. On the 27th of July this same gentleman, while in Delagoa Bay, landed in green velvet shooting-coat, tight jockey-trousers, and neat regimental cap—quite a *swell* in comparison with his master; but though he was considerably blacker than the natives there, and very probably came originally from the same stock,[6] he told me that he did not understand a word of their language—a curious instance of negro affectation. These Delagoa men were the first genuine Africans I had made acquaintance with—bright-witted apparently, slim, and very ugly, with a wild avaricious look, eating and drinking anything you chose to offer them, and scrambling for the fag-ends of your cigars—all in strong contrast to the gentle Hindoo. What surprised me was, that near their conical grass huts they kept pigs, which

[1] Neither the mules nor the soldiers were to prove themselves suited to conditions in East Africa.

[2] That is, Gurkhas.

[3] The *Brisk* was a screw steam corvette of 250 horsepower under the command of Captain Algernon F. de Horsey whose seniority dated from 1857. *Navy List,* 1860, 1861.

[4] From the 18th century to the present, men of the Kru, a coastal people of the region of West Africa from Liberia to the Ivory Coast, have served as sailors for various navies and shipping lines.

[5] 'Hottentot' was a derogatory term long used by Europeans for the people encountered near Cape Town, now more correctly known as one of the San peoples.

[6] Not so: the San were older established in Southern Africa and distinct physically and linguistically from the Bantu people whom Grant saw at Delagoa Bay – probably Ronga or Chopi. Even though Grant seems to acknowledge that his servant was correct, he writes of 'negro affectation'.

are rarely seen near an Indian village. The breed was a very good short-nosed black kind. Two vessels in the harbour, manned by East Indians, were pronounced by the "Prince of Wales," and others who boarded them, to be fitted up for slaves; but the Portuguese governor assured us that no slaver had visited Delagoa since the last English man-of-war was there a year ago. This did not remove our suspicions, for the flat-roofed houses in the bazaar had every appearance of being receptacles for slaves.

On the night of the 1st August the Admiral indulged us all by landing on the uninhabited coral island of Europa. He was the first to "turn a turtle," and in low water capsized and sat upon the animal all alone, while a jolly middie, named O'Rouke, ran for help. The beast was so strong that he was carrying the "light weight" out to sea by the use of his flappers, which acted to some purpose on the making tide, and on the Admiral's legs in particular. The doubtful struggle lasted an hour and a half, when some sailors came up and towed the vanquished turtle ashore—weight, 360 lb. The birds here were so tame and insensible to danger that the men were able to knock them over when on the ground with sticks and stones. Four living turtle were brought on board and placed on their backs, with a swab each as pillow. When the ship was at anchor they were lowered with a rope attached to them, and swam about playfully below the stern of the vessel, coming to the surface for air every thirty seconds. The butcher, while killing one by cutting its throat all round and opening holes in its groins, remarked that its thick blood felt "cooler than a sheep's," and I observed it to be two degrees less than the atmosphere (78°). He also entertained the common belief that turtle will only die at sunset.[1]

On the 7th of August we lay off the wooden pier of the island of Mozambique, an extinct coral formation. Here Speke and I were able to converse, in their native tongue,[2] with Indian traders living away from their wives and families, whom they had left behind in India. We saw an interesting sight at a ship-provisioner's: in his back premises we found a sewing-school of negro boys and girls, presided over by a black sempstress; the boys were on one side and the girls on the other, Quaker fashion, all very neat and orderly, and engaged in making shirts. Farther on, in a dirtier quarter, women stood at a millstone grinding wheat, while others were alongside sifting it. One, a handsome gypsy-looking girl, had through her upper lip a large button of wood, which she sucked into her mouth most adeptly, in order to create a laugh and coquet for money. The cooks and henmen[3] were of a lower grade; and two lads, who also begged hard, were in chains, having a rod of iron between their ankles. They probably were recent investments, and could not be trusted at large. But what shocked us most deeply was seeing a poor woman brutally struck across the chest by her master, a black half-caste Portuguese, for attempting to go out without leave. Such are some of the vicissitudes in the life of a slave!—submission may obtain kind treatment, but even this is not always sure

The Portuguese troops in Fort Sebastian have Hindostanees amongst them, and they observe the pleasing (Spanish?) custom of doffing their caps during the "beat off" at sunset, and I understood from a sentry that they paid this respect also to the rising sun. The governor dined with the Admiral. He was in plain clothes, and wore a star. His crew

---

[1] There are seven species of marine turtles; *Chelonia mydas* is common in this part of the Indian Ocean but Grant did not identify the capture further. The size of the specimen suggests it was mature and thus probably at least 20 years old.

[2] Presumably, Hindi, as it is known today. Grant was qualified in Hindustani.

[3] 'Henmen' is not a term found in works of reference but presumably means a keeper of fowls.

of ten negroes had to wait in their boat during the operation of dinner. They were in man-of-war costume, and, remarkable enough, the head-dress was a black Highland bonnet with crest.

On the 10th of August a slave-vessel, Sunny South or Manuella, was captured with upwards of 500 slaves on board, 75 of whom were women. The scene they presented of nakedness, despair, disease, and hunger, was too loathsome to describe;[1] while, to judge from the ham and preserves I saw with Long, our mule attendant, who had been sent on board and made good use of the opportunity, the captain and officers must have fared well.[2] The crew were brought on board the Brisk for the Admiral's inspection. All came willingly, with the exception of one or two, who were a little rusty, requiring the assistance of one of our big marines to bring them to order. They continued smoking till stopped by the stern discipline of the ship's corporal, who received and ranged them in formal line to take their names. Eventually they dispersed over our ship, and, after some days, might be seen working quietly with the other sailors. The slaver, one of the fastest and most beautifully-proportioned vessels ever put together, went to the Mauritius, losing 105 of the poor starving creatures during the passage, and was afterwards wrecked near the point at which she was captured.

At Johannah Island (about 12° S. lat.)[3] we stayed four days taking in coals. To a rambler or lover of picnics by clear brown mountain-streams, margined by a most luxuriant flora, I know of no such charming spot within the tropics. Its harbour, however, is a dangerous coral basin or lagoon.

On the 17th August the island of Zanzibar came in sight; also four smaller isles, looking like great arks whose bows and sterns hung bushing over the waters. The island has a low appearance. The town, running along the shore for a quarter of a mile of flat-roofed warehouse-like buildings, is not imposing, its mud fort-towers and the flags of four consulates[4] being the only prominent objects. The bay is perfect, and we anchored close to shore in seven fathoms, this being the 108th day since we departed from England.[5]

The greatest heat encountered—and it was felt to be excessive—was when in 16° S. lat. at Mozambique, the medium temperature in the shade being, on the 7th August, 78°. Lat. 37° S., long. 21° E., on the 22d of June, after a storm during the night, shows the lowest recorded medium temperature, namely, 46°. Many a pleasant hour was whiled away during the two voyages—shooting, band-playing, rubbers at whist, amusements with the various dogs,—Tawny, a clever collie; Ossian, a deerhound; and Lumpus, a retriever, &c.;—sketching and photographing, drying botanical specimens, and picking up daily instruction in nautical observation.[6]

---

[1] In his journal, NLS, MS. 17915, 10, 11, 12 August 1860, Grant does record more details.

[2] For Grant's depictions of the crew of the slave ship, see Figures 17, 18 and 19, p. 97.

[3] The correct form of the name is Anjouan although its modern name is Nzwani. The latitude is 12° 15′ S, longitude 44° 25′ E.

[4] At this time, Britain, France, the United States and Hamburg.

[5] Grant photographed the harbour and the British Consulate; see Figures 8 and 10, pp. 89 and 91.

[6] During the subsequent Expedition, it does not seem that Grant took observations for position although he did record his results during the voyages. NLS, MS. 17915, p. 51. On the mainland, astronomical observing for position was Speke's province; his results were set out as Appendix D to his Journal, pp. 620–22.

CHAPTER II

[Pages 11–21]

Zanzibar and Bagomoyo [17 August–2 October 1860]

After anchoring at Zanzibar,[1] the Brisk had complimentary salutes from the men-of-war in the harbour namely, the Sultan's, the French, and H.M.S. Lyra. Next morning at eight the Admiral had a special salute from one of the Sultan's frigates; and again, as he put his foot on shore to attend a durbar, another was given in honour of our country—our ships returning each and all.

Colonel Rigby, an officer of the Bombay army, H.M.'s Consul,[2] entertained us with true Indian hospitality during the thirty-nine days of our stay; and his exertions greatly contributed to our getting away so quickly. He, having passed in six languages, acted as interpreter at the durbar, where the Sultan[3] was most affable, shaking hands with all.

Extracts from Journal: Meetings with George Rae[4] and Von der Decken[5]
Rae, of Livingstone's Exp*editio*n, his Engineer, came in and had a long talk x [with] him. Said the Zambesi can only be navigated 80 miles then you must go up the Shiré. I was amused at his idea of shooting. Never shoot Elephants out on foot–always from the Steamer. Two herds of 120 & 80 were one day seen. A bull hearing the steamer came towards it making a noise. The battery of rifles were opened on

[1] See Figures 8 and 10, pp. 89 and 91, for Grant's photographs and Figures 20 and 21, p. 98, for his sketches of boats in the harbour.

[2] Colonel, later General, Christopher Palmer Rigby (1820–85) was, as Consul, answerable to the Foreign Office but at this time his function as Agent for the Indian Government was more significant. Rigby was a noted linguist and also a resolute opponent of the slave trade who had raised the tricky issue of whether the Indian merchants in East Africa were British Indian subjects and, if so, whether they could own slaves. In the disputes between Burton and Speke which had broken out, he was an ally of Speke. For a full account of his life, see the work by his daughter, C. E. B. Russell, *General Rigby*.

[3] This was Sultan Seyyid Majid bin Said who ruled Zanzibar from 1856 to 1870.

[4] Perhaps true to his remit from Speke for his book, Grant included little on the European visitors to Zanzibar but more probably he thought that to report Rae's views on navigational possibilities in the Zambesi would be an implicit criticism of David Livingstone. George Rae (1831–65) was Livingstone's engineer on the Zambesi Expedition and was bound for Scotland to get a new river steamboat (the *Lady Nyassa*) constructed.

[5] Baron Claus Von der Decken (1833–65), an adventurous nobleman from Brandenburg, had come to East Africa in the hope of contacting Albrecht Roscher (see below, p. 81). Thwarted by Roscher's death, he climbed the slopes of Kilimanjaro in 1861, visited the Pangani Valley in the following year and then was killed on a subsequent foray into Somali country. In view of Grant's involvement with the execution of Roscher's alleged murderers which he chooses to describe in some detail, and Roscher's link to Von der Decken, whom he noted in his journal and also photographed (Figure 11, p. 92), it is odd that he does not mention encountering the Baron in his text.

him. Up he charged to the St*eamer* and in getting him 80 bullets were in his head. Rae approved of no other but the special bullet as it made a greater hole in the animal ... but not near so killing for antelope or Buffaloe ... With him went next door to Hamburgh House. Had cigars & there met Baron [*blank*] whom I heard of in London as a sporting character – he goes in a month from here to try to recover the journal belonging to Roscher a young traveller killed in Af*ri*ca: a few months ago. [NLS, MS. 17915, 17 August 1860]

Though the streets of Zanzibar are too narrow for a wheeled carriage, and the supply of water deficient, everything looked clean and neatly kept; and the shopkeepers, chiefly Indians, were respectful even to a painful degree, rising as we passed them. The bazaar is very abundantly supplied with vegetables, fruit, and dried fish; little butcher-meat, but liquor-shops abound, and water has to be purchased—the best quality being carried fully a mile from a hot spring, which bubbles from under rock, and tastes unpleasantly warm. Men in the marketplace have an odd way of hawking about their goods for sale. Goats, carved doors, beds, knives, swords, &c., are all paraded up and down, and their prices shouted out. The market for human beings is a triangular space surrounded by rickety huts, thatched with cocoa-nut leaves; and the parties of slaves (negro men and women brought originally from the interior of Africa), on being exhibited, are guarded by men with swords.[1] Some of the unhappy groups sit calmly in the marketplace, looking very clean, well fed and dressed, but with a depressed anxious look, saying to you with their eyes, "Buy me from this yoke of slavery!" It is a very striking though most humiliating sight to observe one of the Zanzibar rakish-looking crafts (felucca-rigged)[2] arrive from Ibo,[3] on the mainland, crammed with naked slaves for the market—all as silent as death. The Arab owners, gaily dressed, stand at the stern, and one holds the colours, in seeming defiance of the British Consulate, as he sails past. The price of slaves was low in 1860— only £3 each; and many Arabs would have taken less, as Colonel Rigby had released upwards of four thousand,[4] who became independent, living in a newly-made part of the town, and gaining a livelihood by fetching water and selling the produce of the island.

The Sultan was most polite in sending riding-horses to any gentleman who might request them from his stud of Arab descent. Colonel Rigby's horse-attendant took me to the spot. The *ménage* consisted of some forty horses and mares of Arab blood—twenty of them packed so close in line under a long shed that it would have defied any one of them to lie down. They stood upon an incline of wood six inches higher in front than behind, with heel-ropes so tight that the poor animals could hardly raise their feet; many of their tails shaved to the bone, others snipped round with scissors; not a sound one among them—broken knees, greasy and gummy legs, mangy skins, bags of bone; and the outer one of all such a skeleton that I listened to ascertain whether he breathed. Certainly

---

[1] See Fig. 7, p. 88, for Grant's attempt to photograph the scene.

[2] That is, with a lateen or triangular sail as in Grant's sketches, Figures 20 and 21, p. 98.

[3] Large numbers of slaves were being captured in the interior near Lake Malawi, as Livingstone was currently discovering, and being brought to ports like Ibo and Kilwa for dispatch to Zanzibar and perhaps on to Arabia. The legal position as defined in Britain's 1847 Treaty with the ruler of Oman and Zanzibar, was that this traffic was to be allowed; hence Grant's feeling of humiliation.

[4] In the end, Rigby released 8,000 slaves from Indian owners. From 1873, trade in slaves became technically illegal in the Sultan's dominions in East Africa following an enforced treaty with the British. Yet the status of slavery was to remain tolerated until 1907 in what had become a British protectorate.

the mares looked more comfortable when picketed in the morning in the open yard upon sand, and tied loosely by the head, with nose bags full of grain; and the picture around them of domestic animals had much the appearance of a home farmyard.

The climate of Zanzibar is very relaxing, owing to the humidity of the air, a great amount of rain falling during the year. The rain comes down in plunges, pelting showers, or like squalls at sea, and in the intervals any bodily exertion is attended with profuse perspiration and lassitude. I may mention that we pitched camp on the 13th September, for our Cape Mounted Rifles, on a rising ground near a pond behind the town, where they remained upwards of ten days. On the 28th, when on the main coast of Africa, three of these Tots were struck down with fever, a fourth was seized soon after, and then a fifth—all on the same day. Speke and I did not sleep in that camp, and our health was not affected. Colonel Rigby mentioned a similar case of the Assaye men.[1] Twenty-six out of sixty who slept inland were attacked with fever; those who had taken quinine recovered, while those who had not died. From this it would appear that risk attaches to certain constitutions from sleeping inland, away from the sea-breeze; although, on the heights of the island, where the soil is a rough red grit or friable clay, I should not anticipate danger.[2] But on these elevated spots there is this disadvantage, that no water is procurable; even in a well forty feet deep I observed there was none.

To one wishing to enjoy good health I would prescribe this recipe: Reside on the shore; be in a boat by sunrise; row to any point on the island, or to the exquisite living formations of coral; walk home between the hedgerows, amongst beautiful clove or mango groves; enjoy the refreshing milk from the cocoa-nut; observe the industry in the fields, the snug country-houses of the Arabs; examine the "diggings" for copal; look at the men washing the elephant-tusks on the sea-shore, or at the immense variety of crazy craft—in short, keep active, and you will find that there are many worse climates than Zanzibar.

The island has two crops of grain yearly, and four of manioc, which, with dried shark, is the staple food of the people. They cook it in every form, making also flour of it. One has only to walk of a morning along the roads leading into the town, to see the productiveness of this beautiful island. Negro men and women laden with mangoes, oranges, plantain, sugar-cane, grass, cocoa-nut, manioc, yams, sweet potato, Indian corn, ground-nut, &c., go in streams to the market. The return of these crowds is, in contrast, utterly ludicrous. Nothing do they then carry but a stick over their shoulder with a cut of stale fish hanging from it; and one wonders at the extreme poverty of the people in the midst of such abundance. Besides the above products, cloves, cotton, bajra,[3] sorghum, dall, coffee, tobacco, sessamum, grass, nutmeg, red pepper, betel-nut, catchoo-nut, jack-fruit, papau, almond, pomegranate, and the castor-oil plant, were all seen growing. To remark upon a few:—The mango-tree, met with everywhere, is splendidly umbrageous, more lofty than the variety seen in Indian topes,[4] and not so brittle. It yields two crops

---

[1] This is a reference to the men who slept in a similar area in 1859 of which complement, 26 contracted fever and 3 died. They were part of the crew of HMS *Assaye,* a steam frigate which had arrived to help thwart a rebellion by Said Thowanee of Muscat against Sultan Majid, whom the British had installed in Zanzibar. Russell, *General Rigby,* pp. 79, 108–11, 335.

[2] The use of quinine as a cure or prophylactic for malarial fever was now common but, as Grant's speculations emphasize, the real causes of malaria were not known.

[3] A form of millet.

[4] An Anglo-Indian term for a grove or orchard, especially one of mango trees: *Hobson-Jobson.*

yearly of stringy fruit; but there are better sorts, such as those from Pemba Island, to be procured. The clove-tree is planted in rows 20 feet apart, and after it has grown to the height of 30 feet, it seems to die, as if from the effects of ants. Cloves[1] have diminished immensely in value; what cost 25 dollars twelve years ago can now be purchased for one dollar; consequently the agriculturists do not replace the dying trees. The spice was being gathered by men on tripod ladders on the 6th September. Cotton we rarely saw. The cocoa-nut is the most common tree in the country—the husk, we observed, being used as firewood, and a capital salad is made from the crown of the trunk. The Arabs allow their slaves to cultivate the manioc or "mohogo" gratis, under the cocoa-nut trees, in payment for gathering the harvests of mango, cloves, &c. The growth of the ground-nut is very curious, creeping close to the ground, with a yellow flower and leaf resembling clover. On the flower withering the pod goes underground, where it matures. The coffee-tree grows luxuriantly, and the sugar-cane is very fine; pomegranate does not seem to succeed. The boundaries of farms are often marked by the castor-oil bush.

Miserable-looking camels drive the oil-press. Cattle do not thrive, though upon the neighbouring island of Pemba a small breed succeeds. Few butchers' shops are seen: the natives adopt the vegetable and fish diet, not being able to afford meat. Goats, when castrated and stall-fed, become very heavy, and their meat is considered a great delicacy by the Arabs.

Trade has considerably increased at Zanzibar. The shipping consists chiefly of large native craft—thirty to forty from Bombay, Muscat, &c., and but three or four ships from Europe and America. The merchants have their Exchange, if the place they daily meet in may be designated by this title. Here human beings, money, ivory, copal, cloves, cloths, beads, rice, cowries, opercula,[2] and goods from all quarters of the world, change hands. The largest single tusk we saw at Zanzibar weighed 165½ lb.; length, 8 feet 7½ inches; greatest circumference, 1 foot 11 inches—all of the purest blue-tinted soft ivory. It belonged to Mr Webb, the American consul.[3] He had also an enormous hippopotamus tusk, nine inches greatest circumference, and turning, like the horn of a Highland ram, once and a half round. As the tusk increases in size, a corresponding rise takes place in its value per lb. Tortoise-shell fetched 15s. per lb.; for hippopotamus ivory there was then no demand in Europe.

Several stirring events occurred while we were at Zanzibar. Once the Brisk got information of a slaver, but on sailing in search could find nothing of her. Again, after she had left, the Sultan requested Speke to take one of his ships of war and capture a slaver at

[1] Cloves had rapidly become Zanzibar's most important export crop. Seyyid Said, who had ruled Zanzibar from 1806 to 1856, encouraged his fellow Omani Arabs to plant the trees which had probably been introduced to Zanzibar and Pemba in 1819 by one Saleh bin Haramil al Abray, having earlier been obtained from the Molucca Islands by French merchants who tried to grow cloves on their Indian Ocean islands. Sheriff, *Slaves, Spices and Ivory*, p. 49; Gray, *History of Zanzibar*, p. 129. Much labour is required to tend and harvest cloves and one important effect was greatly to increase the need for slaves from the mainland.

[2] 'Opercula' are discs of various kinds. *OED*. To Grant it would have meant the discs taken from certain kinds of shellfish for use as ornaments or rendered into material to be burnt as incense. Opercula were, and still are, exported from Mumbai (Bombay). Sundaram and Deshmukh, 'Gastropod Operculum', pp. 20–22.

[3] The American traders from Salem in Massachusetts who sold cotton cloth (*merikani*) in return for East Africa's ivory, gum, hides and other products were the crucial spur to the development of East Africa's external trade in the earlier 19th century. See Bennett and Brooks, eds, *New England Merchants in Africa, passim*. On William G. Webb (1832–96), see ibid., p. 508n.

Panganee; but this also proved a fruitless chase; and as we were anxious to return to the preparations for the march, we left the Sultan's corvette at sea, and proceeded homewards, at 10 A.M., in an open boat of ten oars—distance to Zanzibar, 40 miles. We pulled till 5 P.M., found the current carrying us to the Indian Ocean, and put in for the night on a coral isle.

Our brave crèw of blacks, the same class of men who subsequently accompanied us upon our expedition, started again at four in the morning, rowing, off and on, till we reached home at eight that evening. The rowers accomplished this great feat without a grumble, singing the greater part of the way, though with nothing to cheer them for the two days but a few biscuits, sweetmeats, and oranges. Who can fail to admire such spirit![1] But we have the same class of African, when roaming amid his native wilds free from all control, committing murder without scruple; and an illustration of this came under our notice here. Dr Roscher,[2] a German gentleman, while exploring near Lake Nyassa, was murdered in 1859[3] by natives who coveted his scientific instruments. The sultan of the country, justly indignant,[4] sent four men to Zanzibar to stand their trial for the murder. Two were condemned, and suffered decapitation on the 23d August. I was present, going to the execution with the "surrung" or boatswain of the British Consulate, who cleared the way for me to get near the two men. They squatted outside the fort wall with perfect composure, naked from head to foot, except a waistcloth; neither tied nor handcuffed, and guarded carelessly by a few jesting soldiers. The Sultan's order to proceed with the execution not having arrived, a considerable delay occurred, during which the most intelligent-looking of the two prisoners stated to me that he had committed the act when in a state of unconsciousness! A jail official here announced that the Sultan wished the sahib to give the order, and I informed Colonel Rigby of the circumstance. He at once saw through the timidity of the Sultan, and said, as the sentence had been passed weeks ago, he could give no orders about it. Returning to the place of execution, where both men still sat, we found the mob had increased. An Arab boldly asked me, "Why should two men suffer for one white?" On my remarking that "Sooner or later the men must suffer—the sun was broiling over the poor creatures' heads—would it not be charity to go on with the execution?" the reply was, "They are mere animals, and have no feeling." Still no one would give the order. Again the Sultan was applied to. A rush was now rudely made on the crowd by half-a-dozen handsomely-dressed Arabs, brandishing their shields and swords. I thought it was a rescue, but kept my place; and it appeared they only wanted to get up to the prisoners, around whom every one laughed heartily at the momentary panic. Here one of the guard with whom I had been conversing laid hold of my arm, and, followed by a noisy drummer, the prisoners, and mob, we pushed on for a dozen yards, and

---

[1] NLS, MS. 17934, the proof copy of Grant's book, shows that the original word here was 'pluck'.

[2] Albrecht Roscher (1836–60), educated at Leipzig University, in 1857 produced a work, *Ptolemaeus und die Handelsstrassen in Central-Africa*, which ingeniously (but in my view entirely erroneously) sought to show that maps based on Ptolemy's information on Eastern Africa could be reconciled to modern discoveries. His object in going to Lake Malawi had been to prove the theory by practical observation. See Howgego, *Encyclopedia of Exploration*, III, pp. 786–7 and the references there. But Howgego, as this account shows, errs in stating that Roscher's killers were hanged. For a full account of Roscher's expedition, see Bontinck, 'Un Explorateur Infortuné'.

[3] The actual date was 17 March 1860.

[4] NLS, MS. 17934 has 'where it took place' rather than 'justly indignant'.

stopped in an open space where some cows were lying. A twig of grass pinioned each man, and they were made to sit on the ground, speaking calmly, while the crowd, all crushing around, joked as if at a holiday rout. Another delay occurred; no one had given the order. On being asked, "Might it commence?" I replied, "Yes, certainly; proceed." The executioner at once took his place, drew his sword, weighed it in his hand, threw up his sleeves, and slipped his feet out of his shoes, while the dense mass all seemed breathless. The executioner was a small man, respectably dressed, looking like an Indian "Nubbeebux."[1] The prisoners sat three yards apart, one slightly in advance of the other. The foremost was then ordered to bend his head, when, with one stroke, the back of his neck was cut to the vertebrae; he fell forward, and lay breathing steadily, with his right cheek in his own blood, without a sound or struggle. The executioner, after wiping his sword on the loin-cloth of the dying man, coolly felt its edge. The other victim had seen all, and never moved nor spoke. The same horrible scene was again enacted, but with a different result; the man jerked upwards from his squatting position, and fell back on his left side, with no sound nor after-struggle. Both appeared as if in a sweet sleep; two chickens hopped on the still quivering bodies, and the cows in the open space lay undisturbed.

Extract from Original Proof Copy Text
The sword was again wiped; two chickens hopped about undisturbed on the living body; the cows still lay in the space, and both men seemed to be in a sweet sleep. One never again moved, and the other, at my request, was put to death by a second slash on his neck.[2] [NLS, MS. 17934]

I left the spot, hoping never to witness such another scene; but I had the satisfaction of feeling that justice was carried out, and that had I not been present those murderers would have escaped punishment, owing to the effeminacy and timidity of the Sultan of Zanzibar. Their accomplices, each with a cleft log on his neck, were taken to witness the bodies: they were to have a free pardon, and to be sent back to their homes.

Extract from Journal: Further Information on Roscher's Killing
[One of the men to be executed] was the headman of his village – a traitor took Roscher into his house as a guest & then [killed him] with his mother-in-law assisting – two arrows from the <u>same</u> bow struck him at once – one in the throat & the other in the chest his only defensive weapon being a swordstick. He had ... two servants and one woman porter under the shade of a tree to cook when this blackguard invited him in. [NLS, MS. 17915, 23 August 1860]

[Much later Grant records] We have three men who accompanied Dr Roscher & friend to the Nyassa in our camp – the former was unwell and was generally carried, had a large telescope, made his observations at night ... had two loads of Botl. drying papers the flora being very rich. Though not hilly in that [area] collected white stones like bullets ... Roscher was killed having no guard with him ... [NLS, MS. 17915, 21 July 1862]

[1] Yule's *Hobson-Jobson* does not record the word in this form but from the entry for *Buxee* it would appear that the term suggests an official, especially a paymaster.

[2] Grant's motive in making the request was no doubt to prevent further suffering but in the final version of his description, he seems anxious not to be seen to be responsible for any of the disturbing events.

We had now a great deal to do in preparing for a three years' journey, in taking observations and working them out. For the benefit of photographers, I may mention that the "developer" succeeded. It was given me by Mr Apothecary Frost, E.I.C.S.[1]

The Sultan very kindly ordered that we should proceed across to the mainland of Africa (only forty miles) in his corvette, the Secundra Shah, commanded by Captain Mahomed Camese. We sailed on the anniversary of Havelock's entry into Lucknow, the 25th September.[2] The wind was ahead; our crew, a rough set of African lads; sandbanks were about; and after splitting our maintop-sail, and many oaths (strange to say, in English) from the native commander, trying to put things to rights, we put back for the night, anchoring close to where we started. The commodore, an Arab gentleman, came on board to see what accident had happened. He remained in charge, and early next morning, taking us as far as Choomba Island, returned in an open boat. The passage to the seaport of Bagomoyo was made in ten hours, but before we could land there was a row of three miles' shallow water, near the end of which two fine stout fellows came splashing through the water, shouldered me from the boat, and bore me like a child, *nolens volens*, in triumph over to the dry shore. These were our own "Seedee boys,"[3] or Africans, and they gave us a warm greeting. Everything was reported by Sheikh, the Arab in native charge, as ready for a start.[4] We tried to march on the 1st October, but the trashy bazaar—all its flints, fish, rice, grog, and sixpenny accordions, not worth more than ten pounds—had too many attractions for our men; and we did not get away till the following day, after having drunk success to the expedition in a bottle of Colonel Rigby's champagne, and seen our kind host into his boat on his return to Zanzibar.

[1] Grant does not in this chapter explicitly state that he himself gave up photographic work and reverted to sketching because of the unpleasant effects of working in the dark tent in tropical conditions. See the Introduction on Grant and Illustrations, above, p. 7.

[2] This was 1857 and a significant date for Grant as he was wounded, losing his right thumb and forefinger during the engagements.

[3] Really an Anglo-Indian term originally from the Hindi for 'Arab' or 'lord' which had come to mean Muslims from the west of Africa but which Grant now applies to any Africans. See *Hobson-Jobson*, p. 806. The Swahili word *sidiboi*, meaning a member of the crew of a warship, is clearly derived from it.

[4] Here Grant's original text in the proof copy noted that 'one of the Cape mules lay dead on the shore, having probably been hurt during debarkation'. NLS, MS. 17934. It is not clear why this information should have been omitted.

CHAPTER III

[Pages 22–43]

Journey to Kazeh [2 October 1860–25 January 1861]

ON the 2d of October 1860, we started from Bagomoyo on the East African coast for Kazeh, 500 miles in the interior of Africa, latitude 5° south. The party consisted of the following:—

Captain Speke, commanding.
    „   Grant, second in command.
Corporal, Cape Mounted Rifles, butcher.
Private "William," bugler and cook.
    „   Middleton, Speke's valet.
    „   April, Grant's valet, cook, &c.
    „   Lemon, useful generally.
    „   Reyters, fiddler.
    „   Peters.
    „   Arries.
    „   Jansen.
    „   "Jacob" Adams.
Said bin Salem, native commandant.[1]
Bombay, factotum, interpreter.[2]
Baraka, commanding Zanzibar men, interpreter.[3]
Rahan, interpreter,
Frij,   do,   } Private servants and rifle carriers
Uledi, valet,
Mabrook, valet, donkey-man.
Three or four women.
Sixty-four Seedee[4] boys,   } Carrying our kit and
115 porters of the interior, } barter.

[1] Said bin Salim al-Lamki (d. 1879) had been with Burton and Speke on the previous expedition. As neither Speke nor Grant could converse with him in Arabic as Burton had done, difficulties arose even before Said left the Expedition at Tabora (Kazeh). The Expedition thereafter became more dependent on its African personnel, especially Bombay and Baraka. See Bridges, 'Negotiating a Way', pp. 105–6, 115–16.

[2] Bombay was a Yao, born perhaps about 1820, who had been enslaved but released on his owner's death in India. He later joined the Sultan of Zanzibar's guard from which he was detached to join Burton's 1857–9 expedition to Lake Tanganyika. Later to serve Stanley and then Cameron, he died in 1885. Simpson, *Dark Companions*, p. 192. For Grant's photograph of him, see Figure 9, p. 90.

[3] Baraka proved to be a great rival to Bombay during this Expedition. See n. 1 above and the references there.

[4] From the Hindi *sidi* and Arabic *saiyid* originally meaning an African Muslim lord but by this time it signified any African. See *Hobson-Jobson*.

Eleven mules carrying ammunition.

Five donkeys to carry the sick.

Twenty-five Belooch[1] soldiers escorted us for the first thirteen stages, and we had the under-mentioned casualties during the journey:—

Private Peters dead;[2]

Five other privates sent back sick;

About thirty Seedees deserted;

One discharged;

113 porters deserted;

Eleven mules and two donkeys dead;

Fifteen out of twenty goats stolen; and

Our native commandant, the Sheikh, *hors de combat.*

The daily stages have been so well and so fully described by Captain Speke[3] that I shall not dwell upon them, but merely mention a few incidents descriptive of our life in the interior, and the fauna we observed. To accomplish this distance of 500 miles in 71 travelling days, of from 1 to 25 miles per day on foot, took us all the months of October, November, December, and twenty-five days of January, struggling against the caprices of our followers, the difficulties of the countries passed through, and the final desertion of our porters.

There being no roads, merely a rough track, no beasts of burden nor conveyances of any kind in the country, our whole kit was put into loads of 50 and 60 lb. each,[4] without lock or key, and the porters paraded up and down with them a whole day trying their weight—a ludicrous scene of confusion and squabbling. Their captain, distinguished by a high head-dress of ostrich plumes stuck through a strip of scarlet flannel, seeing all ready, led the caravan in single file with great dignity during the march. The pace was never more than three and a half miles per hour. When the captain put down his load for as many minutes as he thought necessary, the rest, a gang of naked, woolly-haired negroes, with only an airy covering of goat-skin in front, would also stop and refresh themselves with pipes, snuff, grain, dancing, and singing choruses. Generally there was an argument to settle how long the march should continue; and many were the excuses found for a halt, no water ahead being a common one. Once camped, and the loads stacked amidst cries of "Bomah!" or ring-fence, and "Posho!" or food, the first concern with every one was to receive his day's wages, consisting of either a portion of cloth or

---

[1] Men recruited from Baluchistan in India because they had a warlike reputation.

[2] See Figure 22, p. 98.

[3] Speke, *Journal*, pp. 16–83. In fact, as will be apparent, Grant's account is useful as a description of the periods when he was separated from Speke and because it has its own insights which are derived from the enormously detailed journal he kept, some extracts from which are interspersed in what follows. In his manuscript journal, pp. 61–116 cover the journey from the coast to Tabora (Kazeh), that is, the period between October 1860 and January 1861.

[4] This was the typical 'caravan' then used to provide trade and other contacts between the coast and the interior. It was based in part on the model of African, especially Nyamwezi, hunting and trading parties but more obviously on Arab traders' practice. Although to a limited extent animal transport did come into use, it was much inhibited by sleeping sickness or other diseases. Effectively, it was not until the railway was built roughly along the route the caravans took to Tabora and Ujiji that porterage was to be superseded. On the general question of porterage, especially as far as the Nyamwezi were concerned, see Rockel, *Carriers of Culture*.

one necklace of beads, while we retired to tents seven feet square, which were generally sheltered under a tree, with the kit and natives all round us, a motley crew.[1] If we had that day arrived at the headquarters of a sultan, an officer would call saying his master must have so many cloths, with various other articles, and he must himself have so many more.[2] Strong arguments and menaces would follow, and it sometimes took several days to the conference, as the sultan would be reported absent, or, more often, tipsy. However, once settled, if no porters absconded, we were free to proceed on our journey. I may here remark that nothing can exceed the noise and jollity of an African camp at night. We, the masters, were often unable to hear ourselves talk for the merry song and laughter, the rattle of drums, jingling of bells, beating of old iron, and discordant talk going on round our tents. No Hindoo dare be so rude in your hearing, but an African only wonders that you don't enjoy the fun.

We passed through three distinct countries[3]—Uzaramo,[4] Usagara,[5] and Ugogo.[6] Now at Kazeh we were in Unyamuezi—translated "Country of the Moon."[7] Our interpreters had been Africans speaking Hindostanee,[8] and seemed to learn the dialects as they went along, their native Kisuahili tongue being to them a useful basis.[9] The four countries were not governed by one king, but divided into provinces,[10] each from 20 to 30 miles across; and each had its despot ruler, the terror of travellers, who were forced to pay whatever tax was demanded without reference to any scale. The aristocrats or chiefs lived in no greater luxury than the poor, although they had a revenue from fines, taxes, a tusk of every elephant killed or found dead in their province,[11] and the produce of large herds of cattle and of farming.

---

[1] See Figure 33, p. 104.

[2] One effect of the increasing caravan trade between coast and interior was that African peoples who lived along the routes attempted to gain some benefit for themselves by claiming 'hongo' – in effect a transit tax. The practice of demanding hongo was one of the reasons why 'chiefs', who probably traditionally had rather limited powers, now increasingly claimed territorial jurisdictions.

[3] Grant's natural instinct was to try to identify 'countries' with territorial limits as he showed on his map (see Plate 1) but in fact, as noted above, pp. 20–21, territorial identities were at best vague.

[4] For the Wazaramo, see below, pp. 114–15, where Grant, following his systematic arrangement of information, deals with the people encountered.

[5] The Sagara are also treated in detail below, p. 115.

[6] This was the region most feared by travellers from the coast because, as is explained later, they had come to rely heavily upon exactions on the caravan trade.

[7] Enormous confusion has been caused by the assumption that this is what *mwezi* implies, not least because some former and even modern commentators have tried to equate Unyamwezi with maps based on Ptolemy's information about the 'Mountains of the Moon'. See Introduction above, pp. 38–43. In fact, the Nyamwezi people were given the name not by themselves but by other peoples; the term implies that they were people from the west where the new moon rises. See Roberts, 'The Nyamwezi', p. 117.

[8] The use of Hindustani by Speke and Grant must have seriously delayed and often distorted communication with both their porters and the local Africans they encountered. See Bridges, 'Negotiating a Way', pp. 106–7.

[9] Kiswahili is in essence a Bantu language with some Arabic and other alien additions and therefore closely related to the tongues spoken by the peoples among whom the explorers now found themselves. The language was in the process of becoming a lingua franca in the interior as well as along the coast.

[10] Again, Grant is trying to impose order to make the situation comprehensible in European terms but, as noted above (n. 3), the notion of 'countries' and 'provinces' is misleading.

[11] This was another manifestation of the territorialization of power but the right was by no means uncontested as the demand for ivory increased. The matter is much complicated by the existence of stores of dead ivory which Grant mentions. See Bridges, 'Elephants, Ivory', pp. 203, 209–10.

Figure 6. Nyamwezi men who had reached the coast where Grant photographed them. They would have been ivory traders in their own right or by 1860 probably porters employed by coast traders. He said they were 'fine muscular men'. RGS Collection, SOO11715. Reproduced by permission of the RGS.

Figure 7.   Photograph of the slave market in Zanzibar and also the scene of the execution of Roscher's alleged murderers. Some women slaves are seen on the right. Other dim figures may be seen but owners ran away rather than be photographed. RGS Collection, SOO11716. Reproduced by permission of the RGS.

Figure 8.   Photograph of Zanzibar harbour seen from the door of the British Consulate. RGS Collection, SOO11717. Reproduced by permission of the RGS.

Figure 9.   Photograph of the all-important 'Bombay', effective leader of the porters, adviser to Speke and Grant, interpreter and frequently negotiator with local potentates. RGS Collection, SOO11718. Reproduced by permission of the RGS.

Figure 10.   Photograph of the British Consulate and the harbour in Zanzibar. RGS
Collection, SOO11955. Reproduced by permission of the RGS.

Figure 11.   Photograph of Baron Claus Von der Decken, the Hanoverian explorer who had intended to search for the murdered Roscher but went on to explore on his own account. See note in Chapter II, p. 77. RGS Collection, SOO19041. Reproduced by permission of the RGS.

Figure 12. Photograph of man in village. Grant's notes do not reveal whether this is a scene in Zanzibar or on the mainland coast. RGS Collection, SOO19042. Reproduced by permission of the RGS.

Figure 13.   Photograph of an unexplained scene. However, the imposing building seen dimly in the background looks large and important enough to belong to the Sultan of Zanzibar or possibly the British Consul, General Rigby. RGS Collection, SOO19119. Reproduced by permission of the RGS.

Figure 14.   Photograph of thatched building and a second unexplained scene. Perhaps this is the same building as can be seen in Figure 13. RGS Collection, SOO26109. Reproduced by permission of the RGS.

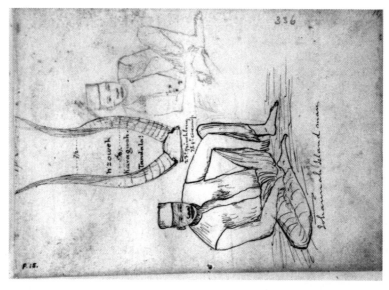
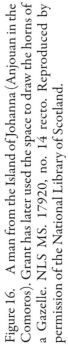

Figure 16. A man from the Island of Johanna (Anjouan in the Comoros). Grant has later used the space to draw the horns of a Gazelle. NLS MS. 17920, no. 14 recto. Reproduced by permission of the National Library of Scotland.

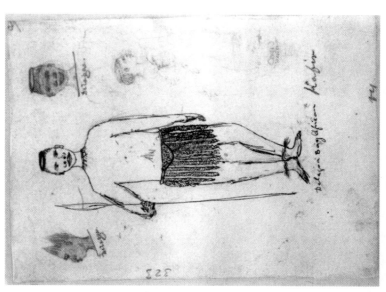

Figure 15. 'A Zulu Kafir' is how Grant described one of the dreaded Watuta (Ngoni) warriors who had moved into East Africa as a consequence of the upset caused further south by the rise of the Zulu Kingdom This warrior was encountered at Delagoa Bay. NLS MS. 17920, no. 12 verso. Reproduced by permission of the National Library of Scotland.

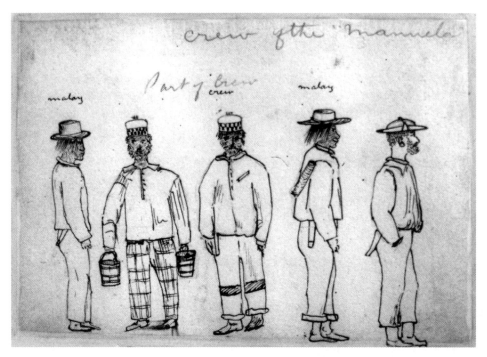

Figure 17.   Some of the crew of the Spanish slave ship, *Manuela,* apprehended by the Royal Navy ship on which Speke and Grant were being carried to Zanzibar. See Chapter I. NLS MS. 17920, no. 14 verso. Reproduced by permission of the National Library of Scotland.

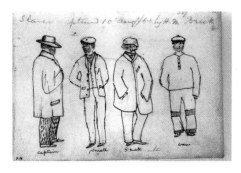 

Figures 18 and 19.   The other members of the slave ship's crew. The captain is first in 18 and 'a surly little blackguard' on the left of 19. Grant received a share of the prize money. NLS MSS. 17920, nos 15 recto and 15 verso. Reproduced by permission of the National Library of Scotland.

Figures 20 and 21. Grant's sketches of some of the boats to be seen in Zanzibar harbour in 1860. NLS MSS. 17920, nos 18 verso and 19 recto. Reproduced by permission of the National Library of Scotland.

Figure 22. Funeral of Private Peters of the Cape Mounted Rifles who had volunteered to accompany the Expedition. The usefulness of these men was limited and the survivors returned to the coast a month or so after this. NLS MS. 17920, no. 19 verso. Reproduced by permission of the National Library of Scotland.

Figure 23. Some Zaramo people pictured c. October 1860. Grant says they were smeared with red clay. NLS MS. 17920, no. 20 recto. Reproduced by permission of the National Library of Scotland.

Figure 24. A scene in Uzaramo. NLS MS. 17920, no. 21. Reproduced by permission of the National Library of Scotland.

Figure 25. 'Hot spring with active and extinct crater' is Grant's not very enlightening title for this scene in Uzaramo. NLS MS. 17920, no. 22 verso. Reproduced by permission of the National Library of Scotland.

Figure 26. 'Smelting furnace of four bellows in Forest' is Grant's title but this picture is a puzzle. Despite being grouped with others from the October 1860 period in Uzaramo, it is apparently dated December 1861. NLS MS. 17920, no. 20 verso. Reproduced by permission of the National Library of Scotland.

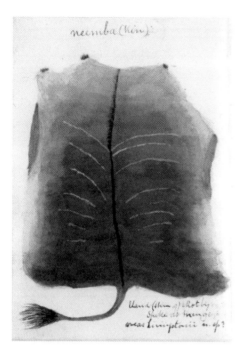

Figure 27. The skin of an eland shot by Speke, November 1860. NLS MS. 17920, no. 23 verso. Reproduced by permission of the National Library of Scotland.

Figure 28. Mountains and huts seen in Usagara, October 1860. NLS MS. 17920, no. 24 recto. Reproduced by permission of the National Library of Scotland.

Figure 29. Hills in Usagara, November 1860. NLS MS. 17920, no. 25 recto. Reproduced by permission of the National Library of Scotland.

Figure 30. A rhinoceros shot by Speke in November 1860 in Ugogo. NLS MS. 17920, no. 25 verso. Reproduced by permission of the National Library of Scotland.

Figure 31. 'Outline of Usagara hills', October 1860. NLS MS. 17920, no. 26 recto. Reproduced by permission of the National Library of Scotland.

Figure 32. African heads, c. October 1860. As Figures 17, 18 and 19 show, Grant found it easier to draw fellow Europeans than Africans but he continued to practise as with these heads. For the small vignette of hills, see Figures 32A and 33. NLS MS. 17920, no. 24 verso. Reproduced by permission of the National Library of Scotland.

Figure 32A. 'Church' hills seen from Kinyenge. Because of their appearance, 'the Church' was the name Grant bestowed on a range of hills near their camp in Kinyenge. His very small sketch appeared among the heads in Figure 32. From these hills, as his note explains, Grant drew the scene shown in Figure 33.

Figure 33. 'Our camp at W. Kinyenge [at about 38°E in Ugogo] with flat range and Useke hills from "the church."' The camp is on the left and not very distinct. For 'the church', see Figure 32A. NLS MS. 17920, no. 29 verso. Reproduced by permission of the National Library of Scotland.

Figure 34. Speke's tent at Inenge, November 1860. NLS MS. 17920, no. 27 recto. Reproduced by permission of the National Library of Scotland.

Figure 35. 'The East Coast Range' at Inenge, November 1860, but it is not clear why Grant chose this title for the hills so far inland. Nor, unfortunately, is his depiction very successful. NLS MS. 17920, no. 27 verso. Reproduced by permission of the National Library of Scotland.

Figure 36. The 'Robeho Pass' at Inenge, November 1860. NLS MS. 17920, no. 28. Reproduced by permission of the National Library of Scotland.

Figure 37.   Tembe (fortified settlement) in Eastern Kinyenge, 21 November 1860. NLS MS. 17920, no. 29 recto. Reproduced by permission of the National Library of Scotland.

On leaving the coast our path ran up a broad, flat, dry valley of grass and trees for twenty marches. At the ninth stage, from a ridge of rising ground composed of small pebbles in rotten sandstone, we saw distant hills to the north-west, and had a good view of the sluggish, winding Kingani,[1] which we did not altogether lose sight of till the thirteenth march. We crossed the East African chain at an elevation of 4750 feet,[2] and got into Ugogo, a plateau without a river, and its "neeka"[3] or deserted land requiring abundant rain to make it look at all green. These hills were tame in general outline; the flora also was poor. We next hailed with delight the country of Unyamuezi, where water was abundant, oozing from under rocks on the surface or from outcropping rock; and there was a pleasant confiding air of homeliness and repose in the people, so different from those worthless races we had found such trouble in passing through.[4]

The climate, with wind behind us on the march, was cooler and less creative of thirst than that of India. Our dress was an English summer one; no turbans were necessary; the evenings were delightfully cool; the sun seldom set in a haze, and one morning of mist, the 24th January, was the only one we had. At night, feeling quite secure from attack, we never slept in our clothes, but covered ourselves with from one to five thin blankets, according to the elevation. During the last week of November, previous to the regular rains, our camp at Ugogo suffered from heavy north and west gusts of wind, which set in at 9 A.M., or from dust-storms lasting two or more hours. In December the rain for the time would almost crush our little single canvass tents, but it afterwards imparted to the air that delightful freshness of the "cold season" in the Punjab. Fine, however, as this country appeared to us, nearly all suffered from an acclimatisation fever,[5] which rapidly undermined our strength. The five Tots were sent back from its effects; all were martyrs to it, suffering from pains in the head, eyes, and limbs—ague, perspirations, drowsiness, startled sleep, and delirium. The only remedies in our power or skill were calomel and jalap,[6] quinine, the first thing in the morning, and strong soup or hot grog when in store. The following is the report, 27th October 1860, and about the same number of men were in hospital every morning:—

William, 10 laud., 2 quinine.

Middleton, 10 jalap, 2 calomel.

Lemon, Corporal, April, Jacob, } 2 quinine each.

Rahan, 2 pills col.;[7] Speke dressed wound.

---

[1] The Kingani was one of those rivers flowing into the Indian Ocean which were to be unsuccessfully tested almost 20 years later as possible water routes into the interior by enthusiasts whose efforts explorations like those of Speke and Grant had encouraged. See Bridges, 'RGS and African Exploration Fund', p. 30.

[2] Or it might be better said, reached the ancient peneplain which characterizes the vast plateau which makes up most of East Africa. Grant's not especially successful attempts to depict the landscapes encountered in this period can be seen in Plate 3 and Figures 25, 28, 29, 31, 33, 35 and 36, pp. 100, 101, 102, 104, 105.

[3] More accurately, *nyika* in Kiswahili.

[4] Grant's attitude gradually changed as he became more understanding of Africans. However, the demands for 'hongo' on the route to Tabora were very trying for travellers.

[5] Presumably malaria. Although the explorers had quinine, its use as a prophylactic was not understood.

[6] Calomel (Mercuric oxide) and jalap (from a Mexican plant's root) were both purgatives.

[7] This is colocynth, a drug derived from the bitter apple, used as yet another purgative. *OED*.

This does not include the doses given to natives in camp, who had the greatest faith in the medicine chest, often sitting round us as it was administered, and asking for the dregs of the glass! We had an amputation case. The men were practising with their rifles at a suspended bottle, and Rahan blew off one of his middle fingers, and came bellowing with rage into camp, saying, "Look here what I have suffered by being induced to come upon this horrible journey! My life-blood is running," &c. He had evidently been drinking. No time was to be lost. I thought from the first that I should have the operation to perform, and Speke requested me to do it. I overcame the feeling of reluctance, and asked for a knife. The Sheikh's razor performed a beautiful flap operation, taken from the inside of the hand, and covering the knuckle. Rahan shrank at first from it, crying out most lustily, and abusing us and Baraka for having brought this misfortune upon him. At last he said, "Go on: do it." When half through, he pulled away his hand, and gave a tremendous scream; but with great coaxing the affair was finished; and, without having tied up any arteries, in a very few days he had the use of his hand, and recovered his temper.[1]

We never could understand the disease that was fatal to the mules and donkeys. Speke and our Tots would have known a tzetze fly had they seen one, and we therefore concluded that their deaths must have been caused by their eating deleterious grasses, for they lived on what they could themselves pick up, having neither corn nor hay. Here are the notes on one case: "30th Dec. '60.—Mule (the last red one) swollen all over the body for the last two days; breathing thickly; discoloured water oozing from the body; on making incisions, blood and water came freely; not relieved; half of tail cut off; no blood, only water came; on pressing the body with thumb, the impression remains. Miracle if he recovers"—which he never did.[2] The donkeys had much more spirit than the mules. We lost only three out of five during the march, though overladen with bundles, pots, and kettles. The wild zebra and donkeys mingled and fraternised by distant neighs.

Some of the daily incidents seemed so strange and interesting to me that I noted them rather fully, and think a few quotations from the Journal now and then may not be unacceptable. Extract: "8th Nov. '60.—Peters reported ill yesterday; teeth clenched, eyes rolling, body rigid, pulse 120; wouldn't speak; had been asleep in the sun. I recommended bleeding. To-day he had ridden the march on a donkey, but could not sit up; had to be lashed to the beast. He now lay on the ground seemingly unconscious, his stomach violently heaving. At 3 P.M. the caravan was under way again. Lashed Peters on the saddle like a Mazeppa![3] Fever still upon me." "November 9th.—'The man is dead,' said the corporal, while we were busy painting. We were all shocked. He had died calmly without the knowledge of his comrades. I had fever to-day." "November 10th.—Funeral, 5 A.M. The body sewed up in an American cloth; carried in a blanket, four Tots with a corner each. The corporal, Speke, and myself formed the procession, the corporal

---

[1] No doubt Grant's own experience of a hand wound was brought into play here.

[2] It is interesting that at this early stage, Grant is able to draw on experience among travellers and local people (including Speke on his previous expedition) that the tsetse fly was associated in some way with trypanosomiasis (sleeping sickness). Perhaps Grant was right to assume this was not sleeping sickness; East Coast fever may be what killed these animals.

[3] Ivan Mazepa (1639–1709), was an influential Ukrainian whose colourful military and administrative career made him a still despised figure in Russia, and also inspired a wholly legendary story that he had seduced a young Countess, Theresa. The elderly husband had his revenge by tying the naked Mazepa to a wild horse. Byron adopted the story for his long poem, *Mazeppa* of 1819, doubtless the source of Grant's knowledge.

carrying a hatchet and two sword-bayonets to extend the grave if necessary. Found only a grave one foot deep, and partly filled in with grass. Hatchets and bayonets were used, and we got a place large enough. I read the service, and afterwards returned to camp.[1] Sketched a 'Goodae' tree.[2] Had fever, no ague, but mind wandering; very drowsy; disturbed rest. All the niggers[3] exceedingly jolly—singing, playing bells, horns, drums, &c."[4]

At our first camping-ground by the coast there was not a drop of water to be seen—a sad calamity! But Bombay, an old traveller, and always ready-witted, relieved the minds of the Tots by telling them that a well would be dug after the camp had settled down a bit, which literally was the case. While near the Kingani—a true African-looking river, with its tall reed edges—we had abundance of water, but mawkish. It was a white, muddy, sluggish stream 40 to 50 yards across, with steep clay banks 16 feet above the water, and winding so much that no steamer could make its sharp turns.[5] Canoes ferried it. One well, or puddle, a short distance from this river, made our plated spoons quite black, and turned blue test-paper red. In Ugogo the wells were from 11 to 15 feet deep, of bluish clay upon rock, the water nitrous, and nearly the price of beer. Sometimes, when there was no water for thirty miles, a small quantity would be carried in gourds, where, from the shaking and heat, it soon became nauseous or insipid.

Extract from Journal: Problems with Water
Scarcely any water today. In pouring out the tea, it comes out literally as <u>black</u> as <u>mud</u> although poured in the pot <u>white</u> ... the plated teaspoons were discoloured with it ... I put some blue test paper into it and it turned blotting paper red. [NLS, MS. 17915, 8 October 1860]

Our Zanzibar Seedees have a very polite custom: when they see any one of the camp arriving fagged, done up, and parched with thirst after a long march, one's thoughts perhaps running on displays of fruit in shop-windows, ices, or lapping water in a stream, they run out, like good fellows, to meet you with a drink. Let it be hot, bitter, or black as ditch-water, thirst is allayed; and, on looking to see whence the luxury came, you observe the men standing in a miry pool, like dogs on the 12th of August, while the poor birds, disturbed by the intrusion, wait their turn in the trees overhead.

There is not a plough in the country; a broad hoe answers equally well.[6] Men with small axes cut down the forest; the trees and rubbish are burned; the long-handled iron hoe, chiefly in the hands of the women, turns over the light soil; and the seed is dropped into a hole made by the woman's toe, and covered up. Manure is seldom used; six months' fallow would seem to be its substitute. Fields close to villages occasionally get manure, or red clay heaps are spread over the dry, drifting sand-soil of Ugogo. We had no opportunity

---

[1] Figure 22 shows the funeral, p. 98.

[2] See Plate 2. It has not been possible to identify the tree botanically.

[3] A commonly used term at the time but even then seen as derogatory; Grant subsequently ceased to use it.

[4] The foregoing extract is not a completely faithful transcription of the original journal entry which, for example, says under 8 November that Peters 'lay on the ground like a dog'. Interestingly, too, Grant originally used a Scotticism 'a thing' on 10 November to refer to the grave. NLS, MS. 17915, 9, 10, 11 November 1860.

[5] See above, p. 107, n. 1.

[6] Hoe culture was the norm and well-adapted to the environment; many soils later proved difficult to plough and there was the added difficulty of finding suitable beasts to pull a plough.

of seeing the reaping.[1] Copal holes[2] are only found between the coast and the African chain of hills. The country produces chiefly sorghum, bajra,[3] sweet potato, and Indian corn, with tobacco, pumpkins, a small quantity of rice, manioc, ground-nut, and grains mentioned in Appendix to Speke's book.[4] Mushrooms grow wild, and are eaten considerably. Tomato is not eaten. Tamarind, figs, honey in hollowed logs placed up trees in the forest, rich and good. The chief staff of life is stirabout, made from the sorghum,[5] and from this grain they also produce a coarse, intoxicating, thick liquor, tasting like wort. In Ugogo they manufacture small pillars of salt by evaporation, but it is dirty in colour, with a disagreeable bitter taste. Fowls, eggs, and goats were occasionally brought into camp to be bartered for cloth, tobacco, or beads, as there was not a coin—copper, silver, or gold—that they would take in exchange for their produce.

We met with no cattle, except those collected for export at the coast, until we had proceeded twenty marches into the interior, at which point, and farther on, we saw a small humped breed, the prevailing colours being white and red—the bulls with large humps and small horns.[6] The goats were of the ordinary short-haired sort, never used as milkers; and sheep, though rarely seen, were of the "doomba"[7] or fatty-tailed variety, the size of a year-old Leicester, costing nine yards cotton stuff. Small bandy-legged brindled dogs followed the Wagogo.

Food was not abundant. As it was the dry season, we had to trust to chance and our rifles. One night our entire dinner consisted of two ears of Indian corn, eaten with salt; nothing besides, neither bread nor rice. Bombay very kindly, in the middle of this repast (which was laid out on our "service" of reversed tin lids placed on the tops of wooden boxes as tables), went and brought a cold grilled chicken, very small, and awkwardly flattened out. Though our hunger prompted us to accept the offer, we declined with many thanks. But, while sitting rather silently over our empty tin covers, he again appeared, having foraged five live chickens—thus securing for us not only that night's supper, but food for the next two days. Our supplies of grain frequently ran out in camp, but the sportsman need never starve in the country we passed through; for although we could not always find large game, there were sparrows, doves, or guinea-fowl to be had; while persons who do not sport may take note of the herbs gathered by the natives, and live upon them at a pinch. The spirit of our men sank, and a deep, gloomy silence hung over camp, when we had no grain, and continuous days of bad sport with our rifles. Not a man would obey orders; they refused to march, and discipline had to be upheld in several instances by inflicting corporal punishment for the crime of stealing cloth to buy food.

[1] However, Grant was later able to review and illustrate the agricultural process in Unyamwezi. See below, Chapter IV, pp. 119–20, and Plate 4.

[2] Copal was an important product of the coast region. Gum copal is the sap of partly fossilized trees and was until later in the century, when oil-derived substances came into use, a vital raw material for varnishes used to protect e.g. steam locomotives.

[3] A Hindi term for a form of millet. *Hobson-Jobson*.

[4] Speke, *Journal*, pp. 625–56. But this was a long, scientifically arranged list of plants compiled by Grant himself. Not to mention his authorship here seems false modesty.

[5] Sorghum is a form of millet and probably the original African grain, more drought resistant than the non-native 'Indian corn' or maize which was apparently becoming attractive to growers.

[6] These were probably the type of zebu cattle now known as 'small East African shorthorn'. Middleton, *Encyclopedia of Africa*, I, p. 50.

[7] 'Doomba' is yet another Hindi term used by Grant, but is rendered as 'doombur' in *Hobson-Jobson*.

One Seedee, a powerful fellow, roared for mercy during the flogging, and disclosed to us who had been his accomplice in the theft. He was therefore excused the third dozen of lashes, and carried away bound, to be expelled from camp next morning.[1]

We foraged zealously for the camp, and succeeded in giving to every one a little meat. The black rhinoceros would rarely charge, even though he saw us standing close to him; but they always afford considerable excitement by the feints they make, and by their deep hoarse grunt. Their ears were often torn and their tails mutilated, apparently in consequence of their fighting with each other. Our whole camp ate heartily of the rhinoceros; but the flesh, though sweet, requires very sharp teeth. Their young would seem to have great affection. Wounding a large female one night, I next day traced her spoor for four miles, and suddenly came on her squatting like a hare in her form, with her back towards me. There was a great deal of whining or puling near the spot, which I took to be her dying cries. Advancing cautiously, a different rhinoceros cocked its ears at me, and I felt for an instant at a loss which to fire at: both barrels from "Blanshard" went at my new *young* friend, who rushed off crashing through the underwood, and I only then saw that the poor old lady was cold dead, and she proved so heavy that three of us could not move her. It was the young one weeping over its mother that caused the plaintive cries I had heard.

Zebras seen cantering in open forests of bare-poled trees without a vestige of underwood, form a beautiful sight; they can be stalked very easily, and, unless made aware of danger by antelopes feeding with them, they will turn round and stare at you, some even advancing a few paces, like the wild horse of Thibet. When I first heard the cry of the zebra I took it for the call of a bird, with a little of the donkey at the end; but, listening for some time, and seeing the animal, I would describe it as a half-bray, or cross between a foal's and a donkey's call. They are perfect in symmetry, and barred jet black to the very hoofs, which are large, wide, and well cared-for by nature's farrier, the grass in the forest. Two of our Tots would not eat them because they had never eaten horse-flesh; but everyone else was glad to get "five year-olds," or even "aged" ones, though of all wild animals I considered it the worst food, tasting so very strong. After the tongue or any portion of the meat had been boiled, it smelt of a stable, and caused instant disgust and nausea. Cut in long stripes, sundried, and toasted in ashes, was the only way of making the zebra flesh lose this flavour. Had we had any salt, probably pickling it might also have answered. The paunches were in several cases lined with clusters of maggots, a disease known amongst sheep in this country.

Buffaloes gave Speke some dashing home-charges; but though I sought them everywhere, I never had a shot. Their meat was as fine as that which any English butcher can produce—the men eating of it day and night as long as it lasted. Brindled gnu is equally good, but far more beautiful in the field. Fearfully shy, they look at you for an instant only, then scamper off, lashing about their switching long tails; and after giving a short spurt, they turn round again, take another furtive glance, and then bound madly away.

Giraffe are such wary animals, their heads peering over the tops of the acacias on which they feed, that only one specimen, a bull, was shot. This was done with a Lancaster ball through the heart, and I thought the latter small in proportion to the size of the animal.

---

[1] No doubt Grant and Speke reacted to problems with their porters as if they were still in the Indian Army; but in a situation where it was easy for followers to desert, the leaders soon found that they must negotiate with their followers as well as with the local Africans through whose lands they were passing.

On asking for the head to be brought for preservation, I found that the Wezee[1] porters had cut the ears off, and were already frizzling them for dinner. The hairs of the tail are so stiff, thick, long, and such a handsome black, that the natives value them very much for stringing bead-necklaces. It being a thorny acacia country, our men benefited by the giraffe's thick skin, which they converted into excellent sandals. For days afterwards, as they passed to windward, the odour of a menagerie was unmistakable.

Lions were fired at once during a moonlight march; others were heard both day and night making short coughing noises, but never "roaring like a lion." They kill cattle, and, if trapped, are carried lashed in a litter as royal property to the sultan. Tracks of the elephant were numerous in Ugogo. Here we saw some hunters, Mukua, from the Lufigi, with long "Tower" flint-muskets, looking as perfect as when new.[2] With these they watch the elephant at night by solitary pools of water, and fire a volley into him; but they consider that the best place to strike him is just in front of the ear orifice. Eland, hartebeest, black antelope, &c., and several smaller species, were shot or observed in our constant pursuit for specimens. There is a charm about the bark and spring of the startled saltatrix, a chamois-sized antelope, or when seen standing proudly on the face of the shelving rock, that reminded us of the goorul or chamois of the Himalayas. Their fore-feet hoofs are immensely long in the heel, enabling them to cling to the rocks. The hirax, or coney, basking on the rocks, is also very interesting: he is about three times the size of the hare. We saw very few of the latter; they were the same colour as the English, but smaller, with ears disproportionately large; they seemed to run more like rabbits than hares. Lungoor[3] and monkey we seldom met with; the latter are hunted for their skins by the common pariah dog in Uzaramo, but the natives do not eat them. Squirrels occasionally cracked nuts on the forest-trees: they were of the usual size and beauty, most difficult to "twig," and having a white longitudinal stripe running down either side. There were weasels, brown ferrets, small foxes with black muzzles, and red foxes, jackal-sized, white-chested, with the perfect bark of a dog, and extremely graceful, with elegant dark brush. Mangy-coloured, impudent hyenas prowled and howled round the camp, much to every one's amusement; they are such wary, cunning beasts that only one was shot, and our men had no delicacy in carrying it into camp for examination and dissection. In India private servants would refuse to touch such a piece of carrion.

The ugliest monster is the wild boar—head narrow and long, with four warty protuberances, and the skin between the two tusks as broad as it is between the eyes. The mane is immense, but behind it there is little or no hair; however, nothing looks prettier or more like a race of Arab horses than a herd in full flight going across the forest with erect heads and straight-up tails. We saw a crocodile, the colour of a tiger, lying on the bank of the Kingani, where the spoor of hippopotamus was visible. We came across very few chameleons or serpents, but saw a puff adder 2½ feet long, with abruptly short tail and four fangs. There were many species of lizards; one twelve inches long, very handsome,

---

[1] This is the shorthand Grant uses for 'Wanyamwezi'.

[2] This is interesting evidence on the nature of the ivory trade: that the Makua should come from such a comparatively long distance north to a region which one might have expected to be dominated by the Nyamwezi, if not Zanzibar Arabs. But this largely Mozambique-based trade did not establish a permanent grip in this region. The Makua had acquired firearms from the mid-18th century. See Alpers, *Ivory and Slaves*, pp. 11–12, 33n., 110–11. Tower muskets were those obsolete British weapons stamped with the Tower (of London) symbol.

[3] 'Lungoor' is the white-bearded ape of India. *Hobson-Jobson*.

with vermilion head and shoulders, and bright-blue body. Shooting two of these amongst some rocks cost us twelve cloths, as I was told that I had encroached on sacred ground. Rats, bugs, and musquitoes seldom gave us trouble. During rain, frogs and crickets were deafening. Insects and white ants (eaten by natives) seemed to enjoy themselves by attacking us and the candle at night; and small yellow butterflies, apple-green underneath, fluttered in suspense over the edges of little puddles.

Of birds of song there were remarkably few: a species of lark on the coast had a short sweet note. Of game-birds, the ordinary guinea-fowl, weighing 3¼ to 3½ lb., was the most common, and ate deliciously after being kept two days. Early in the morning they roost lazily in tall trees, and in the evening they may be found near cultivations, chasing insects or grubbing up sweet potato. We killed one rare species, red round the eyes and on the throat, having a standing-up purple collar of loose skin, a ridge of ostrich-like black feathers from the back of the head to the nostrils, weight about 3 lb., and in running it seemed to have a more compressed body than the ordinary species. There is something peculiar about the shape of the "merry-thought,"[1] which differs from that of a fowl. The best-flavoured bird we found was the florikan,[2] which has a rough gritty call; but few were shot, as they were extremely shy. Green pigeons are handsome, and after they have fed on the wild fig, no bird looks plumper on the table. Rock-pigeon, snipe, quail, plover, and several species of partridge, we shot occasionally; also a very pretty species of pintailed dove found in Ugogo. Pigeons, generally white, and not differing from those at home, are sometimes kept as pets by the villagers. Of ostrich we saw only one gang on the bare plains of Ugogo, where the natives make handsome wreaths of their plumes; and among the other birds seen were crested cranes, hawks, a solitary raven or two, a few parrots, but scarcely any crows. The natives capture all these beasts and birds by means of pitfalls and nooses. The former are cut like a wedge, most disagreeable to look down upon, eight feet deep, and but one foot across the top, which is coyly covered over. The nooses were formed of an elastic bough, stripped of its branches, with the noose hung perpendicularly, neatly concealed and placed in an antelope-frequented track. Diminutive traps were set for partridge, quail, &c. and if intended for soaring birds, the noose is laid on the ground horizontally. The animals are struck with spears and killed, and are eaten by all; while the tendons are made into bowstrings, the horns used as charms, and the skins rudely dressed for wear.

Fish are rarely met with. On the coast, women standing in a circle up to their waists in the sea use their cloths as nets, and encircle small fish. Stakenets in the form of the letter U, turned in at the apices, were seen. In the interior, upon the clear, gravel bottomed river M'gazee, a party of fishers were seen wading down the stream, the men leading with handnets, while boys in their rear thrust spears into the holes in the banks. A number of slimy-looking fish, 18 to 20 inches long, had been caught, and were slung by their heads to a cord tied round the waist, surrounding the wearer like a Highland kilt.[3]

---

[1] A now little-used alternative for 'wishbone', i.e. the furcular bone of a bird. *OED*. See Plate 44 for Grant's depictions of florikans and partridges.

[2] 'A name applied in India to two species of small bustard'. *Hobson-Jobson*.

[3] The forgoing enumeration of the wildlife by Grant is evidence of his great interest in Natural History, especially ornithology. Also clearly in evidence is the fact that Grant was someone who had learned to participate in the almost obsessive custom of hunting wild beasts which had been copied from upper-class landowners in Britain by the official and military classes in India. Grant's account is also affected by the everyday problem which confronted the leaders of expeditions of providing food for the members of their caravans.

The four native races were as follows:—

I. *The Wazaramo.*—A smart, dressy (though nearly naked), well-to-do-looking people, with a most self-possessed air, and fond of ornaments in beads, seashells, or tin.[1] Their heads are covered with wool, elongated with bark fibre into hanks, and their bodies smeared with an oily pomade of red clay, which soon soils their only covering—a cloth wrapped round the loins. The dress of the women is slightly longer, but they leave the neck and chest uncovered. Their arms are spears, and bows and arrows, with a few flint-guns. As they do not allow strangers to camp within their villages, we saw few houses, but those into which we were admitted were very tidy, with mud-and-wattle walls and thatched roofs. The appearance of these people was prepossessing. The attentions of the men to their women were very marked. A man might be seen in a field performing the office of hair-dresser to his lady-love; or, spear in hand, he would join a party of women going to draw water, pitcher on head, and escort them lest any of our camp should fall upon, steal, or seduce them away. A very pretty girl and her beau were coaxed to sit for their likenesses, and went away with a smile; but two hideous old women screeched at the pitch of their voices because they got but one necklace of beads as payment for sitting before the camera.

Extracts from Journal: Photography Problems
I took five plates ... they all failed. [NLS, MS. 17915, 12 September 1860]
Sent back all my chemicals in three large cases with <u>deep regret</u> but saw the necessity of keeping camera & paper ... safe in one load instead of six. [NLS, MS. 17915, 2 October 1860]

pitched tent. Did photos: heat overpowering – 4 to 5 drops [of sweat] falling from my face in shirt <u>in</u> tent. The chill after it not pleasant. All photos got spoiled. [NLS, MS. 17915, 26 October 1860][2]

This partly exhibits the boisterous nature of the people: they killed a European named M. Maizan,[3] and I have no doubt that it was only the warning guns fired by our Belooch guard every night that prevented an attack, for which, however, we were not unprepared.

The villagers *en route* turned out to see the white men; amongst them, during a single march, we saw two albinos, one of whom had black woolly hair. Again, of an afternoon, we considered it an extraordinary occurrence if our camp was not thronged by people, curious and well-conducted, some bringing their produce to barter. Women would sit at our tent-doors suckling their infants while cracking jokes at our expense. We saw no places of burial, but by the roadside the skeleton of a traveller lay; and also at other places single

[1] The Zaramo were a matrilineal people who lived on the coastal plain opposite Zanzibar and who had already become largely Islamized. Predominantly agricultural, growing rice and millet, they tended to live in stockaded villages. Beidelman, *Matrilineal Peoples*, pp. 15–22. See Figures 23, 24, 25 and 26, pp. 99–100. There is little anthropological information on this people.

[2] Grant is somewhat reticent about his photographic failures but it seems to have been at this early point in the Expedition that he gave up the practice and reverted to sketching and painting only.

[3] Lt Maizan was a French naval officer detached from Captain Guillain's ship in 1843 at the time when France was negotiating a treaty with Zanzibar. He aimed to travel inland to Unyamwezi but delayed until 1845. Apparently prosperous but ill-guarded, he was murdered by a Zaramo village chief named Mazungere. See Coupland, *East Africa and Its Invaders*, pp. 353–7; Bennett, 'France and Zanzibar', pp. 607ff.

tombs, with large dolls of wood or some broken bowls of delf,[1] standing as *immortelles* at one end of the graves, which were those of Seedees from Zanzibar. The only superstitious observance we noticed was in a field at the foot of a tree; a grass model of a hut was erected for the rain-god, as our men told me, and called, as usual, a "M'ganga."[2] The worst features in this Wazaramo race are, that they will give travellers no aid, and will pounce upon stray men. They are polygamists;[3] their only faith is belief in the "black art;" and though residing on the borders of civilisation, they have no curiosity or ambition.

II. *The Wasagara* population[4] live such an outcast life on the tops of their conical hills,[5] above the path of the traveller, that we saw little of their manners or customs. Parties from the coast attack them, to capture their people and cattle; and as we were considered of this class, our followers had great difficulty in getting supplies. We also suffered from a set of coast slave hunters, who gave orders that we were not to be supplied with anything, because we had come into the country to put down slavery. However, it being a sporting country, we were more or less independent. Guides were got with difficulty, but a short, sharp fellow took me over a very fine range of streambeds and shady spots for buffalo and rhinoceros, showing great cleverness and intelligence as a tracker. We met with nothing but beds of lilac convolvulus in the woods. My guide's chat, and his archery at a leaf ten paces off, beguiled the time very agreeably. He made me laugh at his sultan, Senga,[6] who had fourteen wives; but he himself, he said, could not marry until his present wardrobe was increased, it consisting only of what he then wore—a rag round his loins.

III. *The Wagogo.*[7]—We did not enter their oblong, walled villages,[8] but I have a distinct and vivid recollection of the people. Among them were smart, wiry, active young fellows, who would make first-rate recruits. Their woolly hair, elongated by working into it hanks of bark fibre, flew in the air as they ran; beads were at times strung on, or an ostrich-feather waved about their heads; their ear-lobes were distended by a plug of wood, &c. Their arms were five-feet-long spears, knobsticks, and oblong shields of leather; dress generally a small loin-cloth. With a gourd cup they drew water from their wells and filled it into

---

[1] Delf is cut turf. *OED*; *Concise Scots Dictionary*. Beidelman, *Matrilineal Peoples*, p. 19, reports that effigies of the dead were fashioned from soil from the grave mixed with water.

[2] A native doctor, especially one who uses charms but in this case, more accurately, these were diviners whose job was to detect witchcraft.

[3] However, Grant missed the key fact that the Zaramo were a matrilineal people.

[4] The Sagara were another Bantu matrilineal people living in a mountainous region some 100 miles (160.9 km) inland from the coast. Agricultural and cattle keepers, they were already much affected by the caravan trade and the coastal influences it brought. As Grant says, they seem to have been victims of slave hunters from the coast. Beidelman, *Matrilineal Peoples*, pp. 51–3; Murdock, *Africa*, pp. 359–63. The Sagara are another people on whom there is relatively scant anthropological information.

[5] See Figures 28, 29 and 31, pp. 101 and 102.

[6] Possibly a minor lineage leader; the Sagara seem to have been little developed politically.

[7] 'Gogo' was a name given to these peoples by Nyamwezi traders although they were not really a well-defined group. They were peoples in an area influenced by the semi-arid environment and nearby Nilo-Hamitic warriors, who taught them the custom of having age sets and loving cattle. They preyed on caravans to obtain iron hoes plus slaves to use the hoes to practise agriculture. Living in a rather marginal area for cultivation or cattle keeping, the patrilineal Bantu WaGogo had thus come to rely heavily upon exactions on the caravan trade. Burton, *Lake Regions*, I, pp. 294–312; Rigby, *Cattle and Kinship*, p. 20 and *passim*. Rigby's book is the only considerable work on them.

[8] That is, *tembes*. See especially, Figure 37, p. 106. For other depictions of Ugogo, see Figures 32A, 35 and 36, pp. 103 and 105.

earthen "gurahs," similar to those in India. Women carried their children on their backs in a skin, with cross supporting-straps; and boys brought music out of a stringed bow attached to a gourd as sounding-board. We were so mobbed by the people in camp that a ring of rope had to be placed round our tents; but this only increased their inquisitiveness. When told to go away, and not keep peeping under the canvass of our closed-up tents, they laughed, telling us the ground we pitched upon was theirs, and that they could take our guns and property from us if they chose. A porter of ours accidentally broke one of their bows; this was immediately turned to account, and a demand made for something ten times its value. I shot a lizard at some curiously outcropping rocks, and was told I had hurt their feelings, and must pay for my folly.

Extract from Journal: Grant Regrets He Cannot Comment Knowledgably on Geology

I am sure [this] is an interesting geolog[ica]l country – so many fragments of different rocks are thrown up. Ashamed of my ignorance of them. I think granite, limestone & mica slate I distinguish. [NLS, MS. 17915, 28 November 1860]

Previously to firing I had thought of the Indian superstition as to sacred spots and marks, and examined the place well; but seeing no trace of them, I reckoned this fine had no connection with any such traditions, but was knowingly imposed on us in the way of extortion. They told us we must not have lights out at night—alluding to Speke making his observations. Like all Africans, if they gave us any information a present had to follow. The settlement of the tax was a most harassing affair.[1] The sultan, after receiving all he had demanded, said the cloths were not suitable to his rank—"you have better ones than you gave me, and my head wife must get some." In short, he so bullied us by threats of attack that our main stand-by of porters, 113 "Wezees," were frightened into the dastardly act of deserting us at the most critical part of the journey.[2]

IV. *Wanyamuezi.*[3]—The 115 porters we left the seaport with were of the class of the Wanyamuezi, and we had good opportunity for observing their habits and character. They were average-sized, slim-limbed negroes, many of them with handsome countenances and incisions of caste above the cheek-bones; they were dressed in goat-skins hanging loosely in their front from the right shoulder; most of them with a shabby small bow and a couple of arrows; a few of the better sort had flint-guns, which they carried awkwardly at the long "trail," and pointing to the men behind them.

They are frank and amiable on first acquaintance, eating or taking anything from your hand, singing the jolliest of songs with deep-toned choruses from their thick necks and throats, but soon trying to get the upper hand, refusing to make the ring-fence round

[1] The Gogo demands became more extreme during rather frequent famines; Speke's account suggests that this was a time of famine. Speke, *Journal*, p. 56.

[2] Speke describes all the difficulties in Ugogo in great detail, *Journal*, pp. 55–83.

[3] The Nyamwezi were and remain the most important people of the central plateau area east of Lake Tanganyika. Grant calls them 'Wezees' for short. Their relatively well-watered land makes intensive agriculture possible. They developed trading links to other regions, especially to the west and to the north and then found a market at the coast, especially for ivory. At this period, their dominance of the route to the coast had already been seriously diminished by rival and better-capitalized traders from the coast and Zanzibar; many of the Nyamwezi were reduced to becoming porters for their coastal rivals and the Expedition's men were essentially of this class. The best short account remains that by Roberts, 'The Nyamwezi'. Grant's photograph of those Banyamwezi he had already met in Zanzibar is Figure 6, p. 87.

camp, showing sulks, making halts, or going short marches, treating with perfect contempt any message sent them even to sit apart from your tent, as the smoke of their fires, the odour of their persons, and their total want of delicacy annoy you. All these grievances my companion bore with great patience, and often got the offenders into humour by suggesting a harangue at night, to be delivered by their captain. On an animal being cut up into shares one day, they so far forgot themselves as to dash upon it with the utmost rapidity, and bore off the whole from our Zanzibar men, who were left in vacant amazement without redress. On killing a goat, I observed they never spilt a drop of blood, but smashed its head with a stick or stone. Out shooting they were invaluable as guides, first-rate spoorers, and never at a loss for anything: a pipe would be made by putting a grit of clay an inch or so into the end of a tube of bark. "Duncan's *smoking* mixture" they preferred stuffing as far as possible up their noses. When an animal was shot they always stole the fat. They had extraordinary knowledge of edible roots and herbs, and under almost any circumstances would not starve. They had no particular superstitions or sacred days, either in the week or year. They were intelligent and amusing enough, but had no claim to honour or honesty—113 of them, although handsomely paid, deserted us, carrying away a considerable quantity of property. Perhaps they treated us in this way in consequence of having been badly paid by Arab traders on former occasions.

A few of their women accompanied us: quiet, decent, well-conducted, tidy creatures, generally carrying a child each on their backs, a small stool and etceteras on their heads, and inveterately smoking during the march. They would prepare some savoury dish of herbs for their men on getting into camp, where they lived in bell-shaped erections made with boughs of trees.

CHAPTER IV

[Pages 44–56]

Sojourn at Kazeh [25 January–16 March 1861]

WE were delayed here for fifty-one days on account of the falling rains, the flooded state of the river ahead, and the impossibility of getting porters to move at such a season, when grain was not procurable.[1] Our arrival was hailed with great delight.[2] Moossah,[3] an excellent friend of Speke's,[4] several Arabs and many followers, all in holiday attire, came out a mile to welcome our ragged-looking Indian file. Guns were fired, yambos[5] and salaams with shaking of hands followed, and we were lodged once more under a hospitable roof.

Extract from Journal: Arrival at Kazeh

This is an immense establishment of Moussah's his tembe[6] being surrounded by a circle of walls within which are servants' houses & ... detached garden enclosures, plantations. The Arabs visit S[peke] to talk over their warring nearby. He gets confirmatory information regarding the source of the Nile. [NLS, MS. 17915, 25 January 1861]

The country is surrounded by low bare hills,[7] which every morning till eight or nine were obscured by an unhealthy coloured mist, filling the wide valley where we lay. There was nothing to cheer the eye—no river, no trees: it reminded Speke of the Crimea. Rills ran here and there through grass, and opened out on white sand: one of these, collecting in a pool, formed the drinking water of the inhabitants. Scarcely a man amongst us escaped fever. We arrived on the 25th of January, and by the 1st February several were laid up. My first attack lasted seven days, the 2d, 4th, 6th, 7th, and 8th terminating in headaches every

---

[1] Grant was afflicted by fever for much of this time and did not play a particularly active part in Speke's efforts to make arrangements for porters to accompany the Expedition northwards and to mediate in the war then intermittently raging between the former ruler of Unyanyembe, Mnwa Sera, and the coast traders who had deposed him. See Bridges, 'Negotiating a Way', pp. 117–19.

[2] The Arabs hoped Speke and his armed men would help them fight Mnwa Sera.

[3] Musa Mzuri (Moses the Handsome) was the pioneer Zanzibar trader to establish himself in the interior from perhaps as early as 1825. Most other traders were Arabs but he was a Khoja Muslim and unusual among fellow Indian merchants in venturing inland. It was probably not until the early 1850s that he had set up his base in the Nyamwezi polity of Unyanyembe. Burton, *Lake Regions*, II, pp. 223–5.

[4] Speke had met Musa in September 1858 just after his 'flying trip' from Kazeh to Lake Victoria and when Musa had returned from a trip to Karagwe. Speke, *What Led to the Discovery*, p. 257.

[5] *Jambo* is the normal form of greeting in Kiswahili.

[6] See Figure 38, p. 138.

[7] See Figure 39, p. 139.

morning. After twelve days another sharper attack, with delirium at night, but no ague, lasted three days. The third and least severe came on fifteen days afterwards, with drowsiness and profuse perspiration, and terminated in three days. All suffered from after-weakness in the limbs; some from blindness of one eye, the eyelid much inflamed and drooping, accompanied with excessive watering; or no inflammation of the eye, but total blindness of it, and no disease or scale observable. Acute pain rarely accompanied this complaint. Our men ascribed their bad health to not having got accustomed to the water of the country. The natives had no efficient remedies for preventing the recurrence of fever, but took pinches of a pounded plant or wood to cure their headaches, or cupped themselves in the following curious manner: A man put some beeswax into his mouth, applied a small cow's horn to cuts made in the temple of the patient, exhausted the air by suction, and with his tongue shut the hole at the end of the horn with the wax. We had only one fatal case. Quinine and applications of blistering tissue behind the ear and on the temples partially restored health and eyesight. During our stay the prevalent winds were the E., N.E., and S.E., but the coldest were the westerly after rain. The mornings were foggy, the grass dripped with the night-dew, which interfered with Speke's observation of the stars by dimming the instruments. The days were often dark and hazy; pelting showers beat down from the N.W., but we sometimes had a fresh English morning, with a clear sky, a N.E. wind, and temperature only 69° at 9 A.M. We had no striking or beautiful sunsets like the equatorial at sea, but in the evening the flowering grasses, gorgeously lit up by the rays of the setting sun, had a singularly fine effect; and such evenings were often followed by a few dry days, and a temperature of 82°. This hot weather occurred when, at the short twilight, the sun appeared to set in the east, and the whole sky was an arched illumination. On an average we had rain two-fifths of the time we halted, and the greatest fall noted in twenty-four hours was two inches. These African rains we did not find followed by the disagreeable steamy or muggy feeling experienced in India; all was cool and fresh after them. We had thunder and lightning, but rain did not always follow.

This province of Unyanyembe has nearly four months of rain, commencing in the end of November, and winding up with the greatest fall in February. As soon as the soil of sand, or black spongy mould, has softened, the seed is dropped, and by the 1st of February all is as green as an emerald. The young rice has to struggle for fifteen days against the depredations of a small black caterpillar, green underneath. It is a precarious time for the agriculturist; for if rain does not fall the crop is lost, being eaten close by this insect. Women walk in the fields, with small handpicks, loosening the soil, clearing it of weeds and worms. There is only one crop in the year, and all the cereals known in Zanzibar are grown here.[1] Cotton was considered by an Indian resident to be as fine as that grown in Kutch, but he said they had no use for it, merely burning it as wicks.[2] As the previous year's corn had been consumed, the poorer classes gathered the heads of a wild grass (*Dactyloctum Ægyptiacum*),[3] and prepared it for stirabout by sun-drying, beating on the

[1] Grant's description of agricultural activity and other occupations in this chapter is disappointingly short but there is compensation in the form of two of his best illustrations – Plates 4 and 5 with the accompanying keys to the objects shown.

[2] Most of the peoples of this region of Africa had some tradition of weaving but the importation of Indian and, at this period, increasingly, the *merikani* cotton cloths from New England, had tended to kill the local industry.

[3] That is, *Dactyloctenium aegyptium*, 'an annual or short-lived perennial up to 2½ft. high ... the grain is sometimes eaten by humans in time of famine'. Eggeling, *Grasses of Uganda*, p. 13.

rocks, and rubbing it into flour on their flagstones. They also fed upon mushrooms, growing amongst the rank "dub" grass, after drying, roasting, and peeling them. They were five inches in diameter, and sienna-coloured. Another variety was white, and half the size. All the cattle and goats in the country seemed to have found their way into the folds of the Arabs, and had been captured in a war still going on between them and the native population.[1] The surrounding country is devoid of game, but within a long day's march a forest was visited, where various antelopes, giraffes, lions, and a few elephants might be met with along the valley of the Wallah river. The scales of an armadillo were seen worn as a charm, three inches across, and striated or lined at one end. Our men had a superstition that the person who found a live armadillo would become a king—meaning, I imagine, that it was so rare. However, we came upon a pet one at 3° N. latitude. About the cultivations near the village no singing-birds are ever heard, but the plumage of those seen is often very brilliant. Flocks of beautiful little birds, with black bodies, golden-tinted scarlet heads and backs,[2] pecked at the ears of corn; or in the rice-fields the favourite of the Cape farmers, the "locust bird," black, and looking like a curlew when walking, went tamely about. Crows, with a ring of white round the neck, were seen in twos and threes. The matting in the houses was full of bugs, or ticks, which pestered one while seated at night, causing considerable irritation.

It is not a country for ivory,[3] the natives seldom if ever bringing any for sale. Grain was so scarce that slaves could be purchased for two fathoms of calico. One day a naked native passed us in charge of three Seedees armed with spears. They had found him stealing, and offered him for sale. No one would purchase him, and he was taken to the sultan, who would, as Moossah said, either spear him, keep him as a slave, or allow him to be sold. Slaves from the northern kingdoms of Uganda, &c., were considered the most valuable, just in the same way as many persons consider a country girl the best servant. They were held to be more trustworthy than men from the coast, made excellent servants, and were famous at killing or capturing wild animals.[4] The most esteemed women were of the Wahumah tribe[5] from Karague; they resembled the Abyssinians.

Let me give the reader some idea of our life here. Moossah, an Indian in whose house we resided, was a fine benevolent old man, with an establishment of 300 native men and women round him. His abode had, three years ago, taken two months to build, and it was surrounded by a circular wall which enclosed his houses, fruit and vegetable gardens, and his stock of cattle. The lady who presided over the whole was of most portly

[1] See p. 123, n. 3.

[2] There are several kinds of black and red weaver birds; possibly this was the black-winged bishop, *Euplectes hordeacea*.

[3] Essentially this was because the 'ivory frontier' had passed further west to Lake Tanganyika and beyond. In other words, most elephants in this region had been killed.

[4] On slavery, and the relationship of Unyamwezi to coastal influences, see the excellent study by Deutsch, 'Slavery and Social Change', pp. 76–110; pp. 81 and 88–91 are especially relevant here. Deutsch draws on Grant's evidence for the 1860s. Grant has noticed what appears to be slavery in its traditional variety with a supposed criminal being enslaved although the option of selling the man to the coast has now been opened. Whether the trade in slaves from the lacustrine kingdoms to the north was long-established or a recent development stimulated by the arrival of coastal influences is not clear. See Plates 6 and 7 for Grant's depictions of slaves in this region.

[5] More properly, the BaHima who formed an elite of pastoralist ruling clans not only in Karagwe but also in Ankole, Toro and other kingdoms. Speke, in particular, regarded them as the harbingers of civilization and so gave birth to the 'Hamitic myth' about African history. See Speke, *Journal*, Chap. IX, *passim*.

dimensions, and her word was law. Moossah sat from morn till night with his "foondee,"[1] or chief manager, and other head servants within sight, receiving salutes and compliments from the rich and poor at the front or *gentlemen's* side of the house, while the lady presided over the domestic arrangements of the interior. We had full access to both, and no house could be conducted with greater regularity. At three o'clock in the morning, Moossah, who had led a hard life in his day, would call out for his little pill of opium, which he never missed for forty years. This would brighten him up till noon. He would then transact business, chat, and give you the gossip at any hour you might sit by him on his carpet. To us it seemed strange that he never stopped talking when prayers from the Koran were being read to him by a "Bookeen", or Madagascar man.[2] Perhaps he had little respect for the officiating priest, as the same reverend and learned gentleman was accustomed to make him his shirts! After a mid-day sleep, he would refresh himself with a second but larger pill, transact business, and so end the day. The harem department presented a more domestic scene. At dawn, women in robes of coloured chintz, their hair neatly plaited, gave fresh milk to the swarm of black cats, or churned butter in gourds by rocking it to and fro on their laps. By seven o'clock the whole place was swept clean. Some of the household fed the game-fowls, or looked after the ducks and pigeons; two women chained by the neck fetched firewood, or ground corn at a stone; children would eat together without dispute, because a matron presided over them;—all were quiet, industrious beings, never idle, and as happy as the day was long. When any of Moossah's wives gave birth to a child there was universal rejoicing; the infant was brought to show its sex: and when one died, the shrill laments of the women were heard all night long. When a child misbehaved, we white men were pointed at to frighten it, as nurses at home too often do with ghost stories.

The most important functionary about this court was the head keeper or foondee, who had been a slave all his life, and now possessed a village with a farm and cattle. His daily duty was to sit within sight of his master. On Speke calling to see his collection of horns, and extract a bullet from the leg of one of his slaves, the foondee made us heartily welcome. Stools were placed, and in gratitude for the operation he produced some ripe plantain, and showed us about his premises. He also took us to one of his favourite shooting-grounds, where he certainly knew how to make himself comfortable. His servants had constructed for him a most luxurious waterproof hut with broad stripes [*sic*] of freshly-cut bark, and a capital bedstead of boughs. At night five fires were kept burning round him to keep off the musquitoes. The grate was most original: three stout pegs of green wood driven into the ground, forming an equilateral triangle, answered every purpose of an iron utensil, and on it a frying-pan, made of bark, frizzled mushrooms and meat to the chief's satisfaction. By his own account, he had shot many a lion from trees; and during the march to and from Zanzibar with his master's property, he, with a staff of under-keepers, used to supply the porters with rations from wild animals, which plan saved the expenditure of bead-money. He had many sporting stories. The lion, he said, seldom killed men; but, not long ago, one had jumped the wall of the building and killed five cows, two of which he dragged over the wall—the natives fearing to impede his course.

---

[1] More correctly, *fundi*, a Swahili word of wide use meaning any person with a particular skill or ability.
[2] *Buki* signifies Madagascar in Swahili.

Moossah's cowherds were a very interesting set of people—so well-featured, tall, and generally superior to the Africans, that I took great interest in them. They were Watusi[1] from Karague. There were ten men and women, all with woolly hair—the men leaving a crescent of it unshaved. Their gums were blackened with a preparation from the tamarind-seed, powdered, roasted, and mixed into a paste with blue vitriol, and afterwards heated until fit for use. Their ornaments were large solid rings of brass upon the wrists, and iron rings, in masses, on their ankles. In walking they carried a bow and arrow, a staff, and long-stemmed pipe. The women were of a large stamp, with fine oval faces and erect figures, clad in well-dressed cow-skin from above their waists to their small feet.[2] Their huts were quite different from any we had seen, being shaped like the half of an orange, and only five feet high, made of boughs, and covered with grass very neatly.[3] There was but one door; the hut had no chimney, the smoke finding its way through the light grass roof. I observed a portable Indian "choolah"[4] or fireplace inside the hut, which was kept tidily floored with hay.

These Watusi are a curious and distinct race. Previous to milking the cows in the morning, they wash themselves, their teeth, and their wooden milk-vessels or gourds with the urine of the animal, as they consider there is some virtue in it, afterwards using fresh water for cleansing. They are allowed half the milk, and Moossah had his half milked into his own clean vessels in the morning at eight o'clock. It took the milk of two cows to fill one good-sized tin teapot. A cow's value was four or five dollars, though a first class one would cost double, or £2. Men milked them into a large crucible of wood or gourd in an open yard; the hind-legs were tied above the hocks with a thong of leather; one of their handsome women sat on the other side with a bough beating off the flies, and with a stick to keep away the calf which stood at its mother's head, a boy sometimes assisting. Should the calf die, its skin is stuffed and placed before the cow, otherwise she refuses her milk. The Wanyamuezi look with great respect on this people. When two of them meet, the Wezee puts both his palms together, these are gently clasped by the Watusi, a few inaudible words are repeated, and they pass on. The form of salutation when a Watusi meets one of his women senior to himself is gentle and pleasing; he places his hands on her arms below her shoulders, while her hands hang by her side.[5]

The way in which an African leads a goat or cow is different from the manner in this country. The fore-leg of the goat is held up by the man, who walks briskly along as if he led a child. An unruly cow is never tied by the head: a man walks behind it, having hold of a rope tied tightly round its hock; this plan seems to subdue or *Rareyfy* the animal most completely. For several days after our arrival, different Arab residents sent us presents

---

[1] The Watusi are assumed to be members of the dominant pastoral castes of Rwanda, Burundi and other parts of the western interlacustrine region. In this case, however, they were not politically dominant. The whole question of the influence of leaders coming from pastoralists variously known as Hima, Tutsi or Tusi on the development of Unyamwezi and other parts of western Tanzania does not have a simple answer. See Roberts, 'Nyamwezi', p. 120.

[2] Grant's somewhat puritanical reluctance to depict women plus his lack of skill in portraying people mean that he did not apparently attempt to draw these women. However, the rather unsatisfactory Figure 63, p. 210, may depict similar people.

[3] Perhaps like the hut shown by Grant in Plate 9 but more likely resembling the hut shown in Figure 40, p. 139.

[4] 'The extemporized cooking-place of clay which a native of India makes on the ground.' *Hobson-Jobson*.

[5] But Grant illustrates two Nyamwezi women greeting one another. See Figure 44, p. 142.

of eggs, some coffee, a fatted cow, rice, or a goat—a very pleasing custom, which was intended as their call upon us. We in return sent each a handsome cloth, which they valued very much. This friendly ceremony over, they freely asked our advice when necessary.

For two years, since the death of the chief of the country, the people of Kazeh had been fighting against the real heir to uphold the puppet appointed by them in his stead.[1] They had killed 300 natives, seized all their cattle and goats, and lost two Arabs and sixty slaves. A severe defeat occurred while we were there, Snay,[2] the chief Arab, and six others, with followers, being killed. A panic ensued, and Speke was requested to patch up a peace by inviting the rebel Manua Sera into Kazeh to attend a conference. "Once," they said, "at our mercy, we can murder him!" We were shocked at hearing this, but Moossah assured us that it was no uncommon occurrence with them. The news of their defeat was brought us by a man who may be allowed to tell his own story:—"I was one of five in charge of cattle; the rebel himself killed three of us; and as I never fight, but run, I threw away everything, and saved my life by coming here." He had a very good sword by him. "Where did you get that sword?" "Oh! it belongs to an Arab who was killed; I picked it up."

It seems that Snay was a very brave fellow, who in the midst of every fight whipped his slaves to prevent them from running away; but this time they got dispersed after plunder: he was left unprotected; and being old and too proud to run like his slaves, he fell a victim. After this severe defeat many plans were proposed for affording relief. "The single cannon must be sent in the morning." Moossah was tired of assisting them. "The Arabs stick at nothing; they had expended twenty barrels of his gunpowder and lost him five slaves; a beautiful gun of his was lost by his late partner Jaffir in this last fight. Jaffir had just been killed, and yet they still ask for aid!" So with true Indian parsimony he despatched five slaves to the war, with only ten rounds of wrought-iron bullets each, to fight the powerful rebel chief!

This long-continued war[3] had driven the natives of the country away from the Arab settlement; the bazaar supplied almost nothing—only one tobacco shop and one or two depots for grain; the most common iron-work could not be made. The villages around had no inhabitants but the sick, aged, dying, and starving, or idiots. We were told not to walk out alone, as a man had been killed the previous month; the country had been made dangerous, and the people were getting exterminated. But when one of our men cut through his hut and ran away one night, having been suspected of theft, Moossah said with confidence, "The Wezees will not harm him, neither will they give him shelter; he'll be found;" and so he was, rifle and bayonet untouched. All the natives were Hywans[4]— that is, unable to count, write, or tell their own ages. Some practised medicine, giving one of our men, who suffered from weakness in the limbs after fever, a black ointment made of roots. The black art of the Damars and the chipping of the Oovamba's teeth are

---

[1] See p. 118, n. 1, above, and the further references there.

[2] Snay bin Amir or, more properly, Thnay bin Amer el Harthi, was one of the first Arab merchants to go into the interior mainland from Zanzibar in about 1842 and had built up the Arab settlement at Kazeh from about 1852. There he became a general agent and leader of the Arabs. Burton had regarded him as a friend and vital source of information, Burton, *Lake Regions*, I, pp. 324–5.

[3] In 1865, Manua Sera, the legitimate ruler of Unyanyembe who had been deposed by the Arabs, was to be killed and so the war would end. However, a new and considerably more successful Nyamwezi challenge to the Arabs was to arise in the person of Mirambo in 1871. Bennett, *Mirambo*, pp. 46–68.

[4] The origin of this term is not clear.

practised here, as noticed in Andersson's Travels.[1] During the illness of the late chief,[2] witchcraft was suspected to be the cause. A fowl was placed in the hands of the suspected, dissected by a seer, and verdict given accordingly. Similar fancies, differing only a little in detail, long prevailed in the Highlands of Scotland, a very common form being to bury a black fowl in the exact spot where a person had been first seized with illness. Moossah had never heard of fowls being thrown up in the air to discover the sorcerer; and but one woman was killed to be placed in the grave with the old king.

Our exploration of the northern kingdoms enabled us to ascertain how far the mass of information gleaned from our good friend Moossah was correct. I can honestly say that, though he had never visited Uganda,[*3] his hearsay, on the whole, was a marvel of accuracy:—"The Egyptian river flowed from the Lake Nyanza. Copper and gold are found in Uganda. [We discovered neither, however.] The king alone wears clothes, killing all others who do so. He keeps slaves, and has 3000 women. The people have 100 each, and the youngest fellow 10 to 20, whom they steal or kidnap in war. The Karague people live entirely on milk diet, yet they are men fit for war. M'tezia, the king of Uganda, is a 'boorra admi,' bad man; but being great friends with Rumanika (of Karague), he will send you from 300 to 400 men to escort you. Smallpox is rife in Uganda yearly. The king has Zanzibar guns. At Uganda and Karague the sultans do not, as in other countries, claim one tusk of the killed elephant. Karague people carry about grog in calabashes; one sort being an intoxicating, fiery liquor, the other mild and good. Rhinoceros (white) are numerous. The king of Uganda makes people kneel in front of him, commanding them not to expose their skin or feet before his 400 or 500 women. The reed-grass huts of Karague and Uganda are so high that strong fires may be burned in them. Musicians of every sort there; king has five clocks sent him from Kazeh. At Karague they have three crops yearly of murwa[4] and sorghum. King of Uganda has a menagerie of 200 wild buffaloes; will give as many cheetah (leopard) skins as you like. The Wahumah of Karague have the most enormous arms, bodies, and legs; cannot walk; always rest on their elbows and knees; hands and feet very small; good noses and fair skins. Karague sultan cannot write, but sends a string of bark-cloth with knots upon it corresponding with the number of elephant-tusks sent."

All this exciting information made us eager for a move, but Moossah kept delaying. However, by the middle of March we had finished maps from observations, made collections, boiled thermometers, inspected newly-purchased presents for the kings ahead, sketched,[5] written reports and letters to wait any chance opportunity for the coast, and

[1] Andersson, *Lake 'Ngami*, 1856, pp. 196, 218–19.

[2] This was Fundikira, the chief in Unyanyembe, who enjoyed friendly relations with the Arabs; he had died in 1858.

[3] Grant's note, which was inserted at the proof stage in this book (NLS, MS. 17934, p. 55), reads: 'At Kazeh I understood that Moossah had never travelled farther than Karague; but I observe that Speke, in his Journal, states that Moossah (or "Mŭsa," as he writes the name) had reached Uganda.' Grant is probably correct in assuming that Musa never reached the capital of Buganda. In fact, Speke, in *Journal*, p. 265, stated only that Musa had reached into the most southerly province of Buganda, Budu (Buddu). On early visitors to Buganda, see Sheriff, *Slaves, Spices and Ivory*, pp. 183–4.

[4] A small grain crop.

[5] Grant rarely alludes in his book to his sketching and painting but it is notable that in Unyanyembe itself, as the foregoing notes will have indicated, Grant produced some very interesting pictures, especially Plates 4 and 5. As he moved north through other parts of Unyamwezi, he was to produce more notable pictures.

recovered from sickness. The rivers would soon be fordable, and a fourth of our porters had arrived; the remainder dreaded coming to us, as war was waging. We pitched camp on the 15th, and marched north without Moossah on the 16th March 1861, leaving the bulk of our kit behind, in charge of Bombay. In return for Moossah's hospitality, Speke gave him five hundred dollars and a beautifully chased[1] gold watch made to order by M'Cabe.[2] We experienced one great privation here, never receiving letters from home; but, odd enough, those despatched by us reached their destination.[3]

[1] Changed from 'chaste' at the proof stage – one of the few instances of spelling or grammatical errors on Grant's part.

[2] James McCabe (c. 1748–1811), originally from Ireland, founded a firm of watch and chronometer makers in London which continued to be run by his family until about 1879. It was regarded as a premier maker. Information kindly supplied by Dr Gloria Clifton.

[3] So, too, did Grant's collection of plant specimens. It is odd that he does not mention this. See the section in the Introduction on Grant's botanical activities, pp. 15–20.

CHAPTER V

[Pages 57–80]

Journey to Ukuni and Sojourn at Mineenga [16 March–27 May 1861]

However great was our desire to push on with the journey, we could not impress the Africans with this feeling. Porters would be ordered, and two days afterwards you found no one had gone for them. A general panic had seized the natives that the plundering Watuta race were on the wing.[1] The villages to the north were busy making defences, or a report had reached them that the Arabs had killed two of their clan; how, therefore, could they take service with *us,* who might do the same? Everything seemed to be against us; they would accept no bribe. None of the slaves of the Arabs would take service, though offered it, first by Baraka, and then by Speke in person, who walked 80 miles to induce them to accompany us. Ultimately we moved off by detachments, and accomplished 90 miles, with 110 men's loads, in 75 days.[2] To describe this country and its inhabitants, I devote the present chapter.

The whole route was fine; never once did we lose sight of trees, wooded hills, or valleys, while water was everywhere abundant. The forest was what might be called "Donkey or Zebra forest"—bare-poled trees and no underwood. The hills, now close, now distant, were richly clothed and exceedingly graceful, reminding me of the Trosachs [*sic*]. Grey rocks looked out in fantastic shapes from amongst the trees. Huge blocks lay one over the other, or abruptly ended a range of hill. The valleys had been cleared by the axe, the wild grasses were most luxuriant, and palisaded villages were often met with. We had not to leave the path in order to pluck the Indian corn. Our way led from one valley to another, or threaded the green forest, which rang with the songs of our followers. Generally the road was of fine sand, which, when lately washed by the rains, was loose and yellow. Once it crossed a quicksand, the only one I recollect seeing in Africa—very shaky and watery—along which a patch of rice grew. Two streams running west were forded; the Gombe, twenty yards across, there only 4½ feet deep—and with

---

[1] That is, Ngoni. Grant's own definition is 'a plundering, restless race, said to be a branch from the Zulu Kaffirs of the Cape. They have spread north as far as 3½° south latitude', *A Walk*, p. xviii. This is broadly correct: after Zwangendaba's Ngoni crossed the Zambesi in 1835, various groups of these marauders in what is now the area of Tanzania, preyed upon the inhabitants, taught new means of waging warfare, influenced politics by encouraging warrior chiefs and also increased their numbers by intermarriage with local people. Similarly, a separate Ngoni group, the Tuta, had much influenced the region and had recently reached the northern area of Unyamwezi which Grant was now entering. See Omer-Cooper, *Zulu Aftermath*, pp. 5–7, 73–5, 173–4.

[2] For details of the porterage problems, see Bridges, 'Negotiating a Way', pp. 120–21.

no current, merely a gentle flow of mud-coloured water; its banks well wooded and shelving: our men shouldered us across, but there were some rickety canoes made of bark lying on the left bank. The other we crossed at night in two channels running also west, but said to be dry one half of the year, although now it was breast-deep, with a current that nearly bore me down in my weak state. Attacks of fever came on about every tenth day, lasting eight and ten hours, with from two to five days of nausea and fevered brain. Speke, who had been so long in Africa, was not subject to them, but our men were constantly laid up. One died, and the poor Cape riflemen were such martyrs to fevers and sore eyes, that they confessed they could not stand the hardships of the journey, and were sent back to Kazeh, saying they were sorry they had come so far.[1] We were told that smallpox was the most fatal disease in this part of the country, but we saw no cases. The general elevation of the country is 3400 feet, rising gently up to the low ranges of hills everywhere around. It is more open than Unyanyembe. Mists rarely lie, except on the hill-tops after rain. The greatest fall measured was three-fourths of an inch in half an hour, after a storm, which burst overhead with fearful concussions of thunder at 3 P.M. of the 13th April. This may be described as the grand *finale* to the rainy season. Every morning the dews lay heavily, and a S.E. wind blew, but the coolest breeze was when from S. by W. The daily temperature inside a hut was 78° to 80° at 1 P.M. During the day the sky was generally clear, with a fierce sun; but the air in the mornings and evenings was deliciously cool, a fire at night being cheery and comfortable. No dust-storms troubled us, otherwise the open huts would have been uninhabitable. Drinking water was always sweet and refreshing. At Mineenga a copious spring gushed out of the shell of a tree lying level with the earth in the centre of a rice-field. This was the well of the village; from its position it was considered a phenomenon, and was looked on with veneration, as it afforded cool water the whole year round—a rare blessing.

The flora was new and interesting;[2] but we were amazed at not seeing better crops, as grasses with pendent panicles grew luxuriantly ten feet high. The surface-soil, however, was very light—merely the washings of the hill-sides brought down in a stream of red clay grit. In this tract of country we came upon groups of palms, not met with since we left the coast: they were converted into many uses—fences, thatching, firewood, and uprights for building, &c. Toddy also was occasionally extracted. The fruit hung down in rich, large, tempting clusters, at the mercy of any hungry traveller. We observed several of these palms, with their leaf-stalks still remaining on the tree, to be the support and life of a species of ficus, growing like a parasite, luxuriantly healthy, its roots not near the ground, but forming a complete network round the stem of the palm. Tamarind-trees, so umbrageous and beautiful in outline, were numerous. There was also the rumex, from ten to twelve feet high;[3] and the tree, a ficus, whose bark affords the Waganda their clothing, was here seen for the first time.[4] The bark is taken off in stripes, according to the size they can get it, then damped and beaten by heavy wooden hammers till pliant,

---

[1] Presumably the nine remaining men, Private Peters having died.

[2] On Grant's botanical activities, see Introduction, pp. 15–20.

[3] Probably *Rumex abyssinicus*. Lind and Tallantire, *Flowering Plants of Uganda*, p. 108. They are large herbs of the buckwheat family.

[4] According to Grant, this is the fig tree, *Ficus kotschyana*. Speke, *Journal*, Appendix G (Grant's Flora) p. 647. Grant, 'Botany of Speke and Grant Expedition', p. 141. Grant shows the tree in Buganda: see Plate 30.

and afterwards sewn into a sheet the colour of chamois-leather, but much thicker; the outer bark is thrown away. Near the villages a few scrubby bushes of cotton were grown upon mounds made by white ants. Looms of the rudest construction converted the produce of these into a hard, very stout, heavy cloth, about four or five feet in size, with one fourth of it a black border, and worn by women only.[1] Sessamum grew in ridges with the sorghum; its oil, and that extracted from the ground-nut, being used by the natives for smearing themselves from head to foot, giving their skins a handsome colour, like the gloss on polished marble. To vary the colour, some red clay is added. The sorghum is sometimes affected with a black blight, but the natives do not think this any deterioration; all goes into the mill. They live upon Indian corn, ulezee,[2] and sorghum, made into flour by rubbing the grains between stones as a housepainter pounds colours. Their vegetables are sweet potato, and the leaves, flowers, and fruits of pumpkins; and they brought us daily ground-nuts, tobacco, and fowls for sale. On the 3d of April the rice-harvest was being gathered in; but we perceived no traces of irrigation as in Egypt. Abundant rains gave an ample crop. The reapers consisted of negro women and girls, who sang pleasantly, though the scene was marred by the sight of a gang of men-slaves, heavily ironed together by their necks,[3] with some superintendents, gleaning. Those who had small knives cut the stalk four or five inches below the grain, and held it in their left hand till the hand was full, when it was placed in a huge tub of bark lying in the field. In this way a three-feet-high stubble was left standing, to be trodden down by cattle. The thrashing of the rice was novel. A quantity of ears was placed upon a cow's hide, slaves in irons were made to work it with their toes and feet, and winnow it in the wind; and after being thoroughly sun-dried upon a clear space of cow-dunged ground, it was fit for the process of shelling in the large pestle and mortar. If a considerable amount was to be thrashed, a bludgeon answered the purpose of the negroes' feet. The stubble would afterwards be turned over with powerful long-handled hoes, beds of the soil made, and the suckers or offshoots of the sweet potato planted there by bands of twenty or thirty villagers, shouting and singing the whole time. If our Seedees had to clean rice in the wooden mortar, a dozen hands would set about the work of two. It could not be done without those who worked beating time with the pestle to their song, the lookers-on clapping hands and stamping with their feet. The work and song never ceased till the rice was pounded almost into dust—such joyous, reckless creatures are these simple Africans! Yams are grown upon mounds of earth placed all over a field, the branches of the plant trained up a stick, or more commonly allowed to crawl over the ground. They do not attain a great growth. Grain is housed under the eaves of stack-shaped huts, or a clustered mass of Indian corn may be seen suspended from the bough

[1] This is important evidence that there existed an indigenous cloth-making craft which had not yet been made entirely redundant by imported cloths as was apparently the case in Unyanyembe.

[2] Ulezi is a form of millet.

[3] The question of whether this was an indigenous or imported form of slavery was raised in the previous chapter and reference made to the two pictures of the slaves Grant drew, here shown in Plates 6 and 7. The situation here in Mininga is evidence of the growing tendency of chiefs in the Unyamwezi area to acquire slaves as their dependants and so avoid kinship constraints. Holding slaves also increased their wealth and prestige. See Deutsch, 'Slavery and Social Change', p. 98. Deutsch sees Grant's evidence as particularly important and also, incidentally, includes on the cover of the Médard and Doyle volume in which his article appears, the composite version of Plates 6 and 7 which was made for Speke, *Journal*, facing p. 102. See also above, p. 120, n. 4.

of a tree, as exhibited in the illustration of 'Unyamuezi harvest' in Captain Speke's Journal.[1]

Provisions were all remarkably cheap upon this route. A fat cow was purchased for four fathoms of calico; another full-sized cow, and four small goats, were got for eight fathoms; a single sheep was dear at two fathoms; but three small goats were a bargain at the same price; a donkey was offered for fourteen, but he would have been dear at half the amount. For a fowl, one native demanded a charge of gunpowder, and would not sell it for anything else; another native led in a goat to camp, saying if we repaired his old flint-musket we should have the animal; he refused to bargain for anything else. For two quarts of impure honey, ten strings of common beads and a fathom of calico were asked, but not given. Milk was not always to be had, the people being afraid to keep herds of cattle, as they would attract the plundering propensities of the wandering Watuta race. Milk sometimes cost three strings of beads per pint; twelve measures of rice, one fathom of calico; sweet potatoes were one-tenth of the price they brought at Zanzibar; a basinful of ground-nuts or a load of wood cost but one string of ordinary beads. In short, our men lived luxuriously on their daily allowance of one string of beads per man. The people preferred keeping a few milk-cows,[2] being more productive than oxen, which were rarely met with, except one or two fattened up to a large size on purpose to be killed on the visit of a neighbouring sultan, or to celebrate some success in war. After the cattle have been brought in at night, a quantity of rubbish is allowed to smoke and smoulder in the centre of their fold. It was amusing to watch how each animal took up its nightly position, never altering it, and thoroughly enjoying the smoke, which prevented it from being annoyed by insects. The sheep were very stupid-looking animals, small, and wanting in rotundity. Their colour was either white and black, black with white, or a bay brown; no wool, but crisp hair; their tails tapered off from a broad fatty base. The head was the only handsome part; and two pieces of skin hung from the throat, as is seen in the long-eared breed of goats in India.

Of wild animals we shot none on this route, though, away from the cultivations, the spoors of buffalo and antelope were seen. A herd of ten elephants had passed through the district, eating up the sorghum crop, but no one went after them. The skin of a leopard was brought us for sale. Its spots were jet black upon yellow ground, and shone almost like a mirror. At this season of harvest the crops were favourable for concealing lions; and after a native had been killed by one, we were recommended not to go out after sunset. When travelling at night, the natives move quickly in bodies, blowing cow-horn trumpets, which sound wild in the stillness. While we were at Mineenga three men were chased by a pair of lions, and just as the last man reached a hut, he was picked off by a horrible man-eater. I went to see the spot.[3] There were the tracks of the poor victim when knocked down and dragged, and where his blood was first spilt; farther on, blood lay in quantities, as the body had been trailed along; but of the body itself only a small bit of bone was left. The incident had happened just after sunset, said to be the most dangerous time.

---

[1] Surely Grant is being unnecessarily modest here in not pointing out that the picture in Speke, *Journal*, facing p. 115, is entirely based on his careful drawing as shown here as Plate 4 and which has been discussed in Chapter IV, above, p. 119. The picture shows some of the operations here described by Grant.

[2] Koponen, *People and Production*, pp. 243–4, finds Grant's information very useful on cattle and their uses and surely might have found Grant's depiction of zebu cattle shown here in the very attractive Plate 13 additionally useful in discussing which types were in use.

[3] See Plate 8.

Here Speke shot and brought in a load of four large black geese, weighing 9 lb. each, having curious horny spurs to their shoulders, and taking to trees on being wounded. Farther south I had seen the same kind flapping their wings and pluming themselves between showers on rocks in the bed of a stream, and I took them for cormorants.[1] Their wings were white outside and black under. The natives came in numbers to see these birds, such a load of them never having been seen before. The wing-feathers were converted into head-dresses, but the meat was rejected. Flocks of wild pigeon and varieties of small hawks were constantly seen about the groves of palms. We shot numbers of the former, but they were not good eating, though plump to look at: a large red wattle surrounded the eyes; their plumage was extremely pretty; wings and rumps blue, with one white bar across their black tails: shoulders and elbows chocolate-coloured; feathers of the crop forked; and legs grey.[2] The crested crane is a slaty black or blue colour, the size of a heron, with shorter hackles. His head is very handsome, the contrasts of colour being beautiful. He has a black bill, a top of rich black feathers, behind it a straw-coloured bunch of four-inch-long fibres, having a few black featherlets near their roots; a chalky-white bare skin on the cheeks, and a hanging scarlet wattle underneath, with quantities of beautiful blue down on the rump; his call at night when roosting is harsh and grating.[3] Fish weighing three and four pounds were occasionally caught by our men in pools, but the natives would not eat them, as they had not come out of the sea. However, with the addition of eggs, we thought these mud-fish (*Makambara*) as good as any we had ever tasted.[4]

The villages of the country are fortified by high palisades; many of them are of immense strength, having a broad dry ditch, a quickset hedge of euphorbia, a covered-way, and then a palisading.[5] Sometimes a very good attempt at a bastion of mud is made, to give a flanking fire of arrows. Outside, opposite the only entry of one village, an old hoe was stuck on a mound, and protected by an awning of bark cloth: we were told this was to repel the evil eye. To give a general idea of these villages, I may mention that, on entering at the low doorway, you see before you an avenue of palisades; to the right and left sets of houses are similarly railed off. Until lodging had been obtained inside the village, we rested with our kit at the 'iwansa' or club-house. It was a long room, 12 by 18 feet, with one door, a low flat roof, well blackened with smoke, and no chimney. Along its length there ran a high inclined bench, on which cow-skins were spread for men to take their siesta. Some huge drums were hung in one corner, and logs smouldered on the ground. The young men of the village gathered at the club-house to get the news. They smoked, pulled out each other's eyelashes and eyebrows, filed their teeth, and cut their marks of caste on the face or temples. Dances would take place in the space in front of it, either by day or night. The regular Wezee dance is as follows:—A strip of bark or cow-skin is laid on the ground, and a line of men, the tallest in the centre, stand on it; the drums commence, a howling

[1] Neither of the two main East African species of cormorants seems to provide a likely identification. In fact, the horny spurs Grant mentions make it reasonably certain that this must be the spurwing goose, *Plectropterus gambensis*. Cave and Macdonald, *Birds of the Sudan*, p. 73.

[2] This would seem to be the red-eyed pigeon, *Columba guinea*.

[3] Appropriately enough, Grant now met the bird which was to become the national symbol of an independent Uganda almost 100 years later. The crested or crowned crane, *Balearica regulorum gibbericeps*, is now said to be under threat.

[4] Possibly *Protopterus amphibius*.

[5] In Plates 10, 15, and 17, plus Figure 43, p. 141, Grant shows the palisades and the layout of the villages.

song joins in, and with hands on their haunches and heads bent down, they thump in unison with their feet. Female spectators look on silently from behind, and men in front join in the chorus. A shout of laughter, or burst of admiration, winds up each dance, and never was there a more truly primitive scene of joyous riot.[1] Our Seedees had a much better performance, which they went through to the music of their voices, hands, and feet. Two stood in the centre of a ring, kicking high at one another like Frenchmen, clapping hands and dodging about most ingeniously, while the mob sang a lively song, clapped hands and stamped, all keeping perfect time, and enjoying it with the most thorough good-humour. They also had a favourite teetotum game. Two sides were formed facing each other, and all sitting on the ground. Each had before him a stump of Indian corn and a teetotum of gourd in his hand. The object was to knock over with the spinning-totum the adversaries' stump, and the efforts on each occasion caused immense merriment.

Extract from Journal: Original Description of the Teetotum Game
The seedees play a most amusing but good game – 6 to 8 on a side squatting with straddled legs at 10 to 12 feet apart – each has an old stump of Indian corn slotted in in front of him, the object is to knock him over on his side with a spinning totum (1) shying it ⑴ out of [the] hand with finger & thumb with a spinning force at the small stump (2). There must be always lots of spinners or its [*sic*] no fun. [NLS, MS. 17915, 22 April 1861][2]

In a Wezee village there are few sounds to disturb one's night rest: the traveller's horn, and the reply to it from a neighbouring village, an accidental alarm, the chirping of crickets, and the cry from a sick child, however, occasionally broke upon the stillness of our nights. Waking early, the first sounds we heard were the crowing of cocks, the impatient lowing of cows, the bleating of calves, and the chirping of sparrows and a few other unmusical birds. The pestle and mortar shelling corn would soon after be heard, or the cooing of wild pigeons in the grove of palms. The huts were shaped like corn-stacks, supported by bare poles, 15 feet high, and 15 to 18 feet in diameter; sometimes their grass roofs would be protected from sparks by "michans", or frames of Indian-corn stalks;[3] there were no carpets; all of them were unswept, and dark as the hold of a ship. A few earthen jars, made like the Indian "gurrah," for boiling vegetables or their stirabout,[4] tattered skins, an old bow and arrow, some cups of grass, some gourds, perhaps a stool, constituted the whole of the furniture. Grain was housed in bandboxes of bark, and goats or calves had free access over the house. The goat-skins worn by the Usagara natives differed from their neighbours in Unyanyembe, being neatly dressed, so as to leave an edging of fur upon them. The cotton-cloth of the country, or a piece of soiled calico,

---

[1] This is presumably what Grant was attempting to depict as accurately as he could in Plate 10. The version of this in Speke's *Journal*, p. 115, has been added to by the artist engraver with a depiction of Grant in Scottish dress dancing with Ukulima depicted as a woman. See the extended discussion on this matter in the section of the Introduction on Grant's illustrative work, pp. 8–11.

[2] The teetotum is in Britain a four-sided disc with letters on the faces which can be spun to act like dice in games of chance. This is interesting evidence that a version of the game was being played in the middle of Africa. Grant's drawing of the teetotum comes from his Journal, NLS, MS. 17915, 22 April 1861.

[3] Grant shows various huts in this region in Plates 8, 9, 15 and Figures 40 and 43, pp. 139 and 141.

[4] Here Grant extends the English term for oatmeal porridge to cover African porridge made of locally available grains or root crops. For an additional meaning, see p. 132, n. 3, on *ugali*, below.

generally covered the loins of the women. We saw here a man wearing the skin of a new antelope, the Nzoe, afterwards discovered in the Karague Lake.[1]

A description of one of the sultans will suffice to give a general impression of the appearance, manners, customs, &c., of the three Wezee clans[2] we had passed through, keeping in mind that this dignitary was the finest specimen we had seen, and was supposed to be enlightened, though he did not know his own age, could neither read, write, nor count beyond ten, and had no names for any day of the week, for any month, or for any year! After we had been about a month in his district, Sultan Ugalee[3]—*i.e.,* Stirabout— arrived at Mineenga on the 21st of April, and was saluted by file-firing from our volunteers, and shrill cries from the women. He visited us in our verandah the day following. He looks about twenty-two years of age; has three children and thirty wives; is six feet high, stout, with a stupid, heavy expression. His bare head is in tassels, black hanks of fibre being mixed in with his hair. His body is loosely wrapped round with a blue and yellow cotton cloth; his loins are covered with a dirty oily bit of calico, and his feet are large and naked. A monster ivory ring is on his left wrist, while the right one bears a copper ring of rope pattern; several hundreds of wire rings are massed round his ankles. He was asked to be seated on one of our iron stools, but looked at first frightened, and did not open his mouth. An old man spoke for him, and a crowd of thirty followers squatted behind him. Speke, to amuse him, produced his six-barrelled revolver, but he merely eyed it intently. The books of birds and animals, on being shown to him upside down by Sirboko, the head man of the village, drew from him a sickly smile, and he was pleased to imply that he preferred the animals to the birds. He received some snuff in the palm of his hand, took a good pinch, and gave the rest to his spokesman. He was led to look at my musquito-curtained [*sic*] bed, and on moving away was invited to dine with us. We sent him a message at seven o'clock that the feast was prepared, but a reply came that he was 'full' and could not be tempted even with a glass of rum. The following day he came to wish us good-bye, and left without any exchange of presents, being thus very different from the grasping race of Ugogo.

The arms of the people consisted of spears, bows and arrows, and leather shields shaped like the figure 8. Boys in the villages were fond of practising war, by pelting each other with Indian-corn stumps, using leather shields of defence.

We had daily visits from the women of the country, who came in parties. They were copper-coloured and flat-featured, and wore round their necks a profusion of pendent bead necklaces of the colour of the mountain-ash berry; their ankles were concealed with masses of wire rings. For hours they sat silently before us, smoking, nursing, and shampooing the limbs and necks of their infants; some wore the heavy cloth of the country, others had soiled robes of calico. Young girls, many of them with pleasing faces and plump round figures, wore merely a diminutive cloth about their loins, and infants had a fringe of beads. These women were rarely accompanied by men, but on Speke having taken a woman's likeness, the husband requested him to write his (the husband's) name on the picture, so that the people of England might know whose wife she was! We saw

---

[1] See Figure 57, p. 207.

[2] Presumably, Grant means three of the chiefdoms among the Banyamwezi, which were not clans in any technical sense, of Usagari, Unyambewa and Ukimbu.

[3] *Ugali* is also the Swahili word for an African porridge. The secondary meaning for 'stirabout' in English is a busy, bustling person (*OED*). One assumes therefore that Speke and Grant made the name into a little joke.

some decidedly handsome N'yambo girls[1] on this route: their men attend upon cattle exclusively, while they stay at home doing household work, cooking, coquetting, and showing off their beautiful feet and ankles. Two, in the bloom of youth, sat by us with their arms most affectionately twined round each other's neck, till asked to sit apart that they might be sketched.[2] The arms were at once dropped, exposing their beautiful necks and busts, quite models for a "Greek Slave". Their woolly hair was combed out and raised up from the forehead and over their ears by a broad band from the skin of a milk-white cow; this contrasted strikingly with their transparent light copper skins.

The Waha[3] women are somewhat similar, having tall, erect, graceful figures even without crinoline, and with intelligent features. They are looked upon as an inferior tribe to the Watusi (described at Kazeh), though wearing the hair bound up, and having naked arms, &c., similar to them; but their cow-skin coverings from the waist to the ankle are different, being of a yellow-ochre colour. We put up one day at the settlement of a trader, Sungoro-bin-Tabeeb, of whom we had heard a good deal, as he travelled always in a double-poled tent, and kept sixty wives, who lived like goats inside his tent. We saw five of his women; one was a Hubshee,[4] or Abyssinian, whose appearance disappointed us. Her mouth was large, and, though fair for a negress, and with distinctly bridged nose, she was a poor specimen of her race. Another was of my favourite caste, always distinguishable by their intelligence and easy, polite manner—a Watusi, a beautiful tall girl, with large dark eyes, the smallest mouth and nose, thin lips, small hands, &c. Speke said she much resembled the Somal;[5] her noble race never will become slaves, preferring death to slavery, and they refuse to touch fowls or goats. It was to be regretted that she had not a better husband, for Sungoro had been in jail for robbery, committed by order of his Arab master. His master, however, by way of compensation, left him his ill-gotten wealth.

Two years previous to our arrival in this district, the wandering Watuta, whose women are said to use the bow and arrow, treacherously inviting up their enemy, had come in thousands to plunder cattle from the villages; but after fighting against the sultan for five days and losing three men, they left, not being able to make way against the muskets of a Seedee named Sirboko. We lived for some days with this excellent man, who was most anxious to get back to Zanzibar, but the sultan would not hear of his departure; because, in return for his having protected his country, he had made over to him a considerable tract of land, on which he was expected to reside for life. This was a rare instance of generosity. While living in his clean, comfortable, thatched bungalow, waiting for porters, Sheikh Said communicated to us by letter from Kazeh that we had better get on with our journey as fast as we could, for the Arabs there had meditated putting us to death, believing that we were the accomplices of the rebel chief Manua Sera! However, on our friend Moossah taking a

---

[1] This is a somewhat puzzling observation because the Banyambo (Abanyambo) are the 'commoner' people of Karagwe region west of Lake Victoria, not the cattle-keeping elite groups. Presumably, they were commoner women who had become the wives and concubines of the dominant Hinda clans. The social structure in Karagwe is complicated. See Katoke, 'Karagwe: A Pre-Colonial State', pp. 530–31.

[2] Yet Grant seems reluctant to illustrate clearly what he goes on to describe about the girls' figures. See Figure 41, p. 140.

[3] The Ha, living to the west of Unyamwezi, are generally regarded as distinct, their affinities being with the interlacustrine peoples and having, as Grant goes on to observe, the same division between the cattle keepers and the commoners.

[4] More correctly in Kiswahili, *Habeshi*.

[5] That is, 'Somali'. Speke had been in Somaliland with Burton in 1854–5.

solemn Mussulman oath that neither he nor we were thus guilty, the affair was supposed to have blown over, but they would not allow Moossah to join us. Since poor Snay's death Mohinna was the chief of the Arabs, and had taken offence at us, probably because he was requested not to beat so brutally his women-slaves, who one day came weeping and wailing to us at Kazeh for protection. The result of our good-natured advice was that, though he promised he should not again offend, the poor women got another and more severe beating, and were put in the stocks to prevent their coming near us to complain. The class of Arabs we met were certainly a most degraded set, and instead of improving the country had brought ruin upon it by their imperiousness and cruelty.[1] All traded in slaves, whom, for security's sake, they were often obliged to treat harshly. At Mineenga, we met several parties or gangs of slaves in chains, and my thoughts reverted to the happy village-life in our own country, a pleasing contrast to such painful and revolting scenes.[2]

Clad each in a single goat-skin, the slaves kept themselves warm at night lying near a fire. Never is the chain unfastened day or night. Should one of the number require to move, the whole must accompany him. All ate together boiled sweet potato, or a spinage made from the leaves of the pumpkin plant, and were kept in poor condition to prevent their becoming troublesome. One day a woman-slave, on seeing our cook casting away the head of a fowl he had just killed, picked it up, and gave it to a poor convalescent slave, who grasped it with the eagerness of a dog. Any meat or bones left over from our dinner were always given them. A small lad, whose ears had been cut off (probably a Uganda boy), watched or accompanied the slaves, and treated them, I thought, with unfeeling coarseness. A sick slave having recovered, it was the boy's duty to chain him to his gang again, and it was grievous to see the rough, careless way he used the poor emaciated creature. Beyond bringing in firewood for themselves and cleaning corn, they were not much worked. The sole object of the owner was to keep them alive, and prevent their running away till sold at the coast. Ten men and five women had lately deserted, chains and all, from Sirboko, so that he did not approve of taking off their irons; "the birds would soon fly if he did". They looked generally sullen and full of despair; but might be seen dancing, and even riotous at times, till a word from the earless imp of a boy restored order. One amongst them was of a cannibal race to the N.W. of the Tanganyika.[3] In appearance he did not differ from the rest, but he was laughed at for his cannibal propensities, which were not entertained by them. Another who had been five years in chains was heard by Speke to say that "life was a burden to him; he could stand it no longer." We had observed him to be a good fellow, the leader and conductor of his gang, and we released him from bondage; his chains were struck off with a hammer while he lay calmly with his head on a block. Once on his feet, a freed man, he did not seem to believe the fact; but when attired in a clean sheet of calico by Baraka, he strutted about, the pet of our Seedees, and came to make us his best bow. His life had been hazardous, as proved by the spear-wounds in his body; he had been captured by the Watuta, who cut off several of his toes, and also some of his toe-nails. This man never deserted us the whole journey. It was his good fortune to reach Cairo, with the character of a faithful servant; and if any of his

[1] Arabs were competing with Africans for control of trading activities. Their access to supplies of cloth and beads meant it was possible to use patronage to get supporters.

[2] See Plates 6 and 7.

[3] Tales of a supposed cannibal race living beyond Lake Tanganyika were common to the east of the lake but never substantiated.

companions attempted to assault his benefactor Baraka, he would instantly fly to defend him.[1]

The curiosity of the people was sometimes trying to our tempers; but it was excusable, as they had never seen white men before. There was not the slightest privacy even inside our tent; they were certain to peer in. Sitting in the open air under a tree was tried, and succeeded best, for they saw you till they became tired of looking, or at your laughing at or mimicking them. Every one, except an old woman, was easy to manage. She would pester you with questions you didn't understand, didn't mind being laughed at, and would not leave till led away by some villager who took compassion on us. Another woman was most anxious to see my feet. "What had I under my shoes and socks? She had never seen such coverings". I told her she could not be gratified till the evening, when I would take them off. The men were generally fawning, very inquisitive, and fond of putting their arms round Bombay's neck to try and get him to give them some present. Little satisfied them; and though we had all our kit without lock or key, we never suffered loss by theft in a Wezee village. At Sirboko's, thieves came one night, were caught, beaten, and dismissed. Exactly one month afterwards they again came, carrying away a tin case with clothes and writing materials, seven ivories of Sirboko's, &c. &c. Our Seedees were as active as policemen, flying about the whole night with torches, looking for the stolen goods, and at break of day they found the tin case, minus some things, including four tusks. To recover the rest a quack doctor or Mganga was sent for, an elderly-looking man, and he found the whole, except an ivory and a flannel shirt, in a couple of days. The thieves, in fear, had placed the articles at the doorway of the village. Our men were most excitable creatures. If a cow attempted to break out of the village by jumping fences and defied capture, they never thought of calming her, but all would arm with guns, spears, swords, and sticks, and chase her down till stupefied with fear. If they had been behaving badly, it did not prevent them from asking to have a cow given them; and on being refused, they never sulked, but took it out of you some other way by studying their own wishes, comforts, and wants in marching, halting, eating, drinking, or stealing whatever they pleased, and at night giving us the benefit of their laughter, shouting, and riots or howling, in imitation of a Wezee who has smoked bhang.[2] Our cooks (Seedee boys) were most difficult to teach, though they had learned a little from the Cape men, who had always done this duty. The only idea these black roughs had of cooking for themselves was to stick a wooden skewer into a piece of meat and scorch it over the ashes, or make stirabout. No great *cuisine* could therefore be expected. Being anxious on one occasion to get some soup after a fever, and knowing the larder to contain only a wild duck, I asked Rehan,[3] "Could you get me some soup for breakfast? I cannot eat meat". "Yes". "What!" said I, "out of a duck?" "O yes". Thinking him a clever fellow, I gladly consented; but his soup was only a thin watery stew, placed before me with the most perfect complaisance. Again, at 7 P.M., he came up asking would I like some dinner? He had not thought of preparing even a boiled potato. Such were the men we had as cooks for our entire journey. On the march a party of them tried, by holding out for three days in not accepting their rations, to extort double allowances, on account of the price of provisions; but finding

---

[1] This man was named Farhan ('Joy'). See Simpson, *Dark Companions*, pp. 30, 36, 193. It is not clear why Grant does not name him. It is notable that he regarded Baraka as his actual benefactor; the reality was that in several respects power in the life of the caravan lay less with the two Europeans than with Baraka and Bombay.

[2] That is Indian hemp, *Cannabis indica*, which was chewed or smoked.

[3] Presumably this is Rahan, as Grant normally spelled the name.

it of no use, they quietly submitted. Again, they told us our donkeys would not live long if they were made to carry beef; and this I believe was only a device to get the meat themselves.

When detained for want of porters at Mineenga, we taught our men the sword exercise for an hour every afternoon. They were apt at learning, did remarkably well, and enjoyed it very much, though kept strictly to it for the time they were out. Not understanding discipline, if a shower of rain fell, they thought themselves at liberty to run off our parade-ground; and when I brought a cane in my hand, they could not resist a titter, thinking I had brought it to enforce orders, and not merely to show the sword positions. On the coast we had taught them the platoon exercise and target practice, but they never would take care of their ammunition, ramrods, or stoppers—always firing them away. On the arrival of a detachment, salutes of welcome must be fired, and always, on new moon being visible, each one would try to be the first to fire his gun. But with six months' drill and strict discipline, we saw that a negro could be made into a good light-infantry soldier; and if he only becomes attached to his officer, there is no more devoted follower in the world.

On arrival outside a Wezee village, generally a set of armed men would meet us, bounding on the grass, running in circles, making feints at our caravan, either in delight, or in attempts to frighten us. A shot in the air would cool their courage, though our porters on hearing it would sometimes drop their loads and fly in fear, but speedily returning when reassured. Men were in abundance in the country, and if a solitary one ran away, he could always be replaced. For instance, a father saw his son carrying a load in our caravan; he led him angrily away, and we soon got another. But to collect one or two hundred we found a most difficult task: they are as fickle as the wind. A wave of a flag will attract them, while one misplaced expression will send them away discontented. They higgle pertinaciously about their hire; and after they have been induced to accept double wages, they suddenly change their minds, think you've got the best of it, and ask for more, or more commonly disappear.

One of the most pleasing sensations in going through an immense forest is suddenly to come upon the traces of man. The Wezee experience this, for, in their forest south of Kazeh, they erect triumphal arches with poles, over or by the side of the path. These they ornament with antelope-skulls, having the horns, or with elephant-dung, bones, bows, or broken gourds. It cheers the traveller, and gives fresh vigour to his wearied limbs, for he knows that camp and water are never far distant, and that the trumpet of the caravan leader must soon sound the welcome "halt." In travelling through these forests, the Unyamuezi[1] rarely loses his way, as he is accustomed to range in woods, and to mark his route either by breaking boughs or noting the position of the sun.

During my fifty-five days' detention at Mineenga, Speke had been away for sixteen days at Kazeh trying to procure porters by means of the Arabs. The third day after his return, the 18th of May 1861, I marched northward with a detachment of forty loads, making for Ukuni. He picked me up on the 21st, and I again went on alone, and reached it on the 27th. The Journal of the last two days[2] may perhaps possess some interest to the reader, as it introduces him to Ukulima, the sultan, in whose place I was detained one hundred and nine days. It is as follows:—

[1] *Sic*. Presumably Grant meant to write 'Munyamwezi' indicating a single member of this people but became muddled over the appropriate prefixes.

[2] There follows the longest extract from his journal which Grant provided in his book. In fact, the text given is faithful to the sense of the original although the mode of expression has frequently been made more comprehensible.

"*26th May.*—Speke keeps the larder well filled.[1] Last night, three guinea-fowl and a large tree-goose. I went early amongst the Watusi; handsome people, beautiful rounded small heads, prominent large eyes, thin noses, rather compressed upper jaws; all so clean and trim; no resemblance to the dirty Wezee, who are coarse and mannerless in comparison. They make their own baskets of osier-like twigs, with a sharpened spear, and work with their feet very neatly. They got a cow down by pulling its hind-legs to a post, and then carefully washed its eye, which had been injured. The blacksmith was working amongst them making wire anklets from long rods of iron; bellows very small, of wood, with cane handles, which a man worked up and down. The hammer was a massive mason's chisel: they worked squatting. A whole family were very curious to hear the tick of my watch. The fighting Watuta had one open-field combat with the Watusi, and obtained a victory over them; both are afraid of each other. I see that the slaves of the Wezees are very well dressed, and treated with great kindness, never doing but what they choose: quite different from slaves at Zanzibar, where, as Bombay tells me, they would be made to work all day, and, by some, be made to steal all night. The orthodox custom at Zanzibar is five days' labour for master, and two days' for the slave himself. Rehan (the new cook) came to say 'there was no grease to roast with'. 'What are you to roast?' He pointed to his breast. 'You ought not to roast a brisket'. He brought a tongue, hump, and double brisket, smelling, all of which had been boiled yesterday, and now he wanted to roast the brisket already done.

"*27th.*—Bombay and I march with 38 porters to make a start of it to Nunda, in Ukuni, and to see Sultan Ukulima. Distance was eight miles through a very pretty country, with rocks jutting out fantastically, and lying now and then one on another; cultivation all the way. Sighted the village when within a mile of it; quantities of spring water coming down from a rocky height to our right. After we had entered the first milk-bush enclosure, there were several cleanly-swept windings. Village nearly empty. A heavy old man sitting on a stool with half-a-dozen men round him, induced me to say 'Yambo'; he returned it, and I went looking for a house. Came to the palace, a very high round hut, smelling strongly of goats and cattle. I asked permission to live here, and the old man, who proved to be the sultan, said, 'Doogoh yango'[2]—'Come along, my brother'. Sweeping out the verandah of goat-dung, my bed was soon made. The sultana, a fat, fair, gentle old lady, welcomed me with both hands as if I had been her son. She was so surprised at the bedding as she sat upon it, and everything she saw, saying 'Eeh, eeh!' and nodding her head: indeed, all were surprised.[3] Bombay got some pombé;[4] the drunken old sultan himself carried a basket-cup of it. He drank first (through a straw), and then I had some, and very good it was. Then he drank again, and I drank again, laughing heartily. People in hundreds came. I went to sleep, though drums beat all day in honour of the arrival. Their politeness was remarkable; they retired as I sat down at meals. Milk very dear, and got with great difficulty. Lads excited with drums, jumping in the air, and flying about. Did not see old man for the rest of the day; he was in a state of pombé![5]

---

[1] The original wording in the Journal is 'S keeps the pot a going.' NLS, MS. 17915, 26 May 1861.

[2] More properly, *Ndugu mwango*.

[3] See Plates 15, 16 and 17, which show the huts and people Grant mentions.

[4] The Swahili word for beer.

[5] Grant seems himself to have become a little intoxicated and was honest enough to include this passage in his book.

Figure 38. The house in Kaze (Tabora) where Grant and Speke lodged for seven weeks when they reached Unyanyembe in January 1861. The house belonged to Musa Mzuri, an Indian trader who had, unusually, chosen to leave Zanzibar and establish himself among the Nyamwezi people at what had become a nodal point for trade. Musa gave the explorers much advice about the territories to the north which they would need to pass through. NLS MS. 17920, no. 30. Reproduced by permission of the National Library of Scotland.

Figure 39. A general view of the countryside in Unyamwezi in March 1861. A village appears in the foreground. NLS MS. 17920, no. 31 recto. Reproduced by permission of the National Library of Scotland.

Figure 40. Grant's attempt to show a family plus its palisaded hut at Mininga, a settlement he reached in April 1861 as he attempted to move northward from Kaze. NLS MS. 17920, no. 33. Reproduced by permission of the National Library of Scotland.

Figure 41. A Munyambo, or peasant-class girl, depicted at an unspecified task but presumably hoeing, in April 1861. NLS MS. 17920, no. 34. Reproduced by permission of the National Library of Scotland.

Figure 42. Silhouettes in Ukuni. Given the difficulty he experienced in his attempts to depict Africans, Grant here seems to have decided to try to produce silhouettes of people in Ukuni, c. May 1861. The experiment was not continued. NLS MS. 17920, no. 37. Reproduced by permission of the National Library of Scotland.

Figure 42A. The chief in Ukuni named Ukulima whom Grant calls a 'Sultan'. Grant was to have a long and close relationship with Ukulima. The silhouette is extracted from Figure 42 and omitted there.

Figure 43. Maulah's village in Ukuni, August 1861. See also Plate 11. NLS MS. 17920, no. 41. Reproduced by permission of the National Library of Scotland.

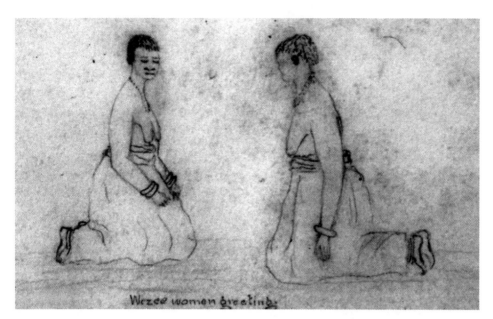

Wezee women greeting.

Figure 44. Two Banyamwezi greeting one another. This sketch was part of Grant's continuing attempts to draw African figures. It was also part of his growing interest in the customs of the people of Unyamwezi among whom he was spending so much time in 1861. NLS MS. 17920, no. 48. Reproduced by permission of the National Library of Scotland.

Figure 45. The execution seen in Ukuni. This is the second depiction in a series of three in which Grant recorded the execution of an adulterer in Ukuni on 17 August 1861. For the first, see Plate 18. NLS MS. 17921, no. 208. Reproduced by permission of the National Library of Scotland.

Scene 5 Sultan keeps back the crowd. His daughter in law with bloody spear point. Mob come on the life & body & trailed out of it. First spear given by some ... by a ... woman.

Figure 46.   The third of the execution series. Grant was sickened by the scene and deplored the role of the women depicted. Nevertheless, he felt bound to complete these pictures. However, they were not included in either of the two portfolios of his illustrations which he had prepared, presumably because he did not wish to show them to family and friends. NLS MS. 17921, no. 209. Reproduced by permission of the National Library of Scotland.

Figure 47.   'Natives of Usui' was Grant's title for this picture. The location of the place is more correctly 'Rusubi' which was a minor chiefdom in the north of Unyamwezi. By 10 November 1861, when this picture was recorded, Grant had been able to resume his march northwards and was nearing Karagwe. Note the supplies of bananas, an increasingly important crop as he entered the 'interlacustrine' group of kingdoms. NLS MS. 17920, no. 43. Reproduced by permission of the National Library of Scotland.

Figure 48.   Scene in Usui (Rusubi). Here the general character of the landscape in Rusubi is shown as Grant saw it in November 1861. NLS MS. 17920, no. 44, part 1. Reproduced by permission of the National Library of Scotland.

Figure 49.   'Rocks in Usui' was Grant's title for this view in Rusubi. NLS MS. 17919, no. 12. Reproduced by permission of the National Library of Scotland.

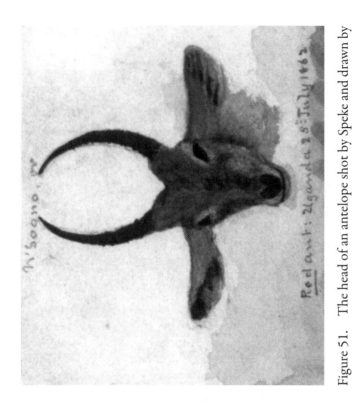

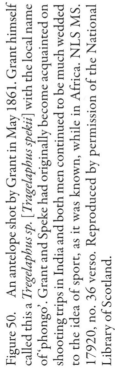

Figure 50. An antelope shot by Grant in May 1861. Grant himself called this a *Tregelaphus sp.* [*Tragelaphus spekii*] with the local name of 'phongo'. Grant and Speke had originally become acquainted on shooting trips in India and both men continued to be much wedded to the idea of sport, as it was known, while in Africa. NLS MS. 17920, no. 36 verso. Reproduced by permission of the National Library of Scotland.

Figure 51. The head of an antelope shot by Speke and drawn by Grant in July 1862. Grant refers to this as a bush bok. NLS MS. 17920, no. 44, part 2. Reproduced by permission of the National Library of Scotland.

CHAPTER VI

[Pages 81–110]

Life in Ukuni[1] [27 May–12 September 1861]

To commence with the country around, I may state that its general elevation above sea-level is 3260 feet. All the lands run southwards, and are cleared for cultivation, while the low hills are well wooded, their ridges capped with huge masses of rounded rock, some single blocks forty and fifty feet in height, balanced on each other, or forming gorges and passes between one valley and another.[2] The village of the smaller sultan of Roongwa, seven miles to the N.W., has some remarkably pretty landscapes in its neighbourhood. Upon gently-swelling lands gloomy peaked masses of granite rise amidst the dense foliage, reminding one of a baronial castle at home, with its parks and clumps of trees. Sometimes large water cavities are seen in those boulders; one contained sweet pure water in a basin fifty feet in circumference and six to eight feet deep, which had been worn out by the crumbling of ages.[3]

During the months of June, July, August, and twelve days of September, we had but one or two slight showers of rain (in July), which were preceded by dull cloudy weather every night, that prevented our seeing a comet in the constellation of Ursa Major. The sun rose and set in a haze, which obscured the sky for 40°. During the day, unless the regular S.S.E. wind blew very hard, a veil of mist lay about. This wind from the S.E.[4] was very unhealthy, making every one sneeze, and giving hard coughs and colds. It generally began about 8 A.M.; but by the 12th of September it changed to a more easterly direction, and brought with it beautiful clear weather. The June mornings were piercingly cold, and at night the naked boy who looked after the calves might always be seen sleeping with his head pillowed upon them to keep himself warm, and our Seedees would lie out for the night with a sheet-covering, and a blazing fire at their backs. By the end of June the trees had shed their leaves. Nothing but evergreens were interesting in the forest; the grasses had been burnt; the fields lay in fallow baked in the sun, or were of powdered dust, where cattle had trodden: the aspect was decidedly wintry. In August the trees began to bud,

---

[1] More properly Bukune; this was yet another minor chiefdom within Unyamwezi. Bukune is about 15 miles (24 km) to the south of the township of Kahama.

[2] See Figure 49, p. 144.

[3] See Plate 12.

[4] The south-east trades in these months bring air from the Indian Ocean but unless there are mountains to produce orographic rainfall, these months are a relatively dry season in this region. Later in the year, from October to December, the north-east trades, having passed over the equatorial zones of the Indian Ocean, bring rain. A second wet season comes in March with the initial onset of the south-east trades.

and the grasses, where they had been set on fire, were sprouting with fresh leaves. I have
alluded to the S.E. wind being unhealthy—not a man of us escaped it. Speke suffered
most dangerously from its effects while separated for three months from me. His heavy
cough had been brought on by constant anxiety, and by his walking about the country
trying to persuade men to lead, or proceed with us in our journey northwards. My fever
came every second day from the 29th of May till the 4th of July, lasting six hours, making
me feel weak and tottering. In July I had colds, discharges of mucus from the nose, and a
large abscess burst—all of which staved off fever for a time; and I had only one or two
attacks, of nine hours each, during the two following months. In the intervals of fever I
generally managed to go for a stroll with my gun to shoot a dove or guinea-fowl for the
sultan or myself. Of ten Seedees who formed my body-guard, servants, &c., only half were
generally fit for duty, or, perhaps, four in ten, at this S.E. wind season. Their complaints
were of the chest, cough, fever, abscess, ulcers, and venereal (the *social evil* was evident
every evening in the frequented part of the village). Our medicine-chest was at every one's
service, but some Seedees applied to an old-lady doctor, who, instead of cure, brought
tears and screams from them whilst applying her remedies to ulcers, bandaging them up
with cow-dung and leaves to exclude the air. To cure headaches, the men cut their temples
and rubbed in a paste of gunpowder. Blood would scarcely appear, but the mark was
indelible, and the cure said to be complete.

The diseases observed amongst the inhabitants were swollen legs, resembling
elephantiasis, itch in children, scales on the eyes, a few smallpox-marked and blind
people, one harelip, and a shrivelled infant without a thumb. One blind man used to
visit periodically, and, without even the guide of a dog, knew every turn in the village;
he was welcomed everywhere, as a smile for ever played upon his lips. By moonlight he
would stand singing for two hours at a time with a crowd of a hundred people, men and
women, the sultan amidst them, all round him, joining in a chorus of almost devotional
music. He had the power, by placing his hand to his mouth, of sending the deep, pleasing
tones of his voice away to a distance, which gave delight to everyone, the women in
particular showing approval by a shrill peculiar falsetto noise, which they make by
tapping the cheek or shaking the lower lip with the forefinger and thumb. Another blind
man, deeply marked with smallpox, gathered the village boys around him and taught the
songs of their country, while he beat time with his foot. They have several fine national
airs.

Their funeral ceremonies are simple enough. Chiefs, and most of the respectable classes,
are buried under the floors of their dwellings,[1] or more commonly in cattle-sheds; while
witches and slaves are thrown into the jungle without interment. I observed one of the
latter lying, tied with his face to a pole, in long grass, with some rags round the waist; the
limbs were trussed up much in the same way as an infant lies asleep.

Though residing in the verandah of the chief house of the M'teme or sultan, or in the
most central part of the village, I rarely saw any men at their meals, unless when assembled
round pombé. They seemed to take pot-luck at any hour of the day, and at any house
where the signs of eating were going on—getting a boiled sweet potato here, a drink of
pombé there, or a snack of beef as a rarity. Women were more regular in their living. The

[1] Grant's evidence was still accepted by the modern anthropologist, R. G. Abrahams; see Abrahams, *Peoples of Greater Unyamwezi*, pp. 75–7, for a discussion of death and burial customs among the Nyamwezi.

lady of my house, seated on a wooden stool in the open yard,[1] had always some guests to dine with her, generally women of her own age and some little children, and never by any chance did her husband, the sultan, eat with her on these occasions. The food—some boiled sweet potatoes—would be brought on a wooden tray, and placed on the ground by a servant-maid, who knelt on one knee, or a bowl full of pombé would be presented in the same way. The sultan had seven wives. Each had her own separate house and establishment, which he visited daily, though at night he always slept in a place not much larger than himself, surrounded by charms and lions' paws. He lived almost entirely upon pombé, drinking it three or four times during the day, commencing as early as seven o'clock, and ending the day, if he was not already stupefied, by having it at suppertime. He was a very hale, healthy-looking old man, apparently about seventy, and most active in his habits. Different houses in his village held daily 'receptions' for him, when he presided, and he was the first to taste the bowl of beer. The female population drank separately, and were presided over by the sultana. The liquor took five days of preparation: the grain (sorghum) had to be cleaned, ground, soaked, boiled, generally with cow-dung as firewood, allowed to cool, and was drunk, without filtration, in a fermenting state, out of bowls neatly made of grass by the women. With honey added it was tolerable, but without it the beverage was coarse and heady to a stranger. Our men were constantly tipsy; but the natives who fed upon it had a healthy appearance, and rarely became drunk. Their active early habits conduced to this result, for all of them were in the fields before sunrise gathering the crop, or were doing varied works inside their enclosures. The women on the 3d June were clipping with a knife the tops of the sorghum, putting them into baskets, and carrying the whole on their heads to the village, where the grain, after being thoroughly sun-dried, was thrashed out by lines of men with long-handed rackets, as seen in the illustration, "Unyamuezi Harvest," of Speke's Journal.[2] They sang and beat the grain to a chorus, winnowed it in the S.E. breeze, divided it into shares, and by the 1st of July all was housed for the year; and porters, had they chosen, might have gone with us to Karague, but they preferred tasting the new year's grain. After the harvest, the poorer people were allowed to glean the potato, ground-nut, and grain fields, glad to have some refuse, as, should the previous season have been a poor one, they must have lived upon dried potato, or what wild herbs they could pick up. Our Seedees, all of whom except ten were away with Speke, could not afford to purchase a cow or goat, and they felt the want of meat considerably, but not to the extent that a European does. My gun almost daily provided a guinea-fowl or pigeon, and the Seedees lived upon stirabout or fish; while, clubbing their daily rations, they could afford to purchase a fowl, or by doing some office for the natives, such as sewing, &c., they always secured friends. The coin we at first used was rose-coloured beads, called "goolabee". These were great favourites; and when exhausted, the price of everything rose to double—in fact, the new coinage of sea-green beads, or "magee bahr" was refused point-blank; they wouldn't circulate. Pure whites, "Kanyera", were tried; they also failed. Indian reds, or "Kudunduguru", were utterly refused, as only taken in uncivilised northern countries! "Kutu'mnazee", cocoa-nut leaves, at last passed muster, and milk was procured for our tea. It was a regular strike in the

---

[1] See Plate 15.

[2] This was, of course, Grant's own depiction of various agricultural operations: see Plate 4. A faithful engraved version appeared in Speke, *Journal,* p. 115.

market. All this rubbish of beads was merely the equivalent to coppers.[1] Silver was represented by webs of unbleached calico, 30 to 32 yards long, 1 yard wide, and weighing 10 lb., stamped in blue, 'Massachusetts Sheeting'.[2] The man who got this stamped portion—"Keerole", or looking-glass,[3] as they called it—was thought a considerable swell, and took care to show it across his loins. Sovereign coinage consisted of coils of brass and copper wire, thicker than that used for telegraphic purposes, and converted into bracelets by the natives.[4] The blacksmith is never allowed to work inside the village, perhaps because he has ample space outside, and it is considered safer—not that his caste prohibits it.[5]

The nodules of ore are generally smelted in the forests, and brought in a lump to the smith, who, by means of stone anvils and stones as sledge-hammers, converts it into a long rod; and finally, by a hand-vice, and grease from a small pot he carries, it is tied between two posts and drawn till it becomes a thread. It is now fit, after being once heated, for being twisted neatly with the finger and thumb round a few hairs from the tail of a cow, or the thicker hair of a giraffe. In this state it is worn in rings ornamenting the ankles of men and women, fifteen of them costing one string of beads, value a halfpenny, and fifteen copper or brass ones being double price. Iron hoes, adzes, grass-hooks, small knives, pincers, &c., are all made up by the natives in the above rude way; and this is the extent of their knowledge in ironwork.[6]

The women have no needlework. The men, if they make a web in the loom, sew it all themselves; but the former are very neat-handed at working in straw and matting. They grind the corn and attend to the house. There is no fine earthenware, such as cups and plates, in the country; they are not requisite. Straw or wooden ones suffice to hold water, beer, or vegetables; and European pots and kettles are represented by earthen gurrahs,[7] like a sphere with a slice off it. Salt is extracted from the soil, as practised in Uhiao,[8] and is considered better than that taken from the ashes of plants.

The forest at this dry season did not afford any amusement in its flora: everything was in a dormant state, and few or no flowers could be gathered, except some jasmine-scented bushes in the stream-bed; the beautiful little seeds of the abrus[9] peeping out of their open curled-up pods, and the plant twining delicately round a small tree; some thorny bushes of a vermilion flowering-shrub, and large umbrageous trees of the ficus order, used for bird-lime by the natives; several sweet plums now ripe, but nearly all stone. The most

---

[1] Burton, *Lake Regions*, II, pp. 390–95 gives a full description of the bead trade and names many of the 400 varieties which he says existed. The names reported here by Grant coincide with Burton's designations. The *kudunduguru* was a dull brick-red colour and little prized; the *ukuti wa mnazi* is a sea-green colour. It is not clear, however, what type of bead was implied by the term Grant printed as 'magee bahr'.

[2] This is important evidence that by this date imported cloth, *merikani*, was beginning to replace locally produced textiles. See Deutsch, 'Slavery and Social Change', p. 79.

[3] The Swahili is *kioo*.

[4] The copper and brass wire mentioned was imported but, as Grant notes, normally fashioned into coil bracelets or necklaces.

[5] In other areas, smiths were often regarded as separate socially but Grant's firm insistence that this was not the case here is important evidence.

[6] Despite Grant's dismissive tone, most authorities draw attention to the importance of the production of iron hoes both for local use and trade.

[7] The Hindi term for an earthen jar.

[8] The country of the Yao people living east of Lake Malawi many of whom became slaves or porters including several in Grant's party; presumably he obtained this information from 'Bombay' or another servant.

[9] Probably *Abrus precatorius*.

useful tree to the natives here is the Miombo;[1] it makes a brilliant fire, and lasts the whole night, just to suit the African, who luxuriates in its heat. Most of the trees are bare-poled, admirably adapted for palisade purposes, and seldom heavier than can be carried by two men. The wands from the Miombo, a kind of banyan,[2] afford the natives the fibre which they attach to their wool. Its manufacture is simple: split the wand longitudinally, separate the inner from the outer bark, and chew it well till the next wand is ready; use soon blackens it. Every tree and fruit has its separate name and use in this country.

The sultan owned three hundred milch cows, yet every day there was a difficulty about purchasing milk, and we were obliged to boil it that it might keep, for fear we should have none the following day. This practice the natives objected to, saying, "The cows will stop their milk if you do so." The calves drank most of it. Butter, except when rancid, we could not procure, the people using it for smearing their persons.[3] They seldom had butcher-meat for their dinners, preferring to economise their cattle; and on my informing them that a cow lay in a neighbouring jungle with its leg broken, and ought to be cared for, a party, headed by the sultan's son, went at night, killed the animal, and brought over the carcass. It had belonged to another village. They kill all their animals with bludgeons, hunting them down through lanes and amongst houses. The goat's head is twisted; it never is killed as is done in this country, because it is thought the skin would thereby be injured for wear. The dogs are no better than the pariahs of India, and quite as prolific; a favourite, which was fed by me daily, had twelve pups, two of which were drowned. Pet pigeons, of the ordinary dovecot sort, flew in circles round the village, or would evince alarm at the sight of a large bird. We met with no new wild animals here, and killed no lions. The natives used to trap game by means of nooses and pitfalls, and the lads of several villages would assemble with dogs, horns, and spears, to have a battue[4] of the different forests—partridges, hares, coneys,[5] and sometimes antelopes, being the result. In my morning walks (I could not leave the property for a single day's shooting) after guinea-fowl, when they had become so wild that a rifle was necessary, I once stumbled across two full-sized rhinoceros; both attempted to run up to me, but at 20 yards' distance turned off, showing their full lengths, hobbling in their canter like little pigs, the leader with cocked tail. A steady aim at the shoulder had no effect, and in case he might charge, I looked for my shot-gun, but my two followers were in full flight. They had observed the animals, and had been calling out to me to take care, but allowed me to go right upon them without a stalk. We tracked, and found that the two had separated. All animals wander so, that you never know which to keep in your hand, the gun or rifle. I was fortunate in knocking over with shot a light bay hornless female antelope,[6] which was new to me: it had four white cuts across its saddle, the spinal ridge and inside of legs white, spotted sides, and tail a tuft of long hair. Altogether I was proud of my prize, as there was nothing whatever in the larder. My single follower made many excuses that he was not able to carry it home, but I

[1] The Swahili term *myombo* refers to *Brachystegia* of various species whose fibrous bark may be used to create cloth as Grant explains.

[2] The term for various Indian species of ficus. *Hobson Jobson.*

[3] The cattle were probably kept by Tusi herders and may have been recently introduced rather than traditionally kept by the Nyamwezi peoples. See the discussion in Koponen, *People and Production*, pp. 244–8.

[4] A drive of game animals.

[5] i.e., rabbits.

[6] As it was hornless this was probably not the species of waterbuck later known as Grant's gazelle.

assisted till close up to the village, when I was ordered to go and ask whether the sultan would allow it inside, my attendant saying, "Wezees generally have an aversion to it." "M'weeko"[1]—*i.e.,* "it's not customary;" "it's a 'phongo,'" "never eaten," &c. Disgusted at having wasted two charges of English shot upon it, I thought there was a chance for me through the sultan. He looked surprised, and flew into such a rage, that the men round him had to explain—"If you eat it you'll lose your fingers and toes, get scab all over, and if it has spat on you the part will become a sore." I begged that the skin might be allowed inside the village; no, not the skin even, nor its tail, so I could only sketch the animal.[2] By-and-by a native caravan, carrying loads of salt, arrived, and the men were glad to get it to eat. Our Seedees said it was called the "bawala" in their country, and was never eaten; but to look at, it was as nice as any antelope I had ever seen. The smaller animals were N'geeree,[3] a pig which the Wezee is very fond of: wells are dug by them in the forests. Another animal of the same size, but which it is not customary to eat, is the N'grooweh; and from the description given of it, it must be an antelope, having no tusks, but teeth like a goat and hair like a buffalo.[4] There are also wild-cats, deep brown, and barred across—very bold, fearless-looking creatures. Troops of that beautiful little animal the mongoose, which becomes so tame in the house, we saw searching for water: they are called "goozeeroo."[5] Their dark bodies are barred across to the tip of the tail. On one of them being wounded by a bullet, another commenced to tear it with the greatest viciousness.

Lions and lynxes are considered the sole property of the sultan, and form part of his right and revenue. When carried in, lashed on a frame on men's shoulders and placed at his door, drums are beat, the women shout, great excitement prevails, and a dance usually takes place about the carcass. I had the curiosity to measure the length of one lion, and found it was three steps from the root of the tail to the nose, and in passing round it I was said to have subjected myself to a fine of two fathoms calico; but this I refused, and never did pay, because I had not stepped over it. The putrid flesh is cut in pieces, and boiled by the sultan in person. All the grease is preserved as valuable magic medicine, the tail and paws are hung over his doorway, and the skin, skilfully pegged out in the sun to dry, is prepared for the sultan's wear, as no one else dare use it. The colour of a young male lion was a pale ochre, with distinct dark spots on his hind-legs. The lynx is even more highly prized than the lion, though only the size of, and a little heavier than, an English fox, with a stumpy, short, curled-back dog-tail, and tips of hair to his black ears. He has immense, powerful, thickly-formed little arms, great length of body, and is said by the natives to kill even the lion and buffalo. This I believe, for he gives one the idea of bull-dog courage. He is said to watch his prey from a tree. The colour of the lynx is a dusty red, indistinctly spotted; a perfect cat's head; white round the eyes and underneath the body. The ceremony observed on the arrival of either a lion or lynx is curious:—The sultan, sultana, and the sultan's wife next in rank, sit on stools placed in the open air, with the dead animal in front of them, the crowd all round, squatted or standing. A small lump of serpent-dung is made into a paste with water upon a stone. Spots of this white ointment are placed by the sultan's own hands upon the forehead, chest, tips of shoulders, instep, and palms of

---

[1] Swahili *mwiko* indicating something deliberately abstained from.

[2] See Figure 50, p. 145. The term 'bawala' which follows does not seem to be a Kiswahili word.

[3] *Ngiri* usually denotes some form of wild boar.

[4] Grant is wrong here; *nguruwe* is a wild pig in Swahili.

[5] The Swahili word is *nguchiro*.

hands of himself and the two wives, and drums and dancing continue afterwards for some hours. The serpent-dung is supposed to have the charm of bringing plenty, or "burkut," to a house, because it gives many young. No one but kings may make use of it.

Vultures always hover where a dead body is thrown out of the village into the grass. This did not prevent the natives from making use of their feathers, or those of the adjutant,[1] for head-dresses on occasions of merriment, or on the march. Another bird of prey is a slate-coloured hawk, possessing a powerful flight, quite able to knock over a guinea-fowl, and altogether of noble appearance. Of eating-birds, there were three species of partridge, a few quail, the florikan,[2] blue wild-pigeon, guinea-fowl, and a knob-nosed duck. The "k'engo," tree-partridge, resembles the painted one of India, has yellow legs, beautiful plumage, and weighs about a pound; the natives trap them in nooses of hair. The "kewtee" or "næne," only half a pound in weight, is a very plump little partridge, found in open places, scratching and scraping the ground like a hen; and in colour it is almost the same as the quail. It has reddish legs, with a button-like pearly spur. A third kind of partridge is the "qualæ"[3] it is more common than the others, and has a handsome blue full plumage and red legs, with sometimes an appearance of a double spur. The most game bird in plumage was the florikan, weighing from 1½ to 2½ lb., and forming even better food than the Indian species. A few parrots, a long-tailed bird of paradise, with the most graceful airy flight, some handsome yellow birds, about the size of the blackbird, and others with black bodies and white primaries, taking languid, short flights, were the most remarkable we saw during a morning or evening walk.[4]

Our Seedees killed nearly all the fish in the country. They were caught by raking the still, waist-deep pools in the stream-bed by means of a hurdle of sticks. The large 20-pounders were often left for another day, but a good load of fifty smaller fish was generally brought in to be split up, dried over the fire, and kept for consumption. Two species, the "makambara"[5] and "gogo," were usually taken—the former and largest is scaleless, large-headed, and lank-bodied; the latter is only ¾ lb. weight, and resembles a stickleback.

Rats, fleas, and ants very often made our nights miserable. The calves alongside broke through their pens, and roused every one, while an alarm of "seafoo"[6] or ants, and "bring a light," would be shouted by our Seedees. In a moment these vicious insects fixed upon our skin, biting and clinging like leeches till killed in their death-grip, and it became a desperate case for us whether we turned out or they turned in! A line of burning charcoal was placed to scare them away, and then you could again recline without further molestation or after-effects. But what was to be done to prevent their return the following night like an invading army? The sultan very properly would not allow the reckless Seedees to place charcoal round his house during the night, but he had about a hundred goats brought in, and kept there three nights and days to pollute the place and make it obnoxious to the ants, and this was found to be an effectual remedy for the time.

---

[1] An Anglo-Indian term for a bird, especially a kind of crane: *Hobson-Jobson*. In this case it was probably, according to Mr Stanley Howe, in a private communication, a marabou stork, *Leptoptilus crumeniferus*.

[2] Or 'florikin' another Anglo-Indian word for a type of bustard, probably here *Ardeotis kori*. See also Plate 44.

[3] The Swahili word is *kwale* and the bird was possibly a francolin.

[4] It has not been possible to identify all the birds Grant mentions, partly because his indiscriminate mixture of Anglo-Indian terms or indistinctly-heard Swahili words creates difficulties.

[5] Presumably *kambare*, the commonest freshwater fish resembling a barbel.

[6] Properly, *siafu*.

These ants are no larger than ordinary ones in England, but bite with the greatest ferocity.

The description given of the sultan at Mineenga will answer for all the natives in the "Land of the Moon," *i.e.,* "Unyamuezi." They are a sottish and unambitious race, even the best of them, though by no means incapable of improvement. My friend Ukulima of Ukuni was a fine old fellow, although he had his failings. As I resided in the verandah of his best house, the inside of which was occupied by the old sultana, some goats, and female servants, he passed or saw me daily, always saying "Yambo," or, if in extra good-humour, calling me "Doogo yango,"[1] brother, or even "sultan." Constantly, till I was tired of him, would he sit by me in my iron chair, greasing it all over, and playing the fool in various ways, such as opening the medicine-chest, helping himself to quinine, which he would put in his beer, or give it to a neighbour, to have a laugh over its bitter taste. Lucifer-matches he delighted in seeing lit, though afraid to light them himself. One day he felt dissatisfied because I would not give him magic medicine, and when he left, he with great difficulty put on my thick shoes, strutted about the village with them, and collected all the little boys as he trailed his feet on the ground. If a pigeon was shot, he would be most childish in begging it of me, saying, "Go and shoot another, as I want two." If this was not done, he would not be content with the one, but leave it in a pet, saying, tauntingly, "There will be pombé to-morrow." My Bible, sketch-book, or the book of birds, he would turn over, smiling at each new leaf or picture, and asking what it meant. When he saw that I never asked a fee for the medicines given to his wives or followers, he thought I must have some object in it, and redoubled his little kindnesses; or, as I was so friendly, he would suggest that I should give him a recipe by which he could distinguish friends from foes! He inquired anxiously why we were going on to Karague; we should get killed. "The people there plant their spears in your foot, and demand, 'What do you want?' You must return to the coast, and I will send my own son in charge of you."

All this was very good; but, on the day of our departure, having already received and expressed satisfaction with the presents from Speke, he showed his true character by demanding a separate present from me. He so far forgot himself as to seize two cases of ammunition and a gun, and drove my porters out of the village with his stick. Poor old man! some cloth and beads sent the following day softened his anger, and my effects were allowed to leave his dominions. He was much respected in the country, and most of the neighbouring sultans visited him with great formality. On these occasions my guns were asked for to fire salutes. The procession would be headed by spearsmen, then followed the lady visitors carrying gourds of pombé, drums beating furiously, shots, shamfights, &c.; and the sultan would ask me to join in the dance. After a time I was called upon by the strangers, and every book, box, blanket, &c., was minutely scrutinised by them.

On the morning of the 8th June, my journal remarks:—"A.M., One shot knocked over two guinea-fowl—a blessing—nothing to eat; people pleased at seeing them. No fever. Sultan still here: whole village at pombé; had a potful sent me, but cat turned it over. Bombay and Rehan asleep all day. Called for dinner at usual hour, fire black out; asked for the roast-fowl of the morning—Rehan had eaten it. Took all this philosophically, and got two fellows to prepare a guinea-fowl by 7½ P.M. Not many drunken men about—all

---

[1] *Ndugu yango* means in Swahili, 'brother mine'.

153

asleep."[1] A batch of tall Watusi men paid me visits; my umbrella was much fancied by their chief. He offered me his pipe for it; and, finding this was not enough, he brought me another day an iron hoe! To get rid of the subject, I asked him to sell me his forefinger, and said that twenty cows wouldn't buy my umbrella, which at last made him understand my meaning, as they value everything by cattle. The natives had great faith in the "Wazoongoo,"[2] white men. Our very paper, which they called "pupolo,"[3] was considered by some to have virtues; but we hadn't much of it to give, having had no communication with England for nearly a year.

The custom of the Arab in this country is to take presents for everything he does, and the same idea was formed of us.[4] For instance, if a gun had to be repaired, a bullet to be extracted, an old sultan to be cured of dimness of vision, or the split lobe of an ear to be mended, for any of these services a cow or cows were at hand to be paid when the task was finished. When slaves were brought us for sale and declined, they could not understand our indifference to such traffic, but would turn from us with a significant shrug, as much as to say, "Why are you here, then?"

Every morning the sultana and myself met, cordially shaking hands and asking how the night had been passed; previously to this her grandchildren had been in to her bedside, bidding good-morning. Every respect was paid the old lady by her family and by the lower classes, who stooped, knelt, or twice clapped their hands as they met her. She was active like her husband, an excellent housewife, gave herself no airs, but still maintained her dignity. She might be seen nursing an infant, kindly carrying it about on her back, or at times shouldering a log of firewood. If I had refused pombé from her husband and son, she would bring me a cupful, put it to her lips, and with a gentle, ladylike curtsy, ask me to accept it; refusal would have been boorish. Her old eyes were getting dim, and on her hearing that I had made up some wash (from filings of zinc), thinking in her ignorance it might have a virtue for impaired vision, she begged for a little. On our getting to Cairo, some beads and trinkets were sent her ladyship *viâ* Zanzibar, which it is to be hoped have ere this reached her.[5]

The women, through my servants, soon found out that I had a looking-glass. They took it into their hands, and held it there, continually looking at themselves, but it was evident they were not altogether satisfied with their appearance. They busied themselves with field operations, even using the flail, and at night a band of them would meet to dance in the moonlight. Their manner was to twist their bodies, stamp, and sing, till, exhausted by their antics, they paused to breathe and laugh. Two quarrelled one day, and came at last to blows, striking out like men, and drawing blood, but they were separated by our Seedees. They are very masculine in several respects; two of them accompanied me as volunteer porters when going to join Speke, and were even more inveterate smokers than the men. Their entire dress was one cloth wrapped round the loins from below the

---

[1] The extract from the journal is more or less faithful to the original although there Grant actually uses the Swahili term *kanga* for the guinea-fowl. NLS, MS. 17915, 8 June 1861.

[2] Properly *Wazungu*.

[3] An attempt to say 'paper'?

[4] To be treated as if the Expedition was an Arab trading caravan was both an advantage and sometimes a disadvantage.

[5] It is not known whether these presents reached Bukune. This is an example of the growing sympathy Grant developed for the Banyamwezi during his long sojourn in the village.

breasts to the calf of the leg, below which, down to the ankle, were immense masses of brass or iron wire rings, as before described. The head wool, dressed with an oily preparation, looked as if they wore a scalp of shining black beetles, among which were interspersed hawthorn-berry-coloured beads or rings of brass; others wore their hair in tassels, with seed-charms, &c. Necklaces of beads, brown or rose-coloured, adorned their necks; they had no rings on their toes.[1] Men often allow the nail of the small finger to grow long. The meeting of two women of unequal rank is a pleasing sight; the inferior sinks on her knee, and droops her head, while the other lays a hand on her shoulder muttering something. Both remain silent for a moment, but on rising they chat and gossip. The curtsy is also observed by them. When the wife hears that her husband is about to arrive from a journey to the coast, she dresses herself in a feathered cap and in the best costume she possesses, and proceeds with other women in ordinary dress to the sultana's, where they sing and dance at the door.

These Wezee women do not practise much tattooing, merely making three lines on each temple, and perhaps a line down the forehead reaching to the bridge of the nose; but some of the Watusi females were observed to have their shoulders and breasts very handsomely tattooed to imitate lady's point-lace in front, and crossed like a pair of braces behind. The waists were also marked in the same way. They prepare their dress of cow-skin to look like thick Irish frieze-cloth: a needle teases the leather fibre into this appearance, and the turn-over part at the waist is made ornamental by strips from the skins of variously-coloured cattle. I have understood that some East African women live in the forests as much as fifteen days before the expected birth of a child, having a hut erected for them.[2] This practice was not observed here, but the children are as fondly cared for by the mothers as in any part of the world, and not an instance is known of one of them selling her offspring, even when tempted to it by famine—they would sooner die. The boys practised many manly games as seen in our own gymnasiums,—such as jumping over sticks—shooting, with bolted arrows, partridge or pigeon, or teaching small birds to sing—making model guns out of cane, going off with a trigger and having a cloud of sand for smoke—copying our double-barrelled guns, and making them, with nipple, hammer, trigger, &c., out of mud, with cotton for the smoke. They had also made cross-bows; and generally they evinced great powers of imitation. Seeing the ingenuity of the little fellows, we could not help longing for the happy day that should introduce amongst them more valuable improvements.[3]

The habitations of the country have been described in the previous chapter. It only remains to add that there were no wells in the villages, water being carried from distant springs—that the dust was very annoying from the dances, &c.—that ground-nuts were not allowed to be roasted inside the bomah—and that outside the village human skulls and skeletons of hands (those of enemies killed in action) were stuck on the tops of the highest trees, or fixed on poles at the top of mounds. When the boundary of the village was to be enlarged, bare-poled trees for palisades were carried from the forest by Watusi,

[1] See Plate 5.

[2] Abrahams, *Peoples of Greater Unyamwezi*, pp. 71–2, has an account of birth practices but does not mention such a custom among the Nyamwezi.

[3] Grant's later life was to be much taken up with attempts to foster the sorts of improvements that he saw as necessary. See Bridges, 'Towards the Prelude', pp. 89ff.

crying like jackals. On putting them into position, skulls of animals (or human), broken stools or baskets, land shells, &c., were stuck upon them.

On the 27th of June we had cries of "War, war!"[1] In an instant the place was alive, and thirty poor-looking creatures, each with a bow and from four to six arrows, rushed out of the village, followed slowly by the sultan, carrying two spears. All got upon a mound, looking in the direction whence the noise proceeded. A party from a distance here joined them, and after skirmishing and larking in the grass, all again turned into the village to have their pombé! There was a second attack on the 4th July. The people of a M'salala village[2] had captured some cattle. A few men with short-handled hatchets, spears, bows and arrows, all the "troops" that could be spared, paraded under the command of a red-robed leader; in ten days they returned all alive and safe, reporting the death of six of the enemy, and bringing the trophy of one head, which was stuck upon the palisading over the eastern gate, with the face to the zenith. Great rejoicing and pombé took place in the evening.

On the 17th [July], at 1 P.M., a dance took place for an hour, after which a court assembled on the same ground to hear evidence regarding the M'salala war. In the centre space lay the tusk of an elephant. Only the sultan and his wuzeers[3] or officers sat on stools. The women were most attentive listeners to the speeches, and all was marked with the utmost decorum. For an hour the sultan addressed the crowd, sometimes stopping to think, and pulling out hairs from his face with iron tongs. There were bursts of laughter at his jokes, and when he had finished, a general conversation began. A wuzeer now spoke very sharply, and after each of his sentences there was a great clapping of hands and assent of "hums." Two of the crowd then delivered addresses, which were received with a single "viva," and the court abruptly broke up. Except the ridiculous part of pulling out the hairs of the sultan's beard, there could not be a more impressive or orderly court. It again assembled two days afterwards: the tusk still lay in the space, and was presented by the chief of M'salala in token of submission to the court's decision against him. Thus, by simple arbitration, ended their war of four-and-twenty days, which had entailed no greater loss than half-a-dozen men.

A great talk and excitement was caused on the 4th August by the discovery of a man throwing a pair of human hands into a bush in the forest. As he could give no satisfactory account of himself, and was suspected of murder, he was at once made prisoner, but unfortunately he made his escape. It seems to be the established rule here, that when such trophies are proved to be those of war, the chief of his village kills a cow and gives a feast. This was sufficient for the prisoner, and for many others, no doubt, to commit murder, and it was the only case I heard of that created any very great sensation amongst the natives.

Owing to such incidental circumstances, trade and travel are very much impeded, as single individuals can never with impunity move from one district to another, and are sure to be plundered, if not murdered. Two of our men fell behind upon one occasion, when their guns were at once seized, and to recover them it was necessary to pay a tax of

---

[1] The journal does not support this version; rather, 'Rehan reported "there is war broken out with the village who have seized the cows of their neighbours"'. NLS, MS. 17915, 7 June 1861.

[2] A village and minor chiefdom a short distance to the south-west, apparently.

[3] Presumably a corruption of 'viziers'; it is not clear why Grant uses the term.

two fathoms of cloth, after which the men were allowed to pass on. War causes retaliation in every direction. A M'salala caravan on its way through Ugogo from the coast was plundered by the natives. The latter on their part attributed their ill fortune to the Arab traders, who had brought war on the country, and to revenge themselves they seized the property of an Arab trader passing through their territory, and meant to treat all foreigners visiting them with the same rigour,[1] until the *lex talionis*[2] was fairly vindicated.

The sepoys of the sultan consisted of about twenty idle young fellows, who tried to dress jauntily, and were the fast men and pick of the place. If an order had to be conveyed from one of the sultan's villages to another, their word was law. If an escort was necessary, they were employed, and when war broke out they collected levies all round the country from their own class or from poorer natives. None of these soldiers would deign to carry a load for us; they were, in their own estimation, the life-guardsmen of the state, consequently led an idle life, playing at pitch-and-toss, bao, beating the drum, &c. Without coins one would imagine that pitch-and-toss could not be played; but has not bark got two sides? Circles of bark were used, also a few leaden discs pitched in the air, while the gamester clapped his hands and let the discs fall upon a cow-skin placed on the ground. My wonder was how they fell so fairly on the skin, and also that the game was not known by our Zanzibar men. The stakes were bows, arrows, arrow-tips, and ankle-wires; the counters were made of pieces of stick. Bao is a coast game, played by two, with a board having thirty-two cups or wells in it, and sixty-four counters of seeds, called "komo." The sultan sat down with any one he could get to play this rather skilful game.[3]

Every large country has its own style of drumming; that of Unyanyembe was more musical than the jumble of drums here. The conductor had always the largest drum; the rest watched him for the time, while at his feet a little black youth rattled as hard as he could, without ceasing, at a wooden trough. If the noise of it was not heard, the music lost its stirring effect! The drums were of wood, three to four feet high, and slung on a beam at a convenient height; the sticks were twelve inches long.[4] At these dances the head men were present to preserve order, and to prevent, as much as possible, the use of spears or arrows in their antics. On the arrival of a distinguished guest, such as the son of the sultan, who owned a neighbouring village, a roll from each of the four drums was given in succession, and as he entered the place every one hid in his house from shyness. If a lion or a culprit was brought in, the "assembly" was beaten furiously. Single taps at short intervals, and gradually increasing to a roll, were given in a case of murder, at five in the morning, and again an hour afterwards. The previous days had been, night and day, celebrated by incessant drumming on the part of a dark set of wandering beggars or gypsy lads, richly necklaced with beads, to commemorate some event which appeared, from the scant information I could obtain from my interpreter,[5] to be celebrated once or twice in

---

[1] This is further evidence of the hostile relations which developed as Arabs took over the trade which Nyamwezi trading caravans from even such minor villages as Msalala had been wont to make on their own account.

[2] That is, the 'law of retaliation' – an eye for an eye and a tooth for a tooth.

[3] *Bao* is the Swahili word for 'board' but is used for the game Grant describes. It is found in slightly differing forms in both West and East Africa. There are suggestions that it was introduced from Asia about 2,000 years ago. Grant is probably wrong to assume that Bao was a coast game; certainly the Baganda appear long to have known a version which is similar to that described here and which they call *omweso*.

[4] Note the drums Grant shows present for the dance depicted in Plate 10.

[5] Presumably, this was Rehan as Bombay was away at the probable time of this event.

three years. This, if true, shows that they mark a period, announced by gypsies, whom I observed but twice during my stay at Ukuni.[1]

Of religion, idols, Sabbaths, or holidays they have none, but of superstitious fears and beliefs they have an ample store. On the occasion of the arrival of Speke with a detachment at a village, the natives shut their doors against him, and for three hours inhospitably kept the party in the sun. They had never before seen a white man, nor the tin boxes that the men were carrying; "and who knows," they said, "but that these very boxes are the plundering Watuta transformed and come to kill us all? You cannot be admitted." No persuasion could avail with them, and the party had to proceed to the next village.

Three stones, placed in a triangular form, surrounded the dwelling-house of the sultan of Ukuni, and within them it was believed no harm could ever happen to him, even if a gun were fired at him. One of our men sitting on one of these stones, jumped off, as if stung, on being told of the sacred character of the place.

The ceremony of driving out an evil spirit, or "Phepo," is elaborate and curious. The sultan sits at the doorway of his hut, which is decorated with lion-paws. His daughter, the possessed, is opposite him, completely hooded, and guarded by two Watusi women, one on each side, holding a naked spear erect. The sultana completes the circle. Pombé is spirted up in the air so as to fall upon them all. A cow is then brought in with its mouth tightly bound up, almost preventing the possibility of breathing, and it is evident that the poor cow is to be the sacrifice. One spear-bearer gives the animal two gentle taps with a hatchet between the horns, and she is followed by the woman with the evil spirit and by a second spearbearer, who also tap the cow. A man now steps forward, and with the same hatchet kills the cow by a blow behind the horns. The blood is all caught in a tray (a Kaffir custom) and placed at the feet of the possessed, after which a spear-bearer puts spots of the blood on the women's forehead, on the root of the neck, the palms of the hands, and the instep of the feet. He spots the other spear-bearers in a similar manner, and the tray is then taken by another man, who spots the sultan, his kindred, and household. Again the tray is carried to the feet of the possessed, and she spots with the blood her little son and nephews, who kneel to receive it. Sisters and female relatives come next to be anointed by her, and it is pleasant to see those dearest to her pressing forward with congratulations and wishes. She then rises from her seat, uttering a sort of whining cry, and walks off to the house of the sultana, preceded and followed by spear-bearers. During the day she walks about the village, still hooded, and attended by several followers shaking gourds containing grain, and singing "Heigh-ho, massa-a-no," or "masanga."[2] An old woman is appointed to wrestle with her for a broomstick which she carries, and finally the stick is left in her hand. Late in the afternoon a change is wrought; she appears as in ordinary, but with her face curiously painted, her followers being also painted in the same way. She sits without smiling to receive offerings of grain, with beads or anklets placed on twigs of the broomstick, which she holds upright; and this over, she walks among the women, who shout out "Gnombe!" (cow) or some other ridiculous expression to create a laugh. This

[1] This information is difficult to interpret; there were no gypsies in East Africa. The wandering group are hard to identify and their function obscure. The most likely possibility is that these visitors were diviners. See Abrahams, *Peoples of Greater Unyamwezi*, p. 79.

[2] The words were probably *Haya, masanga*. The first is asking someone to appear and one meaning of the latter word is 'evil spirit'. A belief in sorcery and in various remedies for it was common among the Nyamwezi; Grant's evidence provides us with one instance of supposed possession and its cure.

winds up the ceremony on the first day, but two days afterwards the now emancipated woman is seen parading about with the broomstick hung with beads and rings, and looking herself again, being completely cured. The vanquished spirit had been forced to fly!

Black-art cases were duly tried, and generally ended in conviction. A cowherd who had sold me some fish died very suddenly; one of his two wives was suspected of having poisoned him; and being tried, she was convicted and condemned. She was taken to the dry bed of the stream, her arms tied behind her, and was killed by having her throat cut from ear to ear. No hyena touched the body, which still more confirmed the belief that she was guilty; for my Seedee cook said, "Has not the hyena the soul of a man? does he not know your thoughts when you determine on shooting him?"[1]

On the 10th of July my servant asked permission to go and see the uchawé.[2] I accompanied him to the outside of the bomah (village fence), where a woman and lad lay on their faces with their arms bound painfully tight, and writhing in torture. Poor creatures! they met with no sympathy from the jeering crowd, but the ropes were slackened at my request. They had been apprehended on suspicion of having bewitched the sultan's brother, who lay sick for fifteen days, and unless they could work off the magic spell they must die. The lad said, "Take me to the forest; I know an herb remedy." On the seventh day from this scene (during which the lad was outside the village, and the woman kept by the sick patient in the stocks) the former was killed and the woman released. I went to see his body the following day, but the hyena (I was told) had taken it away. Nothing remained but blood and the ashes of some hair by a fire. Could they have tortured him by burning? A case of adultery was punished in the most horrible manner, too painful to describe minutely.[3] They had no Divorce Court! The strapping young fellow who had found his way into the harem of the sultan, was tied to railings, stripped, certain parts of his person were smeared and covered with rags, then set fire to by the sultan in person, and he was dragged to the fire outside the village; but before he could reach it, assigais from the hands of the son and daughter-in-law of the sultan pierced his neck and chest, and he was drawn out by one leg like a dog through the gate. The woman who committed this act came in fear to me at night, saying, "Give me protection: it is said I am to be killed for stabbing the adulterer." Though for the moment I detested the woman,[4] I endeavoured to calm her by saying my guns would be her protection, and my men should sleep in her house. On asking her "Why did you soil your hands with such a deed?" she replied, in the most animated way, "Oh, did I not glory in it! did the fellow not

---

[1] Hyenas (and owls) are associated with sorcery by the Nyamwezi. Abrahams, *Peoples of Greater Unyamwezi*, p. 79.

[2] *Mchawi* or 'sorcerer' – one who practises bad magic.

[3] And yet Grant proceeds to make clear what happened. Moreover, he drew and painted three scenes from this gruesome happening although these were not bound in with the majority of all his artwork. See Plate 18 and Figures 45 and 46, pp. 142 and 143. The journal extract below gives some indications of his attitude at the time of the atrocity.

[4] This phrase was inserted at the proof stage; Grant had originally written: 'Though I now loathed the woman and all her brutal race.' NLS, MS. 17934, p. 108. This phrasing was closer to the original entry in his journal: 'In my gallantry, though I now loathed the woman ...'. NLS, MS. 17915, 17 August 1861. Perhaps Grant's softening of the condemnation was because he wished to show that he now could see some virtues among the Nyamwezi. Nevertheless, he found the woman's behaviour even more worrying than the sultan's treatment of the adulterer.

come to my bedside one night making propositions to me, and I never could get hold of him since?" The following day she, as usual, wished me good-morning, but I shuddered to think that so handsome a woman and so kind a mother, with four beautiful children who must have seen all, could have committed such an act. The woman who had offended was a middle-aged good-looking person. Nothing whatever was done to her, though she had once before been the cause of a man's death under similar circumstances. Previous to this event she would come often to look at herself in my mirror, but afterwards I did not see so much of her.

Extracts from Journal: Grant's Reactions to Brutalities He Witnessed
Outside the bomah a woman lay on her face on the ground in the torture position of having her arms from the shoulder to the waist lashed behind her – the most cruel sight I ever beheld [NLS, MS. 17915, 10 July 1861]

I saw a strapping young fellow they had brought in with arms pinioned to the palisade – find out he had committed adultery – the Sultan arrived ... and went up to the fellow as if he would release him, no, it was to lash him with all his power round the body by the legs more securely to the palings ... the hellish vengeance of the Sultan was working. [The victim] showed such signs of consciousness he was twice threatened with a bludgeon across the face which made me [consider] interference ... to beg [for] his forgiveness but women [arrived] some with spears and making a tremendous noise. ... [As he was dragged away] the crowd followed & I after them. I was anxious to know what was to be done with him – as I walked out of the village I met the sultan's daughter in law a fair handsome creature with a bloody spearhead in her hand, the shaft was broken off – Good God, the ground was in pools of blood. Could that woman have murdered him? A few yards on I tracked the young fellow's dead body ... the man who was pulling at him was my shikari[1] I left [the body] reflecting on my position out here amongst such a set of fiendish savages ... The sultan's son Keerenga whom I have often mentioned ... struck him first then that handsome woman with two needle like assegais pierced him all over ... I did not witness the brutal murder itself ... [NLS, MS. 17915, 17 August 1861][2]

Several of our men made brotherhood with the Wezees, and the process between Bombay and the sultan's son, Keerenga, may be mentioned. My consent having been given, a mat is spread, and a confidential party or surgeon attends on each. All four squat, as if to have a game at whist; before them are two clean leaves, a little grease, and a spear-head; a cut is made under the ribs of the left side of each party, a drop of blood put on a leaf and exchanged by the surgeons, who rub it with butter twice into the wound with the leaf, which is now torn in pieces and strewn over the "brothers'" heads. A solemn address is made by the older of the attendants, and they conclude the ceremony by rubbing their own sides with butter, shaking hands, and wishing each other success. Ten rounds of ammunition are then fired off; a compliment from each of the four drums is sounded,

---

[1] That is, his guide and assistant on hunting forays.

[2] The savage punishment for adultery described and illustrated by Grant was meted out by other Bantu societies, including the sophisticated Baganda. See Roscoe, *The Baganda*, pp. 261–2, who reports that the torture was designed to make the culprit confess.

160

and they parade the village all the afternoon. This was the form observed by the Wanyamuezi. An Uganda lad, the magician of the sultan, made brotherhood with Rehan, the cook, by cutting marks on his chest and rubbing in the fat of lions. This young wizard of Uganda, with his bamboo tube, could blow away all the enemies of the sultan, or, if persuaded to go out shooting with you, a second blast from his trumpet would make the animals of the forest stand before you! The last of their unintelligible customs I shall mention, was that of a number of men amusing themselves by running fast through and about the village, singing, at every third or fourth step, "Queri" or " Hairy," and "Queri Mahamba." [1] I had seen the same custom across country, outside the village; and on the nights of this great stir, dancing would also take place.

To give a description of the difficulties and disappointments we experienced for nearly four months in procuring men to carry our luggage, would be tiresome.[2] I shall only mention a few instances. Speke was away sixty miles in advance of me with a portion of the property: neither he nor I could proceed a step; we were like two planets compelled by a fixed law to preserve our distances. He resolved on making a flying march to Karague, in the hope of sending me relief from thence. Our own Seedees mutinied; they would not hear of this plan, as the country of Usui was dangerous,—it was certain death to accompany white men, who were considered sorcerers of the deepest dye, and they insisted that we had not enough of presents for the chiefs. Speke, ever active, to my utter surprise, walked back the sixty miles to announce this failure to me. "What has happened? I thought you were in Karague!" What was to be done? Our beads and cloth were running short; *my* sultan would not give us a man. Unyanyembe and the Arabs must be appealed to, and carpenters might be got to proceed to the south end of Lake Nyanza, make a raft, and so escape the danger of Usui. This plan was carried out with success. Speke returned on the nineteenth day from the Arabs, having, in going and returning, accomplished a journey of 180 miles. He had ordered from Zanzibar a fresh supply of bartering goods, of which we heard nothing till our arrival in England two years afterwards. The raft scheme had been dropped, and he had brought with him trusty guides and interpreters for Uganda. Here more than a month elapses; his guides desert, his men are more mutinous than ever, and Bombay is on his way for new guides, as his master is struck down with illness, which I knew nothing of for twenty-seven days, and had no prospect of seeing him. Suddenly a party of coast men arrive from the north, saying, "Every chief there waits you; go on, get porters; the road is clear;" so, after days of obstinate resistance and final outbreak by my old sultan, on the 12th September I was able once again to be on the move to join my companion.

[1] Presumably *Kwa heri, Masamba* meaning 'Goodbye, those leaving'.
[2] For details, see Bridges, 'Negotiating a Way', pp. 108–9, 115–16, 120; Speke, *Journal*, pp. 114–38.

CHAPTER VII

[Pages 111–36]

Ukuni to Karagwe [13 September–25 November 1861]

Karague! how charmed we were to get there; its fine hills, lake scenery,[1] climate, and, above all, the gentleness of the royal family, were all in such contrast to what we had experienced elsewhere of Africa and Africans, that, if surrounded by our friends, we should have been content, for a time at least, to take up our residence there. But before describing the country, the thread of our narrative must be taken up to show what had to be undergone to reach this haven. In September 1861, when preparing to move, I found that before a start could be made on an African march, particularly after a long halt, there were hundreds of annoyances unknown in other countries. No one believes you wish to move till a display is made of your beads, by counting them out, stringing them, and packing up the loads. The sight of these rouses the sultan: he, his family, and all the people of the place, begin to pester you for presents, and you would give worlds to be away from such intolerable bullying. Half your number of porters at last being collected to receive their pay, a momentary suspense takes place: the first man hesitates to accept the hire he had agreed for; each man strives to lay the responsibility upon another; but as soon as one accepts, instantly the rest scramble for it. Here are some extracts from my Journal[2] previous to the march:—

"*8th September.*—Attempt to push all the engaged men ahead with their loads, in charge of Said, but fail, and half the day is lost by the native procrastination.[3] Said no better than the rest of them.[4] After a long day of it, started off 40 loads and three donkeys ahead to first march, where they will wait for us. Ten paid-up porters not present. One says, 'My wife is ill; I return my hire:' another, 'My father and mother won't allow me to accompany you.' I chastise him; he puts himself under the protection of the sultan, and bolts, leaving his hire of calico blackened by one day's wear. A third will not go because I refuse him the leadership. Last night my men returned from searching for porters, saying, 'None will go unless you give them four times the usual hire.'

---

[1] See Chapter VIII below, p. 182, and references to illustrations there.

[2] The extracts are from very much longer and more detailed entries in the Journal for the dates mentioned. The wording has been altered to some extent; see e.g. following note.

[3] The original wording of this clause was: 'lost by the African's cursed procrastinations'. NLS, MS. 17915, 8 September 1861.

[4] It is not clear who this is; Said bin Salem had left the Expedition in Tabora. However, Speke records a porter called Saidi who was recruited during the journey but deserted in Bunyoro. Speke, *Journal*, p. 616.

"*9th.*—Three of my men have been away all day, and have not brought back a man. Wezees had promised to come, but I have no faith in what they say; others ask triple hire. Twelve loads sent out by men of the advanced camp.

"*10th.*—Cannot see a prospect of marching from here. Ordered Manua to Roongwa for porters; saw him at night. 'Have you been for porters?' 'Yes, there and back.' I laughed at this cool assertion, and asked, 'How many did you get?' 'Four are coming in the morning.' This was too much, as all the Seedees satisfied me that he had never been out of the place; I therefore ordered him to receive two dozen. Rehan (cook) said, '*I* won't give it.' 'You must,' I said; but ultimately the matter was settled by Manua running away, all the Seedees after him! (Manua afterwards became a great friend of mine, as he knew the names and uses of every plant and tree in the country.)[1]

"*11th.*—Yesterday sent a note to Speke, but find the bearer did not start, because he had a Wezee lady in tow. Verily these Africans are a self-pleasing and most trying set. Two men off for porters. My leader reported sick. Manua (the man I ordered to be flogged yesterday) not to be found. Four porters arrive, but won't start till to-morrow, as they feel tired!

"*12th.*—Start three loads; fourth man not present;[2] he had gone away to sleep in another village. Ten men came in from camp ahead to carry away my remaining traps. Sultan demands a present, but on consulting my men, we all agreed that as he had already got eight fathoms of cloth, a large quantity of beads, some gunpowder, and had lost four cows placed in his charge, no more was necessary for him. At this decision he struck my porters and drove them out of his village, and seized some cases of ammunition and a rifle. The quarrel was made worse by the drunkenness of my chief interpreter, Rehan, who in this state threw his gun and accoutrements at my feet, spat upon one of my men, and gave his support to the sultan. After bearing these insults, and seeing the powder, &c., recovered, I walked outside the village and sat down, feeling sick, sore at heart, and exhausted from the detestable strife, but thankful to God that I had so much command of temper. A servant reported that he and another must sleep that night with their loads in the village, as security for my paying some cloth and beads. Anything to get away, and I marched to my advanced camp, eight miles off, regretting that I had not bid adieu to the sultana.

"*13th.*—Sent back the cloths to the sultan by Uledi. So jolly and civilised-like to have a note brought me by three or four Seedees from Speke, wanting me up sharp! Uledi returned at sunset, having satisfied the sultan. Said, Rehan, and Baraka sent word they would be up in the morning; so like an African's system of[3] procrastination, winning the mornings and evenings from us, and saying the day is too hot to move.

"*14th.*—March three miles to a wretched village. A number of men hanging on for hire; one man promised for Karague, and backed out of it because I frightened him by writing his name down. Tried to make an afternoon march, but no one would stir; besides, three loads were behind.

"*15th.*—Under way outside the village by six A.M.; eight loads still on the ground, no porters to carry them, and loads in the rear belonging to men sleeping in other villages.

---

[1] This is probably Manua listed by Simpson as a Munyamwezi, *not* Manua Sera also known as Uledi. Simpson, *Dark Companions*, p. 195.

[2] 'Like an African sleeping in' had been inserted here in the original text but was removed at the proof stage. NLS, MS. 17934, p. 113.

[3] Originally, Grant had written 'African's impudence and ...' NLS, MS. 17934, p. 114.

Every day seems to be won from me. Countermand the march till the afternoon; a panic had struck the porters. The Watuta are at the next ground from camp. I took the chief porter, walked there and back, 20 miles, by 3½ P.M., and found this much-dreaded tribe had left that morning.

"16th.[1]—Having aroused my camp, a noisy conversation soon began with some strange armed men, who had been sent by Sultan Myonga[2] to insist on my visiting him with my caravan; but as I saw yesterday that his residence was completely out of my route, and as Speke had laid down that no further present should be made to him, his 'soldiers' were told this; but, at the turn to their master's village, they planted their spears in defiance, and dared us to proceed by any but their way. We laughed at them, and held on our road for seven miles, when out of some thick cover came a howling of voices. I was about the third from the head of my Indian file, when a troop of about two hundred, with assigais, bows and arrows, burst upon us, springing over the ground like cats. Passing the van, apparently without any intention of molesting us, or 'showing their colours,' no one stopped even to look at them; but of a sudden they broke in upon the centre of our line, and, with uplifted assigais and shouts, frightened the porters to give up their loads and fly, if they could escape the hands of the ruffians who were pulling their clothes and beads from them. Seeing my goods carried off, I tried, without bloodshed, to prevent it; for they were too numerous to attack, as I had but one of my gun-men and two natives. On searching for others, I found Rehan with rifle at full cock, defending two loads against five of the men. He had been told by Manua that he was 'a fool to think of the loads; fly for your life!' but the property, he said, was his life. On making for the village of the Sultan Myonga to seek redress, I was told not to fear; all would be returned me; 'to go and reside in the village of his son, where all would be brought.' On proceeding thither I found that the natives had dressed themselves out in the stolen clothes of our men. I felt like a prisoner; my bright hopes were wrecked; and they all laughed at me as I stood amongst the mob of insolent marauders jeering and exulting at their triumph. Very little at that moment would have set things in a blaze; but though honour was dear, the safety of the expedition was so also, and one false step would have endangered it. They threatened, presenting assigais at my breast; but though I was defenceless, my rifle in its case resting harmlessly on my shoulder, they did not venture to strike, but scattered over the place.[3]

Fifteen of my 55 loads were returned during the day; 15 of 56 porters reappeared; two Wezees were reported killed, but instead of finding even a trace of them, I came upon three others concealed in the grass with their loads. Myonga was said to be infuriated at his people; he had cut off the hand of one of his men, and promised that all, except the property of my porters, should be restored.[4] The following night the sultan sent, saying everything in his possession had been given up, but by my account there were still wanting six bead-loads, some cloth, my teapot, looking-glass, basin, pewter mug, a saw, a goat, &c.

[1] This is the last of the supposed extracts from his Journal but Grant forgot to indicate where the quotation should be taken to have ended.

[2] Apparently a minor chief among the Nyamwezi peoples known as the Sumbwa.

[3] This last sentence was originally worded: 'When threatened with assigais at my breast, they dared not strike the blow though I was defenceless, my rifle in its case being harmlessly on my shoulder; but I felt that God defends the right.' NLS, MS. 17934, p. 116.

[4] At this point, Grant had written a letter to Speke in which he reported his being in 'utter despair' before Mionga made some amends. See Speke, *Journal*, pp. 159–60.

Every load was partially plundered; our most private keepings had been ruthlessly handled; and cases were destroyed by rocks and stones in trying to break them open. My porters, who had received their full hire to Karague, deserted; the march was delayed; and we had all been dishonoured. On making this representation to the sultan, he expressed great sympathy at first, saying, 'Your property will all be restored, and you shall have men from me to convey your goods to Karague.' This was a mere ruse. In four days after the attack I was in a position, by aid sent me from Speke, to march ahead; but the Wezees said, 'If you attempt a forced march, and leave without obtaining the sultan's permission, we will run away.' In reply to my request to be allowed to leave his country, saying I was satisfied with having recovered so much, he very coolly replied, 'I want no present from you, but must have your Seedees with their guns to aid me in an attack against a neighbour of mine.'[1] But though two of my men volunteered to go, intending to escape from him during the night, the proposal seemed preposterous; and, to settle the affair, a scarlet blanket was taken from my bedding and sent to the sultan, along with some other cloths. These were returned contemptuously, with a message that I must aid him with men and guns. The Seedees would not hear of my going to see this ruffian of a sultan, neither could they manage him themselves; their remonstrances and pleadings had become stale. The natives in the mean time were boisterous, refusing our bead coinage.[2] I tried to make use of my rifle in the jungles, but failed to get anything. In my rounds I only saw the brutality of the people towards travellers in pouncing upon a party of four women and two men, demanding their bows and arrows, which I saved by interference. Again, the coarse fellows struck so brutally a donkey which Speke had with him on his former journey to Lake Nyanza, that the animal, then in foal, died. For this no redress could be obtained, because the offender was said to belong to a different village. But how were we to get away from these annoyances, which were exhausting to one's strength and patience? Our porters began to desert, saying, what was the use of staying there—there was nothing to eat? I was almost driven to giving up a gun or more, as I had seen the country traversed without them; but on reference to Speke, who lay prostrated with sickness twelve miles from me, I was told on no account to give guns, but to settle the tax, and join him at any sacrifice. Some Seedees under Baraka, who had a great deal of native bluster about him, arrived with a bound and dash, bringing Speke's message; and having armed himself and a dozen followers with ten rounds of ammunition each, Baraka[3] went to the sultan, carrying an offer of forty fathoms of calico and ten wires of copper. The chief did not see why he should be treated so stingily! 'Other men of his rank get much handsomer presents; he merely asks for twenty coloured cloths, no guns, but he must have four barrels of powder, and don't forget the gentleman's blanket!' To settle the matter, as we had been delayed seven days, one case of gunpowder, double the quantity of cloth, the scarlet blanket, and a bundle of beads were sent sorrowfully, but in the full hope of success. No; we could not leave his country till one case of powder was given; so the case was rendered, and his men were requested to take it to him. They then got up a noise because a box of percussion-caps had been taken out, and before going to their sultan they requested each

[1] See Bridges, 'Negotiating a Way', pp. 120–21. Mionga may well have been seeking 'insurance' against marauders or enemies. The narrative later shows why Mionga wanted protection.

[2] 'We lived upon sweet potatoes.' This was in the original text but removed at the proof stage. NLS, MS. 17934, p. 117.

[3] Baraka was a key member of the party because of his negotiating skills.

a cloth for their trouble. Baraka again went to appeal; the box of caps was not wanted; the men were rebuked; one goat was given by the sultan to Baraka; and we marched that afternoon, the 23d September, having been detained seven days, with wounded feelings, and with every howl of the exulting natives sinking deeply into our hearts.

Some remarks upon the Watuta[1] race may not be out of place here. They had lately been assisting Bolæma, a chief of the district, to defeat my friend Myonga, and had succeeded in capturing thirty of his cattle, and striking terror into the country. Although we never saw one of the tribe, we came upon their deserted camps, and had two men amongst our followers who had once been taken prisoners by them. To these two I am chiefly indebted for the following information. Their M'foomoo, or sultan, M'Tookoolla, has his headquarters at Malavie, a province bordering on the north-west shore of Lake Nyassa. A brother of his, called M'Tumbareeka, has wandered north to Utambara, and there formed a royal residence.[2] They seldom go themselves in search of cattle and slaves, but send their wuzeers or officers, with several thousand followers, roaming over the country, leaving nothing but waste behind them. If they find a village without cattle, they demand slaves instead, never giving up the siege till some tax has been extorted. Some cases are told of their besieging a place for months, with their superior numbers encircling the village to prevent escape; those who were so fortunate as to break through this Watuta cordon being looked upon by the country afterwards as having had a charmed life. The only race in the south that ever mastered them, and can pass through them, are the Wabeesa,[3] living to their west. We had one of these people in camp, a young lad, so bold that he would show fight against our strongest follower. Men from the coast are sometimes found to enter their camp fearlessly; but, as a rule, every race in the interior is in continual dread of their arrival. They have large boats, with which they navigate the Nyassa lake, landing and making raids on the people of Nyassa and Uhiao.[4] The pure race adopt the costume of the Kafir in their extraordinary coverings; but as they are made up of many who love a life of freedom, or had been captured from villages in childhood, the race must be a very mixed one. Their arms are two or three very small short spears, which they never throw, but, with a leather shield in the left hand protecting their own bodies, they close upon their foe; and, if he resists being captured as a slave, stab him. We once were encamped in a village when, at night, the drums beat the alarm—tap, tap, slowly, increasing to a tremendous roll. This was to warn all that the Watuta were on the move in the vicinity, and might take this village on their way; however, they did not come to it till some days after we had left it, when the people got warning and escaped. We saw their camp in a circle of fence, completely surrounding a village, at a distance of 200 yards. Forked sticks were stuck in the ground to support the cow-skins which their women carry

[1] See above, Chapter V, p. 126.

[2] Grant's information is slightly confused, not surprisingly, given the complicated histories of the six Ngoni groups which had emerged from the Zulu kingdom. 'M'Tookoolla' must be Mtambara son of Ntabeni, a brother of the great Zwangendaba. Mtambara's brother was M'Tumbareeka, (more properly Mtambulika). The succeeding account of the Tuta tactics records a significant development in the region's history, not least because Ngoni tactics were copied by others such as Mirambo of the Nyamwezi. See Omer-Cooper, *Zulu Aftermath*, pp. 74–5.

[3] The Wabisa live in what is now Zambia to the east of Lake Bangweulu.

[4] The rumour about the Ngoni (Watuta) having boats is entirely wrong; possibly Arab slave traders' attempts to navigate Lake Malawi are the origin of the story. The Nyassa and Yao people, however, did suffer both afflictions.

to shade them during the day from the sun. Most comfortable beddings of grass lay on the ground; or, when long in one place, their huts were a half-orange shape, very low, and surrounded by a fence made from the euphorbia, which is imagined to be poisonous, and only fit for the use of the Watuta.

The chief Myonga, who plundered my caravan, and the eight or ten other petty chiefs whose country we had to pass through afterwards, were not a whit better than the Watuta, and the wonder is they did not take everything from us. It was only because they feared being shot or bewitched, or come down upon by their neighbouring chiefs, that they desisted. When one is known to possess wealth, obtained by tax or by plunder, jealousy and quarrels are the certain result. We no sooner heard the vile sound of the war-drum to collect the natives, and intimidate our party into the settlement of the tax, than our porters would desert; and when the drums beat a "receipt" for all demands, and we were free to move out of their clutches, our Wezee porters would get up a row with us, and demand more cloth, thus causing us to suffer as much annoyance from friend as from foe; and often they would run away in a body as soon as they got what they wanted. Nothing we could devise seemed to succeed, till their bows and arrows were seized, and they had got so far on the journey that going back through these boisterous races to their homes without arms would have been as bad as death to them. One trouble over, we had others: our Seedees, who had been engaged and paid at the British Consulate of Zanzibar to accompany us, struck for double pay and increased allowance for rations. Their complaints were calmly listened to; and when it was told that they might leave our service but lay down their arms, they surrendered them, but thought better of it the following morning, and only three of them deserted. These constant drains upon our resources had one good effect—they lightened our baggage; and after the enormous tax levied by the sultan and under chiefs of Usui, we were far in the interior at Karague, with certainly not enough of beads to last us six months.[1]

The first sixteen marches from Ukuni were through very pleasant undulations of tall soft grass and umbrageous forest-trees, spots here and there being cleared for cultivation, and capable of yielding grain for one or two thousand travellers throughout a season. On getting into Usui[2] the watershed had changed; all ran to Victoria Nyanza. Our path crossed three or four escarped hills, tailing gently off to lower ground in the north. About Lohagattee[3] there was picturesque scenery. Delightfully wild rocks and crags interspersed with trees overhung the valleys, reminding one of the echoing cliffs over the Lake of Killarney. A waterfall, too, added a rare charm to this part of the journey. The water fell upon hard, black, volcanic-like boulders of conglomerate, in a cascade of two cubic feet from the top of the escarpment seventy feet in height. Amongst the spray beautiful ferns and mosses grew in great luxuriance, recalling many a ramble at home for plants and objects of natural history; but though crabs were about the water, no land-shells were found. The natives came into camp asking why the fall had been visited by the white man. Did he mean to stop the water that supplied the whole valley, by turning its course or drinking up its waters? Their chief, we heard, when rain is required, goes through a

---

[1] The lack of resources to pay their way helps to explain why, later, Speke and Grant became so anxious to get support from Petherick whom they supposed to be coming south to meet them.

[2] That is, Rusubi.

[3] This is difficult to identify on the modern map.

propitiatory ceremony at this spot to bring it in abundance; but as this year rain had fallen at its usual season, their fears were easily calmed. The rain-doctor had put out his magic instruments under a tree by the 20th October, and expected it abundantly at new moon, fifteen days afterwards, when his year would have expired. He begged for a piece of paper to assist him, and on getting half a sheet of foolscap, said he would prefer paper written over! From the 26th of September, and during October, we had very pleasant showers and slight thunderstorms. At new moon, on the 2d November, as the doctor predicted, we had a heavy wind-storm, with pelting rain; but by the 5th, *our* magical horn, the rain-gauge, had worked its charm and stopped the rain! When in low ground, or where water was lying near the surface, the mornings were so cold that gloves would have been a comfort. During the day the sun was oppressive, but in the shade, with a N.E. wind generally blowing, it was agreeably cool. Water was everywhere abundant the first half of the journey, in wells dug outside the villages, and in the boggy dips which drained the country to the north in the latter half. For the first time in Africa, we got clear crystal water bursting from under the hard stratified rock of the parallel ranges of Usui; and whether it was that the water was purer, that the season had changed, or that we were in a finer climate, the men suffered less in health during the months of October and November than during any previous time of the year. Speke was rapidly recovering from his dangerous chest complaint; and instead of my fever visits, I had only periodical nausea in the morning, occurring about every ten days during the march.

Geologically, the country of Uzinza has a great deal of interest, being broken up into so many varied forms. One day, from the path of splintered rock, you may contemplate the face of a long, bare, sloping hill, the surface of which is half rock half bog, giving it the wild dreary look of a Highland moor in the heart of Africa, but with this difference, that a garden of plantain forms part of the landscape. Again, pick up a walnut-sized nodule of iron, covered with a rusty red dust, and think how rudely, how quietly, they turn it into a spear that glistens like steel![1] Again, see the long high escarpments, and wonder at the power that had raised them into such a position. The volcanic mounds in Kishakka, seen from the spur above Vihembé, were most curious, so many of them rising in one part of the horizon like mole-heaps on the earth's surface, some of their tops nearer us being sterile and of red grit, their sides strewed over with white quartz fragments; others clothed with pale green grass to their very summits, and dotted with trees sweeping down to, and shading with verdure, the valleys below. Their forms were saddle-shaped, horse-shoes, and frustums of cones; many were crowned with rock, and nearly all had stratified splinters bristling from their sides.[2] The eastern slopes below the escarpments, where the debris lay, were more cultivated than the western rocky parts. The natives bestowed great care on their fields, hoeing them up by the 8th October for the expected rain, collecting the weeds in heaps with a forked stick, and burning them. Fields of plantain trees were grown, each tree six feet apart. From the fruit a sweet spirituous wine is made, tasting somewhat like still hock, and quite as pleasant. The decayed leaves and stems of the plantain were allowed to remain on the ground to preserve the roots and soil from the heat of the sun, and afford nourishment to a crop

[1] Or a hoe; the WaZinza were famous for their hoes which were widely traded.
[2] Grant tried to draw some of the landscapes described here. See Plates 13 and 14 and Figures 48 and 49, p. 144..

of beans, "maharageh,"[1] peculiar to this country, and often grown in the shade of the trees. The other crops seen ripening in November, were Indian corn and manioc;[2] sweet potato was ripe and abundant; sorghum, "M'tama,[3] at that season, was scarce and dear; tobacco, fowls, goat, and cows were more expensive than we had found them in Unyamuezi.

The cattle looked wildly at our dress, and were here a different breed—namely, the heavy, ungraceful, large-horned variety of Karague, without humps,[4] and many of them probably from Unyoro, hornless, like the Teeswater breed, but bony and gaunt from bad grazing. All night the people allow their cattle to remain in the field, without any fence, standing round smouldering fires by their habitations. I observed at cow-milking time the skin of a calf placed in front of one cow, when she licked it all over, and while her hindlegs were tied with a thong, the milk was taken. In a goat that was killed, a black glazed ball of hair very much resembling its own was found inside: no cattle diseases were heard of. The manner our men had of getting hold of a vicious cow was quite African. A noose is laid on the ground, she is driven over it till by perseverance she is caught; or if she is to be killed, they chase her with a sword-bayonet, and either hamstring or break the bone of a hind-leg.

In the southern forests of Uzinza, hartebeest, eland, zebra, pig, and various species of antelope might be shot from horseback or on foot, as there is a wide range of fine country for them; but the greatest number and variety of animals I saw in Africa were in the valley of Urigi,[5] which is the boundary between Uzinza and Karague; all the above animals, with the rhinoceros and giraffe, might certainly be seen any morning by the sportsman. The valley or plain is covered with four-feet-high grasses, is from three to four miles broad, and probably twenty miles long, evidently once forming part of Victoria Nyanza. We counted fourteen rhinoceros upon the plain below; they were so numerous that while marching they were often within gunshot, affording us excellent sport had we chosen to follow them up. Instead of being frightened, one of these rhinoceros walked up towards me till I whistled at sixty paces, which was close enough; but the bullet from one of the men's rifles only made him put a twist in his tail and trot off proudly over the grassy plain for three miles, tripping repeatedly, and halting for an instant to give himself a shake, as if he had been stung. No elephants were seen—it was too open a country for them; hyena were rarely heard; porcupine-quills were picked up in the woods; serpents, we saw few or none; beeswax was never met with, though hives made out of logs were occasionally. Of game-birds the most plentiful was the guinea-fowl[6] near the cultivations. The natives of Usui will not eat the fowl, but the Walinga, a class of people who work in iron and its nodules,[7] have no objection. Florikan were shot; also a species of partridge quite new to me. I was attracted by their curious gait in running with their bodies thrown back: their

---

[1] But this is simply the general Swahili term for bean plants, properly, *maharagwe.*

[2] That is, cassava, a root crop.

[3] *Mtama* is a general term for millets; sorghum is the essentially African and traditionally most common grain crop.

[4] As distinct from the humped zebu cattle. However, cross-breeding produces many intermediate types. For a discussion of cattle and their usage in East Africa, see Koponen, *People and Production,* pp. 242–9.

[5] The River Ruigi.

[6] Perhaps *Numidia meliagris.*

[7] Blacksmiths often came from separate clans.

call, too, was strange—"cock, cock, ko-cock," or "chick-a-chick, chick-a-chick," not unlike the Himalayan cheer-pheasant's voice; our Seedees called it the "Booee." Its throat and round the eyes were an orange red; one was double-spurred, and weighed 1½ lb.[1]

While delayed by the sultan of Usui for fifteen days in settling his tax, we found the above partridge amongst the bushes of the valley; also numbers of pretty birds of no value except as specimens. We observed three fine species of swallow on the wing; the prettiest was entirely black, except on the forehead and under the lower mandible, where it was snow-white; a smaller was black all over, and both had forked tails, and frequented craggy ground. A larger species have red belly and chest, whitish throat, some white under the wings, long forked tail and general colour black, frequenting ground covered with brushwood. The smallest seen was black with white belly, red over forehead and under the lower mandible, with forked tail.[2] Black birds the size and shape of robins flew from tree to tree; water-wagtails[3] were familiar with our camp; creepers hopped amongst the bushes; smaller genera were in flights; and a peculiar-looking bird, with plain brown plumage and long tail, was shot amongst the rushes. Though mentioned last, our Seedees considered this the king of birds. He is called the "M'linda,"[4] and he moves escorted by a staff of little birds, whose duty it is, should a feather fall from the king, to tear it to pieces, thus preventing its being put upon an arrow. A similar tale is told with reference to the tippet-monkey, who is said to believe his handsome skin so much coveted, that when wounded he tears out all his beautiful long hair, to prevent your making use of it! The skin of the M'linda is as thick as that of a mouse, the feathers might be called hairy, the bill is stronger than a linnet's, and the feet are soft and red. Our men were much pleased during a march to meet with a bird they called the "kong-ot'a:"[5] we were certain to have luck attending us when it was seen!

The most powerful chief on our route through Uzinza was Suwarora of Usui[6]—a Wahuma by caste, but a superstitious creature, addicted to drink, and not caring to see us, but exacting through his subordinates the most enormous tax we had yet paid. His chief officer or "sirhidge"[7] was a Watusi; and when he called upon us dressed in the most ridiculous costume—a woman's crimson cotton gown, a red-check turban, and "saharee" thrown round his shoulders—he was treated with every respect, and got a chair. We had time to make his acquaintance. He was middle-aged, with a dissipated, reckless look, full of animated conversation, very black, with flat nose and prominent teeth. His legs were masses of iron wire, fitting as tight as a stocking. He had many favours to ask; he would like so much to have a pair of our shoes, &c. He had sent two men, bearing the royal rod of his "M'kama"[8] or sultan, to convey us with safety into the country. He hoped they had done their duty, for no Arab had ever such an honour paid him. There were ridiculous

[1] Presumably one of the francolins, perhaps the red-wing, *Francolinus levaillanti* or *F. afer.*

[2] These swallows are difficult to identify precisely from Grant's brief descriptions but with the expert authority of Mr Stanley Howe, it can be suggested that they are, respectively, *Hirundo angolensis, H. daurica* and *Psalidoprocne albiceps.*

[3] Possibly *Motacilla alba* but it is more likely these were *M. aguimp.*

[4] The Kiswahili word signifies a guard so this is a guard bird – perhaps a goose such as *Aliopochen aegyptiacus.*

[5] A term which seems to indicate a heron or, perhaps, a woodpecker.

[6] That is, Rusubi.

[7] Perhaps *msiri*, a close adviser.

[8] *Omukama* is the term for a ruler in areas with Hima overlords.

stories going about regarding us—as that we were possessed of supernatural powers, that we killed all the inhabitants of the country we passed through, and that we took possession of all countries; but, on his consulting the M'ganga, these reports were proved to be false, and we were admitted into the country. He paid us a second visit, dressed in a much less gaudy suit; and while he sat, eating coffee from a little basket he carried, we suggested that the tax had better be settled soon; but he treated the matter with great indifference, saying, "Oh, don't press it; let it take its time! My brother will arrange it the day after to-morrow, because I have to go into the district to see some patients; and now I must bid you adieu." The previous night he had sent us a message that some handsome cloths would be acceptable if we would have the kindness to present them. We did so, and in return he gave us two goats, and we saw no more of him.

The brother of the sirhidge, a more morose person, now came into the field, and said, "Before I can even broach the subject of your arrival here to his highness the M'kama (sultan), I expect a present;" and so the treaty dragged its length for several days, till officers appeared in camp pronouncing the demand, with little sticks to represent each article. About five men's loads of copper were paid and carried away for the chief by our men. Although the tax was heavy, it was conducted in a gentlemanly, quiet way, and much quicker than we had expected, on account, it was said, of their fear to detain magicians longer in the country. The last extortion was, that guides must escort us to the frontier, and they had to be paid a load of copper between them.

The people of the country,[1] generally called Wanyambo,[2] dress in nothing but goat-skins, the length and shape of the tails of a shooting-coat, without pockets or buttons; a thong of leather ties this smartly round the waist, right side uppermost, and is slackened on sitting down; this forms their entire costume. With a variously-shaped spear or a bow and arrow (sometimes poisoned), they looked very active, slim fellows, having a far greater air about them than the Wezee. A tuft of wool is often left on their crowns; sometimes the teeth are entire, or the two upper incisors filed inside, but none are ever extracted. Some of the people cover the body and arms with artificially raised solid blisters, in circles, waves, or lines. Their address, when it suited them, was that of cringing politeness, showing great respect every morning; but they could also be boisterous and insolent. The Wasui race can seldom be induced to carry loads; but amongst them numerous Wezees, driven from their homes by the Watuta, reside, and the traveller receives aid from them. A M'sui will carry a load on his head, but not upon the shoulder. On coming into camp to see the novelties, all the better class had a gourd of pombé in one hand, and generally chewed coffee-beans. Round their ankles was a profusion of wires, generally more upon one leg than another. One stranger I saw wearing round his neck a flat piece of stone, which I thought to be malachite.

In this country we were more troubled by thieves than we had been anywhere else. After sunset our porters when beyond camp were assaulted, and their cloth coverings torn from them. At night they made several attempts to get inside our ring-fence of thorns, and the thefts became so numerous that we had to shoot two or three found plundering. The

---

[1] Grant does not provide a description of the landscape but he did depict it in Figure 48, p. 144. The picture shows the effects of burning the vegetation to clear the land.

[2] That is, the commoners, members of non-Hima, clans. Figure 47, p. 143, depicts the people of Rusubi but the description here does not seem consistent with the depiction.

people rather approved of our doing this, and complimented us on being so alert and watchful during the night. They seemed generally to be an industrious people, with comfortable "crofts" round their houses.

The Walinga are workers in iron, scarcely distinguishable in dress from the Wasui.[1] Their furnaces are in the heart of the forest; charcoal and lumps of iron cinder (like a coarse sponge, and of a "blue bottle" colour) usually mark the spot; and four lads, squatting under a grass roof with a double-handled bellows each, blow at a live mass of charcoal which has the nodules of metal intermixed with it.[2] In this calcining nothing else seems to be used, and the metal melts, descending into a recess, much in the same way as I have seen at the Cumberland lead-works.

One morning, to my surprise, in a wild jungle we came upon cattle, then upon a "bomah," or ring-fence, concealed by beautiful umbrageous large trees, quite the place for a gypsy camp. At the entry two strapping fellows met me and invited my approach. I mingled with the people, got water from them, and was asked, "Would I not prefer some milk?" This sounded to me more civilised than I expected from Africans, so I followed the men, who led me up to a beautiful ladylike creature, a Watusi woman, sitting alone under a tree. She received me, without any expression of surprise, in the most dignified manner; and, after having talked with the men, rose smiling, showing great gentleness in her manner, and led me to her hut. I had time to scrutinise the interesting stranger: she wore the usual Watusi costume of a cow's skin reversed, teased into a frieze with a needle, coloured brown, and wrapped round her body from below the chest to the ankles. Lappets, showing zebra-like stripes of many colours, she wore as a "turnover" round the waist; and, except where ornamented on one arm with a highly polished coil of thick brass wire, two equally bright and massive rings on the right wrist, and a neck pendant of brass wire,—except these and her becoming wrapper, she was *au naturelle*. I was struck with her peculiarly formed head and graceful long neck; the beauty of her fine eyes, mouth, and nose; the smallness of her hands and naked feet— all were faultless; the only bad feature, which is considered one of beauty with them, was her large ears. The arms and elbows were rounded off like an egg, the shoulders were sloping, and her small breasts were those of a crouching Venus—a perfect beauty, although darker than a brunette! Her temporary residence was peculiar—it was formed of grass, was flat-roofed, and so low that I could not stand upright in it. The fireplace consisted of three stones; milk-vessels of wood, shining white from scouring, were ranged on one side of the abode. A good-looking woman sat rocking a gourd between her knees in the process of churning butter. After the fair one had examined my skin and my clothes, I expressed great regret that I had no beads to present to her. "They are not wanted," she said: "sit down, drink this buttermilk, and here is also some butter for you." It was placed on a clean leaf. I shook hands, patted her cheek, and took my leave, but some beads were sent her, and she paid me a visit, bringing butter and buttermilk, and

---

[1] Nevertheless, as is commonly the case in this region, the iron workers are in a separate clan because, as some authorities have suggested, their skills in transforming ore into useful objects, may be a form of witchcraft. Those who smelted, rather than forged, iron were likely to be fenced around with more ritual. Koponen, *People and Production*, p. 259.

[2] Plate 5 shows the smiths and the boys and some of the utensils produced, of which the hoes must have been the most important. Nevertheless, Grant's illustrative work provides important evidence that other iron tools were made.

asking for more presents, which she of course got, and I had the gratification to see her eyes sparkle at the sight of them. This was one of the few women I met during our whole journey that I admired.[1] None of the belles in Usui could approach her; but they were of a different caste, though dressing much in the same style. When cow-skins were not worn, these Usui women dressed very tidily in bark cloths, and had no marks or cuttings observable on their bodies. Circles of hair were often shaved off the crowns of their heads, and their neck ornaments showed considerable taste in the selection of the beads. The most becoming were a string of the M'zizima,[2] spheres of marble-sized white porcelain, and triangular pieces of shell, rounded at the corners. An erect fair girl, daughter of a chief, paid us a visit, accompanied by six maids, and sat silently for half an hour. She had a spiral circle of wool shaved off the crown of her head; her only ornament was a necklace of green beads: she wore the usual wrapper, and across her shoulders a strip of scarlet cloth was thrown; her other fineries were probably left at home. The women of the district generally had grace and gentleness in their manner.

The plump little negro girls who came about our camp, standing with crossed arms and looking very frightened, are never allowed to shave their heads till they get married, consequently the hair is in matted tufts or mops, very ugly, with a triangular or square space shaved on the crown: if ornamented with cowries, the black wool appears to more advantage. They are not allowed to wear the usual clothing of women, but have the skin of a goat, with the hair inside, round their loins, and so arranged that from the waist to the knee it remains open, exposing completely the right thigh. Not having lived in their villages, we could not see any of their customs. The chief of Usui's residence, entitled Quikooroo,[3] was a set of grass huts, encircled by three concentric fences of thorn, the largest one being two to three miles round. The other huts in the valley had no fence whatever, except where planted round with a dense quickset of euphorbia, growing from twelve to twenty feet high. Sometimes by the pathway we observed cairns of stones, such as are found all over the world, and our leading porters generally threw their mite on the heap. In Hindostan they would be called "Peer ke jaggeh," places of devotion;[4] and our Seedees called them "M'zeemoo."[5] A rock was also passed, on which our porters placed pebbles.

The language of the country was quite unintelligible to our men—I mean as spoken by the Watusi, who are the reigning race here; but they did not find it difficult to pick up some words and phrases. It was not so hard as the dialect of Unyamuezi, which they considered more "bharee" (difficult).[6] If one Seedee wishes to address another by saying, "I say," or "Old fellow!" he calls "Somoh!"[7]—if a Muezi, "Doogoh yango!"[8]—if a M'sui,

---

[1] The Introduction discusses sexual attraction and the travellers. Youngs, *Travellers in Africa*, pp. 94–5, sees this passage as not only romantic but also an example of the Western visitor bringing about an endorsement of capitalist values. See also above, pp. 50, 54.

[2] See Chapter VI, above, pp. 148–9, and Burton, *Lake Regions*, II, p. 393, where the *mzizima* is described as a large flat bead of glass either of a blue or whitish colour..

[3] Or *Kwikuru*.

[4] *Peer*: a holy person or his tomb. *Hobson Jobson*.

[5] *Mzimu* is the Swahili word for a spirit or the place where offerings are made to ancestors and other spirits.

[6] Or, more accurately, to be avoided.

[7] This indicates a close friend.

[8] Grant means a Munyamwezi and the greeting means 'my brother!'

"Kunewani!"—if a M'ganda, "Awangeli!"[1] There is no similarity in these; consequently, to speak to any M'ganda, two interpreters were at first necessary, until our men picked up some of their language; but in their numerals they were almost the same.

The style of dance at Myonga's seemed to be peculiar to the country. It was conducted, without arms or any rough coarseness, by moonlight, in an open space, all the lads and lasses collecting without music. A circle was formed, singing and clapping of hands commenced, and either a woman made her most graceful curtsy to a favourite in the crowd, and retired skilfully backwards to her place, or a young fellow bounded into the centre, threw himself into attitudes, performed some gymnastic feat, bowed to the prettiest, and then made way for the next champion or fair lady.

After I had joined Speke at Bogweh on the 7th October 1861, a letter was received by him from Colonel Rigby, the consul at Zanzibar, dated 31st October 1860, advising the despatch of brandy, biscuit, and cigars, &c.; and that our letters were in another packet. We, of course, were delighted at receiving this news—a whole year had elapsed without any communication whatever from the outer world; but where were the letters and supplies? "Oh, they must have been lost in Ugogo, where the Arabs had gone to fight!" Whatever was the cause, our letters were cut off from us for the period of twenty-seven months—viz., from October 1860 to February 1863, when we got to Gondokoro. We had consequently to content ourselves with the news of the countries around us. Stories from men who had seen snow on the top of Kilimanjaro; with accounts of a tribe to the south of it who rode on horseback, and a salt lake called Lebassa[2] in that direction; or the appearance of a M'ganda, tall, stout, broad-nostrilled, seen for the first time, gave me a longing desire, from his manly and true African look, to reach his country. The dress of this people was formed of gaily-coloured goat-skins and bark cloths, well arranged, striking, and becoming; their accoutrements and drums were got up with neatness and simplicity; their drapery perfectly concealed the whole body, except the head, feet, and hands; and once a strapping girl, of a tribe still farther off, was shown to us as an Unyoro.[3] Having since then seen her race, known by the extraction of the lower incisors, I can state that we were not imposed upon.

In the next chapter will be described the country of Karague, which reminded me of the English Lake district. An Arab caravan, like our own, but of 250 loads, had got ahead of us, and having settled their tax with the Usui chief, the men were plodding on to the ivory and slave mart. In their file two men and a girl were in chains together—no doubt recent investments. Our Seedees, by their curious ways, continued to amuse us. Our table-attendant, Mabrook, or Burton's "bull-headed Mabruki,"[4] was a thorough African, so opposite to what an Indian servant is. Ever naked from head to waist (and looking gross with fatness), he would come up to "lay the table," whistling or singing, with a bunch of knives, spoons, and forks in his hand; having placed the tin lids and pots at our feet, he

---

[1] In the interlacustrine region, Bantu peoples were affected in culture and language by non-Bantu overlords who ruled them.

[2] Porters who had accompanied Krapf or Rebmann might have the story of snow; the horseback riders must have been mythical; the salt lake is one in the Eastern Rift Valley, possibly Lake Natron. See Map 6, p. 31.

[3] Strictly, Grant should have written 'Muganda' and 'Munyoro' for the individuals from Buganda and Bunyoro whom he now met.

[4] This is 'Mabruki Speke' who, before his death in 1875, became one of the most experienced men who served European travellers in East Africa. See Simpson, *Dark Companions*, pp. 28, 195.

would squat on the ground beside them and dole out our dinner. Should he have to clean your plate, a bunch of grass or a leaf is generally within his reach; and, if he has to remove the plate, he seldom returns without wiping his mouth. He chaffs his comrades as he sits by you; and dinner over, you see him eating with your spoons and drinking out of the teapot or the spout of the kettle.

CHAPTER VIII

[Pages 137–87]

Karagwe[1] [25 November 1861–14 April 1862]

Extract from Journal: Arrival in Karagwe

March 6 miles to the Sultan's residence – halted on hill top in sight of it – beautiful and half hidden by other hills, lake, the distant margins being invisible from Rain & mist – sight most pleasant one, quite repaid the disappointments we had had. Moosa's men came to meet us & walked us straight to the Sultan himself. [NLS, MS. 17915, 25 November 1861]

THE royal family of Karague consisted of three brothers and their families. Their father, Dagara, had died about eight years previous to our visit. He had lived to a good old age; was almost a giant in height, with leprous hands, of the Wahuma caste; was esteemed a wise and sagacious prince, and was very popular with the people. On his death, his body was sewn up in the skin of a cow, and placed inside a hut, with several women and cattle, who were there all left to die and moulder to dust. The question of succession was disputed by three surviving sons, and the test as to who should ultimately rule was that some sacred emblem would be placed before all, and whoever should raise it from the ground would become the reigning sovereign. Rumanika,[2] not the eldest, was found to be the only one of the three competent, or who felt conscientiously that he could support the dignity of the position by raising this weight from the ground; consequently he was elected. From that time a younger brother, Rogærah, became his bitter enemy, and fled to a corner of the province, taking with him a great proportion of the people with their cattle, as he was the more generous and the greater favourite of the two brothers. But Rumanika's mother had to be got rid of before he could properly hold the reins of government; and by some magic medicine she was killed, and he was declared "M'kama of Karague."[3]

---

[1] Grant spelt the name 'Karague'. The months spent here were an extremely important part of Grant's experiences because his long illness forced an extended stay in the country when Speke had departed. He thus became the principal authority on the kingdom. At this period, Karagwe was at the height of its importance as the gateway to the northern kingdoms but later declined both because of internal dissensions and the fact that traders from Zanzibar began to use water transport across Lake Victoria to Buganda. See Sheriff, *Slaves, Spices and Ivory*, pp. 183–4, 194; Katoke, 'Karagwe, a Pre-Colonial State', pp. 539–40.

[2] Rumanyika Orugundu was probably born in the 1820s; he came to the throne c. 1853 and committed suicide at an uncertain date after 1878; Katoke, *Karagwe Kingdom*, p. 99, believes that it was 1882 or 1883.

[3] Rumanika's position was not entirely secure as his brother, Rogero (Rwegira), with the support of the Hima (Watusi) clans, continued to dispute the succession.

Although illness prevented my seeing so much of Rumanika as I should otherwise have liked, I could not but notice that he was the handsomest and most intelligent sovereign we had met with in Africa.

Extracts from Journal: Rumanyika

[Rumanika] asked to be shown the guns, powder flask, leather bag, telescope ... looked at our shoes, told us of the lake crocodile, did we think it big, how we liked Karagweh hills! How we knew there were people here etc. so intellectual all his queries were in comparison to any African I had ever expected to see. [NLS, MS. 17915, 25 November 1861]

Painted a map of the world for the Sultan. [NLS, MS. 17915, 1 December 1861]

He stood six feet two inches in height, and his countenance had a fine, open, mild expression. There was nothing of the African look about him, except that he had wool instead of hair. His dress was a robe of numerous skins of small antelopes sewn together, and knotted over one shoulder, with a loin-cloth underneath; or an Arab cloak or shawl of bark-cloth hung from his shoulder, reaching below the knee. Going about with nothing on his head, his arms bare, except common ornaments of beads or brass, with painted porcelain beads on his ankles, and carrying a long staff,[1] he was altogether the picture of the gentle shepherd of his flock.[2] His four young sons, of ages from sixteen to twenty-four, were tall, smart, nice-looking young fellows—quite gentlemanly in their manners, and very cleanly in their persons and dress. There was a younger son, an infant, always kept at the royal residence, and not allowed out. The five wives of the king have been described by Captain Speke:[3] several were of enormous proportions, unable to enter the door of an ordinary hut, requiring a person on each side to support them when moving from one place to another, and expressing great delight at any present the "Wazoongo" (white men) should send their lord and master. Their diet, and that of the sons and daughters, was generally boiled plantain or milk. They considered their existence depended on the latter article of food, and certainly they all throve admirably upon it— the sons were full of vigour, and the women were fat and healthy, though not prolific. On Captain Speke asking to be allowed to take a young prince to England for education, the cry was, "They had never been more than ten miles from home; how could they go?— there would be no milk for them—they would die." Probably they had also some dread that the lads would be made slaves of. All of them were very particular and fastidious as to their diet.

The sultan drank milk; thought the meat of goat and sheep unclean; would not eat fish, fowl, or guinea-fowl; rarely or never touched stirabout; and merely sucked the juice of boiled beef. He drank very little plaintain-wine,[4] and was never known to be intoxicated. He had many superstitions; he would not drink out of the vessel that we or

---

[1] Grant attempted two sketches of Rumanyika neither of which was coloured. See Figures 52 and 66, pp. 205 and 211.

[2] The very favourable view arose in part because both Grant and Speke developed the idea, later dubbed the 'Hamitic myth', that non-negroid immigrants from the north, from whom Rumanika was descended, had brought some measure of 'civilization'. Speke devoted a whole chapter of his book to the idea: Speke, *Journal*, pp. 246–60. See also Sanders, 'The Hamitic Hypothesis', *passim*.

[3] Speke, *Journal*, pp. 209–10.

[4] The spelling mistake here was not picked up either by Grant or by his original publisher.

any commoner had used, and he combined the offices of prophet, priest, and king. As prophet, he would place the tusks of an elephant upright on the ground, fill them with charms, seal them, and predict rain, although his calculations were not always correct. As priest, three days after new moon, he sat concealed, all but his head, in the doorway of his chief hut, and received the salutations of his people, who, one by one, shrieked and sprang in front of him, swearing allegiance. His head on these occasions was wonderfully dressed, and made to look quite patriarchal, with a crown of beads and feathers, and a false white beard of considerable length, giving him the look of an Indian "khitmutgar"[1] or Jewish rabbi. He was very fond of curiosities, and amongst the collection he had obtained from Arab visitors were stuffed birds, an electric battery, looking-glasses, a clock with eyes in the cast-iron figure made to roll with the movement of the pendulum, &c. He expressed surprise that we had brought nothing to amuse him, so that all our ingenuity was put to the test in order to try and gratify his highness. A jumping-jack made of wood was sent him for his infant son, and he said he must have me make him one the size of life before I left the country. He had a three-pounder brass gun brought him unmounted from the coast; and on a picture being sent him, showing how we in India drag guns into action by means of elephants, nothing would satisfy him till he had ordered fifty men to cut down trees, to be made into a gun-carriage. I protested, saying, "You have no iron—no elephant; who is to make the wheels?" Here was a dilemma—a wheel to make before I could be allowed to join my companion, and nothing to make it with but a penknife in my pocket! Luckily my friend Rumanika was not pig-headed, and had compassion on me when it was explained to him that ropes of bark, and men to drag the gun, would not answer the purposes of iron and elephant.

This sovereign several times came to call while I lay sick, one day bringing me a fish alive in a jar from the lake;[2] this pleased me, as the Wahuma have a prejudice against fish. But his chief delight seemed to be in medicines and pictures. It was an anxious moment when our tent was emptied of all listeners, and we were pressed for a medicinal charm to bring about the death of his brother Rogærah.

Extract from Journal: Rogero
S[peke] told them his life was in the hands of God, we do not practise witchcraft; the only thing was for the Sultan to strengthen his Govt. by encouraging trade and putting down the villainous taxes enforced by the Usui Sultan – no more was said. [NLS, MS. 17915, 26 November 1861].

Then, during the visit, the weight of the mercury, its reflections, &c., were looked at in amazement; the compass—"was there water in it?"—our shoes, our bedding—all were marvels. With the sextant he looked through at the sun without fear; and when consulted one morning by my servant about some strange large animals that came in at night to our camp, he recommended that the next time they appeared we should challenge them three times, and if no answer were received, to fire at them; for "depend upon it they were enemies sent by his rebel brother to lay a trap for him." Should they, however, prove to be leopards, they were not to be molested. For all leopards they have a great reverence, as

---

[1] *Kitmutgar* is a Hindi word derived from Arabic which came to mean, especially in Bengal, someone who served at table: *Hobson-Jobson*.

[2] Presumably, the lake which the travellers called 'Little Lake Windermere'. For an illustration, see Plate 21.

Dagara, the late sovereign, is believed to be still protected by them; and on an invading army coming from Uganda, this sultan had the power to send leopards to disperse them. Their skins are only worn by royalty or its followers. The sultan, on seeing the picture of some of his milk-carriers, sent for the sketch-book, turned out all idlers, and showed them to a few favourite servants about his family. His wives were quite clamorous about seeing them, asking why Rumanika had not been drawn. The back view of a naked young prince, enormously fat, with clotted long hair concealing his neck, gave them great amusement, and they clapped their hands and laughed with joy at the resemblance to the original.[1] All the princesses living in separate houses got jealous unless they saw the sketches, so that my servant was several times detained a whole day by them; and it became so fashionable to look at the pictures, that for days my camp was beset with people wishing to have their curiosity gratified. M'nanagee,[2] the brother of the sultan, a man of six feet three inches in height, brought his favourite bow to be ornamented with pictures. There never was a prettier bit of stick; it was exactly his own height, of ash-coloured wood, bent merely at the ends, balanced beautifully, not a curve in it that could hurt the eye, and it was strung with the sinews of a cow. He could with ease throw an arrow, by giving it a high flight, 150 or 200 yards. Wishing to enlighten and amuse Rumanika, I sent him coloured pictures of our soldiers, and of men in ordinary costume; these he admired very much, but could I not show him how our ladies looked? Certainly. Figures of three ladies were painted—one in morning costume, one at an archery meeting using the bow and arrow, and a third in ball costume. He immediately hung all up on the wall of his small hut; and on inquiring which figure pleased him most, the palm was given to the evening costume.

Whenever he wished to spend the day at a spot on the hill across the lake, where I think his father had been interred, he was carried in a basket, made of osiers, by four men. The band led the way with music; several hundred followers surrounded him; and if he was on the return journey, small fat boys, having their heads wreathed with water-lilies plucked in the lake as they ferried over, danced and skipped up the hill the whole way to the sound of the pleasing drum and bugle band.[3] His revenue was said to be one jar out of every three of plantain-wine; and all his guests coming from the neighbouring provinces had to be fed by the farmers around. It has always been the custom of Uganda, Usui, and Karague, that when any one of their chiefs sends messengers to the other, the royal bearers are free to settle where they like, and to provision themselves as they require from the stores of the people, no payment being ever taken for anything. Plantain is so common that nothing is said if a stranger is seen plucking a bunch from a tree; but at night many disturbances and frequent fights occur when a raid is made for goats. Stones fly, spears are thrown, and all is in confusion, if anything beyond a bunch of plantain is attempted to be carried off.

We were asked to witness a new-moon ceremony.[4] This generally takes place three days after the first appearance of the luminary, and it was celebrated as usual by our men firing volleys in the air. The sultan assumes the priestly garb, and dons his long, false, white beard on this occasion. His whole body remains concealed behind a screen, and he has beside him his insignia of office, either a small drum, or an instrument which no one but

---

[1] See Figure 58, p. 208, for what proves to be a single milk carrier and, on the right, the naked prince.

[2] See Figure 60, p. 209, for Grant's depiction of the man with whom he was to have much to do during his stay.

[3] Figure 53, p. 205, shows the band.

[4] This was on 8 December 1861; see Figure 54, p. 206, for Grant's depiction of the ceremony which he goes on to describe. He shows 33 drummers just as his description specifies.

himself can raise. The drums, generally thirty-three, are on the ground, in a line, each having a large white cross on its head—a strange Crusader-like custom. A man stands behind each, and the leader, with two small drums, is in front to give the time. On his raising the right arm, the thirty-three drummers do the same, then the left arm, and they gradually beat the drums quicker, till ending in a tremendous roll. This continues for three hours, with intervals, and is repeated the day following. A band of hand-drums is near the sultan's hut, giving lighter dance-music for the amusement of the boys and girls, who must make merry as the new-moon term comes round.

Rumanika was on excellent terms with the neighbouring kings of Uganda and Unyoro, often exchanging presents with them.[1] He had sent to M'tesa of Uganda a book printed in English ("Kaffir Laws"),[2] which we saw on getting to Uganda; and they would send to him for powder, cloth, &c., he being supposed by the chiefs living further north to have easier access to the coast. In return for these favours, or for the gift of a porcelain cup, or neatly-made ankle or wrist ornaments in brass or copper, &c., he would expect to receive ivory, cattle, or slaves. Curious enough, none of these kings had ever visited each other, consequently their ideas of foreign countries were very limited, and they believed any story a designing traveller might choose to tell them. Rumanika, for instance, expected to have seen us always dressed in white cambric shirts, instead of which we had no soap to wash our flannel ones! Was it true that we made doors out of his ivory? He told us the road to the north was a most dangerous one; we could not march through it without 200 guns! One race we should have to pass through were pigmies; others lived in trees, and seized women; dogs we should come across with horns, sheep with three horns, and men travelled about with a stool tied behind them. This last was partly true, for we found the Wagani carrying little stools on their arms; and "those living in trees" may allude to M. Du Chaillu's gorilla![3]

We could not trace any distinct form of religion amongst this interesting race, but there were certain indications or traces of Jewish worship.[4] A piece of copper, made up in the form of a grapple or anchor, two feet long, lay near the door of the sultan's hut. We were told this was to represent the horns of cattle, and had a sacred signification. It was placed upright in the ground on the occasion of the monthly festivities, and looked like what the Brahmins of India might have assumed as an idol. The cleanly huts of the Wahuma race reminded me of Indians; also the superstition of not drinking out of the same cup with you. The moon in its different phases was thought to laugh at us. A tree was considered the greatest object in the creation, not even excepting man. Lions protected the mausoleum of Dagara, the former sultan! "No kingdom was so powerful as this; no one dare attack us! Lions guard us!" Captain Speke could not kill any

---

[1] As noted above, at this period, Karagwe had a key function in linking the two major interlacustrine kingdoms to the coast-based system of trade routes.

[2] The two explorers did not give very full information about this book but it must surely have been *A Compendium of Kafir Laws and Customs*, published in 1858, the work of Colonel J. MacLean, a Commissioner in what was then known as British Kaffraria in South Africa. Oddly, Grant does not mention that it was Speke who had given this book to Rumanika: Speke, *Journal*, p. 233.

[3] Paul Du Chaillu (1831?–1903) was a Swiss- or French-born explorer who had apparently emigrated to the USA. It was American money which sent him to western Equatorial Africa where in the late 1850s he claimed to have seen gorillas. He was widely disbelieved and what he actually achieved has since remained a subject of controversy.

[4] This was an entirely erroneous idea.

hippopotami in the lake, because he had made no present to the invisible god, or "deo," who lived upon it; and the sultan of Unyoro could divide the waters of the lake with a rod!

A younger prince, M'nanagee,[1] was equally tall and erect with his brother Rumanika, and he was even a greater prophet and priest. The natives had unbounded faith in his powers as a diviner. Daily did he walk to a stone on the face of the hill, or he might be seen going to visit some stuffed elephant-tusks placed in the ground within an enclosure, for the purpose of daily consultation with his gods. Although M'nanagee had these peculiarities, he was friendly and gentlemanly, always ready to give any information he might possess; rather formal at first, with a haughty air, but ever kind in getting us provisions, assisting in the knowledge of plants and herbs, and very modest in his requests for presents. His dress did not differ much from the people of the country; the usual short leather wrapper hid his loins, and a sheet of cotton check kept his shoulders and body warm. The head was shaved bare, and a strap, holding a charm, was tied round the back of it. Bunches of charms hung on his arms and from his neck and below the knee, and huge masses of wire were on his ankles. He always carried a long walking-stick, with a charm of wood tied at one end. A small boy, very fat, carried his chowrie, or fly-flapper, and a huge black pipe, the size of half a goose's egg, with a long stem. On paying me visits he was seldom accompanied by any one. His eldest son measured six feet five inches; but, though quite as gentle as the father, was not so good-looking, and seldom came to visit me. A younger one, not more than two or three years old, died while I was at Karague, rather suddenly, and the father mourned greatly for the child, crying most grievously. The body was buried, the sultan said, in an island on the lake, whereas his barber told me it was placed under rocks on the face of the hill. I am inclined to think the former statement correct, as the islands in the lake are considered sacred ground; while the Wanyambo (the peasants of the country) deposit their dead in the waters of the lake. M'nanagee had a firm belief in evil spirits. He knew them to be about his country, and felt certain as to the fact; but it was possible, he thought, for clever people like those at Zanzibar to confuse their designs for certain periods.

A third brother, to whom we had to make presents on our arrival in Karague, was named Roazerah. On sending a gift of a red cloth and some beads, &c., he asked what he could give in return. "Would a tusk be received?" "No." "Would they like a slave?" "No," said Bombay; "give them a couple of cows, that their men may have a feast." Though older than either of the other brothers, he could not succeed to the throne of his father, because he had been born before his father became a crowned king. In like manner, none of the princes at present in Karague can succeed to their father, as all were born while he was a prince.[2]

The chief possessions of this family are bounded on the north by the river Kitangule.[3] The valley of Urigi divides the kingdom on the south from Usui,[4] and its total extent is from 3000 to 4000 square miles of hills, dale, and lake, standing at a general elevation of 4500 feet above the level of the sea. Entering it from the south, the hills, rising 200

---

[1] See Figure 60, p. 209.

[2] See Katoke, 'Karagwe, a Pre-Colonial State', pp. 537–9, for the princes and the succession problem at this period.

[3] The river is usually known as the Kagera; Kitangule is a place on its southern bank.

[4] More properly, Rusubi.

to 300 feet above the valleys, are covered with waving grasses; a few trees run in lines with certain strata, almost with the regularity of plantations; and very often dense brushwood, the refuge of the rhinoceros, crowns two-thirds of their tops, or runs down the ravines or water-cuts to the valleys below. They have a very desolate appearance, all the habitations being in the lower grounds: a traveller is seldom met with. On the more precipitous hills, rock-fragments and jutting-out masses of sandstone-shingle lie at a steep angle on their slopes; and the path, of splinters from these, goes up and down, or makes long circuits to get round the spurs, seldom displaying any pleasing scene except the freshness of the young grasses after having been burnt. These reminded me of the "Emerald Isle," and when the view on reaching the residence of Rumanika, the reigning king, burst upon us, all hardships and trials were forgotten and forgiven. As you stand on the greensward, you see, 1000 feet below you, and two miles distant, the sweetly-lying lake of Karague, "Little Windermere,"[1] reposing in oval form amidst gently-swelling grassy hills, so surrounded as to puzzle one to think where the waters come from, and where they make their escape. On its western shore, trees hang over its clear sweet waters; wooded islands dot its glassy surface, and a deep fringe of the papyrus borders its southern side. But the most interesting sight to us was looking away to the far west over four distinct parallel ranges of hill, with water (Lakes Kagæra, Ooyewgomah, &c.) showing here and there between them; and occasionally about sunset, after the foggy mists had cleared away, appeared a sugar-loaf mountain, known to the natives as "M'foombæro," or Cook.[2] It is the largest hill in the country, and caused, on first view, quite a sensation, attracting our intense admiration by its towering height. Two brother cones, but lower, lie to its left, and all are so steep, that the natives said few attempt their ascent, having to do it on hands and knees. Their distance from where we stood was calculated at fifty miles.

Extract from Journal: Mfumbiro

[at bearing] 295° saw a high sugar loaf mountain some 40 miles off beyond Ruanda – quite excited us as country has been enveloped in hanging clouds since we've been here – called "M'foombæro" has two brothers bearing to its left. [NLS, MS. 17915, 28 November 1861]

Unfortunately they could not be reached, as they were off our direct route, and in a different kingdom, and many obstacles intervened; so that our only privilege was to look at them when not veiled in mists, at sunset.

The capital of Karague[3] is 1° 40′ south of the equator, within a complete belt of vapour the whole year round. Fruitful showers seemed to fall continually. There are no very

---

[1] The lake's real name is Lweru Rwabishonga, one of a string of lakes along the poorly-drained here south–north flowing Kagera River which today constitutes the boundary of Tanzania and Rwanda. Speke, *Journal*, p. 202, claims that it was he who named the lake 'Little Windermere'. For Grant's depictions of the lake, see Plate 21 and Figure 56, p. 207.

[2] In fact, Grant was seeing the Virunga volcanoes of the Western Rift Valley. The assumption that there was one major mountain persisted until the early 1900s and bedevilled arrangements for the partition in this part of Africa. Britain wanted to have Mfumbiro despite not knowing precisely where it was. 'In some ways the story reads like a farce'. Louis, *Ruanda-Urundi*, p. xvi. See pp. 41–64 for the detailed story. The fact that modern Uganda's boundary in the south-west extends south of the 1°S line of latitude owes something to Grant's report.

[3] Bweranyange, which lies east of 'Little Windermere'.

marked seasons, as winter and summer. On the same day, sowing, gathering, and reaping may be seen, and from November till April the fall of rain increases or diminishes according as the sun becomes more or less vertical to our position. The natives had their reasons for knowing this also; for when asked, on the 2d December 1861 (when we were having abundant showers), "How long is this to last?—when does your rainy season commence?"—they at once said, "With the new moon," which corresponded with the time for the sun to return towards its more vertical position. Again, when asking them, "When have you your heaviest rains?" the reply was, "At the time the Mohammedans call Ramezan" which is equivalent to our equinoctial period in March, when the sun crosses our zenith. A note about this time is as follows:— "17th March 1862. The weather looks black, peals of thunder with lightning; 1.65 inches of rain fell straight and thick, with occasional hail, in one hour."[1] The fall increased in quantity from this day till it reached its climax about the 10th of April, when it began again to decline. In December till January 7, the usual maximum temperature in a grass hut open to the south was observed to be 81°, and the minimum 56°, at an elevation of 5000 feet above the level of the sea. We had a great number of dull English days, very few bright ones, never an Italian sky, as too many vapours hung about this equatorial region.[2] The dews were heavy, and lay long, and the mould getting amongst plants was very disheartening to the collector, obliging him to discard many a souvenir.[3]

Extract from Journal: Getting Plant Specimens
Taken to having plants brought to me, writing their descriptions & sketching them. A young Muhinda assists. [NLS, MS. 17915, 26 February 1862]

Brushwood was used instead of firewood, which was scarce and dear, otherwise the chilly mornings and nights might have been cheered by the watchfire. The country was luckily so hilly, that, though the rain dashed with the N.E. wind into the red clayey soil, making the hill-sides stream with muddy rivulets, one hour after the "pelt" all had run down, and a gleam of sunshine made the ground not unpleasant to walk upon. The health of the men did not seem to suffer from wet. Zanzibar people are accustomed to getting ducked. It keeps them occupied in repairing their grass huts, collecting firewood, and making merry over it, rather than causing despondency. With one case of ophthalmia, and a few of fever, there were no other cases of sickness amongst the half-dozen men left by Speke on the 10th January, when he departed for Uganda, leaving me behind sick. At first sight this appeared to some persons at home as an unkind proceeding, leaving a helpless "brother" in the heart of Africa; but my companion was not the man to be daunted; he was offered an escort to the north, and all tender feelings must yield to the stern necessities of the case. "Strike while the iron is hot," applies to Africa more appropriately than to any country I know; another such opportunity might never occur, and had the traveller's determination of character been softened, and had he not proceeded without me at that time, we might never again—so little upsets the mind of an African chief—have had the road opened to us.

[1] The wording in the original journal entry is slightly different but the sense here is true to the original. NLS, MS. 17915, 17 March 1862.

[2] As noted in the introductory remarks on Grant's scientific work, he did attempt to say something about the climate of this equatorial region as well as to comment on the weather.

[3] For Grant's important botanical work, see Introduction, pp. 15–20.

Extract from Journal: Speke departs for Buganda

I am on my back while Speke marches away towards Uganda in charge of a swell Mookoongoo[1] & Gang. Mtesa had sent them down for us as he heard we were in Usui & a lot of boys were to take him up a gun and ammo from S[peke] who said <u>no</u>, my guns you don't [get] but here's some powder – the boys went ahead with it. [NLS, MS. 17915, 10 January 1862]

The following account of my own ailments I give, not with a wish to parade them, but in order to convey information:—Having had fevers twice a-month, in December my usual complaint assumed a new form. The right leg, from above the knee, became deformed with inflammation, and remained for a month in this unaccountable state, giving intense pain, which was relieved temporarily by a deep incision and copious discharge.[2] For three months fresh abscesses formed, and other incisions were made; my strength was prostrated; the knee stiff and alarmingly bent, and walking was impracticable. Many cures were attempted by the natives, who all sympathised with me in my sufferings, which they saw were scarcely endurable;[3] but I had great faith—was all along cheerful and happy, except at the crisis of this helpless state, when I felt that it would have been preferable to be nearer home. The disease ran its course, and daily, to bring out the accumulated discharge, I stripped my leg like a leech. Bombay had heard of a poultice made of cow-dung, salt, and mud from the lake; this was placed on hot, but it merely produced the effect of a tight bandage. Baraka was certain that a serpent had spat upon my leg—"it could not have been a bite." Dr M'nanagee, the sultan's brother, knew the disease perfectly; he could send me a cure for it—and a mild gentle peasant of the Wanyambo race came with his wife, a young pleasing-like person, to attend me. With the soft touch of a woman he examined the limb, made cuts over the skin with a penknife, ordered all lookers-on outside the hut, when his wife produced a scroll of plantain leaf, in which was a black paste. This was moistened from the mouth and rubbed into the bleeding cuts, making them smart; afterwards a small piece of lava was dangled against my leg and tied as a charm round the ankle. Two days afterwards he found no improvement, and, having repeated some mystic words behind me, another charm of wood and goat's flesh was tied above the knee and round the ankle, much in the same way as a kind lady-friend in Scotland once sent me a string of soda-water corks to be worn at night as a cure for cramp! Paste, very like gunpowder, was rubbed into fresh cuts, and this was repeated without any result, although the charms had been on for two days. M'nanagee, seeing his medical adviser had failed, sent an herb to soak in water and rub over the part; it had a very soothing effect, but did not allay the pain. He had seen me apply the leaves of the castor-oil plant as a hot bandage, and forbade their use a second time as being injurious, having given me a delirious fever, and causing a counter-action of profuse discharge of water from the limb.

---

[1] A chief or official: a term used in Buganda and Karagwe (Mkungu).

[2] John Hayman, MD, has provided a most useful account of the affliction to accompany the Wikipedia article on Grant. He says it was a case of *Mycobacterium ulcerans* infection, a disease prevalent in this part of Africa. http://en.wikipedia.org/wiki/James Augustus Grant.

[3] Grant's journal makes it clear that the intense pain which he mentions often made it impossible for him to sleep.

Extracts from Journal: The Onset and Progress of Grant's Affliction
[7 December 1861]
Drank two pints of most delicious raisiny tasting & flavoured wine from plantain; if aerated would be as fine as the sparkling hock my [?] once imported from Germany – sent me to sleep, making one feel jolly; previously thirsty whole day.
[8 December] Seedy feverish and heavy head ... by noon scarcely able to keep up my head and eyes open – may have been too much pombeh!
[9 December] Fever all day & all night.
[10 December] have some soup ... fever and restless all day and night – blind boils out over right leg ... not able to put it on ground.
[12 December] Managed + intense pain to hop out of tent and lay there whole day – leg red and deformed with inflammation.
[13 December] Could not walk to my tent; had my bed brought out.
[16 December] Leg still unaccountably bad.
[17 December] No rest.
[19 December] Excessive pain.
[20 December] Sent for medicine cow dung, black mud & salt which Bombay recommends ... made a hot poultice of ... moist mixture & covered my leg with it.
[21 December] Poultice has done no harm. M'nanagee examined [leg] so did Kiengo; both knew the disease.
[23 December] No rest nor improvement in leg.
[25 December] Xmas day. Leg improved for first time.
[29 December] Blister and poultice no use: ankle and foot still as sodden as dough.
[30 December] Nothing but time will cure it. Pain decreased but no sleep.
[3 January 1862] Slept several times during last night ... during day returned as bad as before ... The last day of the year; altogether it has been a most happy one but this leg keeps me much depressed often wishing England & home were nearer.
   Begged M'nanagee to give me medicine for my leg as being so long in its bent state is alarming, besides the constant pain is hardly endurable.
[18 February] M'nanagee – a long consultation on my sickness ... delirium off and on all day.
[19 February] Eighth day that fever has never left me.
[21 February] A severe night of delirium, shouting for old Speke & awakening my servants – a madhouse would have been preferable.
[22 February] Slept without fever or delirium, thank God.
[23 March] Struck with delirious fever from 6 to 9 a.m. after taking quinine about 5. Never had such a severe bout. Foot too puffed out and buboos paining much ... Could not read S[*peke*]'s letters.
[3 April] Much better and getting strong. [NLS, MS. 17915][1]

By the fifth month the complaint had exhausted itself; at last I was able to be out of the hut inhaling the sweet air, and once more permitted to behold the works of God's creation in the beautiful lake and hills below me. Never did I experience a happier moment! During

---

[1] In fact, Grant remained subject to fevers and unable to walk until well after he had left Karagwe on 14 April 1862. Even his own published account of the illness hardly shows just how distressing a period he endured. Hence the extracts.

this illness, the family at the palace were very kind in coming to sit by me; the young sons brought me plants in flower, birds' nests, eggs, or other things which they thought might interest me; while I sketched for them or their father, and sent a servant to get the news, and ask for the king every morning. Since Speke had left, there was considerable difficulty in getting supplies, and the sultan was not so kind in this respect as he might have been; but, African like, he had received his presents, and until more were given him he withheld sending goat, fowls, or other necessaries, which my men had to hunt the country for.[1] One poor fellow lost his life in doing so. Two were together; the natives set upon them while bringing home loads of grain; they shot one with arrows, the other ran for his life, and slept all night up a tree, afraid to go near a village. On asking him, "Did you sleep?" "O yes, I tied myself with rope to the boughs, and slept several hours." The sultan sought for redress from the village, but all the people had decamped in fear. Several other natives paid me almost daily calls—officers, barbers, ivory-traders, musicians, &c., in whom a good deal of character could be observed. At night my few men would gather round their fire, and, particularly after having an extra allowance of plantain-wine, sing a ditty about my health. Frij on the single-stringed zeze or guitar would commence—"I am Frij, I am Frij; my brother Grin (meaning Grant), my brother Grin, is very sick, is very sick; we'll get a cow, we'll get a cow, when he gets well, when he gets well," to which the others would all subscribe in a louder voice, "Ameen," with the most perfect solemnity.

My couch or bed, the height of a table, was formed of the trunks of plantain-trees covered with grass and blankets. This was roofed over with a low grass hut, having its gable end wide open to the south, where no wind blew from at that season. Much to the surprise of the natives, there was no fence round our encampment. By day, dogs walked into our huts, and by night hyena often carried away our fowls. Indeed, while lying awake, one came sniffing with his nose in the air up to my couch, and ran sulkily away on my shouting at him. One cannot say whether he would have sprung upon me had I been asleep, but the precaution of a trap was taken for several nights following.

The most curious disease known in this country was a case of dropsy brought to be operated upon. Some days after having seen it, and declined the operation, a number of watery globules, the size of common marbles, were brought me upon a leaf, said to have been extracted from the person afflicted. This operation they performed generally without fatal consequences, and the disease was not uncommon. There were several leprous people, favourites about the court. One, an old woman, who saluted us with "Vihoreh," had flesh-coloured hands and colourless patches on her arms. M'nanagee complained of not being able to drink his usual fare of milk; and though his knowledge of herbs was very extensive, he could not cure himself. One of his favourite medicines was a preparation from the long roots of nettles found growing in the shallow end of the lake. These, I was informed, were used in decoction as purgatives. On my requesting him to give me his tapeworm medicine, it was obtained with considerable difficulty. The servant was told to go to a certain bush on the hillside, never to look back on his way thither, but to return without plucking the plant if he should meet a dog! Through the kindness of M'nanagee,

---

[1] Rumanyika may have had better reason than mere desire for presents for becoming less encouraging to the travellers. Speke had spoken of his desire to open up a Nile route from the north to the lake region and its peoples; this would have greatly diminished Karagwe's importance as the gateway for contacts with Buganda. Speke, *Journal*, pp. 208–9, 239; Bridges, 'Negotiating a Way', p. 123.

his nephews, and others, a species of frankincense and many interesting plants were examined and preserved.

The country of Karague rarely affords space flat enough for a single tent to be pitched, but there are thousands of acres now in grass which are perfectly capable of profitable cultivation. Captain Maury, of the United States navy, at the British Association meeting in 1863, stated his opinion that this region, from its equatorial position and moist atmosphere, would make an excellent coffee-growing country; and as many parts resemble portions of the Himalayas, where tea is grown, and there are no frosts at Karague, I think it is admirably adapted for the culture of tea as well as coffee.[1] Wild grapes were occasionally gathered in the lower grounds, but no beds of gravel similar to those at home or on the Continent, where the vine flourishes in such luxuriance, are to be seen. A few clumps of wild date-trees grow in the valleys, but the natives are ignorant of the sexes of the trees, and never have any fruit. Sugar-cane is seldom or never grown. There are two heavy crops in the year—sorghum and plantain; while pease (English garden), a species of bean or calavance, called "maharageh,"[2] Indian corn, &c., are grown at other seasons. All these we saw ripe or ripening, and fresh shoots of plantain were being set, while other fields were prepared for the heavier crop of red sorghum, sown in March. Then squads of men and women assemble, probably only one-fifth working at a time, the rest standing, lounging, and laughing. The men, with a hook having a three-feet-long handle, slash down the weeds, women hoe them up, collect the stones, clear the ground, and give it the tidy appearance of a garden. In February great care is bestowed upon the plantain, which affords one of the staples of life in this country throughout the year. Acres of it cover the hillsides, a rivulet sometimes dividing the field; the trunks are trimmed of the leaves which have been torn into shreds by the wind; fresh shoots are planted; and the whole orchard is industriously superintended.

The natives asked us ludicrous prices for their products. Our beads, the manufacture of Venice, were of little value, from fourteen to twenty-five (size of pigeon-eggs) being given for a single goat, and a proportionate number for a cow. This our Seedees thought a great contrast to their native country of Uhiao,[3] where a bucketful of flour, with a fowl on the top, could be obtained for one necklace of ordinary beads. But here the women were double the size round the waist that they were anywhere else, and they must have beads enough to begird them once before a goat can be parted with. They would refuse us milk and butter, because it was not their custom to sell them, and because we eat fowls, and the bean called maharageh; but on making them a present of several coils of brass wire (thirteen), we could procure a quart-sized wooden jar of butter. In November, grain is scarce. The natives brought salt to exchange for it; and on being offered meat instead, they have been known to refuse it, because the allowance was not so large and satisfactory to them as grain. When marching, the head-men of the villages had orders from their sultan to supply our camp with sufficient provision for the day. A quantity of

---

[1] Grant was certainly right about coffee: what became known as Bukoba District was a significant producer of Robusta coffee with over 10,000 tons produced annually by 1939. However, most was grown by the neighbouring Haya rather than the Banyambo of Karagwe. Moffett, *Handbook*, pp. 96, 118, 193. See below, p. 190, for the contemporary use of coffee beans. Tea was not grown in the colonial period.

[2] More correctly, *maharagwe* which is the plant and *haragwe* the bean itself.

[3] Most of the porters were Yao people who had been slaves or ex-slaves brought down from near Lake Malawi to Kilwa and then Zanzibar.

sweet potatoes, some pumpkins, fowls, and a goat, were generally given, and a present of cloth and brass wire was made them in return. Plantain-wine was seldom presented: it seemed to have conveniently run dry on our arrival! English garden-pease were first seen in this part of Africa by Speke, and with the aid of the sultan we were able to lay in a supply of this delicacy, not in their green form, but dry and dead ripe, boiling and making them into a mash. They were grown broadcast in considerable quantities about Meegongo. Tobacco, ripe in April, we could always procure, but it was extravagant in price—six pipefuls of the finest description costing the daily ration allowance of one porter.

Extract from Journal: Tobacco
Had some of the finest tobacco I ever tasted – said to be & was very like one got from the Sultan the other day – my dear six pipes full for one khete [*measure of beads*]. [NLS, MS. 17915, 26 November 1861]

The sultan smoked a very full-flavoured description in his large pipe. We tried to discover from an old man, his one-eyed tobacconist, the secret of its preparation; but he would not divulge it unless a handsome reward was given. It had a rich mellow aroma, more pleasant than any tobacco we had ever smoked; and whether it was from rubbing the leaf in his perfumed hands, using a secretion from the cow, or that honey was mixed in it, we never could discover. He would not allow that any ingredient was used—the tobacco when green was merely rubbed in his hands.[1] In December beautiful granulated honey was offered for sale. Though there were few bees to be seen in this country, their produce was always procurable in small quantities, and it was of excellent though sometimes of highly flowery flavour.

Plantain-wine, called here "marwa," was made by every family that had an orchard of the trees. It is a sweet raisiny-tasting wine; if aerated, nearly equal to sparkling hock in richness of flavour. A quart could be taken with comfort, but after the third day it becomes dead, sour, and intoxicating; our men got so riotous from it that the sultan was requested not to send us the daily allowance of one gourdful. Ridiculous scenes of drunkenness would sometimes occur. One Seedee with a gun would in his intoxication chase another through the fields; others with guns would fly to prevent bloodshed. At last the original offender would have so many guns pointed at him that he would surrender, and then his gun would be found not loaded!

The process of making plantain-wine in Karague takes generally from two to three days. A huge log scooped out, and looking like a canoe, is essential for a large quantity. It is tilted at one end, and dammed up with grass in the centre. Ripe fruit has clean grass put amongst it. A woman mashes all at the upper end with her hands or feet. The liquor strains through the dam, and is again strained with grass till clean. All the liquid is then placed for fermentation in the "canoe" freshly cleaned. Some burnt, bruised sorghum is placed in it; all is covered up from the air, and allowed to remain in the sun or near a fire for two or three days, when it is skimmed and fit for use.[2] Wine is never exported or bottled, and probably not a drop of the brewing can be obtained after the lapse of only four days. All,

---

[1] Tobacco has continued to be produced for local consumption but did not become an export crop in this part of Tanzania.

[2] Grant illustrated the very similar production process in Buganda; see Plate 30.

even the youngest children amongst the peasants, drink it, carrying gourdfuls of it about with them wherever they go, as regularly as we carry our purses.[1]

Of the natural products of the equatorial regions, such as slaves, ivory, salt, copper, iron, bark-cloths, coffee, and sugar-cane, Karague scarcely yields any, but it is a great depot for trade.[2] Arabs and coastmen bring up beads, cloths, and brass wire, and meet people of all the nations around, and trade with them for ivory and slaves.[3] Copper and salt are brought from beyond Paroro[4] to exchange for brass wire. N'kole is justly celebrated for its tobacco, though every hut here has its garden of it. Ruanda sends her painted matting, goat, salt, and iron wire, and requests the sultan, who drives a stiff bargain, to fix the price of each article—as, 160 ankle-wires = a single necklace; a goat = twenty necklaces. The Wanyamuezi carry salt from their country to exchange it for the ivory brought by the people of Unyoro, N'kole, and Utumbi. Bark-cloths are not made well in Karague: the people of Uganda, Kittara,[5] and Uhia excel in them. They are sewn in four stripes, each a foot to 18 inches broad, and, when well greased by the Wanyambo, make a most comfortable, becoming square shawl to keep out the cold and rain. During the 1861 war in Unyanyembe (at 5° S.) a slave might be purchased for something under one shilling sterling, or, if estimated in beads, ten necklaces. If a number of them were brought up (as they have been in several instances) to the equator and beyond it, they would each fetch a frasila, or 36 lb. weight of ivory, equal to £12 in Zanzibar. This is one of the inducements for Arabs and Africans to speculate, but the instance is exceptional.[6]

Trade encounters great difficulties in such a country, where there are no regular laws, no roads, no carriage conveyance, and the caravan is liable to losses from heavy taxes, desertions, and attacks. For instance, two traders, named Sungoro and Joomah, left Karague while I was there for the south with a considerable supply of ivory. On reaching the borders of the first province (Usui), they sent forward to ask the sultan's permission to pass through his country. A demur was made that the party was too strong, but they would be permitted. When once in the chief's power, he demanded half their ivory as a tax. Provisions were very dear; they resisted, they complained, all to no purpose; and they were told to cultivate the soil if they chose, but that they would not be allowed to depart till the demand was paid. Rumanika interfered and got them out of the trouble, otherwise they would have been detained there for many months. In Ugogo and Unyamuezi the

[1] In the colonial period, the drink was categorized as a 'light beer' and regarded as an essential part of the local diet. Moffett, *Handbook*, p. 193.

[2] Grant's evidence here is very important data on the economic history of Karagwe emphasizing, as it does, an entrepôt function as the main characteristic and little original production.

[3] It was in the interest of Buganda to exercise control on the trade route into Buganda from the coast by dominating Karagwe; trade goods might otherwise have gone straight to the rival kingdom, Bunyoro. Sheriff, *Slaves, Spices and Ivory*, p. 184.

[4] Grant probably means Mpororo, a minor kingdom to the north said to have become extinct after 1759 and which is now part of Ankole in Uganda. President Yoweri Museveni of Uganda is a Hororo and some of his critics believe he is trying to revive Mpororo as a political entity.

[5] That is, Bunyoro-Kitara. Utumbi was apparently another mini-kingdom nearby to the north. For 'Uhia', see below, p. 190.

[6] Grant's evidence indicates that the slave trade operated in both directions. But most of the trade must have been in 'raw' slaves from the north to the coast; those brought from Zanzibar to the interlacustrine region presumably had particular skills. See Médard, 'Introduction', pp. 11, 17, 21, who says Karagwe is under-researched in respect of the slave trade.

chief claims a tusk of every elephant found dead or killed; he gets the tusk from the cheek that lies nearest the ground. There is no such law in Karague.[1] Amongst the curiosities in tusks, we heard of one so large that it could not be carried to the coast, and that one elephant had been seen with four tusks! Both stories, like those about fences being made of them in some countries, are, of course, among the fables of the natives.

Between Karague and the Victoria Nyanza there is a country called Uhia or Mohia,[2] whose people are traders to the north. They also bring coffee to Karague for sale in bundles covered with plantain-leaf, containing two handfuls, which they sell very dearly at one necklace of beads.[3] It takes a handful to make a pint of very inferior coffee, as the bean, when the loose husk is taken off, is not larger than half a grain of rice. In this state the natives chew it as a sailor does tobacco. It is pleasant, inducing saliva, and leaving a comfortable flavour in the mouth. When our store of tea and coffee was consumed, we found this, when roasted and infused for drinking, a substitute, but very inferior, because the bean had not been allowed to come to perfection when it was pulled. The natives do not make use of it as we do, but refresh themselves on a journey by throwing two or three beans, husks and all, into their mouths. Several of these Wahia traders were seen—sturdy, very black, middle-sized men, with bare, unshaven heads and beards. Their dress was a cow-skin, having the leg parts neatly rounded off, of a saffron yellow, and friezed inside, knotted over the right shoulder, and hanging to the middle of the thigh. This dress is sometimes worn with the hair outside: above it they generally wore a brick-coloured bark-cloth, well greased. Their ornaments were a sheep or goat's horn, tied jauntily with a strip of leather round their bare heads, and a few solid rings, crow-quill thickness, worn round the ankles. Their arms were differently shaped, as was their dress, from those of any race we had met with. The spear-shaft was six feet long, and the spear was heart-shaped, or like the ace of spades. Jumah,[4] a coast-trader, called them a bad, unsafe set of people, probably because they were rivals in his business. He also abused the Ruanda people, because they refused to allow any coast-men into their kingdom, which, he said, was even more populous than Uganda.[5] The specimens seen by us were merely men from its borders, who had come with produce by water in three days from the west. They were tall, lean men, with the shortest loin-cover of skin I ever saw; of the same pattern as, but even smaller than, those worn by the natives of Usui. The above native gentleman, Jumah, had

---

[1] Perhaps the reason is that, as Grant's other evidence shows, there were few if any elephants in Karagwe. Elsewhere, as chiefs endeavoured to territorialize their power, to claim one tusk from each elephant killed in their areas became more common.

[2] Grant here refers to the Haya people among whom there had been some 'kingdoms' created but who were essentially very diverse politically. Katoke, 'Ihangiro', p. 700, mentions eight kingdoms. On the question of identities in this region, see Cory, *Bukoba District, passim*, and his *Law of the Haya Tribe*, pp. 281–7, where the clan structure is explained.

[3] Koponen, *People and Production*, pp. 119–20, points out that the trade in coffee beans and other items in this region was semi-formal and lacked institutionalized markets. Cowries were used as currency. As noted above, p. 187, n. 1, coffee became an important cash crop in the colonial period.

[4] Jumah arrived on 6 January 1862 bringing news from Buganda that the kabaka, Mutesa, wished the explorers to be sent on to him; as noted above, pp. 183–4, Speke set off four days later having arranged to send Baraka to Bunyoro to seek news of Petherick. Speke, *Journal*, pp. 243–4; Bridges, 'Negotiating a Way', p. 123.

[5] No. doubt also because they were off the main route from Unyamwezi to Buganda, Rwanda and Urundi were not explored by Europeans until Oscar Baumann's expedition of 1892 and Graf von Götzen's in 1894; rather unusually, exploration followed political partition. Louis, *Ruanda-Urundi*, pp. 101–6.

travelled a great deal, had sailed on Victoria Nyanza, had attempted the ascent of Kilimanjaro, had made great friends with the king of Uganda, and said he could converse in at least ten different African languages. I begged to differ with him as to their being distinct languages; but he insisted that each was as different from the other as Baniani is to Hindoo.[1] He was of East Indian origin,[2] though he could not speak its language, and had acquired all the superstitious notions of the Seedee. However, during my illness he paid me constant visits, afforded me a great deal of amusement, and was a kind, hospitable man.

Extract from Journal: One of Jumah's Stories

Joomah here ... he tells me that in a fit of drunkenness, Burton shot an English woman at Zanzibar and also a wangwana. Everyone knows it to be a fact! Speke never told me of it so I disbelieve it. [NLS, MS. 17915, 5 February 1862]

He told strange tales about the snow-capped mountain Kilimanjaro, which has since been ascended by my friend the Baron von der Decken, gold-medallist (with myself)[3] of the Royal Geographical Society for 1864. When encamped at Chaga, Jumah could see it change colour "five times during the day. First it was white in the early morning, then changed into black, green, brown, and, lastly, scarlet, like a red blanket. He thought the colours were not reflections from snow—the sun was too hot for any to lie there—they were stones! and he picked up several carnelian-coloured pebbles at its base. He and all Arabs firmly believe that the mountain can never be ascended by either black or white man. Though gold is there in abundance, no one dare dig for it—a demon has possession! Even Speke could not go up it, unless the devil should take fright at the face of a white man! He mustered courage one day, and determined to try the ascent, but he was struck with a huge swelling in both limbs, which disappeared as suddenly as it came. Was not this a caution? and did it not show that it was possessed?" Jumah was full of these tales, and of his brave fights with supernatural characters. Of Uganda he gave me a great deal of accurate information, describing the numbers of people who are daily killed there by order of the king; and he thought if M'tessa were asked not to rule so cruelly, that a greater sacrifice would be the only consequence. "It was not from any love he had for destruction of life, as he was an amiable young man, but from its being the ancient custom of the country; and were it not done, the fear was that the people would become rebellious. Besides which, was not the country swarming with people? did it not abound with food? did they not love the king's rule, and prefer his sentence of death to a natural one, as being

---

[1] Grant was right if the languages were those of Bantu peoples.

[2] Speke, *Journal*, p. 243, calls this man a 'semi-Hindu-Suaheli', a confused description and an unlikely one. Grant's own description in his journal is somewhat better: 'a Hindoo ivory trader from Mombas'. NLS, MS. 17915, 6 January 1862. Unfortunately, the continuing account below, p. 203, muddies the waters by describing Jumah as 'my Mahommedan friend'. Much later, in 1872, Grant added the information that Jumah was the agent of a house in Zanzibar and that he had met Burton and Speke at the time of the 1856–8 expedition at Ugogi. Grant, 'Summary of Observations' p. 237. Neither Burton, *Lake Regions*, I, pp. 241–3, nor Speke, *What Led to the Discovery*, p. 197, mentions meeting Jumah at Ugogi. It is a pity there is not better information on such an apparently well-travelled merchant and certainly an unusual one if he was or had been a Hindu 'Banyan'; these men seldom left the coast.

[3] The words in parentheses were added at the proof stage: NLS, MS. 17934, p. 162. It is odd that Grant does not acknowledge meeting and photographing the Baron when he was in Zanzibar at the outset of the Expedition. See Chapter II, p. 77, n. 5, and Figure 11, p. 92.

more princely?" Jumah had made M'tessa a considerable present, which will illustrate the manner of trading in this part of the world. A gold-embroidered silk scarf or deolee, value $50, a "mucknuff,"[1] a gold-embroidered vest, two men's loads of blue beads, half a load of brass wire, a small tiara, value $1, and two flint-muskets without powder, constituted his gift. The king, in return, gave him 700 lb. weight of ivory (some of the tusks weighing 90 lb.), seven women, and fifty cows; besides which Jumah asked for his two guns to be returned. In receiving these he considered himself well repaid, as one-third belonged to himself, the rest to his master in Zanzibar. He had been trafficking for three years in this way without ever visiting the coast, and meant to remain another year, when he would have completed collecting 500 frasila, equal to 17,500 lb. of ivory. This mode of fair dealing is very different to what takes place at the Nile trading-marts to the north of the equator. There guns and bullets, in the hands of Nubians employed by European, Turkish, and Armenian masters, assist in capturing the herds of cattle used in paying porters and purchasing ivory. If a tax is asked, all that is given, as one of them told us, is the muzzle of a gun. It seems marvellous, therefore, that the Zanzibar traders who pay as Jumah did, or buy tusks at the market price of weight for weight in Venetian beads, can bring their ivories into the same market as the Nile men, who actually *pay nothing* for the tusk. But this is the explanation: although they have been purchased by plundered cattle, the master of those plunderers has to provide guns and ammunition; he has to pay the men, and also the freight of the ivory, and its duty to the Egyptian Government. These are the expenses which bring the price of Nile ivory up to that which is taken to Zanzibar. But on either the one or the other side of the equator no *honest* man would have a chance against the present field of traders, who do everything in their power to keep the country as a preserve for cattle, slaves, and ivory.[2]

As our narrative has here touched on the Nile, I may as well mention what information we received regarding it from the many travellers coming to Karague for the purposes of trade. On the 2d of January 1862, while Speke and I were together, we were thrown into a state of excitement by being told that a man had arrived from a country far away to the north, bringing tidings that "a party having guns which knocked down trees had been attacked by the Wagani race, one hundred of them killed, the most of their property seized and made over to one Kamarasi, a king." The extraordinary part of the story was, that the strangers had not left the country, but still occupied their ships, which were reported to be large enough to contain cattle. Our firm impression was, that this could be no other than Petherick, who had promised, when we parted with him in England, to meet or have boats for us in November 1861 and until 1862. Plans were at once formed to send him a letter, and Rumanika gave us every facility, as the king above mentioned was his connection, having exchanged sisters with him. Although this intimacy existed, nothing would induce Rumanika to allow us to march there till a reply had been received. We were to be kept for months in suspense, until Baraka, the bearer of the despatch, should return. Although we told Rumanika repeatedly that we expected boats on the Nile for us, on the receipt of this important information he would not allow us to advance—it would

---

[1] What this is, I have not discovered. However, Dr Johnson's *Dictionary* had an entry for 'muckender' which he says means a handkerchief. See McAdam and Milne, *Johnson's Dictionary*, p. 256.

[2] Grant's condemnation of the Nile traders was certainly justified. His evidence on the ivory trade is insightful and important. On the ivory trade generally, see Beachey, 'East African Ivory Trade'; Bridges, 'Elephants, Ivory'.

not be etiquette toward the northern kings! Meanwhile the king of Uganda luckily sent a message that he was most impatient to see the white men, and as a story was got up that no sick people nor donkeys were allowed to enter his territory, I had to remain till sufficiently recovered to march. Speke left on the 10th of January; and Baraka, having bought the disguise of a native—a bark-cloth and spear—consulted magicians to find out whether this march would be prosperous; he started on the 29th with several companions, and letters for the ships supposed to be Petherick's. These turned out to be a perfect myth—no such boats were there; the nearest point that any lay at was Gondokoro, a place known in Europe for thirty years. But the Nubian soldiers of M. de Bono had worked their way from Gondokoro by land far south by means of their guns, and gave origin to the report we had heard.[1] Feeling anxious about Baraka, my head man Frij went repeatedly to the sultan's brother, M'nanagee, asking whether anything had been heard of him. No intelligence had actually been received, but M'nanagee had consulted his magic horns, and they told him that "Baraka was perfectly well, but his companion Seedee was suffering from a chest complaint!" M'nanagee was so confident about this telegraphing on his own part, that he said, "If it does not turn out true, I'll give you that goat." Months afterwards, on our reaching Kamarasi's, we were told that the man had been ailing slightly!

Of Speke I could hear occasionally by letter; his men were discontented at getting nothing to eat but boiled plantain; but they ultimately found out that there was nothing else to be procured in the country. He had crossed a body of water four hundred yards wide, running to the north. What a pleasure it must have been to him to come upon the first flowing waters of the Nile![2] In a previous letter, dated 12th February, from the borders of Nyanza, he wrote saying he was to return for me in a boat along the lake. On mentioning to Rumanika that an Uganda boat was to arrive in his lake to convey the baggage and myself away, he replied, "It was all practicable except for two miles, at the Kitangule, where the river is shallow, and the boat must be carried." I added, that as the waters we then looked upon mingled with those in my country (alluding to the Mediterranean), the day might come when a traveller could go from Karague to London and *vice versa* by water! Since saying this, we have discovered that cataracts are the only obstacle to this grand tourist route.[3]

The cattle of this country resemble those we saw at Cape Town—all horn, with staring ribs.[4] The sultan kept 400 of such animals at his residence on the high grounds. He had perhaps 10,000 more on the grazing-grounds on the banks of the Kitangule,[5] where they had better feeding, and looked more sleek. Some horns were two and three feet long, and eighteen inches round the base. No use seemed to be made of them, unless by Seedees and Arabs, who converted them into powder-horns. At nine every morning these 400

---

[1] For the activities of this Maltese trader, Amabile de Bono, and his uncle Andrea, together with the Italian explorer, Giovanni Miani, see Howgego, *Encyclopedia of Exploration 1850–1940*, III, pp. 866–7; Langlands, 'Early Travellers', p. 57.

[2] The travellers had not yet seen Lake Victoria.

[3] The cataracts on the Nile are certainly formidable and the Kagera, here alluded to, is only fitfully navigable by small craft. However, the comment reflects the constant hope of men like Grant and Livingstone who wished to improve Africa, that rivers could be found which would be the means of utilizing European technology in the form of steamboats to solve the problem of reaching the interior of the continent.

[4] That is, the longhorn variety with small humps favoured in the interlacustrine region; most of the cattle Grant had seen up to this point would have been the shorthorn humped zebu variety.

[5] That is, the Kagera.

cows were trotted down the hill to their grazing ground, sometimes accompanied by one of the princes, and they were walked back to be milked after dark, having been allowed to drink once at a trough of clay filled by an osier bucket from a well on the edge of the lake. Every tenth day the lanky creatures were driven down (at 7 A.M.) two hours earlier than usual, as they had to go farther, for the purpose of receiving a drench of brackish water some distance away. On the hillside by the path shallow pits are dug in horizontal lines, to allow water to collect there for cattle or wild animals. They are wretched milkers, only giving half the quantity of the plump smal-horned breed of Unyanyembe. Two were set apart by the sultan for our use, as no one would drink from the same cow that supplied us; and whether it was that the animals were less cared for, or that they soon became dry, our supply of milk latterly became reduced to almost nothing. No doubt this was attributed to our bewitching the cows by boiling the milk! Daily, men carrying five or six prettily-shaped "chanzees" or jars of yellow wood, browned from use, slung from a stick on their shoulders, would pass my hut with milk for the palace. It was the staff of life— the children and women fattened upon it; and the butter, sometimes of a good quality, but never rich, was used merely as a pomade on their bodies, to soften their skin-coverings, and as an external cure for everything. We had considerable difficulty in procuring any, because we ate it. However, a handsome present now and then would induce them to give us some. The sheep (lambed in the month of November) were a smal species,[1] without wool, generally white, and only half-a-dozen would be seen in a tract of ten or twenty miles. Within 200 yards of them we have observed the white rhinoceros grazing, looking like a solitary stack in the middle of a hay-field. We did not take the trouble to shoot him, because his flesh is worthless, and shooting interfered with the march. Sometimes our men fired, which made both them and the animal run in opposite directions. Every hunt had its little flock of short-haired goats, whose skins were so valued as an article of dress that the natives could seldom be induced to sell them. One roan-coloured goat presented to us was fancied for its colour by the sultan, and exchanged, as he longed for it to assist in some ceremony.

There were pet dogs about the palace, used in going after small antelope and tiger-cats. The breed was like the pariah of India, leggy, with smooth red hair, but much more domestic, giving a paw, lying down quietly by your side, or always ready to walk with you, having been taught docility by the young princes. They are said to run after game by scent, but this we did not observe. This particular breed is always gelt, the natives believing that they are thereby rendered more keen in the pursuit of sport. One, a great favourite, answering to the name of "Keeromba"—a wild, beautifully-sounding, musical name— became much attached to our camp. To give an idea of the sport here, Speke bagged three white rhinoceros in one day, much to the delight of the native princes, who never will forget the enjoyment it gave them. They would not eat the flesh; but some Wezee porters—poor starved-like men, belonging to the Arab traders at Kufro—carried it away in enormous loads; but when seen by their Mohammedan masters, the meat was sent out of camp as being unlawful, not having been regularly killed. On our mentioning to the king that we had heard of an extraordinary animal like a goat living in the lake, he ordered his people to capture one. Canoes of logs, two paddles each, and 18 feet long, were collected to beat the papyrus rushes, driving the animal into the water, when he was chased

---

[1] Probably the broad-tailed of the two varieties identified by Koponen, *People and Production*, p. 251.

(as we were told) and captured alive, care being taken by outside canoes that no crocodiles attacked the men while in the water. A procession of singers walked up the hill, passing our huts, carrying the live animal neatly lashed upon a frame of wood to the sultan, who sent him to us "fresh from the lake." He (a young male antelope) was very timid, and lay *down* with a rope about his neck for a whole day; but on a dish of water being presented to him, he dashed his head into it as if he felt himself once more in his native element. As he seemed to pine, refusing his natural food—the tops of the papyrus—he was killed. His coat was of long, dirty brown, rather soft hair. His horns, from five to six inches long, were commencing to spire; the hoofs were of the true waterboc, immensely long, and widely separated; height more than three feet. This species of antelope is called "nzowe" by the natives, and lives altogether on the borders of lakes.[1]

We never heard of elephants while residing here.[2] There are no forests for them on these heights and valleys. Hartebeest, and rhinoceros or "faroo,"[3] are the common animals of the chase. The former, called "nyamœra,"[4] in the rutting season become highly combative. Two stags fought in the plain with unflinching determination, calmly halting to breathe between each round. The force of every butt as their heads met, and as they fell on their knees, sounded distinctly, the energy and impetus of the attack sending their small bushy tails over their backs. After a battle of twenty minutes, one became the victor, and chased the other into and out of a herd of hinds, when I was obliged to leave the interesting chase. Several antelope were wounded this day, but they were very wild in the open plain of grass, and it required accurate shooting at 300 and 400 yards to bag one. Of other game animals there were several varieties of antelope. The mountain gazelle bounded very prettily over the bare hills, and did not seem very wild. Pigs were in the low grounds, and hippopotami swam in the lake. But Karague is not a country of sport; and although the sultan imagines that lions garrison the country, and mount guard over his father's remains, we never saw one, dead or alive. The natives told us that otter, called "gonejeh,"[5] of the ordinary colour, live in the lake, and that their king (concerning whom they have some superstition) is as white as an old man's beard. The manner in which a Wezee prepares a skin for wear is very simple, and seems perfectly efficacious. Straw is laid on the ground, the skin is pegged out neatly over it till thoroughly dried by the sun into the state of parchment; it is then doubled and pressed in every possible direction, and a few integuments are pulled off. It is hand-rubbed, and smeared with grease, and then becomes fit for wear.[6] Great numbers of moles, larger than English, were caught in our camp. Their fur was black or brown, and some were white. The natives seemed to make no use of them.

Of game-birds the most numerous are the guinea-fowl, the "boee" and "qualee" partridges.[7] The natives shoot at long distances with their arrows, and must destroy great

---

[1] This was not a waterbuck but what was subsequently called Speke's tragelaph, *Limnotragus spekei*, or *Tragelaphus spekii*, which spends most of its days semi-submerged in water. For Grant's drawing of the very one which was caught for him, see Figure 57, p. 207.

[2] Hence Karagwe's part in the ivory trade, as noted above, was only as an entrepôt.

[3] More correctly, *kifaru*.

[4] The word *mnyama* can be applied to any animal.

[5] Perhaps what Grant heard was *mnyama mgongo* which would indicate an animal with a hump.

[6] Grant later painted some skin costumes in Buganda: see Plate 22. Other crafts existed of which he seems not to have been aware, e.g. pottery. Koponen, *People and Production*, p. 266.

[7] *Mbuki* means goose but perhaps Grant heard *mbuai* meaning wild; *kwale* is the Swahili word for partridges. For Grant's pictures of these sorts of birds, see Plate 44.

quantities of game. They also use springes,[1] for during the march a small boy was met carrying on a string some birds he had caught. We said to him, "Come to camp—you'll be paid for them;" but he naively replied, "Catch me going to your camp! you'd put chains upon me, and make me a slave." On the 10th of April a nest of guinea-fowl, "kanga,"[2] eggs were brought me; this was in the middle of the rainy season; but they most probably breed all the year round. Small red sparrows were also picking up feathers; and a nest made of one species of grass, with two unspotted white little eggs, was brought in, showing that incubation goes on at this season. On the lake there were varieties of duck, which came in flights every night about the beginning of December from the east, flying over our camp with the sound of a passing shell. An Egyptian goose,[3] to us particularly interesting from its name and connection with the Nile, was shot by Speke, and sent to the sultan, who was more delighted with its splendid plumage than with the English table-knife, fork, and spoon he had that day been presented with. He, no doubt, had never seen the bird before, although it was shot by his own lake. We, of course, observed the rhinoceros bird, which sits as calmly on the animal's back as a man does on the top of a coach; he is the size of a "mina" or a blackbird, and has black wings, with a grey or white rump;[4] they are partly gregarious, three being seen together; and they must feed upon the tics which infest the skin of the rhinoceros. Here we came across a new swallow skimming the grasses of the hillsides—black or dark-brown wings of a slate tinge, white belly, black ring at neck and round the rump, tail-feathers not forked but slightly convex, body sparrow-size, and not so fish-shaped as swallows generally are.[5] The golden-headed and crimson-backed little finch perched here, as in Unyanyembe, on the stalks of the Indian corn near dwellings.[6] Another bird had, as Speke described it, a black coat and plush waistcoat; its colours harmonised beautifully with the tree on which it sat, a thorny species of jasmine, then (December) in rich pink-and-white bloom. We had no songsters at Karague, but we had a "bugler," who had one very rich note. There never were more than from two to four crows (handsome birds, with a ring of white round the neck) seen together, and the natives like killing them, as they eat up the red bitter sorghum, and prevent the people from sowing the white or sweet variety. The crow was used here by the sultan as supposed to be useful in divining events. The crops are protected from the barn-door fowl by a barbarous practice—the toe-nails of the fowl are cut off to prevent them from scratching the ground. This is done also in Zanzibar, but here it first attracted our notice in consequence of the peculiar crippled gait of the poultry.

A snake was caught amongst the rocks, measuring six feet five inches; it was of a bluish-black colour. M'nanagee brought it in a wicker basket to show me. He said he had had it for three days, and meant to keep it as a pet. Although one of his men held it fearlessly by the neck, they were afraid to allow me to do so, because they called it poisonous; however, no fangs were visible. It was one of the few snakes seen in Karague. Rats were in swarms, and were *very* troublesome to the traders, stealing their beads and cowries in considerable quantities, and concealing them in their holes; unfortunately we had no poison with us

---

[1] A snare for catching birds.
[2] That is, the common guinea fowl, *Numida mitrata*.
[3] *Alopochen aegyptiaca*.
[4] The red-billed oxpecker, *Buphagus erythrorhyncus*, has a white rump.
[5] Possibly a little swift or a spinetail, *Telecanthura ussheri*.
[6] Possibly the African fire finch, *Lagonosticta senegala*.

when asked for some by M'nanagee. This shows that the natives have no means to rid themselves of them; some pills of flour and pounded caustic were made up, but we never heard whether they were effectual. In the low flat valleys near the lakes, large grey-legged mosquitoes bite through your socks and trousers, keeping your limbs in constant motion; but on the higher ground, where wind blows, we were never annoyed by any. The bee that produces the honey of the country resembles our common hive-bee at home; and although beautifully granulated honey was brought for sale, we observed no hives. It certainly is not a productive country in this respect—the hills are barren of flowers. There are quantities of fish in the lake; but during my residence no fisherman was ever seen or heard of. Except one fish, the makambara, brought me by the sultan as a curiosity alive in a jar, and a half-pound-weight macquareh,[1] caught by a Seedee in the Kishakka lake, saw no fish, and the natives never eat them. The macquareh attains a great size, has immense large scales, no feelers, and a ridge of sharp-pointed fins along its arched back, and eats very sweetly. These notes must not be accepted as a list of what the country contains, but merely a notice of those which struck me as strange or interesting.

The population of Karague may be divided into two races: the reigning race or Wahuma; and the peasantry, who originally owned, and now cultivate, the soil, called Wanyambo, alluded to in the preceding chapter.[2]

The king and his brothers, of the former race, have already been described; a few remarks on their Moheenda[3] or young princes may be added. This royal class or caste have slight marks cut below the eyes; but they neither extract their teeth nor file them into any particular shape. Their diet of milk seems to make the men a tall active race, while the women get out of all proportion with obesity. The grown-up sons of the king (according to seniority) were Chundera, Kienj, Kananga, and Kukoko. First, Chundera,[4] twenty-five years of age, was a smart active young fellow, about five feet eight inches in height, with a somewhat effeminate figure and expression of countenance; he was fair for a negro, and except that his lips were rather thick, and that his wool was in regular pepper-corns, he might be taken, from his straight features, for a slim East Indian sepoy. He affected the dandy, being more neat about his loinskin cover and ornaments than the other brothers. He lived a gay life, was always ready to lead a war-party and to preside at a dance, or wherever there was wine or women. From the tuft of wool left unshaven on the crown of his head to his waist he was bare, except where decorated round the muscle of the arm and neck with charmed horns, stripes of otterskin, shells, and knobs of wood. The skin covering the loins, which, with the Karague people, is peculiar in shape, reached below the knee behind, and was cut away in front. From below the calf to the ankle was a mass of iron wire; and when visiting from neighbour to neighbour, he always, like every Karague person, carried in his hand a five-feet-long staff with a knob at the end. He constantly came to ask after me, bringing flowers in his hand, as he knew my fondness for them; and at night he would take Frij, my head man, into the palace along with his "zeze" or guitar, to amuse his sisters with Zanzibar music. In turn the sisters, brothers, and followers would sing Karague music, and early in the morning Master Frij and Chundera would return

---

[1] Possibly, the *Polypterus senegalus*.

[2] The Abanyambo may be regarded as *Bairu* or serfs; the Bahima are pastoralists of non-Bantu origin.

[3] The Bahinda are the ruling castes of the Bahima.

[4] Drawn by Grant: see Figure 61, p. 209. The drawing illustrates the shape of the loincloth he goes on to describe.

rather jolly to their huts outside the palace enclosures. This shows the kindly feeling existing between us and the family of the sultan; and although this young prince had showed me many attentions, he never once asked for a present. The second son, Kienj, was by a different mother (the sister of the king of Unyoro, I believe); he was six feet high at least, very black, and so ugly and disproportionately long about the head, that we called him the "camel." He was a slow, stupid fellow, very simple, and a bumpkin in comparison with the others. Like his brothers, he was married, and had one child, but lived in the palace enclosure. Previous to my leaving he made bold to beg for my only umbrella, because his own was past mending! The third son of the family was so shy that he only came near me when told to sit for his portrait; and the fourth, Kukoko, was such a pet, and was so nice-looking, that the father never went anywhere nor did anything without taking the young prince along with him. He was mild and gentlemanly in manner,[1] and would come to us every day, putting out his left hand when wishing us good morning, and remaining to chat quietly for an hour at a time. After we left Karague we sent him a comfortable blanket as a reward for his attentions. Although none of these lads had more covering than a sheet of leather round the loins, it was so neatly put on, their ornaments were so becoming, their persons so bronze-looking, their gait so polite and *distingué*, that we quite forgot their nakedness; more particularly when we saw the effect produced by pulling on a pair of white kid gloves upon Kukoko's hands, and seeing him strut away with the air of a Bond Street swell! Their food was chiefly a bowl of milk once in the morning; no grain, nor mutton, nor fish, nor fowl, but a small quantity of boiled beef or goat at night. They looked after the cattle belonging to their father, had M'koongoos, or agents of their own, who went to neighbouring countries to traffic for them; and so domestic were they that they never were known to sleep out of their own country.

The Wanyambo are the ryots, or peasantry.[2] In the low grounds of Urigi, where there was a great deal of swamp at the very doors of the people, they are very black and rather lanky. All grease their bodies to prevent the skin getting dried in the sun, and smoke themselves with sweet fuel having a peculiar heavy odour. The Wakungu, or district governors, possess probably one sheet of calico, or a scarlet blanket, in excess of the skins usually worn by the people. The men about Urigi seemed a depressed race, and though superior in position (being cultivators of the soil)[3] to the Watusi, who tend cattle, they surprised me by their appearance of misery; this, however, may have been assumed. They have the sultan's orders to furnish all travellers with sufficient provision for themselves and followers free of charge; and in return for this a present is generally given of some coils of brass wire. Some of our Wanyambo porters showed spirit on the march by refusing to be led by an Unyamuezi. On this occasion it was alarming to see the fellows using their spears and arrows at one another; the whole caravan joined in the fray, which became a party one, and had to be settled by our men threatening to shoot them: one cut finger was the only casualty. Again, if a Seedee or two wandered away from camp amongst the

---

[1] Yet when succession disputes later engulfed Karagwe after Rumanyika's suicide, Kukoko (the name is rendered Kakoko by later authorities) was said to have put out the eyes of one of his brothers and murdered 17 relatives. Ford and Hall, 'History of Karagwe', pp. 11–12; Cory, *Bukoba District*, pp. 29, 31–3. See Katoke, *Karagwe Kingdom*, pp 103–15, for a full discussion of the 'Regency of Terror'. Kukoko is depicted with his father in Figure 52, p. 205.

[2] See the left-hand illustration shown in Figure 58 and the middle portrait in Figure 59, both p. 208.

[3] Grant here makes his own assumption; in this kingdom, the pastoralists were regarded as superior.

Wanyambo, they were in some danger, for this tribe were so drunken and excitable that several instances of their boisterous nature proved serious to our men when out purchasing provisions. About the palace, however, they were very civil, constantly advising me as to my health, telling me to keep my weak limb shut up from the air, to eat plenty of meat, &c. They never carried arms when near the palace, neither did our men, which was different to our practice in the badly-governed district of Usui, where no one dare go about unarmed. The only weapon was a five-feet-long knobstick, generally carried across the shoulder; and in wishing good morning to a comrade the end of the stick was presented to be touched. The bows of Karague are the finest I have seen in any part of the world, 6 feet 2 inches in height, and of immense power; the arrows are about the length of the arm, seldom or never poisoned, with their tips shaped like a spear-head. There is no particular character in the spear: the handle is from six to twelve feet long, and the iron part indifferently made, the people prizing themselves more upon their bows. Guns are unknown, except amongst the princes. As has been mentioned, the Wanyambo are fond of carousing over drink, singing and chanting wild airs till early morning; but tottering drunkards such as we see at home are never met with—the people have more self-respect. The food of those who possessed cattle was chiefly milk; others lived upon boiled sweet potato, the flour of Indian-corn or millets, and various calavances or beans. Meat they eat when they can get it, but fowls and fish are forbidden them, though the prince M'nanagee told me the Wanyambo would eat the former "on the sly."

The princesses have been well described by Speke, who had more opportunities of seeing them than I had.[1] One I saw walking, enormously fat, obliged to rest every few paces, by sitting down or reclining in a stooping position, one hand grasping a long staff. When seated, her head was uncovered, the wool allowed to grow into a mop neatly tied off the face with a thong of leather, and having a bouquet of bird's feathers in the centre. The face was a handsome oval, with fine intelligent eyes, and the flesh of her arms, bare from the shoulder, hung down like a fashionable sleeve. They had few employments, their mode of life forbidding this, and most of them could not move without the support of a person on either side. In some respects they reminded me of Hindoo women. In visiting us, the better class, from modesty or custom, had a shawl of bark-cloth covering all their persons except one eye, while they wore the ordinary friezed cow-skin from the waist to the ankle. They were very fond of pictures, the sultan always indulging them by sending my sketches for their amusement. They could make caps of cane stuffed from the outside with their own wool, like moss in a summer-house. Their children were very handsome, with large shining black eyes: the wool was never shaved off their heads nor cut till after marriage, and no covering was ever on their loins till the age of puberty, or even later. Boys and girls would come to look at us, careless or unconscious of their nudity, and chatting without the slightest shyness. A wet-nurse is provided for the infant prince or princess, who is generally suckled away from home, as was the custom amongst Highland families in the last century. Their after-diet is altogether milk: they are whipped into drinking and fattening themselves with it. No marriage ceremonies were observed, but on two occasions we saw a couple of women walk together without any followers, one of them hidden in bark-clothes; and we understood that the veiled one was being conveyed to her betrothed. The dead of the Wanyambo, as has already been mentioned, are deposited in

---

[1] Speke, *Journal*, p. 209; Grant's illustration of women, Figure 63, p. 210, shows ordinary women.

the lake, and princes alone receive burial on the island. On one occasion we observed inside a village enclosure two sticks tied to a stone, and lying across the pathway; and this was done, as we ascertained, to prevent people walking over the spot, as a woman had died there.

With respect to the habitations of the people, suppose that on the face of a bare hill overlooking a lake we place forty or fifty low dome-looking huts of cane, covered with grass; divide them into sets of twos and threes by screens and gates of cane; throw an embankment round the whole, and have a dense hedge of euphorbia trees on the top of the embankment, screening the view of the lake and the country around, and you have the Palace of Rumanika, containing his five wives, sons, four hundred cows and their calves, &c. Except a hut or two outside this "bomah," nothing but a curl of smoke in the valleys showed that there was any population in the country. Descend to the valleys, and you find neatly-formed huts of grass inside the plantain-groves. Their interiors are plastered for five feet with cow-dung and mud; the ceiling is of cane, blackened by smoke, for there is no fireplace. The temporary huts made for us by our Seedees were gable-ended, made of props from the meelomba[1] or bark-cloth tree, and roofed over with grass and the decayed leaves of plantains, the whole made water-tight by India-rubber sheeting being placed on their roofs—the last a requisite which the traveller should never forget.[2] The sultan generally received us in a tidily-kept hut, carpeted with the silky leaves of the papyrus, and loopholed in several places for visitors outside to make him their obeisance by clapping their hands and addressing him. Here, seated on his warm bedding, we chatted and laughed with him, paying long and pleasant visits, his majesty at the same time smoking his large black pipe. Screens of cane, placed as gates, prevented our interviews being interrupted, and permission was required before any one could visit him or pass those barriers, where men always stood, like porters at the Government offices. The ordinary mode of salutation of an Unyambo or ryot of Karague, when he reached a circle of people seated, was to present the end of his staff to each acquaintance, who touched it, saying, "Verembe, verembe, verembe kooroongee," *i.e.,* How do you do, how do you do, how do you do? are you very well? The same answer would be given, and the same salutation exchanged, if two met upon the road. To a superior they also hold out the stick, but it is only acknowledged by a nod from him.

Crime was seldom observed or heard of, but the people had their distinct punishments, and traders had the protection of the sultan. A caravan of Moossah's was plundered by the Urigi chief, who was at once arrested and made over as a slave, to be dealt with at the coast as Moossah chose. The property lost or destroyed was doubly repaid by the sultan in ivory, and the chief, in gratitude to Moossah for not making a prisoner of him, promised a present of ten tusks every time his caravan should pass through his district. I am indebted to M'nanagee, who judges all cases for his brother the king, for the following list of offences with their punishments:—An ear is cut off for adultery; if the case occurs with a slave or a princess, the offender is tortured, as in the Ukuni case, and his throat is cut. Simple theft: kept in the stocks from two to ten months. Striking and assaulting with stick: ten goats. Assault with spear, bow and arrow: property confiscated, half going to the sultan and half to the injured party; if the culprit has no property, he is put into the stocks.

[1] More properly, *Myombo*, that is, *Brachystegia*, which has eight species.
[2] See Grant's depiction of his camp, Figure 55, p. 206.

Murder: all property made over to the relatives of the murdered person, and the eyes of the murderer gouged, or he is thrown over the precipice below the palace. If a husband comes upon a case of adultery, he is permitted to kill the offender on the spot. Unnatural crimes they regard with horror, but these are said to be known only amongst the "wæroo"[1] or slaves; so that the Karague laws are as strict as our own, and, without statistics, I believe there is far less crime. The punishments at Muscat and Zanzibar, under Arab government, were described to me by Frij, and are barbarous in comparison with the code at Karague. For theft, the hand is cut off; if the property is recovered, the thief at Zanzibar is buried in the seashore up to his neck, to allow the tide to reach him—a mode of punishment that will remind the reader of the case of the alleged Wigtown martyrs.[2] Some silver and clothes were stolen from the sultan of Zanzibar, and the thieves being detected were pulled up to the top of a flagstaff and thrown to the ground. At Muscat the tongue of the thief is cut off, and owing to this severe punishment there are few cases of theft. The Arabs are hard masters, and train their servants (several of whom were with us) in a system of rigorous discipline. To enforce despatch, a master will spit on the ground, and say to his servant, "If that dries up before you return with an answer to my message, you'll get flogged."

Musical instruments were in greater variety in Karague than we had previously met with, and the little plaintive native airs could be picked up and hummed, they were so sweet and pleasing to the ear. There was stringed, wind, and drum music. Their most perfect instrument was the "nanga," of seven or eight strings; it may be called national. In one of these, played by an old woman, six of the seven notes were a perfect scale, the seventh being the only faulty string. In another, played by a man, three strings were a full harmonious chord. These facts show that the people are capable of cultivation. The "nanga" was formed of heavy dark wood, the shape of a tray, 22 by 9 inches or 30 by 8, with three open crosses in the bottom, and laced with *one* string seven or eight times over bridges at either end; sometimes a gourd, as sounding-board, was tied on to the back. Prince M'nanagee, at my request, sent the best player he knew. The man boldly entered without introduction, dressed in the usual Wanyambo costume, and looked a wild, excited creature. After resting his spear against the roof of the hut, he took a "nanga" from under his arm and commenced. As he sat upon a mat with his head averted from me, never smiling, he sang something of his having been sent to me, and of the favourite dog Keeromba.[3] The wild yet gentle music and words attracted a crowd of admirers, who sang the dog-song for days afterwards, as we had it encored several times. Another player was an old woman, calling herself "Keeleeanyagga." As she played while standing in front of me, all the song she could produce was "sh," "sh," screwing her mouth, rolling her body, and raising her feet from the ground; it was a miserable performance, and not repeated.

Of wind instruments we had the fife and horn. The fife is more common with the Uganda than the Karague people. It is an 18-inch-long hollowed reed, about the thickness of a German flute, is held like a flageolet, has a slit at the top, and six finger-holes. As the

[1] That is *Bairu*.

[2] The Wigtown martyrs were two young women who supported the Covenanting movement in Scotland but were executed for their faith in the reign of James VII and II in 1685. A monument had been erected in 1858 as Grant would have been well aware.

[3] The scene described was sketched by Grant: see Figure 65, p. 211. The incompetent lady musician he goes on to describe is shown in Figure 63, p. 210.

Waganda walk smartly along the road, with a light load on their heads, they often while away the time with this rude instrument, out of which some of them bring soft, sweet, flute-like music. The bugle they have is shaped like a telescope, and is made of several pieces of gourd fitting into each other, and covered with cow-skin. It is 12 inches long. An expert performer on this bugle can produce a whole chord, which is varied by the thumb acting as a key.

Drums are of different shapes, according as they are beaten by the hand or by a stick. The drum made for the hand is a 4-feet-long log, hollowed out in the shape of an inverted dice-box, open at the lower end, and covered at the top, which is 1 foot across, with the skin of an ichneumon.[1] It is slung from the left shoulder, and played by tapping and stopping with the fingers.[2] The thirty-three drums seen ranged in line at the ceremony after new-moon[3] were of every possible shape, except round, which they all tried to be. They were trunks of trees hollowed out, and covered over with skin. Two copper kettle-drums had found their way into the collection. The sultan had an excellent band, of its kind, composed of 16 men, who performed several tunes before us. The instruments were 14 bugles and 2 hand-drums. Three ranks, the drummers in the rear, formed in front of us, and played, with great spirit and precision, bugle music in waltz and march time. While "trooping" they advanced, swaying their bodies very gracefully to the music; and as they neared us all halted except the bandmaster, who, as he played, being an active, well-made little man, advanced to our feet, kneeling nimbly on alternate knees in time to the music. The drummers were energetic, smart, mirthful fellows; and their music, sounding so sweetly among the hills, was more pleasant than any performance I had ever expected to witness in Africa. It was called Unyoro music, but at Unyoro we heard none of it in consequence of the moroseness of the king. All the time we were at Karague we saw no dance worth noting; they did not seem much given to dancing, and the war-drum was never sounded. Long may this continue! On such occasions the men take the field and the women beat the drums. An alarm of cattle having been captured was once spread, and the men rushed about in hot haste, armed each with a single spear and their faithful bow and arrows; but it proved false, and the bold Prince Chunderah was disappointed of a raid.

The only alarms we experienced were caused by the hyena or other animals stealing from us. Twice an infuriated mob came shouting into our camp, the voices of the women being above all others. A woman had a child, and two men fought for it. Each claimed it; the woman wouldn't give it up; she couldn't settle the dispute; would the white man do it? I was not for some time made aware of the circumstances; but my Seedee servant appointed himself arbiter, and, after looking at both the men and the child, decided who was the rightful father, after which they all scampered off in noisy confusion. A second case was soon after decided in the same way, but with a different result, for the man who lost the suit took his spear and threatened to stab the infant. The African, however, is more prompt in speech than in action.

Of religion, the only approach to it has been mentioned in the various superstitions of the king and his brother, who made idols of horns filled with various charms. To these they

---

[1] An ichneumon is a small mongoose-like mammal.
[2] Grant shows musicians in Karagwe and Buganda in Figure 53, p. 205, and Plate 32.
[3] See Figure 54, p. 206.

appeal for aid against an enemy, for the blessing of health, for the discovery of men's inward thoughts, for rain, &c. In the event of a war or a journey, the mysterious horn was consulted as to the probable success of the expedition. Another belief is that certain animals are possessed of devils, but are in the power of soothsayers.[1] We found that amongst the Wahuma kings it was lawful to cohabit with a brother's wife, or with his own sister.

They have no knowledge whatever of reading, writing, or arithmetic. A printed book to them was like a picture-book to a child; its leaves were turned over one by one carefully by the most intelligent, and immediately shut up by the more ignorant. For twenty years Arabs have been amongst them, but Mohammedanism has taken no hold of the king or his people. The country presents a wide field for commerce to pave the way for regenerating an intelligent race.[2]

Extract from Journal: Education in Britain?

[Rumanika] was asked a second time to allow a young son to accompany us to England – said it was not the custom of his caste to part with a blood relative even for a few days but he'd give a Muhinda or prince whom we might depend upon – S[peke] did not want. Sultan urged for some Mganga to prevent war in his country! Told we did not possess such a thing – send a son to England & you'll enrich yourself & enlarge your territories. [NLS, MS. 17915, 4 December 1861]

On reading the ten commandments to my Mohammedan friend Jumah,[3] who dealt in slaves, ivory, &c., often complaining that his slaves were under no control, he shook hands with me after each commandment, saying how true and excellent they were, he believed in them all. "But do you practise them?" I asked. "Read 'Honour thy father and thy mother,' and tell me how can the slaves honour their fathers and mothers if you tear them away from their families?" "Oh, I am a father to them." "How can you be a father? Are the affections of a parent not as strong in Africa as anywhere else?" He felt the force of the argument, asked me to desist from pressing the matter, as it was not convenient to adopt these sentiments at present. He would return to Zanzibar, never again keep slaves, study the Bible, and go to England. I wished to believe that he said this in sincerity, for the conversion of one influential man in such a land would be of importance.

By the end of March 1862 there were some hopes of my leaving Karague to join Speke in Uganda. The king had sent an officer and forty of his men to convey me up to the kingdom I so long wished to see. Rumanika had received his presents of a Whitworth rifle, Tranter's revolver, Inverness cape, cloths, beads, japanned box, a compass, pair of binoculars, &c., to conciliate him; and he had acted the part of a kind friend in giving us all the information in his power. An Unyamuezi M'ganga, or priest, named Kiengo, was to join my party, but until he had completed his arrangements the march could not take place.[4] The Waganda who had arrived for me were clamorous to get away, but they refused

---

[1] Grant as a son of the Manse is perhaps too bound by his own religious ideas to enter fully into the nature of the beliefs of the people he now encountered. For a useful discussion of religious practice and belief in 19th-century Tanzania, see Iliffe, *Tanganyika*, pp. 26–32.

[2] Grant was to spend much of the latter part of his life trying to bring about that regeneration; see Introduction, pp. 61–2, 64.

[3] Confusingly, Grant now says that Juma was a Mahommedan.

[4] Kiengo was conveying a tribute from the ruler of Rusubi to Buganda. More generally, he carved out a career for himself as a trader in the region. Bridges, 'Negotiating a Way', pp. 122, 131n.

to carry the luggage; and as Rumanika could provide no porters, three-fourths of it were left behind in his charge. Being unable to walk, I was placed in a wicker stretcher (April 14, 1862),[1] and was trotted off on the heads of four Waganda. Wishing to shake hands with Rumanika, I ordered the carriers to convey me into the palace, but nothing would induce them to leave the path—it was not their duty. My adieus were therefore sent through Kukoko, his favourite son; and I left Karague, its hills, lakes, and groves, feeling intensely curious about the next kingdom of Uganda, where I hoped to rejoin my fellow-traveller.

[1] Grant himself pictures his painful conveyance in Figure 67, p. 212.

.13. Rumanika, King of Karagweh, and his son Kukoko.

Figure 52. Rumanika, the ruler of Karagwe, the first of the sophisticated 'interlacustrine kingdoms' encountered by Grant. He treated Grant well during the very long period the explorer had to remain there because he was badly incapacitated by an ulcerated leg. Perhaps because of his illness, Grant seems frequently to have employed the outline system of drawing he used here. NLS MS. 17919, no. 13. Reproduced by permission of the National Library of Scotland.

Figure 53. 'Bugle and drum band' drawn in December 1861. Grant was considerably interested in music and this interest certainly extended to the bands he encountered here in Karagwe and later in Buganda. The kinds of instruments utilized are more easily seen in Plate 32. NLS MS. 17919, no. 15. Reproduced by permission of the National Library of Scotland.

Figure 54.   'New moon Celebration'. Grant witnessed this on 8 December 1861 in Karagwe and he saw it as another sign of the relative sophistication of the kingdom. NLS MS. 17919, no. 16. Reproduced by permission of the National Library of Scotland.

Figure 55.   Grant's 'Standing Camp' in Karagwe. Given his long stay, it is not surprising that his followers made the camp into what was almost an African village with Grant's tent becoming a large hut while the porters had their own small huts. This view was taken at the end of his stay in March 1862. NLS MS. 17919, no. 17. Reproduced by permission of the National Library of Scotland.

Figure 56. 'Little Windermere'. Grant was most attracted by the 'Lake District' character of Karagwe and this is only one of the views he attempted of the lake he dubbed 'Windermere'. This was sketched in December 1861. NLS MS. 17919, no. 19. Reproduced by permission of the National Library of Scotland.

Figure 57. *Tragelaphus spekii* drawn on 5 December 1861. Grant notes that these antelope feed on the rushes beside the lake. NLS MS. 17920, no. 47. Reproduced by permission of the National Library of Scotland.

Figure 58.   People in Karagwe. Again using his outlining technique, in February 1862, Grant depicts some of those he met in Karagwe. To the left is a milk carrier, then a man and woman who are somewhat misleadingly labelled but appear to be from the Hutu or servile and agricultural people of Ruanda dominated by the Tutsi. A prince, yet another son of Rumanika, is on the right. NLS MS. 17920, no. 49. Reproduced by permission of the National Library of Scotland.

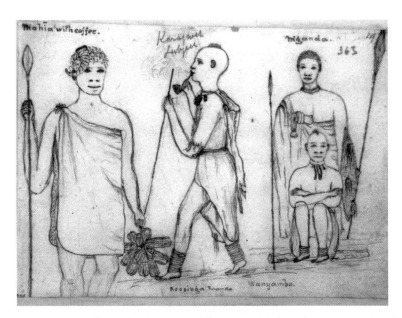

Figure 59.   More people seen in Karagwe. They are a Muhia, that is, someone from the sub-chiefdom to the north of Karagwe, an ordinary Karagwe subject and two Baganda, presumably from the party who had been sent from Buganda to fetch Grant. NLS MS. 17920, no. 50. Reproduced by permission of the National Library of Scotland.

Figure 60. Mnanagee, brother of the King, shown here in February 1862 with some of his followers. Grant said he was a 'prophet and priest'. NLS MS. 17920, no. 51. Reproduced by permission of the National Library of Scotland.

Figure 61. One of Rumanika's sons, Chundera, is in the centre of this picture with a man from Ruanda to the left. Whether the cow is connected with either is uncertain. NLS MS. 17920, no. 52. Reproduced by permission of the National Library of Scotland.

Figure 62. 'Roadmaking' and Frij. 'Clearing a path' is the title Grant gave this sketch which was probably made as he was being carried from Karagwe to Buganda. In the centre is Frij, Grant's 'private servant' and the African in the party with whom he probably had the most converse. This seems to be the only picture of him Grant attempted. NLS MS. 17920, no. 53. Reproduced by permission of the National Library of Scotland.

Figure 63. Some women of Karagwe depicted just before Grant left in April 1862. NLS MS. 17920, no. 55. Reproduced by permission of the National Library of Scotland.

Figure 64. An old woman in Karagwe. Grant was attempting to show the holes pierced in her lips. NLS MS. 17920, no. 46 recto. Reproduced by permission of the National Library of Scotland.

Figure 65. A member of the lower class in Karagwe with a 'nanga'. Grant said that the music produced by many of the musicians he met was 'so sweet and pleasing to the ear'. See Chapter VIII, pp. 201–2. NLS MS. 17920, no. 57. Reproduced by permission of the National Library of Scotland.

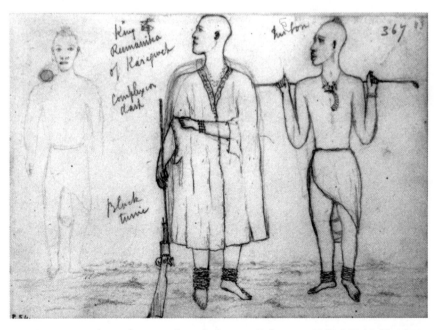

Figure 66. Rumanika with an unidentified son in February 1862. NLS MS. 17920, no. 54. Reproduced by permission of the National Library of Scotland.

Figure 67. Grant leaving Karagwe in April 1862 carried on a litter by four of the Baganda sent to fetch him. He said the shaking gave him intense pain and he regretted that the men would carry him head first so that he could not see where he was going. NLS MS. 17919, no. 18. Reproduced by permission of the National Library of Scotland.

CHAPTER IX

[Pages 188–218]

The Uganda March [14 April–27 May 1862]

Having been detained at Karague for so many months, I was right glad to have a prospect in the end of March of getting away to join my companion.[1] A party of Waganda, under an officer named Mariboo, arrived to take me as far as the Kitangule[2] river, four marches, where large boats were said to be lying to convey me by the lake to Uganda. This, however, was not the case; no boats had been sent,[3] and the journey of twenty-nine marches was performed by land, much to our disappointment, as Speke had previously been over it, and we missed the navigation of the Nyanza.[4] Day by day the Waganda escort deluded me with the idea that we would come upon boats by the side of the Nyanza; and Mariboo ordered the march as he liked, halted when it suited him, got tipsy whenever he could, but in the end compensated for all by conveying me safe to his king.

Rumanika had a sort of litter made up,[5] on which the Waganda lads were to carry me; my half-dozen Seedees could not have done it, as the country afterwards proved to be precipitous, and full of swamps and marshy drains. On the morning of the 14th April, when a start was made from Karague, Mariboo came into camp with his thirty or forty men, making a noise and saying they had been starved while waiting for the Unyamuezi doctor and myself during the last fortnight, and were determined to move to-day whether I was ready or not. "Bring out the white man. Where is his bedding? Let him get into the conveyance." The property, however, had first to be despatched. I lost sight of it for two days, but none of the loads were plundered. On our journey, the stretcher was changed from the head to the shoulder of the Waganda, who went at the rate of six miles an hour, jostling and paining my limb unmercifully. The coach and four, as I may term it, was put down every mile, or less, that the bearers might rest, laugh, joke, and make a deafening noise with their mumbling language, beating their tongues to the roofs of their mouths. They seldom spoke when in motion, only when one stumbled the others would cry out

---

[1] Perhaps the kabaka, Mutesa, feared that Grant might open up a direct route from Karagwe to Bunyoro unless he were brought into Buganda. See Bridges, 'Negotiating a Way', pp. 124–5 for a discussion of Mutesa's strategic interests in relation to other powers in the region.

[2] That is, the River Kagera.

[3] Grant had originally written: 'These boats proved a myth; none had ever been sent.' NLS, MS. 17934, p. 188.

[4] So opening the way for Speke's critics over the Nile sources controversy later to say that his 'Lake Victoria' was not proved to be one large body of water but might be several smaller lakes.

[5] See Figure 67, p. 212.

against him, recommending greater care of their charge. Certainly it was not a safe position to be perched such a height on an open frame of sticks, with rocky precipices, small footing for the men, and very often water below. One great difficulty was to make them carry the conveyance so that the country in front could be seen in travelling; this they, for some reason, refused to do, and persisted in carrying me head first, instead of feet. If a grove of plantain was by the side of the path, it could not be resisted; off all would dash at the fruit, eat, and carry away as much as they were able, sometimes politely offering me a share, or more frequently remaining so long away, as I lay on the stretcher, that it became irritating. The best way was to join as much as possible with them in their frolics; my men did so, and enjoyed the march extremely.

At these groves, a single bunch or cluster of as many as 150 ripe plantains could be got in April,[1] and their juice drunk from them al fresco. The large leaves of the tree, green, and soft as satin, were spread on the ground as a table-cloth; a wisp of grass, well softened by rubbing, enclosed a quantity of luscious ripe fruit, and what the men seemed most to enjoy was to bite and suck the fruit through the grass. During the march they all carried some small load on their heads, never more than 20 or 30 lb, rolled in the form of a web of cloth, neatly bound round, and having pipes and flutes stuck into it. Each man had a spear and shield over his back; the latter served as an umbrella when rain fell; and thus, with their bark-cloths kilted up, their dress was secure from rain or boggy ground. On arrival in camp, the march costume was changed for a clean suit of bark-cloth as stiff as silk, or for a set of many-coloured goat-skins, with scalloped, pierced edges, in which they made themselves smart, and strutted about like gentlemen. Those who had been able to find dogs led them with strings tied to their waists or wrists as they ran along. Very ridiculous they appeared, for the animals (not accustomed to it) always refused to be led in this way. On coming near habitations, the men shouted and sang, as if carrying some object of triumph. Had I been a dead lion, they could not have made greater noise; and on getting near camp, regardless of cultivated fields, they would plunge into them with malicious delight, trample them down, slash away branches or plantain-trees which came in their way, and deposit the litter inside a grove.

When morning again came, the gay Mariboo, always scrupulously clean and proud of his dress, would appear, followed by his drummer-boy and dog, to announce, by beat of drum, a march or halt. If the former, the shouts of his men coming to join him would be heard in the distance, and Mariboo would answer and receive replies, till one by one all rushed up, spear in hand, as if to attack him, shouting allegiance, and causing their "captain" to spring and bound with delight, while I looked on with admiration at the strange and wild spectacle. After several exhibitions of this sort, it became evident that presents were expected, and if the march was to be a success, a little "tipping" was necessary; consequently, the captain was summoned to receive a gift of beads. His delight, as he handled the beautiful small beads, knew no bounds; his spear was flashed up to my face, while his left hand held his shield, and he finished with a number of nimble antics. His arms laid aside, he repeated, "N'yans, n'yans" (thanks, thanks), perhaps fifty times in succession, with a diagonal motion of both palms at each repetition. This over, another

---

[1] Bananas are not seasonal and ripen constantly. The subject of plantains, *Musa x paradisiaca*, in the interlacustrine region is a complicated one with over 30 species of the cultivated type which are used for various purposes. Argument has taken place whether cultivars were introduced from Asia or developed locally.

mode of thanks was adopted, and was even more agreeable; he drew his flute from his waist, played some soft music, making his eyes twinkle with delight, and swayed his body as if charmed with his own sweet strains. They certainly are a most joyous race. On our third march from Karague, the ground was so steep, and there was so much danger of my falling off the stretcher, that I was obliged to get out, and be half-carried up the rocky side of the hill, never dreaming that they would run away with my conveyance, which they did on seeing that I was able to put my foot to the ground. For a couple of hours they allowed me to wait there, while they, like a parcel of wicked boys, kept throwing rocks down the precipice, listening in perfect quiet till they heard the last sound of the stones reaching the bottom of the ravine, when all would shout together.

From the capital of Karague to the right bank of the Kitangule, the distance *viâ* Meegongo was forty miles over flat-topped bare hills, and across valleys with swamps. On emerging from these to the river plain, the flat country became studded with mounds from six to eight feet high, raised by the ever-working white ants. Thorny shrubs, cactus, climbing aloes, with pink flowers, covered them, or the jungle of grass was varied by circles of brushwood, giving shade to the rhinoceros; the older trees were veiled over with silvery grey moss, which drooped gracefully, like the pendent branches of the weeping willow. The plain extended for ten miles, with several "back-waters" upon it, covered with the thorny mimosa and papyrus, through which we had to cut our way. Emerging from it and going towards the river, we came upon higher land—a dry grassy plain three miles across, kept short by cattle, and just the ground on which to find a florikan.[1] There were several huts, which gladdened the eye after a dreary march. The first sight of the river Kitangule,[2] which had been so often named to us as an old ivory depôt,[3] and the stream by which wood was floated down from Ruanda, was rather disappointing. Standing upon its steep shelving bank of white gravel, the stream is almost hidden by the papyrus, which lines its sides in a depth of from twenty to sixty yards; but when ferrying it, its majestic flow is seen. The canoes here were of one log of timber hollowed out, fifteen feet long, the breadth of an easy-chair as you sat in them, and capable of carrying fifteen Waganda, with their loads, dogs, spears, and large shields.[4] They were propelled by poles through a winding channel closely shut in by the papyrus, and by paddles when in the stream, a man at each end holding one about five feet long. I had obtained from the Waganda lads several of their neatly spun coils of rope, which they carry on their heads; three or four of these were knotted together and a stone tied to one end as a sounding-line; but on the ferryman noticing what was to be done, he objected, saying his sultan Rumanika would not permit any stone to be placed or thrown into the sacred Kitangule. A bribe at last softened him; but Mariboo now interfered, saying, in his superstition, that he had an equally sacred charge from his king—namely, that he was to convey me in safety to him, and he would allow no pranks to be played with the river, for "suppose in the middle of it some spirit

[1] As in many other contexts, Grant used a term derived from his Indian experience; a *florikan* is the Indian or Anglo-Indian name for a bustard.

[2] Clearly, the use of the same name for both the place and the river must have been usual; Speke, *Journal*, p. 262, refers to the Kitangulé Kagera and his map has the same usage.

[3] Kitangule was probably the earliest coast traders' ivory depot but by this time it had been superseded by Kafuro in Buganda itself. Sheriff, *Slaves, Spices and Ivory*, p. 183–4. Mutesa had allowed or perhaps forced the coast traders to base themselves in Buganda.

[4] See the attempted illustration, Figure 68, p. 259, which also has written on it 'Kitangulé Kagera'.

215

were disturbed by a stone, and rose to upset the boat, what would his king say?" In short, after wasting words and time, the project was given up, and we commenced the passage of the river at a reach four hundred yards long, having paid beforehand twenty strings of beads for my men, and an extra handful of cowries were given by the Waganda to the ferrymen. Poling for twenty yards through a winding channel cleared of the tall papyrus, and not broader than our canoe, we reached the stream, fully eighty yards across, judged to be five to six fathoms deep, looking as if any man-of-war could sail up, and flowing majestically at the rate of about three miles an hour. The strength of the current was so great that we had to pole up its right bank inside the fringe of papyrus for thirty yards, and then the two ferrymen, with a paddle each, made the canoe glide across diagonally down to the opposite channel in the reeds, which they reached with great precision. Poling for fifty to eighty yards was now adopted, landing upon mire which nearly sucked us into its hold; beyond this, the old line of the river rose abruptly like a railway embankment. At that level the country extended far away in a pleasant grassy plain, giving it the appearance of an Indian parade-ground; but the footing was treacherous, being full of ant-holes, and dotted with cactus-trees, white-ant mounds, with their usual vegetation, thistle-looking plants, and a scarlet-flowering shrub. In the distance to the north were rocky hills.

We observed that the waters of the Kitangule are accumulated from the lakes Karague, Kagæra, Kishakka, Ooyewgomah, and water from Utumbi. This river is, beyond comparison, the greatest body of water met with from the south of the Victoria Nyanza all round its western shore to its most northerly point, where the Nile was seen by Speke to make its exit from the lake. It reminded me, when ferrying it, of the Hoogly ten miles above Calcutta. Every other stream entering the lake was walked across, none had to be ferried; and they were so numerous that nine and ten might be forded in as many miles; this was a daily occurrence when marching on the western shore of the lake. The accumulation of these streams, and the rivulets (no rivers) known from Arab information to be in the eastern or unexplored portion of the Victoria Nyanza, form a boundless sea of 20,000 square miles, never traversed from one side to the other. All these arteries throw in an immense mass of water, and though the greatest of them is the Kitangule, still it is 160 miles distant by water from the point whence the Nile issues from its parent reservoir, the Lake Nyanza, at 21 miles north latitude.[1]

The country between the Kitangule and the Katonga, a distance of 100 miles, is a parallel series of grassy spurs tapering down to the lake's shores on the east. There are many beautiful spots on the route—high grounds from which, for a quarter of the horizon, are seen the waters of the lake, or the country undulating and park-like, covered with tall waving grasses, and overlooked by rocks. The curves, sweeps, and inclines of the hills often blended together in great beauty—never making the path inconveniently steep or too long in ascent or descent. All the cultivation was on these slopes, as the plains between them, sometimes six miles across, were ankle-deep in water and mud in this

---

[1] In other words, the Kagera, which rises in Rwanda, could be seen as the ultimate source of the Nile. These comments, which were clearly made as Grant prepared his book and after all the controversies had begun about Speke's identifying the Ripon Falls outlet as *the* source of the Nile, could be taken to be an oblique devaluing of the importance of his companion's discovery. See the Introduction, pp. 47 and 52, on the Nile source arguments and the possibility that Grant did for a time abandon his unquestioning loyalty to his companion. Nevertheless, the common-sense position is that the Ripon Falls constitute the source of the Nile; otherwise almost any stream which flows into Lake Victoria could be claimed as the source.

month of May; or where the valley was narrow, water would have accumulated in a drain four feet deep, across which the Waganda carried me on their necks, or, like a child, in their arms. On some marches we had to cross ten different waters, and, to avoid others, long detours were made to get upon higher grounds.

The now famous Victoria Nyanza, when seen for the first time, expanding in all its majesty, excited our wonder and admiration. Even the listless Wanyamuezi came to have a look at its waters, stretching over ninety degrees of the horizon.[1] The Seedees were in raptures with it, fancying themselves looking upon the ocean which surrounds their island home of Zanzibar, and I made a sketch, dotting it with imaginary steamers and ships riding at anchor in the bay.[2] On its shores are beautiful bays, made by wooded tongues of low land (or points such as Boonjacko and Surree Points, guarding the Katonga river) running into the lake, with very often a rounded detached island at their apices. The low islands of Sesseh lie on the western shore of the lake. A deep fringe of the papyrus generally hid the view over its waters. When standing here, the hoarse tromboning of the hippopotamus, wishing to come out to graze, echoed from out these rushes. The harbours of the natives were cleared spaces composed of a spongy mass of seeds, rotten reeds, sticks, and roots. In front, for twenty yards, a short rush with a circular leaf grew, breaking the small surfing waves on the lake from two to three hundred yards, showing that it was of no depth. In the distance, large boats paddled along from the mainland to the islands of Sesseh. One, of five planks sewn together, having four cross bars as seats, was brought to convey me to Uganda; but after four of us had got into it with some loads, the craft was so cranky[3] that such a voyage would have been madness, the water streaming in. Her bows and stern were pointed, standing for a yard over the water, with broad central plank from stem to stern, rounded outside, answering for a keel, and well adapted for gliding through papyrus.

The flora along this tract did not afford much variety. The most graceful tree on the route was the wild date-palm, growing in clumps of three and four upon the bare green hills: its crested plumes waved in the breeze, giving almost animal life to the silent scene. Birds' nests, or clusters of Indian red fruit, hung in pendants from the branches. We met with a new acacia, whose thin pods were broad and numerous; on looking at the tree, the crop was so abundant that the leaves were all but hidden by the fruit.[4] Few large trees were seen; they probably got killed by the different varieties of lichens and parasites which covered them. One acacia with a flat top was netted over with bushes of them, as if they had been planted on the tops of the branches. The north-east sides of trees were observed to have the most moss upon their trunks, denoting that it was the dampest wind at that particular locality and position. On the 14th of May I was sheltered from the rays of the sun by the boughs of the coffee-shrub, then with clusters of green berries bowing down

---

[1] Grant first saw the lake on 27 April but the extensive view described here came on 9 May. NLS, MS. 17915, 27 April, 9 May 1862. In his 'Summary of Observations', p. 267, Grant quotes his journal and gives the compass bearings he made from this spot. Pratt, *Imperial Eyes*, pp. 205–6, rather unconvincingly seizes on this episode to claim Grant's reaction was of the 'monarch of all I see', variety.

[2] This sketch can be seen as Figure 75, p. 263.

[3] 'Unsteady, insecure, unreliable': Robinson, ed., *Concise Scots Dictionary*.

[4] There are 750–800 species of *Acacia* and it is difficult from this description to tell which species Grant now saw. However, his later flora refers to *Acacia hecatophyla*; 'Botany of the Speke and Grant Expedition', p. 67. See also Turrill and Milne-Redhead, eds, *Flora of Tropical East Africa. Leguminosae (Part 1) and Mimosoideae* (1959), pp. 49ff. and p. 87.

its branches till within reach. Each yearly growth or produce could be seen by looking at the number of knots in the branches. No care or pruning was observed, and the roots near the trunk grew very much above the soil. On the grounds facing the lake, 20 or 30 miles south of the equator, quantities must be grown, as some houses there were found full of sacks containing very large berries of it.[1] The sacks were remarkably stout and well made—somewhat similar to Calcutta rice-bags. Two fruits, new to us, were seen growing—one, the colour and size of the Indian loquat, with several stones, but growing on a lofty tree with sombre foliage and densely-close branches. The other was an underground scarlet fruit, growing in sets of five and six clustered together like bananas, and of the same size. After being peeled, the pulp, with numerous black seeds, tasted refreshing as a lime, and was much enjoyed by the Waganda, who carried them strung as necklaces. The stalk of this plant (an amomum) grows four feet high from a creeping knotted root, like that of many grasses; and the scarlet fruit does not show above ground till ripe, when it forces up the soil like a mole.[2]

Food was abundant, plantain particularly so, and might be had by the king's guests for the mere pulling; but if fowls, goats, or animal food was required, the natives charged almost London prices, preferring cowries,[3] which we had none of, to beads. In the houses different grains were slung, in plantain-leaf coverings, from the posts which support the roofing. The staple food of the people is green plantain, a particular variety, boiled, when the peel comes off freely, and eaten like mashed potato.[4] A piece of meat boiled with them made both very savoury, but plantain alone is not satisfying to a European. The various uses made of this tree surprised us. A chip from the bark was so watery that the hands could be well washed with it, but it was said to crack the skin: thread, wrappers, and stripes like ribbons were taken from the trunks, and the leaves were made into screen-fences, &c.

The wine I have before mentioned; two quarts of it could be drunk without any injurious effect. Every large hut seemed to have a trunk of a tree scooped out like a canoe, leaving a narrow opening. Several of these are collected in the grove when sufficient fruit has ripened, and the plantain juice is put in them to ferment, with some grain, and heaped over with leaves.[5] The scene at opening these, after three days of fermentation, was quite a festive one. The immense gourds of the village were brought to be filled; cups were made from the leaves to taste the new beverage, and all was merry as at a carnival. A species of wine was made by the Waganda boys, very simple in its mode of manufacture, and excellent to drink. A small cavity was made in the ground, plantain leaves were placed

[1] There are several species of *Coffea* which grow wild but it is clear from his flora, 'Botany of the Speke and Grant Expedition', p. 87, that Grant regarded the bushes he now saw as cultivated *Coffea arabica* which is the only *Coffea* he mentions. Coffee beans were certainly traded into Buganda by the Haya. See Koponen, *People and Production*, p. 119. Grant's evidence on the use of sacks suggests the trade was more formalized than Koponen allows.

[2] The first of these plants was probably not a loquat or *Eriobotrya*, which seems to be confined to East Asia, and it is difficult to guess its identity; the second is *Amomum augustifolium*. Grant, 'Botany of the Speke and Grant Expedition', p. 152. The plant is now referred to as *Aframomum;* it is in the Zingiberaceae or Ginger family.

[3] Grant's evidence here confirms Burton's hearsay evidence of c. 1858 that cowries were in use as a currency in the interlacustrine region, which is rather earlier than Koponen appears to assume: Burton, *Lake Regions*, II, pp. 185, 416; Koponen, *People and Production*, p. 119 and note.

[4] This, the staple food of Buganda, is known as *matoke*.

[5] See Plate 30.

flatly into it, so as to make a basin for liquid. Fruit, mixed with leaves, was pressed with the hands, some water added, and the leaves ultimately thrown away, leaving the "togweh"[1] in the basin ready for drinking.

In travelling through this country our Seedees never received any pay as in the southern provinces, for the king of Uganda gave orders to his people to provide and cook for us. This was not always done: it more frequently happened that as soon as our approach was seen the natives fled, leaving almost all their goods and chattels at our mercy. No persuasion would bring them back, they are so accustomed to be surrounded and captured by troops of men sent by the king. Several influential officers in charge of districts were seen on this route—Simjabee, Kittareh, Kuddoo,[2] and some of the Wazeewa or Wahia[3] race. All brought presents of fowls, buttermilk, sugar-cane, and wine. Simjabee was a tall, thin, long-faced man, with small beard, and very much marked on the forehead with smallpox. His caste was not a particular one, for he ate honey, boiled beef, goat, sheep, antelope, water-boc [sic], beans, and grains, and drank boiled milk and wine. He was a gentle old man, and begged for wires and large beads, which I did not possess. His present was several fowls and some buttermilk, which I thought strange to see in this part of the world. Kittareh called, bringing a bunch of the richest plantain I ever saw, actually dropping juice. Before presenting it he went through the Uganda custom of smoothing it over with his hands, and rubbing it on his face. We became great friends,[4] and he took me over his neatly-kept premises enclosed trimly with high fences of plantain leaf. In his hand he held by a cord a red pariah dog, and a liver-and-white beagle(?) followed at his heels. This animal was the only one of the kind I had observed. Kuddoo, a fine intelligent young fellow, was my companion up to Uganda: it was his duty to see that the various district officers on our route provisioned us properly. He was very fond of looking at pictures, a hunting-knife, or any European-made article. On my showing him a paper of pins, and strewing numbers amongst a crowd for them to take as curiosities, I was surprised to see all collected most carefully and returned to me, because their king did not permit them to keep anything so strange.

They are under extraordinary control these Waganda, and obey their king through fear, making as smart obedient soldiers as any in existence. Two on our march quarrelled one day, and fought in the most manly manner—not with spears, knives, or bows and arrows, as an Unyambo, Seedee or Wanyamuezi would do. They planted their spears, tucked up their bark clothes, and wrestled until one knocked the other down, and held him till he gave in.[5] Previous to our leaving the finely-kept grounds of Kittareh (the man owning the beagle), he brought out a stirrup-cup of wine and some boiled plantain-squash for the Waganda lads, who, having finished all, knelt in a body before the old man to thank him

[1] This is the Swahili word *togwa* rather than the Luganda term, *omwenge*.

[2] It is not clear whether Grant is recording the titles of the offices held or the names of the holders but later remarks suggest the latter. None of the three terms appears among the titles listed by Roscoe, *The Baganda*, pp. 248–57. On the complicated subject of 'chiefs' in Buganda, see Chapter X, p. 238, n. 1.

[3] As noted in Chapter VIII, there were perhaps eight minor 'kingdoms' among the Haya, who live in the area between Karagwe and Lake Victoria. Grant here seems to be referring to those listed as Basiba and the Heia by Murdock, *Africa*, p. 348. See also Katoke, 'Ihangiro', p. 700.

[4] Such statements raise the question of Grant's attitude to the Africans he encountered. See the Introduction, p. 54, where the rather hostile view of Tim Youngs is discussed.

[5] Wrestling was traditionally a popular and carefully regulated sport in Buganda. See Roscoe, *The Baganda*, p. 78.

for his politeness. This they did by diagonally swinging their hands placed together, and repeating the words "N'yans, N'yans," or "M'wambeea, M'wambeea,"[1] in a loud chorus—after which, all sprang up, looking grateful and happy. The upper class are in the habit of making speeches. On a present being put into their hands, they hold it, and talk for five minutes expressing thanks. The Waganda mode of salute on meeting a friend is peculiar: neither party smiles until the words "Nyo, Nyi, Nyogeh,"[2] are repeated alternately by each many times, when one makes bold to address a sentence, then resumes the "Nyo" once or twice, and after these formalities a conversation may with propriety commence. When the women wish to show respect to a superior, they kneel before him like the Wanyamuezi women. All these social forms are as scrupulously attended to in Africa as the ceremonies at the most polite court of Europe.

On the march we never knew where we were to halt for the day. The men did not know themselves; they could not tell the probable time of arrival, so that the dinner-hour was always uncertain;[3] and if our baggage was tied up by seven in the morning, we seldom left before eleven: once off, we continued wandering till sunset. They were like a parcel of hungry hounds, darting into every hut, spear up, and shouting at places where they thought they could safely plunder, eating and drinking on the way perhaps five or six times a-day. Mariboo, although in charge of me, would be absent for days drinking, allowing me to get on as I best could; consequently, on several occasions, my conveyance, bedding, and writing materials were nowhere to be found. Some villagers, instead of presenting our party with wine, would in excuse make an offering of half-a-dozen cowries to me, and on having it explained to them that the white man did not exact presents, they would express great surprise. The Wezee[4] doctor (Kiengo) of our party had Rumanika's orders to seize the officer of the Kisuere district for having committed two misdemeanours. The man had been to present me with a gourd of wine, and did so very hurriedly, slipping away from my sight. Soon after, chase was given, a party following him up to his house, but the alarm had preceded him. The cattle that were to have been taken as forfeited to Rumanika, and the wives who were to have become the wives of Kiengo, were both driven to the jungles, but the plunder that fell to the lot of his pursuers was brought into our camp. The case was an illustration of the uncertain life of African men and women. The home they have lived in since the day of their birth, may in an instant, by the caprice of another, be wrested from them, or they may return to find it a ruin. My Waganda were careful not to plunder too much in their own country, for fear of the wrath of their king;[5] but when in Rumanika's territory, or on the borders of their own, they never hesitated to seize what they could. In the same way the Karague race of Wanyambo, now that they were of our party in the strange land of Uganda, were the most expert of thieves, making travelling painful and annoying from the cries of the sufferers. On inquiring of an officer whether

[1] More accurately, *nyanze* and *webale*. Grant does not add, possibly out of delicacy, that in such a situation, the partaker of a feast was supposed to belch loudly to show his appreciation to the chief. Ibid., p. 45.

[2] Ganda greetings are very formal and vary according to the status of those meeting or the length of time they have been separated; *nyoge* is used after a long separation. Ibid., p. 43.

[3] 'a glorious uncertainty' was the phrase changed at the proof stage. NLS, MS. 17934, p. 201.

[4] Having used the proper term 'Wanyamwezi' several times in this chapter, Grant here suddenly reverts to his own contraction, 'Wezee'.

[5] On Grant's evidence, Kabaka Mutesa clearly did control the system of 'plundering' at this time although that control was to falter later on. See Hanson, *Landed Obligation,* p. 101.

such plunder was permitted by the king, he replied that the order was that the natives should quit their houses as soon as a guest came into the country, and take to the hill-tops. Numerous instances of this were observed, and on my wandering up a hill to beckon them back, they retired as we approached. On this occasion I had an instance of the taste of the Waganda race. The sun was setting (it was the 13th of May 1862), when one of them, having pointed out to me the various directions of the countries around us, quickly turned, and eagerly directed my attention to the full moon rising out of the Victoria Nyanza, sending its glittering rays over the beautiful placid waters. Here was a lover of the picturesque!

Extract from Journal: Grant's Varied Experiences on 13 May 1862[1]
Rainfall morning but marched to Kibogo – seven miles of sharp but short ups & downs towards the lake not ten miles from [sic] and a half away ... stood on a high open ridge, its curved sides the steepest I <u>ever</u> <u>saw</u> (nearing perpendicular) grassed of course & probably of stiff clay the surface soil. The hills[?] looked as if washed round by a river ... Three Wan[yambo] when alone during the march were assaulted ... for their loads, spears held up &tc but when the loads were putdown and <u>empty</u> guns levelled, they fled. (?Waganda chased) after them down the hill. Here there are no boats at any point of embarkation! & that I must go 3 marches more before we find any. Good heavens what liars they all are dragging me all this way, the excitement of being so near the boats & made me walk this whole march & played mischief with my leg ... A young smart Mk[ungu] [who] came to call and see pictures. He took me to top of hill above cult[ivation] & eagerly pointed out many places he knew while I took their bearings. He gave me a fabulous account of a people to W[est] (as the sun set) who use bows of great thickness arrows like sticks, spears of immense length & are very fierce ... A Wag[anda] when on the height called my attention to the rising moon shining its glittering rays on the lake while the sun set behind us. For a savage the Ug[andan] is not so unobservant.[2] [NLS, MS. 17915, 13 May 1862]

On the slopes looking towards the lake the climate was delightful, quite English; only once, in a confined valley, did the temperature show a great heat—viz., 97½°, falling during the night, with the cold damp air, to 50°. We had showers, on an average, almost every third day between 15th April and 19th May, and but one severe N.E. storm of wind and rain. On the 14th of May, our Seedees predicted that no rain would fall if Dr Kiengo's magic horn of an antelope were placed in the sun; "for," said they, "is not the M'ganga out? No rain ever falls when it is in the open." Sure enough, when rain was threatened, the horn was taken in to prevent its getting wet. The contents of these idol horns must be renewed periodically, as the charm within them is supposed to live or have power only for a certain period of time. Some other superstitions were observed on this route:—By the path a pole was stuck into the ground, with a large land-shell or some relic on the end of it; or the same relic was placed on the tallest branch of a tree. In the same way that we sometimes place a horse-shoe behind our front door, they hang a small charm of rush and

---

[1] This passage illustrates the fact that Grant was by this date able to walk again. It also shows something of his attitudes while on the Expedition as compared with the gloss he gives his account in the published version.

[2] Yet a third version of this observation worded in 1872 was 'This shows that those who live in a state of nature are not blind to the beauties of nature'. Grant, 'Summary of Observations', p. 268.

feathers, or have a magic wand in the house. The Waganda had anklets of seeds, wood, &c., which were supposed to keep away snake-bites; but few or no snakes were seen. Their other charms and ornaments consisted of tiaras of the abrus[1] seeds, tiaras of large snowberries, necklaces of the scarlet amomum fruit, tusks of the wild boar, horn-tips of antelope, and a square or kidney-shaped pendant round the neck, covered with the skin of a serpent.[2]

The industry and wealth of the Wazeewa or Mohia[3] (a race mentioned in the Karague chapter), amongst whom our camp was pitched for a few days, was very marked. Some of them had migrated from the right to the left bank of the Kitangule, and were now cultivators under the king of Uganda, bringing all the grains of the country for barter into our camp. They seemed a very cleanly race, using little or no grease pomade on their bodies, and never sitting down unless some grass or leaves were placed between them and the ground. Many of their bark-cloths were coloured red crimson, having zigzag marks of black upon them. They dressed their cow-skins very beautifully, placing them stretched on a huge upright square frame to be thinned by scraping with a hatchet; this was observed in Bogweh also. One chief amongst them came to see me, leading his fat brindled dog, partly of bull-dog extraction. He wore a silvery roan-coloured cow-skin down his back, and slung from the neck—a most handsome garb, almost lustrous, and of which he seemed very proud. Their women were comely; and although they had an objection to allow me to drink out of their gurrahs[4] or earthen jars of water, one of them, while her husband, an officer in the king's service, was absent, wished to accompany me on the march; but even this pleasure had to be declined, and the pretty Wazeewa had to console herself, as many others did, without even a lock of my straight hair, which was the wonder of them all. These people paid great attention to their plantain orchards. The bunches sometimes contained 200 large fruit, bending the stems, which had to be supported by a forked stick or ropes. On the fruit being ripe the tree is cut down, to permit the growth of the young shoot, which comes from the parent root. All the groves are of bare-poled single trees, which makes the fruit much finer than if the trees were allowed to grow in clusters; and should the leafstalk droop too much from the trunk, the natives bandage it up to prevent rain from beating into the heart of the tree. They use large circular trays, four feet across, made of osiers, and covered with cow-dung, for drying their grain in the sun. An article of diet not seen before was locusts; a number of them were brought in by a woman to be roasted as food. They were one inch long, had two pairs of wings, and antennae 1½ inches long. White ants also, when young and freshly fledged, were caught in a framework placed over their mound of earth, to be eaten by the people.

In concluding these remarks upon the country lying between the two rivers Kitangule and Katonga, which is occupied by Wanyambo, Wanyoro, Wazeewa, and Waganda, it may be mentioned that "Khass[5] Uganda," or Uganda proper, has yet to be reached when

---

[1] Grant, 'Botany of the Speke and Grant Expedition', pp. 59–60, noted identifying two species of the Abrus or Bean family (*Papilionoideae*). See also Lind and Tallantire, *Flowering Plants of Uganda*, p. 84.

[2] See Plate 37.

[3] As noted above, a people usually classified as being part of the Haya.

[4] This does not appear to be a Swahili word. Perhaps it is a Hindi term but it does not figure in *Hobson-Jobson*.

[5] An Anglo-Indian term denoting 'particular' or 'most important part'. *Hobson-Jobson*.

the Katonga river is crossed;[1] and as the dwellings, domestic and wild animals, &c., had nothing about them peculiar, we shall not stop to describe them, but cross the arm of the lake at the mouth of the above river.

Letters from Speke announced that the king of Uganda, as well as himself, were impatient for my arrival, and that I was expected to come by water. The king, he said, now dressed in English clothes, and our men were regularly supported by him. Uganda, however, was not a land of milk and honey. Grain could not be had to make bread, and I was, if possible, to lay in stores of flour and pease among the Wazeewa people.

By sunrise of the 20th May 1862, I had packed and was ready to cross the equator at Katonga Bay. Seeing a new face seated apart from, but within sight of, Mariboo's little wife, for the sake of speaking to the downcast-looking creature I advanced and asked her the way out of camp; she suckled an infant, was very pretty, with deep black round eyes, and she smilingly gave the information. She was so interesting that on getting into camp for the day I inquired her history. She had been captured by my Waganda the previous day, and was now their prisoner, for our party was strong, and her relatives, had they come to claim her, would also have been made slaves. She had not been brought into camp: we never again saw her, and my Seedees told me she must have been sold, as the Waganda would never give her up for nothing, or they might have killed her.

Extract from Journal: Reaction to News of a Slave Trade Victim
I'm told the M'Ganda has either sold her or killed her for he'd never give her her freedom; how horrible! [NLS, MS. 17915, 20 May 1862.]

On the 20th of May, as I sat on a height admiring the beautiful Katonga Bay, one mile across, and looking at the sweep of richly-wooded land on its other side, with hills in the background, the king of Uganda's order arrived that I was to proceed to his capital by land, and the pleasure I had long anticipated of being conveyed by water was doomed to disappointment. My heart sank within me. I descended, however, to the edge of the bay, where our men were amusing themselves, and where five or six canoes were ready for the party. The Waganda and our Scedees got into them to splash and duck each other. The fowls belonging to the ferryman were seized and killed previous to crossing over, because, if the hippopotamus heard them crow, the canoes would be upset! Hours of larking were spent, and at last fourteen of us, with ten loads, sat in my canoe of four paddles, and we emerged from the winding channel of tall rushes into the bay; here we were joined by two other canoes, all well laden. Racing commenced, the paddlers facing to the front, scooping the water with all their might as they sat on the *sides* of the canoe, and, for a marvel, not splashing us, for three-quarters of a mile over rippled water. Here, for the first time, I met with a plant whose leaves looked very beautiful in the water, growing by those of the lily of the Nile—namely, the *Trapa natans*,[2] the roots of which the Waganda eat. There was no shore to land at; a floating mass of tangled grasses prevented the further progress of the canoe, and we had to jump out into the water. One leg went down four feet to hard sand, while the other had to be pulled out of the grasses. A mile of this disagreeable wading, with a mid-day sun on the equator, was dreadfully fatiguing. On getting out of the swamp, we

[1] In fact, Grant had been travelling through Buddu which was undoubtedly a province of the Kingdom of Buganda. His assertion is justified to the extent that this province had been one of the most recent territories to be added and he was now proceeding to the original heartland on the northern shores of Lake Victoria.

[2] That is, the water chestnut. Grant, 'Botany of the Speke and Grant Expedition', p. 75.

found the country flat and grassy, with cleared cultivated spots and huts. Here, in the shade of some plantain, while resting till the loads arrived, I saw Mariboo's wife enter the houses, quite alone, bringing out a large bundle, which she placed on the ground, and she was immediately surrounded by her servant-girl and two Waganda. I also made one of the party. The bundle contained boiled plantain, sweet potato, and a species of solanum[1]—the dinner of the people whose house she had entered! All seemed to enjoy it so much, eating it in such a refined way, with a leaf in their fingers to prevent them getting burnt, that the little woman, without any Hindoo ceremony, enticed me to join them, and I never made a better luncheon. Everything was cooked in the most savoury way, and I learned that African cooking is as cleanly and quite as wholesome as our own. It seemed strange that we should be so calm and unconcerned, when the tall spears of the inhabitants watching our movements were seen in the distance; but Mrs Mariboo must have known that the natives dared not attack any party belonging to the king.

The journey from Katonga Bay to the capital of Uganda—named Kibuga—was without exception the most disagreeable I ever made. Climbing over hills is bad enough for a lame person, but when a broad miry bog runs between each range, and there is no means of getting through it but by sinking into mud and water at every step, disgust is superadded. Most of the valleys were a quarter of a mile wide; others were square, and four miles from hill to hill—a dense mass of sombre foliage concealing their swamps, musquitoes, and low grounds. Ravines, dells, and gullies, formed by the waters from the hill-sides, were veiled with impenetrable thickets; above these the inhabitants dwelt, surrounded by groves of the plantain at considerable distances from each other. Occasional red clay ant-heaps, boulders, and a few trees dotted the middle height of the hills, and the sky-line was a vegetation of waving grass, from three to six feet high. The general elevation of these hills above their valleys is four hundred feet. On their flat tops the air was fresh and delightful. Whichever way you looked, from your feet to the horizon was a sea of these flat-topped ridges and conical hills.[2]

The Waganda make first-rate pioneers; one is struck with the direct cuts they make across the hills: perhaps their duty of conveying messages, or bringing in cattle and slaves to their king, conduces to this quickness of movement. When carrying me, if a hill, however steep, was to be crossed, they went directly over it, or if a bog was to be forded, it was all one to them—they would dash right into it. We had never seen a road in Africa till coming into Uganda; here they were so broad that a carriage might have driven along them, but they were too steep for any wheeled conveyance.[3] No metal was used on them, but the grasses had been trodden down by the constant driving to and fro of cattle and slave-hunting parties. Attempts at bridges had been made, but we found them in a state of dreadful disrepair. Originally, in the late king Soona's time, piles with a forked end had been driven into the bog, and logs of wild date-palm, &c., were laid parallel with the run of the valley upon the piles, forming a passage about twelve feet broad. These had sunk and rotted, and walking over them with bare feet was annoying and painful. The trees and deep green foliage in the moist dells were densely thick and lofty, some with straight

---

[1] The very large family of *Solanaceae* or Nightshade of which Grant himself recorded 12 species. Some have edible berries. Grant, 'Botany of the Speke and Grant Expedition', pp. 118–19.

[2] Figure 79, p. 266, shows Grant's drawing of such hills.

[3] 'Each District-Chief had to maintain in good order a road, some four yards (3.7 metres) wide, reaching from the Capital to his country seat.' Roscoe, *The Baganda*, p. 239.

unbranched stems, towering higher than any ordinary palm. Ferns, mosses, creepers, climbers, &c., hid or covered their trunks and branches, making shade for the wild buffalo and elephant, who, unconscious of a stage erected overhead to watch them, would come to escape the heat of the day.

An extraordinary-looking tree, of the plantain family, was seen growing wild outside a cultivation. I brought home its seeds, and they have been pronounced to be the *Ensete* of Bruce, first discovered by him in Abyssinia. From its similarity to the plantain I had almost passed it unnoticed, but was attracted by its marvellous stoutness of stem and disproportionately low appearance, its shape being as if one big drum were placed over another, with gigantic single leaves growing from their sides. The natives wore necklaces made of its seeds, which were called M'seegwah by our Seedees.[1] At 3°N. they were again met with, growing upon broken rocky heights, but they were seen nowhere else. The leaves were much eaten by the goats.

The stretcher which carried me part of the way from Karague had been discarded, as the Waganda saw my only ailment was lameness and stiff knee-joint. Through such a rough country walking was very tiresome and a severe exertion, and it was made more so by the pace these excitable Waganda travel at. But they were very civil in assisting me through difficulties, a sergeant and two privates (if we may call them so) being in constant attendance, leading the way or at my heels. They were Mariboo's chief men, fine fellows, very polite in lending a hand or even bringing water to wash off the pair of black boots of mud I had got in coming through the bogs. The marches varied from 9 to 11 miles daily, occupying from 7½ A.M. till noon, or later, according to circumstances. If it was a populous country, and our long line passed through a grove having dwellings inside it, more time was taken. Each hut was entered and ransacked; cautiously a Seedee or Waganda, musket or spear all ready, would go to the door and call, "Ho, ho!" and, gaining admission, come out with what he had picked up—tobacco, or a good bark-cloth. Every house passed was in this way plundered, while the inhabitants watched us in the distance. Travelling was most disagreeable, and sometimes our men suffered for their rashness. The light-hearted gallant little Mariboo came for the aid of two guns one day, because one of his men had been wounded on entering a hut. My Seedees were up in an instant, ready to leave the baggage and myself to take care of each other, but no more than the number asked for went, and they returned without a combat. At another camp we were told to have our guns ready in the morning, as the natives were up in arms; a boy amongst them had been, the previous night, captured, and ransomed for two goats and four bark-cloths. Not understanding that Mariboo was the entire cause of such injustice, I ordered the guns of the Seedees to be filled with shot-sized pebbles instead of bullets; but we did not require to fire them. Even my men became as bad as the Waganda at this trade, their guns making them daring; but it never came to my knowledge till it was too late. For instance, seeing one of Mariboo's boys lead two timid villagers to the grass hut occupied by my Seedees, I watched the result. A conversation ensued, the men afterwards passed me with two naked little girls with strings and tassels to their waists, looking dreadfully frightened. They had been stolen by my men, were

---

[1] The *Ensete* seems to be regarded as part of the *Musaceae* or banana family but a wild variety with dry inedible fruit. Bruce's plant, the 'Abyssinian banana', is *Ensete venticrosum*. See Grant, 'Botany of the Speke and Grant Expedition', pp. 19, 152–3.

the daughters of one of the two villagers, and had no doubt been recovered by paying bribes to Mariboo, his boy, and their captors.[1]

The streams and bogs crossed may be alluded to. All those going towards the Lake Victoria Nyanza were fordable, of white muddy water, rarely brown or mossy, having their bottoms and edges of black mud, the accumulations of decayed vegetable matter. Those which ran north and away from the lake,[2] within two marches of the Uganda capital, had a hard firm footing of sand, with dry edges, and little or no mud. The difference was very marked, and pleasant to observe. The passage of these Uganda bogs is most trying. Imagine a flat valley, a mile across, looking like an osier-bed, but covered with the gigantic papyrus and reeds, &c.; cut a narrow winding passage through it, leaving the roots in the water, and walk through this barefooted. The tears almost came into my eyes, the suffering from the sharp roots was so severe.

Extract from Journal: A Difficult Road to Buganda's Capital

in the middle of the march the path is above the knee in water <u>for a mile or more</u> & only 3 or 4 feet wide – of white, muddy water its sides of gigantic [?] reeds &tc. The footing was such torture to my game leg & bare feet for I can't yet wear a shoe, [that it] made me groan in torture. It consisted of holes of mud, sharp roots, entangled grasses, reed stubble as sharp as razors and so, fumbling and falling through it, at last got on dry land to find both feet swollen like lobsters. Waganda [?] were kind in sticking by me and did their best to pull me out of holes I stuck in. In the middle of it met a large party of a hundred (strapping fellows chiefly) with no loads but holding overhead their shields and spears. They made way for me & looked afraid but, terrible of systems, they were a slave party from the palace going to fetch as many men, women, children and cattle as they could capture for the king! [NLS, MS. 17915, 22 May 1862.]

Being carried was almost impossible, for even the natives, with the soles of their feet hard as leather, bearing their loads, dogs, spears, and shields on their heads, had enough to do to keep their footing. In my lame state, my feet, after having been covered with mud, came out of these bogs red and inflamed, too large to wear shoes with comfort; or where the valleys were free from the tall rushes, the chill of walking in such mire with a burning sun overhead was quite stupifying; but, strange to say, none of us suffered in health.

The Mwerango, twenty miles west of the Uganda capital, was the first large body of water we found flowing towards Egypt.[3] The centre part of the bridge over it had long since fallen into disrepair, and as the river was too deep for wading, we had to swim across about twenty yards of its width, which was from 300 to 400 yards. You could not look up or down the stream, as the reeds hid everything; neither could it be crossed anywhere but

---

[1] Grant was grateful to the Baganda for the help they gave him but thoroughly disapproved of the system of plunder by which parties sent by their ruler met his and their own needs. He could do nothing about it; to a much greater extent than earlier in the journey he was subject to African authority and unable to exercise any independent power.

[2] See Map 8, p. 33, for the complicated drainage pattern in Uganda.

[3] Part of the river system of the Mayanja which flows north to the Kagu and then into the Victoria Nile. Understandably, in a region of such confused drainage and with the added linguistic problems, the names Grant picked up were not entirely accurate. The proof copy of the book shows that Grant originally said that the Mwerango was found 'going to the north'. NLS, MS. 17934, p. 213.

at this spot, or at other openings made in the bed of papyrus. In one hour our baggage was all across, and everyone was freshened by a bathe. This stream and a sister river, the Moogga Myanza, join and form the Kuffoo,[1] which flows to Unyoro, joining the Nile to the north of Kamarasi's residence. Regarding the rise of these two rivers there were various opinions among the Waganda. The Mwerango, they said, had its rise from rocks one day's journey to the S.S.W. of Namagoma. The other was honoured with a poetical tradition. It was named "Moogga," after one of the wives of the late king Soona. She, on becoming pregnant, was sent, for medical advice, to the S.E. of Namagoma. Accompanying the birth of the child there was a flow of water, which has run ever since, and was christened "Moogga," after the queen![2] This river, or rather bed of rushes, was 500 yards across, and breast-deep. As we waded across it, on either side, within reach, the papyrus grew arching beautifully overhead. Its waters were clear, and sounded sweetly as they trickled through the rushes to our left, contrasting pleasantly with the bogs we had previously been crossing. When asked at Namagoma how long it would take to reach the source of the Mwerango, my friend Mariboo replied figuratively by saying, "A pot of plantain would not be boiled by the time you returned from its source," meaning that it would take a very short time.

As my caravan daily shortened its distance from the residence of the king, messengers came to inquire for me, where I was to sleep each night, and to hurry on, because the king had heard I was *beautiful*, and he could not eat till he had seen me! These parties were sometimes commanded by boys of thirteen years of age—smart little fellows, who travelled very quickly over the country, never getting fatigued. If they met our caravan on the march, complimentary taps and rolls were sounded by their drummers, and returned by ours. It was not considered etiquette for any of their number to mingle with our baggage-party while moving along; because, if anything should be missed, they might be made answerable for it.

Pokino, the governor of a large territory,[3] was one day announced while I was dressing. His name had been constantly quoted as an authority by Mariboo, and I had a strong desire to see him. On coming out of my hut, he sat surrounded by twenty Waganda in considerable state, and I could not help saying aloud, "Hallo! is this Pokino?" At once all grinned at the mention of the name; no one moved from their seated positions, and my iron chair was placed outside the red cow-skin, on which he alone sat,—a determined, sly-looking functionary, with a bad expression of mouth, and just the man to have an order obeyed. His dress was the ordinary one of the country, robing him in graceful folds of bark-cloth, salmon-coloured, which harmonised well with his dark complexion. Round his bare head he wore a wreath of creepers (*Coccinia Indica*),[4] which made me inquire whether his head ached. A laugh from him, and suppressed titter from his men at my

[1] Now written 'Kafu'. See Map 6, p. 31.

[2] According to Kaggwa, Suna had 148 official wives among whom was Muganzirwaza, the mother of the current kabaka, Mutesa. Kagwa, *Customs of the Baganda*, pp. 44–6 (later works and references use the spelling 'Kaggwa').

[3] *Pokino* was the name of the office of the chief of Buddu, the large district or province through which Grant was now passing.

[4] The capitalization of the species name is a mistake the proof readers did not spot. In his flora of 1873–5, Grant, or his advisers, call this *Cephalandria indica*. It is a creeper of the Cucurbitaceae family. Grant, 'Botany of the Speke and Grant Expedition', p. 77.

ignorance, immediately followed, and he wished to see my pictures and lucifer-matches; of the former he preferred the buffalo's head, and one representing some slaves in chains;[1] these amused him more than any of the others, and he soon took his departure, walking away slowly with considerable style, as if proud of his tall stout manly figure.

The dwellings on this route were superior to any we had met with in Africa—loftier, better constructed, and more cleanly. Having command of immensely tall reeds, and beautiful grasses for thatching, with, in most places, tall spars, they could readily make themselves comfortable dwellings; besides which, they are a very neat-handed race. A M'ganda has a double roof of reeds to his house, like the two "flies" in an Indian tent. The outer "fly" has a steeper slope than the under, and is covered to the ground with a thick thatch of long broad-bladed grass, a species of wild sugar-cane. This roofing appears when new white and clean from the inside, and is placed with perfect regularity, and supported by more poles than are generally requisite, as there are sacks of grain, dried flesh or fish,[2] &c., to be slung from them. The interior is partitioned off into front and rear compartments, by means of high screens of the plantain leaf. The better class of houses have a raised bedstead in the dark interior, which has but one door as an outlet for smoke, goats, and inhabitants. They also have their summerhouses, generally in a shady spot, where men meet to chat, smoke, and drink. It was amusing to see such comfort in these "barzahs,"[3] which only required a table, and to be seated round, to look like a remarkably neat summer-house at home.[4] Two huts on a height appeared devoted to the remains of the dead. On getting over the fence surrounding them, a lawn having straight walks covered with gravel soil led up to the doors, where a screen of bark-cloth shut out the view of the interior. Conquering a feeling of delicacy, I entered one of the huts. I found a fixed bedstead of cane, curtained as if to shade its bed of grass from the musquito, spears, charms, sticks with strange crooks, tree-creepers, miniature idol-huts of grass, &c. These were laid in order in the interior; but no one was there, and we were told it was a mausoleum. These, or similar places less pretentious, might be seen on the bare hill-sides; the latter merely square enclosures or fences of tall reeds, which my Waganda orderlies called "Looaleh,"[5] or sacred ground. Occasionally one of their men, to amuse us, went through a strange unnatural antic. Placing both elbows at his sides, with the hands pointing upwards, like a position in the dumb-bell exercise, he commenced glimmering with his eyes, writhing the muscles of his shoulders and back, never drawing breath, and gradually sinking to the ground till he apparently lay dead, as if he had worked himself into a trance, or sleep of death.

Within a radius of thirty miles from the palace nothing is allowed to be plundered, as a number of government annuitants reside there. It was a great pleasure to get amongst them to see order once more. Sheep, goats, and cattle were safe grazing at the roadside—not one of my escort dared touch them. It must have been very trying to them, for provision was scarce, and could not be purchased. We passed some small lakes, and the residence of the present king when he was a youth—all was now a wilderness, but pointed

---

[1] Presumably Plates 6 and 7.

[2] Important evidence that river fish were an important part of the diet. Reid, *Political Power*, p. 67.

[3] Grant means the Swahili word *baraza* – a reception area or verandah etc.

[4] See Figure 73, p. 262, for Grant's depiction of some of these features.

[5] Perhaps Grant misheard this for *Lubaale*, a term used for various deities. On sacred places etc., see Roscoe, *The Baganda*, pp. 331ff.

to with as great reverence as we should regard a sacred or historical spot. When within one march of the capital, Mariboo refused to convey me nearer "till an order came, because all travellers remained there a fortnight and more—it was the custom of the country!" However, the detention was only for one day, and on the morning of the 26th of May a dashing party of Seedees came with their usual joyful demonstrations, bearing a letter and a fore-quarter of goat from my friend Speke! Cheering thought, to have him once more so near! We now heard a great deal of news. First, "there was no food, only boiled plantain, in Uganda, and this could only be had by risking their lives! My arrival would be celebrated by a great deal of bloodshed. Captain Speke was a favourite with the king, because he was not, like the Arabs, particular about having the cattle or goats killed according to Mohammedan rites." This last bit of news led me to ask Frij whether all Mohammedans ate fish. His reply was, "They do not eat every fish—only those that have the finger and thumb mark of God making them lawful." They continued: "Baraka, who had been sent to the north with letters for the boats from Egypt, had been seen in Unyoro all safe, but its king would not allow him to come to join us *viâ* Uganda. The ships were still at Ugani.[1] The Nile went to Misr (Egypt). The men and women killed daily by a blow on the back of the head are cut in pieces by knives made from the common reed; the pieces are then put into a cloth, and thrown to the birds; Masoongo,[2] the head executioner, reserving for himself all their hearts! Speke had saved the lives of four or five people. If a man is seen being led away with his hands tied in front, he is marked for execution—if they are tied behind, he is under sentence of a fine."[3]

We shall by-and-by see whether this gossip, brought me by the Seedees, had any truth in it. And it may not be uninteresting to mention here, that at a private audience given me by his Holiness the Pope in 1864,[4] when I submitted to him a map of our route, explaining the general configuration of the country upon the equator, he remarked with animation, that my description tallied with what he had observed in the country of the Amazon, where he had passed many years of his life as a missionary,—a fact I had not known before. The Amazon is in the same parallel of latitude as Uganda.

---

[1] For the reason for Baraka's mission and the general problem of Petherick's supposed presence, see Bridges, 'Negotiating a Way', pp. 110–11, 123–4.

[2] Usungu was one of the executioners at Mutesa's court. Ibid., p. 129.

[3] These reports Grant has copied almost verbatim from his journal for the stated day.

[4] Pius IX who was Pope 1846–78.

CHAPTER X

[Pages 219–35]

Buganda [27 May–7 July 1862]

Extract from Journal: Arrival at the Capital of Buganda, 27 May 1862
27 to H[ea]d Q[uarter]s of Uganda 12 miles from 8 till 3 p m 8 streams. I walked round the head of the 9th. The 4th ran to the left so also did the "Mogga Nyanja" a 500 yard body of clear water waist deep & in places up to our armpits with reeds arching overhead ... The others were not above the knee & all had clear sides ... On the way to my left on a height came tall thatched houses some the residence of the royal family ... S[peke]'s men hearing my coming came to meet me. S had gone to the Palace. I found his camp within half a mile of it, a hut enclosed with reed fence & the Wangw[ana]'s huts in line inside. Made myself at home till he came but neither <u>pombe</u> nor <u>plantains</u> were to be had, none even for nearly a month. Thought this so shabby of the King. S heard two guns fired by his men to announce my arrival & came looking pale and ill, once he said very thin, wanting good living to eat one up. A goat was [sent?] & I dined in company & felt thankful to God for having again united us. King sends pages to say the Mzungu must visit him tomorrow. I say a rest must be had first, no, I must go. The morning would settle it & if I went I must be carried and have a chair to sit upon. 28th Halt. Pages arrive saying King must see me today and I can bring my chair ... [NLS, MS. 17915, 27–28 May 1862]

THE day of my arrival at the Uganda capital, the 27th of May 1862, was one not only of intense joy, but deep thankfulness. I felt that my prayers for our safety had been heard. Speke and I had been separated for upwards of four months, and on being led by some of his men to the small hut he occupied, we were so happy to be together again, and had so much to say,[1] that when the pages[2] of the king burst in with the royal mandate that his Highness must see me "to-morrow," we were indignant at the intrusion.[3] The morrow,

---

[1] By this time, Speke's affair with the young woman, Meri, which Jeal, *Explorers*, pp. 157–62, describes in detail, was over. Whether Grant, who must have been familiar from his Indian Army experience with such liaisons, learned of the affair and if so, what his attitude may have been, does not emerge from his book or journal. See Introduction, p. 50, and also Kennedy, *Last Blank Spaces*, pp. 195–8.

[2] The subject of the 'pages' in Buganda is an important one. They were young boys and men sent by clans or prominent chiefs to gain favours from the kabaka by serving him in a notable fashion. They might hope to become the elite officials of the next generation.

[3] As may be noted above, Grant's immediate description of his arrival does not mention the long talk nor any indignation at the interruption and it is reasonable to assume that this is a later recollection. The proof copy of his book shows that Grant had first written 'we were very sorry for the intrusion'. NLS, MS. 17934, p. 219. Speke

however, came, and with it the same sharp, intelligent boys, to say that my stool might be brought to sit upon in the presence of the king. Accordingly, the present of a gun and some ammunition having been graciously received by him, at three o'clock, dressed in my best suit—*i. e.,* white trousers, blue flannel coat, shepherd's-plaid shirt, a helmet, and a red turban—I sallied forth with Speke and some Seedees to make the call. It may be mentioned, as a curious custom of the court at Uganda, that when I told Speke that I meant to wear knickerbockers[1] at the levee, he warned me that I should not be considered "dressed" if any portion of my bare leg was left exposed. This costume, because my stockings were not long enough, had therefore to be abandoned for white trousers. In proceeding to the palace we had to make one short descent, cross a bog, with grass thrown over it to keep the feet from being soiled, and rise on a broad road to the top of a hill, on which several hundred houses were built, each surrounded with a screen of tall reeds.[2] The outer gate, having iron bells behind it, was slid aside, and we entered under a cord strung with charms. Here was a wide oblong space, screened all round; one steep-roofed house, beautifully thatched, was the only dwelling visible.[3] Inside its wide threshold sat a single figure; and on the open space in front a mob of bare-headed, well-dressed Africans sat, forming a crescent, and facing "His Majesty M'tessa." Our approach was abruptly stopped, and we were directed to halt. Some minutes elapsed, the court broke up, and the mass of people ran quickly through a wicket that had been opened. We followed, but the doorkeeper closed the gate, and ten minutes elapsed ere we were admitted. We next entered a similar place, but smaller, and stood in the sun, uncomfortable enough, till permitted to be seated on our stools, with our hats off and umbrellas up. M'tessa sat upon a bench of grass, with a dog behind him.[4] His kamaraviona (commander-in-chief)[5] was the only man allowed to sit at his feet; a sister and several women were on his left, also seated on the ground under the shade of the lofty cane-and-grass building. His quick eye detected that part of my hand had been cut off. "How did this happen?" He no doubt fancied that some offence had been committed by me, as it was the custom of his court to maim people by cutting off fingers, feet, or ears for even slight offences. He spoke in whispers to his pages, when Mariboo, the officer who had charge of me from Karague,

---

wrote: 'How we enjoyed ourselves after so much anxiety and want of another's company need not be described ... I was only too rejoiced to see Grant could limp a bit and was able to laugh over his picturesque and amusing account ... of his own rough travels.' *Journal*, p. 421.

[1] 'Short loose-fitting trousers gathered in at the knee or calf.' *OED*.

[2] See Plate 29. Plans showing the layout of the whole capital with each chief's or official's residence designated and, separately, the *Lubiri* or royal enclosure, were later drawn by Sir Apolo Kaggwa. See Roscoe, *The Baganda*, pp. 523–5 and plans, and also Hanson, *Landed Obligation*, pp. 70–71, who has a somewhat modified version of the Kaggwa plan.

[3] Grant much admired this reception house and similar buildings and carefully depicted it in Plate 33.

[4] Grant did not himself attempt to depict this assembly but it appears in Speke's *Journal*, p. 421, as shown in Figure 108, p. 385; the engraver, Zwecker, has used Grant's picture of the reception house and figures from other sketches to produce a composite illustration. This picture, frequently reproduced, is thus not a direct representation of what Grant experienced; it appears to be based on Plates 33 and 34 and Figure 77, p. 265.

[5] A more accurate term might be 'Chief Minister'. 'Kamaraviona' was the title which Speke and Grant used; the word is actually *kamalabyonna* – 'one who finishes all things'. As Kiwanuka, *History of Buganda*, p. 140, explains, it was a nickname denoting military prowess given to chief minister Kayira by the kabaka Suna but the real title of the office was *katikkiro*. See Reid, *Political Power*, p. 208. His real power came from controlling access to the king. There is considerable doubt as to whether Kayira still held the office of *katikkiro* during the visit of Speke and Grant. Bridges, 'Negotiating a Way', p. 128.

informed him that I had received the wound in my hand in action; he also told him of the difficulties he had in bringing me to his majesty. The people listened with the most perfect decorum, only once interrupted by a sudden arrest. Maulah, the chief "detective," observing some breach of etiquette—probably a man speaking above his breath—suddenly seized the offender, and dragged him away. The look of anguish of the miserable creature thus apprehended was most painful. No one ventured to show sympathy; and Maulah soon returned alone, looking pleased and satisfied.

Conversation is never interrupted by these scenes; music from drums and other instruments drown any noise made by a poor prisoner, or it is continued to please the ears of those attending the levee. The mode of testifying allegiance was curious; the mob suddenly stood up *en masse,* with their long sticks balanced in the air, and charged towards the threshold several times, with shouts of praise for their king, who made no acknowledgment.[1] The court broke up, after an hour, by the king walking away on tiptoe, with the most ludicrous swagger, through a screen leading into another enclosure.[2] The doors were opened and shut by men, who watched every movement of the king, for fear they should be discovered off the alert, and punished according to his caprice. A short time afterwards, a third scene was prepared for us. On entering the courtyard, M'tessa leant in a studied, affected attitude against the portico; about two hundred women sat on the ground on one side, and we were told to bring our chairs to within twenty yards of him, facing the women. No men except our Seedee interpreters were present. The remarks of the great potentate, who regarded us with a kindly surprised air, were confined to his favourite women, and seemed to be concerning our appearance. After a time, the thought seemed to strike him that we all ought to remove to some more shaded place. This was the only sensible thing he had done. Making us draw our stools close to the iron chair on which he sat, the conversation turned upon sport, our expedition, &c. A woman ran to fetch the gun he had that day been presented with; two others held spears beautifully polished. He signalled that I was to show my head uncovered to the ladies; a titter followed, and all of us laughed heartily. Another signal, and I was told to place my hat on; this made us all feel less restraint; and the women were not afraid to return our smiles at the ridiculous formality of the scene. As the sun was approaching the horizon, this "drawing-room" was ended by M'tessa walking away, leaving us to reflect on the strange events of the day. He was a tall, well-built young fellow, sprightly in manner, very vain, his woolly hair dressed with the greatest care; small head, remarkably prominent clever-looking clear eyes, good teeth, and long nails to his hands and feet; the instep of the latter was, as in most of the Waganda, highly arched, indicating a well-moulded sinewy leg. His barkcloth "toga" had not a speck upon it, and was neatly knotted over the right shoulder,[3] concealing his whole body. His ornaments of beads were made with great taste in the choice of colours; the most minute beads of white, blue, and brown were made into rings and rosettes, which he wore round his neck and arms. Each finger had upon it a ring of brass; on the third finger of the left hand he wore a gold ring, given him by Speke; with

[1] See Plate 24.

[2] See Plate 26. What the engraver made of this and Grant's description appeared in Speke, *Journal,* p. 292, and is shown in this edition as Figure 109, p. 386.

[3] Plate 26 shows the 'toga' knotted on the kabaka's left shoulder; for the necklaces and beads etc., see Plate 37 which does have the 'toga' gathered on the right side of the figure.

these he played while sitting at his levees, occasionally receiving a golden-coloured gourdcup of wine from a maid of honour sitting by his side; after each sip, a napkin of bark-cloth was used by him to wipe his mouth. The only unseemly vulgarity he was guilty of while on his throne was to use his napkin to rub away the perspiration from his person. On leaving the court, and getting outside the last gate of the palace, a woman's screams made us look back; a cord was tied round her wrist, and a man dragged her, almost naked, down the hill to be executed; she screamed "N'yawoh! n'yawoh!" (Mother! mother!) in the most bitter anguish.[1] A second, similarly tied, followed slowly, but not uttering a sound. A shudder of horror crept over me. Had we been the cause of this calamity? and could the young prince with whom we had conversed so pleasantly have had the heart to order the poor women to be put to death?

The road to our hut was crowded by files of men dressed as "Neptunes," in tattered leaves of plantain, their limbs coloured with ashes and vermilion, and girdles of long-haired goatskin (from Usoga)[2] hanging from their backs and waists. Daily these wild-looking creatures shouted and rushed with all their might along the roads, spears and shields being held high in the air; they were M'tessa's men preparing and drilling for a slave-hunting campaign.[3] The day after my first visit to the king, he came to return the call without giving us any warning. We heard a noisy crowd passing outside our enclosure, and immediately, through the fence, came the young king in a tremendous hurry. He was not the puppet of yesterday, but dressed, like a negro sailor, in an open coat of bed-curtain chintz, loose white trousers or "pyjamas," having a broad stripe of scarlet; his feet and head were naked. He was shown into an iron chair, and seeing some books he turned over their pages as a monkey would; asked to see the picture of Rumanika,[4] and said he would like to know when his own portrait was to be done. His brothers, a mob of little ragamuffins, several in handcuffs, sat behind him chattering very familiarly, and tearing all the while at sugar-cane. I was told to show them my hair by taking off my hat. We were asked if we did not admire the leather wideawake[5] made by one of the brothers?—and the vulture, the dove, and the horn-bill his highness had just shot? This scene over, the king rose, ordered Speke to follow him, and, led by the mob of brothers, all rushed madly away. On following them, the chained lads, escorted by two servants, were very much in the rear, and hobbled along, poor little fellows, in perfect good-humour, looking as strong, healthy, and contented as any of the others. It was said that the king, before coming to the throne, always went about in irons, as his small brothers now do. Where could they have got this custom?[6] Wishing to know what had become of Speke, I went in search of him, and found on the way a *flight* of pages—there is no other name for it, as they always go at

---

[1] Grant illustrated this directly in Plate 25.

[2] Busoga was in effect, a tributary state of Buganda. Kiwanuka, *History of Buganda*, pp. 140–43.

[3] Buganda was in a state of almost constant warfare in the form of predatory expeditions into neighbouring territories. Reid, *Political Power,* pp. 179–81, 198–9.

[4] Presumably the sketch in Figure 52, p. 205.

[5] Normally a hat with a wide brim, low crown and made of felt with no nap – hence the punning title. *OED*.

[6] Grant's report here is regarded as important evidence that, when Mutesa came to the throne, all the other princes (his brothers and half-brothers) had not been killed as had been the previous practice at least on some occasions. Wrigley, *Kingship and State*, p. 227. Hanson explains the problems caused by the presence of princes and the reasons for the increasing use of 'coercive violence' by Mutesa and goes on to point out that, ultimately, 11 princes were starved to death by his mother, thus leaving only two alive. Hanson, *Landed Obligation*, pp. 85, 110.

full speed, their robes flying, when serving the king. They were going with torches to light his highness home; but they knew not what route he had taken. It afterwards appeared that he had entered a house to dine upon boiled beef and wine, a share of which he offered to Speke; then, taking a suit of clothes out of the tin box he had got from us, and which was carried to this picnic, he cast aside his torn and dirty suit for another, and went home by torchlight and drums.

Extract from 'Summary of Observations' on Mutesa

M'tessa is one of forty sons besides many daughters born to the late King Soona, of Uganda, by many wives. His family are said to be a branch of that from Unyoro, and they extend as princes and nomads as far as Kazeh. He is the ninth king,[1] and the names of all the previous kings are known from the fact that their tombs are protected and preserved by the Crown to the present day. In these tombs the lower jaw-bone and the bones of the thighs are deposited. At each new moon the present king has the bones of his father conveyed to him, and a ceremony, lasting two or three days, is gone through on the occasion.

He is not the eldest son, but was selected by the people, or by his court, for his noble bearing, and as a likely successor to his father ... He has a remarkably quick perception often showing kindness and mercy to those he rules over, but the existing law of his country obliges him to assume the fierceness of the lion when he has to execute or punish criminals, events of frequent occurrence, and often for very trivial offences. We daily observed three or four men or women being led away to be killed[2] ... [Grant, 'Summary of Observations', 1872, p. 272]

My introduction to the king's mother took place on the 1st of June. Captain Speke and myself went with five or six Seedees carrying pads of grass (stools not being permitted), with our gourds of pombé, our sucking-reeds, and umbrellas. The dowager lady had been informed of our intention, but took her time as to seeing us. Walking over one hill to the top of another, in three-quarters of an hour we were at her royal highness's gate. On getting as far as the second courtyard, we were told to wait, with the other visitors, in the drum or ante-house. Here for an hour we were left to smoke, drink, and doze. A musical instrument in the place was new to me—a harmonicon of twelve blocks of wood, which, on being struck, gave out notes as glasses do when played. They rested upon the trunks of plantain, and were isolated from each other by thin reeds. We took our hats off on approaching the old lady, who laughed most heartily, and welcomed us with great cordiality, telling us to sit in front of and near her.[3] She seemed to me like a Tartar woman, being fair-skinned, stout, and short. Her head was shaved, and had a cord tied round it. Conversation was kept up briskly for an hour or so, during which she fondled in her lap a plaything the size and shape of a hedgehog, studded with cowries and beads. She sipped

---

[1] This is essentially Speke's information, *Journal*, p. 252, which, clearly, Grant had no reason to doubt on the basis of his own knowledge. Wrigley regards it as important evidence which may be nearer the truth than the later king lists numbering up to 30 kabakas posited by Kagwa, *Customs of the Baganda*, pp. 18–67, and accepted by Kiwanuka, *History of Buganda*, pp. 93–110, 280, 285. The earlier kings and their shrines may have been mythical but essential validations of kingship. Wrigley, *Kingship and State*, pp. 20–34 and *passim*.

[2] Grant's ambivalent attitude to Mutesa is evident. Although deploring the cruelties of Buganda and its ruler, he was by 1872 hoping that Mutesa could be an agent of Christian modernization.

[3] See Plate 34.

at wine, looked at herself in a small mirror, smoked, and, like any housewife at home, gave orders to her domestics. Quantities of plantain neatly tied up and arranged in line, several basketfuls of boiled beef also tied round with leaves, were laid out as a present for Mariboo and myself. Each basket of beef was tasted by one of her officers tearing a bit away with his teeth, and we took our leave, very much pleased with her good-humour and homeliness.

Extract from Journal: Seeking Favours from the Queen Mother

told her I had no presents to give because all belonged to S[peke]; that we were most thankful for her presents as our men had received no food for nearly 20 days except a few plantains, finally that we wished to have the road to Ugani[1] opened. She replied very promptly she would like a present from the small sahib however bad it might be, that our men might come every day for food & she would speak to her son over the Ugani question but the water route there was rather impracticable; however it might be opened while Grant went to Karag[ue] for the remaining traps. This was right [?] trying me by the leg & again separating us: it made my heart sink. [NLS, MS. 17915, 1 June 1862.]

Many other calls were made upon her by invitation; but although we sat waiting the dowager for hours amongst steaming natives, she did not always give us an interview, saying she was too busy or too tired.[2] Her brother, Katoonzee,[3] an officer of high rank, and with a most *distingué* Uganda air, pointing his toes and showing off his high instep as he walked, was treated with as much ceremony as ourselves, generally being obliged to sit so far distant from her that he had to bawl out to make himself heard. However, the dowager would allow him to whisper jokes into her ear, and be familiar enough when few were present. Any wine intended for us her majesty always tasted before it was presented. This was a condescension on her part not shown to every one.

The people of Uganda require to have the permission of an officer before the barber can use his razor. The women seen about the queen's residence had no hair, neither had she; all were shaved, and only a few in M'tessa's court were allowed to dress their hair in the same aristocratic fashion as the king. One of these women, in the bloom of youth, we one day saw led to execution. She was the fourth female victim that had passed that day. Her back was covered with scars, and blood appeared on her neck. She wept bitterly. Notwithstanding this circumstance, when we went and had an interview with the king, we found him as gay and cheerful as ever. His detective Maulah lived next hut to ours, and the shrieks of poor people, night and day, were quite heartrending. Not only were their cries heard, but each lash of the stick was distinct; and being in such close proximity to the place of torture was a severe trial. When Maulah captures women, they are asked, "Will

---

[1] This is really a reference to the area occupied by the Acoli (Acholi) people who live in what is now North Central Uganda and includes a section known as the Gan. See Murdock, *Africa*, p. 329. Girling, *The Acholi*, *passim*. Nomenclature among the Nilotes peoples is extremely confused. Middleton, *Encyclopedia of Africa*, IV, p. 308.

[2] Nevertheless, the visitors, whether they realized it or not, were right to gain the help of this alternative locus of power in Buganda. Bridges, 'Negotiating a Way', pp. 128–9; Hanson, *Landed Obligation*, pp. 49–50, explains the position of the Queen Mother.

[3] That is, the office *kitunzi* which was, indeed, a high rank and included chiefship of the *ssaza* or 'county' of Gomba. Roscoe, *The Baganda*, p. 233. His actual name was Nakamali. Kagwa, *Customs of the Baganda*, p. 52.

you live with so and so?" if they object, the rod is applied, and consent in this way is forced upon them. He and other chief officers were very jealous of Speke's influence with the king, for they knew he could at times obtain an interview, while they had to wait for days.[1] On seeing us return from the palace, Maulah would inquire, "Have you seen the king?" and when we wished for an interview, and asked how it could be brought about, he would coarsely reply, "Are you kings, that you always expect to be received?" Certainly our influence had a most beneficial effect. Not only did Speke save the lives of many, but men about court got him to intercede with the king on several occasions. The executioner Konzah had a favourite son, who was under sentence. The boy, through Speke's intercession, was pardoned, and it was thought he would never again be punished; but on Bombay asking this high functionary "how the son was; had anything more been said of it?" the father replied, "My boy was killed yesterday for another offence." A child-page whom we took an interest in, and whom Speke had dressed up very gaily, named Loogohie (or cloth), got into a dreadful scrape one day for coughing while the king was at dinner. It was thought his little ears would have been cut off, and he laughed very much when he found he had escaped, but he did not expect to live long, as he was always getting into hot water. On my asking what the king had killed when out shooting, Loogohie's reply was that, "As his highness could not get any game to shoot at, he shot down many people."[2]

The king had become so fond of the gun,[3] that, like a young sportsman, he seemed to dream of it. In the early morning his gun or the rattle of the diminutive drums which always accompanied his movements was heard. Interviews were difficult; his whole time was occupied. He had received so many presents from us, he had made so many promises to open the road, and his pages had stolen for him so much of our ammunition, that he at last was ashamed of himself, and suddenly permitted us to leave.[4] For several days neither of us could visit him, being unwell, but Bombay, by showing some pictures to his servants, conveyed such accounts of us that communication was sometimes obtained. In a book he had received from Rumanika, 'Kaffir Laws,' his highness wished all the birds he had shot to be painted in imitation of our sketch-books. His pages pestered us, and became bold and insolent, walking into our hut, taking up anything they saw to examine it, or coming with the king's orders that our very beds, chairs, guns, shoes, &c., were wanted by the king, and saying there must be no delay about sending them. The union-jack which we had got from Admiral Keppel was also demanded. All these indignities, added to the brutal treatment of the women, made us feel that Uganda was not the "garden of pleasure" we had heard it called,[5] and that the conduct of the king was a worse form of plundering than we had experienced in the Ugogo and southern territories. Here,

[1] Some had wished to have Speke killed. Welbourn, 'Speke and Stanley', p. 221. Access to the kabaka was undoubtedly the key to influence or importance in Buganda.

[2] The kabaka's power rested on a brutal tyranny which seems to have been accepted by his subjects.

[3] Guns with percussion caps were subsequently known as *Makoowa Speke* and Mutesa formed a corps of musketeers. Bridges, 'Negotiating a Way', p. 130 and references there.

[4] Mutesa's precise reasons for this concession are difficult to discern. Possibly increasing hostility towards the travellers from some of his chiefs, prompted by jealousy, made it politically necessary. Perhaps, too, Mutesa had real desire for more European contacts as Speke and Grant promised for the future. Unfortunately, Grant's journal for the early July period when permission came is even more difficult to read than normal, possibly because he was suffering from some sort of eye complaint.

[5] Before he died, Speke tried to arrange for 'civilizing' initiatives to be organized and it is significant that he saw Bunyoro as a better starting point than Buganda.

by robbing us of our ammunition, they had placed us in a defenceless position; and though we did not want their offered hundreds of women and hundreds of cattle, it induced our Seedees to become mutinous, saying, "Although *you* don't take them, we will, for as yet we have received nothing but broken bones for the 2000 dollars' worth of property given to M'tessa." They refused to march with us until they obtained sufficient ball-cartridge. This occurred just previous to our departure, up to which time our men had been gathering a precarious existence from what could be plundered from the gardens.

No beads were allowed to be taken here by the natives, although privately they would always purchase sufficient provision for ourselves and men.[1] Cowries were a more current coin, one hundred of these shells making one string = a bunch of a hundred plantain = the skin of a goat; and a single large gourdful of wine cost a sheet of bark-cloth. We fortunately received goats now and then from the king, and sweet potatoes from one of the gardeners in exchange for beads. There was no flour nor milk used in the country, the natives living entirely upon plantain boiled, or made into wine, which they called "m'wenge." There was very little drunkenness visible. Cattle were rarely seen: the hills all round were such a mass of tall reeds and grasses that they could not penetrate them; even a dog would have had difficulty in hunting through these thickets. Pleasant walks were cut through them, and kept from being grown over by the constant transit of slave parties. Katoonzee returned from one of these during my stay at Uganda. He had captured 130 women, chiefly old, and only fit for weeding the fields. Some few, fitted for wives, stood apart, to be given away to men thought deserving, or whose services were to be rewarded. Each woman of this class was worth three cows. An instance occurred of the king having given a single slave to one of his officers for some service performed, and the man being bold enough to ask for another, was cut to pieces with the usual reed knife. His limbs were carried away openly, while the trunk was wrapped in a cloth. There were several executioners, men of rank, who were the privy councillors of the king. These men had numbers of followers, distinguished by wearing their mark of office—a short turban of cord—and sometimes carrying a peculiarly-shaped bludgeon. Konzah has been mentioned; another, named Oozoongoo, was always carried to court in a litter, being an invalid. On meeting him, he would stop to speak, and in expression had nothing repulsive; but when seen with a wreath of black fringe encircling his head, hiding his eyes, and hanging down to near his mouth, his appearance was completely changed, and he reminded one of a black Highland bull looking fiercely through his forelock. Both these executioners were really polite men, always frank when met at the palace—much more so than the kamaraviona (commander-in-chief), who was a proud, haughty young fellow. One day I had the curiosity to follow a poor woman who was led by a boy to be killed. She carried a small hoe, balanced upon her head. No one told me she was under sentence, but the cord on the wrist was sufficient; and after travelling for half a mile, I followed her down to the executioner's gardens. Waiting outside for some time, not a sound was heard, nor a person seen. A lazy, yellow-beaked vulture, the cannibal of Uganda, sat perched on the stump of a broken tree; others hovered high overhead, looking on the scene below. This circumstantial evidence was enough for me, and I returned.

[1] Reid, *Political Power,* p. 158, sees this as important evidence that the royal control of trade by the people was not always complete.

One of the sights at the capital of Uganda was to watch the crowds of men on the highroad leading to the palace; all were under officers,[1] perhaps a hundred in one party. If wood is carried into the palace up the hill, it must be done as neatly as a regiment performs a manoeuvre on parade, and with the same precision. After the logs are carried a certain distance, the men charge up hill, with walking-sticks at the "slope," to the sound of the drum, shouting and chorussing. On reaching their officer, they drop on their knees to salute, by saying repeatedly in one voice the word "n'yans" (thanks). Then they go back, charging down hill, stooping simultaneously to pick up the wood, till, step by step—it taking several hours—the neatly-cut logs are regularly stacked in the palace yards. Each officer of a district would seem to have a different mode of drill. The Wazeewah, with long sticks, were remarkably well disciplined, shouting and marching all in regular time, every club going through the same movement, the most attractive part of the drill being when all crouched simultaneously, and then advanced in open ranks, swinging their bodies to the roll of their drums.[2]

At every new moon M'tessa went through an examination of his idol horns; but I should not suppose him to be much of an augur: he was too light-headed and fond of field-sports, of boating, swimming, and music, to give much attention to making rain, &c. He left all these things to the Witchwezee[3] race who were about him, and seldom denied himself to visitors at the time of new moon. On the very day that four of his women were going to execution, at an audience given to ourselves and in our presence, some maidens were offered for his harem.[4] He had detained us in an outer court for a long time, and probably brought us in to enjoy our surprise at the poor naked offerings. Each held by the upper corners an open napkin in front of her, and all were smeared with grease and decorated with girdles and necklaces of beads. After being reviewed without a smile, they were told to face to the right, and march to the "zenana."[5] As was customary, the king then sat on the knees of the matron-like woman who had presented the maidens, and, having ordered all away but ourselves, the interpreters, and some young lads, a conversation began about men and women in general.[6] It is, however, worthy of remark, that M'tessa never behaved indecently by word or deed while women were present; his language was uniformly correct. On his complaining of sickness, medicine was brought him by a page, one of our men having first to taste it. In all probability the page was made

[1] That is, *batongole.* Grant's definition of them as 'officers' is probably as good as any; there is no suitable equivalent term to indicate their status, below that of the *bakungu* or 'county' chiefs yet powerful because directly exercising the power of the king. Reid, *Political Power*, pp. 103–4, adds that Grant's evidence shows that there was, in effect, a militaristic organization of state labour. Hanson, *Landed Obligation*, p. 66, also quotes this passage as evidence of the 'strategic exchange of goods and services'. Incidentally, neither of the quoted scholars is aware of the illustration in Plate 24.

[2] See Plate 24.

[3] It is interesting and significant that Grant reports the *bachwezi* as if present in the kingdom as they were the supposed ancestral rulers in the interlacustrine region now known only in spirit form. Probably Grant was really referring to the mediums at shrines who kept the cult alive. Mutesa's attitude, I suggest, was not his 'light headedness' but part of his campaign to overcome the influence of the traditional priests in Buganda. Bridges, 'Negotiating a Way', p. 127.

[4] This was a normal procedure: clans offered him women hoping that one might become the mother of a new kabaka and so gain favours for that clan.

[5] Once again, Grant uses an Anglo-Indian term meaning the secluded area of a house for the women: *Hobson-Jobson.*

[6] Mutesa hoped for a cure for venereal disease.

to swallow the pill instead of the king! He and all his people were less suspicious of us than of any traders; our presents were received without the usual form of preparation; whereas, when Dr Kiengo, the native of Unyamuezi, gave his offering of five giraffe tails, a mould of Kittara copper, &c., all were dipped into plantain wine or "m'wengé," which had to be drunk by the Doctor to show there was no impurity connected with the presents. A pill, having great virtues, was licked all over for the same reason by Kiengo.

The ingenuity of the Waganda in imitating our chairs, mode of walking, dress, gun-covers, &c., was very striking. Having seen so many of our pictures, they at last took to drawing figures of men in black upon their bark-cloths.[1]

Extract from Journal: First Attempts to Draw Pictures
Last night, (8½) a kanga & crested crane shot by king were brought to have entered in his Kaffir Law Book! [sic] given him by Rumanika.[2] They already have attempted pictures of men in black on their loongas.[3] [NLS, MS. 17915, 1 June 1862]

At light work they are highly ingenious. Their spears, knives, drums, shields, ornaments, houses, &c., are made with great taste and exactness.[4] Their barkcloths are cut from several varieties of ficus, beaten upon a log with a mill-headed wooden hammer, and sewn beautifully together into large shawls, ranging in uniform tint from salmon-colour or maize to a brick red. These are very becoming on an African skin, and when worn by our Seedees as a turban, the harmony of colour was pleasing. Our men in Uganda could not be distinguished at a distance from the natives; for their Zanzibar clothes being worn out, they dressed like them in bark-cloths, or the skins of cattle and antelope prepared by leaving on the hair. The skins of small antelope, made white and soft as kid, are put together so well that the sewing with banana or aloe fibre is scarcely observed. They have not attained the art of the brazier.[5] The habits of the people are so simple, that the fresh green leaf of the banana serves them as a plate. Wine they drink out of a corner of their cow-skin coverings; shoes, hats, and gloves they have not yet obtained; and a strip from a reed is their knife, as we have often seen when the palace guards were at their excellent meal of good boiled beef, mashed plantain, and wine. Their dinner was a strange good-humoured scramble, the strongest keeping meat from the weakest by snatching it away or tossing it about. They are excellent cooks, cutting butcher-meat up into very neat joints, wrapping them with fresh plantain leaves, and boiling all in a large earthen pot full of plantain, to which, by this process, a rich flavour is added.[6] Our Seedees missed many a good dinner by not partaking of this fare, on account of their profession as Mussulmans. They could not eat plantain that had been boiled with unlawful meat.

Lightning was said to be very much dreaded at Uganda, but no cases of death occurred from it during our stay. One of the king's houses was burnt down, the accident causing a

[1] This is surely a key observation; Grant and Speke had not only introduced the idea of two-dimensional visual representations to many East Africans but had now inspired the first desires to draw.
[2] This is the work referred to above and in Chapter VIII which, no doubt finding it useless in East Africa, Speke, *Journal*, p. 233, reports he had given to Rumanyika. Grant's evidence shows that the latter had felt bound to pass this unusual treasure on to Mutesa.
[3] The Anglo-Indian term is *loonghee*, a web of cloth wrapped round the body: *Hobson-Jobson*
[4] See Plate 37.
[5] That is, welding metal together.
[6] See Plate 35.

great commotion, because on the occurrence of such a calamity it is every one's duty to render aid. We did not call that day (the 30th June),[1] because an interview would have been impossible. The storm had commenced by rain at 1 P.M.; during a lull we had thunder, lightning, and hail; by 5 P.M. all had cleared away, and .82 inch of rain had fallen. During June, misty showers fell almost every day, but not enough to measure in a rain-gauge. The valleys were veiled every morning by a dense fog, and very often we had no sun the whole day. The heaviest shower noted was in the following month of July (4th), when 1.04 inches were measured.

Extract from Journal: Preparing to Leave Buganda and the Kabaka
In palace by 7 a boy having been sent to see our arrangements, had hardly [finished?] the king asked us into a private interview. We had seen three women tied round their waists being led to execution all looking [miserable?] enough. He gave us full permission to leave today, not at first replying to our request but afterwards brought it about himself ... while saying "goodbye" he returned by placing his hand in ours ... We had a pleasant parting and got away by 8 a.m. [NLS, MS. 17915, 7 July 1862]

[1] The journal for this day is largely indecipherable.

CHAPTER XI

[Pages 236–76]

From Buganda to Bunyoro and 'Captain Speke Proceeds to the Lake Nyanza'[1]
[7 July–9 September 1862]

Although the distance from Uganda to Unyoro by a direct route was reported not much above eighty miles, we were not confident of the fact.[2] The marches given by the natives can seldom be depended upon.[3] A M'ganda without a load will march the whole day, stopping at every hut where he can get anything to eat or drink. A laden Seedee thinks six miles, or even less, a day's work. How, therefore, could we anticipate that Unyoro was so near to us as eighty miles? The journey may be divided into three sections: the first, from Uganda to Karee, when Speke and I travelled together; the second, when Speke tried the water route and I the land; the third when we joined our forces and marched into Unyoro headquarters.[4]

I. Uganda To Karee,[5] Four Marches; Camps United.

The country at first was hilly. As we proceeded north, it gradually assumed the appearance of parks and grazing grounds, dotted with trees and clumps of bushes, favourable for stalking. Water was abundant in the sandy-bottomed streams and miry swamps. With this change of outline, we had no longer the gigantic reed of Uganda; it was replaced by a waving grass three feet high. The trees were small, the same as those species met with 5° south of the equator. Scarcely one-tenth part of the route was under cultivation. Plantain

---

[1] This quotes one of Grant's chapter sub-titles which, like much else of what follows, may appear to be a somewhat muted response to what was, after all, the crowning moment of the Nile Expedition.

[2] In fact, the distance from Kampala, the Buganda capital, to Masindi Port, near where Kamarasi, the *Omukama*, or monarch of Bunyoro was then based, is, as the crow flies, about 102 miles (164 km).

[3] The original phrase, before proof stage, read 'can never be depended upon unless you know your man thoroughly'. NLS, MS. 17934, p. 236.

[4] This first paragraph of the chapter is misleading. Although it states accurately what was to happen, it implies that the journey to Bunyoro was planned in this way. In fact, as becomes clear later, the original intention was that the two men would remain together, both visit the actual source of the Nile and then proceed to Bunyoro. See Speke, *Journal*, pp. 453, 458. The entries in Grant's own manuscript Journal confirm this and in his 1872 account, Grant writes, 'After receiving permission to leave for the north from the king of Uganda, we determined to visit the outlet of the lake ...' 'Summary of Observations', p. 284.

[5] This point is difficult to identify precisely. Reid, *Political Power*, p. 43, says it is a cattle grazing area in Bulemezi *ssaza* (county) near its boundary with the northern tip of Kyaggwe. This would accord with Speke's narrative (*Journal*, p. 459) and with the map showing 'Early Travels' in the *Atlas of Uganda*, p. 73, which gives a position of approximately 0°51′N 32°45′E.

groves were more abundant than fields of sessamum and Indian corn; and in the houses we occupied, bundles of seeroko and jooggo[1] (a pulse and bean) were found. It was a disagreeable march in one respect; for as soon as our caravan halted at a grove, the cultivators fled, and when we entered their houses we found the fire burning, with earthen pots, grain, and vegetables, and their beds and bark-cloth bedding undisturbed. All the etceteras about their snug little domiciles lay at the mercy of our men. Knives, shields, shells, beads, skins, pipes, tobacco, &c., hung from the roof, or were stuck into the rafters; and, on our leaving, it was not a rare occurrence to find that our men had ruthlessly burnt some of the supports of the hut to make themselves a fire to cook their food. This they would do most wantonly, although they had the best of the country, paying nothing for the plundered goats and other property permitted to be taken by M'tessa. The dwellings were not different from those already described, but each had over its doorway a diamond-shaped charm of rush, hung horizontally, and generally stuck with feathers.

The cattle seen in the low grazing country were almost "prize" animals. They were made hornless when young—not by sawing off the horns of grownup animals, as still barbarously practised in Scotland, but by searing with a hot iron. They were most docile, handsome creatures. The general colour was grey, their faces and inside the ears black; they had little or no hump, and were larger in bulk than an Ayrshire cow.[2] The cowherds were the lanky Wahuma, called here Waheema, who might be seen tending herds of several hundreds at a time.[3] These people were never afraid to come out and look at our caravan, even when it passed their ring fences in a secluded tract of country several miles away from any cultivation. The Waganda, on the contrary, on meeting us, would fly off the road, leaving whatever they might be carrying to be plundered by our followers. This difference in the two races is accounted for by the Wahuma never being made slaves, although their women are very much prized for their beauty as wives. M'tessa had given orders that we and our escort were to receive sixty cattle and ten loads of butter. Half-a-dozen cattle were first brought as an offering. Those made over to our Waganda disappeared the first night, and as ours, having been tied up, were all safe, we were called magicians. When the number was completed, our share was marked by squaring their tails, so as to distinguish them from those taken by the Waganda. During the night they were placed within a fence made to surround the only door of a hut occupied by a M'nyamuezee, Manua, who constituted himself their guardian. On receiving an order to slaughter one, our table-knives were called into requisition because the common country knife had no guard to it, and was not considered lawful. The Seedees, though knowing nothing of the Mohammedan religion, the majority not being circumcised, were much more particular on those occasions, and offered more opinions than a "moulvie,"[4] or Mussulman priest, would. "The animal must lie facing a proper direction;" "a certain man must officiate," &c.

The tracks of elephants and buffalo were numerous, but none of the animals were seen; neither did we shoot any lions, but we heard them at night. It was not a roar, neither was

---

[1] The Swahili terms are *choroko*, signifying a small green pea and *njugu*, a kind of groundnut.

[2] These were shorthorn zebu-type cattle probably of the kind the Baganda called *nganda*. See Roscoe, *The Baganda*, p. 415.

[3] For a full discussion of the place of cattle in relation to the Baganda and the Wahima herders, see Reid, *Political Power*, pp. 40–55, 68.

[4] Another Anglo-Indian term meaning, strictly, a judge or doctor of law. *Hobson-Jobson.*

it the sound a lion makes in a menagerie; at the time I considered it to be no more alarming, even to a novice, than if one were to blow through a cow's horn. Two zebra were shot by Speke, and eaten by the Waganda escort, and the skins, being the property of royalty, were simply left in a hut, the proprietor of which was bound to have them conveyed to the palace. Pallah,[1] hartebeest, and other antelope were seen or shot, and might have been hunted on horseback at certain seasons. The n'jezza,[2] whose horns curved over the brow, was new to us. None of these animals were ever seen in herds; a dozen together would be considered a large number. As it was also a great cattle country, the natives tried to trap the lion by means of a number of logs raised high on end. When the animal came under them for the bait of a live goat, all the logs, guided by piles on either side, fell in a mass, crushing him, somewhat after the fashion of the triangle of sticks and stones adopted in the Himalayas to kill tigers, leopards, or bears. Never having seen the contrivance in this form, my curiosity was raised to enter; luckily some Seedees called out in time to tell me of my danger. Three of our cows were less fortunate; one was killed, becoming food for our Waganda escort, because the Seedees would not touch it, and two were dragged from under the logs much bruised. The natives were eager sportsmen, netting the smallest or largest antelope, which they ate or conveyed alive to their king. Nets were made of beautiful soft and strong fibre, from the aloe generally.

A most simple, ingenious foot-trap for wild buffalo we observed here for the first time. It was set generally at salt-licks, where these animals were known to scratch the ground, and consisted of two small circles of wood, placed immediately one over the other; between them a quantity of stout acacia thorns pointed to a common centre; all were lashed strongly together, and the trap, when completed, was several inches larger than a buffalo's foot. This was fitted over a hole made in the ground, and a noose (attached to a block of wood) laid over it, and concealed with earth. On the buffalo putting his foot upon it, the trap fastens, and the more he struggles the tighter the noose becomes.[3] The former king of Uganda was said to have kept a large menagerie of animals caught in this way.[4]

Birds were not numerous; the cannibal vulture of Uganda, now that we had left the capital, was a rare bird.[5] Guinea-fowl and florikan were the only gamebirds observed, the grass being too tall to discover partridge, &c. An owl of very handsome plumage, weighing six pounds, was shot.[6] A graceful bird on the wing—a new goatsucker—with a single feather of each wing twice his own length, and since named *Cosmetornis Spekii*,[7] skimmed amongst the plantain trees at night. These long feathers probably sweep up flies as they float behind him.

---

[1] The pallah is a large type of antelope, *Aepyceros meampus*.

[2] I have not been able to identify this animal. Dr Clifton suggests it might have been a gnu, i.e. a wildebeest.

[3] See Figure 87, p. 332.

[4] This presumably refers to Suna II who reigned from c. 1825 to 1852. Kagwa, *Customs of the Baganda*, p. 51 records him as extremely fond of hunting.

[5] For Grant's sketch showing the three vultures of Uganda, see Figure 71, p. 260. They are identified below, p. 252.

[6] Given its size, this may have been Verreaux's eagle owl, *Bubo lacteus*.

[7] This bird is illustrated from a specimen in Speke, *Journal*, p. 462. 'Goatsucker' is the former name for nightjars, falsely thought to suck goats. This species is the pennant-wing nightjar, still known by some authorities as *Cosmetornis* but *C. vexillarius* not *spekii*. An alternative name is *Semeiophorus vexillarius*.

Fish were not to be had on this route, although cruives[1] or basket-traps, the shape of an Egyptian water-jar, and made of flags or papyrus, were constantly found in the houses of the people. The way of placing them was as follows:—Two long parallel ditches, six feet apart, were cut in a swamp; here and there their waters were made to communicate. At these points the baskets were laid on their sides, and the fish driven into them, whence there was no escape.

While detained at Karee receiving a portion of the cattle ordered to be given us by the king, we had several exhibitions of the temper of the people. As was customary, we took possession of their houses, and dwelt in them for eight days. This so exasperated them, that, on our Seedees going to fetch water, or leaving camp, they were threatened; a spear was thrown, and one of our men, named Karee, was killed. No redress could be obtained till the king had been communicated with. His reply was, "Allow it to pass over for the present, and when the villagers have returned to their houses I will send a party to seize them all." The night previous to our leaving, two huts occupied by Seedees were set on fire—the natives throwing in a bunch of burning straw at the doorway. Egress through the flames was impossible; but, having secured their guns, they cut their way through the side of the hut, losing a bayonet and their bark-cloths. Precautions were taken against any further alarm; and, on leaving in the morning, after they had fired the hut, our Waganda escort took a delight in burning down all the houses they had occupied. The spear that had been thrown at our men was brought in as a trophy; its handle was 7 feet long, having a blade of 16 inches. This is the size of the common Waganda spear; and one wonders that they ever throw it, as you can always see it coming, and get out of its way. With guns unloaded, no ordinary Seedee would have a chance with a M'ganda, his movements through the tall grass are so rapid. Our men got to know this after the death of poor Karee, who had been the spokesman of the camp. He was a tailor by trade, and had made several suits, after English and Arab patterns, for the king, who never paid him his bill—namely, four cows. His body was buried by moonlight, in a grave dug with bayonets,—the men remarking that they never saw such a march as ours was, we did not even carry a hoe. The truth was, they had lost or thrown away all our pioneer implements. The men were very crestfallen on the night of this death, the younger Seedees being afraid to carry the body, and the older remarking, "Suffr maqueesha," "Oh, the march is now done for."[2]

The villagers had a dread of keeping anything left behind by our men. An old bit of calico was brought us by a woman, accompanied by two servant-girls carrying m'wenge and plantain for us. She sympathised in our loss of Karee, and, having accepted a present of beads, thanked us in the most gentle way by moving her hands and slowly repeating in a soft low tone the word "n'yans," thanks. Her attendants then fell upon their knees, and bashfully, with down-cast eyes, went through the same form of acknowledgment. Another instance of the honesty of the people may be mentioned. Manua, the cowherd, wished to return to the last camp for a cloth he had forgotten. On telling him that it would be brought to him, he hesitated, but the wild strains of a tambira[3] were heard

[1] A chiefly Scottish term for a fish-trap.

[2] More correctly, *Safari mkwisha*.

[3] Or *tamboura*. The local name was *nanga*. The instrument, a kind of lute, was illustrated by Grant; see Plate 32.

approaching the camp, and the rag was produced by the party, along with a gourd of wine for the Mazoongoo. In this case the instrument was played as a token of truce, to show that the arrivals were friendly. On the other hand, the natives often betrayed fear. If a few huts were passed by us while out shooting, first the children, then the women, and afterwards the men, armed, would fly from their houses, and conceal themselves in the plantain groves. This order was invariably observed—the children were the first care of the parents. Once, on calling to some men running away, a single man came up and sat by us; others became equally bold, and did so also, till a mob gathered round us, and the women returned to their several vocations in and out of the houses. To test their hospitality, I asked for as much tobacco as would fill my pipe. A handful was given me with the greatest readiness. It was like the coarsest-grained black tea in appearance and consistence; and, after obtaining information about the game to be procured in the country, we parted excellent friends—so much so that the day following they paid me a visit at my hut, and brought me some more tobacco, for which they received a present of beads.

Budja, the chief officer or M'koongoo,[1] whom the king had sent in charge to deliver us over to the king of Unyoro, was a very handsome, intelligent man, clean in his dress, and never sitting down unless a carpet of cowskin was laid for him by one of his attendant boys. Like all his race, he was impetuous; if sent for, he would come leisurely with the haughty airs of M'tessa, sit for a moment, pretend to listen to what was said, and before any business about the march could be negotiated, would rise abruptly, making some silly excuse, that the cattle must be looked after, &c., and then disappear. He travelled with three wives—tall, fair women—and about twenty young lads, who anticipated his every wish. One amongst them always looked after the ladies, whether on the march or in camp; another had both ears and fingers cut off for adultery. These men without ears had a very curious appearance—one old man in particular, his head looking like a barber's block, with black holes bored in it; not a fragment of the external ear was left. Whether the operation ultimately affected their hearing we could not ascertain, but apparently it did not; they had the sharp look of pug dogs. As Budja and party will accompany me into Unyoro while Speke goes to look at the exit of the Nile from the lake, his name will appear often in this chapter. He was a great authority on the road, being the mediator between the kings of Uganda and Unyoro.[2] On asking him what relation a certain man was to the queen-dowager of Uganda, he replied by placing his left hand on his own right shoulder, thereby signifying that they were full brother and sister. I had never before seen any race that adopted this mode of expression, and it would imply that they, like ourselves, think the right hand of more importance than the left. Budja, however, could use either hand equally well. On his arm he carried a reed-whistle three inches long, but it seemed to be more for ornament than use.

---

[1] The term *mkungu* can mean any important person in Buganda. It seems unlikely that Budja was one of the dozen or so *bataka*, that is, *ssaza* or county chiefs; indeed his name does not appear among those listed by Kagwa, *Customs of the Baganda*, pp. 56–7. More likely he was a *mutongoleh*, one of the chiefs directly responsible to the kabaka for particular tasks or missions.

[2] Relations were tense. Bunyoro was the relict of the once much more extensive 'Empire' of Bunyoro-Kitara but from 1750 or earlier had been in decline with Buganda having taken much of its territory. See Kiwanuka, *History of Buganda*, pp. 136–7. By this period, new factors had entered the situation since Bunyoro was now athwart the Nile route to the outside world.

In Uganda were both wind and stringed musical instruments, and the natives excelled in whatever they attempted. Night and day, in the palace precincts, the sound of drums was heard from the hill-sides.[1] Every officer who commanded fifty men was allowed a kettle-drum. These were neatly made of wood, and when carried were slung on the back by shoulder straps; the short drumsticks were stuck in loops outside, and a loose cover protected them from sun and rain. Each party of men had its regimental drumcall. Budja's was a certain number of taps in quick time, which we all soon got to distinguish from any other. But none sounded such a loud tenor "doogoo, doogoo, doogoo," as the king's small drums when he was out for the day. They were beaten so as to make the sounds swell from double piano to forte, and *vice versa*. At all levees bands of reed and bugle players attended, and also danced. The reeds, held like flageolets, were never without decorations of blue, white, and scarlet beads, with hair at their lower ends, and they sounded sweet and pleasing. Sometimes an enormous kettle-drum,[2] slung over a stout Waganda's neck and shoulder, was allowed to join the wind instruments. It was profusely decorated with shells, beads, brass bells, bouquets of long goat's hair, &c., and beaten by single taps, the drummer throwing back his head and body, and giving a deep long "Bah!" after each tap. The harmonicon has been mentioned, also the stringed "nanga" or tambira, their most elegant instrument, looking, while laid in the lap to be played, like a harp in miniature. The queen generally had a blind musician performing on the harp, and the king was most expert at all these instruments, sitting for hours playing or listening to others. There was not much singing among the Waganda, though a great deal of instrumental music. During the march they sang in a quivering voice, slurring the notes and words in an odd manner, only heard in Uganda. They could all whistle through their fingers, and snapped them curiously when wanting to speak with emphasis.

On parting with M'tessa, he gave rather indefinite orders to Budja, who was in charge of our march, to take us to the exit of the Nile from Victoria Nyanza, nearly east of his residence. This route was not adhered to by Budja, and for four days, in the most obstinate manner, he led us more north than east. Having got so far out of the line, it became a question whether it was really of importance to visit this point.[3] Speke did not see any great advantage in it, and many would have been of the same opinion, because we had seen the lake daily from above our quarters at Uganda, and knew, from all accounts, that after making a few more miles we should come upon an immense river, with which we were now running parallel.[4] However, in order to avoid any reproach or charge of indifference at home, we resolved—Budja being overruled—to see the river issue from the lake, and thus leave nothing undone. Speke asked me whether I was able

[1] Grant took a great interest in the musical instruments. See Figure 53, p. 205, and Plate 32.

[2] This is shown in Plate 32 as what Grant calls a 'kooleywala'. Grant's depiction of the drum took on a life of its own as illustrators in Britain used the image; see Bridges, 'Images of Exploration', pp. 72–4.

[3] That is, the point where the Nile flows out of the lake.

[4] Grant is somewhat disingenuous here. As noted at the beginning of this chapter, it is apparent that both men had wanted and intended to see the actual source of the Nile. Speke, *Journal*, p. 455 makes it very clear in his own case. He goes on to explain on p. 458 that, 'as it appeared all-important to communicate quickly with Petherick, and as Grant's leg was considered too weak for travelling fast, we took counsel together and altered our plans'. As noted here in the extracts which follow, Grant's own record at the time does not support the cast given to this vital stage in the exploration in either of the published accounts. There seems to be no evidence of any formal or informal 'taking counsel together'.

to make a flying march of it along with him, while the baggage might be sent on towards Unyoro. At that time I was positively unable to walk twenty miles a-day, especially miles of Uganda marching, through bogs and over rough ground. I therefore yielded reluctantly to the necessity of our parting; and I am anxious to be explicit on this point, as some have hastily inferred that my companion did not wish me to share in the gratification of seeing the river. Nothing could be more contrary to fact.[1] My state of health alone prevented me from accompanying Speke to set at rest for geographers the latitude of the interesting locality, as to which we were perfectly satisfied from native report.

Extract from Journal: Problems over the Route to the Source

8th [July 1862] We have been much tricked in this journey – every day our Wakonongos saying we'll reach the river which is easterly whereas they take us due north!

9th march 7 a.m. to 11½ we've been so tricked on the route that S[peke] threatens to return and go from Palace to the Ghaut[2] east … and so see the Nile's source but he'll probably go up the river (if practicable from the cataracts) and by land along Usoga from the Ghaut we are making for. My game leg gives considerable trouble. I have to make such <u>exertion</u> in marching & I doubt being able to make S's intended flying trip to the source.[3] [NLS, MS. 17915, 8–9 July 1862]

Extract from Journal: The Parting of the Travellers

18th [July 1862] Kill the first of the twenty cows … S[peke] shot another deer … The Sekibobo[4] made his complaint that Budja wd give him no meat … S off shooting at 3PM. About an inch of rain fell & some very large hail so we caught it all.[5] 19 [July] Our men's shouts awake us both by 8 we marched as was our intention. Our men and the Wag[anda] taking savage delight in burning down the huts. Took an hour to separate the loads going Speke's route to source from all going direct to Kamrasi's. this arranged we marched three miles together, halted for the ostensible reason of getting the Wakonongo's permission to march on but it <u>actually</u> was to secure some cows for Budja who, not coming when called, got into a row x S which was settled amicably & we parted in opposite directions, he E. and me W.[6] [NLS, MS. 17915, 18–19 July 1862]

---

[1] In 1878, when perhaps he was considering a second edition of his book, Grant at this point inserted the further comment: 'It was on <u>my</u> strongly representing to Speke, that the people of England would not be satisfied with his explanation if he did not actually see the Nile flow from Victoria Nyanza, that he undertook this trip.' NLS, MS. 17934, p. 248. As has been noted, Grant's record of the day in his journal does not support this claim.

[2] Here meaning a range of hills.

[3] This shows that doubts about Grant's ability to get to the Nile source had begun to emerge, at least in his own mind at this early stage in the march from the palace. Clearly, his leg was not yet fully healed.

[4] The *Sekibobo* is the title of the chief of Kyaggwe County, the richest and most fertile part of Buganda which was east of the capital and bordered on Lake Victoria. Roscoe, *The Baganda*, pp. 250–51.

[5] This is the date on which Speke, *Journal*, p. 458, says 'we took counsel together' but Grant's evidence here makes no mention of any discussion unless 'as was our intention' in the next line indicates that there had been one.

[6] Grant records no emotion of his own at this point although he must surely have been bitterly disappointed. Nor is there any record of the two men wishing each other well.

II. CAMPS SEPARATED, FROM JULY 19 TILL AUGUST 19.

On the 19th July Speke left with a light equipment for what he afterwards named the "Ripon Falls,"[1] where the Victoria Nyanza discharges itself to form the main waters of the White Nile.[2] He intended to have joined me at the headquarters of Unyoro[3] by proceeding there by boat, but was repulsed in the attempt.[4] Budja, the majority of the Seedees, the baggage, and myself, struck away in the opposite direction towards the capital of Unyoro. The chief incidents of the first few days' marching have been embodied in the previous part of this chapter. But I will now, to vary the narrative, give the events as they occurred daily during Speke's absence.[5]

22d July.—Marched N.N.W. through nothing but meadows of tall grass from 7.30 till 10 A.M. seven miles—from cultivation to cultivation. Rain during the night. The district is in charge of the queen of Uganda's brother.[6] During the march a large black animal, looking back at us, glancing in the side way that an elephant does, ran fearlessly past some huts occupied by Wahuma in charge of cattle. No one turned out to give chase or showed much alarm; on this account I fancied that elephants are not uncommon in these parts. Manua, who has charge of our cattle, came crying, and bleeding from a jagged cut on the back of his head. A Seedee, twice his size, had struck him with a bludgeon for refusing to give up his hut. The offender, who generally was well-behaved, expressed great penitence.

Extract from Journal: 'My First Serious Row'
I was horrified, had them both up, warned him [the offender] if he did so again I'll put him in irons till we come to the first jail & have him in it for five years ... It had never struck me (being my first serious row since leaving the coast)[7] to apply the articles of war to the case. [NLS, MS. 17915, 22 July 1862]

The truth of the story could not be arrived at; and after threatening the Seedee with confinement in irons (which we hadn't), all seemed satisfied except Manua, who could not brook the insult of having been taunted for being "only an Unyamuezi." Blubbering most bitterly, he said, "It is not the wound that pains me, but here, here," violently beating his heart. Poor little fellow! he felt his honour at stake, and swore he would take the other's life; but nothing further occurred.

We were to receive the remainder of our present of cows from M'tessa at this ground, which is on the borders of Uganda. Some cows are brought, but Budja pronounces them

[1] The Earl de Grey and Ripon (1827–1909), later Marquis of Ripon, was President of the RGS in 1859–60 when Speke and Grant set out. Speke, who had reached the Falls on 28 July, contradicts Grant by saying that he chose the name on the day of reaching them: *Journal*, p. 469.

[2] This is surely a very brief record of the fact that, as Speke himself wrote, 'The Expedition had now performed its functions'. Speke, *Journal*, p. 467.

[3] At that time, Kamarasi's headquarters appear to have been nearer the Nile than the present-day capital, Masindi, presumably because of hostilities with a rival claimant to the throne, Ruyonga. See Chapter XII, pp. 277, n. 4, 281, n. 1.

[4] See Speke, *Journal*, pp. 475–81. Problems with his own men and hostilities at the frontier meant his boats could not proceed.

[5] However, what follows is an epitome of Grant's journal entries (which are, in fact, extremely lengthy) not direct quotations.

[6] That is, the Kitunzi; see Chapter X, above, p. 235 and n. 3 there.

[7] This is a somewhat surprising claim since there had been many cases of Grant endeavouring to maintain order and discipline among the porters.

no better than goat. A particular favourite of mine, Ooreymengo, the goat-boy,[1] reported having seen a herd of Waganda villagers sweep away all our goats. I ordered an armed party of men to proceed in pursuit. Half an hour afterwards our goats were discovered grazing close by camp; no one had stolen them—the boy had invented the story because he could not find them! He was sentenced to receive twenty lashes, having lost three goats for us some time before. On his hearing my order, he exclaimed, "I don't want to be flogged;" but Mabruk tied him to a tree and gave it him well with a long switch.[2] On asking the latter, whose duty it also was to keep count of the cattle, how many cows were now left, he took a half-inch rope which he wore on his head as a turban, and told me to count the knots upon it; "Chumsa-thillatheen"[3]—35—all right.

23d.—*Halt.* Budja, on seeing the baggage packed for a march, says that if I go without receiving the complement of cattle, his king will kill him for not obeying orders. One of the women of camp being unwell, this is also brought forward as an excuse for halting. The district officer pays me a pleasant visit, and afterwards sends a gourd full of m'wengé.[4] Went shooting from 9 till 12, wading up to the knees through bogs[5] after elephant or buffalo (Bogo[6]): plenty of their spoor, and several large game-traps were seen—also fish-cruives set; but nothing was bagged. We had a cow killed to-day. Although all its "joints" were at my disposal, the Seedees cut them so small, and into such cross-grained-looking pieces, that when served up they were very uninviting; there was no carving them, because the meat was cut up while warm. The Waganda, on the contrary, cut as neat joints as we do at home, the Seedees calling their cooking "Kissoongoo," or "à l'Anglais," meaning that solid joints are always cut. When boiled they are surrounded by plantain leaf; a layer of peeled plantain is put in a bundle at the top, and all placed in an open earthen pot, which is covered with leaves as a lid. I took to this cookery, and found it answered admirably.

24th, A.M.—*Halt.* Cattle not yet arrived. Chief officer presents another gourd of wine. Thunder, lightning, and heavy rain about noon. Leopard and lion must be common about here, as one of the former was seen by our men while fetching water, and there are three lion-traps (of logs) within a short distance. The dogs kept by the Waganda rarely run loose after their masters; they are tied to the elbow, hand, or toe (when seated) with a cord, which cannot be bitten through, as a stick is generally attached. If they have to run through grass, however long, even with a basket of chickens swinging at their backs, the poor dog is dragged after them in the most ludicrous way. The breed would be shot down in England, but here they value them very much, castrating them as at Karague. Our goatherd was offered 250 cowries for a playful dog he had picked up, but refused every offer under 300!

[1] Ulimengo (born c. 1841), also known as Farjallah Chalinda, presumably after he became a Muslim, received an RGS medal for this Expedition and one for serving Livingstone. He lost his life in 1875 whilst serving Stanley. Simpson, *Dark Companions*, p. 197.

[2] Jeal, *Explorers*, p. 166, says this was 'a shocking punishment for a minor offence' and implies that Grant must have been upset at being excluded from the trip to the Nile source itself. Neither this text nor Grant's journal supports such an interpretation. By the standards of the time this caning with a switch was hardly worse than schoolboys in Britain experienced.

[3] More correctly, *thelathini na tano*; '*chumsa*' must be a language other than Swahili.

[4] Plantain wine.

[5] This raises the question of just how lame Grant actually was by this date.

[6] Correctly, *mbogo*.

Some cattle arrived by 3 P.M., and a march was ordered; but Budja said, "There are no habitations; nothing ahead but jungle full of lion! We will march early to-morrow." A meeting took place to discover who had stolen some property at our last ground; until this is settled, I am told, we do not move from here. My men quarrel with Budja about the unfair distribution of the cattle; we were given not only all the bad ones, but were short of our number.

25*th*.—By daylight I had everything ready-packed for a march, to avoid disputes about the cattle. Budja came saying we could not march till evening: the cows must be looked after. "We must go now," said I. An hour passes, then I am told we cannot move, as the men have just commenced cooking. A second hour, and Budja's drum will sound the advance. It now looks cloudy, and a M'ganda comes to say, "After the shower we will move off." Not being able to stand this any longer, I walked off hastily to Budja's little camp, got a guide, and we all marched together for five miles; they refused to go farther, camping in a grove, fenced round to protect it from wild animals. By noon I was shooting in a swampy meadow of tall grass, and succeeded in bagging a beautiful red buck, the "n'soono" or leucotis, which we christened afterwards the "noble buck."[1] Plodding through the deep water, full of a network of grasses, was uncomfortable; the wounded game was lost, and no other species could be seen. The proprietor of the house I put up in came timidly to get out his large game-nets, in order to save them from being injured by my men. About his house were the spoils of eland and "phongo" or bush-boc;[2] so that this is a sporting country.

26*th*.—Marched nine miles, getting into Unyoro territory immediately after leaving camp. Nothing marked the boundary between Uganda and Unyoro. The country rolled in waves, had many pretty glades, and was covered with tall grass and trees. At the fourth mile an arch of boughs was thrown across the path, seemingly the work of the previous day. My Waganda did not pass under it for some unknown reason, probably because they suspected treachery on the part of their bitter enemies, the people of Unyoro; but nearly all the Seedees and myself did, as we took it for the Unyamuezi sign that dwellings and water were not far distant.

At yesterday's camp a native fell upon his knees to Budja, and presented him with the lid of a tin canister, and a rag of cloth which my men had purposely thrown away. This was the third instance of their returning things through fear of their king M'tessa. Being now in the kingdom of Unyoro, it was considered necessary to halt here, and send some men in advance, to obtain permission to proceed further.

Two Seedees quarrelled, and fought with sticks for the heart of the cow just killed. I tried to separate them, but made matters worse, as the whole camp took up the quarrel. My side won; and the two were placed in different huts, but unfortunately not sufficiently apart to prevent their abusing each other. The result was, that they challenged each other to fight it out alone in the forest with sticks; and I saw the silly creatures march away with a bludgeon each to have their round out. No one followed, and no damage was done.

27*th*.—*Halt*. Budja and five of my men have gone on a march to ask permission to advance. The rule will be very different to what we experienced in Uganda. If the people desert their houses, there will be no one to take payment for anything; but should they

---

[1] Presumably, the white-eared cob, *Cobus leucotis*.
[2] *Tragelaphus*.

remain, everything, even plantain or sweet potato, must be purchased, and nothing plundered. The day was a weary long one of expectation; but by three o'clock in the afternoon the taps of Budja's drum in the distance were recognised, and we went to meet him returning from Unyoro.

All the villagers except one man had run away at the sight of the Waganda; but this person told them "to return for orders to-morrow, as the district officer was absent; they must not advance, otherwise there would be a fight. When they reach the king's, the white man, as he is a cannibal, will have an albino to eat, and the Waganda the back-bones of an old cow!" It seemed odd that they should consider us cannibals; but my valet Uledi told me that in his native country of Uhiao[1] the people there imagined that "all foreigners eat human flesh; and that cloth was dyed scarlet with human blood." It seemed to be a favourite joke against the Waganda, "the bones of a cow"—they are so constantly plundering the people of Unyoro of their cattle that it is not to be wondered at that this taunt should meet them.

28*th*.—Halted by order; probably for several days. On requesting[2] a certain number of my men to proceed and find out whether we could advance, they refused through fear, and lecturing them was the only remedy. Appealing to Mabruk, who had some months previously been sent to Kamarasi as an envoy,[3] whether *he* would go, he replied that, although the king had called us names, such as "cannibals" and "buttereaters," &c., he would willingly obey orders; therefore he and some Waganda went, returning in the afternoon. They had seen a M'koongoo, or district officer, who said we must remain where we were till orders arrived from headquarters. He particularly inquired, "What could have made the other white man go by water while I proceeded by land? for it looked as if he was approaching the country by a forbidden route." This made me anxious about Speke, of whom I could hear nothing. The natives were laughing and shouting during the night, and in the morning three of them, with spears covered up, came to call, begging for some beef; but my Waganda were very angry with them for appearing armed in camp, though they seemed poor harmless creatures. The Wanyoro I have seen are all dull, stupid-looking men, with heavy foreheads and eyebrows, without the gentlemanly appearance or smartness of the Waganda.[4]

New moon was seen to-night. Seedees uttered their prayers as they looked at it.

29*th July*.—*Halt*. Coarse, rainy morning and afternoon. This month, when no rain is falling at 5° south lat., we have had several heavy showers; rain seems to fall here every month in the year, which accounts for the continuity of crop. A dozen armed Wanyoro, with capped spears, pay us a visit, their chief bringing me two bunches of plantain as a present. They get some beef and beads, and say that Speke will never be allowed to proceed by the water-route he is trying. He will have to return and approach by the regular beaten track on which I had travelled. On my appealing for aid to Budja, he says it is impossible to communicate this information to Speke; he will find it out himself, and there is no fear of him.

[1] The country of the Yao people east of Lake Malawi.

[2] Grant had originally written 'ordering'. NLS, MS. 17934, p. 253.

[3] Mabruki, a very experienced porter and friend of Bombay, reported that Kamarasi, the monarch of Bunyoro had treated him civilly and given the party two cows and three pots of pombé. NLS, MS. 17915, 26 July 1862.

[4] Exactly 40 years later, the British Commissioner for the Uganda Protectorate, Sir Harry Johnston, said the Banyoro were 'rather nice-looking negroes, tall and well-proportioned'. *Uganda Protectorate*, II, p. 581.

My valet, whom I considered honest, I found helping a brother Seedee to some m'wengé. On reprimanding through an interpreter, he begged pardon for the offence, while lolling on his bed with a quid of tobacco in his mouth. These Seedees are not to be trusted unless the most rigorous discipline is enforced.

Two of my men start with their guns, carrying beef and cowries with which to purchase plantain or potato from the villagers. They meet a party of Waganda there, who say to them, "You fools! what do you mean by paying for food, when you can get it like us for nothing?" The custom was for the Waganda to go to the Wanyoro and make a polite request for provisions, which were generally given free.[1]

An infectious disease has broken out amongst the cattle. One of them has the roof of its mouth so affected that it cannot eat. Its tongue has become discoloured, and there is an appearance of irritation between the hoofs.[2] This does not prevent the men from wishing to eat it before it should become worse.

30*th.*—*Halt.* Rain during the night. We are haunted by three different coloured vultures. The first is the ragged-looking, wedge-headed vulture of Uganda notoriety, the "m'ssega," easily caught in a trap by a bent bough and two nooses. His plumage is a dull sepia colour. The whole neck is red and bare, with a ruff of white feathers circling the root of the neck. The second, probably the female, is a much bolder bird, larger, and of a dun colour, with a bare, dark grey, or black neck, called "m'foongoo" by the Seedees. The third was a very shy bird, quite as large as, and plumper than the last, and much handsomer than either. His plumage was jet-black, with the rump, thigh feathers, and rear half of the wings snowy white.[3]

The hut I am in is full of small lizards about six inches long. In fighting, two chased each other round and round, with intervals, in a small circle, keeping their tails everted, for fear of being bitten off. The largest got hold of the other's foot, held it most viciously, while the other, struggling, made its escape. They live by stalking up to flies, and suddenly pouncing on them. At night they have the power, like flies, of sleeping while on the ceiling of the hut.[4] After rain, when small red centipedes were on the ground, I have seen these little animals make a rush at the insect, shake it as a dog would a rat, leave it there, and run back to the hut. On examining the insect, which remained motionless, its head was found to have been eaten off.

31*st.*—*Halt.* I was roused out of a fast sleep by shouts and screams from my men in the hut. My first thought was to look whether a fire had broken out; and finding this was not the case, I inquired whether Wanyoro had attacked us. The bleating of a goat disclosed the fact that a hyena had carried away the fattest of our flock. Torches were lit and search made, but nothing was recovered till morning, when the paunch and one kidney of the poor animal were the only traces found. He must have been a bold hyena to have broken

[1] Presumably because the Banyoro in this border area between the two kingdoms were fearful of raids from their now more powerful neighbour, as Grant notes below.

[2] This would seem likely to be rinderpest. If so, Grant's evidence is important as many authorities have suggested that the cattle disease which was to have such devastating effects did not reach East Africa until the 1880s although another gives 1864 as the first instance. See Kjekshus, *Ecology Control*, p. 127; Koponen, *People and Production*, p. 169.

[3] As noted above, Grant sketched the three vultures shown in Figure 71, p. 260. They are, respectively, the Egyptian vulture (*Neophron percnopterus*), the African white-backed vulture (*Gyps africanus*) and the white-headed vulture (*Trigonoceps occipitalis*).

[4] Presumably these are geckos, perhaps the common house gecko, *Hemidactylus frenatus*.

through so strong a fence close to where we all slept, and in size he must have been a monster, for his spoor was as large as my hand. The Seedees complain that all the plantain and sweet potato about the place have been eaten up—"they are starving;" although every third day a cow is killed for them!

Not far from this hut there are three caverns dug, looking like the hold of a ship, in which the natives secrete their grain, &c., from their plundering neighbours, the Waganda, but at present they are empty. The Unyoro M'koongoo sends a message, bidding us not to be impatient for the king's reply, as it will certainly arrive to-day or to-morrow; but I am more anxious about Speke, who should have joined us by this time, and nothing has been heard of him.[1]

A storm of thunder, lightning, and rain, blew in gusts from the south, then veered round to N.W., dashing like waterspouts upon the ground. It began at 4, with an interval at sunset, and lasted till 8 P.M. About two inches of rain fell.

1st August.—*Halt.* A bait of a cow's head was placed last night for the hyena that had stolen the goat, but no shot was obtained, as it rained. In the morning, however, it appeared, from the tracks of the animal that he must have been dancing about it on his hind legs like a bear. Our cattle, though in a perfectly open fold, the hyena never attacks, as the cows would kick him out of the place.

My men, without permission, went to Budja, requesting him to get vegetables in exchange for the beef of a blind, lame old cow, that was killed to-day. He sent some of his boy-pages with them to the villagers, with an order that two loads of potatoes for each mess should be made over to them without payment. This was done.

I sketched the two Wahuma girls belonging to my camp.[2] The prettiest, "Sikujua," is young but very black, and her history is curious. When at Uganda, Speke's men had to forage, seizing what food they could lay hands on. One man got his head broken, but he succeeded in making a prisoner of this little girl, and took her home with him as *his* mode of redress. No one ever came to claim her, and she remained his property. She had the pretty oval face and large ears of the Wahuma; and no doubt, as those with a dark skin thrive best at Zanzibar, she is considered there a great beauty. The other sketch was of a younger girl given to Speke by the queen of Uganda, and now the property of Bombay. She had a yellow skin, fine eyes, and a rather droll face and figure.

2d and 3d.—*Halt.* A man who had gone from Unyoro to Kawalogeh for salt, brings intelligence that Speke had gone far up the river.[3] This afterwards proved to be quite true. No tidings from him or the king of Unyoro. Slight shower about noon. Leg stiff again. One of Budja's men, who had been to sell women near Karee, confirmed what we yesterday heard about Speke's movements. This man had obtained ten cows in exchange for two women kidnapped on our march.[4] At Uganda capital they would have fetched only five cows. We have a few of the African tribe, called Mukooa,[5] in camp. They are

---

[1] Speke was actually still at the Ripon Falls enjoying the area and not apparently feeling any great need to hurry. *Journal,* p. 470.

[2] See Plate 36.

[3] Presumably, this was news that Speke had gone up to the Ripon Falls.

[4] This and other evidence in this chapter on the behaviour of Grant's escort of Baganda suggests that slave raiding and trading was prevalent every day.

[5] That is, Makua, a people who live in the Malawi/Mozambique area and akin to the neighbouring Yao; like them, they were frequently enslaved.

marked on the forehead with a stamp resembling a horse-shoe, called "real" or dollar, and three horizontal cuts are made with a knife on each temple.

Being out of smoking tobacco, I sent a man with half a brisket of beef to purchase some from the villagers. In exchange he brought back four packets, each the size of an egg. Others were bought for ten cowries each, or its equivalent, a single necklace of common beads.

Seedees have strong attachments. Separated from their parents in childhood by slavery, they are cast upon the world, and become devoted to some one—it may be their first master—whom they look upon as their protector and adviser for years, or even for life. Instances of this often occurred. On my directing that a party of five should proceed ahead for orders, one man stepped forward and volunteered; his pupil, child, or "m'toto," at once made another, as he would not see his patron risk his life, or be put to inconvenience, without sharing the danger himself. A story told me by Frij also illustrates this attachment: Some years ago he was proceeding to sea from Zanzibar, when four boys were placed under his charge by their relatives, to learn their duty. A storm struck the vessel while a boy of his was aloft in imminent danger. Frij went up the rigging, tied the lad to a rope, and lowered him down all safe, but the difficulty now was with himself. The mast had that day been greased, and while lowering himself by a rope it gave way, and he fell upon the spare anchor, and from thence, much cut, overboard. Two of his boys threw themselves after him. Frij had gone down, but they succeeded in tying him to a life-buoy, to which all three clung till picked up exhausted. He added, that for their devotion the captain gave them 15 and 11 dollars respectively.

One of our men became possessed of a devil, as was believed, for several hours.[1] He was seized with fits so violent as to require being held down. In this insensible state he was asked where Speke was? Would this march end successfully? To which he replied, that "Our journey would be prosperous, but there would be delays." All Seedees believe most firmly that devils have this power, and that there are a great variety of them, some English, some Abyssinian, others Mombas, &c.—in fact, every country or district has its devil, some more difficult to get rid off[2] than others, the English being about the worst. Is this African idea a remnant of tradition? It has some resemblance to the Jewish notions mentioned in Scripture.

The moon shone bright and inviting to-night, though we had a shower during the day, and the men till 11 o'clock made a playground of the space in front of my hut, singing, mimicking, and acting with considerable grace and great humour. The operatic song of the Unyamuezi, from the gesticulations and perambulations of the performer, who invented words as he proceeded, was highly amusing. They were chiefly in compliment to myself—that God had sent them the white man, or "Mazoongoo,"[3] who gave them beef to eat, and did not, like Dr Kiengo, make use of divination by the horns of antelopes and the entrails of fowls to procure food.

4th.—*Halt.* Started a second set of men ahead for information. The reply we received from them was, that Kamarasi was a great king, and that it took many days before a

---

[1] 'As was believed', was added at the proof stage whilst 'today' had originally appeared at the end of the sentence. NLS, MS. 17934, p. 259.

[2] *Sic.* One of the few typographical errors in the text.

[3] Mzungu.

question could be referred to him. Such is the way that travelling is delayed in this country! However, I sent a message to say that two days hence we meant to march to the north, even without permission. Heavy rain, thunder, and lightning in the afternoon. Guinea-fowl crying all round camp. I went shooting them with ball from the trees in the forest, and succeeded in getting one. The grass at present is too tall to see beyond twenty yards; and no antelopes have been seen. Water is a mile away from our huts, in a puddle surrounded by rushes, in the low part of a glade running to the north.

6th.—Halt. Sent a party ahead to inquire why we are detained. A portion of them return, saying they had met a number of armed Wanyoro, who asked why we were parading up and down the road every day—we'll get a thrashing one of these days! By noon of the 7th, the remainder of the men returned without further news. Their commander, Mabruk, had seen a lion in a trap last night. The Waganda threw their spears into the dead animal; while the brave Mabruk discharged his gun at it, to show its effect upon the Wanyoro, who immediately dropped their spears, and ran, never having heard the report of a gun before.[1]

8th.—Halt. By noon a king's messenger arrived, with followers having their spears capped with leather and tufts of hair. He informed us that the king did not wish to see the white men because they had insulted him by approaching his country by two different routes; they had also come *viâ* Uganda, the king of which is an upstart. If they choose to return a year hence, with a recommendation from Rumanika, he will see them with pleasure. No remonstrance would be listened to; we might march back as soon as we liked. This was startling, but I still had hopes.

9th.—Halt. A meeting, which lasted three hours, was held to-day to discuss the subject of our visit, and whether we could advance. There were present Wanyoro, Wanyamuezi, Waganda, Karagues, Wungwana (Seedees), and myself. Every possible argument failed; entreaties and presents were of no avail; and my most valuable possession, a double-barrelled rifle by Blisset, presented to me by a kind old friend, Blanshard (formerly governor of Vancouver Island),[2]—even this was refused as a bribe to the king. He had sent his messenger merely to see the strength of our party, and to ascertain, if possible, whether we were in the habit of stealing cattle and men, and ultimately to desire that we should retire to the Uganda frontier, where, after eight days, we should have a reply. This appearing to have considerable reason in it, and all supplies having run short, I reluctantly gave my consent[3] to retire next day, but only to the Uganda frontier, where I should wait for my companion. To show the wicked spirit of the men, and their utter want of sympathy at this critical time, a few commenced wantonly cutting down some sorghum which was growing close to my hut, saying they were hungry. The only notice I took of it was to prevent the further waste of the crop. The same men had often exhibited symptoms of mutiny, and not many days elapsed ere they finally deserted.

*10th.—*March back nine miles to Uganda frontier, agreeably to Kamarasi's orders, though much against my inclination. Two Seedees were speared by Waganda villagers

---

[1] Firearms were not yet common in Bunyoro as it was Kamarasi's policy to restrict them to his trusted chiefs. Doyle, *Crisis and Decline*, pp. 25, 42–5.

[2] Richard Blanshard (1817–94) had been in the Indian Army with Grant but became Lt Governor of Vancouver Island from 1849 to 1866. *ODNB*.

[3] 'Before evening' had appeared in the original and 'reluctantly' was omitted. NLS, MS. 17934, p. 261.

255

while taking possession of houses. We in return took four prisoners, chased and kept at bay others; and, to prevent a sudden alarm, cut down all the plantain-trees growing within thirty yards of our huts; but except seeing numbers hovering around us, we had no further annoyance. The wounds were slight, but made much of by the Seedees, who said that one of the women prisoners was necessary as a nurse. This was a mere ruse to be allowed to keep the woman, whom I had made over to Budja, and I would not hear of it.

11th.—*Halt.* Fever and ague all night. Fifteen armed villagers came to pay their respects, but they had no sooner entered Budja's camp than he demanded what right they had to come there carrying spears. A row, in which my men joined, at once took place, and all were disarmed. I saw here the male prisoner of yesterday, a district officer, in the stocks. Perfect torture the creature seemed to be in; he sat upon the ground, with two long sticks, forked at both ends, between his feet and hands. The neck and waist were tied tightly to a post, so that all night long he could not lie down, nor have the use of either hands or feet. However, in the afternoon Budja released him, on promise that the men who committed the assaults should be surrendered, otherwise his wife, now our prisoner, would never be given up. What a mode of coercion! But ever since Budja has had charge of affairs he has shown very great tact, doing his duty most conscientiously. His defences,[1] in comparison with the slovenly ones put up here by the Seedees, really seem erected with the eye of a general. He is very proud of his position, will not associate with his own or my men, neither will he eat meat that has been killed by Mohammedans. All his cattle, I may remark, are killed by a blow on the back of the head.

12th.—*Halt.* Sent eight Seedees and eight Waganda to inform Speke of my compulsory retreat. They did not know where he was, but had orders not to return without having seen him. They all returned at sunset, giving us a surprise. An officer had told them their errand was useless, for Speke had gone to Kidi, far, far away. Budja was infuriated with his men for being such poltroons as to return; besides, what would his king say if Speke had proceeded to Kidi, where he had no permission to go? He (Budja) had been imprisoned three times by M'tessa, and thought if a fourth offence were committed he certainly would not escape.

After sunset, cries came from Budja's camp, about 200 yards distant. I found that the cries were those of one of his good-looking wives, beaten on mere suspicion for having been outside the house after the sun had set. Such severity to guard the honour of the wives is not unlikely to have a quite opposite effect; and, so far as my observation went, the husbands had no great cause to complain. Adultery is severely punished; mutilation is not uncommon; and the Wakoongoo, or officers in charge of from fifty to several hundred men, have power to order these punishments, and even to put the offenders to death.

13th.—*Halt.* Twelve men are sent in search of Speke. A Seedee had fever from bathing after noon, which is thought by them an unhealthy time. Out shooting after "noble buck," with a dozen villagers as guides. The animals were very wild; and the bogs, with a broiling sun overhead, were disagreeable.

14th.—*Halt.* Fever and ague all night. Frij and all Seedees believe that the Jews, or Yahoodee, living in Calcutta, seize people, and tie them up by the heels till blood falls

---

[1] The thorn hedges put up round a camp.

from them into a dish, when they are released, but rarely survive. The blood so obtained is prepared, and sold as a most valuable chest-complaint medicine called Moomcean. Frij had, while in Calcutta, once been seized, but escaped while the Jew went up a ladder. Also one of his comrades he had seen tied up by the heels, gave evidence to the police, and had the Yahoodee put in prison for eighteen months. These silly stories helped to pass the time.[1]

The cowherd Manua knows his duty thoroughly, for the day he herds the cattle he brings them home full and sleek-looking, being acquainted with the grasses the animals like best—those that are green and succulent, in deep shade. The other herd, not knowing a cow from a horse, drives in the cattle from their grazing as lean in appearance as when they went out.

We lost three cows some days ago; and Mabruk. who keeps count of them, now stands every night, with his rope in his hand, at the door of the cowfold, passing a knot as each cow goes inside; in this way he counts easier than by the usual enumeration, and the animals walk in to enjoy the volumes of smoke rising from the fire in the centre of their fold.

15*th.—Halt.* Feel anxious for news; by noon it came. Speke could not be found; he had gone up the river. The chief Wahuma officer would not give an audience to my Mussulmans, in case the sight of them would make his cows run dry; and men who sat upon chairs before kings—meaning the "white men"—would not be received in Unyoro.

Shot two guinea-fowl with one bullet, and also two "n'soono," or noble bucks, accidentally with one ball. The second one could not be found, although he went away dangling his broken leg, followed by dogs. I stood in admiration of the villager who, with his spear-head, skinned and cut up the animal into saddle, brisket, leg, and other joints, laying them on the pure leaves of plantain as quietly and cleverly, and with far less mess, than is to be seen at the abattoirs of Paris.

16*th.—Halt.* The time has arrived for Kamarasi's reply, and none has come. My men all press me to retire. There is not one in the camp who wishes to go the north or Egyptian route; and I long most anxiously for Speke. Here we are, not more than seven days, it is said, from the place where boats lie to take us down the Nile; yet nothing will move those around me to push on. It is most tantalising. I asked Budja to join me in forcing the road, but he could not be induced to leave his country. "Let me then communicate with Captain Speke, *wherever he is.*" It was impossible, as his men had no permission to visit Oogoongoo, on the other side of M'tessa's,[2] where my companion was; but if I retired for two marches, and halted there, he would ask leave from his king. In the afternoon he anticipated my wish to send ten men into Unyoro to demand a reply from Kamarasi. To dispel the anxiety we both felt we went out shooting—Budja having dressed himself very smartly in cow and antelope skins.

---

[1] 'Amuse one at the time' were the original words ending this sentence, NLS, MS. 17934, p. 264.

[2] 'The palace of' omitted from the original. NLS, MS. 17934, p. 265. This whole sentence is puzzling as it stands but it makes sense if one assumes that Grant meant to refer not to 'M'tessa's' but to *Kamarasi's* palace as Bugungu is an area within Bunyoro near where the Nile enters Lake Albert and where Speke might be assumed to be if he were travelling by river (which in fact he was not). Grant's journal entry refers only to 'beyond the Palace' thus confirming his original information was about the Bunyoro ruler's palace. NLS, MS. 17915, 16 August 1862.

At night I assembled all the men to explain our difficulties, and to intimate to them that our rations of butcher-meat must be curtailed, otherwise there would be disgrace and starvation for us. They agreed to my proposals.

17th.—*Halt.* Having now been twenty-two days without a message from the king, as a last resource I sent a dozen men ahead, carrying some wires as a bribe, to ask why we had received no definite reply. In the mean time I went shooting some distance off, and had a shot at a leucotis buck[1] standing knee-deep in water—the tall grasses almost concealing him. This animal is always to be found in ground of that nature, though he has not the hoofs of a waterboc. Rain commencing, we returned shortly before the sun had set, twenty-five villagers having accompanied us, and been entertained by my burning some powder in the bare palm of my hand. They told me it was no use sending men so often to Kamarasi, as he had determined on not seeing us.

18th.—*Halt.* My men all return from the Unyoro frontier,[2] bringing back the presents of wire I had sent. The district officer said, "How can I receive these gifts if the king, my master, refuses to see the white man?" and he added, that if I stayed ten years where I was the road would not be open to me. So. after a dismal day, I determined—having been attempting this route since the 26th ult.—not to stay a moment longer, but to make search for Speke, whom we had heard nothing of for thirty days, and to try the route to Unyoro *viâ* Karague.[3]

19th.—Marched eight miles south, crossing a bog five hundred yards wide, and knee-deep, and camping on the second crest of land beyond it. No sooner settled down than Bombay and three Seedees arrive with a note from Speke, who had that morning reached the ground we passed! I at once walked joyfully[4] over to his camp. He had gone out shooting. His servants were got up like M'tessa's pages—heads all shaved, except cockade-like tufts left to grow above each ear, giving them a knowing look. In the absence of their master they gave me a cordial greeting. I waited in the camp till Speke arrived, and I need not attempt to describe our joy at meeting once more.

III. OUR CAMPS UNITED.

Each of us had met with a reverse. But Speke had accomplished his object, and seen the first cataract of the Nile at the point where it flows from the Victoria Nyanza. He had been attended by only a dozen Seedees under Bombay, himself a host,[5] and a few Waganda. Our further plans could not now be decided upon without a conference with Budja. It was proposed, if everything else failed, to induce M'tessa, by enormous bribes, to give a thousand men, and with this force try the Kilimanjaro route to the east coast.

[1] Grant originally used the local term 'n'soonoo'. NLS, MS. 17934, p. 266.

[2] 'Direction' in the original text, which makes more sense as Grant was in the frontier region. NLS, MS. 17934, p. 266.

[3] This would have been an enormous retreat and diversion.

[4] This word was inserted at the proof stage. NLS, MS. 17934, p. 267, where there are other trivial changes.

[5] The meaning of this phrase is not clear.

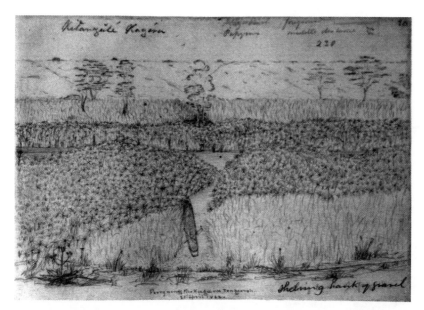

Figure 68.   Crossing the Kagera. Grant's attempt to show the difficult ferry crossing of the River Kagera as he was carried towards Buganda. He was confused over the name of the river, initially thinking it was known as the Kitangule. Grant had been carried to this point by 21 April 1862. NLS MS. 17919, no. 20. Reproduced by permission of the National Library of Scotland.

Figure 69.   The Kagera as source of the Nile? Another attempt by Grant to show the Kagera. The river is the major affluent of Lake Victoria which discharges into the lake just north of the current Uganda-Tanzania border. It rises far to the south-west in present-day Burundi. Many regard it as the ultimate source of the Nile and Grant himself hinted at some sympathy for this view. NLS MS. 17919, no. 21. Reproduced by permission of the National Library of Scotland.

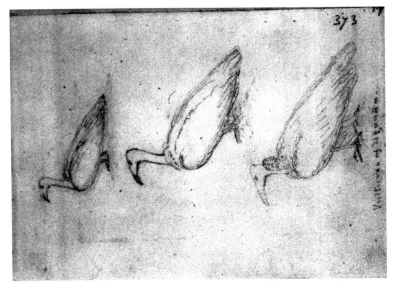

Figure 71. Three different kinds of vultures seen in Buganda. Again, this is an unfinished sketch. NLS MS. 17920, no. 60. Reproduced by permission of the National Library of Scotland.

Figure 70. More African heads. A sketch for some heads Grant made in April 1862. However, he does not indicate who these people were. NLS MS. 17920, no. 59. Reproduced by permission of the National Library of Scotland.

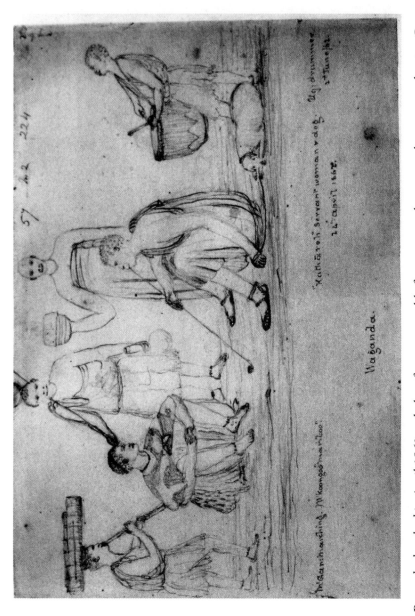

Figure 72. Baganda sketched in April 1862 and, therefore, presumably from among the group who were conducting Grant to their king. From the left, a bearer, marching, called 'M'gan', Maribu, a mkungu, i.e. a chief who was in charge of the party, another bearer, a servant woman, another man with a pipe and a dog. The drummer on the right seems to have been added later, in June. NLS MS. 17919, no. 23. Reproduced by permission of the National Library of Scotland.

261

Figure 73. The baraza or reception area and residence of 'Kabureh', whom Grant believed to be an uncle of the Kabaka of Buganda. But there is confusion. Initially in his journal for 23 April 1862, Grant named the man 'Kithari'. Clearly, however, he was a chief of some standing in the southern part of Buddu, the province of Buganda Grant was entering. This attractive pencil drawing reflects the fact that Grant found this the 'neatest' residence he had so far seen. NLS MS. 17919, no. 24. Reproduced by permission of the National Library of Scotland.

Figure 74. Distant hills. A block of hills in what Grant calls the 'Kittara plains' or the area to the north of Buganda, which kingdom he assumed was confined to a narrow strip along the northern shore of Lake Victoria. NLS MS. 17919, no. 40. Reproduced by permission of the National Library of Scotland.

Figure 75. Grant's first view of Lake Victoria at Mwengaruka Bay on 9 May 1862 when he was at the north-west corner looking towards the Sese Islands. The steamship and two other large vessels were imaginary: Grant inserted them to amuse his African companions and to forecast what he hoped would be the future. NLS MS. 17919, no. 25. Reproduced by permission of the National Library of Scotland.

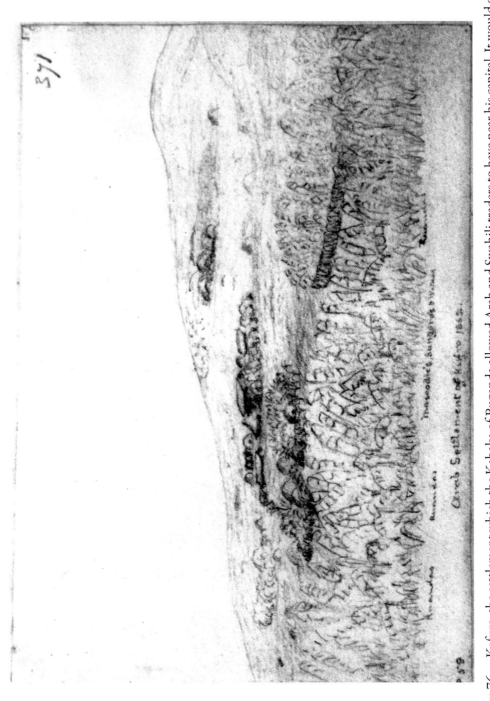

Figure 76.   Kafuro, the settlement which the Kabaka of Buganda allowed Arab and Swahili traders to have near his capital. It would seem traders from Ruanda were also there or nearby. Although the details are unclear, this is important as apparently the only representation of the Arab establishment. These Muslims were to become a crucial element in the subsequent troubled history of Buganda. NLS MS. 17920, no. 58. Reproduced by permission of the National Library of Scotland.

264

Figure 77.   Some Baganda. Grant was obviously trying to improve his human figure drawing and recorded these images before he left Buganda in July 1862. Extracted from NLS MS. 17921, no. 289. Reproduced by permission of the National Library of Scotland.

Figure 78.   Further Baganda types extracted from NLS MS. 17921, no. 289. Reproduced by permission of the National Library of Scotland.

Figure 79. Murchison Firth, as Speke had called this arm of Lake Victoria in honour of Sir Roderick Murchison, the dominant figure at the RGS. Grant saw little of the lake and so, when he could, was anxious to prove that the lake existed; Burton and other critics had doubted it. NLS MS. 17919, no. 31. Reproduced by permission of the National Library of Scotland.

Figure 81. Kamarasi, the Omukama of Bunyoro, depicted on 5 November 1862. This is a version of Plate 38, made a little earlier and shown to Kamarasi so that his 'autograph' could be obtained. NLS MS. 17919, no. 42. Reproduced by permission of the National Library of Scotland.

Figure 80. Kimenyi, a dwarf encountered in November 1862. His picture coupled with the sketch of the monkey makes the inference about him obvious. NLS MS. 17919, no. 43. Reproduced by permission of the National Library of Scotland.

Figure 82.   The explorers' encampment at Kamarasi's capital in Bunyoro. Speke's hut and the Union Jack are prominent, with the King's houses beyond and hills in the further distance. NLS MS. 17919, no. 44. Reproduced by permission of the National Library of Scotland.

Figure 83.   'Wakidi', as Grant calls them, depicted in November 1862. He clearly noticed how different they were from the Bantu peoples he had hitherto met in East Africa. They are part of the people known more normally as Langi. NLS MS. 17919, no. 47. Reproduced by permission of the National Library of Scotland.

Figure 84.   Mothers and infants among the Madi as seen in January 1863. The Madi are a Nilo-Saharan group who live in the far north-west of modern Uganda. NLS MS. 17919, no. 49. Reproduced by permission of the National Library of Scotland.

Figure 85.   Members of the Madi group herding cattle in January 1863, but the picture is more interesting for showing how a hut's framework could be carried to a new location for the herders. NLS MS. 17919, no. 50. Reproduced by permission of the National Library of Scotland.

Figure 86. Elephant tusks destined for the Egyptian market; whether they were willingly sold by the Madi or ones they were forced to provide by Khartoum-based raiders is not clear. Grant later said he had made the tusks look too large. NLS MS. 17919, no. 51. Reproduced by permission of the National Library of Scotland.

Extracts from Journal: Frustration then Reunion with Speke[1]

18[th] [August 1872] <u>Halted.</u> Our prospects are as black; they continue to haunt me while my men seem to have no cares but their bellies. ... My men all returned today far ahead they had seen Kam[aras]i's spokesman ... [who] has told them if we waited ten years where we were we'd not get an interview with Kam[arasi] ... who is afraid of our witchcraft ... All this made me very downcast and sullen; while the man was sitting I was told of Kanga[2] close by but did not start till almost dark, when suddenly, I called in one breath for my gun ... & off I walked rather determinedly telling no one. My men saw all this and watched my movements, every fellow in camp, even the laziest who had shammed sick when wanted, turned out armed. I pushed though the Wag[anda] camp. When they asked my men what was up, no one knew and took it into their heads that I was off to fight Unyoro as with shouts of "Wambea", "Wambea"[3] they handed me with spare shields ready for anything. On finding I was after kanga, my men had a good laugh and my anger was somewhat soothed. I determined on not staying a moment longer, my only anxiety now being to find Speke – the sooner we go the Karag[we] route the better ...

19th. March at 7½ miles on the Ug[anda] road ... No sooner settled down than Bombay [brought] a note from Speke ... I found Speke's camp ... Both our journeys had met with reverses ... S[peke] & men returned to the camp by 10 pm ... He had seen the first Nile cataract ... the 150 yard stream, broken by rocks and with brushwood, a fall of 12 ft.. Bombay said the height of a man. Fish skipping and jumping in the fall and men all about catching them, the scenery beautiful, the banks gently receding in swells covered with acacias. Above the fall the river widens into the lake but the main waters were not visible from there.[4] Bombay had been to the palace, saw Mtessa, got his order for boats to descend the river ... [NLS, MS. 17915, 18–19 August 1862][5]

20th.—Return to my yesterday's ground along with Speke. Having discussed whether we could again send messengers into Unyoro, the plan was considered impracticable, as the natives had threatened us. Besides, we did not know what impression had been produced by the fight on the Nile with Speke's men, where several of the natives were killed. Probably their king was enraged at this disaster. In our difficulty we are saved by the arrival of Kamarasi's factotum, who brings us an invitation from his king. The relief and delight experienced at the moment were inexpressible—everything had happened for the best. We had evidently been on trial, closely watched, and, most probably, the fact of our having been so submissive obtained for us the royal favour. The king had ordered that our Waganda escort should quit us as soon as we entered the Unyoro territory. They

---

[1] As will be noted, Grant's original description of the reunion with Speke does not refer to any joyful feeling. His reception of the news about the Expedition's crowning moment at the Nile source is equally unemotional.

[2] That is, guinea fowl.

[3] From *amba* and meaning here 'let us follow and support'.

[4] Grant's interest in what had been seen is apparent but he did not transfer this sign of his interest to his book.

[5] Presumably the hope was that boats would enable the two travellers to go by canoe through Bunyoro without Kamarasi's permission but obviously nothing came of this scheme because Kamarasi decided to allow them into his kingdom. He had been understandably suspicious given his internal difficulties, Baganda hostility and encroachments by Khartoum traders from the north. See Doyle, *Crisis and Decline*, p. 50.

refused to obey, thinking the order was insulting to them; but I considered it a very wise policy, as they are such a wild plundering race, and apt to quarrel.

On the march I struck a zebra with a bullet, which made him, curiously enough, rear twice in the air. A second ball did not take effect, but he separated from other three, and went away limping through the long grasses, which hid him from our view.

21st.—*Halt.* Something stops the way. We cannot move as we should, but in Africa no one ever can. Budja distrusts the Wanyoro, and does not want to give us up to them. The Seedees get up a complaint, refusing to march because they have not enough of powder; they observe the Waganda leaving their heavy baggage here, and suspect treachery on the part of Kamarasi, who is said to be enraged at having his men killed on the Nile by Speke's party. All this was a mere pretence, and they were distinctly told that they might go back to Karague if they chose, but their guns must be surrendered. Their cool reply was that they would talk it over in the morning, treating the matter as if time were of no value.

22d.—Hurrah! we march again some miles nearer England, and encamp on the northern boundary of Uganda. Seventeen of the mutineer Seedees delivered up their guns, their names were noted, ammunition was served out, and they had the guns returned—a very simple expedient, accomplished without any further misunderstanding.[1]

Went shooting in a swamp. My first shot was at a leucotis buck, but he bounded away untouched. Again we came upon him lying immersed in water, all but his noble head. On being alarmed he stood for a shot, which penetrated both shoulder-blades, and lodged under the off-skin. Budja was in such ecstasy that he jumped through the water up to him, with all his lads following. A Seedee got well butted before he could cut the buck's throat; but after the Waganda had talked and laughed over the powers of my rifle, eight of them raised the animal with the greatest care out of the water, preventing his beautiful skin from being soiled, and placed him upon a bed of clean grass, where he was left to be cut up *à la* Waganda. Budja's eyes glistened when told that he might have the skin; there was no end to his "nyans, nyans," thanks, &c. We heard elephants screeching and trumpeting near some acacias to the far north, but my Waganda dreaded going within sight of them, and stole away home. We could not find them, but during the night heard their musical cry as they browsed in the moonlight.

Between the 23d August and 2d September we only made four marches, but fortunately they were all in the right direction. The country waved in gentle long swells of land covered with tall grass and thin forest, with a few low conical hills. The clearances for cultivation, generally fenced against wild animals, were few; and in the low grounds sweet potato, ooleyzee,[2] and a few plantain were grown. The houses were of grass, perfect domes, but dirty, ill-made, and without door-screens or frames to their single entrances.[3] The people, as we marched past, appeared inanimate and unconcerned; they stood listlessly gazing at us, so different from the reception given to a regiment passing through an English town, when every handkerchief waves a welcome. The natives deliberately carried away everything out of their houses and allowed us to take possession, but at the same time showed sullenness at our intrusion. Our Waganda did not mind this. Wherever

---

[1] Originally 'noise' was written rather than 'misunderstanding'. NLS, MS. 17934, p. 269.

[2] *Ulezi*, i.e. millet.

[3] Doyle finds this passage one of the few available descriptions of Bunyoro's landscape in the pre-colonial period. Doyle, *Crisis and Decline*, pp. 17–18.

they go they know how to enjoy themselves, living always like a party of jolly brigands, by plunder. Numbers of natives came out to see the Wazoongoo, and never having seen boxes before, they believed that the white men were carried in our japanned tin cases!

The Wanyoro would seem to be penurious. The cowries which circulated amongst them were generally covered with earth, as if they had been hoarded up, and kept concealed underground. This coin had reached them through Karague; and Kidjweega, an officer not more than thirty-five years of age, recollected the time when ten cowries bought a cow, and thirty secured a woman. Times have changed. It now takes half a load to purchase a cow. Here, at the division between the commerce coming up the Nile and that of the east coast of Africa, beads were little used, and cloth and coinage were unknown. But Kamarasi had received, four years previously (reckoning five months to the year), some beads from the traders on the Nile, and it is to be hoped that, the road having once been opened, trade and civilisation may advance.[1] The natives manufactured ornaments of ivory for the wrists and ankles. These, and rings, were split at one part, not formed in entire unbroken circles, probably for the reason that they could be slipped on more easily by being divided. The price of their smallest ring was twenty-five cowrie-shells, which I considered expensive. They had also spear-blades, two spans long and two inches at their greatest breadth. The Waganda purchased several of them at five hundred cowries each, and one cow would buy ten, or bark-cloth would be taken in exchange. While here a good deal of business was done, the natives purchasing meat from our men; but if any butter had been used in cooking it, they would reject it as food. Men and women wore anklets made of hair covered with twisted brass, iron, or copper wire.

Manua made brotherhood with the officer Kidjweega, as he had done with Bombay at Ukuni, but after a different fashion. A Wanyoro made a slight incision to the right above Manua's navel. His blood was tasted by Kidjweega, who had the same done to him by a Seedee, and Manua partook of his blood. These brotherhoods are synonymous with our masonic institutions, and do a great deal of good, as from that time forward friendship is sworn; and I must say that until the last moment these two men remained excellent friends. The work of civilisation may be promoted by this means, as the natives have no objection to make brotherhood with Europeans.

We had not much rain during the last week of August. After a shower one morning, upon the space cleared in front of our hut appeared hundreds of white maggots with black heads, curling themselves into an arc, jumping and throwing themselves over the ground as if set upon springs. The morning dews, as we marched in Indian file through grasses higher than and thick as a field of wheat, made everything uncomfortably damp. The Wanyoro, fearful of getting wet, or having their rags of skins and bark-cloths injured, carried in front of them an immense broom made of plantain-leaves to brush the dew off the grass, which they considered injurious to health, causing the itch. At first we could not understand why unclad natives should carry about these besoms, and the sight of so many of them by the side of the path perplexed us.

M'tessa had sent a large party to inquire how we were getting on. Imagining this was all they wanted, we thought they might disperse; but their leader produced four little

---

[1] Grant's note of the importance of Bunyoro's position is perceptive but he did not know as yet of the rapacity of the Khartoum traders. He shows in what he goes on to write the importance of the regional trade between Buganda and Bunyoro despite the hostilities. See Reid, *Crisis and Decline*, pp. 139–40.

pieces of wood, saying with emphasis, one was for a double-barrelled gun that would last the king his lifetime; a second was for gun-wads; a third for strengthening medicine; and a fourth for anything the "Bana" (meaning Speke) liked to send. We returned our kindest regards to their king, and told them that all they asked, and even more, would be sent from Ugani[1] should an opportunity ever offer.

A touching incident occurred here. A woman, of the village recognised amongst our Seedees her brother, whom she had not seen or heard of since they were children at their home in Uhiao, fifteen hundred miles distant to the south-east.[2] Both had been captured as slaves in infancy. On seeing her brother the poor woman burst into tears, but did not, through timidity, make herself known the first day, merely leaving a message that he should be asked whether his name was not so-and-so when he was young. The following day her owner came for the brother (called by us Barootee, or Powder), and led him away. Several Seedees went to witness the scene, and I felt much inclined to be equally intrusive. They reported that the girl, who was very like her brother, fell at his feet, got into hysterics, but could not communicate with him, as she had forgotten her native language, and Barootee did not know that of Unyoro. This was the only interview they had. She would willingly have followed him, and she sent him all she could to show her affection—namely, an immense dish of porridge and three fowls boiled into soup! Her husband or owner accompanied us on the march for several days; but Barootee said he had no present to give his sister, and she therefore was left behind.

On the 31st August, a party of Waganda came with an important message from the king that we were to return at once to him, even if we had got within a march of Kamarasi. He had something very particular to say to us, and would allow us to proceed by whatever route we chose. Budja said the order could not be disobeyed, it was imperative; but after four hours' consultation, neither side would yield, except the Seedees, who said, "We go to Uganda whether our masters like it or not." On being told they were welcome to leave, but they must not take their guns, as they were Speke's property, they got up abruptly, saying, "The guns are ours, and we march to-morrow with Budja to M'tessa." They insolently beat the drum at night for a morning's march. Kamarasi seems to have had information of this, for nearly two hundred men, all armed, were collected and gathered round our hut next day to resist, if necessary, any attempt made by the Waganda to take us forcibly away. However, they were not required, as by six o'clock of the morning of the 1st September twenty-eight Seedees deserted with Budja, who took with him the rain-gauge as a present for his king. Thus we were well rid of all the disaffected of our camp, and left simply with Bombay and our best Seedee servants.[3]

2d to 9th September.—The great events of this week were elephant-shooting and our arrival in sight of Kamarasi's residence.

Let us note the former. A number of Wanyoro led the way out of camp to a forest covered with tall grasses like wild oats, and with ordinary-sized shady trees. Mounds of earth, the formation of white ants, were here and there visible. After a time the boughs bore marks as if lightning had struck them, they were broken so wantonly; the grasses underneath were trodden as if they had been passed over by a roller. All the spoors were

---

[1] In other words, when Petherick had provided new supplies.

[2] This shows that some slaves from the coastal trade had been brought *inland* from Zanzibar.

[3] By the end of the journey, only eighteen 'faithfuls' were left. Speke, *Journal*, p. 611.

fresh, so that every moment we expected to see the herd, and not a little excitement prevailed. A low whistle from a sharp-eared Wanyoro made us all exchange glances. He had heard the cracking of branches, and soon, sure enough, about three hundred yards distant, in the open grass, were the blue backs of about forty elephants. I had never seen such a sight,[1] and Speke wished me to have the first shot; but another herd appeared in an opposite direction, and I preferred going alone, with a single follower carrying a spare gun. Here, whichever way we looked, for three-fourths of the horizon, elephants were seen, all grazing quietly, perfect "lords of the forest," and so unconcerned that I walked boldly upright through the grass to a tree within fifty yards of twenty of them. It was a beautiful sight; all were mothers with their young; none so large as the Indian breed, but short, stumpy, handy-looking animals, with small, long, and uniform tusks. The most game point and the most striking about them was the peculiar back-set of their enormous ears. While waiting to get a close shot by their coming nearer me, I looked round for my man with the second rifle. Master Seedee was nowhere! so putting up my Lancaster rifle, and aiming behind the shoulder of an old female with long tusks, I fired: she merely mingled with her comrades, who stood around in stupid alarm. In an absent fit of gazing, I forgot to reload till they were approaching me. I then changed my position to another tree, within thirty yards of a full-sized animal, whose shoulder-blade wrinkles I could trace distinctly, and brought her down on her hind-quarters with a small bullet. Up she got, rushed in amongst some others, who, with tails erect, commenced screeching and trumpeting, dreadfully alarmed, not knowing what was taking place. At last, some head wiser than the others took the lead, and off they all scuttled into thicker cover. I ran after them, but the jungle got so dense that there was some fear I should lose my way, as no one was within hail. Returning to more open cover, a female elephant was coming diagonally towards me, and she passed so close that I saw her wink her eye; but the bullet behind the shoulder, though delivered at eleven paces, only frightened her into a bowling amble with her tail half cocked. A low whistle now announced Speke close by. He had been trying their heads as well as shoulders, and had no better luck than myself. The Wanyoro guides joined us, as all the elephants had left, and kept saying to us in compliment, "Weewaleh, muzoongoo m'saeja"[2]—You white men *are* men. The same compliments on our bravery awaited us on our arrival in camp, where we were looked upon as wonderful sportsmen for having gone so near elephants. During the night we heard their wild music, first to the west, then to the north, gradually dying away in the distance. The herd had very wisely marched, taking their wounded along with them.

[1] Evidence that elephants had been cleared from the areas the Expedition had so far traversed as a result of the tremendous demand for ivory.

[2] Perhaps more correctly, *Wale wazungu m'shuja*.

CHAPTER XII

[Pages 277–300]

Bunyoro, the Omukama Kamarasi and Embarking on the Nile [9 September– 9 November 1862]

The country, for a few marches before reaching the residence of King Kamarasi of Unyoro, was gently undulating and evergreen, with tall grass and trees. On the light and higher grounds the grasses grew six feet high, with large panicles which adhered to one's dress. Where the richer soil had been washed down to the low grounds the vegetation was shorter but more luxuriant. Nothing could be more desolate than our encampment at the capital of Unyoro.[1] I can only compare it to a bare and dreary common—not a tree nor a garden to relieve the eye or afford shade from the equatorial sun. The vast plain was covered with tall grass, through which at this season we could not walk without wading, so that we were completely hemmed in by water.[2] The northern half of the horizon presented a few small detached hills, the most interesting being in Kidi. They sloped away to the north from a high bluff point at their southern extremity.[3]

Our huts were within a few yards of a sluggish stream, the Kuffo,[4] from Uganda. Its depth, its mud-coloured water, and the tall rushes with which it was fringed on each side, prevented us from seeing the crocodiles with which it is said to swarm. In the third week of October its waters had swollen immensely, and bore along with them islands of the papyrus which it had torn away in its course, and on which I often wished myself embarked, as they were on their way to Egypt. Several times, when a gleam of sunshine broke upon the hills of Kidi, we could see from a height near camp the river Nile, looking like a mirage, but we were prohibited from going nearer it.[5]

While fishing upon the Kuffo I was rather surprised to find that its bottom was pebbly, while its banks were formed of retentive clay, about ten feet in depth, through which no water seemed to percolate. The soil upon the pathways, after it had been thoroughly

---

[1] See Figure 82, p. 268.

[2] The Expedition was on the western fringes of Lakes Kyoga and Kwania, an extremely ill-drained area of rather indeterminate drainage. See Introduction, pp. 43–5, and Maps 6 and 7, pp. 31–2.

[3] This seems to refer to the hills between the Victoria Nile and Aswa valleys with the high point possibly being Ngeta at 4,069 ft (1,240.2 m) near present-day Lira. What Grant called Kidi is part of the territory of the Lango people.

[4] The River Kafu here flows to the north-east and debouches into the Nile just south of Masindi Port; it lies in the same valley as a stream flowing westward into Lake Albert – another oddity of the drainage in this region. See Map 6, p. 31.

[5] This gave critics of Speke grounds for claiming that he had not proved that his 'Nile' coming from the Ripon Falls was the Nile of Egypt. See, e.g. Burton, *The Nile Basin*, p. 16 and *passim*.

washed with rain, became of pure white sand, without gravel, and formed a pleasant walk. It was a loam, with from 40 to 70 per cent of clay, and, if closely drained, would make excellent land for growing wheat.

Of the surrounding countries we obtained a good deal of geographical knowledge; for the people here were not afraid, like those about M'tessa of Uganda, to state what they knew. We had fully expected to receive letters from Egypt, but saw only some beads quite new to us, which must have been brought from thither. Until Bombay should return with a letter from a party of Egyptian ivory-traders to the north, we did not feel that the two hemispheres[1] had been thoroughly united by our efforts. Our first move was to make the junction with these traders at Faloro. We were told that the water route was impracticable, and we afterwards found this to be the case, owing to the cataracts on the river between Chopeh and Madi.[2] Were it not for these, our informants told us we might proceed the whole way by water. This intelligence, together with our own observations of the level nature of the country, enabled Speke to map the bend of the Nile,[3] which we were not able to visit, it being entirely off our direct route, and within the province of a rebel chief.[4]

One of the king's officers had travelled to the Masai country, to the east of Kamarasi's, and he said we might do the same, if his king gave us a particular horn filled with charms to be carried at the head of our party. This, with 600 iron hoes, giving two to each chief of a district, would enable us to get through the unexplored country without molestation.[5]

This man also spoke a good deal about the Lweetan-zigeh (the Luta-nzige of Speke), an immense body of water some marches away to the south-west, and extending back towards Karague.[6] He thought we should take twenty days to reach it; but a M'ganda would go the distance in half that time. This is the lake whose position we expect the enterprising Sam Baker[7] to ascertain, as we gave him a map of its general direction, and he would also be enabled to verify the latitude and altitude of that portion of *our* journey

---

[1] That is, north and south of the Equator.

[2] The Karuma and the Murchison Falls. Chopi is the northern part of Bunyoro then inhabited by people who were basically Acoli. See Johnston, *Uganda Protectorate*, II, pp. 581, 591. Madi is the northern part of Acoli territory adjoining the east bank of the Albert Nile.

[3] Of the many bends in the Nile in the region, Grant possibly means the great more than right-angled bend east of the Karuma Falls at approximately 2°16′N 32°20′E. Alternatively, this is a reference to the major gap left in the Expedition's coverage of the Nile by reason of the two men proceeding north-west from near the Karuma Falls to near the confluence of the Aswa with the Nile, so missing the Murchison Falls, the head of Lake Albert and the upper part of the Albert Nile. See Map 10, p. 66.

[4] That is, Kamarasi's cousin and rival, Ruyonga, with whom Samuel Baker was later unwisely to ally himself. Beattie, *Nyoro State*, pp. 29, 65, 69. For Baker, see below, n. 7, p. 284, n. 1, p. 325, n. 4.

[5] Whether there had been such a journey seems doubtful but the supposedly fierce Masai were known by hearsay in many other parts of East Africa.

[6] More correctly in Runyoro, Mwitanzige, the water later named (inevitably) by Samuel Baker during his visit to Bunyoro of 1864–5, Lake Albert. Many, including Livingstone, erroneously thought that an ultimate source of the Nile further south than Speke's Lake Victoria might be found to flow into Lake Albert whose actual size Baker greatly exaggerated.

[7] Samuel Baker (1821–93), whose later knighthood Grant rather resented, was to meet Speke and Grant at Gondokoro. Armed with the information from Grant's map (Plate 1), he was able to go on to discover 'Lake Albert' as well as involve himself in Bunyoro politics. Later, Egypt appointed him 'Governor of Equatoria' as the attempt was made to annex the interlacustine region. Baker grossly exaggerated his own achievements and concealed the harm he had done, but obtained fame and fortune at home as a result.

over which he might pass. When last heard of, he had manfully gone back on our track and reached Kamarasi's. God grant that he may be spared to return.[1]

Far to the north-west of our position, at Unyoro, are people named Ooreea-Wantu—translated eaters of men, cannibals the Walæga, perhaps.[2] We saw some of them, but were told they had drunk or tasted the blood of Kamarasi in the same way that Kidjweega and Manua had made brotherhood.

We had a considerable quantity of rain during our stay here. The showers were very partial, appearing to fall from six or seven different points of the heavens at the same moment, while the small river by our camp had been rising for three days, though we had no rain. There were no regular prevalent winds at this season; three violent storms, all from different directions, the north, south-west, and south, were noted.

An observation of the weather, from sunset of the 7th November to 8 P.M. of the 8th, is here given:—

Sunset.—A bank of clouds collected in the south-west.
Night.—Still and fair.
7 A.M.—Perfect calm; the grasses arching with the weight of dew.
9 A.M.—A breath of air. Last night's clouds rising. Clear horizon from north to east.
Noon.—Heavens fleeced over with cloud. Gentle breeze.
3 P.M.—Breeze increased to freshness. Temperature, 82° in the shade.
Sunset.—Wind dying away. Heavy clouds over the south horizon.
8 P.M.—Still and calm. Sky half covered with watery clouds.

Every morning and every day seemed alike, only varied by occasional falls of rain. The mornings were dull, with fogs hanging low, the paths wet, and the tall grasses dripping with dew. A fire was very comfortable at night, particularly when the rain trickled through the roofs of our small grass huts. We suffered no inconvenience from the heat, being always sheltered.

We had no sport while here. The king was such a morose autocrat he would not allow us to go beyond our dwellings; but this was no great loss, the country being mostly covered with water. It had been said of this country that the fences of the huts were made of elephants' tusks; but we found that the natives rarely killed the elephant,[3] and when they did, used only the rudest uncertain methods. No pitfalls were seen, merely a heavy wedge of iron suspended from a tree.[4] A leopard-kitten was one day brought us; he had been caught in the rushes, and Speke desired to buy him and make a pet of him, but his owner would take nothing for him in case he should happen to die; if, however, he survived, a present would be acceptable. The little animal seemed to pine away for want of its natural food, and died in a few days, when it was given back to be eaten by its original owner.

The king had a large coarse breed of dogs, foxhound colour, although he never seemed to employ them for any purpose. He wished us to give him a medicine to prevent disease amongst cattle; but our own soon became affected, and we knew of no remedy. The

[1] Of course, he had not done so before Grant's book was written and published.

[2] The Walega are a group within those classified as Equatorial Bantu who, surprisingly according to Murdock, have a 'notorious addiction ... to the practice of cannibalism'. Murdock, *Africa*, pp. 278–80.

[3] Sheriff draws attention to this evidence and adds that it was not until 1877 that coast traders managed to outflank Buganda and get ivory directly from Bunyoro. Sheriff, *Slaves, Spices and Ivory*, p. 184. Doyle dates the change from 1872. Doyle, *Crisis and Decline*, p. 44.

[4] Such a trap is shown in Figure 87, p. 332.

complaint attacked grown-up animals of all ages; they became thin, with a staring coat, refused food, sometimes frothed at the mouth; and as certain as they were attacked, although showing no signs of actual distress, their death was inevitable.[1] The natives always ate the carcass, but the meat looked fly-blown and discoloured. Calves appear to suffer from a weakness in the limbs. Our cowherd came, with a five-days-old calf following him, to our door, asking for a thread to tie round each of its hocks. On being asked what charm this had, the reply was, "Don't you see that he cannot put his hoofs flatly on the ground; that he is walking upon his toes? This thread will give him strength!" The calf actually did become strong. We found that some meat would not keep beyond a single day; this was not attributed to the heat, but to the man who had performed the operation of killing the cow. "He must be a dirty fellow, sleeping cuddled up with his hands between his knees." "If Baraka had been there to kill the animal, the meat would have kept for four days." Goats were never healthy; the soil stuck between their hoofs, making them foot-sore, dejected, and unable to graze with any apparent satisfaction.

We were unsuccessful in fishing with the hook. The natives had a better system; they set creels, into which they drove the fish in numbers. At the Ripon Falls, while Speke was there, the Waganda plied to considerable purpose a barbless hook, baited with roasted plantain cut in dice. On trying the fishing in the Kuffo, first with entrails, and afterwards with worms from the mud on the banks of the river, none would take properly, and the stream was too muddy for the fly. Four loads of dried fish, as black as tar, were sent us by the king. Our men did not recognise them, but called them "mamba," the name for crocodile, because they had large teeth, and were supposed, from the rounded form of two of their fins, to suckle their young. Manua, on being asked to have some replied that he had never tasted fish, and did not see why he should begin then; our men also had some objection to them; and when the women of the country were shown them, they ran away. In fact, some of these very species were purchased at the Ripon Falls, but the women refused to cook them. I tasted both a bit of the tail and shoulder; the former had been dried to a stick, and the latter was tough and tasteless. All had been caught in the Nile, and were eaten by the male population alone.[2]

On my asking some of our Seedees, four in succession, if they had eaten rats, all pleaded guilty, saying, "We have eaten every living thing except hippopotamus, dogs, snakes, and cats. Rats were better food than beef, tasting sweetly, like tender chickens, and frogs were also very excellent! But now that they had become Mussulmans, they had given up living upon these animals." None had ever eaten human flesh, but they stated that when a person in their country of Uhiao dies from having been bewitched, the wizard eats part of the body to complete his incantation. In our huts the number of rats and lizards living on friendly terms together was immense. Every house had two or three traps, but these did

---

[1] Presumably, this was rinderpest. If so, it is evidence that the disease was already prevalent before the outbreak of the 1890s which affected so much of Eastern and Southern Africa, compounded as it often was by the changes brought on by colonial conquest. British and Baganda interests were to combine to make the Banyoro suffer grievously at that time. Doyle, *Crisis and Decline*, pp. 2, 90–91. However, see Koponen, *People and Production*, pp. 168–70, on early examples of rinderpest and the likelihood of the presence of other cattle diseases in the pre-colonial period.

[2] It is not clear what kind of fish this was. Although it might seem to be the Nile perch, *Lates niloticus*, Grant's assertion that it was the same species as obtained at the Ripon Falls throws doubt on this as the Nile perch was not introduced to Lake Victoria until a hundred years later.

not keep them down, or prevent their annoying fowls, in consequence of which the latter could not hatch on the ground, and were suspended, like flower-pots, from the ceiling in a tray made from the leaf of the plantain. Lizards fed upon cockroaches and other insects, and much enjoyed picking the bone of a fowl. There were two species; the largest was dark, covered with bright spots, with a white fish-like belly; the other and more handsome one had a bright stripe down either side, from the arch of the eye to the tail. Rats fed like rabbits on grass, or flour when they could get it. Whenever we camped near swamps the musquitoes were in myriads, working their way even through bed-curtains of net.

Nine days elapsed before the suspicions of the king would permit of our seeing him. Our servants had many interviews before his highness would grant us an audience. But it was at last brought about by informing him that, as he seemed to prefer black to white men, we would shave our heads and beards, blacken our faces, and present ourselves! His messengers at once brought a reply, that we must not do so, for the king was preparing a house and throne where the reception would shortly take place.

Extract from Journal: Negotiations with Kamarasi, the Omukama of Bunyoro
11 [September] Kidg[wiga] and co arrive from the Palace where they had spent the whole day, with the K[ing]'s compliments telling us not to [complain?] at our not yet having seen him ... They said the king, wishing to show his visitors, many having collected from all the countries about, what dangerous people we were to meet on land or water, having instruments to kill anything at far distances, was quite ashamed when three shots were fired at a cow standing, that it was not even touched ... However, Bombay arriving, explained all ... they had fired over the cow purposely. [NLS, MS. 17915, 11 September 1862]

His excuses were, that he had heard many bad reports of us through Waganda, who said we required several men and women for our daily food; that we drank up rivers and ate up mountains; that he did not know exactly what to believe; but we must have patience, and we should be gratified.

Extract from Journal: The Baganda Tell Scare Stories
12 [September] B[ombay] said the King asked why do they need to see me in such a hurry? They'll see me but wait a little; it was I who ordered them back out of Unyoro for the Wag[anda] said of the English that they devoured mountains and swallowed up lakes ... He did not mind this but thought it took six people daily to satisfy them eating ears & cheeks & private parts of men & women. Fearing this & to spare his subjects, he forbade our visiting him; he wished us every success but would not hear of us going to Ugani until his men from there arrived; if anything happened to us, he'd get blamed ... [He] wished to be taught the use of guns[1] and to send us in among the Wakidi to frighten them. [NLS, MS. 17915, 12 September 1862]

He had some Wanyamuezi guests whom he made swear, by stepping over their arms (bows and spears), that we did not do these things. They became answerable for us, consenting, as a punishment, to be circumcised if we should commit a fault. Although the king, from suspicion and timidity, took these precautions, he would daily inquire for our health,

---

[1] On the next day, apparently, Bombay did shoot a cow. Speke, *Journal*, pp. 503–4.

sending provisions occasionally; and on being asked what he would do if the Waganda carried out their intention of rescuing us from him, he replied, seizing a stick and holding it like a spear, that he would not allow them to touch a hair of the white men's heads. If they came, he would put us in boats, and send us away to our own country. He was lost in admiration of our hardihood in coming to such a far-away land. We must be devils; we must fight his rebel brother,[1] and also fight the Kidi—a race of people who constantly annoyed him.

His highness's residence, for the last seven years, had been where we now saw him, in a naturally strong position, on the point of low flat land between the Nile and the Kuffo.[2] About three hundred huts of grass stood here, covering an area of two square miles. One dwelling was conspicuous amongst the rest, from its size, and in it his highness resided, with his cattle and followers around him. This station had been chosen in preference to his proper residence, three marches south, as a greater security against the attacks of his rebel brother Reonga, living upon an island down the Nile.

Extract from Journal: The First Meeting with Kamarasi

18th [September] By noon a Wezee came calling us for the King is quite prepared ... Our marches start[ed] with the Union Jack at our head and after 100 [yards] [we] came to this little river where lay two immense single-logged canoes. In these we were ferried over after all our guns were fired ... Then [we] got hoisted out to a small landing ... 20 yards to the door of a twelve-feet high circular hut. Fronting the entry was a three-foot high throne of grass covered with leopard & cow skins. On a higher step was Kamarasi. [After limited talk], Kamar[asi] intimated that we had permission to leave. No goodbye took place & we left the cold reception for the canoes & home reflecting on its contrast to Rumanika's warm friendly one and the gay scenes at M'tessa'a palace. Not a drum nor a note of music & the only interruption to the slow affair was many of his subjects standing outside the door shouting allegiance ... [NLS, MS. 17915, 18 September 1862]

In appearance the king was fair for an African, of slender figure, nearly six feet high, and about forty years of age.[3] His features were good, with soft gentle eyes; in sitting he would often rest his head upon his hand, with his elbow on his knee, and having long arms, this position did not seem constrained. As was the custom of the natives of his country, all the lower incisors and eye-teeth had been extracted in his youth, and the dentist to his father received the handsome sum of one hundred cows for the operation. The teeth are probably taken out by the head of a spear or small knife, as no more refined weapon, such as a dentist's key or pinchers, was observed in the country. His forehead was disfigured by black patches where it had been burned or cauterised for headache or other ailments; on his nose he had a similar mark, which he wished us to take off because it disfigured him. We never saw him wear any calico or silks; a bark-cloth covering, tied round his body tightly from above the waist to his heels, was his only raiment. It was the usual salmon

---

[1] Ruyonga was constantly in revolt against Kamarasi and the latter's successor, Kabarega. Ruyonga was a prince who was Kamarasi's father's brother's son's son. Beattie, *Nyoro State*, pp. 64–5.

[2] The position would appear to be near but south of the modern Masindi Port, presumably on or near the eastern bank of the Kafu River.

[3] Grant's two depictions of Kamarasi are shown in Plate 38 and Figure 81, p. 267, with the dates being 29 October and 5 November 1862. On the problem of Figure 81, see below, p. 290.

colour, but had small pieces of black bark-cloth, sewn very neatly with a looping stitch, dotting it all over. His head was periodically shaved, scissors being unknown; and small tufts of wool, the size of black pepper-corns. were the only protection. A single necklace of beads, worn very long, was his most conspicuous ornament. By his side a spear rested against the wall; its blade was neatly capped over with leather, laced like a shoe with two long strips from the skin of a leopard.

Our presents of beads, boxes, guns, cloth, &c., were received by Kamarasi very coolly, with no sign of pleasure, only an occasional remark. He sat, as Bombay said, "like a cow," showing neither astonishment nor delight. A pair of spectacles put on by Bombay created a titter amongst the men, but he remained perfectly solemn. Nothing was examined by him, or handled with that eagerness which all other Africans were in the habit of showing; all was affected indifference. None of these things were new to him; he had seen all, except the double-barrelled rifle, and the watch which he saw Speke take out of his pocket. This watch, a valuable chronometer, was yielded to him at our second interview; and whenever he received it, he told us that we had better leave—it was going to rain! Though he now followed us to the canoe in which we embarked to cross to our huts, and stood on the shore, spear in hand, till we had landed on the opposite side, he neither bade us adieu nor smiled; and even the natives accompanying him squatted or stood unconcerned. However, we paid him every honour, standing up in the canoe, with the union-jack floating high over our heads.

At the other interviews it was constant begging; he must have table-knives, musquito-curtains, our pots and pans, our medicines, finger-rings, &c., and most of them had to be rendered up. Once, when we had got into our boat after an audience, he followed and ordered us out into one with water in it, because he required the best canoe for himself. All was done so roughly, and with such a total want of grace and hospitality, that, at the moment, I felt inclined to throw myself into the river and swim across it, but the effect would have been lost upon such a cold-blooded mortal.

Extract from Journal: Introducing the Bible[1]

29 [October] While working out time, messengers came saying the King wished to see us in the hut just erected on the left bank of the "Kuffo". The usual chilling reception took place ... S[peke] asked how he was. K.V.[2] said "If he were not well he would not be here" What coarseness. [Speke said] I have brought a book (the bible) in which the history of your forefathers is written. They and we were descended from Adam. After [the] Flood, Ham Shem & Japhet ... were talked of. He signed for the book to be given to him when he commenced seeing whether there was a page of the History coinciding with what S[peke] said was the age of the book [by counting the leaves]. He grew tired before he was ¼ through it. K.V. counting also & conversation joining in. He was pleased with its gilt edges ... Mtessa's rule talked of, his succession to the throne, stealing two of our men ... We asked to leave at once [to go] next to the Lake to the West. What Lake does he mean? ... They mentioned the name of a place when I took out his tablet of ivory and wrote it down.

---

[1] See Plate 38.

[2] Grant's abbreviation for 'Kamaraviona' meaning Chief Minister. He is using the term they had learned in Buganda although the offices were not really comparable. Kamarasi's leading adviser was a man called Kategora. Doyle, *Crisis and Decline*, p. 53.

K[amarasi]'s eye caught it & he must play with it & the pencil. Tired of this ... he said why have they not brought the medicine chest. I want to see everything they have got. I'll steal nothing. This was the first damper we got – the commencement of fleecing ... [NLS, MS. 17915, 29 October 1862]

Extract from Journal: Kamarasi Sends Entertainment

3d [November] Halted. Sent our men to King begging to be allowed [to] march. They soon returned having seen the King superintending the milking of his cows after which he listened [to our message], saying you will receive our answer by K.V. A dwarf nearly two [?] high or 37 inches & 30 years old was brought to us. [He was] deformed, bandy-legged, big headed, face like a monkey ... waddled in walking [with his] long staff and went through antics ...[1] [NLS, MS. 17915, 3 November 1862]

On his sending to announce that he would pay us a visit,[2] Speke prepared his hut as nicely as our means admitted, by ornamenting it with antelope-horns, blankets from our beds, the union-jack, &c. A japanned tin case was covered for his highness's throne, and a donkey-rug placed for his feet. Salutes were arranged to announce his arrival, and all our men had donned their best to pay him every honour. But our preparations were not seen to advantage, for a wooden stool and some leopard-skins were placed for his majesty to sit upon, hiding our decorations. On being asked to change his seat for the one we had prepared, he eyed it suspiciously, and in a coarse voice asked what it was—what was underneath? and on being shown that it was no more than a box such as he had previously received in a present, he sat himself down upon it. The conversation turned upon trade. "Did he desire traffic by opening the road to the north?" With his usual chilling stiff manner, though seeing the advantage to himself, he replied that all the ivory of his country now goes to Zanzibar,[3] because he is constantly at war with the tribes to the north: two days he is at peace, and five days at war (curiously enough indicating the division of time into weeks). Changing the subject, he commenced to scold a swarm of boys who were naturally peering in at the door. He ordered all but a few listeners to withdraw, and now commenced begging everything he saw in the hut. Pointing to his cheek, head, and back, he said that all his children after a certain age die; we must give him a cure for this. A quantity of medicine was tied up in a veil, and he left abruptly, saying to his men, "Erokh togendeh."[4]—Let us go. Although we accompanied him to his canoe, he took no notice of us, and was paddled across by some naked boys. No influential persons were around him, and when one of the scullers fell overboard the canoe was not stopped. The creature swam ashore, and commenced to scrub himself without any ceremony before his highness the king of Unyoro.

---

[1] See Grant's depiction of this man, named Kimenyi, Figure 80, p. 267. His caption, however, amends the age of Kimenyi to 48. The same page of Grant's illustrations shows a monkey; the implicit and unfortunate comparison was probably intended as the text may suggest.

[2] This had been on 25 September 1862. Grant's text here fairly closely follows his original journal entry for that date. NLS, MS. 17915, 25 September 1862.

[3] This situation was to change abruptly with the arrival just after Speke and Grant had left of the rapacious Khartoum-based ivory and slave raiders.

[4] Perhaps the phrase was *Nakwenda*. Whether this is a sign that Kamarasi had become familiar with Swahili is not clear. Most of the negotiations with him were through the medium of Bombay's interpretations.

With all his apparent rudeness, Kamarasi was not unkindly. Though his neighbour, M'tessa, ordered his subjects to be butchered, no such savage custom prevailed in Unyoro; men were admonished, and told how fortunate they were under the king's lenient rule. Murderers, however, were flogged or speared, and their bodies thrown into the river Kuffo. Scarcely a day passed that we did not receive a little flour, some drink (very coarse and bad), sweet potato, or other remembrance; but the great present was made soon after our arrival, when we each had ten cows and five fowls sent us, with an explanation that the king thought it necessary to send us separate presents, as we had approached him by different routes. Before leaving, we solicited, and were presented with, a few more cattle, and a tusk was offered to each of our head-servants. In return for his presents, Kamarasi received English and foreign goods to the value, in England, of £150 sterling; this included a double gun and rifle, a chronometer, &c. Besides these, he obtained a considerable quantity of property left behind at Karague; so that it is confidently hoped he will treat all future white men with due hospitality.[1]

Kamarasi was constantly visited by men of far countries coming to trade with him for cattle, slaves, and ivory.[2] By his permission, the Waganda who had accompanied Speke to the Ripon Falls arrived with a message for us from their king. When they appeared, in their beautifully clean dresses, our hearts quite warmed towards them as old friends. Their orders, they said, were to accompany us through fire and water as far as we wished, only they were not to go to England! Kamarasi would not hear of this, telling them, until he heard farther from M'tessa, he would not risk their lives amongst the wild people of Kidi and Madi;[3] so they had to return to their king with a messenger from us in the form of a tin-lid, which was supposed to convey our kind remembrances. We gave them some salt, which they licked like sugar. Unfortunately they would not eat our beef, as it had not been killed by one of themselves, and had been boiled in our pots; however, they got some porridge, some m'wengé, and a cow. Before leaving, after having knelt to "nyanzig" (return thanks) at our door, they expressed themselves devoted to us; "their lips had been sweetened and their hearts warmed in our society." The skins on which they had been seated in our hut were smartly bundled up by boy-pages, their court-dresses exchanged for marching costume, and away the merry creatures went back to their king. I learned with regret that my good friend Budja had died from the fatigues of marching back and forward between Uganda and Unyoro. The report was that the "black art" had accomplished his end. A thorough soldier the poor fellow was, with good tact and spirit.

People from Gani to the north often paid Kamarasi visits: they and the Kidi were similar in one respect—neither, in their own country, wore any covering around the loins,

[1] Unfortunately this did not happen because Baker, who was the next European visitor, was associated with Khartoum raiders and, on his 1864 visit and a subsequent one on behalf of the Khedive of Egypt, undermined any goodwill that Speke and Grant may have created, to the long-lasting detriment of Bunyoro. See Beattie, *Nyoro State*, pp. 62–9. On the way in which events on the ground and the interests of African peoples can affect the *narrative* produced by the Western participant or observer in the particular instance of Baker and Bunyoro, see the important article by Wisnicki, 'Rewriting Agency', pp. 1–27.

[2] The list of goods was far more extensive than Grant learned, including locally produced salt, many foodstuffs, cattle, goats, tobacco etc. See Doyle, *Crisis and Decline*, pp. 29–30. Reid, *Political Power*, p. 117, sees Grant's evidence as an indication that Kamarasi's capital was an important slave-trading centre from which Buganda obtained large numbers of its slaves.

[3] See following footnote.

and their language was a perfectly new one to our men, as well as to the great majority of the people of Unyoro.[1] They used to come with strange presents: for instance, a small tusk, the skin of a tippet monkey, a string of handsome beads procured from Egyptian traders, and the tail of a giraffe, formed one present received by the king while we were there. They returned to their homes with a few cattle in exchange.[2] The Wagani had conveyed and brought back Bombay from the camp of Nubians, and for this service they received a cow. After it had been skinned, the muscle that lies on either side of the backbone was neatly taken off in a long ribbon, the meat scraped off, and eaten before us without being cooked. A portion of the entrails was also eaten raw at the same time. It seemed quite a *bonne bouche* to them after their journey; and on the following morning, when they were seen wearing the fat of the animal twisted in a coil round their bare necks, they looked fresh and well after their dinner of the previous day. This custom of eating a little raw meat from an animal immediately after it has been killed is not an uncommon one, but I do not think they are fond of it after the meat has been allowed to become cold; they then have it cooked.

The language of Unyoro, as spoken by its natives, although it differs but slightly from that spoken in Karague, was not understood by our Seedees until they had been some weeks in the country. It had not the mumbling sounds of the Uganda dialect, where their d, g, k, &c., and most consonants, are doubled in pronunciation. The dialect of the Chopi, Kidi, and Gani was perfectly unintelligible to our Seedees. They said it sounded in their ears like English; but there was no resemblance, every word uttered being guttural, and not thrown smoothly out from the lips, but kept in the mouth by closing the throat with the root of the tongue. Many of the names of our Seedees, such as M'kate, Uledi, and Sirboko, all coast words, were heard in Unyoro applied to men of the country. We also found this in Uganda; and Kamarasi is the name of an Indian Bunnea, or corn-dealer, living at Pangani on the east coast of Africa. These names are diffused over the country by means of the slave-trade.[3]

The wives of the king lived upon milk, and were of enormous proportions—drinking the milk of from five to fifteen cows daily. They were slovenly and listless, not able even to make butter, or assist in any household work, and never appearing at any audience given us. In the fields, while at work, the women wore a neat kilt of bark-cloth to the knees, and had nothing on the head or above the waist. One came to our hut while it rained, saying

---

[1] Grant now begins to refer to the Chopi, Gani, Kidi and Madi. As he comprehends, they are linguistically distinct from the peoples whom he has so far encountered. In other words, they were non-Bantu and are now normally referred to as 'Nilotic' although there has been much debate about classification and confusion over nomenclature. The Chopi are a Lango-related group who lived in what is now Bunyoro District south of the Victoria Nile; the Gani are part of the Acholi living 3°N east of the Nile; the Kidi part of the Lango is 2°N also east of the Nile; while the Madi are a somewhat different 'Central Sudanic' people living in 3°50′N just west of the Albert Nile. See Girling, *The Acholi*, pp. 237–8. For a succinct account of the Banyoro and Nilotic connections, see Wrigley, *Kingship and State*, pp. 74–5. Grant depicts the Kidi and the Gani in, respectively, Figure 83, p. 268, and Plate 40. The Banyoro themselves are shown in Plate 39.

[2] In bringing tributes to Kamarasi, the peoples referred to in the previous note may have been acknowledging their once having been part of the much larger forebear of Bunyoro, the Empire of Bunyoro-Kitara and perhaps having provided its semi-legendary ruling dynasty, the Babito. See Nyakatura, *Anatomy of an African Kingdom*, pp. 49–57; Beattie, *Nyoro State*, p. 29.

[3] This is certainly a false assumption; any similarity of names and words all over the vast region occupied by Bantu peoples long pre-dates the slave trade and Kamarasi's name is local from Bunyoro.

she feared being seen if coming at any other time, and wanted medicine. They are of an average height, and appear healthy, though their husbands complain that their offspring do not survive many years. An officer made a sad complaint to us, saying that if his wife had a child to a servant it always lived, but any she had to himself died. An extraordinary little old man, not more than three feet in height (correctly drawn in Speke's 'Journal'), paid us a visit.[1] He was perfectly sensible, though very restless while sitting for his portrait, constantly moving his head or holding up his fingers close to his one eye. In contrast to this dwarf, the king had a man who looked a giant in strength, though scarcely six feet in height. He was employed in conveying messages to us, and could go through all the motions of a warlike attack, wielding his spear with grace and agility, struggling with his enemy, planting his foot triumphantly on the dead body, snorting, and finishing off by wiping his spearhead upon the grass to free it from his supposed antagonist's blood.

A class of mendicants or gentle beggars called "Bandwa," allied to the Wichwezee,[2] seem spread all over these kingdoms. They adorn themselves with more beads, bells, brass, and curiosities than any other race, and generally carry an ornamented tree-creeper in their hands. Many of their women look handsome and captivating when dressed up in variously-coloured skins, and wearing a small turban of bark-cloth. One man amongst them wore, from the crown of his head down his back, the skin of a tippet-monkey, to which he had attached the horns of an antelope. They wander from house to house singing; and are occasionally rather importunate beggars, refusing to leave without some present. A set of them lived near us at Unyoro, and seemed to have cattle of their own, so that they do not entirely depend upon begging for subsistence. The natives all respect them very much, never refusing them food when they call, and treating them as religious devotees. Any one may join their number by attending to certain forms; and the family of a Bandwa does not necessarily follow the same occupation. I knew one of them the captain of a band of soldiers. This whole country was once occupied by people of this class, called Wichwezee, who, according to tradition, suddenly disappeared underground!

The arms used by the Wanyoro were the poorest we had anywhere seen. Bows and arrows are unknown, although their neighbours at Karague make them their chief weapon. The spear is small and weak, with a thin six-feet-long handle of ordinary wood. Excellent spear-heads are hawked for sale in the southern borders, but the Waganda, a richer people, buy them up.[3] A party of soldiers, wretched representatives, dashed into our camp one day to rescue us from the Waganda. They wore each a handkerchief of bark-cloth tied round the head, high in front like a Highland bonnet, and dirty rags of the same material covered their loins. Bead ornaments round the neck were worn by such as possessed means to obtain them. Others wore flattened pellets, larger than garden-peas, made of polished iron or ivory, and strung round the ankles.

The huts or hovels of the country were wretched; but there was this excuse for the people that no wood grew in that out-of-the-world corner—and most of the habitations

[1] See Figure 80, p. 267, for Grant's original drawing. The engraver's version, based very closely on the original, appears in Speke's *Journal* at p. 550 and the information about him on the following page shows that he was from Chopi.

[2] The Bachwezi, originally a dynasty, have in myth become spirits and these mendicants presumably claimed to be their mediums. Wrigley, *Kingship and State*, pp. 39–40.

[3] The trade deficit in arms noted by Grant reflects perhaps Kamarasi's inability to control trade. Doyle, *Crisis and Decline*, p. 30; Reid, *Political Power*, p. 140.

seen by us were temporary. Their floors were never swept, but bedded with grass, which, when it became soiled, was left there to rot like a dunghill, and fresh grass laid over it: vermin of every description swarmed.

The cultivation is carried on chiefly by women, who cut up the stiff soil with an iron hoe, and plant the various crops. We missed the shady plantain-groves of that garden of African neatness—Uganda. No fruit of any description is grown near the palace. Coffee is brought from Uddoo.[1] The vegetables are pumpkin, sweet potato, and the grains sorghum, sessamum, ooleyzee,[2] and the other ordinary varieties. The bread and porridge made from these grains are miserable; and butter being scarce, and no plantain to moisten the flour, we had very poor fare. The cowries were the chief coin of the country; two hundred of them bought a small bag of flour; and in selling the meat of a sick cow to enable us to buy fowls (for thirteen cowries each), we obtained ten foondo, or one thousand cowries. The natives were sometimes induced to sell butter by our making up necklaces with alternate-coloured beads. A string of these five times round the neck purchased three-quarters of a pound of butter, which was brought neatly tied in the broad fresh green leaves of the sorghum. We had fallen upon the man who procured this treat for us in a simple manner. Seeing him pass, his body glistening with grease, we accosted him, and gave him the commission which he executed so well. Our men killed a cow as food for themselves and us every third or fourth day. The natives, on hearing that meat was for sale in our camp, would bring their flour, tobacco, or sweet potato to barter. In this way sufficient variety was generally to be had, and both parties were accommodated. We could obtain milk daily from our own cows, though they were but poor milkers.

The intoxicating drink sent us pretty often by the king was called "m'wenge", and made from the millet murwa. Kamarasi's officer, on presenting a jar of it, would say, he "had brought it with the king's compliments," and that "we should find it as pure as water," but it tasted like the dregs of a beer-cask,[3] and I wonder how his highness could get tipsy upon such coarse spirit. The person who brought the jar always went through the form of tasting it, and the vessel was never required to be returned, as was the case in Uganda. Near the king's residence a market for this "grog," and for meat, fowls, firewood, &c., was held almost daily, our servants calling the place a bazaar; but we were never allowed to cross over the Kuffo river to inspect it.

A visit to the blacksmith's shop in any country always repays one, and there the gossip is usually heard. In Africa it seems to be the same, and idlers always lounged about the Unyoro blacksmith's. The "shop" was a ten-feet-high awning made of the stalks of sorghum. One lad sat on the ground and blew a double-handled and double-nosed bellows, the air from which passed through a detached earthen tube upon the live charcoal. Two men squatted naked all but a leathern waist-cover, hammering, talking, and smoking all at the same time. Their anvil was a flat boulder, and the hammers bolts of iron, the shape of large chisels. The only other instruments were bent sticks as pincers, and a wooden handle like that used at home for a firing-iron. One man had three iron hoes in various states of preparation; the other was making needles. When the bellows-

---

[1] Buddu, a province of Buganda.

[2] Ulezi is a form of millet.

[3] This condemnation is quoted directly from Grant's Journal. NLS, MS. 17915, 15 September 1862.

boy forgot his duty staring at me, and allowed the fire to get too brisk, the smith gave him a lecture, and some water from a brush of straw damped the flame.

One of the commodities which, being rare, we much enjoyed, was salt, brought from Kivro,[1] a place to the north-west upon the Lake Lweet-an-zigeh,[2] and which was perfectly pure in colour and taste. The natives there are said to extract it from the soil by boiling and evaporation.

The amusements of the people are few, but our Seedees remarked that the dancing of Unyoro was superior to what they were accustomed to see at Zanzibar. We had the opportunity of seeing a few of their dances, at which the men wore all the beads and shells they seemed to possess, and, forming a circle, sang and clapped their hands while going through some graceful figures. The nights were often enlivened by soft-sounding duets coming from the harmonicon and drum played across the river.

Superstition is prevalent, from the king to his lowest subject. Some straws out of the thatch of a house occupied by an enemy of Kamarasi's were to be brought us, that, bewitched by our supernatural powers, they might bring calamity upon their owner, who lived miles away. When our rain-gauge was missed, at the hour for observing it, the theft was communicated to the king, who sent a one-eyed man with a cow's horn in his hand to detect the thief.[3] The horn was capped over with a rag of bark, and had an iron bell tinkling from its top. This instrument was shaken roughly in the face of each of our Seedees as they sat down; all seemed to change colour at the suspicion, and the old man proceeded to the spot where the gauge had been taken from. He found it lying a short way off. A hyena had removed it, as his tracks were visible. This did not shake the faith of our men, but only the more strongly confirmed their belief in the "black art." Manua wore wood tied round his ankle, which he had received from some of his Waganda cronies, who told him it was a charm against snake-bites. Upon Bombay ridiculing him, he sharply replied, "Why do you take medicine from the Bana or Sahib? my charm answers the same purpose." At cross roads we several times came upon a dead frog or fowl; and in such places, if the party is wealthy enough, a goat is laid. The animals are split open, with some plucked grass beside them, and are placed there for the purpose of curing any sick member of a family. Wonderful stories were related of a dog having a single horn, and of the horn being long preserved by one of the king's officers, and used, when war broke out, to be stepped over by the troops as a good omen previous to going into action. One superstitious belief struck us as very remarkable—that Kamarasi, if he chose, could divide the waters of the lake! It seemed a long-enduring and far-spread tradition from the time of Moses.[4]

No funeral was ever seen by us in Africa, and human bones were remarkably rare. The dead are buried somewhere near the house or under the cattle-fold. The body is wrapped in bark-cloth or the skin of a cow. The king's corpse is dried with heat, and the lower jaw-bone ornamented, buried, and a tomb-house built over it. The hands and hair of kings' officers are preserved in a similar manner. The umbilical cord of male children is buried inside the doorway, and those of females outside, as was the custom also at Zanzibar. We

[1] That is, Kibiro. The Banyoro were very sophisticated salt producers using techniques which gave them sodium chloride of 97.6 per cent purity. Doyle, *Crisis and Decline*, p. 29.

[2] Lake Mwitanzige is now generally known by the name bestowed on it in 1864 by Samuel Baker, Lake Albert.

[3] Grant's sketches of some of the Banyoro include this magician with his horn. See Plate 39.

[4] There are various versions of this myth; one of the Bachwezi kings is supposed to have done this.

had not much sickness while at Unyoro, but there were some cases of tertian fever and dysentery. Amongst the inhabitants there were no remarkable diseases; the only complaint of the men was that their progeny did not always live; they could not have the number of children they wanted—a fact which can only be explained by the poverty of their diet and the abuses of polygamy.

Our situation was little better than that of a prisoner in a solitary cell. We certainly had our "morning post" after breakfast—the king's messenger—but there was seldom any news, and the day hung heavily. No one was allowed to visit us but these postmen coming to ask how we had passed the night. Natives from interesting countries all round would visit the king, but *we* could not see them! Dances and parties went on, and we could not attend them. Rain was felt as a relief, as it employed one in reading the gauge every morning. The insects at night were interesting, particularly a species of glow-worm half an inch long, seen amongst the roots of the grasses. If placed upon the hand or sleeve, it travelled quickly, throwing out a constantly twinkling light at shorter intervals than the firefly, which also was numerous. We slept in separate huts. Mine was occupied by my two servants, who, though only screened from me, talked incessantly to themselves or to me, and sometimes got up to eat in the middle of the night. The head-servant was an intelligent Seedee, named Uledi. On asking his opinion as to copal, which is used as varnish, he said it was not the production of an insect, although an insect is always seen inside; but is a formation from the roots of decayed trees, called "nango," plentiful in Utumbee.[1]

The march to the north from the capital of Unyoro was effected, as before mentioned, by sending Bombay and Mabruk in charge of some northern men, with a letter to find out whether Petherick was upon the Nile with boats for us. Kamarasi would not hear of our accompanying them: besides which, he said that, when we did leave, he meant to keep five men of each of the three races we should pass through, as hostages, till he heard of our safe arrival! After many days of suspense, on the 1st of November, when working at some lunars,[2] a gun was fired in the direction of the king's house, then another was heard. In the distance a man, it was reported, was seen with trousers on. It was Bombay; and his dress was hailed by us as a substantial proof that he had come in contact with civilisation. For a moment there was a feeling of disappointment, as if we had nothing further to do.[3] Our expedition seemed over, and we tried to scan or predict the far-distant future. What would be our next duty? What our destiny?

Extracts from Journal: Problems over Behaviour of Frij and Making Pictures during Last Days in Bunyoro

4th [November] Last night, Bombay, Frij & [?] were drunk and riotous in camp, KV coming to us to complain Frij tried to get into his house and when his wife went at him with a spear, he [broke?] it with his sword. Quite indignant he was when Frij

---

[1] Copal in East Africa is fossil resin found at the root of resin-producing trees called in the coastal areas *mnango*. East African copal was found to yield exceptionally hard-wearing varnish in use on steam locomotives. See Burton, *Lake Regions*, II, pp. 403–7, for full details.

[2] That is, astronomical observations of the distance between the Moon and Sun or a planet which can be used to determine longitude. Speke made Kamarasi's palace 32°19′49″E. Speke, *Journal*, p. 622.

[3] This feeling arose because the two men assumed that Petherick was now reasonably close with supplies and the means of getting them back down the Nile quickly; their subsequent disappointment and sense of anti-climax explains, in part at least, the bitterness towards Petherick that Speke, in particular, was to display.

came and insolently ordered him away.[1] 5th Halted ... the rain constant and I caught 4.6 inches in the tea tin. Wachopeh[2] guide came with the Inter[preter]. Both were treated for bloody discharge in urine, drank their prescriptions like men. King sent for us and after asking after his health, the conversation commenced by Speke saying "as we are about to move, what message would we carry to our Queen?" K.[amarasi] made a long speech during which I could not look at him for fear any word I misunderstood was [understood ?] in my mind into some detention[3] ... he said he would open the road for us but leave at least two of our men here with him as the whole country may hear of his strength as if we were here in person ... S[peke] asked me to take my pencil now there to sketch him, three times was he asked, twice gave no answer & the third time said am I to have myself made an image (Nosimoo)[4] No no and he then told us to go through his Inter[preter].[5] What a coarse savage! ... 6th Halted sketched the country about ... 9 Nov [1862] ... We may go today by sailing down the river & changing ground which we did, the Wany[amwezi] first disgusting me by taking two hours to pack and then leaving ten loads on the ground. The King arranged that we go down the stream in a large canoe for two miles to our camp on the left bank because he did not wish the people to see us! However, the bank was lined with several hundred people ... [NLS, MS. 17915, 4, 5, 9 November 1862]

In gratitude to Kamarasi, we sent him everything we could possibly give away, asking whether he had any objections to our leaving. He replied that a couple of our Zanzibar Seedees, with their guns, must be left with him, as he required them to deceive his enemies into believing that we were still his guests. Many other excuses about the unsafe state of the road were laid before us, but Speke's *suaviter in modo,* no less than his *fortiter in re,*[6] won the day. A parting souvenir of two spears was sent him by the king, and on the 9th November we glided down the river Kuffo. The banks of the river were lined with crowds shouting and waving adieus as we shot down the stream. Amongst them was a woman conspicuously dressed, and recognised by our men as a maid of honour, who generally sat at the feet of the king. She was the only female of rank we had seen, and she seemed plain and flat-featured. Her dress of yellow bark-cloth was striped with black, and her hair was dressed in a ridge-like form, after the fashion of the Uganda court. We enjoyed excessively the boating down stream, going at the rate of four miles an hour, and driving fish before us. The Kuffo was so broad that two "gigs" might race abreast of each other. The sides seldom admitted of landing, being margined with rushes and reeds, hiding completely the country behind them. Delightful to us was the prospect of the water route!

[1] It seems that relations were repaired later that day.

[2] That is an Acholi from Chopi in the northern part of the kingdom.

[3] This passage is difficult both to read and to comprehend but Grant perhaps feared Kamarasi would find some excuse for detaining them even longer.

[4] Perhaps the Swahili word *sanamu* was misheard.

[5] Despite this refusal, Grant did in fact produce a picture of the Omukama which was embellished with a squiggle said to be Kamarasi's 'autograph'. Presumably this was made with the pencil which, according to Speke, Kamarasi had asked for on the same day. Nevertheless, neither Grant's journal nor his book explains the way in which the picture was made or the squiggle added. Figure 81, p. 267; Speke, *Journal*, p. 554.

[6] 'Gentle in behaviour, determined in action' might be a translation of the Latin.

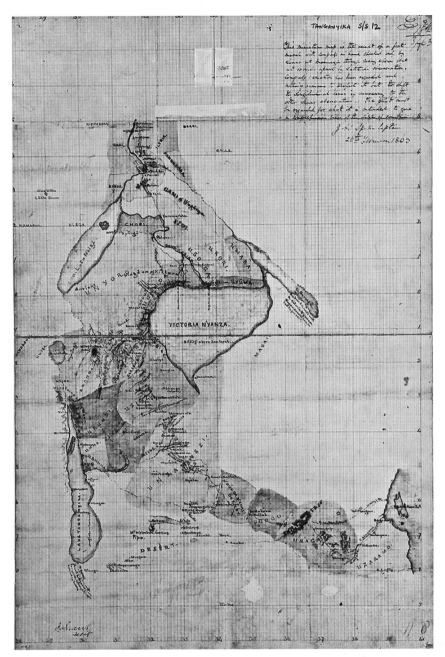

Plate 1.   'Route from Bagamoyo to Gondokoro on the White Nile'. Dated 26 February
1863, this is a map drawn by Grant when he and Speke reached Gondokoro (near present-
day Juba in South Sudan). Printed here at two-fifths size, it cannot be used as a detailed
guide to the Expedition but does show how Grant saw East Africa immediately after
leaving the Nile source area. Only four years before, maps showed the region as blank.
The work of Burton, Speke and himself now revealed great lakes, the Nile source and
previously unknown peoples. When S. W. Baker arrived in Gondokoro, the depiction of
the lake 'Little Luta Nzige' encouraged him to go on south and visit that water and name
it Lake Albert. Note how Speke takes over the map in the note on the top right yet it is
clearly Grant's work as the bottom left ascription shows. *RGS Reproductions of Early Maps*,
8, 1964, no. 5. Reproduced by permission of the Royal Geographical Society.

3. Usagara and a "Goodæ" tree.

Plate 2. 'Goodae' tree. This was depicted by Grant early in the Expedition as they went through Usagara in November 1860. In his Linnean Society List of 1875, pp. 9, 18, Grant describes this as having 'a straight trunk, and yellow, slippery bark; the trunk twists with the sun'. Oddly, he does not identify it botanically. In Swahili this is the *mparamuzi* which exudes a gum used medicinally and whose wood is used for boats and drums. NLS, MS. 17919, no. 3. Reproduced by permission of the National Library of Scotland.

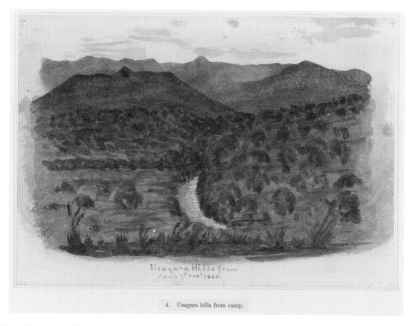

4. Usagara hills from camp.

Plate 3. Scene in Usagara. A more general view of the vegetation in the hills of Usagara. Grant took the view from the Expedition's camp on 7 November 1860. The party was now steadily ascending from the coast to the plateau at about 4,000 feet (1,219 metres). NLS, MS. 17919, no. 4. Reproduced by permission of the National Library of Scotland.

7. Unyamezi harvest, 1861.

Plate 4. The harvest in Unyamwezi. Drawn c. February 1861, this and Plate 5, following, were Grant's depictions of African material culture and were intended to make a contribution to ethnology as it was then understood. Shown here are grain storage methods, threshing, cutting sorghum, separating corn and chaff, and grinding. NLS, MS. 17919, no. 7. Reproduced by permission of the National Library of Scotland.

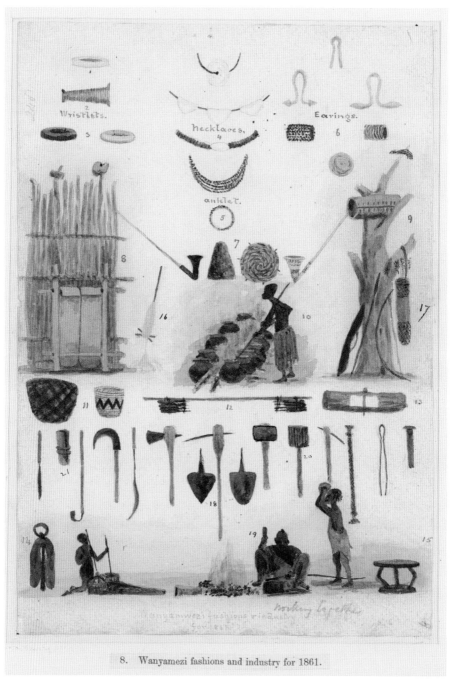

8. Wanyamezi fashions and industry for 1861.

Plate 5. Wanyamwezi fashions and industry, February 1861. Shown are: 1. ivory amulet; 2. brass wire wristlet; 3. bracelets of brass and copper; 4. necklaces of beads; 5. iron and cow's tail anklet; 6. earrings; 7. tobacco and pipes; 8. village doorway with human skull and wood; 9. beehive; 10. old woman making beer; 11. creel and drinking cup; 12. load of locally made iron hoes; 13. stocks; 14. double-toned bell; 15. sultan's seat; 16. cotton spinner; 17, quiver, bow and shield; 18. hoes; 19. blacksmith and boy at bellows. NLS, MS. 17919, no. 8. Reproduced by permission of the National Library of Scotland.

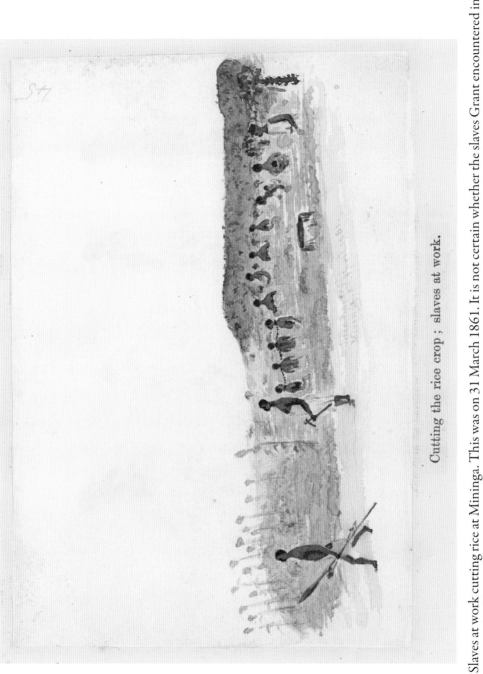

Cutting the rice crop ; slaves at work.

Plate 6.   Slaves at work cutting rice at Mininga. This was on 31 March 1861. It is not certain whether the slaves Grant encountered in this minor Nyamwezi chiefdom a few miles north of Tabora were in a traditional servile relationship or were newly captured victims of war who were being treated according to practices learned as a result of contacts with Zanzibar and the coast. The fact that they were chained together may suggest the latter explanation. NLS, MS. 17920, no. 31 verso. Reproduced by permission of the National Library of Scotland.

Within the image (handwritten annotations):

74

316

19

74

Gang of slaves with firewood.
Mininga 31st March
1861

collar open

Chain from them the rings't
clay sled tak the under.

p.20

32. Gang of slaves with firewood at Mininga.

Plate 7. A gang of slaves carrying cut wood at Mininga. These men who had been set to cut wood were also seen by Grant in Mininga on 31 March 1861. Here it is even more obvious than in Plate 6 that the slaves are chained together in a fashion which seems to reflect the way slaves were kept at the coast. As Grant makes clear in Chapter V, he believed these slaves to be owned by low-class Arabs who merely kept them alive until they could be taken to the coast. These were, Grant said, 'painful and revolting scenes'. NLS, MS. 17920, no. 32. Reproduced by permission of the National Library of Scotland.

3ʳᵈ During last night (7 or 8) three men were chased by two lions, one was victimised just as he reached the back of this hut out of the cultivation. Mininga, Ukuni 4ᵗʰ April 1861.

35. Spot where lions killed a man at Mininga.

Plate 8. Charming scene of a tragedy, 4 April 1861. The charming scene in Mininga conceals a tragedy. 'Last night (7 or 8) three men were chased by two lions; one was victimised just as he reached the back of this hut'. After nearly two months' wait in Mininga for more porters, Grant went on to Ukuni. The tree appears to be another Goodae (see Plate 2). NLS, MS. 17920, no. 35. Reproduced by permission of the National Library of Scotland.

42. Lumerezi, Sultan of Bogweh, and his palace.

Plate 9.   A minor potentate: Lumerezi of Bogwe. One of the minor 'chiefs' Grant visited on 10 June 1861, during his long sojourn in Ukuni, was Lumerezi the 'Sultan' of Bogwe as he terms the man here portrayed. NLS, MS. 17920, no. 42. Reproduced by permission of the National Library of Scotland.

The "dance at Doondah, Ukuni.

38.   The dance at Doondah.

Plate 10.   The dance at Doondah in Ukuni, 23 June 1861. This is the original of the picture which was misrepresented in the version which appeared in Speke, *Journal of the Discovery of the Source of the Nile*, p. 138, with Grant wearing Scottish-style clothes inserted as dancing with a female. See the discussion on Grant's illustrations in the Introduction, section 1. pp. 8–11. NLS, MS. 17920, no. 38. Reproduced by permission of the National Library of Scotland.

6. Maulah's village in Ukuni.

Plate 11. Maulah's village in Ukuni. Another Nyamwezi settlement visited by Grant on 23 July 1861 during the long stay in Ukuni. During this period of 1861, Grant had more time to create his pictures. He also began to learn more of African life. This is clearly a defensive site so necessary in the somewhat disturbed conditions in Unyamwezi at this time. NLS, MS. 17919, no. 6. Reproduced by permission of the National Library of Scotland.

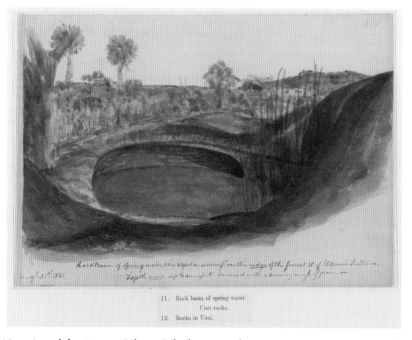

11. Rock basin of spring water. Usui rocks.
12. Rocks in Usui.

Plate 12. A rock basin near Ukuni. The basin, with pure spring water in it, was depicted by Grant on 31 August 1861. The depth came up to a man's armpits. Grant was not well versed in geology and was unable to explain the phenomenon. NLS, MS. 17919, no. 11. Reproduced by permission of the National Library of Scotland.

9. Hill of M'Phonza, Ukuni district.

Plate 13. The hill of M'Phunza with zebu cattle. Drawn near Ukuni on 27 July 1861, this is one of Grant's most successful watercolours as far as artistic competence is concerned. 'Marooned' in Ukuni for such a long period, perhaps he had more time to concentrate on his drawings and his botany. The cattle shown appear to be the small East African zebu. NLS, MS. 17919, no. 9. Reproduced by permission of the National Library of Scotland.

Plate 14. Some of the hills encircling the the Doondah valley. Another view, taken three days after Plate 13, of the hills encircling the Doondah valley in the Ukuni District of Unyamwezi, 30 July 1861. Again, this is an artistically pleasing production. The animals shown here are wild ones. NLS, MS. 17919, no. 10. Reproduced by permission of the National Library of Scotland.

August 3: 1861. The Ukuni Sultan's house = an every day scene = old Sultana entertaining some friends —

The Ukuni Sultan's house in which I lived. — Sultana at her dinner.

39. The house of the Sultan of Ukuni in which I lived. — Sultana at her dinner.

Plate 15. House of chief of Ukuni with chief's wife 'at her dinner'. The picture dates from 3 August 1861. The house of the 'sultan' or chief of Ukuni was where Grant stayed for three months. This is another successful picture from the very productive few days at the end of July and beginning of August in 1861. Note the strong palisade around the settlement. NLS, MS. 17920, no. 39. Reproduced by permission of the National Library of Scotland.

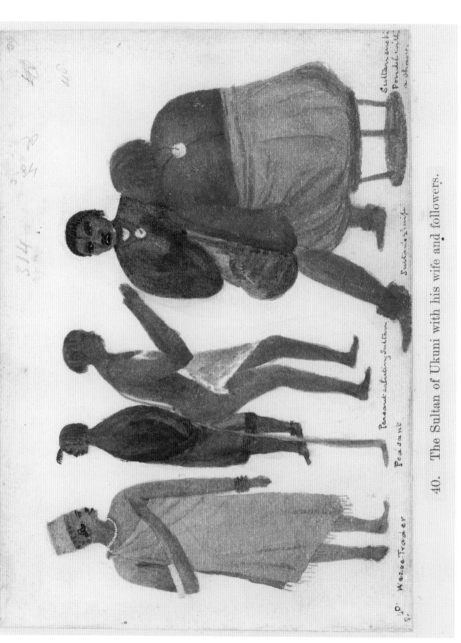

Within the image (handwritten labels): Waze Trader · Peasant · Peasant saluting Sultan · Sultan's wife · Sultan and his Pombé, wild & clear.

40. The Sultan of Ukuni with his wife and followers.

Plate 16. Chief of Ukuni with wife and other followers. The date is in August 1861. Grant found drawing human figures difficult, especially Africans, at this stage in the Expedition. From the left are shown a Nyamwezi trader, presumably from Tabora and perhaps having been a visitor to the coast as he appears to be a Muslim; a peasant; a peasant saluting the Sultan; the Sultan's wife; and the Sultan himself sucking pombé through a straw. NLS, MS. 17920, no. 40 recto. Reproduced by permission of the National Library of Scotland.

Sultan of Ukuni's village.

Plate 17.   Village of Ukuni with palisades. Another August 1861 view showing the whole village of Ukuni with its two palisaded areas – one for cattle, the other for humans. This was typical of the way settlements were arranged given threats from the Watuta or slave traders, not to mention wild animals. NLS, MS. 17920, no. 40 verso. Reproduced by permission of the National Library of Scotland.

Plate 18.   A gruesome execution for adultery, August 1861. Grant's growing sympathy for Ukuni's people was badly dented when he watched this execution for adultery. He recorded it in some detail on 17 August 1861 in two or three pictures, perhaps on the ground that it was ethnographic information. It is nevertheless difficult to square this interest with his normal outlook. NLS, MS. 17921, no. 207. Reproduced by permission of the National Library of Scotland.

Plates 19 and 20.   Depiction of a lake in Karagwe. The left and right ends of a lake seen from Grant's vantage point. There are many small lakes in Karagwe, the kingdom the Expedition had reached by November 1861; which lake is shown is not clear. Grant was most attracted by this lake area as it reminded him of the English Lake District and of Scotland. NLS, MSS. 17921, nos 11 and 12. Reproduced by permission of the National Library of Scotland.

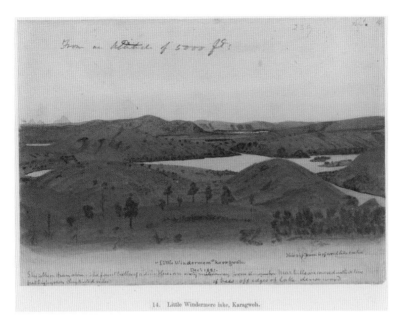

14. Little Windermere lake, Karagweh.

Plate 21. 'Little Windermere' lake. Grant thus dubbed Lweru Rwabishonga, the lake near the ruler of Karagwe's palace. His notes concern the actual tints of the colours in the picture which, using the guidance in Aaron Penley's book, he strove to make as true to life as possible. Grant's view is to the west with the intriguing line of hills he would have liked to visit. See the Introduction, section 1, and Chapter VIII. NLS, MS. 17919, no. 14. Reproduced by permission of the National Library of Scotland.

56. The gay skin costumes of Uganda.

Plate 22. 'The gay skin costumes of Uganda.' Depicted on 30 March 1862 were some of the party the Kabaka of Buganda sent to Karagwe to fetch Grant. In the centre is a boy with his drum while the figure on the right was the leader, a Mkungu, or district chief. The Baganda did wear some skin clothes but the normal dress was made of barkcloth. NLS, MS. 17920, no. 56. Reproduced by permission of the National Library of Scotland.

59. The Waganda mode of salute. M'yambo figure on the right.

Plate 23.   Salute by Baganda soldiers, 19 April 1862. How Baganda soldiers (here wearing barkcloth) salute a superior officer. Unusually, Grant has added himself (or is it Speke?) to a picture; why is not apparent. On the right is also a sketch originally made a few days earlier, of a 'Munyambo' or ordinary citizen of Karagwe who had been to the coast. NLS, MS. 17920, no. 59 recto. Reproduced by permission of the National Library of Scotland.

27. Waganda recruits at drill.

Plate 24.   Baganda recruits at drill, June 1862. Like all visitors, Grant became fascinated by the sophisticated social and political arrangements of the despotic kingdom. Here recruits to probably a raiding party pledge their loyalty: 'our hearts are true', they chant. NLS, MS. 17919, no. 27. Reproduced by permission of the National Library of Scotland.

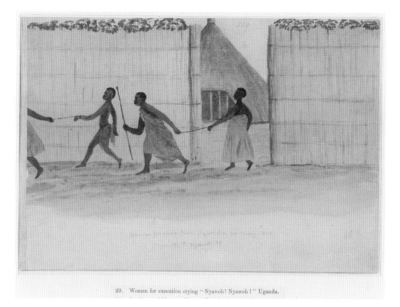

29. Women for execution crying "Nyawoh! Nyawoh!" Uganda.

Plate 25. Women dragged away for execution, 28 May 1862. One of the earliest experiences Grant had of events at the Kabaka Mutesa's court was to note how people were executed for what seemed to him the most trivial of infringements of court etiquette or other shortcomings. Here he shows women being dragged away by executioners despite their cries for mercy. NLS, MS 17919, no. 29. Reproduced by permission of the National Library of Scotland.

22. M'tessa, the King of Uganda, and his commander-in-chief.

Plate 26. Grant's first attempt to depict the Kabaka Mutesa. But he is not confident enough yet to attempt the monarch's face. The figure on the right, wearing small antelope skins sewn together, is the dominant official Speke and Grant called the 'Kamaraviona' and regarded as 'Commander-in-Chief' but his correct title is *Katikiro*. He was suspicious of the explorers and unhappy about Mutesa's interest in them. See Chapter X. NLS, MS. 17919, no. 22. Reproduced by permission of the National Library of Scotland.

Waganda skipping along the roads near the Palace, shouting "Kaveea, Kaveea, Kaveea." June 1862.

26. Waganda skipping along the palace road shouting "M'kaveea."

Plate 27.   Baganda skipping along the roads near the Palace, June 1862. Probably these are 'pages' – young men sent to the Kabaka's court in the hope they would gain advantages for their clans as they were given various jobs to do. These bright young men were to be the first to embrace Christianity a dozen years or so later. NLS, MS. 17919, no. 26. Reproduced by permission of the National Library of Scotland.

King M'tessa with an M'Koongoo and Page.

Plate 28.   Mutesa sitting, 22 June 1862. Grant now attempts to show the Kabaka's face but the note below says it is a 'bad likeness'. However, the mkungu or major chief approaching his lord and the attendant 'page' were both 'good likenesses'. NLS, MS. 17919, no. 33 verso. Reproduced by permission of the National Library of Scotland.

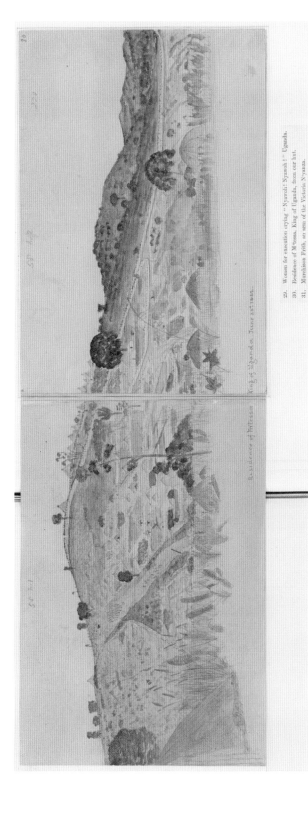

Plate 29.　The capital of Buganda. The Kabaka's capital area in Buganda known as the Lubiri at Mengo drawn by Grant on 23 June 1862. Apolo Kaggwa later drew a plan showing how various officials and wives had designated houses within the whole enclosure. The plan may be seen in Roscoe, *The Baganda*, p. 526. NLS, MS. 17919, no. 30. Reproduced by permission of the National Library of Scotland.

Pouring off the Plantain brew
Kittara 2d aps 1862.

These men are drinking
from cups made of
plantain leaves the Kitta funnel
is also of the same leaf.

Bark cloth tree
barked & showing
depending roots.

39. Pouring off the plantain brew in Kittara.

Plate 30. Beer and barkcloth. In Buganda, various kinds of plantains, or bananas, afforded the basic diet and various dishes. As is shown here by Grant in April 1862, a special kind of plantain, *mbide*, was used to produce beer, the pulp being placed in the troughs Grant depicts and squeezed to produce the liquid fermented in the pots also shown. Grant adds a view of the trees which produced barkcloth, with their characteristic depending roots. NLS, MS. 17919, no. 39. Reproduced by permission of the National Library of Scotland.

Waganda drinking Pombe
at the Queen's [June 62]

28.   Waganda drinking plantain wine at the Queen's.

Plate 31.   Drinking the beer. Here Grant shows the plantain beer (see Plate 30) being consumed, in this case at the court of the all-important Queen Mother, in June 1862. Clearly, one man has already drunk too much. It would seem that Grant was still finding it difficult to draw African faces but the details of dress can be seen. NLS, MS. 17919, no. 28. Reproduced by permission of the National Library of Scotland.

Jamēvoo   makondére   mīwēngé   kooleywāla   mʼwengé   mirrére   nenga.

Waganda Instruments.

32.   The musicians of Uganda.

Plate 32.   Musical instruments of the Baganda, June 1862. Grant had a great interest in music and tried to learn about African modes and his best chance came in Buganda. The names he gives here, however, are puzzling. From the left, 'Jamevoo' which is really the *amadinda* a kind of log xylophone, second only to the drum in importance; 'makondéré', a kind of fife; 'mwengé', a small drum; 'kooleywaalá', a large drum, but there were many types of drums and officials to look after them and Grant's word, 'mwengé', is not recognizable; 'mirréré', a kind of flute; 'nanga' properly *ennanga*, a kind of harp and another of the more important instruments. NLS, MS. 17919, no. 32. Reproduced by permission of the National Library of Scotland.

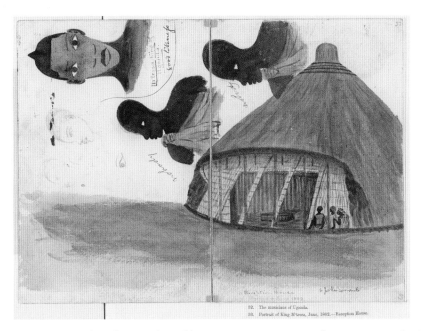

Plate 33.   The Kabaka of Buganda and his Reception House. At last, in June 1862 Grant managed what he considered a 'good likeness' of Mutesa. The depiction of the Reception House is also important as it was used for an engraving in Speke's book (p. 421) which has been widely copied ever since. NLS, MS. 17919, no. 33. Reproduced by permission of the National Library of Scotland.

Plate 34.   Grant's first meeting with the Queen Mother, 1 June 1862. The 'lassie' is bringing a pipe and a rug to spit on. The Queen Mother was an alternative locus of power in the kingdom. Like her son, she had an elaborate hierarchy of chiefs and officials. To a certain extent, Speke and Grant realized that they could use her influence to further their ends which were to get permission to go on to the source of the Nile. NLS, MS. 17919, no. 34. Reproduced by permission of the National Library of Scotland.

35. Palace guards at dinner in Uganda

Plate 35. 'Palace guards at dinner', June 1862, is Grant's title for this watercolour. On the left is a gate with bells. On the right is shown 'planks covered with [a] cage (& cowskins at night) for the guards to recline upon'. NLS, MS. 17919, no. 35. Reproduced by permission of the National Library of Scotland.

37. Two native girls belonging to our expedition.

Plate 36. 'Two native girls belonging to our expedition' is the title Grant gives to this study. The date is 1 August 1862. Chapter XI explains that the dark girl from the Wahuma was captured by one of the party during a foraging raid; the 'rather droll face and figure' of the second was a girl given to Speke whom he passed on to Bombay. There were many women in the party attached to the porters and guards. NLS, MS. 17919, no. 37. Reproduced by permission of the National Library of Scotland.

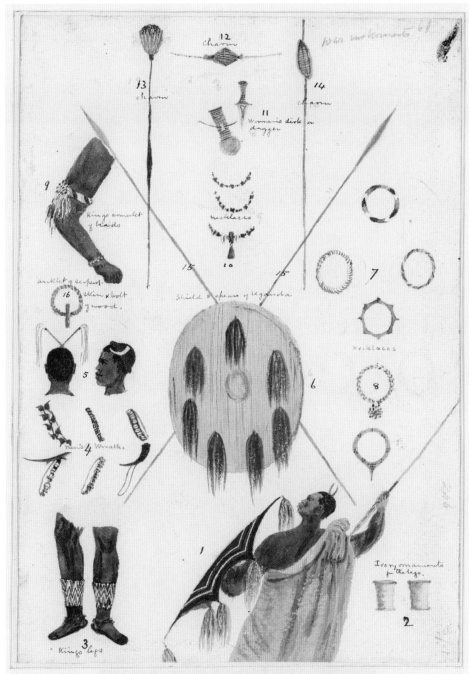

38. Waganda fashions in 1862 : arms, charms, necklaces.

Plate 37.   Arms and charms in Buganda. Depicted in June 1862 by Grant, with no doubt ethnographic data in mind, are: 1. warrior and shield; 2. ivory leg ornaments; 3. the King's legs; 4. and 5. head wreaths; 6. and15. shield and spears; 7., 8. and 10. necklaces; 9. King's amulet of beads; 11. woman's dagger; 12., 13. and 14. charms; 16. amulet of snake skin. NLS, MS. 17919, no. 38. Reproduced by permission of the National Library of Scotland.

41. King Kamarasi's first lesson in the Bible.

Plate 38. 'King Kamarasi's first lesson in the Bible', October 1862. Kamrasi, the *Omukama* of Bunyoro, ruled a kingdom which had once been the ancient 'Empire' of Bunyoro-Kitara dominating most of the interlacustrine area. However, internal strife plus the rise to the south of the much more effective and aggressive Buganda had reduced the standing of the kingdom. At the time of Grant's visit, Kamarasi had to contend with a rival trying to get his throne, raids from Buganda and now incursions from the north by Khartoum slave and ivory traders. Not surprisingly, the two explorers found him difficult to negotiate with for their passage northwards. NLS, MS. 17919, no. 41. Reproduced by permission of the National Library of Scotland.

46. Natives of Unyoro. Dwarf, conjurer, chief and soldiers.

Plate 39. 'Natives of Unyoro', September 1862. The Banyoro shown by Grant are two dwarves on either side of a chief, a woman with a partly goatskin 'bandivah'. The pencilled-in soldier has cowrie and bead tassels. On the right is Mandua with a colobus monkey skin and the horns of an antelope and then a *m'ganga*, a witch or magician, with his magic horns. The pencilled-in figure is a puzzle: Grant says his skin on his back is like a lizard; from ankle to calf are black. In the background, is one of Grant's party with the Union Jack. NLS, MS. 17919, no. 46. Reproduced by permission of the National Library of Scotland.

48. Wagani at their rock village of Koki.

Plate 40. Wagani at their village of Koki, 1 December 1862. The 'Gani' are actually a group within the Acholi, a Nilo-Saharan people very different from the Bantu people encountered up to this point. From the left, an old woman with heavy iron anklets; a warrior with Bluelead centre and egg border [*sic*]; Chongee's son and other men with amulets etc. all of 'most polished' iron. Note the grain store in the background. NLS, MS. 17919, no. 48. Reproduced by permission of the National Library of Scotland.

45. Karuma Falls on the Nile, at 2° 15′ north latitude.

Plate 41. The Karuma Falls on the Nile at 2° 15′ north latitude. Had Speke and Grant gone on westwards, they would have encountered the far more spectacular Murchison Falls. The falls are because the Nile flows steeply down into the Western Rift Valley containing Lake Albert. However, from just beyond this point, the two men turned north towards Gondokoro. NLS, MS. 17919, no. 45. Reproduced by permission of the National Library of Scotland.

53. Tusks being carried through the Madi country.

Plate 42. 'Ivory hunters on the march in Madi, February 1863'. As Grant walked further north along the Nile Valley, he encountered more and more parties of Khartoum-based ivory hunters. The Madi, who were much affected by these rapacious hunters, are a Nilo-Saharan people who now live in the far north of the modern state of Uganda. NLS, MS. 17919, no. 53. Reproduced by permission of the National Library of Scotland.

Remains of the Austrian mission house.
Gondokoro Feb 15 1863.

57. Remains of the Austrian mission-house at Gondokoro.

Plate 43.   The remains of the Austrian Mission at Gondokoro. Drawn on 15 February 1863, the mission house was right beside the Nile which can be seen together with the masts of boats. The Catholic Mission, originally in the charge of Dr Ignaz Knoblecher, who had died in 1858, was closed in 1860. See Chapter XV. NLS, MS. 17919, no. 57. Reproduced by permission of the National Library of Scotland.

36. A Floriken and three kinds of partridge.

Plate 44. 'A Floriken and three kinds of partridge', March 1861. This plate highlights Grant's strong interest in scientific Natural History, in this case the ornithology which Professor MacGillivray at Marischal College taught him. The first partridge, a qualia weighed 1¼ lb (567 g), the second 1 lb (454 g) and the third ½ to ¾ lb (227–340 g). The francolin, *Francolensus gariesseris,* weighed 2 to 2½ lbs (907–1134 g) and measured 3½ feet (1.1 metres) between wingtips. Its colour is given as 'grousie' with brilliant wing spots. NLS, MS. 17920, no. 36 recto. Reproduced by permission of the National Library of Scotland.

CHAPTER XIII

[Pages 301–26]

From Bunyoro to an Egyptian Encampment at Faloro [9 November–3 December 1862]

MY first sail on the *river* Nile—the White Nile—was made upon this journey, but my companion, Captain Speke, had sailed on it at Urondogani.[1] We entered it on this occasion in a log canoe, a few miles below Kamarasi's residence, at the point where the Kuffo[2] joins it; and we floated upon its sacred waters during a portion of four days, making the rest of the journey to the Falls of Karuma by land, along the left bank. Though the mode of transit was not dignified, the water route was extremely pleasant, from its novelty and interest.

Extracts from Journal: Problems of Boating on the Upper Nile
11th [November 1862] By boat for an hour and a half. After the usual din & row at starting, we went off bag & baggage in three boats. Seized two jars of pombe from a boat we met on the river as the king had ordered it for us. Went down the stream about a mile an hour ...

16th Nov The M'K[ungu] (Veeároowanjo) here [has] a slight stutter. Came in with a host of spearmen (I counted above 90) soon after our arrival. A very handsome young fellow of Rumanika's caste of countenance, straight nose, [?] mouth, compressed upper teeth, large jowl & neck, ears ordinary but slightly turned back, neat eyes & hands.[3] He could not contain himself for laughing at us but was sedate enough in presenting his pot of pombe. Asked whether he'd give us boats down the river, excused himself saying the Wachopeh would steal a boat. When we reminded him that it was all Kam[arasi]'s country, he said all would be ready for us in the morning. The language here is perfectly diff[eren]t to any thing I have ever heard[4] ... Guttural, it is the Chopeh lingo.[5]

---

[1] See above, Chapter XI, p. 248.

[2] That is, the River Kafu.

[3] Grant had clearly embraced the 'Hamitic myth' and his careful note of physical characteristics informed his judgements on how 'civilized' were those he met.

[4] In other words, Grant had crossed the 'Bantu Line', probably the most fundamental socio-cultural divide in Africa, between the Bantu peoples to the south and the Nilo-Saharan and Afro-Asiatic peoples to the north.

[5] The Chopi were a Nilotic group normally classified as part of the Lango living just inside the north-east corner of what is now regarded as Bunyoro; their chief had thrown off his allegiance to Bunyoro early in Kamarasi's reign. See Nyakatura, *Anatomy of an African Kingdom*, pp. 98, 126; Girling, *The Acholi*, p. 237.

17ᵗʰ [November] Found S[peke] had touched at a ghaut where we were told other boats w[oul]d be provided.[1] I sent to the M'K[ungu] "Phoobee" while I waited by the river bank. My men then brought him ... he refused to provide a boat. By bullying, talking & [?] they forced him to provide one which I could not get manned tho' while I sat in it urging the fellow to paddle me ... the load carriers rush at their spears and a shout was heard, guns presented ... spears thrown &c but all escaped except one. This now alarmed my only boatman who jumped back into the water &escaped in the reeds. Rage made me desert traps & my men at this. I left them, taking my rifle ... saying "God knows where I'm to sleep or whether a guide will come near me now but I'll try the upper road." Going 2 miles I sat waiting for them to follow me. [NLS, MS. 17915, 11, 16, 17 November 1862]

Having emerged from the channel of the smaller stream, we suddenly found ourselves in a large lake, to all appearance without an outlet, being surrounded by rushes; and without a pilot it would have been hard for us to guess which direction to take. After proceeding for an hour the scene changed: we were upon a river a thousand yards wide, and in certain parts so large that we had a sea horizon. The waters struggling past myriads of moving and stationary islands, made the navigation very exciting, particularly when a strong head-wind blew, and hippopotami reared their heads in the water. Having passed these, there was no perceptible current; but by watching the floating islands rolling round and round like a tub in the water, we saw that the stream moved about a mile an hour. These islands were perfect thickets of growing ferns, creepers, small trees, &c., hiding one-third of the stems of the lofty papyrus rush. It occurred to me at the time, seeing such masses of these islands, some being twenty yards in length, that the delta of the Nile could easily be accounted for by an accumulation of their sediment.[2] During a smart breeze, with all their vegetation yielding, and lying over to the wind, they looked like a fleet of felucca-rigged vessels racing, and continually changing their relative positions. No sight could have been more striking as the crests of the waves dashed against them, and the sky looked black and stormy. It was a beautifully wild picture; the slender stems of the tall papyrus, with their feathery tops, now erect, then waving to and fro, or crouching before the sudden blast, as if prepared for a spring.

By the third day all the islands had disappeared: they had melted away into floating fragments, or had got ashore, and lay over—wrecks—the leaves and fronds drooping in shapeless disorder.

Where the river was above 500 yards wide, the colour of the water in the centre was quite muddy from the freshes;[3] that of the sides a clear brown. The greatest depth was eighteen feet, which it preserved, with a hard bottom, till within a boat's length of the side, where it became nine feet deep, with a bottom of mud. As it narrowed between steep banks to 200 yards, there was no impediment to landing; the waters then became of a uniform dark colour, and were shallower, flowing with a current of about half a mile an hour. We landed daily to sleep ashore, and had to pass through a long channel of water vegetation, as the sides in most places where the river was of such immense width were walled in by a depth of reeds, rushes, and convolvuli. An interesting custom amongst the

[1] Speke had gone by river, Grant overland on this day.
[2] This was an incorrect notion.
[3] Fresh or freshet – a rush of water in a stream. *OED.*

boatmen was observed as we paddled past an old pensioned canoe of huge size which lay in the rushes. A boatman patted my shoulder, and then sprinkled water upon the veteran boat. I did the same, which pleased the natives, who never pass it without paying this mark of respect.

Many fine scenes were come upon at reaches and bends of the river. One with a precipitous double-coned hill called M'kungurru, on the right bank, was remarkably pleasing, the river sweeping majestically round its wooded heights. This hill was reckoned to be 800 feet above the water, and for a long distance it served as a prominent landmark.[1] The Kidi side of the river was undulating, wild, and uninhabited, covered with handsome trees overspread with a network of flowering creepers, then, in the month of November, in rich bloom, and presenting every contrast of colour. It was the hunting-ground of the Wanyoro and Kidi people.[2]

We had some exciting chases after canoes seen on the river, the king having given the officials who were in charge of us orders to procure food by seizing any provisions they might find. Immediately any canoe came in sight, all our energy was applied to the oars.[3] The "chase" on seeing us would double and race with all his might, till, finding it hopeless, he would strike his colours by standing up in his canoe, when a yell of delight burst from the conquerors, though still several hundred yards from the prize. No sooner did we come in contact than the prize was at once rudely boarded. Bark-cloths, liquor, beads, and spears were taken and concealed by our Wanyoro followers, while the poor owner looked on powerless. The sequel, however, was delightful: the Seedees, of their own accord, recovered all the stolen property from the hands of the Wanyoro, and restored it to the proper owners, who then laughed with ourselves at the joke. The largest canoe carried a ton and a half, and was hollowed out of the trunk of an immense tree—not made of planks, like those on the Victoria Nyanza. Our kit was placed in the centre, or formed a seat for us at the bow or stern. Some cows we had received from the king were sent by the land route, and had to pass through a boisterous people, who twice tried to plunder them. While a few goats were in charge of my valet Uledi, four Wachopeh threw their spears at him. He could not see the men coming on account of the long grass, but he captured a spear and a stick, losing none of his herd, thus showing his tact and bravery. He carried an unloaded gun, with ten rounds in his pouch; also a spear, which he broke by throwing at the enemy. We fortunately caught another thief driving away our goats to the jungle. Two of our men brought him into camp with his arms tied behind, and a rope round his neck. On seeing him each Seedee took a savage delight in slapping his face, and then covering his body with a mixture of mud, ashes, and water. They also tortured him by binding his body tightly with cords; but during the night, though the door-screen was fastened, his comrades came and released him.

When marching across country, we required aid from the inhabitants as porters, but they showed great unwillingness, never agreeing until their women or cattle were seized. Kidjweega had the king's orders to collect a force of forty men as our guard. He had, however, much difficulty in procuring even half the number, the natives making excuses

[1] Grant depicts this hill in Figure 82, p. 268.

[2] The Kidi as Grant called them were, like the Chopi, part of the people known today as the Lango. Grant depicts them in Figure 83, p. 268.

[3] Perhaps 'paddles' was intended.

that the country of Kidi was dangerous to pass through. Our route was thus rendered circuitous, as we had to zigzag from village to village in order to obtain relays of porters. Even when the distance to the nearest village was only a mile or two, most of them insisted on being relieved, and the more refractory were compelled to carry loads by our seizing their spears. On the line of march they were lively and polite enough. When any obstacle occurred on the path, such as a sharp rock or hole, they, with their disengaged hand, would slap their thigh to warn those behind them to look out. No remark was made, merely this simple signal given. The Seedees had a different mode of giving warning: they called out "M'wiba,"—that is, thorn; "cimo," hole; or "jiwee," rock.[1]

To return to the Nile, its scenes and sports. One day's journal notes "four hippopotami, two crocodile, two dead fish, and numerous small gulls," seen in and over the waters as we glided down the stream. The hippos required sharp shooting, as they seldom gave us time for an aim, sinking their heads the moment the boat was steadied. The natives harpoon them with barbed irons stuck loosely upon heavy poles longer than capstan-bars; and use trimmers of "solah," or pith-wood,[2] attached by long ropes to the barbs. It must require expert swimmers to get up to a hippo in the water and deliver the thrust. We saw small gulls flitting about and darting at them. The dead scaly fish upon the water were about seven pounds weight, the shape of a thick short cod, but with a well-forked tail, above which, as Speke observed, there was a small rounded fleshy fin, like that seen on salmon or trout. The boatmen eagerly picked those up that floated along, even though they were stale. We could not account for their being found dead, except that they had been poisoned by the decayed matter which filled the river. At every place where a creel-trap was set, our men pulled in to extract the fish, but got little for their trouble. One morning we had some "Macquareh"[3] for breakfast, and enjoyed them very much; they had as little bone as a sole, and tasted like trout. Where the banks were high and covered with trees, monkeys occasionally jumped from bough to bough, and did not seem alarmed even within sight of habitations. They were grey, with long tails, white beards and eyebrows, black faces and ears.[4] The largest birds were the Batteleur[5] eagle and the Buceros: the former, when seen soaring and circling in the heavens, resembles a bat in figure, and has a black body, with the wings white underneath; the Buceros[6] is a large black bird, walking awkwardly about the cultivated grounds, having short legs, and his three toes almost of equal length.

The people were generally civil and hospitable, sending us small presents of their produce—plantain, or perhaps a goat; but they did not relish our passing through their country, and they gave up their houses with great reluctance. This was no wonder, for our Unyoro escort plundered wildly like the Waganda, and escaped capture by running away. On one occasion they cunningly got up an alarm in camp, and took the opportunity,

---

[1] The Swahili words are *mwiba*, *shimo* and *jiwe*.

[2] A corrupted Hindi word for the material used in the making of pith helmets or 'solar topees'. *Hobson-Jobson*. Grant depicts the 'harpoon' and also another form of killing hippos in Figure 87, p. 332.

[3] Grant's own explanation of names described this as 'a flat, broad, sweet-tasting fish'. It is difficult to identify it biologically or the other fish Grant mentions here.

[4] Presumably vervet monkeys, *Chlorocebus pygerythrus*.

[5] *Terathopius ecaudatis*.

[6] 'Buceros' refers, strictly, to Asian species of hornbills; what Grant saw was possibly the ground hornbill, *Bucorvus leadbeateri*.

when the inhabitants were in a state of fright, to seize their property. But in districts where the population was numerous, all turned out to look at us, rejoicing most heartily, leading the way in a crowd, shouting and saluting. Some of our men became so drunk from their good wine, taken while resting in the middle of a march, that the natives tried, by applications of water, to bring them to their senses. They actually wished to carry one man, and never attempted to rob him of his clothes or gun, which he kept brandishing about. We were addressed indiscriminately as Wazoongo (white men), M'kama (sultan), Nyans-wengeh, and Witchwezee.[1] Those who knew us best used the two former titles, while others spoke of us as Nyans-wengeh, meaning, probably, strangers, sailors, or Nyanza men.

The women wore a sort of double kilt, as if a short one had been put over a long one. Some had tightfitting leggings of iron beads, as bright as steel, and very becoming on their fine limbs. The quantity of brass wire round some of their arms surprised me. It seems that their husbands take ivory to the mart of Karague, and exchange it with the Wazeenja or people of Usui, which is on the road to Zanzibar. This metal was more commonly worn than copper; being an importation, it seemed to be in greater favour.[2]

The dwellings were detached grass huts, generally in the middle of plantain orchards, and forming three sides of a hollow square, with some charmed poles[3] outside. A store-hut raised upon piles is built in the centre space, to contain their grain, hoes, &c. The bark-cloth tree, or ficus, which we had not seen for several months, abounds in the district, but never grows to any great size. The people collect the flat linear leaves of a rush growing on the river-bank, and extract salt from them. After being dried and burnt the ashes are washed, and the water, which becomes impregnated with salt, is used to boil potato or plantain. Some leaves of this rush measure fourteen feet. The papyrus is here converted into door-screens (like a hurdle). Strips from its stem bleach white in drying, and make beautiful fish-creels, while its pith is converted into wrappers or coverings for jars of wine. The pith-wood supplies floats, door-bolts, and oval-shaped shields to the people. A tree with compound leaves was an object of Phallic worship—the only instance of the kind we knew of.[4] These, with the universal bottle-gourd,[5] were amongst the most useful plants we observed.

Extract from Journal: Linguistic Problems and 'Phallic Worship'
My guides were two Wakonongo; they had a great deal to say about the islands, trees &c but the nuisance of not having a linguist kept my curiosity unsatisfied. A fine compound-leaved tree I had explained [to me] after I returned to camp. If a man cannot copulate, he ties the tree with a cord, saying to it 'give me strength'. He

---

[1] The former title perhaps derives from the Lunyoro or Luganda terms for those deserving respect; the latter implies those with notable powers (the Bachwezi).

[2] This is important evidence that contacts existed to the Zanzibar trading network avoiding Buganda by direct communication west of Lake Victoria with the WaZinza people and via Rusubi. At this same period, however, as Grant was to discover, Khartoum-based traders were coming in from the north to impose their very much less peaceful mode of trade. See also Doyle, *Crisis and Decline*, pp. 43–5.

[3] Meaning that the poles were adorned with charms or decorative objects.

[4] Grant seems to have derived this doubtful notion from the story he heard recounted in the extract which follows.

[5] *Lagenaria siceraria* is common throughout southern and eastern Africa although whether it was originally indigenous is disputed. See Van Wyk and Gericke, *People's Plants*, p. 46.

looks at it till he has an erection when he unties the cord releasing the tree. [NLS, MS. 17915, 20 November 1862]

We found fresh eggs placed in the forks of trees near houses, said to be put there as medicine or M'ganga. None were rotten, though several placed similarly in the ceilings of the huts were shaken, to try them, and then replaced. The spoil of hippos, their skulls, tusks, &c., lay in small heaps near the houses of those who possessed tackle for killing them. It was not thought lucky to throw these away, and a beautiful convolvulus (*Argyreia sp.*) with immense mauve flowers, was planted by their side.[1] With a branch of this plant in the hand of the hunter, it is believed that he is certain of sport.

The millstone in use here is a slab from the brick-red, rough-grained granite[2] seen along the pathways, and it is placed inside a hut, embedded in and edged round with clay. Any round stone in the hands of a woman, who kneels to her work, rubs down the grain. These stones had not been seen in Uganda, as the people there seldom grind corn. Another slab, with irregular fracture, seemed of hornblende, as waving lines ran through it.

In our short experience we did not observe much disease amongst the people, and the country, where it sloped down to the Nile with an eastern exposure, appeared very healthy. Wens[3] on the forehead and behind the ear were noticed upon some men; and a woman, whose hand had been cut off, probably for some misdemeanour when in Uganda, was the only maimed person we saw. She appeared to be an old vixen.

Exposure in an open canoe during the heat of the day is very trying, and told on both of us, causing sick headaches. There was nothing, when the river was broad, to rest the eye upon but its glassy surface, consequently we were glad to come upon cataracts and proceed by land. On the eighth and ninth days from the time we embarked, both of us had attacks of fever, sickness, and dysentery.

Extract from Journal: A Feverish Day and Night

19th. [November] After my morning coffee, I had severe stomach sickness and purging, vomiting a small quantity of jellied blood. This quite took my appetite away however I would march & after severe sickness ... I lay down in a hut 2 to 3 miles on while S[peke] went on with all the kit leaving five men in charge of me. I fainted as I was going to the rear. Spent a most wretched day of strong fever in my cot but the good pombe of which I drank (from thirst five pints) set me up. By [?] PM when I determined on going ahead. All my men were drunk ... however villagers armed with staffs & spears turned out ... and I had a triumphal journey [arriving] after sunset. 20th Halted. No rest during night, feverish, vermin, mosquitoes bothering me all night. Went to the cataract, a noble sight as I stood a 100 feet above it ... [NLS, MS. 17915, 19, 20 November 1862]

After a severe day of illness during the march, I arrived in camp exhausted, at dusk of the 19th November, and found Speke also unwell, but with the delightful sound of a

---

[1] This is the plant now named after Grant – *Astripomoea grantii*. Lind and Tallantire, *Flowering Plants of Uganda*, p. 126. It was identified as a new species of convolvulus by Professor Oliver from Grant's specimen. See Grant, 'The Botany of the Speke and Grant Expedition', pp. 116–17, and the illustration there by W. H. Fitch, Tabula 80, reproduced in this edition as Figure 5, p. 18.

[2] This is more likely to have been a gneiss from the very ancient igneous and metamorphic rocks of the Pre-Cambrian basement complex.

[3] A wen is a 'sebaceous cystic tumour under the skin, occurring chiefly on the head'. *OED*.

cataract on either side of his position. The night air conveyed this sound to us distinctly, and when morning came, after a night of fever, vermin, and musquitoes, the noble sight of the Karuma Falls quite revived us. It was health and joy to convalescents! There were three cataracts upon less than a mile of the river at this point, and each had its own music. Seated upon the rocks of the central fall of Karuma, we were strongly impressed with its grandeur. The cloudy sky tinted the river a mossy brown, and the water was broken into white foam by a fall of six feet over three channels worn in the rock. On the centre block a hut has been daringly placed to commemorate some event. Below the falls, upon an island, other huts are erected, but they are uninhabited, and approachable only with considerable difficulty. They may have been placed there as stores for grain, as the Kidi people on the opposite shore are constantly plundering. The trees upon the island had their branches connected by cords, on which were slung the wings and feathers of birds, giving it the appearance of a charmed spot. Looking up the river from this fall, there is a long reach, broken by foam in two places; but what gives enchantment to the scene is the view of the steep banks densely covered with tree foliage, forming a frame to the picture, and recalling similar scenes on our wildest Scottish rivers.[1]

Immediately below the Falls, where the water eddies amongst rushes, we observed several baskets suspended from trees; they were put there to contain fowls as a bait for hippopotami, or rather as an inducement for these animals to come and fall under a trap placed not far off. Across their track a cord is placed, with creepers twined round it; and over this a short log, shod with iron, is suspended from a bough.[2] On the cord being touched, this weight falls upon the animal, transfixing him till the arrival of the villagers, who come for water. We tried to catch some fish with Palmer flies, moths, and hooks dressed with red rags, but nothing would take; although, however, we were thus unsuccessful, the natives brought us large fish they had caught in their creels.

We were not sorry to be detained here by the officer of the district for three days, as ferry-boats were not ready for us, and supplies had to be laid in for a journey across the Kidi forests. As I was one day trying to sleep after breakfast, the natives outside commenced shouting with excitement. On going to see the cause, Frij coolly told me to "Nenda indani"—*i. e.,* Get inside—get inside![3] Two distinct parties had collected for a fight—the Seedees, with their Tower[4] rifles at the "ready," with bayonets, &c., and their adversaries with spears, shields, and sticks, in position for attack. All were on the point of fighting, but a gun going off in another part of the camp caused them to disperse, and we heard no more of the intended battle. A woman, it appeared, had been insulted, and the men got excited on the subject, but the affair was soon over. We constantly had these little alarms.

In the afternoon of the 22d, the loud sounds of the stringed tambira (a large harp) announced the arrival of visitors, and it was not long before the Kateekeero or governor

---

[1] Grant waxes somewhat unusually lyrical over these falls which are situated at approximately 2°15′N, 32°10′E. They became a tourist attraction but are now to be the site of a power station. Speke, perhaps because he had seen the Ripon Falls, was rather dismissive – 'a mere sluice or rush of water'. *Journal*, p. 568. Grant's depiction of the Falls, a version of which appeared in Speke's book on the same page, is here Plate 41 and there are three less successful versions in Figures 88, 89 and 90, pp. 332–3.

[2] See Figure 87, p. 332.

[3] More correctly, *Kwenda ndani*.

[4] That is, 'tower muskets' which were obsolete British weapons having the Tower of London stamp on them.

arrived with a squad of rather well-dressed Wanyoro. This official had leprous hands, looked dull and stupid, and would give no direct reply to our questions. He was muffled up all but his head in a yellow bark-cloth with black horizontal stripes. He presented us with a small bull, some flour, and three jars of m'wengé,[1] for which on the following day he received some beads and pills, with the promise of a handsome necklace when we reached M. de Bono's camp.[2] On his second visit this governor wore a different costume, and another variety of beads, thereby wishing to impress us with the idea that he was a man of importance. He was commander-in-chief of the district, and constantly fought his men against Reonga, the brother of Kamarasi, residing on an island one march below the Falls. The interview was not over when it was reported that a large party of travellers were walking down the opposite bank of the river. Through the grass we could see a line of people going like a train, each one with a load on his head, and some wearing white skin coverings. They were Kidi going to assist Reonga in fighting against the governor with whom we were conversing, and they marched along with perfect security, as a wide and rapid river divided the belligerents, and the distance prevented the possibility of an arrow reaching across the water.[3] No one proposed to have a shot at them, as we were to ferry the river, and cross their track as soon as the party had passed. We issued orders that our twenty cattle should be first sent across, but Africans always reverse everything. The cattle were not over till after the sun had set, and we were put across in the first canoe. The canoes were of hollowed logs, eighteen inches out of the water, very rotten, and obliged to be caulked with the roots of the papyrus. We had three men paddling with spoon-shaped sticks, who worked hard to get us across the one hundred yards of stream, as delay on their part would have caused us to miss the landing-place, and probably carried us down to the next cataract. Kidjweega, who had charge of us, brought over a small goat as a sacrifice to the rocks, and to propitiate our march. A "M'ganga," having some boughs in his left hand, killed the animal, and spread it out upon the path, with its head laid in the direction we were to take. Speke was then asked to step over it, in order that we might have a prosperous journey, and all followed his example. Another goat, I understood, had been similarly sacrificed on the left bank. While waiting for the cattle being brought across, we ascertained the altitude to be 2970 feet above the level of the sea.[4] The manner of swimming the cattle was very simple. Men in the canoe held ropes tied to their horns, and those wanting horns were tied by the lower jaw. There was considerable delay on account of the tricks of the ferrymen, who, had they chosen, might have taken four cattle over at each trip; but when about three-fourths were crossed, a message came that, until we gave them one cow for their trouble, over and above the amount of their agreement, which they had already received—namely, a hatful of beads—the others would be detained. This was acceded to, but another messenger arrived saying they must have a larger one in exchange. On getting this, they brought us a quantity of ripe plantain for our

---

[1] The equivalent of pombé.

[2] Grant's control of his narrative slips here as he has not explained de Bono. Grant and Speke were still expecting to meet Petherick but he had sent to find them, Amabile de Bono, a Khartoum-based ivory trader who had reached Faloro. Not hearing of the explorers, de Bono withdrew. He was the nephew of Andrea de Bono (1821–71), a more important trader who had been associated with Giovanni Miani. See Howgego, *Encyclopedia of Exploration*, IV, p. 866 and the references there; Langlands, 'Early Travellers', p. 57.

[3] For Ruyonga, see Chapter XII, above, p. 277, n. 4, and p. 281, n. 1.

[4] This level, i.e. 905.2 m, taken with a boiling-point thermometer, was remarkably accurate.

liberality, and we encamped for the night a mile from the Falls, in the middle of a forest of tropical vegetation. A storm of wind and rain blew with violence, making the boughs above us creak, and our unprotected camp-beds became pools of water. But notwithstanding these and other discomforts, in the midst of vivid lightning and bursts of thunder, our Seedees kept up a cross fire of shouts and songs. A sudden cry that our cattle were wandering away, put every one on the alert, as the beasts were to be our mainstay for the journey of six days which lay before us, through a country destitute of habitations. A fire was lit for the poor animals, and they enjoyed it like ourselves, till moonlight and the break of day.

The evening before we ferried the Nile,[1] our Wanyoro escort got very tipsy, and came to salute us with presented spears, after the manner of the Waganda, but not with such grace; neither did they find such ready use of their tongues. After laying down their spears, they stepped over them, and back again, as much as to say that they were prepared to die for us! This over, while Kidjweega hopped a dance on his tiptoes, all his followers performed a Highland fling round him, to the music of a humming song. The effect, as seen by the light of a blazing grass fire, was ludicrous and wild.

Kamarasi sent us, as his last request, that we should go and fight his brother, who was not more than a few hours' walk off our track; but Kidjweega, his messenger, was not very pressing, and we marched under the guidance of an active little man of Chopeh, called Luendo. For three days we were in forest, broken occasionally by a serpentine bog, along which the path was a gutter with grass eight feet high, and so close on either side that we had to push our way through it. Emerging from this forest, the country to the north was covered with tall grass, undulating from our feet to the horizon, where the low hills of Gani were visible twenty or thirty miles off in the far distance. It was a cheering sight, for there we expected to come upon civilisation. My field-book, dated 27th March 1862,[2] at this point notes: "From a red-clay ant-heap saw the Gani hills to the north. Country to the right a plain of withered waving grass, without trees. The same kind of country lay to the west, in the direction of the river." This note I look upon as important,[3] for it may be held to be a proof that the chord of the arc to the bend of the Nile, which we actually followed, was a plain, offering no hilly obstacle to the flow of the Nile from the point where we ferried, till reaching it again ninety miles farther north. Marching through this tall grass was harassing and monotonous; the tread-mill could hardly be worse. If you held up your head to look for trees, none were to be seen. If you looked for the man who walked in front of you, he was generally hidden. If you walked in your ordinary manner, without stooping, the sharp grasses went into your eyes and nose, blinding you for a moment, or drawing blood; and if you did not keep your eyes and ears open, and take the warning of the hole, rock, or log ahead, you hurt your limbs, or tripped and stumbled in the most vexatious manner. Several times we lost our way, but little Luendo would good-naturedly

[1] That is, crossing to the north bank of the river which flows westward at this point towards Lake Albert.

[2] 'March' is clearly a mistake since the trek described was taking place in November 1862. The journal for 27 November does indeed refer to seeing the Gani hills 'which kept our spirits up'. NLS, MS. 17915, 27 November 1862.

[3] It was certainly an important point because, rather than follow the river to Lake Albert and then northwards, the explorers were taking a short cut to Faloro (near modern Nimule) in 3°36′N so missing out the whole Albert Nile section of the river. This made it easy for critics to say they had not proved the river coming from Lake Victoria was actually the Nile. Hence Grant's attempt here to meet this criticism.

jump upon an ant-mound, take his bearings, and put us right again. In going through bogs he was most careful in taking off his sandals, which he slung upon his wrist; the Wagani, whose only covering was the skin of a kid in front, also took this precaution. As the journey was nearly at an end,[1] and a prospect before us of renewing our wardrobe, we were becoming extravagant, and walked through everything with our shoes, socks, and trousers on; but this was a mistake, as sand got into our shoes, and the grass cut our socks or gaiters. When we came to a pool, the scene was like that of a number of boys bathing. The Wanyoro first plant their spears upright in the ground, then take the load from their heads, doff their small coverings, and proceed joyously to splash each other in the water. Older stagers sit on the banks enjoying the sight, smoking or eating meat cut with their spearheads. This lasts for nearly an hour, and then we move off again through the tall grass, till we arrive in camp, where arbours or huts are made wherein to sleep. Huts left by previous travellers were sometimes met with, their fires still burning; and we were informed that the people of Chopeh and Kidi came there to sport. Speke shot a buffalo, which afforded great excitement. On his wounding him, the natives, with spears erect, rushed at the animal, who charged and drove them away like flies; at last, however, several shots and spears pierced him as he lay wallowing in the water. Not an inch of the buffalo was wasted: though the Wanyoro had our loads to carry, all was brought into camp as food. Many of their spears were broken and bent, showing the softness of their iron. Afterwards, in our march, we saw a knot of elephants, heard the lion, came across some hartebeest—here also called "gnamœra"—and were informed that the people of Chopeh can creep up to the wild buffalo and spear him while he is asleep. This is strange, but is quite credible.

On the 29th of November our party of eighty souls stood upon the face of a rock, large enough to form the site of a garrison. Here we had the satisfaction of seeing in front of us another height, on which houses were actually discovered. All our rear men and cattle having come up and refreshed themselves from a cool spring in the rock, after half an hour's walk we stood by cultivated ground, and in sight once more of habitations. How delightful the feeling after the monotony of the forest! I could not resist a "hurrah," and had a strong inclination to bound forward and see this new race of the "Gani,"[2] amongst whom we were that night to sleep. Patience, however, was requisite. Our men walked along in Indian file, led by Luendo sounding his small horn to convey the tidings that we were upon a friendly mission. Knots of natives appeared on the heights above us, and we halted under a tree, waiting permission to ascend to the village. Although we had had men of their own race to guide us from Kamarasi's, and they had burnt grass on the downs the previous day to intimate our approach, and that they might prepare pombé and lodging for us, we had to wait till the "lord of the manor" invited us to his residence. By-and-by relief arrived. Two naked young fellows, their faces whitened with ashes, came rushing like mad "jogees"[3] or devotees down the hill with spears balanced, and pulled up beside us. Their bodies had two coats of paint—purple and ash colour—the latter scraped as a painter imitates mahogany—and this colouring gave to their thin tall figures a very grotesque look. They were soon joined by others, no two painted or ornamented alike;

---

[1] Because they expected shortly to meet Petherick with new supplies and the ability to take them quickly down the Nile and home.

[2] See above, p. 285, n. 1: the Gani are an Acholi group.

[3] A Hindu ascetic. *Hobson-Jobson.* Grant depicts the painted warriors in Plate 40.

and some of them vermilion all over. Even boys affected gay colours, and dressed their heads with single feathers of jays, &c., floating like a vane in the wind. Brightly polished iron rings were worn round the fleshy part of the arm, a pendant of iron-wire hung from the under lip, large rings of copper and brass were in their ears, and all of them carried spears with bamboo handles. Bombay and Mabrook, who had passed through the district some weeks previously,[1] were gladly welcomed with "Verembé, verembé" sounded in a guttural tone of voice. They had stools offered them to sit upon, and after some delay permission was given us to advance.

Having mounted the side of the rocky height to its top, we were surprised to come upon a flat cleared space, surrounded with huts of bamboo and grass. In the centre stood a single "miloomba," a bark-cloth tree, with two idol-huts of grass, and horns of wild animals on the ground by its trunk. An aged man with grey hair advanced, with other "elders" and women, carrying a white chicken, some m'wengé, and a handful of a plant with a white flower. This old gentleman was Chong'ee, the chief of the place. While holding the fowl he addressed us, then waved it over the ground, and passed it to his chief officer, who did the same. The body of our guide, Luendo, who had conveyed us from the Karuma Falls, was now rubbed over with m'wengé from the plant; the liquid was also sprinkled on us, and we were invited to sit upon the cow-skins placed in the shade of the miloomba tree, and were presented with m'wenge, called "water," to quench our thirst.

The first impression made by the appearance of the little colony was very pleasing. Their beehive-looking huts were cleanly swept and tidy, and their stores of grain were raised upon rough pillars of granite, smaller, but resembling those circular erections in our own country known as Druids' temples.[2] These grain stores consisted of an enormous cylinder made of mud and wattle placed on the top of the stones, and covered with a roof or lid of grass and bamboo, which could be raised sufficiently with a pole to admit of a man entering them. A rough ladder or stick with forks enables the women to get to the top for the purpose of taking out grain.

The women, married and single, old and young, wear only a bit of fringe suspended from the waist in front, and a pendant of chickweed, or a bunch of long leather thongs like shoe-ties, behind. They have no other clothing. Enormous heavy rings of iron sometimes ornament their ankles, and a few beads their necks; and they are not nearly so smart in appearance as the men, who may be seen sitting upon the rocks in the shade of trees dressing each other's hair with shells, beads, feathers, or turned-up queues covered with fine wire. Their whole employment would seem to be ornamenting their persons; and they are generally seen standing in conceited and ridiculous attitudes.[3] The women carry their children on their backs, tied by straps, and the mother has thus the free use of her hands. The infant is shaded from the sun by a gourd placed over its head and shoulders. This custom is said to be common also with the Watuta race. Here also the people sleep upon the skin of a cow or goat placed on the clean-swept floor of mud, and have no covering. The doors of the huts are so low that ordinary people would have to go upon their knees to enter, but the natives are so supple that they can bend their bodies until

---

[1] Because they had been sent ahead to seek news of Petherick.

[2] The term widely and wholly inaccurately still used in the early 19th century for prehistoric stone circles of which there were many in Nairnshire and Aberdeenshire whence Grant had come. Grant shows what seems to be one of these grain stores in Plate 40.

[3] See Grant's depiction, also in Plate 40.

within two feet of the ground, and still be able to walk. The women make a superior description of basket, of close workmanship, from osiers or wands brought from the rocky dells. It may be mentioned that we had not seen the bamboo tree growing since we were in the seventh degree of south latitude, and we were gratified to come upon our old acquaintance again. Many of the trees gladdened the eyes of the botanist of the expedition, Manua,[1] who knew most of them, as the same species grow among the rocks rising out of the forests in his native home of Unyamuezi. Again Bruce's *ensete* [2] was found here, of a small size, greedily eaten by goats; also several plants hitherto undescribed or unknown to science, giving a double interest to the colony of Gani. Strolling along amongst its ravines, and wandering far in search of plants,[3] I came upon traps set with slabs of rock and cord: only small animals, such as weasels or birds, could get under them, and the circumstance shows that all races are fond of trapping. A native from the heights above shouted and beckoned to me; in return I beckoned to him, and though we could not understand each other, he was most polite in leading the way, knocking down the thorns and branches that obstructed us, or lending a hand over the rugged rocks. He understood my sign that he should accompany me into the camp, but before doing so he left his spear in a hut, probably for fear his chief should find fault with him for appearing armed. In return for his kindness I presented him with some beef. Chong'ee, the morning after our arrival, harangued the people of the village, telling them they must be kind to his guests: and that whatever we wanted—meat, drink, house-room, &c.—must be provided.

The beer made by the natives was strong and pleasantly bitter, so that Bombay and others showed the effects of it, becoming rather noisy towards night. The beverage is manufactured from Murwa,[4] roasted, pounded, soaked, sun-dried, and boiled. When cooling it ferments slightly, and it is more agreeable to the taste in this lukewarm state than afterwards when entirely cold. It appeared to us a wholesome, though coarse, heavy drink. The other grains here were sessamum,[5] *Hibiscus*,[6] and *Hyptis spicigera*.[7] The last is called "neeno;" we had never seen it before, but the natives cultivate it, eating its seeds roasted, or making oil of them. Although the fields were well weeded the crops were poor, and often appeared full of the *Crotolania glauca,* or "m'cæwæ," of whose inflated pod, leaves, and flowers, the natives make a dish resembling spinage.[8] We had entirely lost the plantain tree of Uganda, and rarely came upon Indian corn or ground-nut, which up to Unyoro had been always procurable.

Like the crops, the cattle are poor, and of a small breed, rather dirtily kept. It was amusing to see the odd way in which our two Gani men, who accompanied us from Unyoro, and who had received a present of some small cows from the king, drove the stubborn animals along. Simple driving they did not understand; one of the horns and the

---

[1] There were two members of the party named Manua. Simpson, *Dark Companions*, p. 195. This is probably a reference to the less well-known porter and is further evidence of the skills displayed by the career bearers.

[2] *Ensete ventricosum*, the 'false banana', the root of which provides food for humans. Grant called it *Musa ensete*(?). Speke, *Journal*, Appendix G, p. 648.

[3] This is one of the few occasions when Grant reveals that he spent much time during the Expedition collecting or studying plants.

[4] Presumably a form of millet.

[5] Presumably *Sesamum indicum* which is cultivated for its seeds.

[6] Perhaps *Hibiscus aethiopicus*.

[7] One of the so-called bushmints whose seeds are said to have healing powers.

[8] An older form of the now more usual 'spinach'.

tail were caught hold of by a man who walked alongside, and in this way the cow was urged along the road. Of a morning, when all the cows are brought to the space in the centre of the village to be milked, the calves tied alongside the mother, the cow, on seeing her milker arrive, makes water into his hands, when, having scrubbed them, he commences to take her milk in a neatly-made oval basin or tureen of wood. The other domestic animals about the village were stupid-looking, long-tailed sheep, with reddish-brown hair. Goats jumped about the rocks, feeding on the leaves of the Indian jujube tree; and dogs were occasionally met with.

Ten hours' marching in two days brought us from Gani to a camp of Egyptian ivory-traders, whose acquaintance Bombay and Mabrook had made some weeks previously.[1]

The small quantity of baggage we had left was carried from village to village, after the manner of the "Begaree"[2] system of India. Our Seedees could have done this, but the villagers, coming forward voluntarily, generally enjoyed the labour. On arriving at a palisaded village where porters were to be relieved, we usually gathered under a tree waiting for the relief. The head man of the place, when wishing to show politeness, had the skin of a wild animal spread, and upon this he placed a wooden stool or two; liquor of the country or sour curd was offered, and after enjoying his hospitality we proceeded on the march. The appearance of the country, with its forests and undulations of grass, and with clusters of habitations every three or four miles, was very pleasing, particularly as it was often intersected by running streams from the hills. Some of these were torrents, and the largest was a river knee-deep, with steep banks and bed of gravel. All flowed to our right. We met with two new trees, both handsome, and one of them, the Sheabutter,[3] called "Meepampa" by Manua, resembled an oak in girth and general outline; its flowers scented the air and were covered with the honey-bee. The other we found to be a new species of *Boscia,* with long lanceolate leaves and terminal inflorescence.[4] The people here, though differing very little in their mode of painting themselves from the Gani, are called "Madi."[5] Their women have the same small fringe in front, and the same appendage behind, formed of fresh green weeds, plucked daily from the edges of water, and hanging from their waists to their knees. Their arms are spears seven feet long, bamboo bows, bound round with leather thongs, and arrows of reed. As many as ten arrows, each with a different-shaped barb, are sometimes carried by one man; their peculiarity is that they have no feathers, and their barbs are as straight as a nail, lance-shaped, or like a broad arrow having hooks; and though none of those we saw were poisoned, all were cruelly notched, to make them more difficult of extraction. The interiors of their palisaded villages are kept very clean; idol horns and miniature huts, near which grow medical plants, such as *Bryophyllum calycinum* and *Amaranthus* (love lies bleeding)[6] are always to be seen. The houses are cylinders of bamboo wicker-work, plastered inside to make them warm, and have steep roofs of bamboo and grass. Game-nets, arms, two-feet-long horns

---

[1] See the conclusion of this chapter and the following one for the 'Egyptian' traders, pp. 304–6.

[2] From the Hindi *begar* which means forced labour. *Hobson-Jobson.*

[3] *Vitellaria paradoxa.* Shea butter is used in food and cosmetics.

[4] Not the well-known *Boscia albitrunca* but what Grant's flora refers to as *B. salicifolia.* Grant, 'Botany of the Speke and Grant Expedition', p. 29.

[5] Grant has moved from the Acholi to a group who may be regarded as separate. They are depicted in Figures 84 and 85, p. 269.

[6] Recorded respectively on pp. 70 and 141 of Grant, 'Botany of the Speke and Grant Expedition'.

(made of gourd, the shape of a telescope), buffalo foot-traps, slabs for grinding grain, &c., are in the interior. The mode of roosting hens is novel; a five-feet-long stick, having three prongs, is stuck into the floor of the house, and the hen hatches upon grass placed upon the forks. A custom which we had not before observed was, that in the early morning a jar of hot water was sent us to wash with; and along with this came a present of some beer of the country.

De Bono's ivory-traders [*sic*] had selected Faloro,[1] a favourable position, for their camp, situated on the concave side of a hill, with a stream below. Our junction with them at sunset of the 3d December was one of those happy epochs which can never be forgotten. We announced our approach by firing guns when within a few hundred yards of the settlement, and a very lively scene ensued. Turkish banners flew, welcome guns were fired, and an army of well-dressed men, "fezzed" or turbaned, turned out with drums and fifes to greet our arrival and escort us the rest of the way. A procession was formed, with music and colours in the van, the two commanders with drawn sabres went next, and then we followed in our rags of clothes, the soldiers bringing up the rear. As we passed outside the village enclosure others joined, kissing our hands; women shouted shrilly with delight, and we were told to be seated upon a bed covered with leopard-skins placed for us in front of commander "Mahomed's" door. The traders all knew Petherick by name, but they either could not or would not tell us anything about him, excepting that he was twenty marches away to the north, and that our letter sent to him from Unyoro had not been forwarded.

Extracts from Journal: Arrival at Faloro

3 [December] Disagreeable night ... March for 6 hours, say, 18 miles, and, thank the almighty, joined the detached camp of Petherick before sunset, all our men and loads being left behind on the way ... [At] the Sultan's large bomah ... the men wanted to stop ... but S[peke] walked ahead, I followed, only five men with us ... crossed a shallow river ... & we saw the Arab position ... our guns brought them out in force ... When I got there no particular recognition was made ... All well disposed, pretty clean. Every description of gun [was fired]. I carried an umbrella till arrival at Mahomed's house ... Petherick not here [but at] Gondokoro, 20 days march north. [NLS, MS. 17915, 3 December 1862]

Everything around us looked strange; we had become such "roughs" that the most common object in this semi-civilised life gave us pleasure. Every one seemed so well dressed, they had all shoes, regular bedsteads, crockery, &c., none of which we had seen for more than two years. The scenes also in a camp of Egyptians were new to us. Mahomed, the commander, seated on a low stool, while being shaved by a barber, excited the wonder of the Wanyoro. A white napkin being placed on his chest, the boy strapped the razor with the rapidity of lightning, and, standing with extended arms, passed his instrument over the whole head and beard at a frightful pace, handing his master a gilt frame looking-glass when the operation was completed. Donkeys were ridden at a sharp amble, without saddle or bridle, driven by a long stick, and the rider seated in the native

---

[1] Faloro is a spot in the eastern part of Madi District of Uganda which Amabile, as a Maltese, the first European to reach present-day Uganda, had attained in 1861. It is about 10 miles (16 km) south-west of the town of Nimule which is over the border in South Sudan near the point where the White Nile has a great bend from a north-easterly direction to a north-westerly. Langlands, 'Early Travellers', p. 57.

fashion on the animal's haunches. Riding-oxen, with halters and ropes through their noses, were exercised about the village by negro lads, who made them go at a fast trot. Our bedding and cooking utensils not having arrived, we requested Mahomed to have some dinner prepared for us. At once he offered a cow, but it was late, and we did not wish to wait till it was killed. Coffee in true Arab style was served, and an attendant stood by offering occasionally tin mugs full of native-made beer. When dinner was ready, a crowd squatted beside us, and a woman stood with water to drink. The repast was minced meat in balls served in a tureen, a roast leg of goat in another tureen, honey and thin cakes of sorghum; all looked inviting, and we longed to begin. We found, however, that there were no spoons, knives, or forks; and we made the most of it without them, and enjoyed an excellent dinner, which we had not done for many a day. But the greatest treat was to come—water was brought us to wash our hands, and, luxury of all luxuries, soap! After the repast was finished, we were gratified to find that the remains were placed before our Seedees; Mabrook was so surprised on receiving a cup full of honey, that he inquired whether it was to be eaten? and after having dined, they all had soap and water served to them by one of the Nubians. A large open shed was made over to us, but we could not retire to rest without a prayer of thankfulness to the Almighty for having preserved us through so many difficulties, and at length, by His all-protecting arm, brought us in safety to the boundary of civilisation, after twenty-six months of unceasing toil and anxiety.

CHAPTER XIV

[Pages 327–60]

Life with the Khartoum Traders and News of Speke's Death [3 December 1862– 11 January 1863]

AT Faloro[1] we found upwards of a hundred men of every Egyptian caste, colour, and costume. They were called by the natives of the country "Toorkee," or Turks; but there was not a true Turk amongst them, and only one or two European countenances. Curly locks were exceptional, and wool predominated. They were adventurers without homes, born in the most northern Egyptian dominions from negro stock.[2] We afterwards ascertained that the bazaar at Khartoum was full of such idlers ready for any employ. The merchants there engage them to go into the interior for the purpose of collecting ivory; guns are put into their hands, an intelligent native is placed over them, and they are sent up the Bahr Abiad (White Nile) as ivory-hunters, not to return perhaps for several years. These were the men we were so glad to meet, but from whom we found it difficult to get away, although they had been at Faloro for nine months previous to our arrival.[3]

The obstacles offered to our departure were many and vexatious. The rivers ahead, we were told, would not be fordable for two months, and we could not cross them without using force; besides which, a party was expected to arrive soon from Gondokoro with ammunition and means of carrying down the tusks in store, and it must be waited for. This we could not assent to. As the streams were getting dry and a march was quite practicable, our Wanyoro men were ordered to be in readiness, but they had deserted to their homes, and we were helpless. Seeing that delay was inevitable, we proposed a trip to the west, in order that we might have a look at the White Nile, which we had left at Karuma Falls. The reply, however, was, that there was no use looking at the river there, because we should see it two marches ahead on the way to Gondokoro.[4] This information

---

[1] Grant gives Faloro the latitude of 3°15′N. For this settlement; see above Chapter XIII, p. 304. At this time it was the furthest south outpost of the Egyptian government but it had been established originally by the trader Amabile de Bono in 1861. Gray, *Southern Sudan*, p. 54; Langlands, 'Early Travellers', p. 57.

[2] From the 1820s onward, the Egyptian Army had needed constant supplies of slaves for the Army and although under Mohammed Said (1854–63) efforts were made to stop slaving, officials and others continued to seek slaves as well as ivory. In the 1860s a 'new ruling caste' of Arab traders and officials were establishing their positions. Gray, *Southern Sudan*, p. 69; Hill, *Egypt in the Sudan*, pp. 62–3, 101–2.

[3] Presumably when Amabile de Bono had arrived in 1861 or just after.

[4] Gondokoro's importance lay in the fact that it was at the effective southern limit of the navigable Nile from Khartoum. It had been reached by a mixed Egyptian and European venture in 1841. It soon became a trading station and the site for an attempted Roman Catholic mission led by Ignaz Knoblecher in 1852 which had been abandoned in 1859. Gray, *Southern Sudan*, pp. 18, 38–44.

was afterwards confirmed by our standing on a rocky height, from whence the river was seen marked by a long line of mist hanging over its course, which ran from the west in a north-east direction. The next event that startled us was the announcement that a party had to go to a district where a quantity of ivory had been accumulated, and that on their return we should all leave together for Gondokoro. There was nothing for it but submission. While we kept their camp eighty started on this razzia or raid, bringing back about a hundred tusks, a herd of cattle, and several slaves. Our importunities to get away were treated as the cravings of children, and we were told, "Do not fear, you'll get to Gondokoro before next moon." We surprised them, however, by packing up our luggage and preparing to start with our remaining twenty Seedees. Our residence amongst the Toorkees reminded me of a military life, for at break of day the *reveille* was sounded regularly with drum and fife; at certain fixed hours we had more music; and at night sentries were placed the same as in a cantonment. But the grand spectacle was their parade every Friday, which was equivalent to our Sunday. We were once requested to attend and see them manœuvre, and anything more ludicrous can hardly be conceived. All were drawn up in line, but no two were dressed alike, neither had they uniform guns. Captain Mahomed stood in front, with drawn "shumshere," in a red jacket and loose Turkish trousers, fez, and silk turban.[1] His second in command had adopted the rifle uniform of green jacket and black braid, loose pyjamas, gaiters, and tasselled fez; he also carried a drawn sword. Speke was the reviewing officer, and I stood on a height in the distance. Bombay, looking very dissipated, thought it his duty to stand alongside of his master; but his appearance, bare-headed, with a dirty shirt worn outside his dress, and holding a spear in his hand, betokened a pretty hard morning's carousing. Our second interpreter, Frij, was also decidedly tipsy, but had not the sense to remain quiet. While the men were marching he would rush wildly at them, flourishing his sword-bayonet, then attempting to show them how to march, blow his boatswain's whistle, repeat the commands, and interfere with the commander, who took it all good-naturedly. The series of manœuvres embraced file-marching, forming square, and open columns of companies—moving in these formations to any flank, over rough ground, to drum and fife music, in slow and quick time. The "general-officer," who had served with Turkish troops in the Crimea, was, of course, obliged to compliment them on their discipline, as their marching and shouldering passed muster; but the commander seemed to be of a different opinion, as any man who lost distance was at once cuffed and shoved out of the ranks, and when one side of the square faced inwards, I thought he would have cut them all down.

After parade, the standards were planted in the open space inside the village, and were there saluted by the men marching round them with drums; or a cow was killed and the colours consecrated by putting some of the streaming blood upon them or on their staffs. This custom was known to our Seedees, who had seen it done by the Sultan of Zanzibar's Mohammedan troops. During the night sentries were posted all over the village, and they performed their duties very regularly, never sleeping, although they sat the whole of their turn of duty upon a stool or stone. This is more than most men could do; but I watched some of them and never saw one fall asleep. Had we asked our Seedees to do this, they

---

[1] This was the trader Mahomed wad el Mek according to Howgego, *Encyclopedia of Exploration*, III, p. 866. His 'shumshere', properly shamshir, is, according to *Hobson-Jobson,* a Persian-derived word used in India to denote 'scymatar, that is, a type of curved sabre'.

would have laughed at us, showing the difference which discipline had made between these two classes of men. The Nubians were seldom idle, employing themselves in curing skins, looking after their cattle, or conducting household matters; seeing this, our men at first were very shy, appearing like savages amongst them, but after ten days the restraint wore off, and they had their usual dances and sport. We could not keep them from getting drunk and quarrelling, until, at the end of a week, we refrained from speaking to them, and then they desisted. One day I saw Frij riding with another man upon a bullock, and he offered me a ride, thinking I should enjoy it after the long journey on foot. There were numbers of riding donkeys and bullocks in camp. On the detachment making a flying march in quest of ivory, &c., the line was paraded with a colour on either flank. At the signal of one gun all moved off, with the three commanders each upon his donkey—the baggage, beads, and ammunition on the heads of natives. Before they returned from this trip, a native brought us information that three villages had been ransacked of their cattle and ivory, and that one more was to be swept before their return. This was pleasant news for us, their allies,[1] as we now felt we were nothing but spies in the camp of a set of land-pirates![2] A circumstantial proof of this was that their chief banner, embroidered in two characters, "Andrea de Bono,"[3] had been left in camp with us. They could not conceal this fact, though they tried to keep us in the dark about their movements; neither could they drown the cries of a girl they had captured. The story of this young captive was curious. Her father had heard and recognised her cries, and brought a tusk to offer for her release, apologising for the people of his village having fled, instead of hospitably entertaining the traders as they passed. The child was returned, and a cow given along with her. They had many more female than male slaves; but there were numbers of captured boys, who, being of naked races, would all their lives be ashamed to return to their homes because they had been marked by circumcision. Grown-up women, generally the best-looking, were prevented from deserting by having a few rings of solid iron tied between each ankle, the links so short that, in fetching water from the stream, they could only advance a few inches at a time. There were about twenty women in this camp of the Unyoro race, distinguishable by all the lower incisors being extracted. Our Seedees could talk with them, and by this means obtain information for us. Some boys also, who were considered more trustworthy than the Nubians, were placed by them over their property of beads and ivory. No doubt they, as well as many other races, were destined for Cairo, and through them information regarding the Nile could at any time be obtained.

The wives of these soldiers were natives of Bari, Madi, &c.,[4] and very industrious. They might be seen, in their only dress of a single petticoat, on their knees cleaning what was equivalent to our doorsteps, in the early morning, by covering the space with a preparation of cow-dung. They kept the interiors of the huts very clean, and employed themselves in

[1] An unusual use of irony by Grant.

[2] Elsewhere Grant uses the term 'plunderer'. Grant and others were later to see the disorder and violence associated with the Egyptian presence in the Upper Nile valley as the consequence of slave raiding. Gray points out that slaving was only a part of a complex situation in which economic or cultural accommodation between the Arab and European traders on the one hand and the mostly stateless indigenous peoples had proved impossible to achieve peacefully. Gray, *Southern Sudan*, pp. 32–3.

[3] The uncle of Amabile.

[4] For the Madi, see Chapter XIII, above, p. 303; the Bari live in the vicinity of Gondokoro on the banks of the Nile. They are regarded as a 'Nilo-Saharan' ethnic group who are mixed farmers and cattle herders.

grinding murwa, making beer, baking cakes, or tending their infants. The women of the villages carried a small knife in their girdle, or stuck into the rings of iron worn above the elbow. This was a curious practice, but not so Amazonian-like as what was told us of a cannibal race nine marches to the north-west, where the women carry ten small knives with leather handles in each side of their girdle. These they hold by the tip of their blades, and throw them at their adversary. Our informant remarked, that after his party had obtained sufficient ivory, and wished to leave this cannibal race, they were told, "No, you are our food, and must not leave us;" but one shot dispersed them, and they escaped being eaten![1] He further added that they were not a nude race, neither did they keep cattle, but they wore the skins of goats. A knife which he had brought from Koshee, three marches to the west, was formed of one piece of iron, and had a round spoon as the handle to its dagger-like blade. He probably exaggerated when he said that the people gouged eyes with it. When a birth took place in the Toorkee camp, drums were beaten violently from break of day; and women assembled to rejoice at the door of the mother, by clapping their hands, dancing, and shouting. Their dance consisted in jumping in the air, throwing out their legs in the most uncouth manner, and flapping their sides with their elbows. One would have supposed the whole to be drunk, but it was their mode of congratulation. When the mother sufficiently recovers, a goat is killed, and she is asked to step over its body, and return again by stepping over its throat; this operation is repeated. Mothers nurse and tend their children with the greatest care, washing them daily with warm water, and licking their faces dry as a dog would her litter of puppies. After this, the body is smeared with a vermilion-coloured pomade, and the infant is laid upon its back on the skin of a goat, which forms its cradle. The four corners of the skin are then knotted together, and the child is sung to sleep while slung in the hand or over the shoulder. When the mother is otherwise busy, the tender burden is hung upon a peg in the same way that we hang a cloak. A wife of the commandant's went through a strange custom with a handful of burning grass. She passed it three times round her body from hand to hand, while she walked to the left of her doorway. The grass was re-lit for her, and the same operation was gone through as she walked in front and again to the left of her door. The whole was performed with perfect solemnity until she saw herself observed, when she returned our smile. This ceremony was connected with the birth of her child. The women of the Bari race cut three horizontal lines on the cheeks of their children, and a black oily paste is rubbed into the incisions, which are kept open, looking raw and inflamed for ten days. I watched the operation upon an intelligent child of two or three years of age. Three deep scars were cut on its plump cheeks; fever seemed to ensue, as the little thing lost its wonted playfulness and its amusing imitation of the mother in her household duties. Ultimately these marks become lines of raised skin, and are cut in different parts of the body according to the race or district. Some have them in horizontal[2] lines on the top of the arm-sockets; others have half-circles on the buttocks; and a very common mark seen at Faloro amongst the natives, was having the temples disfigured by barb-like cuts pointing to the eyes.[3]

---

[1] This is clearly not a credible story; people at the limits of real knowledge are often dubbed cannibals.

[2] *Sic.* This was a typographical error which the proof readers did not spot in 1864.

[3] Cicatrices or raised scars are the norm among most of the Nilotic cattle-keeping peoples. Middleton, *Encyclopedia of Africa*, I, p. 121.

The people of Madi, to whom the village of Faloro belongs, did not seem happy under the yoke of the Turks.[1] Their head men only showed contentment when presented with Arab gowns, pyjamas, &c., and they walked about the villages with canes or whips of buffalo-hide, like the Turks. However, they had their enjoyments of dancing and drinking. Their most pleasing performance was when a band of young men, usually about thirty, each with a hand-drum and a single stick (looking like kangaroos), danced in a circle to a lively quick tune, closing to a centre and retiring again at particular parts of their music.

By moonlight of the 5th December, we witnessed a most extraordinary dance in the village above where we resided. Some three hundred nude men and women were assembled. Six drums, of different sizes, slung upon poles, were in the centre; around these was a moving mass of people, elbowing and pushing one another as at a fair, and outside these a ring of girls, women, and infants, faced an outer circle of men sounding horns, and armed with spears and clubs, their heads ornamented with ostrich-feathers, helmets of the cowrie-shell, &c. Never had I seen such a scene of animated savage life, nor heard a more savage noise. As the two large circles of both sexes jumped simultaneously to the music, and moved round at every leap, the women sang and jingled their masses of bracelets, challenging and exciting the men facing them to various acts of gallantry; while our Seedees joined in the dance, and no doubt touched many a fair heart. But although these night scenes are enjoyed by the inhabitants as well as the Turks, they are during the day oppressed by their masters, and compelled by the lash to labour. Instances of this were constantly seen: a Toorkee thought nothing of giving a woman a cut with his cane if she stood the least in his way; and to escape such cruelty, we saw the people removing the *materiel* of villages for a new erection on a spot more distant from the Toorkee encampment.[2] Any information regarding the neighbouring countries could not be obtained, because the natives feared the Turks, who in turn were jealous, and asked us what business it was of ours to interfere with their subjects? They had also their guests who came on private affairs. These affairs were generally connected with razzias for cattle and ivory, which it was their object to conceal from us.[3] Having been at Faloro for three successive seasons of nine months each, the Toorkees had collected an immense store of ivory, purchasing it with plundered cattle, and occasionally with a few beads—sixteen pounds of ivory fetching but two strings of large blue beads with cut sides. During this their third season, about one hundred monster tusks, and three hundred small ones, called karashas at Zanzibar (averaging sixteen pounds weight each), had been gathered together. All these were easily distinguishable from the eighteen that had been shot by the party, as they were red, and blackened with the flames of fire, applied by the natives in extracting the tusk from the elephant's head. When about to march, sets of tusks were securely lashed together with thong, cut in a single continuous stripe from the hide of a cow. One man could carry from fifty to sixty pounds weight on his head, and when the load was heavier, two men carried it slung to a pole between them.[4]

---

[1] In view of the first-hand description which Grant here provides of the activities of the Khartoum 'traders', this is hardly surprising.

[2] See Grant's depiction in Figure 85, p. 289, which he entitles with the Scots term 'flitting'.

[3] Presumably because of the official Egyptian prohibition of the slave trade as well as the reputation the British had for opposing it.

[4] Figure 86, p. 270, shows how the tusks were tied together. Grant's note with the picture indicates that his drawing exaggerated the sizes of the tusks.

In discharging our Gani guides by payment of beads at Faloro, we gave one of them, in addition, a pair of trousers. He at once put all his small beads loosely into the pockets, but on sitting down, in his usual native manner, the beads kept dropping out, causing much laughter amongst us. To make him still more happy, Frij tied a turban of red rags round his head, which was much admired; but the knowing African rubbed his arms, as much as to say, "Where is the coat?" This man's father, Chong'ee of Gani, a decrepid [sic] old man, with wrinkled skin and dull eye, had received some small beads in return for a cow he presented. They did not satisfy him,—he must have others, the ingenious excuse being that he was too old to see such small things! Other beads much less valuable, but larger, were instantly given and accepted in exchange.

A common disease amongst the natives was a large permanent swelling or growth below the knee-cap of one leg or both. Though the size of a cricket-ball, it was soft, and did not incapacitate the person from sitting, kneeling, or walking, and grown-up women seemed more liable to it than the male sex. Dr Murie (whom we met at Gondokoro) imagined from my description that it might have been brought on from exposure to cold. The only death that occurred while we were with the Turks was that of one of their own number, arising from fever and general exhaustion. His funeral took place at sunrise inside the village; a silent mass of soldiers surrounded the grave, which was dug within the shell of a hut accidentally burnt down a few days previously. And on the occasion of this fire, I may remark that we were all saved providentially by the stillness of the day. The huts being made of grass and bamboo, huddled close together—ammunition and property in every one of them—and water half a mile distant, the alarm was frightful. No one knew what to do, as the unmanageable flames burst through the roof, or kept creeping onwards for more prey. Nude men could not approach it; in their attempts to quench the flame, they held skins of animals to screen them from the heat, which we in our clothes could hardly bear. Its further progress was happily stayed, but the hut with all that it contained was soon a heap of ashes.

In December, the people burn down the grass on the hills and dales. The black ashes fill the air for some days till laid by rain, serving the purpose of manure for the following season. The dews are very heavy at this time of the year: one night my knife was left on a bank, and next morning it appeared rusted all over. After eight in the morning it was too hot to walk out with comfort before the afternoon; and although no musquito troubled us, the place was infested with flies, which stuck to our faces and clothes during a morning walk. The small stream below the village dried up as our rivulets at home do in summer, and, during January, scarcely afforded sufficient water for the cattle. There were nine separate herds, and probably fifteen hundred cows, to be seen daily. They belonged chiefly to the Turks, but the country being overstocked, the animals were small and poor, and many of the calves were not able to follow the flocks. While housed in the villages, each animal was tied to a peg in the ground; and when released, in order that they might be taken to graze, all rushed to a salt bank of earth which had been scooped out by their tongues. We obtained provision here by sending our men with a cow to a neighbouring village, where they killed it before the natives, who exchanged their grains or vegetables for the beef. Very often, when a fowl was required, the natives, though they would not take beads in exchange from us, were obliged to submit to see the Turks knock them over with sticks, and walk away without payment. The vegetable products were tobacco, murwa, a few sweet potatoes, and the stringy seed-vessel of a species of mallow, called here *bamea*.

311

The cultivations were all at least a mile away from where the people dwelt, probably to allow a cleared space for their cattle to range. The field-hoe had a handle as long as the English one; it was large and heavy, but preferred to those made in Unyoro, which were refused here when offered in exchange for sweet potatoes.

As has already been mentioned, the situation chosen at Faloro by the Turks was a very pleasant one. We were surrounded by low hills, the country afforded delightful rambles by rocky streams, through forests, and over downs, with distant prospects. The plants gathered were many of them new and interesting. A plum-tree, having fruit larger than the green-gage, was found in the woods, and large black caterpillars of great beauty, armed with rows of white porcupine-like spikes, fed upon its leaves. A species of silver bush (*Protea sp.*), its flowers spread out like a silvery sunflower, with its scaly calix a pink colour underneath, was interesting. A tree-climber (*Landolphia florida*?)[1] lay with its trunk winding like a huge snake, and then serving as a bridge to the stream. If traced further, you found it had mounted a lofty tree, and spread itself into innumerable branches, covering with luxuriant white flowers the highest foliage. The natives of Uhiyow[2] convert its milk into playing-balls, like those of india-rubber, and consider the rubber superior in quality to that obtained from another tree, M'pira, which has not such adhesive properties.

A very handsome branched lily (*Crinum* sp.)[3] was one day brought in by Speke, who had found it on the bank of the stream-bed. We could find no other in flower, but succeeded in preserving and bringing home this single specimen, which is now in the Kew herbarium. Later—probably by February—their bulbs would throw out fresh shoots for the year. A variety of resinous trees were also found—*Boswellia, Balsamodendron, Khaya, Soymida,* &c.[4]

Trees of the "Sheabutter," and others of similar dimensions, sometimes had diminutive seats placed against their trunks, with the ashes of fire alongside. The seats had been placed there for some idolatrous purpose, to produce rain or probably to remove sickness. The only other trace of superstition we saw was in front of the chief entry to the village. Here a slab, two feet out of the ground, with a circular hole across, faced the entry in an upright position. A pole with a branch of the meelalla palm *(Borassus)* flying from its tip, was planted alongside it.

We had no sport at Faloro, killing only one bushboc, which we found feeding in the jungle of sweet pasture and shrubs by a stream. Further up, amongst rocks, we saw two descriptions of monkeys—one the Lungoor, with black face and bushy head of hair, which barked angrily at us; and the "Yanee"—so called by our Seedees—a smaller monkey, red behind, and said to be so vicious that he will return a spear thrown at him! Both were wild, and changed their ground so often that we did not obtain a shot. The way the Turks have of inflating a sheep or goat after it has been killed appeared strange to our Zanzibar Seedees. A rattan was passed, from an incision in the hock, to the stomach; air was blown in, not with a bellows as in France, but from the mouth, till the animal became distended.

[1] The identification was confirmed. See Grant, 'Botany of the Speke and Grant Expedition', p. 107, where he gives a full description of the example encountered here in Madi.

[2] That is, the Yao people, many of whom were in the caravan as porters.

[3] Grant, 'Botany of the Speke and Grant Expedition', p. 156.

[4] Ibid., pp. 44, 45. Grant mentions here bringing home specimens but does not allude to the fact that he also sent to the Kew Herbarium his illustrations of many of these plants. See Introduction on Grant's major interest in botany, pp. 15–20.

Where the air had not reached, a passage was made for it by striking the part, and the skin by this method was drawn off with greater facility.

The bustard, or "cock of the woods," was occasionally marked down.[1] On starting him he would get up with the usual hurried flight and noise, make a majestic sweep over the woods, and disappear in low ground, or, folding his wings, alight on some cultivated spot. He is a noble bird, with rich game plumage, and nearly the size of a vulture. The other game-birds were chiefly quail and guinea-fowl, but our supply of shot being almost finished, we did not disturb them. Flocks of guinea-fowl were running in the fields three marches north of Faloro. I had never before seen them so numerous; but they were wild, being killed by the inhabitants with bow and arrow. A few rooks, with peculiarly short tails, were now and then observed. They took swift cutting flights from tree to tree, calling like crows, and cleverly evading the darts made at them by kites.

We left Faloro on the 11th of January 1863, our loads being carried by our remaining Seedees, twenty in number. We then travelled without the Turks for a few days to the north, and were joined by their headquarters on the 31st.

Extract from Journal: Reuniting with the Turks

31st [January 1863] Halted. The wild firing of guns, their bullets flying through the air, announced Mahomed's arrival by noon; the man is a kind of ninkimpoop [sic] – so light-headed. [NLS, MS. 17915, 31 January 1863.]

In this interval we employed the time in shooting over the desolate-looking undulations of grass jungle. Rhinoceros, buffalo, gnamæra,[2] n'soono,[3] &c., were killed; and elephant, giraffe, eland, pig, the white-eared antelope of Petherick, and other smaller fauna, were observed. The natives would not eat the rhinoceros. Giraffe were numerous, but very wild, they being in open cover, over which they could, by means of their long necks, see the sportsman. Nothing is more handsome than their bright-yellow black-spotted skin when seen shining in the morning sun; but as you approach to shooting distance they canter away like camels and lash their sides with their tails. Gnamæra or hartebeest are also most provoking animals to stalk; they allow you to approach within three or four hundred yards, when they wheel round with a whisk of their tails, take a canter, and turn back to look at you. The Turks shot a crocodile, and carried him into camp to extract his teeth, which are used by the natives of Madi as necklaces. They are like the long incisors of a sheep, and being pierced, are strung to be worn on the neck. Most of the Turks ate of the crocodile, but our Zanzibar men regarded it with disgust. We ate their eggs to breakfast; and although they were sweet and good without any particular flavour, we had no desire to try another. Ninety-nine of them had been found buried a foot under ground in the sandy bed of a stream, all laid in very neat order. They were longer and larger than the eggs of a turkey, pure white, and uniformly shaped at both ends, with one-third of them an air-chamber.[4]

[1] There are nine species of bustard known in North and South Sudan. From Grant's description, it is difficult to identify what he saw; possibly it was Denham's bustard (*Neotis denhami*). Cave and Macdonald, *Birds of the Sudan*, p. 125.

[2] Grant himself in his glossary, p. xv of the original *A Walk*, gives 'Nyamæra' as an alternative rendering of a word which he says means a 'heartebeest [sic] antelope'. Perhaps one can assume by analogy that, like gnu, it is a Khoisan word from South West Africa transmitted via Cape Dutch.

[3] This seems to be the Luganda word, *ensunu*, which is the Uganda kob.

[4] The forgoing passage about the Turks and crocodile eggs is transcribed almost word for word from the Journal, NLS, MS. 17915, 31 January 1863.

The stream below the village of Apuddo,[1] where we encamped for several days, had cut a wide channel through the plain. Observing some shining scales on its sandy shore, they so much resembled gold that I thought I had made a discovery, and washed the sand for several hours. The result was, glistening black sand resembling iron filings, and a mixture of these gold scales, probably mica, but which remain to be analysed. (*Vide* Appendix B.)[2] While at this operation of digging, a number of bees of the ordinary size came round me, and I could observe them alighting on the sand to enter burrows they had made. They were of two colours, green and yellow, the latter predominating, and barred with black stripes. A few inches underground, a cocoon of the tender leaves of the *Stereospermum sp.*—a tree with pink-white blossom—was found neatly wrapped round some scented yellow substance, having the faintest taste of honey. It may have been liquid wax, as the natives told me that the bees ultimately transport this preparation to their hives. But the curious thing was to see it lying in the wet sand, and almost in water, probably put there to keep it cool from the hot winds. The natives dig wells in the sand and take their drinking water from them. At first we imagined they had been digging for gold, as numerous little pits were in the ground, each with a tumblerful of water; but we observed that the natives filled their earthen "gurrahs"[3] from them in preference to taking water from the running stream close by.

The strong barricade of sticks and logs placed round the villages had numerous openings for entrance. At night these were closed by pulling thorny bushes into them; and during the day one had to stoop to gain entrance. Even their women, when carrying a pitcher of water on their heads, were obliged to go on their knees to pass inside the village. The huts had not room for a camp-bed, not being of greater diameter than seven feet; but, luckily, at this season, quantities of ripe grass were stacked for thatching purposes, and we could always get a temporary shed made to shelter us from the sun. The inhabitants of Panyoro,[4] on seeing our small party arrive, showed a disinclination to admit us inside their villages, and the Turks tried to dissuade us from living there; but in our previous travels we had always fraternised with the natives, and wished to make no difference in the present case.[5] The consequence was that the people confided in us, bringing their property to be placed in concealment under our beds lest the Turks should come and rob them. They also gave us small presents of milk, flour, ears of grain, &c.; and one chief kindly brought us a basin of soup and a mess of porridge. The soup was very nitrous in taste, too much salt of the country having been used. Another dish they had was a mixture of uncooked flour and water, savoured with the fruit of a date-sized plum, the

---

[1] Apuddo is not a place name which appears on modern maps. Grant may have mistaken the name or, as is more likely, the settlement simply disappeared in the numerous wars and raids which have beset this region. The area is now known as Galuffi. In fact, Speke and Grant were just to the south of the present Uganda-South Sudan border, a few miles south of the modern Nimule (3°36′N, 32°03′E).

[2] See Appendix B, p. 384. Needless to say, perhaps, there was no gold and, as Grant surmised, the 'scales' were merely mica.

[3] A *ghurry* is a Hindi-derived term for a certain kind of cup. *Hobson-Jobson*.

[4] Another settlement not to be found on a modern map. In fact this is shown by Grant to be south of Apuddo; his account is not giving his experiences in strict chronological sequence.

[5] Grant's claim gives the impression that a philanthropic policy was in place; perhaps this was partly true but the reality was usually that the travellers had no option but to depend on local people for accommodation, food and other services. Grant no doubt made the comment because it was becoming clear to him that the 'Turks' were not, after all, bringers of civilization but a considerable blight on the land.

Balanites Ægyptica, Dal. The chiefs had a singular mode of salutation, which the common people did not venture to copy; they took our hands successively in theirs, lifted them up as high as they could, and then allowed them to drop. This custom was never seen in Unyoro, Uganda, or south of the equator; and although the hands of the chiefs were not very clean, we were glad to submit to the ceremony. After the natives had become familiar with us by our shooting animals for them, they got up dances similar to the Madi "quadrille." The men held spears over the heads of the women, pointed their elbows at them, and bent their heads to the right and left in time to the drum-music. The Toorkees did not join our men in these dances; they were encamped outside the villages, and thought it was too much like savage life, and beneath them, to participate in the festivities.

As there is no conveyance in the country except by porters, the Turks found it very difficult to get their two hundred loads of ivory carried. The natives on several occasions refused to aid them, saying they were not slaves to be made to carry their property. Resistance being continued, active hostilities were resorted to, and disastrous results ensued. What between the firing of guns and discharge of arrows, three Toorkees were wounded, fifteen natives were killed, and seven made prisoners, the village was burned to the ground, and about one hundred cattle captured! This was told us by some Seedees we sent back to find why the Turks were not coming to join the party. The women captured on these occasions remain the property of the captor, while all cattle and ivory must be shared by the master and his soldiers.[1]

Within sight of Apuddo stands a tamarind-tree, three or four miles from the right bank of the Nile, at 3° 34′ N. lat. and 32° E. long.[2] The Turks informed us that a European had, two years previously, accompanied them from Gondokoro as far as this point, and had returned to Egypt from hence, because the rains were heavy, and he had not sufficient escort to push further south. They did not know his name, but they described him as having a long beard, and said we should find his name cut upon the tree. My notes on the 1st February 1863 are as follows regarding it: "I visited the tree on which a European had cut some letters, but they were so indistinct, that I walked twice round it before I could distinguish them,—they were grown over with a thorny creeper and bark, and had been merely scratched in the wood. They appeared like—ΛIAΛ; the centre letters were I and A, and the outer ones either A *without the stroke,* or part of W. Nails seem to have been extracted, and to read it properly, I had to stand upon some lower branches."[3] I at once

---

[1] Grant's paragraph graphically illustrates what was happening as the Khartoum traders sought ivory and slaves. For details, see e.g. Holt and Daly, *History of Sudan*, pp. 47–82.

[2] Grant's latitude and longitude seem remarkably accurate.

[3] Grant's transcription is not altogether faithful to his original wording in NLS, MS. 17915 for 1 February 1863 and he has added the emphasis. Speke, at the appropriate point in his *Journal*, pp. 598–9, does not mention the tree at all. Giovanni Miani (1810–72), was a Venetian who had fled Italy after the 1848 risings and established himself in Egypt where he gathered information about the Nile Valley which impressed Napoleon III. He set out to find the source of the Nile in 1859 and, with the help of the Maltese merchant Andrea de Bono, in March 1860, he reached the point (just north of the current Uganda-South Sudan border) where Grant found his carving. He was forced to retreat and later disappointed to learn that Amabile de Bono had reached even further south. He then abandoned a further expedition of which Grant later heard plans. His publications in Italian disputed Speke and Grant's Nile source discovery. Later, he explored the Niger-Congo watershed among the Azande people but died of fever in 1872. See Langlands, 'Early Travellers', p. 57; *Atlas of Uganda*, p. 73; the best account in English is by Howgego, *Encyclopedia of Exploration*, III, pp. 624–5, where the available Italian sources of information are listed.

concluded that the traveller was not English, because his letters were not deeply cut into the tree as an Englishman would have done it, and also because the letters were curiously formed. The illegible letters without strokes were scored in thus—∧∧—as a foreigner writes the capital letter M. Not until we reached Khartoom did we find out for certain who this traveller must have been. His name was **MIANI** (Miani), a native of Venice, who has protested against *our* Nile being the proper Nile, because we have placed his tree in a position of latitude and longitude (obtained by daily observations) different to what he made it, without scientific instruments. His assertion is bold, considering the above evidence; but as M. Miani is trying to organise another expedition, I have no doubt he will discover, and perhaps ultimately acknowledge, his error. In the mean time, Mr S. Baker will in all likelihood have passed the spot, and taken the exact position of the tree and river. The Nile at 3½° N. lat., had quite changed the wild character it possessed at Karuma Falls. Its banks were tame and flat, with but few trees. The opposite, or left bank, rose into three blocks of lofty bare hills, almost mountains, called "Jubl Kookoo." Round their north-east bluff end the majestic Nile made a sweeping turn from the west to the north; and looking down the stream from this point, the scene appeared wild and romantic like the Highland Pass of Glencoe.

At this point of my narrative[1] I was arrested by startling intelligence: the first dark cloud connected with our African journey had suddenly appeared. In a moment, without warning, the devoted leader of the expedition was cut off in his prime, and just as he had told the wondrous tale of his adventurous life! On the 17th of September,[2] when engaged as usual in transcribing from my Journal, my apartment was entered by my brother-in-law, the Rev. Peter Mackenzie, whose countenance wore an unusual expression of grief. It was to break to me the sad news that my fellow-traveller—poor Speke—had been shot by the accidental discharge of his own gun. I could not realise the fact. Could he possibly be dead? Was there no hope? The telegraph gave us none. A few days only had elapsed since he and his brother invited me to their home in Somersetshire to be present at the meeting of the British Association at Bath, and had I gone thither and been with my friend, this calamity might have been averted. Innumerable such thoughts hurried through my mind on the first shock of the melancholy tidings. It was hard to believe that one who had braved so much had thus fallen, and that his career of usefulness was run! I reproached myself for having silently borne all the taunts and doubts thrown upon his great discovery, the truth of which will ultimately be acknowledged by all but those determined to cavil. We had corresponded on the subject, and agreed that controversy on my part was to be avoided. Any attempt of the kind might only weaken his cause, and I felt that no assertions of mine were necessary to bear out the facts which he had recorded. Truth in time would conquer, and bear down all gainsayers, while that grand reservoir of twenty thousand miles—the Victoria Nyanza, with its fountains and tributaries—would speak for itself. Knowing that on our travels my attention was more directed to the habits of the people than to the

[1] In the original book, the text for the next two and three-quarter pages (pp. 347–9), is surrounded by a black border to indicate mourning for Speke.
[2] That is, 1864.

316

geography of the country, he expressed a wish that I should write an account of our camp life in Africa. I complied, and part of this narrative lay on his table on the day of his death. It now goes forth without his revision or suggestions—a public loss; for my fellow-traveller had a thorough knowledge of the country, loved its inhabitants, was a practical ornithologist, and would have aided me with his views on all topographical questions. Added to a singular adaptation for the work he had made choice of,—arising partly from his imperturbable temper and great patience,— Captain Speke was, in private life, pure-minded, honourable, regardless of self, and equally self-denying, with a mind always aiming at great things, and above every littleness. He was gentle and pleasing in manner, with almost childlike simplicity, but at the same time extremely tenacious of purpose. This was strikingly displayed in his recent efforts to prosecute his work in Africa, which, had he lived, he would ultimately have accomplished. But God has ordained it otherwise. His will be done! To Captain Speke's mourning relatives and friends, there remains the consolation that though he died in the prime of life, he had attained to immortal fame, and now rests in his own beautiful native district, lamented by all who knew him, and a brilliant example to the youth of future generations. His remains were laid with those of his ancestors in the family vault of the parish church; and had the toll of the funeral bells reached the shores of the Nyanza as it touched the hearts of those in the valley of Ilminster, there is one at least—the King of Uganda—who would have shed a tear for the untimely death of the far-distant traveller who had sought and found his protection. I must now resume the course of my narrative, which has been so painfully interrupted.[1]

At Apuddo gales blew hot and powerful enough to melt any number of glaciers. The "Kousee" wind from the N.E., carrying dust with it, blew as if through a funnel during the latter half of January; it was no doubt reflected with greater violence on account of the proximity of the Jubl Kookoo range of mountain to our N.W. While sheltered from its blasts we perspired profusely; but by sunset it had lulled away, and we were able to walk about with comfort. A coat was then bearable, and during the night we wore sheets of serge to keep us warm. Rain was noted in my journal on the 12th of January from the N.E., and another note mentions at this time, wind "all day N.N.W., blowing with great freshness."

Provisions—namely, koonde,[2] murwa, and jowari—were scarce and dear in the villages opposite Jubl Kookoo during the month of January, which was their winter season. Large figs, called M'kooyoo, though thick-skinned and full of seeds, were now sweet and palatable. No crops were seen growing—all looked desolate wastes and covers. Even the stream which flowed past Apuddo, for three miles up its tortuous course had not a thicket to mark its windings through the plain. The banks dropped straight down fifteen feet to its sandy bed, which was sometimes broken by grass-topped and fissured rocks, and in places by ridges of rock, making a cataract or waterfall. Above this, in one reach two

---

[1] The implications of this passage are discussed in the Introduction, pp. 52–3. It seems to have been inserted at the proof stage of the book as it does not appear in the original version available in NLS, MS. 17934.

[2] 'Vigna luteola. A grain eaten when dead ripe; its leaves are dried and eaten as a vegetable'. Grant, 'Botany of the Speke and Grant Expedition', p. 10.

hundred yards long, the water lay deep and almost still, teeming with fish two and three feet in length. We had no means of catching them, and the natives did not use nets, but most likely they had basket-traps.

The people dwelt in villages surrounded by palisades. Some of these villages contained two hundred souls, young and old. It would not be considered safe to have a much smaller settlement, as their neighbours to the east, the Kidi, would come down to plunder them of their herds of cattle. We observed a leper with white hands and limbs. Whether he had succeeded by right to his position of "M'koongoo," or head of a district, or whether from being looked upon as a favoured man he was elected president, we could not say, but the latter is not unlikely; for the natives of Africa have a respect for men with spotted skins. The Turks generally applied to us for medical advice. One day a tooth had to be drawn; a rag was tied round each half of a pair of scissors, and I had to make these answer all the purpose of a forceps. Again, a disease which very much resembles diphtheria, and which was said to be fatal unless cut, was treated in an odd way. The patient had a white abscess in the throat, and it required to be cut. They had no instrument for the purpose, and we had only a penknife, and there was further the difficulty of reaching the seat of the disease. The natives, however, are ingenious; they pulled out the tongue so far that a hair noose could be put round the abscess, and it was then cut, much to the poor man's relief, who speedily recovered.

It has been mentioned that the people of Madi wear the teeth of crocodiles as neck ornaments. The natives of Bari do the same, and the pearly white colour of the teeth is most becoming to their deep bronze complexions. Another ornament seen here was new to us: the thigh-bones of sheep and rats were pierced at one end, and slung from the neck. I had seen nothing like this since leaving Delagoa Bay, where the Zulu Kaffirs, called in Central Africa "Watuta," wear bones, bird's-feet, &c., as charms round the neck.

On the 1st of February 1863, we marched in a caravan or troop of no less than three hundred souls from our camp at Apuddo to some villages fifteen miles distant on the route to Gondokoro. Having to cross the river Asua,[1] a wild rocky torrent, the journey occupied six hours and forty minutes, our escort consisting of two hundred ivory-carriers, the Toorkees, their wives, women, slaves, donkeys, cattle, &c. The route lay above the right bank of the Nile, and although the country was uninhabited, I do not recollect ever making a more interesting march. At the fourth mile, and to the west, we heard from the heights on which we stood the White Nile sounding below us, like the ocean, but we could not see it until we had proceeded two miles further. The beautiful noble stream was breaking now and then into foam upon hidden rocks; or running at the rate of about four miles an hour past islands so laden with trees and vegetation that we could only partially discern the opposite bank, and obtain occasional glimpses of the river. On our side we had several species of acacia, the double black thorned and the white; with other trees in lilac bloom, wild figs, &c.; and, had the underwood of thorny scrub been cleared away, the place might have been deemed a paradise. The ivory-carriers marched steadily

---

[1] The River Aswa (or Asua, or Achwa) is the major river draining the northern plateau area of present-day Uganda and flows north-westwards to join the Nile some way north of Nimule. Regrettably, the maps in both Speke's and Grant's books showed the Aswa as having its origin in Lake Baringo (which is actually an Eastern Rift Valley lake) with that lake linked to Lake Victoria. The data was thus physically impossible on two major counts and caused needless confusions. Speke's unconvincing explanation is in his *Journal*, pp. 467–8, where he says the 'tophead' of the Nile must be the south end of Lake Victoria, further south than Lake Baringo.

onwards, but I longed for the halt,[1] that we might have a drink of the water that appeared so inviting. At the eighth mile a happy break in the thicket gave us this opportunity; and we who had traced the stream from the Victoria Nyanza were so glad to see our Uganda acquaintance once more, that we addressed it in the language of that country, exclaiming, "Awangeh! awangeh!"—old friend! old friend! While resting on the rocky bank, the views across, up or down the river, were of great interest. At our feet, by the side of a foaming rapid, fish rose like porpoises, showing their backs in a whirling black pool, where reeds, rushes, branches, and logs floated about, making it impossible for any but an adept to attempt fly-fishing The shore was strewed with fish-scales, and remnants of fires showed that the natives had been enjoying dinner at an appropriate spot. Looking across, an island, covered with grass and aquatic vegetation, hid the other branch of the river. For a quarter of a mile at this point no boat could live at any season; it would be dashed to pieces on the bed and sides of sunken rock; and the immense body of water is so strong that no boat could sail up it. Looking down stream, the river ran in a deep one-sided gorge, the left bank being the Jubl Kookoo range, forming a straight barrier of escarped hills, probably two thousand feet in height. They were bleak and barren, diminishing in size and breaking into cones as they receded into the blue distance to the north. At the ninth mile of this march, we suddenly dropped into the bed of the Asua river, and crossed to its right bank. Our first remark was, "Is this the Asua we have heard so much of?" The fording was fifty yards across, waist deep in the strong middle current over sharp slippery rocks, painful for bare feet. The water was good, though not refreshing nor transparent; it ran through five-feet-high rushes (*Cyperus longus*), on the right shore. During December, this river, judging from the appearance of sand lying above its present water-mark, must be a wild torrent, impossible to cross; but we were disappointed with its small appearance when we came to ford it. Our large *cortège* amused themselves for two hours in crossing the cattle and laden donkeys, and in bathing. At this place I saw the brutal nature of the ivory-traders. One of them, in getting upon his laden bullock, mounted so awkwardly, that he tilted the load over to one side, and the animal would not start with him. He belaboured it on the head with a loaded life-preserver, till the poor animal sat down. Immediately he dismounted, and in rage put a bullet through its head; and the men around him cut off the hump and legs to carry with them as food, while the owner sat gloomily apart looking on: anything more revolting I never saw. Having forded the river we encamped in a village, the inhabitants flying at our approach. We had been from sunrise to sunset on the road, having passed several deserted villages and a jungle of thorny wood. The path along which we had travelled was on the top of vertical strata, pointing to the north-west. It was of slaty blue rock, cleaved into loose squares and oblongs, with quartz veins.

One morning I walked, along with three of our Seedees, due west for two hours, to have another look at the Nile. We tried to get guides from the villages, but after promising they generally slunk back into their huts. However, when approaching the river, past the dwellings, I induced a native to give me tobacco, when an escort of about forty men, well armed with bows, spears, and handfuls of arrows, accompanied me to the water's edge. For two miles the calm river ran in a straight reach, unbroken, as far as I remember, by rock or cataract. Its breadth appeared to be about eighty yards, and the current four miles an hour; both banks were dead-level, and of stiff clay. Beyond these, rather barren hills rose

---

[1] Grant was able to depict the Nile in this region at later stops; see Figures 92, 93 and 94, pp. 334–5.

abruptly. While sitting on the bank, my feet almost touched the water; and the level ground was dotted with tamarinds, fig, palm, plum, and jujube trees, the soil itself being then, in parts, lying under cultivation. The people had a ferry-boat—that is, a log of wood scooped out to form a boat; and they tied together large bundles of the jowari straw, and ferried over upon them. I had never seen this before, but further down the Nile it is a common practice. On my way back from this excursion, the villagers at several places invited me to partake of milk, and the guide, on being rewarded with a single string of beads, in a coaxing and familiar manner asked for another. One of the Seedees whom we had picked up in the heart of Africa, was convicted at this encampment of Madi of having stolen a cloth belonging to a Toorkee with whom he lived. The offence was a grave one, bringing dishonour upon our Zanzibar party; he, therefore, was awarded fifty lashes. Bombay administered forty with a whip of buffalo-hide, and Frij the remaining ten. The offender, after receiving the first few lashes, cried, "Kill me! kill me!" meaning that death was preferable to the pain; but little Bombay, who was flogging him, said, "Are you a woman that you scream in that way?" The fellow was at once silenced; but though his back was scarred, he ate his dinner before us and carried a load the following day. He was a hardened culprit, and deserted from us in Egypt, after being detected in stealing from a comrade.

The sick of this district of Madi were not allowed to reside within the enclosure of the village; but huts or hospitals were erected outside for all who were diseased. It was curious to find such a civilised precaution taken in Africa. But the huts were also remarkable for neatness and cleanliness; bamboos were numerous, so that they had the material for making themselves comfortable. The floors were of red clay, packed hard, and the thresholds of the doors the same, but paved or macadamised, with fragments of earthenware neatly inlaid. Many of the doorways had gateposts, with bamboos as movable bars, which prevented goats or cattle entering. Upon the grass tops of the huts in Barwudi numbers of large univalve shells lay bleaching; they were the same large, spiral species as those seen five degrees south of the equator. The natives cut them into circles the size of shirt-buttons, and string hundreds of them to be worn as ornamental white girdles round the waist. They formed the ordinary coinage, and if beer or fowls were required they were used in the purchase. The value of labour was estimated in cows. The porters engaged by De Bono's party to carry their ivories were paid one small cow each for a journey of four marches, and they were expected to carry a return load; so that travelling in these parts is a difficult matter, unless you have plenty of camel and donkey carriage: the hire is always paid beforehand. It was amusing to observe the distribution of the cattle, but it presented much the same scene as that witnessed at home in a cattle-market. Here the naked natives, mingling with the well-dressed Toorkees, as soon as they received their "one-cow hire," chased it away to be tied up in some secure place till their journey was completed. On arrival at one of the villages, I asked the Sheikh what his beer was like; he made no reply, but at midnight he stole into our camp, passing our Seedee sentries, who were fast asleep, tapped Speke on the head, and then shook his hand to awake him. Speke immediately called Frij, to find what the old man meant by coming at such an hour, when it appeared that he had brought us a taste of his beer. It seemed raw and spiritless, but as soon as the sun had risen, the old Sheikh generously brought us a large jar full of the beverage.

The country was populous: but in this month of February, though displaying pretty undulations or downs, dotted with shady tamarind and fig trees, and though the double-coned hills have wooded tops, all had a parched appearance. The brooks were dry. During several of our marches we met with no stream, and what water was obtained was procured by digging holes in the dry and rocky beds. Sometimes wild-fruits would refresh us, such as the fig; it was the size of a strawberry pippin, and tasted excellent. The natives gathered quantities of the fruit of a *Cucur bitaceæ,* the size and shape of a fowl's egg: its yellow rind was dried and eaten by them. Their grain they stored in separate houses from their dwellings, and built or placed them upon a few piles of wood or rough pillars of stone. On arrival in a village the Toorkee always made his way to these stores for the purpose of pillaging. On my desiring one of them to desist, he coolly laughed; but Bombay succeeded better with him. As soon as our caravan arrived at a village for the day, the Turks formed camp outside of it by removing the roofs of the houses, and making their owners carry them for them! If resistance was shown, the buttend of the musket was applied to the poor owner, or the muzzle of the gun was presented to his stomach. One consequence of this system of coercion and plunder was that, whenever the people of Madi or Bari had the opportunity, they retaliated and stole from the Turks freely.

The country was too open and populous for game. Along our route we saw none; but the men often wore ornaments of the wild boar's curved tusk. This was tied with a thong above each elbow, and looked very jaunty on their well-formed arms. Their spears were some inches taller than most men can stretch, with handles of bamboo and handsomely-shaped iron blades. Each was shod with a sharp point of iron, or had its end like the leaded end of an Indian hog-spear. Their iron weapons were of superior construction, and were chiefly made on the spot, as there were traces of smelting. The earthenware was very ordinary; but we remarked an unusual article of luxury, a strainer actually of earthenware—the only *civilised* bit of crockery we had seen since leaving Zanzibar: it was chiefly used for straining beer. The perennial cotton-bush grew 8 feet high, without irrigation, close to the houses; the pods, thick and numerous, were now ripening. Three or four bushes give sufficient cotton to each family for all the use made of it; the women dye it brown, and make their scanty dress—waist-belts and tails—of the fibre. The men practised archery a good deal, placing a number of the large seed-vessels of *Kigelia pinnata* on end and aiming at them at 40 and 50 yards' distance. They must be practised shots, as a villager was brought us in a sinking state with an arrow-mark in his side. The wound was covered up, and plastered all over with leaves—their remedy for everything. He had, in all probability, been struck by a poisoned arrow, as they sometimes use these in Madi.

We had very little sickness, and all were in high glee at the thought of going to Egypt in boats. Some men had arrived from Gondokoro reporting that three boats were lying there; we concluded they must be those of Frith,[1] Petherick, and De Bono, and we were delighted at the prospect of meeting Petherick. The time we were detained by the Toorkees, because they had difficulty in procuring porters to carry their ivory to Gondokoro, was occupied in botanising or gossiping with our men. Manua, the "Man of the Moon,"[2] was forming his plans as to what he would do after he got paid for the journey. He said, very truly, that Zanzibar life would not suit him; he could not afford it; because if he retired there, he would have to pay for water, food, drink, clothing, and house-room. His plan, therefore, was to purchase beads and cloths and take them for sale

[1] Possibly a reference to the photographer Francis Frith (1822–98) who had visited the Nile in 1857–9.
[2] He died in 1871. Simpson, *Dark Companions*, p. 195.

to his native land of Unyamuezi—a resolution which shows the mercantile nature of his race. This little fellow was very intelligent, and a great traveller. He talked in high praise of his late king, Foondeekeera,[1] and was quite in raptures when he mentioned his name. It seems that before the king's death a man and woman were suspected of having worked an enchantment upon him, and they were slain; but the king died nevertheless; none of his wives were buried with him, and a house was built over the grave. The chief of Wakeembwah,[2] to the west of Unyamuezi, is laid in the bed of a small stream when he dies, and fifty living women (his wives), and fifty men, are tied to frames and drowned in the same stream to commemorate the event. Their race practise the rite of circumcision, which is exceptional in Central Africa.

Between the district of Madi and Gondokoro there is a tract of country 40 miles long, inhabited by the Bari,[3] who are the terror of all ivory-traders, as they are an independent and powerful race of people. In passing through their country we were told that our guns should always be at hand, that we should not drink any water, as it was poisoned, and, above all, that we should move across the country in a compact body, and not in procession. On seeing the nipple of Bombay's gun blown out, I inquired how he was to get through the Bari?—was the gun safe to fire in its patched state? Oh yes, he'd fire it, because the gun was strong—it had stood the proof of three cartridges! How was that? "It's some time ago now; but Ubede, Abdulla, and a man who deserted, had a spite at me, and each of them put a cartridge into this gun, thinking it would blow my head off, but the nipple was only blown out." He was such an excellent little fellow that he never told us this when it happened; and when asked whether he had suspected his enemy Baraka to have played him this trick, he generously replied, "No, I never suspected him." One other instance of the Seedee character may be mentioned before giving an account of our travels through the Bari people. Our cook boy, M'kate, a very tall good looking lad, ever obliging and good-humoured, one day left a cooking-pot twelve miles behind. He was admonished by Frij, and took the matter so much to heart that he travelled back for it alone that same day and returned during the night, having recovered the old pot, which was certainly not worth the journey. It only proves what men will do with kind treatment; he was not asked to go back, and had walked by himself thirty-six miles through a strange country.[4]

---

[1] Fundikira of Unyanyembe had co-operated with Arab traders from the coast but after his death in c. 1858, relations deteriorated. Roberts, 'Nyamwezi', p. 131.

[2] Presumably, the Wakimbu.

[3] A Nilo-Saharan group who are farmers and herders with a social system dominated by generation sets. Middleton, *Encylopedia of Africa*, III, p. 178.

[4] Youngs, *Travellers in Africa*, p. 95, analyses this incident in some detail arguing that Grant has inculcated in this man a respect for service and for property which will prepare him for subjection. Whether Grant's writings exhibit such conscious or unconscious prejudices is a subject for discussion.

CHAPTER XV

[Pages 361–73]

Passage through the Bari Country, Gondokoro and the Meetings with Baker and Petherick [11 January–26 February 1863]

The Bari country was a series of gently swelling downs, sloping to the Nile a few miles to our left. The downs were covered with grass now ripe and only a foot high. During the bright mid-day sun, with a fresh, hot breeze, the grass, when set on fire, burns with alarming rapidity; but in the darkness of night, when the air was still, it burned quietly but brilliantly, and we dined by its light: no theatrical footlights or exhibition of fireworks could compare with the brilliancy of the consuming flame. Densely foliaged tamarinds covered with ripe fruit, wild plum, sheabutter, and several other umbrageous trees scattered over the landscape, gave it the appearance of an English park, for here no palms nor other tropical genera were to be seen. We had to step over numbers of running rivulets whose channels and banks were generally of rock. In the rainy season these torrents must be difficult to cross, as they have all worn deep beds for themselves; but now in fording the largest they only reached to the knee, and with bare feet we enjoyed the wading. Their waters were rather insipid and tasteless.

We dared not rest at any of the Bari[1] villages, as the Toorkees distrusted the people; but Bookhait, the second in command of the traders, beckoned to a Bari, and he frankly joined us. He was a tall, erect, thin man, naked from head to foot, but with all the airs of a well-dressed beau, for his body was smeared with a red clay pomade. Above each elbow he wore a massive ring of ivory, upon one shoulder he carried a diminutive stool of one piece of solid dark wood, and he had a rope-sash which possessed a five-finger-like charm; he was unarmed. Next morning he brought into camp a very fine tusk, for which he received in exchange a female goat and its kid—cheap ivory certainly. The women wore each a long apron of leather to the knee and a separate broader one of sewn leather behind: these skins they colour with clay, and they seem to wear no ornaments; however, there was not much opportunity for observation on our part, as they ran away on observing us watch them. It seems strange that these people, who for the last thirty years have been

---

[1] The Bari are a Nilo-Saharan (or 'Nilotic') people who live on both banks of the White Nile at about 5° N. Although stateless, they traditionally regulated relationships between different groups through mediators. Living at the approximate head of navigation on the Nile, they became an obvious target for the Khartoum ivory and slave traders. Their reaction to a slave raid led to a violent confrontation in 1854 when Alexander Vaudey was killed and they subsequently had a bad reputation with the slavers. Hence the unwillingness of the 'Turks' with whom Grant was now travelling to consort with them in their villages. See Middleton, *Encyclopedia of Africa*, III, p. 328, IV, p. 178; Santi and Hill, *Europeans in Sudan*, p. 121.

only from twenty to thirty miles distant from the Austrian mission-station at Gondokoro,[1] should still be so wild; but the missionaries state that the ivory trade has spoiled the country for civilisation, and whenever the inhabitants see a foreigner, white or black, they look upon him as an enemy, come for no other purpose than to seize cattle or whatever else he can.

In travelling through the Bari our large caravan was astir at the rattle of the drum in the morning, and marched the whole day, except the three hottest hours, which were spent under shady trees. During the march the colours led the way, no one was allowed to precede them, and a complete cordon of armed Toorkees surrounded the moving mass and kept order. In this way we proceeded across country at a smart pace, allowing no straggling, but making many halts. Sometimes, at several fields' distance, or outside their palisaded huts, or under trees, knots of the people watched us. A favourite position with them was to stand on one leg, resting the foot of the other leg against the standing limb above the knee. A spear balanced them more firmly, but the posture would be most uncomfortable to a European.[2] We passed through one body of the men, and they showed no fear till they saw our white faces, when they ran wildly away. While halting to drink and refresh at a stream, after I had quenched my thirst, seeing some large branches of the *Euphorbia antiquorum* placed in the water with stones over them, I inquired what could be the cause of the branches being so placed, when they replied, "Oh! have you drunk of the water? that plant has been placed there to poison it." The Toorkees laughed when told that I had been drinking heartily, but as the stream ran as clear as crystal I had no hesitation in partaking of it again, and felt no bad effects. The natives preferred digging holes in the sand of the stream, and drinking from them. The Bari are no doubt a dangerous people. We had two porters wounded by their arrows, of which they carry numbers, and they showed such a front on the occasion of my umbrella being accidentally left behind, that, although thirty of our men went back to recover it, they thought it prudent to abandon my old and trusty friend! Our most serious affair with them was on the night of the 14th of February 1863, the day before getting into Gondokoro. A most anxious night it was: we were all lying encamped upon a grassy slope round a large tree within a mile of the Nile, when, having dined, Frij came to us, saying, "Have you heard that the natives are coming to attack us? Mahomed says we must be prepared with our guns for a fight." "Do you hear that, Speke?" "Yes," was the calm reply. On reflection, we remembered having, shortly after our arrival, seen the porters and Toorkees go to the village and take away a quantity of palisading, and whatever other articles they could carry. The smoke of two guns had also been seen; but whether any natives were killed, the Toorkees would not say. The people had fled at the time, and their return accounted for the present alarm. Darkness soon fell on the camp. We ascertained that the sentries were unusually alert, so we retired to rest; but about ten o'clock my servant Uledi awoke me, saying that "the natives were about to attack us. Do you not see their fires?" Sure enough one-third of

---

[1] Following the founding of the Apostolic Vicariate for Central Africa in 1846, this Roman Catholic mission had been set up in 1852 by Mgr Ignaz Knoblecher (1819–58), an impressive linguist and scholar. However, sickness among the priests, the death of Knoblecher and the hostility of the Khartoum traders as well as the suspicions of the Bari led to the closure of the mission in 1860. Hill, *Biographical Dictionary*, pp. 205–6, 145; Hill, *Egypt in the Sudan*, pp. 79, 98; Howgego, *Encyclopedia of Exploration 1800–1850*, II, p. 326.

[2] Grant shows the pose in a vignette in Figure 97, p. 337.

the horizon was a flame of burning grass, and my first impression was that we should immediately be surrounded by the spreading fire. The natives screamed and beat drums, and men carrying torches made of grass collected from other villages. We now dressed, placed our rifles by us, and sat watching the scene. Dances in circles were performed to drum-music beaten in the most furious manner, and the women's shrill voices sounded loud amidst the bargoma[1] and other horns. Overcome at last by sleep we lay down again, and at daybreak awoke to find the rest of the night had passed without further disturbance. This was very fortunate, as had the maps, journals, and collections of our expedition perished on this occasion, the loss to us would have been irreparable. During the night, Captain Mahomed was asked to send them by a bearer to Consul Petherick at Gondokoro, but he replied that no one dare travel at night, and that the fires and dancing we saw were only an intimation that we would be attacked in the morning. Twice the enemy had come up to our camp, but the click of the sentries' gunlocks frightened them away.[2]

We all moved off in a compact mass by daylight of the 15th February, and were not molested, though we passed villages, outcropping rocks, and jungle of low trees, all favouring attack. After proceeding seven miles the features of the country completely changed from highland to lowland. As far as the eye could reach, there was to the north a dreary plain, dotted with the Punjab madar,[3] growing upon firm and heavy sand. As we approached Gondokoro, a white speck was pointed out to us as the keneessa,[4] or church, the spot where the Austrian mission-house stood. Afterwards we could see the masts of Nile boats,[5] the appearance of which increased our excitement—I could have flown to them; and when our band of Toorkees drew up a mile from them to form line and fire a *feu-de-joie*, I had great difficulty in submitting to the delay. However, Speke was tolerably cool, and we all marched in together. Entering the first respectable hut we reached, we inquired for our friend Petherick, and were informed that a gentleman had been there only a few minutes before. The inmates offering to conduct us, we proceeded in quest of the gentleman referred to, and soon had the happiness to see a sturdy English figure approaching. With a hearty cheer, we waved our hats and rushed into the arms, not of Petherick, but of Baker,[6] the elephant-hunter of Ceylon, who had bravely come in search of us. All England, he said—nay, all Europe—believed that we should never get through the tribes! Here we were, however, grateful for our preservation, and grateful also for the sympathy of our kind friends and countrymen. Baker led us to his "diabeah," or Nile

---

[1] It has not been possible to discover precisely what sort of horn this was.

[2] The story of these happenings on 14 February 1863 is almost word for word copied by Grant from his Journal entry for that day, NLS, MS. 17915.

[3] *Calotropis procera* as listed in Grant, 'Botany of the Speke and Grant Expedition', p. 111; Lind and Tallantire, *Flowering Plants of Uganda*, p. 120. This plant has been called 'Apple of Sodom' given its bitter fruit and poisonous sap, according to *Wikipedia*.

[4] More correctly, *kanisa* in Swahili.

[5] Grant illustrates this scene very precisely in his dated painting, Figure 95, p. 336; the preceding picture, reproduced here as Plate 43, shows the former mission house more clearly.

[6] Samuel (later Sir Samuel) White Baker (1821–93), achieved great fame as an explorer of the Nile tributaries and Lake Albert and later as an agent of the Egyptian Government's in its attempted annexation of the interlacustrine area at the head of the Nile. Arguably, however, he complicated the Nile source debate by grossly exaggerating the size of 'his' Lake Albert. He also grossly exaggerated what he had achieved for Egypt; in fact his efforts seriously antagonized African peoples, especially the Banyoro.

pleasure-boat, and we found him surrounded with many of the comforts of civilised life long denied to us—tea, sugar, coffee, bread, wine, &c.[1] We had had no English news later than August 1860, and now it was February 1863; so that there was much for us to hear of national affairs, as well as matters of private interest.[2] But where was Petherick? Had he made no preparations for us? Or, finding we had not been able to keep to time, had he despaired and given up the search? A handsome diabeah and luggage-boat of his were here, but there were neither letters nor instructions for us. He himself was not at Gondokoro, and had never been there. Instead of co-operating with our expedition, he had gone to his own ivory depot in the west, and only arrived at Gondokoro four days after ourselves.

Extract from Journal: The Encounters and Reactions of 15 February 1863

March 4 hrs = 11 miles N. to Gondokoro ... a tent pitched at Gondokoro was seen far away, nearer and the masts of some boats showed, an exciting time certainly. A mile out the Turks formed line, fired their guns most dangerously and advanced on their course by drum and fife. Led us to a Circassian[3] but where is Petherick, he was here not five minutes ago and will return soon, we load again and were off to his boats. Seeing him advancing, I took off my hat and waved it but it was not Petherick but Baker ... who like a brave little fellow[4] had come to search for us! And here was pleasure & disappointment to him that he had done nothing to get us out of our difficulties. Entering his budgerow[5] we had the luxuries of civilization all around us ... We heard for the first time of Prince Albert's death and the Civil war in America, Noah's Ark[6] and many adventures by sea & land from Baker. Kilimanjaro ascended by the Baron von der Decken and Thornton, late of Livingstone [Expedition][7] to 8000 ft where glaciers, snow and rocks obstructed further advance up the steep mountain which was supposed to be 22,000 ft high ... A donkey was killed today by the rascally Turks, firing in marking [?] our arrival, who fire their guns without cause never looking where they fire in the most reckless way ...

Petherick keeps a shop of the most poor description selling chains, guns, boxes, shirts or [?] cup. I saw a note of his charging 4/2, for this, 8/6[8] for a box of caps. Good heavens, we thought him merely an ivory trader in England & introduced

---

[1] '&c' may be taken to include Baker's then mistress, Florence von Sass, later his wife, whom he had purchased at a Balkans slave auction. Jeal, *Explorers*, pp. 182–3, tells the story. Presumably out of delicacy, Grant does not refer to her, even, as far as one can see, in his private journal.

[2] Baker himself reported that 'Grant was in honourable rags; his bare knees projecting through the remnants of his trowsers ... He was looking tired and feverish.' Baker, *Albert N'yanza*, I, p. 101.

[3] Presumably Khurshid Aga, a Circassian trader.

[4] This was an odd comment since Baker was a large man.

[5] Here in his journal Grant used the Anglo-Indian term he knew for a 'lumbering, keelless barge' (*Hobson-Jobson*) but amends it in his book to the Arabic *diabeah*.

[6] Probably a reference to one of the many claims that the remains of Noah's Ark had been found.

[7] For Von der Decken, see Chapter II above, p. 77, n. 5. Richard Thornton (1838–63) was a young geologist, unfairly dismissed by Livingstone from the Zambesi Expedition, who then joined Von der Decken's Kilimanjaro climb in 1861. He was subsequently taken back by Livingstone only to die. Tabler, *Zambezi Papers of Thornton*, pp. ix–xx.

[8] That is, 4 shillings and 2 pence and 8 shillings and 6 pence; there were 240 old pence and 20 shillings in £1, and a shilling was worth 12 old pence.

him into society! What presumption in him.[1] He has gone west with his wife to 'search' for us and a party has gone to say we were remaining ashore [?] as a detention of ten days must take place here … [NLS, MS. 17915, 15 February 1863]

We learned from Baker that kind friends in England had placed £1000 in the hands of Mr Petherick for our succour, and were doubly surprised that he had made no effort to meet us. It was to M. de Bono's men, and not Mr Petherick's, that we were indebted for our escort. I feel it due to the memory of my companion to state these facts,[2] and to say that I had the same feeling of disappointment which he had, and that our meeting with Mr Petherick was by no means the cordial one we anticipated.[3] Having been previously supplied with all necessaries, and three return boats by Baker for conveying us to Khartoom, we required nothing save a few yards of calico to replace the barkcloth rags of our twenty Seedees, and this we obtained from the stores of Mr Petherick.[4]

Extracts from Journal: The Arrival of Petherick

Petherick arrived on left bank here by 6 p.m. with his wife and Dr Murie[5] all looking filthy dirty. Two 3lbers[6] saluted him I don't know how often from the shore. P had brought them from the Austrian Mission establishment who have sold off everything at a mere song … There were letters for us, & they had Burton's book[7] but we got neither the whole day and thought this very unkind. P. had seen a male crocodile so high that he stood taller than the table and also at least 25ft long … [NLS, MS. 17915, 20 February 1863]

21st [February 1863] Halted. After breakfast call at P.'s boat, full of ILNs [*Illustrated London News*], Punches, Papers & Speke communicated to me the death of my

---

[1] This passage might seem to serve as a good example of Youngs's contention that British travellers in Africa were mainly informed by their domestic class prejudices and insecurities – in Grant's case, a 'higher-class disdain of trade'. Youngs, *Travellers in Africa*, pp. 93–4.

[2] As will be noted, as he wrote this, Grant had recently heard of Speke's death and now would say nothing of the differences of attitude discussed in the Introduction, above, p. 51.

[3] Although he felt bound to support Speke, Grant never showed the vindictiveness characteristic of Speke's subsequent campaign against Petherick. Nevertheless, Grant clearly did share much of Speke's disappointment that Petherick was not at Gondokoro to greet them; after all, they had both for at least a year looked forward to a meeting with Petherick solving all the many difficulties they had encountered in getting through the territories of Karagwe, Buganda and Bunyoro, even sending messengers ahead to contact Petherick whom they believed to be in the Upper Nile region. It is worth noting that the RGS contract with Petherick was imprecise over key matters of timing and that Speke and Grant were ignorant of that contract. As European traders lost out to 'Turks' in the Nile trade, there was much back-biting among them which Baker no doubt reported at Gondokoro, while Petherick was unpopular with both them and the local traders because he tried to prevent the slave trade. For a full analysis of the controversy, see Bridges, 'Speke and the RGS', pp. 33–9. Both contemporary writers, especially M'Queen, 'Captain Speke's Discovery', *passim*, and recent writers, such as Udal, *The Nile in Darkness*, pp. 504–46; Jeal, *Explorers*, pp. 183–95; Humphries, *Nile's Source*, *passim*, and others, continue to take sides over the controversy.

[4] It is notable that, in his 1872 summary of the journey, Grant chooses not to allude to Petherick at all and mentions Baker only very briefly. Grant, 'Summary of Observations', p. 294.

[5] James Murie (1832–1925) was a naturalist and doctor who published much zoological material. Hill, *Biographical Dictionary*, pp. 282–3.

[6] That is, three-pounder field guns.

[7] That is, Burton, *Lake Regions*, with his account of the earlier expedition to Lake Tanganyika with Speke, published in 1860 after the departure of Speke and Grant at the end of April.

brother Alick ... the poor fellow died happily on 4th of Sept [1860].[1] [NLS, MS. 17915, 21 February 1863][2]

We halted at Gondokoro from the 15th till the morning of the 26th, so that Speke might find the moon in lunar distance for the longitude, which he ascertained to be 31° 46′ 9″ east, and latitude 4° 54′ 5″ north.[3] During this dry season it was very hot, the thermometer ranging from 94° to 100° in the shade; but it was thought a better climate and more pleasant residence than Khartoom, there being only two hot months, January and February, during the year. Between Gondokoro and Khartoom the White Nile is reported unhealthy; and amongst its many European victims was a distinguished French naturalist, Dr Penny,[4] who had explored farther south than any previous traveller. His loss was deeply felt at Khartoom. Many of the servants of the traders were suffering from ulcers, having been in swampy countries; and on the tenth day of my arrival at Gondokoro I had an attack of fever. Nearly all our Seedees had tapeworm disease, contracted on the journey.[5] The animal generally appeared in single white portions, one inch long and one-third of an inch broad. It gave them no pain, nor did it reduce the men in flesh, but it was very inconvenient. Bombay vomited one, which measured six to nine inches in length, with pointed head and tail. This happened several times to him; but he thought that until he got rid of the great one, which he called their "mother," the disease would stick to him. On our arrival at Khartoom I prescribed half a tumbler of salt dissolved in water; but having once tried my remedy, the Seedees pronounced it too nauseous to try a second time. Speke, half-a-dozen of our twenty Seedees, and myself, were the only men of our expedition who escaped this disease.

The Nile at Gondokoro is in two branches; the main one lying on the right, and a small low island, on which cattle feed, divides it from the left branch.[6] The old banks were at this season fifteen feet above the alluvial deposit of the river, which again was four feet out of water. There seemed a greater body of water, because it was spread over a larger surface, than when we had seen it thirty miles farther up. Here the strongest current, bearing to the right, was about three miles an hour, and the breadth a hundred and fifty yards. Standing upon the bank, and looking around, the country presents a flat Egyptian aspect, with the solitary hills of Rujub, Beeleenja, &c., to the N.W., S.W., and S. The water was full of lake debris, making it muddy and disagreeable to drink until allowed to settle. All

[1] Grant's elder brother Alexander (1820–60) had also been an officer in the Indian Army. It was actually Mrs Petherick who had brought the sad news but she felt unable to pass it on as she now first met Grant. Petherick, *Travels*, I, p. 311.

[2] This passage shows that there was friendly enough contact with Petherick once he had arrived. In fact, Petherick himself and his wife, as he reported, found Grant 'throughout *the gentleman*'. M'Queen, *Captain Speke's Discovery*, p. 86. Petherick also said that Grant was 'most friendly at Gondokoro'. Petherick, *Travels*, II, p. 128.

[3] Gondokoro's position is now reported to be 4°54′26″N 31°39′41″E so Speke was remarkably accurate in his observation and calculation.

[4] Alfred Peney (1817–61) was a French doctor employed by the Egyptian Government as a medical officer who attempted to explore south of Gondokoro in company with Andrea de Bono but died in the attempt. Hill, *Biographical Dictionary*, p. 304.

[5] Grant identifies this as *Tænia solium* (?) no doubt aware that there are many species. He reports they had no remedy although they had tried local ones. Grant, 'Summary of Observations', p. 303.

[6] Although Grant sketched several views of the Nile's course earlier in February and later in March, his depictions of Gondokoro do not illustrate this description. Figures 92, 93, 94, 95, pp. 334–6, and Plate 43.

day long parties of three and four natives swam across, resting upon a log of the pith tree or ambadj. They do not swim as we do in England, but stretch out their arms alternately over the water, crowing loudly "ow, ow," as they go merrily across. Although there were small canoes on the river they were not often used, even when produce was to be conveyed from one bank to the other. They got sooner over by swimming, and when a cow was killed on the opposite bank, its meat was placed inside the inflated skin, and propelled through the water by the man swimming behind it. Crocodiles were no doubt numerous, but we saw no accident; they must be frightened by the number of people who daily cross at this point. We heard from Petherick of crocodiles as high as a table, and twenty-five feet long. At night the stillness was often broken by the trumpets of the hippopotami, which sound softer and more musical than when heard during the day. Baker had an excellent fishing-net, with which, in a jolly-boat, his men would cross the river to still water, and in a couple of hours bring back half-a-dozen species. Some resembled herring in shape, but the best for eating was a large flat fish. Of birds, the most interesting was a scarlet and green fly-catcher,[1] which nestles in the perpendicular banks of the Nile like a swallow. We had not met with it on the journey. It took short flights, rapidly skimming the air, and then resting for a moment on the brink of the bank. From the Nyam Nyam[2] country to the west very handsome black goats are brought, remarkable for their small size and long hair. It may be worth mentioning that we here saw leeches, which we had not met with in any previous part of our journey; whereas, in the Himalayas, one cannot go through the grass returning from a day's sport without having a dozen of them fastened on one's legs.

Gondokoro presented quite the appearance of a seaport, there being twenty large boats anchored there. We had understood it to be an outlandish place—dangerous and almost inaccessible. But for the last five-and-twenty years or more it has been a mission-station and place of trade. For about fourteen months previous to our arrival, it had never been without Egyptian boats and boatmen. A sailing boat, "diabeah," or a "nægur," leaving Cairo in November, can reach Gondokoro, with a north wind, in three months. On the 19th February, Baker received English news dated 1st November. The return journey to Khartoom is made so as to insure arrival by June, with the advantage of the south wind; but we made the voyage much earlier, and landed on the thirty-third day from Gondokoro. To give an idea of Nile travelling in these regions, I may mention that a boat which conveyed Baker, with his crew, attendants, and four horses, was hired by him at Khartoom at eight pounds per month—a most comfortable boat, with two cabins. The pay of his sailors was lower than what we paid our Seedees for the journey—namely, two dollars per month, and the helmsman and carpenter seven dollars each. Their food, "doora," grain—*i.e.,* jowari—would cost, say, ten dollars monthly; so this, altogether, was cheap travelling on the Nile. He had also brought up several camels and donkeys; and the former gave an Oriental look to the scene around his encampment. Koorshid Aga,[3] a Circassian gentleman, lived here for some months, and was noted for his hospitality.

[1] Perhaps not a flycatcher; Mr Stanley Howe informs me that these birds were more likely to have been swallow-tailed bee-eaters, *Merops hirondineus,* sub-species *heuglini.*

[2] An alternative name for the Azande, mixed farmers who produced a number of politically successful kingdoms. They were the subject of the classic 1937 study by Evans-Pritchard, *Witchcraft among the Azande.*

[3] Khurshid Aga was one of the many people of various nationalities attracted to the Egypt of Muhammad Ali and his successors and especially to ivory and slave trading further south after the establishment of Khartoum in 1821.

Plainly dressed, and living in the most simple style, he would produce to his friends sparkling wines and other luxuries in profusion, for which we could make no return. Here he remained in security, with his guard-ships at anchor in the Nile below his premises, while his three or four hundred dark Nubians, armed with beautiful, though cheap, percussion guns, were on their beat for ivory in the interior. He had his tract of country or "preserve," like all other traders. "Latiffe's beat," "Petherick's beat," "Koorshid Aga's," "De Malzac's,"[1]—all were known by these names, just as we know the "Black" or "Braemar" forests.[2] A trader who attempted to go upon another's beat was considered a poacher, and a fight would certainly ensue if this etiquette were violated. Events taking place in these wide ranges of country are little known, as every party is a world to itself, and all are jealous of one another. But if the stories of "White Nile trade" be true, it is considered disreputable for any European to engage in it. The "Blue Nile trade," on the other hand, is esteemed respectable; but here also there is some jealousy when a new competitor enters the field. The reports we heard at Faloro of Mahomed's men attacking villages by surrounding them at the hours of deepest slumber, and capturing their people and cattle, &c., were here confirmed to us, and these raids had taught the men of Gondokoro the most lawless habits and practices. Life was unsafe, guns loaded with bullets were constantly fired out of bravado close to our boats, the consequence of which was that fatal accidents occurred, and there was no government or police, and no river steamers to stop the slave-trade. Consul Petherick was looked on as an interloper; he tried to put down this illicit traffic, but he was opposed by a clique, and his men saw no advantage in his service or that of any European. They could not keep slaves, so there was great discontent.[3]

We saw with Koorshid a splendid and well-shaped old tusk, which weighed one hundred and thirty-five pounds, and which at Khartoom would fetch 114 dollars. Every country has its own particular quality; and I should imagine the ivory produced from the tall reed grasses of a forest country like Uganda would not be so favourable for forming huge tusks as the vegetation in a lower and more swampy country, although the ivory would be of firmer texture. We were told that the ivory of Kitch on the Nile, at 6° 49' N., was of a superior description;[4] the country there is swamp and covered with reeds to the horizon.

The mission-house at Gondokoro had been built some thirty years ago. Dr Knoblecker, a very eminent man, had long laboured in it, but now it is a mere shell, and its garden of lime, pomegranate, and orange-trees is a waste for cattle to graze in. We met a kind hospitable gentleman, Mr Moorlang[5] of the Austrian mission, on his way to Khartoom:

[1] Alphonse de Malzac (d. 1860), a French hunter and trader, was regarded by some rivals as a 'scoundrel' although Petherick had co-operated with him. His trading beat had passed to an Austrian, F. Binder (1824–75). Hill, *Biographical Dictionary*, pp. 80, 228; Santi and Hill, *Europeans in the Sudan*, pp. 125–6.

[2] The comparison is presumably with deer hunting in Scotland.

[3] Here Grant shows that in fact he had come to understand the realities of Petherick's position, but out of posthumous loyalty to Speke refrains from a fuller vindication. For his part, Petherick remained bitter that Grant had not removed the unfriendly references from this account. Petherick, *Travels*, II, pp. 128–9.

[4] Clearly this was information from Moorlang who had been in charge of the Austrian Mission house at Kitch. However, the suggestions Grant makes to account for different qualities of ivory are almost certainly erroneous.

[5] For Knoblecher, see above, p. 324, n. 1; Grant very considerably exaggerates the length of time the mission and its buildings had existed. Franz or Francesco Morlang (for some reason not to be found in Hill's *Biographical Dictionary*) was a Catholic priest of Italian extraction who had been part of the Austrian Mission and had worked at Kitch further north. But following the decision to withdraw the whole mission, he seems at this time to have

his station had been at Kitch. He gave a mournful account of his labours, and was now recalled because the influence of the traders had checked his endeavours to propagate the Gospel. He had found the natives always civil, but if they or their children were not presented with clothes and beads, they kept aloof from him, and ultimately looked upon the missionary as having paved a way for the Nile trader to traffic in slaves.[1]

In walking about Gondokoro, the natives always addressed us with "Adhoto," which may mean Good-morning; some got as far as to say, "Salam alek." They were all nude like the Bari, and carried a small basket, in which were a few pieces of charcoal with which they lit their pipes. A baron, very highly spoken of, was killed by them a few years ago; his men had accidentally, when firing their guns at random, shot a native, and as no redress was given, the men were attacked, and sixteen of their number slain. The poor baron was away shooting ducks at the time, and, returning in the middle of the tumult, was killed.[2] A missionary, whose boat was close by, was not touched.

At Khartoom it was not expected that we would ever succeed in crossing Africa, but Madame Tinne, her sister the baroness, and Miss Tinne,[3] had more hope of us, and in the most philanthropic manner, braving the malaria of the White Nile, they reached Gondokoro in a steamer expecting to aid us. The natives will long remember their humanity and generosity; but the deadly swamps have since proved fatal to poor Madame Tinne, and also to a medical man of her party, and several European servants. Mr Baker, too, was full of hope, and had told the people of Khartoom that, as Bruce had discovered the source of the Blue Nile, our party would decide that of the White. At length it was time we should leave Gondokoro. By the 25th of February 1863, Speke had found the moon in proper position for taking lunars. We had heard all the English news from Baker, we had shared his hospitable table during our stay, seen his spirited sketches, and listened to his animated conversation. Our boats were filled with the necessaries and comforts of life, and everything was prepared for our starting with the stream in the morning.

---

been making a valedictory visit to Gondokoro. His diary, in German, was translated and published in Italian in 1973. Santi and Hill, *Europeans in the Sudan*, pp. 32, 145. Howgego, *Encylopedia of Exploration 1850–1940*, pp. 650–51, records Morlang as dying in 1875.

[1] This neatly sums up the dilemma facing those attempting to introduce Christianity along the Nile valley at this period.

[2] This was one of the many wild stories which circulated among European traders on the Nile; it is possibly a reference to the death of Jean-Alexandre Vayssière (1817–61). Santi and Hill, *Europeans in Sudan*, p. 125; but see Hill, *Biographical Dictionary*, p. 373.

[3] Grant's information is somewhat confused. Alexandrina P. F. Tinné (1835–69) was a rich Dutch heiress who devoted her short adult life to travel; the Baroness was her mother, not her sister. 'Miss Tinne' was actually her aunt, a Miss A. van Capellan. All these companions died in the course of the expedition to Gondokoro but Alexandrina Tinné herself actually died in a later excursion into the Sahara where she was killed by the Tuareg. Hill, *Biographical Dictionary*, pp. 359–60.

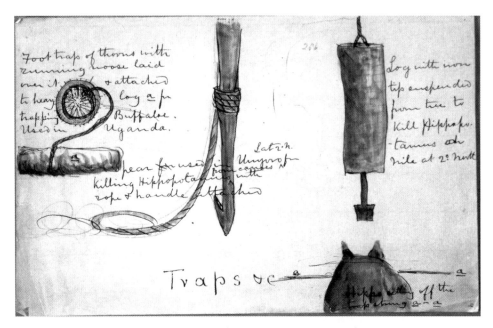

Figure 87. Traps in use in the region of the Upper Nile as noted by Grant in November 1862. NLS MS. 17921, no. 286. Reproduced by permission of the National Library of Scotland.

Figure 88. The Karuma Falls on the Victoria Nile as it begins its descent to Lake Albert. Grant was clearly fascinated by the Falls and made several attempts to picture them. NLS MS. 17921, no. 13. Reproduced by permission of the National Library of Scotland.

Figure 89.   The Karuma Falls again with Grant trying to depict the fierce flow of water. Had the two explorers kept to the Nile and followed it to Lake Albert, they would have discovered the far higher and more spectacular falls which Baker was to dub the 'Murchison Falls'. NLS MS. 17921, no. 304. Reproduced by permission of the National Library of Scotland.

Figure 90.   A third attempt to show the Karuma Falls. How the artist conveys movement was clearly a problem for Grant. NLS MS. 17921, no. 305. Reproduced by permission of the National Library of Scotland.

Figure 91.   A Nile view in December 1862, one of several Grant attempted. It is not clear quite where he was but probably on the Nile at about 2°N. Part of NLS MS. 17921, no. 14. Reproduced by permission of the National Library of Scotland.

Figure 92.   'The Nile and "Jebl Kookoo"' is Grant's title for this view but this is not the modern Jebl abu Kuku but further south in the vicinity of the great bend in the Nile near present-day Nimule. Grant gives the latitude as 3½°N which seems remarkably accurate. NLS MS. 17919, no. 54. Reproduced by permission of the National Library of Scotland.

Figure 93.   A view down the Nile in February 1863, again near Nimule where the travellers had rejoined the river after cutting across country from the Karuma Falls to avoid the large bend westwards in the river north of Lake Albert. Grant said he was reminded of the pass of Glencoe. NLS MS. 17919, no. 55. Reproduced by permission of the National Library of Scotland.

Figure 94.   Another view of the Nile and the 'Kuka Hills', as Grant calls them. This is to the west of the Nile's course near the point where he and Speke had rejoined the river in February 1863. It is almost as if Grant wishes to reassure himself that the Expedition is, indeed, exploring the Nile. NLS MS. 17919, no. 56. Reproduced by permission of the National Library of Scotland.

Figure 95.   Reaching Gondokoro. The exciting sight for Grant on 15 February 1863 when they reached Gondokoro, near present-day Juba, the effective head of navigation on the Nile. The sight of sails promised the presence of the long-expected John Petherick, fresh supplies and an end to walking at the end of the Expedition. In the event, it was Samuel Baker who met them. The mission house was now deserted. See Chapter XV, pp. 330–31. NLS MS. 17919, no. 58. Reproduced by permission of the National Library of Scotland.

Figure 96.   View from the dahabeah sailing to Khartoum. These hills were seen from the boat in which Grant and Speke now sailed down the Nile towards Khartoum. They were no longer directly involved with the landscape or the local people in the way they had been before reaching Gondokoro. Extracted from NLS MS. 17919, no. 59. Reproduced by permission of the National Library of Scotland.

Figure 97. Three scenes near the confluence with the River Sobat. These were depicted in March 1863 in the region of the Nile Valley north of the Bahr el Ghazal, near where the Sobat flows into the Nile from the East at 9°22'N. The confluence is the subject of the main picture. Above are a hut 10 feet (3 metres) high on the river bank, a Nuer man in a typical pose with stacked grass, a tower hut built of reeds and a Shilluk village. NLS MS. 17919, no. 60. Reproduced by permission of the National Library of Scotland.

Figure 98.   A Shilluk pilot pictured on 15 March 1863. A Nilo-Saharan people with a sophisticated political system, the Shilluk lived along the long straight stretch of the Nile south of Khartoum in about 10°N to 12°N. NLS MS. 17920, no. 61. Reproduced by permission of the National Library of Scotland.

Figure 99.   The Baggara Arabs live in the same region as the Shilluk and relations were not (and remain not) always very happy. NLS MS. 17920, no. 62. Reproduced by permission of the National Library of Scotland.

Figure 100. Two scenes near Khartoum. These were observed from the deck of the boat as Grant neared Khartoum at about 14°N at the end of March 1863. NLS MS. 17919, no. 66. Reproduced by permission of the National Library of Scotland.

339

Figure 101.   Sand hills seen on the right or eastern bank of the Nile as the travellers neared Khartoum on 26 March 1863. The note says there is a bazaar above the Gat (Ghaut or, in this case, landing place). NLS MS. 17919, no. 67. Reproduced by permission of the National Library of Scotland.

Figure 102.   Reaching Khartoum. Grant reached this key point on 30 March 1863. His very unsuccessful attempt to draw the city was made on 5 April. NLS MS. 17919, no. 61 recto. Reproduced by permission of the National Library of Scotland.

Figure 103. The Coptic Christian church in Khartoum. Grant and Speke remained in Khartoum until 15 April 1863 but Grant regarded it as something of a 'modern Babylon' and recorded few scenes there although he was clearly interested in the Copts and their priest Gabriel (seen on the left), who served the 500 Copts in Khartoum. NLS MS. 17919, no. 62. Reproduced by permission of the National Library of Scotland.

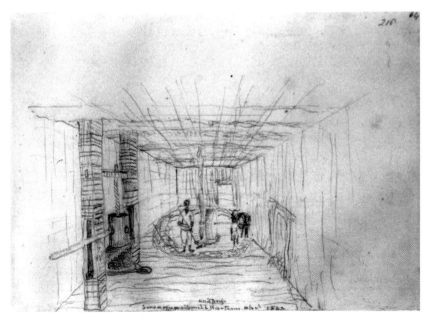

Figure 104. A press for oil from sesamum seeds. It is not clear why Grant made this drawing as only his second depiction of life in Khartoum. NLS MS. 17919, no. 68. Reproduced by permission of the National Library of Scotland.

Figure 105. The confluence of the Blue and White Niles. This very important place was sketched by Grant on 5 April 1863 but it cannot be said that the result is very successful. NLS MS. 17919, no. 63. Reproduced by permission of the National Library of Scotland.

Figure 106. 'Mount Rooeeyan'. Grant and Speke left Khartoum on 15 April and this sketch of 'Mount Roeyan' was made on the next day. NLS MS. 17919, no. 64. Reproduced by permission of the National Library of Scotland.

Figure 107. The bank of the Nile seen on 4 May 1863.This rather uninteresting sketch seems to have been the last visual record of the Expedition which Grant made. There were no more pictures from the river trip to Abu Hamed, the trek across the desert to Wadi Halfa, the further boat trip to Cairo and the journey home from 4 June. NLS MS. 17919, no. 65. Reproduced by permission of the National Library of Scotland.

CHAPTER XVI

[Pages 374–400]

From Gondokoro to Khartoum by Boat [26 February–29 March 1863][1]

Our Seedees were divided among the three return boats furnished by Baker to convey us to Khartoom. Two were nægurs or baggage-boats, made roughly of the *Acacia Arabica* or soonud, and having each an unwieldy sail, without awning or cabins. The third was a diabeah, which we and our private servants occupied. Her build was lower in the water than the others, the hold was neatly boarded over, and upon it was built a poop-cabin. She drew three feet of water when unladen, and had the peculiar Nile rig, with twelve rowers, a helmsman, and a captain or "nakhoda" named Diab. Two of the other hands were not forthcoming, preferring to lead a roving life with their former master, Baker; but at two in the afternoon of the 26th, having bade adieu to all, we shoved off, and floated down with the current. The oars were rudely tied with rope to the gunwales, and the men only required to keep the boat in the stream and prevent her getting ashore on banks of sand. When any exertion was required, they rose from their seats, laying the weight of their bodies on their oars, and joined in a pleasing monotonous song, led by the "stroke" of the party. Proceeding in this way against a slight headwind seemed no labour to them; they rowed, joked, sang, or munched dry "dooro," bread and garlic, from sunrise to sunset. By noon of the third day we had made great progress—namely, one degree of north latitude—notwithstanding that we lay-to during the night on account of the shallows. We had reached a station of Koorshid Aga's in the Shir country,[2] and passed through a corner of the Berri country.[3] The banks were grassy and flat, and the trees were covered with creepers, giving them the appearance of old towers or abbeys. The river was divided by islands into four branches, and it required all the knowledge of our captain to decide which of them to choose. Some of the islands were covered with cattle, which ran off as they saw our boat approach. In the dry season, the natives bring down their cattle to graze and water them near the river. Their rustic settlements, of a conical form, with numerous

---

[1] At this point in the Expedition's progress, Speke chose to conclude his full narrative on the grounds that the subsequent experience did not 'directly relate' to the solution of the Nile problem and no doubt because he was under pressure to get his text to the publisher. Speke, *Journal*, p. 609. Similarly, in his later account, Grant provides only the bare details of the transit to Alexandria in tabular form. Grant 'Summary of Observations', pp. 296–301. Hence this is the only existing published narrative of the period from February to June 1863. Grant's manuscript journal for this period is as detailed a record as at any other point in the journey. Nor did his sketching activity cease.

[2] The Shir are a sub-group within the Nilotic group known as the Mondari; traditionally, they were entirely pastoral. Murdock, *Africa*, p. 330.

[3] The Berri, also a Nilotic, pastoralist people, are a branch of the Anuak. Ibid., p. 329.

people about, were built upon the very banks of the river, and were so small that a single man could hardly lie at length in them. The people sometimes spoke to us, wishing to get beads; but possessing so many cattle, they certainly were not objects of compassion. Nearly all of them were covered with ashes, as if they had lain in them during the night.

Sitting on the poop-deck, we watched the scenes on the river. Pelican flew in solemn procession, or marked the water's edge by a line of white. Myriads of the Indian paddy-bird perched upon the trees. There were cranes, divers, and sometimes a fish-eagle. At one time I counted the heads of twenty-two hippopotami, a perfect shoal of them, packed as close as they could swim together, looking like monstrous retriever dogs in the stream. Some were spouting water, others dipping, others snorting, and others rearing their heads and shoulders; but as we got near them, all dived to come up again scattered. This packing seemed common, as at other places we came on them in the same order, with cranes perched on their heads.

We saluted Koorshid's colours with two guns from our deck at a Shir village where we lay-to for some hours. Two of his soldiers, holding possession of the place, were posted with a supply of beads, &c., with which they purchase ivory. The village chief came to call on us; he was dressed like a Turk, with a fez and long-sleeved gown of pink striped calico, but the crowd of natives who sold commodities on the bank were nude, only that their skins were covered with wood-ashes.

They made here an excellent basket, shaped like a finger-glass,[1] from the fronds of the doom palm. Its fruit and flour, tasting of gingerbread, as also tobacco, were exposed for sale, in exchange for our men's provisions of doora-grain. Many of the nude natives had been circumcised, and all had their lower incisors extracted like the Wanyoro. On entering the village we found it clean and tidy; the part before each doorway plastered as a space to sit upon. Here, sitting by some standards, three women received us graciously by shaking hands and saying, "Adoto." They were the last race that we saw wearing only fringes and switch tails of corded fibre. They smoked clay pipes, in shape like a reversed cone, with two resting-prongs, each holding half a handful of tobacco; and their long stems had mouthpieces of iron, quite fashionable in comparison to those seen in Uganda. The young men sported a two-feet-long piece of solid Dalbergia wood, the shape of a marline-spike, but tapering at both ends, and often nicely milled longitudinally. There was nothing further to remark about this Shir village, but that the cattle were comfortably housed under sheds made of the fronds from the doom palm—a tree we had not seen since leaving the Zanzibar coast.[2]

The next race we came among were the Aliab,[3] known at once by their women being partially dressed. Here they slung a goatskin over the shoulder, like the Wanyamuezi, to hide their chests, and two other skins were tied round their waists, depending in front and behind. We were told, however, that only married women were allowed to wear all this clothing. The men were also distinguishable by a tuft of wool on the crown of their heads, a circle of very white mud plastered round it, and their faces and bodies covered

[1] Grant provides a small sketch in his journal. NLS, MS. 17915, 28 March 1863. A finger glass is 'a small vessel to hold water for rinsing the fingers after dessert'. *OED.*

[2] *Hyphæne thebaica*, perhaps more properly the 'doum palm' of which there is a full description in Grant, 'Botany of the Speke and Grant Expedition', pp. 187–8. The palm furnishes wood, leaves for baskets and fruit.

[3] The Aliab are part of the large and important cluster of Nilotic peoples known as the Dinka, originally pure pastoralists, who for the past 150 years have suffered grievously at the hands of slave traders and their successors.

with ashes. They did not seem at all afraid of us, for they assisted in pushing off our boat. Their diet is said to be almost entirely a milk one, and they have numerous herds. We put in to the left bank at the settlement of Shenooda, a Khartoom merchant, and found the latitude to be 6° 5′ 9″ N. Another station, where there were forty men and a boat, was low and unhealthy, the musquitoes at night being in myriads. Our crew were somewhat lazy, and stopped nearly a day at this point under pretence of laying in wood, but in reality to talk with the people, and kill a cow. However, we were rewarded for the delay by getting a favourable breeze near the point where we again joined the main stream.

From thence to the Austrian mission-station of Kitch the banks did not present any landing-place; we were hemmed in by reeds, and not a tree was to be seen. The station consists of a few round huts, with doors and glazed windows—a miserable place for the clergyman, the Rev. Mr Moorlang, who had there spent three years of his life. To land we had to be carried through swamps which lined the banks, and as we touched the tall grasses, clouds of musquitoes rose from the vegetation. Here was the good Christian's little glass-roofed chapel, surmounted by a cross of wood; there was his schoolhouse too,—but all desolate and forlorn, for not a native would come to learn. The mission was therefore about to be forsaken, as Mr Moorlang had informed us at Gondokoro.[1] On his passage down to Kitch, the natives had fired poisoned arrows into his boat in open day; one man had been wounded, and was since dead. This story elicited from our men mention of a similar incident. They also had been attacked while in rear of our larger boat, but it was during the night, and the arrows and spear fell harmlessly into their boat. To remedy such evils, I should say that the frequent visits of a river steamer would be highly desirable, both as protecting the natives from being plundered by the followers of traders and travellers, and as tending to civilise the people themselves.[2]

Mr Moorlang, in the fulness of his heart, was unbounded in his kindness and liberality. Candles, wine, and goats were pressed upon us by the generous Tyrol mountaineer. He was to be in our wake to Khartoom; and Speke having taken the latitude of Kitch, we roused our crew, asleep on the shore, and rowed during moonlight to Abu Kuka station. Here was another miserable swampy spot; not above six huts of grass, closely surrounded by water; not a tree, only high grass and reeds. The place was unworthy of the name of a station. From this point Consul Petherick had gone across the country to his trading depot of Neambara, in Moro. We came upon another station in this Kitch country, known as Mr Binder's, late De Malzac's;[3] its latitude was 7° 8′ 18″ N. It was rather pleasantly situated on flat ground, and consisted of a dozen round huts, plastered outside, and having a neat thorn fence surrounding them: but the natives were about the most wretched I had ever seen. They brought us their small loads of firewood to exchange for grain, and seemed like living skeletons. They had bead ornaments upon them; but of what use were they?— there was no grain for them to purchase. Before reaching this point the river had been winding in the most fantastic manner; a gentle breeze blew; and over the tops of the tall

---

[1] For the Austrian Mission and Fr Morlang, see Chapter XV, p. 330, n. 5, above.

[2] Grant here foreshadows some of his later thinking as part of what I have called an attempt to set up an 'unofficial empire'. Bridges, 'Towards the Prelude', pp. 102–6.

[3] Franz Binder (1824–75) was an Austrian trader operating in the mid-1850s, Alphonse de Malzac (d. 1860) a French trader and hunter accused of being a scoundrel and a slave trader. Hill, *Biographical Dictionary*, pp. 80, 229.

reeds we could perceive by the sails of our other two boats that we three were sailing in a circle, or that the stream ran in the shape of the letter S.

From the 5th till the 9th of March, while passing the Nouer country,[1] we lost sight of our two other boats. The wind had been contrary, and the hands were reduced by sickness. A breeze luckily came from the south, and brought our fleet together again. They had been alarmed, and expressed a wish for gunpowder, as the tribe of Shillock[2] had lately killed a trading party three hundred strong, and were bent on attack. Some traders' boats we met "kedging"[3] up stream conveyed us this news. It must be extremely tedious going up the Nile where the shores do not admit of landing to tow the boat. The plan adopted is this,—ten men being engaged, a row-boat goes ahead with a cable and anchors, and the large boat is then pulled up to the smaller, much in the same way as they "kedge" on the Ganges. We observed that the huts in the Nouer country were numerous and large; they lie in open plains, which are dotted with cattle and goats, at some distance from the river bank. The papyrus, the pith-tree, or ambadj, and reeds, line the sides of the river, and beyond them was a forest of acacias, which afforded us an opportunity of laying in a supply of firewood. The tracks of elephants were numerous; and the damage done by the gigantic brutes in eating the pods of the trees and breaking down the branches is very great. While in the Nouer country we had the extreme pleasure of seeing the polar star for the first time after nearly three years, as bright as ever, and in the old place!

On reaching the Bahr-el-Ghazal, an affluent of the Nile,[4] our boatmen fired a single gun as a salute. They told us this was done both on the up and down voyage. Our river, which had lately been averaging eighty and a hundred yards wide, kept its course, not mingling its waters with the Bahr-el-Ghazal, which here was without debris or apparent current, looking more like a back-water or still pond half a mile square. After their junction there was an evident increase in depth and breadth; the waters, also, were less like a sewer in colour,—they had become clarified to a certain extent, and the rate of current was estimated at two miles per hour. The sides were rushes to an unknown depth; indeed, from the accounts given by our captain, the Ghazal must at one time have been almost choked with water vegetation. He mentioned that the first explorer of it took three months to penetrate through reeds a distance which can now be reached in five days. I expected to have found it looking more like a river; but instead of this, had we not been prepared for it, we should have passed it without notice. The White Nile was at once pronounced by our captain to be the nobler stream; and he added that, with a favourable wind, it takes ten days to reach the Ghazal from Khartoom, and one month more of fair wind to reach from the Ghazal to Gondokoro.

While waiting at the junction, our cook, M'kate, discovered a crocodile's nest with seventy-seven eggs. They were nearly all presented to us; but their taste being disagreeable, we made them over to our boatmen. Rowing for nineteen hours almost due east, at the

---

[1] The Nuer are another Nilotic people akin to the Dinka.

[2] The Shilluk, living to the north of the Nuer, are classified by some as 'Prenilote'. They were sedentary agriculturists who have been much discussed by later anthropologists because they developed 'divine kingship' institutions. Middleton, *Encyclopedia of Africa*, IV, pp. 75–6. See also Figure 97, p. 337, for a Shilluk man and a village.

[3] To 'warp' a boat by dropping an anchor ahead and then hauling on the attached hawser, as Grant explains.

[4] The junction is with the here east-flowing Nile about 80 miles (129 km) west of the modern town of Malakai.

rate of two miles per hour, brought us to another stream, the Giraffe,[1] coming from a south-east direction. It seemed to flow with rapidity—probably four or five miles an hour—was from fifty to sixty yards across, and bore down with it quantities of the pretty rosette called *Pistia Stratiotes L.*,[2] which was first gathered in the Karague Lake. Our captain, who was an authority, said of this river that it had received its name from the circumstance that cameleopard[3] abound in the country through which it passes. "It is a large river, and if you were to sail up it for fifteen days, you would only be half way to its source in the Bhor country." The character of the Nile changes soon after the Giraffe joins it; the current becomes scarcely perceptible, the width increases from one hundred and fifty to two hundred and fifty yards, and you can generally land, there being acacia trees on the right bank. We observed on both sides of the Nile distant mole-like solitary hills, the first seen since leaving Gondokoro, which may give some idea of the flatness of the land. There were several large islands also,—one in particular, to our left, dividing the stream above the junction of the river Sobat, which joined us from the right almost at an angle of ninety degrees. The Sobat (lat. 9° 20′ N.) was a hundred yards across from bank to bank—a large body of water, its surface undisturbed by current or weeds, and sweeping round to the left in a remarkable manner as you looked up its stream. The left bank of the Sobat was abrupt, and from twelve to twenty feet high, with a few acacias. Its right bank was lower—say eight feet—had more slope, and down to the water's edge grew a dense thicket of reed vegetation.[4] From general appearance, I judged that the body of water thrown into the Nile by the Giraffe during four-and-twenty hours was equal to that contributed by the Sobat in the same time.[5] The distance between those two rivers was calculated to be sixteen miles. We had rowed it in 9½ hours, not including the time we rested while a gale blew from the east. These gales came on suddenly, and detained us generally from nine till three o'clock; the boats stood them well; but, from the impossibility of quickly lowering the yard, to which the immense sail is securely fastened, the boat was often very unmanageable. The crew found the yard so unwieldy, pivoted as it was on the top of the mast, catching the wind and nullifying their rowing, that it had to be finally lowered, the operation taking three-quarters of an hour!

Our course improved after we were joined by the Sobat; instead of sailing east, we were going north-east. The river varied in width from two hundred and fifty to five hundred yards; sometimes it branched round long stripes of islands, or a beautiful reach of water was presented. We had no longer the low swamp on either side; the banks rose boldly ten feet above the water; we could land anywhere,—either in the Shillook country, which was a plain clear of all vegetation, or on the opposite or right bank, the country of the Denka,[6] where firewood might be obtained. Hippopotami in such a locality were scarcer than where there were reeds, but they were met with even here; and at night, between those steep walls, their lowing reverberated pleasantly from bank to bank. An oarsman by chance struck one while sleeping in the water. The sport it afforded caused quite a

---

[1] 'Giraffe' is a translation of the Arabic name, Bahr el Zaraf, for the river which joins the White Nile at 9°41′N from the east.

[2] The water cabbage, a widespread member of the Arum family of aquatic plants.

[3] A term once used as a result of confusion of Latin terms for the giraffe.

[4] Grant attempts to show these features in Figure 97, p. 337.

[5] The Sobat is said to bring white sediment which accounts for the 'White' Nile.

[6] The Dinka are closely related to the Nuer and are cattle-keeping pastoralists.

commotion in our boat, for after being touched, the animal arched his back in self-defence, sending himself half out of the water.

On the wooded banks of the Nile, about 10° N. lat., opposite the Sultan of Dainab's territory, we found thirteen boats at anchor. They had come to demand redress from the sultan, and to settle some political matters regarding the annihilation of a whole zariba, or station of Arabs, in the interior. Their commander, we understood, was one Ibraheem. He and his party of three hundred soldiers, foot and horse, formed a picturesque encampment under some beautiful large soonud trees—*Acacia Arabica*. The Bagara Arab horsemen[1] reminded me of the wandering tribes we read of in the Bible; the listless way all walked about in their long gowns, the docility of their pony horses, the Oriental-like saddles, the women grinding corn, all camped so close together looking in amazement at the white men, wondering where we could have dropped from, and smiling as we walked amongst them. These boats had been two months on the voyage from Khartoom, and had been joined on the route by upwards of a hundred Bagara cavalry, who with fifty camels travelled by land, keeping pace with the fleet. The Bagara wear no covering on their heads; their hair is straight, black, and silky, worn off the face in long broad plaits pinned flat down behind. Their horses, though small and thin, were well cared for, having no galled backs, as might be supposed on looking at their awkward-shaped saddles. With these animals, and their long-handed, broad-bladed, glistening spears, wonderful feats are said to be performed by them in elephant-hunting, although no guns are used. At night, their camp was guarded by sentinels, who called out at intervals, instead of our custom of going the rounds. Music was indulged in to a late hour by incessant beating on drums. An interesting funeral scene took place in this camp, on occasion of the death of one of the Khartoom natives. The body, veiled in white linen, was laid on the brink of a grave, and a line of well-dressed Arabs stood over it reading prayers from a slip of paper held in their hands, all in the most devout and solemn manner.

The canoes of the natives are small, and made of planks, with pointed bows and sterns. Rafts of grass or ambadj are used for ferrying the Nile, the natives standing up to their knees in water while paddling or propelling them with a stick. After coming out of this raft, they place it on end to dry on the shore. The Shillook men, residing in a large tract of country about 10° N. lat., are nude, and, looking at them from behind, the hair is so trained that it resembles a black fan. We took one of the men as a guide to conduct us in searching for our two rear boats that had not come up, as we believed, and had caused us some uneasiness and alarm. Sailing up stream, he landed to speak with the people of Shillook, who immediately flew away in fear of us, commencing to drive off their cattle. Our boats had passed us during the night unobserved, and we found they had preceded us twenty miles. This may give some idea of the size of the river. The guide was not satisfied with two yards of calico, saying, "If I were not alone, you dared not offer me so little;" he was very impertinent, and before leaving the boat exchanged his calico for a spear.[2] We had now got to about 11½° N. lat., where the territory of the true original Shillook race ends, and that of the mongrel Shillook and Bagara horsemen begins. On the

---

[1] The Baggara Arabs have become pastoralists who live west of the Nile but are prone to raid those in the Nile valley. A depiction of these Arabs and their horses is seen in Figure 99, p. 338.

[2] This was on 15 March; Grant depicts the man in Figure 98, p. 338.

left bank was an Arab station called Kaka,[1] its two hundred huts being fenced and ditched against the hostile natives. For the first time we came upon irrigation in the true Egyptian form—a large pole weighted at one end, with a leather bucket at the other. Indian corn, tomato, onions, and plantain were grown here in great luxuriance. The native who commanded at this post was carried on board of our boat to be treated for a swollen limb. From our remnant of medical comforts we were able to give him some plaster, and he went gaily away on one leg, so pleased, that he sent us a plate of rice and some tomato. I have a recollection of seeing strewed on the broken ground about Kaka, curious formations, which may have been ancient relics, or concrete; but, in order to direct attention to them, I may mention that Dr Falconer, the fossil authority of the day, suggests that they may have been fossil remains. The whole depot of Kaka turned out to greet our captain, calling him by name "Diab." They intrusted him with messages, billets-doux, and money, till he seemed astonished at their number. Even after we had sailed, two men ran along the shore with letters, which were thrown at our boat, and cleverly caught by one of the crew.

The evening before our arrival at Kaka we saw twenty boats at anchor in a river said to be a branch of the Sobat, on the right bank of the Nile. They lay one mile up its stream, and the people were on their way to punish some Denka, having with them camels, donkeys, and ponies. I could not learn the name of this unexpected river, but our captain assured us that it was not a branch of the Nile, which, indeed, it did not appear to be. Hence Captain Speke has written of it as a second Sobat; while Consul Petherick asserts that it only exists in Captain Speke's imagination.[2] The windings of the river in this latitude, about 12° N., were very eccentric: sometimes our "head" was west, at other times direct upon the polar star, as when passing a solitary hill, a strange sight in the Denka country. The heat was excessive—94° in the shade, making the bilge-water very disagreeable, though causing no sickness. Indeed, the native sailors considered the smell to be healthy. Our boat was full of cockroaches, climbing about at all hours; musquito also abounded. Our crew were sometimes put into a flutter by seeing a harmless water-snake making for the boat with head erected out of the water. These creatures steer along so direct that they seem to see nothing before them; but the natives imagined that they were purposely making for the boat to get on board! The shores were often lined with thousands of black and white geese, or the solitary fish-eagle[3] might be seen standing apart. He is a bird of remarkable beauty; his general colour is black, but his head is white, and the shoulder-tips and feathered thighs are a glossy red.

Although highly favourable for cultivation by means of irrigation, not a single field or village is to be seen as you glide down the splendid, almost lake-like stream some 400 yards wide. Either side is a flat dry country of alluvial soil, covered with natural bowers of climbers connecting the trees. The banks reminded me of the beautiful Garden Reach on the Hoogly at Calcutta. One evening, in the distance, I thought a range of swelling hills was visible, but their outline seemed suddenly to change into a cloud! This mystery was

---

[1] Kaka exists as a modern settlement.

[2] This is a reference to the veteran 'armchair geographer' James M'Queen's vitriolic review of Speke's book in which he quotes a letter from Petherick. M'Queen, *Captain Speke's Discovery*, p. 173 and note. M'Queen, more usually known as 'MacQueen', was a friend of Mrs Petherick's father, D. B. McQuie.

[3] *Cuncuma vocifer*. Cave and Macdonald, *Birds of the Sudan*, p. 99.

soon explained: the forms I had seen were myriads of finches covering part of the horizon: the creatures were migrating, and resembled swarms of bees in the air, quite darkening the sky. A day or two afterwards, one night on deck, I was startled by a sound as if wind blew through a forest, and was about to beat upon our boat; but we had only disturbed the birds, which in their flight had rested for the night in the tall reeds of an island; the wave of air caused by their motion and their twittering reached us, though we could not see them in the darkness.

We travelled without an accurate chart of the river, and the beautiful parts of it cannot therefore be mentioned by name; but about 13° N. lat. five hills ("Jubl Denka," or "Jubl Nyamat'ee" of the maps)[1] appeared three-quarters of a mile from the right bank. Some were ridged with vertical strata, and descended to the river; but none appeared above water.[2] From this point we may say that civilisation was fairly entered upon, for we were addressed in friendly Arabic from both banks. Boat-building went on in the forests of "soonud" or acacia, and hundreds of camel and cattle stood upon the receding banks of white sand, or drank the waters of the Nile. Women were clothed from head to foot, and carried water-pitchers on their heads—forming a peaceful and pleasing sight after the hardships and anxieties we had endured. The last trace of our jungle life was seen in the acacia forests, where trees lay prostrate, and where occasionally some antelope, new to us, with large horns bending over their shoulders, browsed on low bushes with the camel. A flight of wild geese, a host of monkeys, and a brood of guinea-fowl gave warning to the antelope, and none of them fell to our rifles. Domesticated animals now took the place of the denizens of the forest, and the trading-boats had driven away the wild inhabitants of the water. The sound of the hippopotamus was rare after we had passed the hills of Jubl Denka. Small grey duck no longer flew in line skimming the water; and the black duck with yellow bill, said to be very palatable, no longer stood packed in hundreds on the banks. The myriads of monster black and white geese were left behind. The familiar quack of the mallard was seldom heard at night. The pin-tailed duck shot past the boat, seeking less busy scenes. The crocodile had been scared; he had lost his boldness, but still watched for a victim. Against his attacks thorn fences enclosed portions of the river, where cattle or goats might drink in safety; and it was remarked that in these more frequented regions wild-fowl were seldom seen upon the water; the Egyptian goose, which floated in scattered coveys near the sides, was the only species which showed no fear amidst the sounds of human voices: he fell an easy prey to the sportsman. These, and sundry other familiar sights and reflections, gave warning that our journey was fast drawing to a close.

El Eis, or the Well, at about 13¾° N. lat.,[3] is an Arab settlement on the right bank, on the highway between the countries of Sennaar in Abyssinia and Kordofan. Its houses are not seen from the river, but the shore is lined with troops of camels, a mounted guard or herd being over each batch, denoting that the country is well peopled. Khartoom, we were informed, could be reached from here on a donkey in six days. The river at El Eis is five hundred yards in width, but increases to a mile of shallow water, with islands, as we float down its stream to Shellai and Al'aga; farther down, when opposite Jubl Musa on the left bank, it becomes narrower, being only twelve hundred yards wide, and sluggish as a mill-

---

[1] It is not clear to which maps Grant refers.
[2] This is also an observation which is difficult to understand.
[3] This is the important town of El Jebelein whose more correct co-ordinates are 12°35′N, 32°49′E.

pond. The next feature in the flat landscape is Jubl Broeme, a table-topped solitary hill, three hours' row from Jubl Musa; and the object last seen before arriving at Khartoom is Jubl Aolee, so called because it is the first hill observed when ascending the White Nile from its junction with the Blue. It is not above a quarter of a mile from the right bank, and rises two hundred and fifty feet in a barren mass of rock, which sends a spur down to the brink of the river and crosses it in a N.W. direction, showing one small peak in the stream. The country is finely varied about this hill; the verdure of the shore recedes under small acacias, or the bush euphorbia dots the streaks of white sand.

The banks of the Nile at El Eis shelve gradually into the water: the soil is so rich from the quantity of floating sediment brought down by the White Nile, that it was no uncommon occurrence to see the goats, which had gone to nibble the short sweet grass and drink the stream, sink up to the knees in the soil, and remain there bleating, quite unable to extricate themselves. Beyond this green line the soil becomes cracked, and strewn with several species of shells, some of which we had seen in the interior. Drifting sand, conveyed by the north winds, spread itself over the rest of the shore, and there the walking is firm, and forms the highway for Arabs proceeding upon ambling donkeys to or from their capital of Khartoom. A curious line of sand-hills margins the river almost the whole way between El Eis and Jubl Aolee. There are none upon the left bank. It is naturally an abrupt wall eight feet high in the alluvium of the country, and these violent north winds, bringing the sand of the desert with them, have given it the appearance of sand hillocks; at Gutoena, this is particularly observable where the sand has not perfectly covered them. The consequence is, that wood gave way to sand; and the voyager has to lay in his last stock of logs from the woods above El Eis. Below this all firewood must be purchased, or stolen from the walls and fences on the banks of the river.

We were all much struck with the industry of the natives, who are called "Hassanyeh Arabs,"[1] and are fine powerful-looking men. Though differing from the Bagara who live higher up the river, and not having so many horses, they arm themselves with the same broad-bladed spear, and have few guns amongst them. The chief dwellings and cultivated grounds are at some distance from the river; they reside there during the rainy season, and migrate with their flocks to the edges of the Nile for the dry season. Temporary abodes are erected, and they trade in salt made from the subsoil of the river. In March we observed bareheaded, good-looking men, with a sheet covering their shoulders and with loose "pyjamas," pulling the ripened pods of the cotton. Towards the equator women would have been employed in this occupation, but here, with a Mohammedan population, they are kept indoors cleaning the cotton, making butter, or out drawing water from the well. The cotton bushes are eighteen inches high, planted in lines a yard apart—very luxuriant, in consequence of the rich clay soil being shaded by drifted sand from the rays of the sun. By this provision of nature the soil does not cake, and the roots are kept cool, and free to send out their branches. The islands vary in length from three hundred yards to that of Marda, which is estimated at five miles. All are strips cleared of their natural vegetation, and flourish under a hard-working people. In the brightest of suns we observed two men, harnessed to ropes, pulling a toothless rake, guided by a third man, over the soft mud, preparing it for seed; and, unlike the Africans, the Egyptians never cease to

---

[1] Or Hasania, a semi-nomadic people, related to the Baggara, living on the White Nile banks south of Khartoum. Murdock, *Africa*, p. 411.

work while a boat passes them. The islands in March were not less than three feet above water; no houses were upon the smaller ones; straw was stacked; a few plough-oxen might be seen; and a small boat lay to ferry the labourers to the mainland at night.

The operation of drawing water from the wells dug in the shore is interesting. Two women, a boy, and a donkey are required: the wells are five feet deep, thirty inches across, and only half-a-dozen yards from the ripple of the river. We saw a fair woman stand down the well and pass the water in a gourd to another, who filled it into a goat's skin. Her beautiful black hair was parted in the centre, and braided in small plaits, which hung over her flushed cheeks and neck. Though her bosom was bare she showed perfect innocence. On my asking for her cup to drink from, it was at once given, apparently without any fear of its being defiled by the touch of a Christian. The water, in comparison with that obtained from the filter on board of our boat, was warm and not refreshing. Two goat-skins or "mussocks" having been filled and allowed to rock about in the river, they were placed on the donkey, the boy jumped up nimbly behind them, and with one hand held the water-bags steady, and with a wand in the other he guided the unbridled donkey to the huts.

The people were listless and indifferent to us if we went near their poor abodes, but their dogs at once challenged the intruder. This struck us, because in our journey through Africa we had rarely heard the voice of a dog. We now found that we could no longer purchase produce with beads or cloth. Money was the mode of exchange. We were amused with Bombay going amongst these Arabs to buy fish with an iron hoe: the honest fellow thought, from their simple mode of life and appearance, that we were still amongst a wild set of people; and so they were to a certain extent, for beyond the produce of the soil, and their cattle, sheep, and goats, they seemed to have no other desire. Great care was consequently taken of their flocks. The large lop-eared breed of sheep are bathed in the Nile by their owners. They are carried into three feet of water and dropped on their backs or sides, then scrubbed to the tail, and allowed to run back to join the flock. The goats are tall, generally black, with immense udders and long hair; they are clipped with a knife, and their hair, with that of sheep, is made into a coarse blanket or bernoose[1] by the women. Powerful smooth greyhounds, indigenous to the country or to the western parts of Abyssinia, are used as we use sheep-dogs, and seem to guard carefully the habitations as well as the flocks.[2]

Our captain, Diab, was known to many of the people along the river's bank. The Arabs would call out eagerly to him, asking after their brothers or husbands far in the interior ivory-hunting. I watched several of these interviews. Once an elderly woman called him by name from the shore while our boat moved down the stream. Without asking for our permission, he landed, and they saluted by each placing the right hand on the other's shoulder, then a solemn shake of the hand took place, and Diab for a moment left her to go and sit upon a dry spot of sand. She followed, sat by him and told her tale, while a boy joined them, and was kissed by Diab on the cheek. Master Frij seeing what went on, thought he had better join the small party, and listen to what they had to say to one another. Taking his place close by them, he sat there with the greatest coolness, without introduction to the lady, or any previous knowledge of her. The Africans are generally a

---

[1] More usually 'burnous', a cloak with a hood. *OED*.

[2] Grant depicts the sights during this part of the journey in Figures 100 and 101, pp. 339–40.

free-and-easy race, and despise the formalities of society. When Mr Moorlang, the Austrian missionary, was pressing upon us the acceptance of some delicacy, Frij, too proud to confess our poverty, found a reply by saying that our larder was full to excess—we did not require anything! He was the Caleb Balderston[1] of the Nile Expedition.

Our passage down the Nile from El Eis to Khartoom, though only one hundred and fifty miles, occupied us eight days. The stillness of the current, the head wind, and the enticements offered to our crew by the bazaars at Shellai and Gutoena, prevented our reaching [it] sooner. Although the diabeah was all that we could wish for in comfort, yet knowing the distance to be so short, the delay was vexatious; the more so as we were told that at that point, or more particularly at Gutoena, the north wind coming from the Dongolo direction sometimes, at this equinoctial season, detained boats for eight days, or even a month. I was astonished with the coldness of the atmosphere, even after the sun had risen, occasioned by these northern winds from Dongolo, and I asked Diab, the captain, regarding them; his reply was, that they and the Cairo winds are colder than any ever experienced at Khartoom. We had to lay-to so often that walking on shore was resorted to as a pastime; and we were glad to renew our acquaintance with the Persian wheel, driven seemingly by the same old bullocks and the same drivers as are seen on the plains of Hindostan; even the squeaking music from the wheels was there to complete the parallel.

The management of the diabeah was left entirely to the captain, who, with his crew, tried every possible means of progress—towing, tacking, sailing, and rowing; but all generally failed. The truth is, they were waiting for a fair wind, and preferred a little quiet society on shore every evening, to making any great exertion to get to their journey's end. When they rowed, the boat was held with its broadside in the direction we wished to take; and when they tacked from shore to shore across the river, which was a mile broad, we stuck as regularly as the tack was made, not getting off till the crew jumped into the water and pushed the diabeah. Instead of making progress by these movements, we generally lost ground, in consequence of the awkward way they had of making the boat wheel a complete circle, or fall off the wind at the particular moment of changing the tack. Towing was willingly adopted by the crew, who harnessed themselves to ropes, and walked at a staid pace on the hard part of the shore. However, at this operation it was often very disheartening to find the wind blow, retarding, and finally stopping their advance. We generally put up for the night by the shore, to enable the crew to eat their dinners, and we were on the move by daybreak. When at Shijr Nagara (literally, tree-drums) we were told that, if we stood by a solitary tree on the island, we could hear the drums of Khartoom. We did not make the experiment, and doubt the truth of the saying, on account of the distance. On the night of the 29th March, having rowed for Shijr Nagara till the moon was well up, we lay-to, our captain not wishing to enter the port of Khartoom at so late an hour, because all *éclat* and firing of guns would thereby be lost. Accordingly, on the following morning, we saw, when looking across a plain as bare as a table, at two miles' distance, a single conspicuous minaret, with an extinguisher top, numbers of mud houses, and groves of the date-palm. This was Khartoom—lat., 15° 36′. Our route was down the White Nile for two miles, and then up the Blue Nile or Bahr Azrak for another mile. Wishing to take particular notice of the junction of the two rivers,

[1] The servant in Scott's *Bride of Lammermore* who maintains the pretence that his master is prosperous.

353

Speke and I were both on deck by daybreak. As the main branch of the White Nile approaches the junction, the current gets strong and rapid, showing a broken surface, with a dangerous sunken rock in its right centre.[1] The crew got excited, and shouted; but in an instant the danger rock was past, and we were carried a dozen yards beyond the junction of the Blue Nile. The sail was here spread, and we soon recovered our lost ground, and proceeded up the Blue, whose waters now, in March, had scarcely any flow, and were so shallow that we had to pole a good part of the way up-stream. The colour of the water at once attracted our notice, being somewhat like the Mediterranean; it was a green-blue, and, on being disturbed, was lively and sparkling in comparison with the muddy waters of the White Nile. The junction of the two rivers, the sweeping curve, and both shores of the Blue river, are not unlike what we had seen at the place where the Sobat joins; but the right bank of the Sobat is of gigantic grasses, while here the Blue river is of shelving, drifted sand. Their left banks resemble each other in being an abrupt break of twenty feet in the alluvial soil. A pier of stone lies unfinished near the confluence of the rivers; and after we had passed it by sailing and poling slowly up, the left bank was enlivened by boat-building operations, irrigations, gardens, date-trees, walled enclosures, &c. Two of De Bono's men, to whom we had given a passage from Gondokoro, fired a salute in our honour from the shore. We had not anchored when Ali Bey, the Wukeel[2] of the Governor, Musa Pasha,[3] arrived with a friend in his boat, and stepped on board. He embraced us in the most affectionate manner before we had even time to learn who it was that had thus welcomed us. We proceeded on shore in his boat, which was shaded with an awning, and carpeted. Ali was very nicely dressed *à la Turk,* in a claret-coloured cloth suit, quite a contrast to the ragged clothes we wore. There was no such thing as a pier or platform. We stepped ashore and ascended the steep incline of the river bank, and then stood upon the level of the town. Proceeding at a great pace, our hands being held by our kind conductor, down lanes and round corners, every one we met on the way showing him great respect, we at last reached a house and garden. A white Arab horse stood eating from the same bundle of grass as a caparisoned donkey, and we were directed to sit upon a charpoy (four-poster) covered with carpet, while the Wukeel bustled off into the interior of the house. During his absence, the friend who had accompanied him to the boat told us (native fashion) that the Wukeel who had taken us by the hand was a man of great influence and importance. As yet we had no interpreters, and it was difficult for us to guess what was ultimately to be done. However, the Wukeel soon rejoined us, and, more mysterious than ever, he beckoned and led us into the first or outer room of his house, where we were shown a quantity of seedy old-fashioned clothes, and told that we must put them on,— they were his. I don't know what possessed me—whether affection for my own tatters, or a natural repugnance to put on clothes that had been worn by another—but I shrank from wearing the garments, and objected strongly to a thick cloth surtout, stating that it was too hot for 94° in the shade. The Wukeel then commenced to put his fingers into the holes and rents of my ragged old flannel friend, and said, that I must really oblige him, because these holes were "ibes" or blemishes, which the expected visitors would observe.

[1] See Grant's not very successful depiction of the junction of the two major rivers which he made a few days after their arrival on 5 April: Figure 105, p. 342.

[2] The trustee; the disposer of affairs.

[3] Presumably Musa Pasha Hamdi (c. 1810–65) the Governor General of the Sudan, who had a reputation for violence and corruption. Hill, *Biographical Dictionary*, pp. 283–4.

I accordingly submitted to being stripped by Bombay and our host, who seized my arms, pulled off my old coat, and replaced it by an extraordinary sky-blue paletot.[1] Speke's costume was ludicrous; he looked as if dressed up for some boyish frolic. His trousers, in front, though short, were passable, being of English blue cloth and cut; but when he turned round we saw an immense piece of calico let in, so as to enlarge them for a figure of twenty stone. The next difficulty arose from his unwillingness to change his comfortable plaid waistcoat for a chintz jacket, which buttoned to the throat and had tight sleeves. He objected, because there was no watch-pocket, but one was found, and he yielded. Over this garment a tight-sleeved frock-coat was pulled on by the good little Wukeel. There was great trouble in squeezing him into it, but it was effected, and I thought all was completed. No; Ali Bey took the wideawake[2] off, and placed instead a tasseled fez on the back of Speke's head; and then, fully equipped, Ali Bey stood back, examined him from top to toe, clapped his hands, and pronounced the whole get-up highly becoming! The ingenuity of the Wukeel was not yet over. Tying a knot on each leg of the cast-off trousers, he crammed into them coats, waistcoats, wideawakes, &c., making a decapitated Guy Fawkes, and bundled them over to Bombay. I thought I had escaped all further dressing, but my toilet was not considered complete until an attempt was made to fit a fez upon my head; and this proving hopeless, we were ushered into a room with sofas all round, to partake of coffee, brandy, and cigars. About twenty fashionably-dressed gentlemen in European and Turkish costumes then came rushing in to welcome us. They had heard of our approach the previous day by a letter which we had forwarded from Gutœna, and they had already despatched the message that first reached England regarding us, announcing that the "Nile was settled." It was the intention of these gentlemen to have ridden out on horseback and camels up the bank to bring us into Khartoom in triumph, but their messenger had failed to find us, and they politely expressed regret at being taken unawares. However, their welcome was most enthusiastic. M. de Bono, commonly called Latiffe[3] by the natives, whose trading depot we had found at Faloro, took the lead in offering us hospitality. We all adjourned to his beautifully fitted-up house, and enjoyed the "chibook"[4] amidst animated conversation, interpreted by Bombay, who stood looking as great a rough as one could well imagine. M. de Bono generously offered us his house as a home during our halt at Khartoom; but there being a British consulate, we considered that it would be more correct to reside under its protection, and therefore we proceeded thither.

---

[1] A loose outer garment for men or women. *OED*.

[2] A soft felt hat with a broad brim. See p. 233, n. 5.

[3] This was Andrea de Bono (uncle of Amabile de Bono). As a Maltese, he was a British subject and sailed under the Union Jack but used the Arabic name Latif Effendi. See Hill, *Biographical Dictionary*, pp. 110–11.

[4] Or chibouk: a long tobacco pipe smoked especially by Turks. *OED*.

CHAPTER XVII

[Pages 401–19]¹

'A Modern Babylon': Khartoum [30 March–15 April 1863]

Half a century ago no town existed where the present Khartoom stands, at the confluence of the Blue and White Niles; but, in the days of Egypt's greatness, a city stood on the plain, on the right bank of the Blue river, not ten miles from the modern site. The origin of Khartoom forty-four years ago was a military post on the Egyptian frontier. Previous to annexation it belonged to Abyssinia: now it is a place of considerable trade, governed by Musa Pasha, and held by fifteen thousand Egyptian troops. The point of land on which the town is built is so low, that every season the streets are flooded by the overflow of the river, and still its locality is not changed, though all agree as to its unhealthiness. The derivation of Khartoom is most probably from the safflower (*Carthamus tinctorius L.*), called here "Gartoom," cultivated all over Egypt for its oil, used in burning. Except where irrigated, the country everywhere presents an arid, uninteresting aspect; drifting sands cover the land; there are no trees or anything green to relieve the eye from the glare. In the distance to the north, about seven miles off, there are a few bare hills—those of Dongola, and a small range to the left. It is truly a land of banishment, cut off by deserts and a river of cataracts from the civilised portions of the world. To this Soudan, or country of the blacks, many whose conduct is questioned by their government are sent to pine without hope of release, unless their shortcomings should be forgiven, or a change of rulers take place, when they might hope for pardon, and permission to return to their homes in Egypt proper.

In April the Blue Nile was twenty feet lower than it is during the months of July and August; the snows in the mountains of Abyssinia bring it up to this height; and I suspect this flood has more to do with the inundations of Lower Egypt than the more constant flow of water from the White Nile. The latter river we saw at its maximum height in November, and it has another flooding season in April. Where do these waters go? A great portion is lost in overrunning a space of perhaps 1000 square miles of lowland; and the White Nile thus robbed, as it were, never displays those sudden changes in height that the Blue Nile, more confined to its bed, presents.

The waters of the two rivers are very different in taste and appearance. Neither is considered first-class drinking water by residents at Khartoom; but after their waters are

---

¹ Although the Expedition was no longer engaged in primary geographical exploration, it seems worth keeping this account of Khartoum as it was in 1863. Grant's less than impressive prospect of the town is Figure 102, p. 340.

mingled well together, the mixture is esteemed excellent. Opposite the town the Blue Nile is two hundred and fifty yards across, and of a greenish colour. Six miles up stream it narrows between steep banks to one hundred and fifty yards. The town being on the brink of the river, and every year its houses getting cut away by the falling in of the bank, there is no room for walking along—no quay, as it were, for the exports and imports. You are obliged for half a mile to brush past the walls of houses, the wells, goods, and animals—a most uncomfortable state of things. During our stay at Khartoom the sun was very powerful, and we had but one shower in a fortnight. Bathing in the Blue Nile was much resorted to by men and women, who appeared to enjoy it thoroughly; but I only attempted it once, because the river was so low that I had to walk thirty yards before getting into water deep enough to enable me to swim. Fish were generally to be had in the town. They are caught in various ways; some by nets nearly fifty yards long, with large meshes and short floats of wood. Irrigation from the Blue Nile is effected by cutting narrow channels in the bank; or the Persian wheel, with its hanging earthen jars, overhangs the river, and so raises the water to the height of the fields and gardens. Fruits and vegetables thrive at Khartoom. The former include a small variety of grape, oranges, limes, custard apples, pomegranate, plantain, dates, and figs; the vegetables are beans and pease, onions most luxuriant, lupin, nole kole,[1] bamea,[2] lettuce, &c. The tobacco grown was different to what we had met with in the interior; here it was the low bushy description called *Nicotiana rustica L.*, that of the interior being *N. tabacum L.*, which grows with a longer leaf. Senna is one of the herbs cultivated, also safflower, already mentioned. The harvest of bearded wheat is cut in March, and the grain is large and rich in colour. No pleasant walks had been made in the neighbourhood; the few groves of date-palms, affording the only shade that existed, are generally walled round; and if you proceed into the country, with one exception there is nothing but a desert of sand. This exception is a "cottage in the wood," belonging to M. Bartolemy. It had been surrounded by a belt of the fast-growing yellow-blossomed *Parkinsonia aculeata L.*, and, when within the grounds, the flowers and vegetation looked so green and fresh, that one might imagine he had been transported to a quiet retreat at home. The other European residents lived in the town. Their houses, generally of one storey, are large flat-roofed structures of mud and brick, surrounded by walls, having a single gateway guarded by a doorkeeper. They reminded me of the serais, or stations made for travellers upon the grand trunk-road of India. In their courtyards tame birds or antelope walked; wild animals lay chained; camels, donkeys, cattle, goats, or horses stood about; lumber and store rooms filled the space; and a corner perhaps was devoted to a shady retreat under the vine. Each consulate—and there were French, Austrian, American, and British—at Khartoom had its elliptical signboard over the main entrance. The principal room of the house is the hall; there business is transacted, and visitors are received in the morning, which is entirely devoted to calling, smoking, and drinking coffee. It has been mentioned that we chose to reside under the British flag, although at that time the consul[3] was absent at Gondokoro. The attentions we received from the various gentlemen residents were such as are perhaps only met with in a foreign country—so friendly, free, and unrestrained. Unfortunately neither of us could

[1] The Anglo-Indian term for Kohl Rabi. *Hobson-Jobson*.

[2] In modern Swahili, *bamia*, that is, okra or ladies' fingers, *Abelmoschus esculentus*.

[3] Presumably he means Petherick who had been appointed 'Consul for Inner Africa'. Bridges 'Speke and the RGS', p. 33.

communicate with them, except through Bombay or Frij; but they had become great adepts at interpreting, and we succeeded pretty well.[1] However, a lady, the Baroness Capellen,[2] sister to Madame Tinne, could speak English fluently, and we enjoyed her society frequently. She had been a great traveller, had reached Gondokoro, and had seen the miseries of sickness amongst the slaves of the ivory-traders. Smallpox had broken out amongst a party when opposite Jubl Denka, and the shocking remedy of throwing the slaves overboard when attacked by this disease was resorted to by these native traders. On making our first call upon the Baroness, we were astonished to see Frij and Uledi follow us into the room, both the worse for drink, and each carrying a rifle and spear. We all laughed at their ignorance of European customs; and having asked them to place their arms outside the door, we were amused at their advancing, rather unsteadily, to the lady, kneeling and kissing her hand—this being the most polite mode of salutation known amongst the inhabitants of Zanzibar. We brought her the three young girls of Uganda, to let her hear their language, and see their mode of sitting and of returning thanks. They were highly delighted, received great kindness, conducted themselves very gently, and gave great satisfaction, making friends with a servant girl whom the Baroness had rescued from slavery. While calling upon another occasion, a steamer arrived from the Bahr-el-Ghazal, having made the passage in fourteen days, and bringing news of Madame Tinne and her accomplished daughter. The Baron Von Ablaing was on board, and was to return with stores and baggage-donkeys, to enable the party to prosecute their journey as far as Fernando Po. Since then we have learned how fatal has been the result of this expedition. Poor Madame Tinne has died, and their labours at exploration have thus been suddenly arrested.

We were hospitably entertained at a large reception by M. de Bono, whose ivory-hunters at Faloro were the first to welcome and render us aid on the Egyptian side. There were present four ladies and upwards of twenty gentlemen, French, Italian, Austrian, German, and natives. After dinner our health was proposed, and a toast by M. Thibaut, French consul, "The alliance of France and England," was cordially pledged and applauded. Our twenty Seedees were introduced, and, to amuse the party, went through a number of antics they had learned in Uganda.

Ali Bey, Effendi—or, to give the address written by himself, Ally Fud(h)lee bek, Wakeel, Hokumdariut, el Soudan bil Khartoom (minister, Government House, country of the blacks, Khartoom)—was most constant in his attentions to us. He was the first to receive us and the last to part with us—showing us over the Government House, the schools, manufactures, and magazines, giving us horses to ride, parading the troops for our amusement, and doing numerous other acts of kindness. He had a white Gulf Arab, the most docile, at the same time fiery, creature I had ever beheld. When caparisoned in blue velvet trappings, richly embroidered in gold, and a Busserah bridle of silver chains and

[1] It seems rather surprising that at this stage in their journey, Speke and Grant had still to rely on their porters and servants as translators; presumably Frij, Bombay and others relied on the Arabic which they had picked up in Zanzibar.

[2] Grant is slightly confused: this was Adrienne van Steengracht Capellen (d. 1864) who had travelled with her sister Madame Tinné (1796–1863), who was actually the Baroness, Henriette van Capellen and mother to Miss Alexandrina Tinné (1835–69) the real leader of this group of Dutch lady explorers. Mother and daughter were currently exploring the Bahr-el-Ghazal where the mother was to die, as Grant notes below, to be followed by the lady he now met not long after he left Khartoum.

hanging tassels, the animal looked the most perfect and picturesque of steeds. The bit was a circular ring placed round the lower jaw. If the ribbon-like rein was slightly pressed, the animal, from the utmost speed, was in an instant sent on his haunches, and continuous working of the bit put him into fits of high spirit. I thought from this instance of horse-management that we have still a good deal to learn in England; for there was no pace or figure that this animal would not go through, even if a child were upon his back. We were brought by Ali Bey to see his private house and family. The ladies, however, did not appear. Ajim carpets and luxurious couches filled his suite of upper rooms; all had been brought from Cairo by boat and across the desert. In his Turkish politeness, he said whatever we fancied was ours! He paraded five hundred troops in line one morning for our amusement. They were black sturdy young men, out of mixed races from the Soudan, and were armed with flint-muskets. The uniform was a white suit, jacket and loose trousers, cross-belts covered with calico. In putting them through the platoon exercise, the officer in front stood giving the commands, which were repeated by another officer in the ranks. They went through the exercise with perfect uniformity, quite as well as any sepoy regiment. Their passing in review and forming squares required considerable practice; but these were mere lads, recruits, Ali Bey remarked; and the old trained soldiers, from ten to fifteen thousand in number, were at present on a tour with the governor of the Soudan, Musa Pascha. Every Saturday, Sunday, and Monday morning they parade for exercise, and march through the town, headed by an excellent bugle or drum and fife band.

Another gentleman, one of the oldest residents in Khartoom, was kind and attentive. This was Michaeel, commonly called Lutfullah, a highly respectable banker and merchant. In advancing us funds, he would not accept the rate of exchange, so glad was he to serve the English Government!

Khartoom being upon the highway to Abyssinia and the countries of the White Nile, it is quite an emporium for the trade and products and animals of those regions. At the residence of M. Thibaut, we saw a happy family of black and white geese, guinea-fowl, a Koodoo antelope, ariel,[1] a Soakim long-horned goat, a Nyam Nyam goat, with immense long hair and short legs, and other genera. In his drawing room, a chetah, a species of leopard, played with a pup-dog; and in the garden a striped hyena, not thought fit company for those in the yard, was amusing himself on his chain. At the British Consulate two ostriches walked solemnly about the yard picking up sand; they had no feathers upon them, having been plucked as bare as the dead fowls in a poulterer's window. At the premises of a Marseille Mussulman, who had been in Khartoom for thirty years, we recognised a great assortment of arms and curiosities brought from the southern counties of Ilyria, Bari, and Shillook, but none of the Uganda weapons had reached him. The most remarkable shield we saw was in the possession of M. de Bono, who said it was used in Ilyria by the "rain-makers." It was of iron, diamond-shaped, three spans long, and above one span broad, with a handle of wood. Of M. Miani, whose name we had seen cut on the tree far up the country, we heard an amusing account. Having proceeded farther up the Nile than any previous traveller, his information was always sought for by gentlemen arriving from Europe. Four Frenchmen asked for counsel and advice; but Miani gave them such an unpromising account of the country that they said they would defer their journey, and returned to Europe. Another traveller sent for M. Miani, and told him he wished to

---

[1] A species of gazelle, *Gazella dorcas*.

go up country; "Very good; but you will find the monkeys up there very savage." "Oh, then," replied the other, "I shall not go." The Signior, I suspect, is somewhat of a "character," or original. In his native town of Venice, one room, with his name in large characters upon the door, is entirely devoted to his collections of arms and curiosities, and the wall is hung round with sketches of his battles, as he has designated them, with the natives. He himself is made to figure very largely in his collection of sketches.

We were much interested with the honest frankness of a clergyman belonging to the Pilgrim Mission from the Swiss Protestant Church, Mr Aipperly. He was under middle age, and seemed to have great determination of character and kindliness of disposition. He had come in from his station at Galabat, Blue Nile, riding upon his handsome camel, to transact business in Khartoom, and, knowing English, he came frequently to visit us. His labours were amongst the Dacrooree[1] people, who originally settled in Galabat, in preference to returning from their Mecca pilgrimage to their own country in Kordofan. These people clothe themselves in coarse "damoor," or calico, made into long "jungeers," somewhat like the trousers worn by the handsomest of races—the Seikhs of the Punjab. They cultivate jowari (or doora), have numbers of goats, but few sheep. Weekly markets are held by this race, at which about 250 camels, laden with cotton for sale, are seen; also cattle and goats. Each camel-load of cotton costs three dollars, and, as there are no Europeans to purchase it, all goes into Abyssinia, where it is made into country stuffs, such as the damoor. Mr Aipperly expected to receive from England a machine for cleaning the cotton. From the market it might be carried by camels a few miles to Aboo Kharaz, on the Blue Nile, and thence, when the Nile is at its height in August, to the Mediterranean by water. This worthy Swiss interested me very much, living, as he did, such a contented and happy life with a single missionary companion. Two servants (a native Christian and a Mussulman) formed their entire establishment—one would not eat a fowl or goat killed by the other, but neither had any objection to eating them when killed by his master. For the last year these two missionaries had together only received £43. Mr Aipperly had learned blacksmith's work, and made friends with the natives by assisting to put up their irrigation-wheels, and other carpentry. I was struck with the docility and obedience of his camel, which he had purchased for fifteen dollars in the Galabat market; a single word from him made the animal kneel, and there was no roughness on his part, as with an Indian Surwan, and no reluctance shown by the camel. He described the wine made from honey as remarkably good. Bees abound; they are kept in trees or houses, and the natives do not kill them, but smoke them away from the honey. The Dacrooree people pay tribute to both the Egyptian and Abyssinian or Mokad'a Governments, as their territory lies between both. Their country is hilly, stony, and cool; the hills of Abyssinia are seen in the blue distance, and the minister's station is on the postal route between Khartoom and his fellow-labourers of the Pilgrim Mission in Hubeesh or Abyssinia.[2]

Our Seedees had been living a life of freedom ever since their arrival in the capital of the Soudan. Manua and the Uganda girls had never before witnessed such grandeur.

[1] That is, Takruri.

[2] Grant's information is substantially correct. Galabat is on the border between Egypt and Ethiopia and has frequently been fought over. The Takruri still cultivate good quality cotton. The Pilgrim Mission had been founded in 1840 at St Chrischona and became closely associated with the pioneer East African mission set up for the English Church Missionary Society by J. L. Krapf. See Bridges, 'Introduction' to Krapf's *Travels*, pp. 8–10.

Bombay and Frij were seldom sober, and went about smoking cigars. The clothes in which Ali Bey had dressed Speke and myself were given to Bombay and Frij, with instructions that it would be indelicate of them to wear them while in Khartoom; but they forgot the injunction, and Bombay paraded the town in a blue frock-coat and fez! Frij contemplated marriage, and on the same evening that he announced his intention, the ceremony was performed by a "Fakee," or clergyman, who was paid the fee of one dollar. The lady had been the property of Bombay, and was given him by the king of Uganda, but, for a trifle of twelve dollars, promised to be paid at Zanzibar, she was made over to Frij, who told me that the clergyman exacted a promise from him to protect her and be a faithful husband for life. However, there was a clause in the contract that, should he tire of her, she was again to become the property of Bombay.[1]

Nearly twenty years ago Khartoom was a cantonment with twenty thousand troops. The regimental officers led a gay social life, and the town increased greatly. In 1863, it had rather a decayed look, with few or no troops; but there were shops kept by Europeans and natives, where nearly all commodities might be had, including such varied articles as guns, ready-made clothes, wines, Bass's pale ale, groceries, hardware goods, &c. All manner of trades are carried on in Khartoom; and on the streets water-carriers and people selling pigeons and fowls plied their vocations. Old Turks sat playing chess and backgammon; and in the uncovered streets and open spaces stalls for cooked fish, trinkets, sweetmeats, and vegetables, were laid out as at a market. One is surprised where all these things come from in such a desert country. Except the irrigated parts, and the senna-plant growing as a weed, Khartoom does not yield a single natural or manufactured export. The river presented a busy scene; all the firewood, corn, earthen jars, bricks, grass and palm-leaves for matting and rope, stones and lime, Berber salt, and European goods, were being landed from boats for the use of the inhabitants. Gum (the best coming from Kordofan), ivory, bees'-wax, cotton, and sesamum (called sin-sin), are brought thither, but merely pass through on their way to Egypt. The White Nile is said to have 250 boats trading upon it yearly, including those on the Sobat and Bahr Ghazal. The Blue river probably has as many more; but we saw only forty-five boats lying off Khartoom, and ten on the stocks, of which the largest measured twenty yards in length. The only manufactures we observed at Khartoom were a few for oil and soap for home consumption. The oil-press was a heavy millstone placed on edge, and pulled round over sesamum-seed by a bullock with blinders. After being well bruised, the grain, now looking like a mash of bran, was removed to a screw-press, made of wood (without a nail), cow-hide, and grass. The oil, so expressed, dropped at intervals into a receiver below. At the soap-factory[2] belonging to Shenooda, an ivory-trader, we saw two boilers busily at work. The lime and sesamum-oil used in the manufacture were both from Azrah. Ali Bey, who kindly showed us over these places, brought us also to the gold and silver smiths' shops. The artificers are celebrated for working in filigree, similar to that of Delhi or Cuttack, and must originally have learned the art from Easterns. Cups with stalks, made for holding the Turkish coffee-cup, are formed of the purest soft yellow gold, found as a dust in the Soudan. Napoleon or sovereign gold would not answer for such fine workmanship, having too much alloy;

---

[1] Because they had no choice, Speke and Grant had to accept such dealings among their entourage. See Bridges, 'Negotiating a Way', pp. 107–14, where the character and attitudes of the porters employed by Speke and Grant are analysed.

[2] See Figure 104, p. 341, for Grant's sketch of the mill.

consequently, when cups are ordered, gold-dust is given to the workman. At the two shops we visited several youths were busy, sitting on the ground, each with a small anvil before him, hammering at threads of pure metal. Handsome small drinking-cups are turned out of the rhinoceros horn, which has this advantage over the horns of cattle, that, in a hot country, it retains its shape, and does not crack.

The coinage of Khartoom was puzzling, on account of the variety of pieces and their names. The following are some of those in circulation:—

1 para, equal to one-fifth of a pice.	
8 pice or 8 five-para pieces,	equal 1 piastre (copper silvered over).
2 ¼ piastres or groosh,	equal 1 thick sixpenny piece of silver.
4½ piastres	equal 1 thick shilling piece of silver.
19¼ piastres	equal 1 Egyptian dollar or a five-franc piece.
20 piastres	equal 1 Maria Theresa dollar.
77 piastres	equal 1 napoleon.
100 piastres	equal 1 sovereign.[1]

Besides these there were small coins of gold valued at 4 and 8¾ groosh or piastres. In Abyssinia, where the smallest coin is a bit of salt, the five-franc piece is valued at 28 piastres; at Galabat, Mr Aipperly informed me, its value falls to 18 piastres; but at Cairo it rises to 34. On Speke drawing £150, the account was as follows, the banker (Lutfullah), with great liberality, remitting the charge for exchange:—

	Piastres	Para
100 napoleons, at 77 piastres each,	7700	0
379 francs or Egyptian dollars, at 19–10 piastres each,	7295	30
4¼ piastres,	4	10
Total,	15,000	0

There is but one public building in Khartoom, the Government House, which overlooks the Blue Nile, and is a substantial brick edifice. A flight of steps leads up to the reception-hall, which is lofty and handsome, hung round with engravings of naval engagements, &c. In the courtyard Lubach-trees (*Acacia lebbek*) give shade to orderlies and officials. Baths and all conveniences are attached to the suites of rooms, and comfortable stabling is provided for cavalry and horse-artillery. We were shown through the powder-magazine, a mile distant from the town; it contains an immense store of ammunition, neatly arranged in cases. A barrack, simply walled round and almost smothered with drifted sand, is in the vicinity. The minaret we had observed on first approaching Khartoom is part of the mosque of the town; it is protected from the houses of the city by a high wall of stone, and sentries guard the gateways.

Walking through the streets with Ali Bey, he led us into a walled enclosure, where there were from twenty to thirty tombs surmounted by crosses. The fumes of frankincense met us, and we began to wonder what sight was in store. We entered an arched building; a man in spectacles read aloud from a volume placed on a desk in the centre, and around him were men wearing large turbans, their shoes placed on one side, and several children, all sitting on a carpet listening devoutly. On the walls were draperies and pictures of our

[1] Grant used repeated ditto marks in this table, but the corresponding words have been inserted here for the sake of clarity.

Saviour, and within a doorway was the high altar covered with a cloth marked by the figure of the cross. We were in a Coptic church. As the service proceeded in Arabic, a handsome old man entered, bearing a staff surmounted by a golden cross. He proceeded to the altar, and knelt at each of its four sides, after which he returned to where we stood, and conversed with us. By his invitation we left the church to have coffee at his house. I have seldom seen a finer face than that of this venerable Copt. His name, we found, was Gabriel; he is at the head of the Coptic church at Khartoom, and has a congregation of about five hundred persons. He showed us his copy of the four gospels, printed in Arabic and Hebrew characters; and on our taking leave of him, he thanked Ali Bey and ourselves for having visited his church.[1]

The Austrian Mission has a large and long-established station at Khartoom. It occupies a few acres of ground upon the river bank, and is surrounded by a wall ten feet high. The main gateway faces the town; it is handsome, and built of sandstone from the Rao.[2] Their temporary church is small but very neat; the front pews are occupied by the men, and those in the rear by the women. Through the kindness of Mr Moorlang, we took our Seedees to church, in order that they might be gratified with the sacred music from the harmonicon. It was a Sunday, and many other natives were present. Mabrook became greatly excited. On seeing the bleeding figure of our Saviour upon the cross, he held his mouth with his hand; he wished to touch the figure, thinking it was real. While at Khartoom Speke was asked to be godfather to a grown-up negress, a servant girl in the Mission establishment. His being a Protestant did not preclude him from officiating in this capacity. The ceremony took place in the morning, and there was an immense gathering. The liberal-minded Ali Bey, though a Mussulman, was present, also the Baroness Capellen, who was godmother to the girl. Another christening took place at the same time, when Madame Bartolemy[3] and M. de Bono officiated as godmother and godfather. During the ceremony loud reports took place outside; probably the fellow-servants of the girls were making merry by firing guns in honour of the event!

The ruins of Soba,[4] on the right bank of the Blue Nile, though as yet not much excavated, repaid us for the trouble of a visit, as we had not seen those of Thebes or Phylæ. Ali Bey kindly arranged a picnic for us, and in our old diabeah, Mr Aipperly, M. Angelo, a moullim or secretary, Speke, and I, rowed and sailed up the Blue river for three hours in the afternoon, accomplishing about six miles. We were then opposite Soba. There were no houses on the bank, and the country appeared flat and dreary. Sometimes the ground swelled up, marking the spot where houses or temples were still entombed. Arriving too late to pay the ruins a visit, we delayed till morning, and had dinner on deck. Ajim carpets[5] were laid out, candles were lit, and we sat round six brass saucers full of pastry, cutlets, and stews, which were eaten with the fingers. The usual coffee, liqueurs, and tobacco followed, and we rested for the night under variegated rezzais or counterpanes on the top of the cupboards. Next morning on the shore there was a curious collection of riding animals brought to convey us to the ruins of Soba. None looked inviting, but we were allotted a horse each, while others rode camels and donkeys. The moullim, a sedate fat

---

[1] For the Church and its priest, see Figure 103, p. 341.

[2] It is not clear what area Grant assumes this is.

[3] Perhaps the wife of the French trader Delphine Barthélemey. Hill, *Biographical Dictionary*, p. 74.

[4] The site of a medieval Nubian city which became Christian for part of its history. *Wikipedia*.

[5] Perhaps Azim carpets from India.

little man with black turban, had by no means a dignified appearance sitting on the donkey without a bridle, and the animal soon dropt down on his knees, allowing the functionary to slide over his head. The first mound we examined had been a room ten feet square, floored with square bricks; at each corner stood a round pillar of granite, seven feet between the capital and square base. The capitals were of three different designs; the most conspicuous being marked with the cross between acanthus leaves. All were now in ruin: the pillars were sunk, and the capitals lay separate. This excavation had been open for some time. The next we visited was opened by Dr Dumichen,[1] a Prussian gentleman, whom we met upon the ground, and who kindly gave us an alphabet of characters. It was a small square building of stone, with two-feet thick walls very neatly built, having two opposite doors, and its floor four feet below the present level of the country. The next and last excavation was a scaly sphinx lying upon a plinth, which, though considerably broken, was written over in Coptic characters, which consist of figures of men, beasts, and birds. The head of the sphinx, and some ornamentation on the chest, had been broken off. The measurements were—

Shoulder to plinth	60 inches	
Centre of chest to tail	115	„
Greatest circumference of neck	122	„
Over the saddle part, from plinth to plinth	140	„
Over the rump do. do.	145	„
Length of the tail	60	„

Although there were other ruins about Soba, we were informed that the above were the only remains worthy of note; so we re-embarked at noon, and returned to Khartoom.

Preparations were making[2] for our departure by boat to Berber, and thence by desert upon camels to Korosko. It was necessary, on account of the poverty of Berber, to lay in supplies of food at Khartoom for both these journeys. Ali Bey procured us a small diabeah which belonged to Government. We had only to pay the hire of the crew to Berber, namely, twenty-eight dollars. We had twenty Seedees, and each required to have two goat-skins, or "girba," to carry his drinking-water; Speke and I had two "rey," or cow-skins, each, for the same purpose, and water-bottles to hang from our camel-saddles. All these were purchased, the small ones for seven, and the large for thirty-eight koorsh each. It was necessary to grease and test these skins before setting out on the journey. A number of lads, each with the skin of a goat, blew into them with all their might, and then tied up the inflated skins for our inspection. Having arranged everything, we intended sailing at noon of the 15th April; but the hospitality of the Baroness, the Austrian missionaries, M. de Bono, and other gentlemen of Khartoom, delayed our departure till the afternoon, when about a dozen of our kind friends came to bid us farewell. The advices we received as to crossing the desert were numerous, and I may here mention them for the benefit of future travellers:—Have a list of the stages by land and water, mentioning what supplies are procurable. Always sling a water-bag and bag of biscuit to the pommel of your saddle. Ali Bey recommended a thimbleful of rum in a good deal of water as the best thing to keep one awake, and prevent tumbling off the camel during night. Always take a sleep for a few hours from nine in the morning. Water is more requisite than food; next to this, abrey (or

---

[1] Johannes Dümichen (1833–94) was an Egyptologist of some note who pioneered the study of Nubia.
[2] Grant's syntax, normally sound, seems to have fallen off at this point.

dry unleavened bread) and hard biscuit are the best. See that your men do not steal your water, or the sailors your ropes. The camels, too, are apt, from thirst, to bite through the water-bags, which must be taken care of, and also covered during the night, to prevent the wind drying them up; and always have something under them. We found all these advices excellent; and I have nothing to add except that a "Hadjeen," or riding camel, is indispensable to comfort.

Extract from Journal: Leaving Khartoum and Farewell to Ali Bey

Obliged to start away without Bombay, Frij & two others who joined us a mile down the river all more or less drunk from the cups of the old Flatimah who had been extremely attentive to us during our whole stay. I consulted with Mukeel [*viz.*, Ali Bey] on his being a go-between in making him [Flatimah] a present of twelve napls. [napoleons]; at once he returned to me saying 5 for him & 5 prs [piastres] among the servants was quite sufficient for him ... He was very happy and stayed chatting till midnight giving information and joking keeping us awake while the boat was proceeding downstream till midnight when we lay to on the right bank of the river [waiting] for his horse to arrive. He wrote a letter of instruction for Mustaf'a whose rosary he pitched into the river for the fish to eat ... After hugging him we bade him a fond farewell. He had often expressed his love for the English in preference to every other nation, even the French included; we laughed considerably when he told us that the Prussian Dr. at Soba was known and spoken of by the natives, not by name, but [by] putting their hand sideways to their forehead imitating his salute. [NLS, MS. 17915, 15 April 1863]

CHAPTER XVIII

[Pages 420–47][1]

From Khartoum to Cairo [15 April–4 June 1863]

We rowed down stream till midnight of the 15th April, and lay-to for the remainder of the night at Halfaya. Here Ali Bey and the sheikh of the place appeared, bringing us a present of two sheep. We all dined together, and afterwards our generous friend Ali Bey took leave of us, and returned on horseback to Khartoom, having left an aide-de-camp to escort us to Berber. Our crew rowed incessantly till sunset. About Halfaya the banks are either of hard shelving sand or perpendicular clay, and low solitary hills are generally in sight. The river was again mud-colour, and surprised us with being so narrow—not more than a hundred and eighty yards wide. On the left bank grew tamarisks, a species of willow, and several other plants we had not met with on our previous journey. While at Khartoom I had an opportunity of seeing a collection of plants from the Bahr Ghazal, made by Dr Steudner (since dead)[2] of Madame Tinne's expedition; they were nearly all the same as those found upon the Nile, but some auricularias were interesting. The sunset view of Mount Roeean and the low chain of mounds to its right, as we looked down a rocky reach of the river about four miles in length, was striking; the slopes of the hills became purple, and the bushes on both banks were lit up in gorgeous tints.[3] The river had quite changed its character; numbers of rocks at the sides and centre of the stream stood out of the water, making the navigation dangerous, and impossible at night. Our rowers had to pull very hard to escape the sunken rocks, which we avoided through the aid of a pilot from the shore.

17th.[4]—Having passed the island of Roeean to our right, the river ran through a narrow pass of hills called "Gherri." Nothing could be more desolate-looking: splinters of black rock lay on their sides, like refuse thrown from a quarry. The river branches on making its escape from these hills. Our boat took the right channel, and had scarcely entered it when we had to pass through a rapid and dangerous cataract, known as the Sixth Cataract of the

---

[1] This final chapter records what was an arduous enough journey but one that was even further from exploratory activity than the experiences recorded in the previous two chapters. Nor, apparently, were any considerable number of visual records made in this final three months of the Expedition. Accordingly, this chapter has not been very heavily annotated.

[2] Herrmann Steudtner (1833–63) was a German naturalist who joined Alexandrina Tinné on the foray into the Bahr-el-Ghazal but died there. Hill, *Biographical Dictionary*, p. 345.

[3] Grant's attempt to depict the scene is seen in Figure 106, p. 342.

[4] That is, 17 April 1863. It is not clear why Grant uses this device; the wording under each of the dates noted here bears no relation to the very full and detailed entries in the journal. Nevertheless, the dates of the main events and notes of places reached accord with the dates in the journal.

maps, and called by the natives Cibleoga. It was so narrow, that while our oars were poised, and we shot down the sluice, guided only by the helm, the oars almost touched the rocks on either side. The pilot, steersman, and boatman saw that one false move would have dashed the boat to pieces, so they did not breathe freely till the difficulty was over. No more rocks were met with till reaching Murnat at sunset, where it was considered desirable to rest for the night.

18*th*.—There are only two large places, or "bunders," on the route by water to Berber— namely, Metamma and Scendi. Nearly the whole distance is flat, bare, and uncultivated, without villages; but numerous flocks of cattle, camels, sheep, goats, and sometimes horses, are to be seen upon the banks. The people were civil in offering us milk and garden vegetables. To-day, although the mainmast of our boat had been taken down, the north wind and storm of sand blew so hard from nine till two o'clock that we could make no progress. We were not, however, troubled with rocks in the stream, and by sunset had made as far as the tame-looking district of Bowalat. From this point we had no rocks, but rowed steadily down, at two and a half miles per hour, as far as some wells and cultivations on the right bank at Go(n)cil Ilm. A native of this place, calling himself a Shygeea, had three lines cut upon each cheek, similar to the custom practised on the Nile at 4° N.; but though an aborigine, he was a Mussulman—converted, probably, at the time the late commander-in-chief, Ibrahim Pasha, conquered the country. The district was reckoned exactly half-way between Khartoom and Berber; but we anchored for the night at the left bank of Metamma. There were no antiquities to be seen; and, having gone down stream for an hour, we lay-to on the 20th at the town of Scendi, a straggling, dusty, miserable place, but which afforded liquor to our sailors, and fresh bread to ourselves.[1] There were mounds of ancient remains in abundance; and three miles to the south-west some buildings and figures in stone were said to exist. In the town there had been a deep shaft dug for a well—evidently ancient, for it is not now in use: a deep stratum of pebbles, with concrete above, forms its sides. There appears to have been a canal or watercourse at this place, for its windings, flooded with water and covered with grass, are still visible. The women, as they carried water on their heads, struck us as having a singular way of dressing their hair; but our Seedees remarked that a race of Central Africans, called the Wabeessa,[2] near Lake Nyassa, adopt the same fashion. The Scendi women, like those of Abyssinia, have a tuft of hair on either side of the head and one behind, and the Wabeessa have the same, but add another tuft, like a high comb, to the top of their heads.

Scendi is a place of some note, being the locality where Nimur (tiger), the former governor of all the blacks, planned the death of Poor Ishmael Pasha. The story was related to us as follows:—After Ishmael Pasha had conquered Khartoom, &c., he returned to Scendi, and asked Nimur what he was to give him. The reply was, "I will give you whatever you name, silver or gold, for I am anxious to make friends with you." After a time Ishmael with some followers became the guest of Nimur, who heaped quantities of provisions and straw for cavalry around the dwelling where Ishmael lived. No suspicion was excited; but

---

[1] Grant's account of the places visited during this part of his sail down the Nile is somewhat confused probably mainly because he misheard names. However, his 'Scendi', properly Shendi, was and is now an important place in Northern Sudan at 16°41′N, 33°26′E.

[2] More correctly, Wabisa who live nearer to Lake Bangweulu than Lake Malawi ('Nyassa'). As they were traders of some importance, Grant's Yao followers would have known them. Wainwright, 'Dangerous and Toilsome Journey', pp. 372–3 and n. 5.

the straw was set fire to one windy night. Ishmael, it is said, was too proud to attempt an escape. His followers shielded him as long as they could from the flames, and one arm only was burned, but Ishmael perished under the ruins. After great difficulty a European recovered the body from Nimur, and it was sent for interment to Cairo. A bad imitation of the mosque at Khartoom marks the place where this tragedy was enacted.[1]

We left for Meroe, the ancient capital of Ethiopia, before sunrise of the 21st. Date-palms, we observed, were here more frequently irrigated, and the doompalm grew wild. The bunder, or port, from which Meroe (called by the natives Tarabil Kobosheea, or Pyramids of Kobosheea) is visited, may be either Kobosheea or Budjerewa; we chose the latter, as the wind was not favourable for landing at the former.[2] The pyramids are seen two miles across a plain, upon the right bank, near some low elongated hills. To visit them during the heat of the day it is desirable to have riding donkeys, which, with common wooden saddles, may be obtained at either starting-point. A man carries water, and you make straight for the ruins over a plain strewed with small pieces of clay of curious shapes and lustrous colours. There are three groups of pyramids. The first group consists of fifteen, dismantled to half their original height, and built apparently, as to site, without any regular system or order. A pyramidal shell of masonry 24 feet square, built without lime, and eight feet thick, had been filled with the rubble of the country. The sandstone blocks with which they had been faced were now so soft that a knife could cut them. The second group, consisting of 18 or more, half a mile farther east, are in a better state of preservation, and have their figures of men and animals wonderfully complete. We ascended one having ten tiers, each tier a span and a half high, and diminishing in breadth as you reach the summit. The porches or entries into several pyramids of this group were arched over with stone, and handsomely ornamented with bas-relievo figures chiselled out of the sandstone. These figures consisted of men driving slaves, carrying sheep, or seated on lion-faced dogs, funeral processions, women carrying palm-leaves, and representations of birds, lizards, and elephants. The third group of five pyramids was across a death-like valley covered with withered grass. Having seen all, and made some sketches of the curious figures,[3] we next visited three sphinxes very much defaced, which remain amongst the ruins of the city. They were not marked with scales like the Soba sphinx; they had been cut out of a rock with slaty stratification, and were defaced by the laminæ having split off. In the city, several old walls and pavements, built of immense blocks of sandstone, are to be seen; but everything is in utter decay. On returning to our boat we

---

[1] Perhaps after some 40 years, the story had become somewhat elaborated but it recalls a very important event. Mek [King] Nimr was leader of the Ja' li people (Jaalyyin), relics of the original Nubian people, not 'governor of all the blacks'. He had, indeed, arranged the assassination of Ismail Kamil in 1822. Ismail Kamil was one of the sons of Muhammed Ali (1769–1848), Viceroy of Egypt from 1805, who organized the invasion of the Sudan and the founding of Khartoum. Nimr retreated eastwards to the Ethiopian frontier after 1822 but continued to oppose the Egyptians. Murdock, *Africa*, p. 410; Holt, 'Egypt and the Nile Valley', p. 32.

[2] Grant was now entering not, as he says, the 'ancient capital of Ethiopia', but the area in the Nile Valley which had, between c. 1000 BC and c. AD 350, constituted the Kingdom of Kush. Its later phases were characterized by what has been called the Meroitic culture. Funerary practices to some extent copied Egyptian-type pyramids and Grant visited the site called 'the Pyramids of Meroe' which is a little to the east of the Nile near his 'Kobosheea', still a modern settlement known as Kabushiya (16°53′N, 33°41′E). The site is in an area between the Nile and the Atbara long known as the 'Island of Meroe'. Confusingly, the modern town of Merowe is 150 miles (241 km) further north-west on the great bend of the Nile.

[3] Grant does not seem to have preserved the sketches.

found a considerable number of people wishing to dispose of curiosities they had gathered. These were relics of stone and copper, some representing the scarabæus, and others human figures, but no coins were produced, for they said the coins were too valuable to show us.

22d.—A considerable number of palm and acacia trees were growing upon the banks we passed to-day, and we saw Jubl Ag'edah on the left bank six hours' distance above the port of Damur.[1] We called to get a letter of introduction, and orders for camels from the Mudir, Ibrahim Bey, to the Mudir of Berber. There are upwards of one hundred flat-roofed comfortable-looking dwellings near the river, shaded by acacias. A market is held every Friday, when cotton, salt, baskets, mats, ropes, cattle, &c., are exposed for sale. The Atbara, a river navigable for a long distance, is not above a few hours' sail from this port. We lay for the night just above its confluence with the Nile, because there were sunken rocks in the bed of the river. In the morning we saw the Atbara, Bahr-el-aswad (Black river), the Astaboras of Ptolemy—the last great feeder of the Nile.[2] We liked the brown appearance of the stream. From bank to bank it looked one hundred and fifty yards across, but now there was not more than sixty yards of water flowing slowly in its bed, with a low rock at its junction with the Nile. It joins the latter with even a more graceful sweep than we observed at the confluence of the Blue and White Nile. For a distance of two miles below its mouth there are sunken rocks very annoying to the boatmen, but at this dry season of April they are generally visible. While detained below the Atbara on account of contrary winds, Bombay brought his wife up to Speke, saying she was very unwell; but as she was too diffident to speak, we could do nothing to help her. An hour or two elapsed, and Bombay came, grinning with delight, to announce that his wife had presented him with a child! One of the girls in the boat had told him of it, but he did not know whether it was a boy or a girl—he would go and ask. This was the second child born to Bombay upon the journey; but both died, and he regretted very much that there would be no keepsake of the journey for him to take back to Zanzibar. The infant was buried on the shore.

Our journey by water had now for the present ended—we had anchored off the bunder or port of Berber.[3] There was some show of trade, and twelve large boats lay alongside ours. The population of Berber and the neighbouring villages is probably five thousand souls. The houses are built in irregular streets and lanes, chiefly near the Nile. A handsome embankment has been constructed around Berber, which forms a pleasant walk at all seasons. On the outskirts of this is the unenclosed burial-ground. The tombs have upright slabs at either end, with white shingle laid between, and a few are built of bricks and lime. From the number of graves and the extent they cover, it would be supposed that the locality of Berber is unhealthy, but the natives prefer this latitude to Khartoom: provisions, also, are only about half the price. Wheaten bread, milk, meat, oats, onions, water-melons, tobacco, salt, fish, &c., are abundant in the market every morning, and other articles can be obtained and work executed in the bazaar. The operation of thrashing wheat is performed in the true Egyptian style. A man sits on a frame drawn by bullocks,

---

[1] Presumably Ed Damer, just south of Atbara.

[2] Ptolemy, *Geography of Claudius Ptolemy*, p. 108. How far Grant was actually familiar with Ptolemaic geographical data rather than displaying this knowledge at second hand is not certain.

[3] Berber, 18°55′N 33°59′E, was important as the point from which those travelling down the Nile took to land travel in order to avoid the great western loop of the Nile. This, however, meant crossing the Nubian desert. Berber was also the terminus of a trade route east to Suakin on the Red Sea coast.

and resting upon three rollers, each furnished with iron discs; the bullocks eat all the while, and the grain is well thrashed, but the work is overdone, as the seed gets bruised in the process. In the bazaars the boys discovered that our Seedees had arrows and other weapons to dispose of, and came offering money. The exchange was very easily arranged, for the Seedees were eager to purchase the Egyptian dates. The inhabitants of Berber are proverbially honest, and their servants are considered superior to those of Khartoom. I went to the market to buy food, and saw the rude way it was managed. The butcher not having sufficient weights and measures, a sheep's head and two broken bricks were put into one scale, and my meat in the other. Having weighed it, he said its price was so much. Upon which, trusting to the reputed honesty of the Berberese, I put into his hand more than the amount, and he told me to come back for the change, as he was too busy to give it me then. This I did, and received the balance. The few troops here were a tidy set of men, in clean quarters, below the town. Their arms were flint-musket and bayonet; their uniform, the fez, white jackets, knee-breeches, long white socks, and red shoes. At a short distance from their barracks there is a magazine with four high walls, a single gateway to the south, a few trees in the interior, and towers with embrasures.

Berber became Egyptian at the same time as Khartoom, about forty years ago, when the army advanced from Wady Halfa, The present Governor-General of the Soudan, Musa Pasha, is the man of whom the story is told that when he was sent to conquer the country he circumcised every one of the Bagara Arabs,[1] and so brought them under his subjection. We were not fortunate enough to have an audience of the Governor-General; he was absent on a tour of inspection, and our friend Ali Bey acted for him. The Vakeel of Berber, Rehan Aga, came to call upon us: he had lived twenty years in Constantinople, and, to my surprise, he had more of the features of a M'ganda than a Turk. He has a comfortable house, well furnished, and he kindly showed us every attention. The Sheikh of the desert, a dark, stout, middle-aged man, we saw more of, as it was through him that we were to obtain camels for our journey. He was handsome, with a long black gown and high white turban. He thought we might get off in a couple of days; and, in the mean time, he would get us a house to live in during the heat of the day. We were accordingly put into a dark inner room without a window, but it had a high verandah outside where we could sit during the day. We engaged thirty baggage-camels, at ninety piastres each, to carry us to Korosko;[2] the party consisted of twenty-six souls in all, and the spare camels were for carrying two guides and two loads of water for Speke and myself. Every other man had to carry his two water-bags on the camel he rode. We tried to get a pair of Hadjeens or riding camels, but failed—all were as rough as they could possibly be. The majority of our Seedees had never seen a camel before, and were somewhat afraid to mount; however, once seated, their pleasure was excessive. All was good-humour and fun the first day's march to El Chore, where we arrived at sunset of the 27th April. El Chore, "the Lake," had no water at this season, but the Nile, which is within a quarter of a mile, overflows the grassy ground immediately below the few inhabited houses. The people were civil in selling us milk, bringing us water, and giving us small cots to lie upon during the night. In the desert, amongst Egyptians, a traveller may always expect to be treated with civility.

[1] The Baggara Arabs were the descendants of the original Arab conquerors of Egypt and the Lower Nile after 1045. Grant pictured some of them in Figure 99, p. 338.
[2] The modern Wadi Halfa, 21°47'N 31°22'E.

28th.—To-day we divided the march into two stages, making one in the morning to El Ab'idy, and the other to Gin'noeet'a—the latter name as sounded by a native is peculiarly Italian. The journey occupied seven hours, generally over a hard road of gravel. Although never far from the river, we saw low hills upon the opposite bank, and travelled amongst tall grass, madar, and palms. From this grass the people make a coarse description of rope. The nights were cold, owing to north winds; but, sheltered by the walls of the small flat-roofed houses, we rested comfortably on the cots lent us by the people. From Gin'oeneet'a we made twenty-two miles in eleven hours, two stages to a point in the desert beyond Aboo Ban, resting during the heat of the day at Wadi Khumar—the bed of a stream then dry. Here there is a bend in the Nile, and we were able to fill all our water-sacks afresh. This route was over ground strewn with splinters, and ridged with quartz and clay-slate dykes. Some of the rocks were cobalt blue, ringing when struck, and bearing marks of having been combed down with rain. Wadi Khumar (which signifies the river of asses) derives its name from being the spot where wild donkeys and zebra come to drink. We rested under some palm-trees in rich foliage, beside the Nile, which, at this point, runs rapidly over a bed of rock, divided into several courses. After leaving the river the march became dreary and desolate; not a sign of a human being; all a waste of heavy sand, dreary valleys in the hollows, and splintered black rock on the heights. We lay down at night in a country filled to the tops of the hills with white sand, not a tree nor a drop of water to be seen, and a kind of fearful stillness everywhere around! However, there never was a desert that had not some living thing to show—some insect, bird, or animal. Several tiny ariel[1] appeared as we passed the peaked height of Aboo Ban. In the morning we set off over the sand on foot to keep us warm, but it proved such heavy plodding work that, after some miles, we mounted the camels and descended from the plateaux of sand to the Nile at Bagoere, where we made our noonday halt. The river may be called beautiful at this point, for it runs at a rate of from three to five miles an hour amongst myriads of rush-covered islets, with high banks about five hundred yards apart, and on the opposite side densely covered with tropical vegetation. The people of Bagosre allowed us to occupy a shed roofed with the leaves of the doompalm. They brought us milk, and for their attention we made them a present of a lantern. Travelling as we all did upon camels, not in file as in India, one camel tied after the other, but like a herd of cattle gently driven by men walking behind them, there was always considerable jostling; and if a camel wanted to pluck a mouthful you could not prevent him, as there was no ring in his nose, only a rope tied round his head, which gave the rider no command over him. Their pace was slower than that of a man, and so rough, that the saddle, assisted a good deal by the cold wind every morning, chafed the skin. The march in the afternoon to Wadi Shiroeg (another dry bed of a stream) was over rough stony ground, to the brink of the Nile, occupying us only two hours, when we encamped under date-palms, and amongst houses, near one of which a rudely-made loom was at work. On this march we passed several cairns of stones four and five feet above the level of the country; our camelmen could not say who had formed them, they were of so old a date.

1st May.—The route to Aboo Hasheem,[2] "the Father of Hospitality," was so smooth and pleasant that one might have ridden, driven, or walked the whole distance, which

---

[1] The ariel is *Gazella arabica,* a small gazelle found in North Africa and Asia. *OED.*

[2] Abu Hashim remains a modern settlement on the road and rail routes beside the Nile at the latitude of about 17°N.

occupied us more than four hours on our baggage-camels. It lay on the outskirts of wheat stubble-fields on the banks of the Nile, and on our right rose the variously-coloured rocks of the desert. The river is about three hundred yards across, and has a current of two and a half miles per hour. When passing a roadside house about halfway, we halted to go through a superstitious ceremony. A burial-ground was close by, with cups upon many of the graves, said to be placed there for receiving offerings of frankincense or money. We all dismounted at the hut, which had no appearance of being regularly inhabited, and found several jars of drinking water, which a boy served to us; the skull of a lion was stuck upon a pole, and stood high over the hut. Our guide received from the boy two handfuls of sand, some of which he strewed over his person, some he put into his pockets, some he licked, some he put on the camels, pistols, and saddles, and he finished off by putting the last grains carefully into the bag slung from his riding animal. This odd custom is common over the desert, and is adopted by camel-men to insure their safety on a journey. We came upon old acquaintances as we made for the north: the white kite, raven, sand-grouse, and stonefinches were recognised after we left Berber, and became the most common birds of the desert. At Aboo Hasheem we were allotted a two-storeyed house to rest in. We observed that here six or eight donkeys in a knot are used for treading out the wheat, and are prevented from eating it by a band tied round the lower jaw, crossing the forehead, and fastened behind their long ears—an artful contrivance. The afternoon march, made to Goegee, on the Nile, occupied us till 11 P.M. We had not seen the river the whole way; the track was over heavy sand, strewed with fragments of rock and pebbles. The hill of Burgul Anak was passed when we were four miles to its left, and on arrival at Goegee we could look back upon it seven miles off in a south-east direction.

2d.—Starting off across the plain at sunrise, our beacon was a pyramidal mass of quartz a few miles distant. We passed a tomb erected by Latiffe Pasha to the memory of a Liverpool gentleman,[1] and at length, picking our steps amongst the splinters from the blue and grey slate rocks, we arrived at Musra Jahoesh,[2] upon a bend of the Nile, which here flows in a westerly direction. There were no people nor houses on our side of the river. To avoid the heat we lay in the deep shadow of the doom-palm, and changed our positions as the sun veered round. Starting again at five in the afternoon, we ascended to a wild dreary plateau, but which became interesting from the colours of the rocks. Every moment I was tempted to dismount and pick up specimens in which blue was contrasted with pure white quartz, or pink was marbled with white, or all three colours would blend together. By seven o'clock we had descended from this plateau by a sandy tract, and reached the high gravel bank of the river again. Here the moon lighted up the rippled blue water and the palms and green vegetation on the opposite bank. The village of Aboo Ahmed[3] looked beautiful in this light, but on reaching it we found it ankle-deep in sand.

---

[1] Grant refers in his journal to the 'Liverpool man' and then leaves a space for the name before adding 'who was born in Italy' and 'had been employed as a scientific man by the Egyptians but died 13 years ago'. NLS, MS. 17915, 2 May 1863. Presumably when he came to write up his journal in the evening, Grant could not recall the name. Neither the various authorities on the history of the Sudan I have consulted nor Grant's own later 'Route March' mention the tomb or the man.

[2] This appears to be a mishearing for Dagash (19°19′N 33°28′E) which continues to exist as a tourist centre.

[3] Abu Hamad, 19°32′N 33°20′E is the point where the Nile takes a great bend to flow in a south-westerly direction before it flows north again. He now had to cross the Nubian Desert to rejoin the Nile at Wadi Halfa, known to him as Korosko. Much British interest in Gordon, the Mahdi and the Sudan in 1884 led Grant to

My camel, which for the first time I had pressed ahead with a cane, showed his fatigue by squatting down without warning, upon my stopping to ask for the Deewan's house. He knew that his journey had come to an end, but the proceeding would not be pleasant were he to try it in a desert. We rode past a large caravan from Berber—traders conveying young camels and home-made camel-cloths for sale to Korosko, whither we also were journeying. They were anxious to know whether we had commenced to stint our camels in water, previous to putting them upon the desert allowance of none at all; they had done so, and were ready to march next day; we had not, and therefore our march must be delayed. I may here remark that travelling in the desert on a baggage camel is far from being comfortable. The usual seat is the same as that of a lady on horseback, but without any kind of stirrup, consequently the legs get chafed, the dry wind chips your hands and nails, and you get cold in the head. Manua, an old and experienced traveller, sat always upon his camel with his nose in a sling, which, he said, was a protection against cold; he had a cloth shutting up both nostrils, and tied on the top of the head.

3d and 4th.—Detained training our camels for the desert journey, and getting ropes and other necessaries. The station of Aboo Ahmed is upon the right bank of the Nile, with the island of Mokrat opposite. An oblong wall of mud, with a tower at each corner, encloses the few huts that are there, and other abodes are placed outside the walls in a straggling line of misery. Sand has nearly banked up the whole place—walls, fort, and all—and the majority of the people live upon the island and opposite shore. We had a call from two gentlemen travelling (not for their pleasure, but till further orders) to that Siberia of Egypt, the Soudan, with a line of camels and horses carrying their worldly effects. They had been fifty-one days coming by land from Cairo, and were the first Egyptian travellers we had met. They could not make out where we had come from, and asked us a number of strange questions. Was it true that the Governor-General of the Soudan, Musa Pasha, had made prisoners of us? had we been serving the Abyssinian Government? were English officers fighting for the Abyssinians? was Queen Victoria to resign in favour of the Prince of Wales? were we the remnant of fifty Englishmen who had left Zanzibar to cross Africa? These interrogatories were all put to us by an Albanian gentleman; the other traveller was a priest, a very intelligent man. He went so far as to say, when told that we had come from the source of the Nile, that the Koran had always said that it proceeded from a lake; but what was the size of it? Had we seen cannibals? What did we pay for these five Seedees and the little girls we had with us? Having answered all these queries to their satisfaction, we saw them depart for Khartoom. In the afternoon we had a visit from a fortune-teller. He sat at our feet, smoothed with his hand the floor of sand, and asked our names, which we did not tell him; however, he commenced to span the sand and to mark it in his own cabalistic way, after which he pronounced the opinion that the fatigues of the long journey weighed heavily upon Speke's heart.

5th.—Intending to start across the desert at noon, we had prepared for the journey by keeping our camels without water for two days, and we now gave them as much as they could drink before setting out. Several of them had pieces of goat-skin sewn to the horny

provide a systematic description of the 'very worst' of all his African journeys, the crossing of 'a desert of 230 miles without one drop of water'. Grant, 'Route March', p. 326. The account adds nothing of consequence to the description in this text.

part of their feet to prevent the sharp pebbles or rock from making them foot-sore. We killed a sheep for ourselves, and hit upon an excellent plan of preserving the meat, by cutting it up into portions the size of a mutton-chop, and boiling all in grease: when cooled, it was put into a leathern bag, and being cooked, it lasted us during the journey. Our caravan consisted of twenty-nine persons, including two guides, all mounted on camels. Each camel, besides grain and baggage, also carried, slung on either side, two girbas or water-bags. We had three men and a couple of lads, over and above the experienced guides, for the purpose of driving on and attending to our camels. They wished us to hire more carriage, saying, our water was insufficient, but we found that we were amply supplied. Setting out soon after noon, we passed to the right of a hill, called Moogeran. The route was as firm as a gravelled garden-walk, not a shrub nor tree upon its whole extent, and grass only where water had coursed after rains. I had always fancied a "desert" to be drifting sand, as is seen in the Overland route,[1] but here it was perfectly level, and swept by the wind. Several doves passed us; a jet-black swift skimmed in front of our troop of camels, and alighted on the ground without fear, as the Mother Carey's Chicken alights on the billows;[2] sand-finches and sand-grouse, &c., flew about. We had two species of lizard to interest us while proceeding on our march, and the ground was riddled with rat-holes. These may be said to have represented life, and we had skeletons of camels representing death. The latter were in every state of decay and position. Few seemed to have died here (at the close of their journey from Korosko) without a struggle. While crossing to the hill above mentioned, we saw at its base what seemed a lake with boats upon it; our Seedees at once said, "Let us go for water, let us fetch wood." It was a mirage, the Bahr Belama, or false sea, seen about two in the afternoon in the most fantastic shapes, wherever there was a hill to obstruct the current of air. There was a good deal of bantering amongst the Seedees after the mirage was discovered, each trying to dupe his neighbour into walking over to it. We had been in the saddle from noon till sunset, when we dismounted for two hours to allow our camels to eat their corn, and then we proceeded again, sailing over the plain of gravel till near daylight. This was our first severe night. I felt as sleepy as if I had been drugged; even walking now and then at a brisk pace scarcely kept us awake.

6th.—We had rested well at Aboo Inteh Shurrut,[3] with the glorious heavens for our canopy, and jumped up off our blankets light and joyous, and were saddled by sunrise, having, with the aid of some of our firewood, got a luxurious cup of coffee. We had two severe days' work before us. First, we had to reach Furoodh, a four hours' morning ride across a hard plain, with solitary hills in the distance, and mirage near them. Then we had an afternoon march to Taboon, or Taban (trouble), where the camels were baited. Here,

---

[1] That is, the route home from India rather than sailing by sea.

[2] These are seabirds – the storm petrels.

[3] This was the first major staging post on the camel route across the desert which made it possible to avoid sailing round the great Dongola bend in the Nile. As will be noted, Grant continues to record the names of succeeding staging posts as he proceeds northwards towards Korosko. All these places are also shown on the map which accompanied his volume in 1864. Later in the 19th century, however, a railway was built by the British military and in the following century a motorable road finally eliminated the need for camel transport. The settlements Grant recorded then lost their importance and appear only on large-scale maps, not in atlases. The waters of Lake Nasser created by the Aswan Dam have submerged some places at the northern end of the route.

the place, true to its cognomen, gave us the benefit of a dust-storm: the bank of cloud rolled on from the east—every one lay upon his face; the camels turned their backs and rested their long necks on the ground; the lights were blown out, and for a minute, while we were pelted with sand and gravel, all was dark. The blast, however, was soon over. We were off five minutes after it, making for the pass called Durb-wait, or Udder-a-wæp (signifying narrow road), and entered it after passing two hills, named Gorebat (solitary) and Abnoogara (the drummer). The pass wound very much, and varied in breadth from three yards to a thousand, being sometimes so rocky that our camel-men cheered up the spirits of the animals by calling out to them "Abdil Ka-a-dr" as much as to say, "God preserve you from harm over the rough stones." But when the sandy level bed of the valley widened, and rugged mountains imprisoned it all round, there was something wildly-grand about the scene. The natives had christened this place Ipseha, or the clouds. We encamped some distance up the valley, where a few acacias, having pods like ear rings, grew upon the plain of sand. We had been for ten hours on the move, and we left again at one o'clock, keeping still in "Udder-a-wæp," or the pass, for six miles. Waves of drifted sand almost buried the higher hills, up whose sides it lay like snow-wreaths. Here, curious enough, were some dead trees which we might have carried in as firewood, but the Seedees were too apathetic. The desert we were about to enter was our first genuine sandy desert; all the preceding had been firm and hard. Nothing but miles of heavy sand, as deep as a lake, was now seen. The camel-drivers and guides again shouted "Abdil Ka-a-dr" to give heart to their camels, and with this short prayer urged the animals quickly over the danger. There was no trace of a path, and the night was coming on, but the sky was clear. The Seedees knew no danger; all were jolly; and as there was no chance of a dust-storm, we lay down for two hours. We then resumed, and continued the journey till three in the morning, not feeling so sleepy as we had done the first few nights. It seemed extraordinary that the Sheikhs could find their way in such a desert in the dark, without the aid of hills or trees as landmarks, but they do so unfailingly. They are extremely careful, and when any of our men lay down for a moment's sleep, the ever-vigilant Sheikh would report him for being so indifferent to his own life as to linger behind for an instant. However, by midnight of the 7th the danger was past, and we walked upon rocky ground where the Morad valleys commence, and where there are springs of brackish water.

As we approached the natron wells of Morad,[1] the country appeared to open, though covered with slaty rocks bristling above ground. Hills and valleys, patched with drifted sand, presented the most dreary, waste-like appearance. The heat was relaxing—a crow appeared, and the Sheikh informed us that it was a good sign—we should certainly find water in the wells. A turn in the road suddenly disclosed a long valley below, running from east to west, with camels, donkeys, goats, and sheep standing languidly around five or six wells. Carcasses of animals were numerous in this valley of death. Our camels showed no anxiety for water, although they had been without it for three days; but they seemed eager to have a roll upon a clear patch of sand in view. The well our party took possession of was protected from sand by a wall on its upper and lower sides. It was dug ten feet below the surface, and had only six inches of water. After having been used all day it had not run dry; but the water was like saltpetre in taste. In this dreary valley several huts built of matting are inhabited by Arabs and their flocks. Who else could live on the spot? Where do their

---

[1] About halfway across the desert.

small long-haired goats get a single blade of grass to feed upon? It would seem as if they could not exist; yet before us is a flock of sixty, which are brought to drink at the well every third or fourth day, and though living on this brackish water, no animals ever appeared more healthy. The people residing here are not different from the natives of Aboo Ahmed, and are not more unhealthy; but one of them begged for medicine to cure a chest complaint. Several of their children were pretty, with intelligent eyes, and looking wild as colts, with all the hair shaved off their heads except a forelock and long tress from the crown of the head. In this valley of Morad there is not an atom of firewood; indeed, for three days' travelling, day and night, we had not met with more than thirty trees; and, being so rarely seen, we took them almost every time for a mirage.

9th.—At eleven o'clock we left the wells *en route* for Korosko, still some days' journey without wood or water upon the way; and therefore we carried the brackish water of the Morad wells with us. It was very unpleasant to wash with, as it curdled the soap, and the exterior of the water-bags became powdered as with flour. The camels did not suffer much from drinking it. Our route was across a series of rocky spurs and dykes, all tapering down to the Nile far away to our left. The strata of the rocks seemed reversed in position, as if they had been uplifted by a convulsion in the north. One of the ridges which crossed our road at Wadi Soofoor was four hundred yards long, and so remarkable that it looked as if a waving wall had been built there as a boundary between two properties, standing up in the sky-line like *chevaux-de-frise*.[1] The colours of the accumulated debris and sand in the gorges of the hill-sides were striking. At the top of the incline the sand was flesh-coloured and fiery; lower down the debris was grey and purple, consisting of slate in various shades, and blue rocks like masses of cobalt; bits of spar were also collected. Between each of these are tempting valleys for a ride, the ground being of firm hard sand.

The connection between each valley is formed by a steep rugged path, sometimes, as on entering the valley of Dullah, with high cliffs on either side; and looking through this vista upon the scene below, the effect is picturesque. There is a line of palm-trees which adds a charm to the spot. At a distance they might be mistaken for the doom-palm; but their fruit, unbranched stems, and leaves are different. We had not seen them before, but Manua had found them growing eight degrees south of the equator, in a country where there are numerous rivulets. Some seeds, brought home by the expedition, were propagated in Kew, but they ultimately died. Having passed the valleys of Dullah, Wadi Soofoor, and Thillatha Jindeh, with its acacias, we rested between six and eight o'clock on the sands of Wadi Mereesha, and were on the move again till three of the morning.

While riding along upon the march, conversation is continued in order to keep each other awake. The topics are generally upon the natural objects around us, whether it be the hills, stream-beds, trees, or rocks. The Seedees laughed, mimicked, and ridiculed each other as they rode along briskly on their camels. We had with us a poor half-witted fellow, or fool, named Mahoka, whom Bombay had obtained for a few yards of cloth, and kept as his servant. He was a hardworking fellow, but would often burst out into fearful rages, refusing to work. There was something of the rogue about his fooleries, and he held his own amongst the men. One night he fell asleep upon the top of his camel, and dropt down upon his back on the ground, his legs, arms, and spear flying in the air. I thought the creature was killed, but he got up, laughed, snapped his fingers, and danced a war-

---

[1] A medieval anti-cavalry device consisting of a series of wooden spikes.

dance. He would not, however, remount his camel for an hour or two. While marching through the picturesque valley of Dullah, a circumstance elicited from Manua in his account of his wanderings, may be mentioned here as noted at the time. I repeated it to Dr Livingstone, who also had received some information regarding it. Extract, 10th May 1863: "While riding along on our camels last night, Manua told me of a tunnel, the work of God, which runs north and south between Loowemba and Ooroongoo (two months' march from Kazeh), which took the caravan of Arab Khamees, with whom he was travelling, from sunrise till noon to march through, and which was as broad as from that white stone to the back hill (a distance which I judged to be four hundred yards). Over this tunnel an unfordable river with rocky sides (here he pointed to the hills around us) runs at right angles to the Tanganyika Lake. If boats were to attempt to ferry this river, the cliffs are too steep to permit of their landing,—the river is forded by passing through the natural tunnel underneath. As to its height, this camel, with me mounted, could march through the tunnel and then not touch its top. No water comes through; it is obtained by digging holes in the sand. The reed from which the Waganda make flutes, grows inside it. The rocks are black, and look as if they had been planed (basalt, from his description). White pebbles are plentiful there. Inside it is not as clear as day, but once within it there is sufficient light the whole way. The natives consider it a m'zimo (namely, wonder or worshipping spot). They have no name for it, but the river above it is called Kaoma." On my interrogating him further, as if doubting his tale, and making him repeat it to Speke, he got nettled, and asked with a sneer, "Did not the people of Wambweh take shelter in it, with their cattle, from the attacks of the Watuta? (meaning a branch of the Zulu Kafir). And if you do not believe my story, because I did not mention it before, ask so-and-so of Unyanyembe, who was of our party." Manua added, that "he went and returned by this tunnel, as it is the regular highway road between Loowemba and Ooroongoo." It will be interesting to know what account was received of it by Dr Livingstone. In the mean time the above description as to size, direction, &c., must be considered vague and general. From Manua's description I understood him to say that this river Kaoma flowed into the Tanganyika Lake.[1]

We went smartly over the Bahr Hut'ab, the waterless sea, in ten hours' marching, and by breakfast-time of the 10th reached Aboo Rakeeb, or father of shade, a shelter-rock of sandstone upon a commanding height. The surface of the country was dotted with black conical masses of sandstone, intermixed with which were volcanic bombs, single and stuck together, varying from one inch to three in diameter. Those that had become detached lay like round-shot on the expanse of the desert. We next marched, for four hours, across the Bahr Belama, descending to a pass called El Bab, where we dined, and then travelled all night between bare abrupt hills, which, as we advanced, broke up into cones, looking like huge redoubts and batteries. The footing in these valleys is of level sand. On arriving at the pass our cavalcade was halted by the Sheikh in command, and his men immediately commenced to rattle and beat the bones of some dead camels that lay on the spot; the men also screeched and shouted, making a great noise. The cause of this demonstration,

---

[1] Grant has quoted very accurately from his journal. However, he does not quote the conclusion he then recorded: 'This story I firmly believed though Speke doubted it.' NLS, MS. 17915, 10 May 1863. The tunnel does not exist. This rather undermines one's faith in Grant but he tended to favour Manua's stories because of Manua's help in identifying plants. What Livingstone thought is not recorded.

we found, was, that we had there to pay a certain footing or tribute, and this being agreed to, we advanced. Frij tells me that the same custom exists on board of an Arab vessel when she is leaving the port for the first time; the new hands amongst the crew are obliged to contribute money, to be expended in a jollification. In ten hours, over firm sand, we reached Oogab Ghowab', where there is a sandstone shelter-rock written upon by foreigners. It protected us during the heat of the day. An effendi (secretary) had dug a well, and surrounded it by a wall, but there was no water. There was, however, some vegetation, giving us an idea that water was not very distant or very deep: the wild senna was growing, and some withered bushes of another plant blew about in balls with the wind. With two rests on the way, we reached Korosko[1] from Oogab Ghowab' after sixteen hours' travelling. In a few places there were slabs of sandstone, and as we neared Korosko we came upon old red sandstone and conglomerate as hard as flint. Our direction during six days had been mainly upon the pointers to the north star, when they are westerly and horizontal. The cry of the Sheikh to rouse us for the march from our comfortable couches upon the desert sand, can never be forgotten; his "Abdil Ka-a-dr," repeated and repeated till he saw us up and saddling, was at the time provoking, but how very necessary with such a waterless country to pass over! In my Journal I have noted, with reference to the Sheikh and his followers, that we should never again meet their superiors for civility, their unpresuming modest manner, their thorough knowledge of their work, and their willingness always to serve. They would assist our Seedees in conveying water during the march, picking up for them whatever they let fall, packing and tying up our baggage, and never murmuring or begging. They left us smiling, satisfied with our treatment of them.

The first indication of the Korosko habitations was the appearance of some date-palms, long-stemmed, like the wild date-tree of Uganda. As we emerged from the sandy wastes there was a general impression that the Nile was amongst the hills we saw; and the old Sheikh confirmed this by stating that shortly we should drink of the waters of the Nile. Bounding a hill, the scattered village of Korosko was full before us in the midst of an amphitheatre of hills, their fiery sides of sand nearly killing every living thing around them. There was, however, some shade by the river bank; and we hired a diabeah, and a party of seven men to convey us to Shellal. It was a luxury to get rid of the camels—to experience any change—and especially to taste a water-melon after such a journey! The effendi gave us every aid; and, as it was not desirable to stay long in a place which he called as hot as hell, with no wood or provisions to be had; our crew, glad to escape, ejaculated, "In Sha Ullah!" or "God be praised," and we floated down old Nilus on the evening of the 12th of May. The song and the sailors' mode of rowing were strange to us; the former was powerful, harmonious, and pleasing, and the men stood two feet above the deck pacing upon planks as they propelled the boat; their language also had a strange twang to our ears—a regular Nile patois. As we glided past the Bar'edy hills, with narrow terraces for cultivation, the country appeared hot and dry; everything was parched and arid in comparison with the green of the Soudan. The present Pasha will, I trust, open up the country of the Soudan, for it might be converted, by draining and irrigation, into a valuable possession. We were beginning to feel that the tourist's route had at length been

---

[1] Korosko was the northern terminus of the camel route. It has now been superseded as a traffic entrepôt by a town on the railway, Wadi Halfa (21°48′N 31°20′E). After Korosko, Speke and Grant followed the well-known Nile route to Cairo via Aswan.

reached, for at Korosko we were pestered for "buxees,"[1] or money. Our captain also made an extraordinary request: provisions were scarce; and, purchasing a calf, the captain demanded, as his right, the head and fore-quarter of the animal; which we, however, refused, although he said it was the perquisite of all captains who had charge of travellers on the Nile. We landed at the snug harbour of Shellal, below Phylæ, and there had the final confirmation of our being on a beaten track, for a host of donkey-boys gathered round us, clamouring and shouting to be engaged.

The day we were to leave Aswan for Cairo in a small diabeah, a steamer came puffing up the river. His Highness the Viceroy, Ismael Pasha, had sent this vessel to bring us down, and we sailed on the 19th of May 1863. The mudirs or governors on the way were politely attentive, and we anchored at Boulac, the port of Cairo, on the 25th, after a pleasant voyage of six days. Few of our Seedees had ever before seen a steamship, and they viewed it with strong interest. Every day fresh wonders were revealed to them. The ruins of Dandoor, Kalap'shce, and Phylse, with their carvings, paintings, and stone roofs, filled them with amazement—"no one at Zanzibar could make such buildings." On our passage down the river, the windmills, the tall chimneys, the tame buffaloes going about the villages—all they saw interested, astonished, and delighted them. At Boulac the naval commander, Latif Pasha, sent for us; and on parting, after a short interview, he presented Speke with a bouquet of flowers which had just been handed to him. Our Seedees were lodged in the public garden at Cairo, as the people were afraid to admit them into their houses. On the 1st of June we saw them, headed by Bombay, depart by train for Suez, *en route* to Aden and Zanzibar. They took leave of us with affectionate regret and many prayers, trusting they would again see us in their own country. On the same day we had a private audience of his Highness the Viceroy, who showed great interest in our journey, and offered to aid Speke in any further exploration. On the 4th of June we sailed in the Pera, Captain Jamieson, for England, where we arrived in safety after our long and varied journey, and an absence of eleven hundred and forty-six days.[2]

[1] More usually, 'bakhshish'.

[2] Grant ends his book in this rather anti-climactic way. His journal is no better: he complains of the inconveniences of the hotel in which they spent their last Egyptian days; it had but one thing to recommend it – 'good WCs'. NLS, MS. 17915, 4 June 1863.

APPENDIX A[1]

[Pages 449–52]

LIST OF PERSONAL KIT TAKEN WITH US FROM ENGLAND FOR THE EXPEDITION.[2]

12 blankets (grey Crimean) and 2 pairs scarlet do., from Grindlay & Co.'s;[3] 73 lb. weight.
  4 leather bags for shooting apparatus, from Grindlay & Co.'s.
  1 set of bits in box handle,   do.
  1 spring balance to 60 lb.,   do.
  2 iron beds, from Brown & Co.'s,[4] Piccadilly; 28 lb. each.
  2 belts for revolvers, from Grindlay.
  2 watering bridles,   do.
  4 packs playing-cards,   do.
  2 iron chairs, Brown & Co.'s; each 12½ lb.
  1 digester[5] for soup, Grindlay & Co.'s.; 15 lb.
  4 eye-preservers (glass and wire).
24 flannel shirts, from Grindlay & Co.'s.
12 pairs flannel trousers,[6] do.
  1 large housewife,[7]   do.
  4 hats, wideawake and glazed, from Grindlay & Co.'s.
12 ink-powder packets (black and red),   do.
   India-rubber and India-rubber rings,   do.
  6 japanned tin trunks, weights 13, 14, and 17 lb., from do.

[1] This printed list is based very directly on the handwritten list which Grant made in his journal. NLS, MS. 17915, inverted pages at end of the volume, p. 47.

[2] In his own book, Speke had not provided such an appendix although it should be noted that he did provide lists of the properties acquired in East Africa for paying porters and meeting demands for 'hongo'. These were bolts of cloth, beads of various types and copper and brass wire. Speke, *Journal*, Appendix B, pp. 617–18.

[3] It is not surprising that the kit for two Indian Army soldiers should have come from Grindlay's. Robert M. Grindlay, a former East India Company employee, set up his company in 1828 near the Company's headquarters in London. He specialized in meeting the needs of both civilian and military British people in India. A branch had been established in Kolkata (formerly Calcutta) in 1854. The firm, under various names, increasingly concentrated on banking, in which guise it still exists. *Wikipedia*. A Copy of Grant's record of correspondence shows that Grindlay's were also his banker. NLS, MS. 17915, inverted pages at end, pp. 1–4.

[4] This firm appears no longer to exist.

[5] 'A strong, close vessel in which bones or other substances are dissolved by the action of heat'. *OED*.

[6] It will be noted that Grant's clothes did *not* include the 'Scottish' outfit put on him in the 'dancing with Ukulima' parody. See Figure 4, p. 10.

[7] Younger readers may be unfamiliar with the use of the term 'housewife' or 'huswife' for the packet of sewing materials carried by soldiers and sailors on active service for mending their clothes.

8 table knives, 6 sailors', 24 three-bladed (Rogers') for skinning
  specimens, from Grindlay & Co.'s.
6 pairs leather leggings, short and long, from Grindlay & Co.'s.
2 pewter mugs without glass.
1 medicine chest, containing Brown's blistering tissue, plaster, quinine,
  lunar caustic, citric acid, jalap, calomel, rhubarb, blue pill, colocynth,
  laudanum, Dover's powders, emetic essence of ginger; 30 lb.
2 mosquito netting.
2 hair pillows.
12 pocket-handkerchiefs.
2 penholders.
6 dozen pencils, Winsor & Newton's,[1] &c.
1 2-feet rule.
2 white serge sheets.
12 pairs shoes, Simnett.
6 dozen socks, half woollen, Grindlay & Co.'s.
2 pairs stirrup-leathers.
4 iron stools, Brown's, and 2 sketching do., Winsor & Newton's.
7 saucepans (a nest of block-tin), Grindlay.
16 table spoons, 8 table do., 8 tea do.
12 sail-needles, large and small.
2 lb. mustard and cress seeds.
2 tents (7 by 7, and 7 feet high).
  Tools—2 hammers, 2 saws, pincers, files, chisels, &c.
8 pairs trousers, drill, unbleached.
2 oval tin teapots.
40 lb. tea, from Sterriker.
2 gingham umbrellas, half carriage size, with white covers, Grindlay & Co.'s.
4 waistcoats of Scotch tweed, Grindlay & Co.'s.
2 veils (green), do.
4 waterproof sheets (white), about 10 feet square, Grindlay & Co.'s.
1 photographic instrument for collodion, Bland & Long.[2]

Instruments for Observing; weight 228lb.
3 sextants of 8½ inch radius, Troughton & Simms.
2 stands for do.,   do.
2 artificial horizons.
1 chronometer (gold), Barraud & Lund.
1   do.   (silver), Parkinson & Frodsham.
1 lever watch (B. & Lund), with double-detaching second-hand.

---

[1] Winsor and Newton still exists and has shown some interest in this edition. The firm was certainly very important to Grant as they supplied most of his sketching and painting materials. Moreover, they published the book by Aaron Penley, *System of Water Colour Painting*, which guided his illustrative work.

[2] It is not clear why this is the only piece of photographic equipment recorded; much more was initially in use as has been made clear in Chapters I and II. Moreover, Grant's 'Photography Notes', NLS, MS. 17915, inverted pages at end, pp. 31–3, show that much more equipment was used.

1   do.   (Dent), with split second-hand.
1   do.   (Jones).
3 prismatic compasses, cardless, with platinum rings, T. & Simms.
2 magnetic compasses (pocket), Eliot.
1 telescope, 1 rain-gauge (travellers'), and 1 rain-gauge (Livingstone's).
6 boiling thermometers.
1 maximum and 1 minimum thermometer, Casella.
1 Massey's patent log; 10 lb.
2 bull's-eye lanterns, with vessels to fit for boiling thermometers, Casella.

Mapping and Drawing Instruments.

2 reams mapping paper, Malby & Sons.
  Tracing paper, black and white, Winsor & Newton.
1 circular brass protractor, Eliott; 1 parallel ruler on rollers, Eliott.
1 case mathematical instruments, Eliott.
1 pocket-compass, 1 50-feet measuring tape, one drawing-board.
½ ream open foolscap, graduated in squares.
2 boxes of water-colours, Winsor & Newton.
4 block sketch-books, 2 Clifford's.

Books.

1 Raper's 'Navigation.'[1]
1 Coleman's 'Nautical and Lunar Tables.'
4 log-books, 12 field-books, and 5 longitude do., F. Galton, Esq.
4 Nautical Almanacks, 1860-61-62-63.
  Tables for measuring breadth of rivers, Galton.
  Maps of Africa, all the recent, foreign and English.

Rifles—Arms and Ammunition—Revolvers.

2 single rifles, Lancaster's elliptical,		–		40	bore.
1 single	Blisset,	–	–	4	do.
1 do.	do.	–	–	16	do.
1 double	do.	–	–	20	do.
1 do. smooth	do.	–	–	12	do.
1 do. rifle	do.	–	–	(?)10	do.

1 six-barrelled revolving Colt rifle.
1 Whitworth sporting rifle.
1 double smooth-bore by —— – 12 do.
2 Tranter's revolvers; 8 lb. each.
500 rounds for each barrel.
50 carbines, with pouches, sword-bayonets, and belts, Royal Artillery
  pattern 1860; each 13 lb.
200 rounds to each carbine; caps in complement.

---

[1] The one piece of information in the original version not recorded here is 'Lost on bd. "The Brisk"'. NLS, MS. 17915, inverted pages at end, p. 47.

Presents.

1 watch by M'Cabe, in sword-belt, for Zanzibar sultan.
3 gold-enamelled lever watches, by M'Cabe.

REMARKS UPON THE ABOVE KIT.

On reaching Egypt we still had a suit of clothes, a single rifle, and some bullets each. Except the scientific instruments, everything else had been given away as presents or was worn out. I may remark that we found nothing wanting in this outfit to make it complete and excellent in every respect. The iron beds and chairs of Messrs Brown & Co. of Piccadilly, were admirable. The digester, very useful. The japanned tin cases stood the wear and tear of the journey to the last; they are recommended as superior for travelling to trunks or portmanteaus, made of wood or leather. Crimean blankets, and sheets of white serge, also sheets of waterproof, are indispensable upon such a journey. The stout lacing-shoes, made by Messrs Simnett, Bishopsgate Street, resisted the wet even without blacking. The nest of block-tin cooking-pots, although in constant use, lasted for two years, so also did our single canvass [*sic*] tents. Our shepherd-tartan waistcoats (both back and front of the same material) were so strong, that at the end of the journey they did not appear to have been much worn. The suits of flannel, though comfortable, were liable to be torn in going through thorny covers.

The scientific instruments were little damaged by the journey, as they were always placed in the hands of trustworthy porters.

APPENDIX B.

[Page 453]

The following is the analysis of the sand found in the Apuddo stream (page 343):[1]—

"LONDON, *17ᵗʰ Nov.* 1864.

"DEAR SIR,—In the absence of Sir Roderick Murchison from town, Mr Francis Galton left with me a small bottle of sand, together with a note from you, requesting him to get the contents tested. This has been done in Dr Percy's laboratory, and Mr Richard Smith (Dr Percy's assistant) reports as follows:—

"'The black sand consists chiefly of titaniferous iron ore (ilmenite), with small quantities of quartz, magnetic iron ore, and scales of yellow mica. The sand is free from gold or silver.'

"Trusting that this information will be in time for your forthcoming work, I am, dear Sir, yours faithfully,

"TRENHAM REEKS.

"CAPTAIN GRANT."

THE END.

---

[1] See Chapter XIV, p. 314.

Speke and Grant at King Mtésa's Levee.

Figure 108.   Grant meets the Kabaka, Mutesa, at his 'levee'. From Speke, *Journal of the Discovery of the Source of the Nile*, p. 421. The artist-engraver, Zwecker, produced a composite picture based on Grant's works. See Plates 28 and 33.

385

King cf Uganda retiring.

Figure 109. A depiction of the Kabaka, Mutesa, entitled 'King of Uganda retiring'. From Speke, *Journal of the Discovery of the Source of the Nile*, p. 292. The depiction is based on Grant's various attempts to picture the Kabaka, especially Plate 33.

Figure 110.   Photograph of Grant's memorial in Nairn. The impressive gravestone and memorial to Grant, in the form of a large Celtic cross carved in red sandstone, stands at the southern end of Nairn's cemetery and looks south to Grant's home, Househill, which is in sight less than a mile away. The memorial inscriptions include the Grant Clan motto, 'Stand Fast' below which comes: 'JAMES AUGUSTUS GRANT / C.B. C.S.I. / BORN NAIRN APRIL 1827 / DIED HOUSEHILL FEB 1892 / LT COL BENGAL ARMY / GOOGERAT MOOLTAN CAWNPORE / LUCKNOW MAGDALA / THE NILE 1862 / Blessed are the pure in heart.' Grant's wife, Margaret Thompson Laurie (1834–1918), is commemorated below, as is a son, Alister, who died in the Boer War, 1900.

EPILOGUE

As indicated in the Introduction, Grant's career was by no means over after the end of the Expedition and his return to Britain. The writing of *A Walk across Africa*, a continental tour and marriage to Margaret Laurie occupied the remaining leave from his Indian military service and he returned to the sub-continent with his bride to become second-in-command of the 4th Goorkha (Gurkha) regiment in 1867. Clearly, it was his African experience which soon led to his appointment, again as second-in-command, of the Intelligence Department attached to Sir Robert Napier's Abyssinian Expedition which assaulted Magdala and deposed the Emperor Theodore. Careful organization and the African diplomacy he had learned in 1860–63 seems to have been in evidence and he was awarded the Star of India. In 1868, Grant finally retired from the Indian Army. Thereafter, he divided his time between a full part in the life of Nairn, where in 1872 he acquired the handsome Househill as his residence, and the 'season' each year spent in London. Through his association with the RGS and publications for various other scientific societies, he became a very respected and influential figure. In ways that have been outlined in the Introduction to this volume, he promoted various scientific and missionary initiatives in Africa. Yet after his death in 1892, his fame faded and, again as has been indicated, he was rather unfairly seen as someone who had simply supported his leader, Speke. There had been talk of a second edition of *A Walk* but this never came. All his attempts to provide a visual record have been seen almost entirely through the medium of the work of the professional artists and engravers who used his work as the basis of illustrations in Speke's *Journal of the Discovery of the Source of the Nile*. These illustrations have been frequently reused but very rarely ascribed to Grant. Examples of these engraved versions of Grant's work in the present edition are reproduced as Figure 3 (p. 9), Figure 4 (p. 10), Figure 108 (p. 385) and Figure 109 (p. 386). The other images in this volume, it is hoped, will, even if displaying rather less accomplished artwork, provide a truer impression of what Grant was endeavouring to record about Africa and its people.

A visitor to the crypt of St Paul's Cathedral in London may pause before the brass memorial plaque to Grant which is to be found there and assume this is just one more relic of Empire.[1] It reads:

In memory of
James Augustus Grant
CB CSI FRS
Lt Colonel HM Indian Army
Born 1827 Died 1892
Mooltan. Goojerat. Cawnpore.
Lucknow. Abyssinia
In company with SPEKE
discovered the source of
1860 THE NILE 1863.

Deliberately, and surely in a perfectly justifiable manner, Grant is recorded as the co-discoverer of the source of the river. Indeed, when Speke stood at the Ripon Falls in July 1862, this was a symbolic moment among the many other discoveries made by the Expedition to which Grant contributed so much. Grant is commemorated in the great window of Marischal College in Aberdeen but most impressively in the memorial cross above his grave in Nairn cemetery which is shown in Figure 110 (p. 387). It looks southwards to Househill and perhaps further south to Africa.[2]

---

[1] Apparently for copyright reasons, St Paul's is unable to allow reproduction of a photograph of the plaque.
[2] The Memorial also commemorates Grant's wife and one of his sons.

BIBLIOGRAPHY

UNPUBLISHED SOURCES

The University of Aberdeen Library and Archives

A copy of 'Botany of the Speke and Grant Expedition', *Transactions. Linnean Society*, XXIX, 1875, presented by Grant to Professor James Cruickshank with a letter to him.

The National Library of Scotland, Edinburgh

(i) *The James Augustus Grant Papers*
The National Library in 1979 acquired the very considerable collection of papers etc. which James Augustus Grant had accumulated during his lifetime. They are catalogued under MS. Numbers 17901 to 17948. Listed here are the materials directly cited or consulted for this study.

MS. 17905, Letters of Grant to his wife and she to him, 1866–71.

MSS. 17909–11, Letters from other explorers etc. to Grant, especially those in MS. 17910 from Murchison, Speke and Rigby.

MSS. 17912–17, Grant's seven journals from February 1846 to October 1891. Most important among these for the present study is MS. 17915, covering the period 23 February 1858–31 December 1863. This includes the period of the Nile Expedition and many extracts have been taken from it to illumine particular episodes or to supplement the text of *A Walk across Africa*. MS. 17916 covering 1 January 1864–29 December 1876 has also proved very useful for questions concerning the reception of Grant and Speke on their return to Britain.

MSS. 17919–21, Grant's sketches and watercolours made during the Expedition. Later in his life, Grant had his pictures mounted in two albums (MSS. 17919 with 68 pictures and 17920 with 62 pictures). MS. 17921 contains 17 unmounted pictures. With seven exceptions, all these pictures are reproduced in this volume, 44 of them in colour. The significance of this visual record of the Expedition is fully discussed in the Introduction.

MS. 17922, Various papers relating more or less directly to the Expedition, including, for example, Grant's initial agreement with Speke.

MS. 17926, Newspaper reports of Grant's death.

MS. 17927, Grant's own annotated copy of Aaron Penley, *A System of Water-Colour Painting*, 17th edn, 1858.

MS. 17931, Further letters to Grant from Speke and other explorers additional to those in MSS. 1709–11.

MS. 17934, Page proofs of *A Walk across Africa*. These are interleaved with blank sheets on which Grant's (few) corrections and further comments appear.

MS. 17935, A 12-page collection of newspaper and magazine reviews of *A Walk across Africa*, cut out and pasted on to the pages.

MSS. 17936–7, Copy of the original 'notes and drawings from life of the plants collected by me during the Speke and Grant Expedition'. For a discussion concerning Grant's botanical sketches and what were thought the originals, see the Introduction.

(ii)   *The Blackwood Papers*
In-letters from Grant:
MS. 4181, 1863, ff. 67–87.
MS. 4190, 1864, ff. 33–35.
MS. 4198, 1865, ff. 244–269.
Grant's correspondence with John Blackwood continued into the 1880s but later manuscripts are not directly relevant to this study.

The Royal Botanic Gardens at Kew Herbarium, Library, Art and Archives.

M-GRA, Notes and Sketches of African Plants, by Col, Grant. 85 leaves plus various loose notes of different sizes. A prefatory note in pencil says 'Found among Dr T Thomson's MSS[?].'
GEB/1/4 1601–1623 RGB, Kew Directors' Correspondence, Vol. 87, documents 105–8. Included are letters from Grant to Sir William Hooker and to Sir Joseph Hooker.
Bentham Correspondence, 1599–1603, 1604–1613 and 1614–1624, including Grant's letters to Dr Bentham of the Linnean Society.

The Royal Geographical Society with IBG Archives and Picture Library

Correspondence File: Grant.
Images from photographs taken by James Augustus Grant.

Other Unpublished Materials

Translations into English of selected passages of Claudius Ptolemy, *Geographia*, provided by Dr G. Patrick Edwards, formerly Head of Classics, University of Aberdeen.

PUBLISHED WORKS

Abrahams, R. G., *The Peoples of Greater Unyamwezi, Tanzania*, Ethnographic Survey of Africa, London, 1967.
Agatharchides of Cnidus on the Erythraean Sea, trans. and ed. Stanley M. Burstein, Hakluyt Society, 2nd ser., 172, London, 1989.
Ahmad, S. Maqbul, 'Cartography of al Sharif al Idrisi', in J. B. Harley and David Woodward, eds, *The History of Cartography. Volume Two, Book One, Cartography in the Traditional Islamic and South Asian Societies*, Chicago and London, 1992, pp. 156–68.
Alegria, Maria F., Daveau, Suzanne, Garcia, João Carlos, and Delano, Francesc, 'Portuguese Cartography in the Renaissance', in David Woodward, ed., *History of Cartography, Volume Three. Cartography in the European Renaissance, Parts I and II*, 2 vols, Chicago and London, 2007, pp. 975–1068.
Alpers, Edward A., *Ivory and Slaves in East Central Africa: Changing Patterns of Internal Trade to the Later Nineteenth Century*, London, 1975.
Anderson, Peter John, ed., *Fasti Academiae Mariscallanae Aberdonensis. Selections from the Records of Marischal College and University 1593–1860, Volume II: Officers, Graduates and Alumni*, Aberdeen, 1898.
Andersson, C. J., *Lake 'Ngami or Explorations and Discoveries in Ten Years' Wanderings in South-western Africa*, London, 1856.
Avibase: the World Checklist of Birds: http://avibase.bsc.eoc.org
Baker, Samuel W., *The Albert Nyanza*, 2 vols, London, 1866.

Barringer, Tim, 'Fabricating Africa: Livingstone and the Visual Image 1850–1874', in John M. MacKenzie and Joanna Skipwith, eds, *David Livingstone and the Victorian Encounter with Africa*, London, 1996, pp. 169–99.

Beachey, Raymond W., 'The East African Ivory Trade in the Nineteenth Century', *Journal of African History*, 8, 1967, pp. 269–90.

Beattie, John, *The Nyoro State*, Oxford, 1971.

Behm, E., 'Dr Livingstone's Exploration of the Upper Congo', trans. Keith Johnston, *Proceedings of the Royal Geographical Society*, 17, 1873, pp. 21–32.

Beidelman, T. O., *The Matrilineal Peoples of Eastern Tanzania*, Ethnographic Survey of Africa, London, 1967.

Bennett, Norman Robert, *Arab versus European. Diplomacy and War in Nineteenth-Century East Africa*, New York and London, 1986.

—, 'France and Zanzibar, 1844 to the 1860s', *International Journal of African Historical Studies*, 6, 1973, pp. 602–32; 7, 1974, pp. 27–55.

—, *Mirambo of Tanzania, 1840?–1884*, New York and London, 1971.

Bennett, Norman R. and Brooks, George E., eds, *New England Merchants in Africa. A History through Documents*, Boston, 1965.

Betbeder, Paul, 'The Kingdom of Buzinza', *Cahiers d'Histoire Mondiale*, 13, 1971, pp. 736–60.

Blaikie, William Garden, *The Personal Life of David Livingstone*, London, 1888.

Bontinck, François, 'Un Explorateur Infortuné: Albrecht Roscher (1836–1860)', *Africa. Rivista Trimestrale di studi e Documentazione dell'Instituto Italo Africano*, 44, 1989, pp. 403–12.

Bridges, R. C. [= Roy C. Bridges], 'Europeans and East Africans in the Age of Exploration', *Geographical Journal*, 139, 1973, pp. 220–32.

—, 'The First Conference of Experts on Africa', in J. C. Stone, ed., *Experts in Africa*, Aberdeen, 1980, pp. 12–28.

—, 'Introduction to the Second Edition', in J. Lewis Krapf, *Travels, Researches, and Missionary Labours, during an Eighteen Years' Residence in East Africa*, 2nd edn, London, 1968, pp. 7–75.

—, 'John Speke and the Royal Geographical Society', *Uganda Journal*, 26, 1962, pp. 23–43.

—, 'The RGS and the African Exploration Fund 1876–80', *Geographical Journal*, 129, 1963, pp. 25–35.

Bridges, Roy C., 'The Historical Role of British Explorers in East Africa', *Terrae Incognitae*, 14, 1982, pp. 1–21.

—, 'James Augustus Grant 1827–1892. African Explorer and Illustrator', in Ian C. Cunningham, ed., *James Augustus Grant in Africa 1860–63, A portfolio of facsimiles drawn from Grant's 'Nile Sketches'*, Edinburgh, 1982.

—, 'John Hanning Speke: Negotiating a Way to the Nile', in Robert Rotberg, ed., *Africa and Its Explorers. Motives, Methods, and Impact*, Cambridge, MA, 1970, pp. 95–137.

—, 'Nineteenth-century East African Travel Records with an Appendix on "Armchair Geographers"', *Paideuma*, 33, 1987, pp. 179–96.

—, 'Explorers' Texts and the Problem of Reactions by Non-Literate Peoples: Some Nineteenth-Century East African Examples', *Studies in Travel Writing*, 2, 1998, pp. 65–84.

Bridges, Roy [= Roy C. Bridges], 'Elephants, Ivory and the History of the Ivory Trade in East Africa', in Jeffrey Stone, ed., *The Exploitation of Animals in Africa*, Aberdeen, 1988, pp. 193–220.

—, 'Exploration and Travel outside Europe (1720–1914)', in Peter Hulme and Tim Youngs, eds, *The Cambridge Companion to Travel Writing*, Cambridge, 2002, pp. 53–69.

—, 'Grant, James Augustus', *Oxford Dictionary of National Biography*, 2004.

—, 'James Augustus Grant's Visual Record of East Africa', Hakluyt Society, *Annual Report*, 1994, pp. 12–24.

—, 'Images of Exploration in Africa: The Art of James Augustus Grant on the Nile Expedition of 1860–1863', *Terrae Incognitae*, 38, 2006, pp. 55–74.

—, 'Towards the Prelude to the Partition of East Africa', in Roy Bridges, ed., *Imperialism, Decolonization and Africa: Studies Presented to John Hargreaves*, Basingstoke and New York, 2000, pp. 65–113.

—, 'William Desborough Cooley 1795–1883', in Hayden Lorimer and Charles W. J. Withers, eds, *Geographers: Biobibliographical Studies*, 27, London and New York, 2008, pp. 43–62.

Brown, Robert, *The Story of Africa and Its Explorers*, 4 vols, London, 1892–5.

Buchan, John, *The Last Secrets: The Final Mysteries of Exploration*, Edinburgh and London, 1923.

Buisseret, David, *The Mapmakers' Quest. Depicting New Worlds in Renaissance Europe*, Oxford, 2003.

Bunbury, E. H., *A History of Ancient Geography among the Greeks and Romans from the Earliest Ages till the Fall of the Roman Empire*, 2nd edn, 2 vols, London, 1883.

Burton, Richard F., 'The Lake Regions of Central Equatorial Africa, with Notices of Lunar Mountains and Sources of the "White Nile"', *Journal of the Royal Geographical Society*, 29, 1859, pp. 1–454.

—, *The Lake Regions of Central Africa*, 2 vols, London, 1860.

—, 'On Lake Tanganyika, Ptolemy's Western Lake Reservoir of the Nile', *Journal of the Royal Geographical Society*, 35, 1865, pp. 1–15.

—, *The Nile Basin. Part I showing Tanganyika to be Ptolemy's Western Lake Reservoir. Part II*, James M'Queen, *Captain Speke's Discovery of the Source of the Nile, a Review*, London, 1864.

—, *Zanzibar: City, Island and Coast*, 2 vols, 1872.

Cain, P. J. and Hopkins, A. G., *British Imperialism, 1688–2000*, 2nd edn, Harlow and London, 2002.

The Cambridge History of Africa, see Flint, John.

Capts. Speke's and Grant's Adventures in Africa. A Thrilling Narrative of the Perils Experienced by Capts. Speke and Grant, Philadelphia, 1864.

Casada, J., *British Exploration in East Africa. A Bibliography with Commentary*, New York, 1979.

—, 'Sir George Grey and the Speke-Grant Nile Expedition', *Quarterly Bulletin of the South African Library*, 25, 1970–71, pp. 137–46.

—, 'The Governor as Benefactor: a Further Look at Sir George Grey's Contribution to the Speke-Grant Nile Expedition', *Quarterly Bulletin of the South African Library*, 26, 1971–2, pp. 41–50.

—, 'James A. Grant: a Bibliographical Survey', Parts 1 and 2, *Library Notes of Royal Commonwealth Society*, 184, 1972, pp. 1–4; 185, 1972, pp. 1–4.

—, 'James A. Grant and the Royal Geographical Society', *Geographical Journal*, 140, 1974, pp. 245–53.

Cave, Francis O. and Macdonald, James D., *Birds of the Sudan. Their Identification and Distribution*, Edinburgh and London, 1955.

The Concise Scots Dictionary, ed. Mairi Robinson, Aberdeen, 1985.

Cooley, William Desborough, *Inner Africa Laid Open, in an Attempt to Trace the Chief Lines of Communication across that Continent*, London, 1852.

—, *Claudius Ptolemy and The Nile or An Inquiry into that Geographer's Real Merits and Speculative Errors, his Knowledge of Eastern Africa and the Authenticity of the Mountains of the Moon*, London, 1854.

—, *Physical Geography*, London, 1876.

Cory, Hans, *Customary Law of the Haya Tribe*, London, 1945.

—, *History of the Bukoba District*, Mwanza, Tanganyika, 1959.

—, *The Ntemi. Traditional Rites ... of a Sukuma Chief*, London, 1951.

—, *Sukuma Law and Custom*, London, 1953.

Coupland, Reginald, *East Africa and Its Invaders from the Earliest Times to the Death of Seyyid Said in 1856*, Oxford, 1938.

—, *The Exploitation of East Africa 1856–1890. The Slave Trade and the Scramble*, London, 1939.

Crawford, O. G. S., 'Some Medieval Theories about the Nile', *Geographical Journal*, 114, 1949, pp. 6–23.

Cunningham, Ian C., ed., *James Augustus Grant in Africa 1860–63, A portfolio of facsimiles drawn from Grant's 'Nile Sketches'*, Edinburgh, 1982.

Dalché, Patrick Gautier, 'The Reception of Ptolemy's *Geography*', in David Woodward, ed., *The History of Cartography, Volume Three, Cartography in the European Renaissance, Parts I and II*, 2 vols, Chicago and London, 2007, pp. 285–409.

Darwin, John, *After Tamerlane: The Global History of Empire since 1450*, New York, 2008.

—, *The Empire Project: The Rise and Fall of the British World-System, 1830–1970*, New York, 2009.

Deutsch, Jan-Georg, 'Notes on the Rise of Slavery and Social Change in Unyamwezi c. 1860–1900', in Henri Médard and Shane Doyle, eds, *Slavery in the Great Lakes Region of East Africa*, Oxford, Kampala, Nairobi and Athens, OH, 2007, pp. 76–110.

Dilke, O. A. W., 'Cartography in the Ancient World: an Introduction', in J. B. Harley and David Woodward, eds, *The History of Cartography. Volume One, Cartography in Prehistory, Ancient and Medieval Europe and the Mediterranean*, Chicago and London, 1987, pp. 105–6.

—, 'Cartography in the Byzantine Empire', in J. B. Harley and David Woodward, eds, *The History of Cartography. Volume One, Cartography in Prehistory, Ancient and Medieval Europe and the Mediterranean*, Chicago and London, 1987, pp. 258–75.

—, 'The Culmination of Greek Geography in Ptolemy', in J. B. Harley and David Woodward, eds, *The History of Cartography. Volume One, Cartography in Prehistory, Ancient and Medieval Europe and the Mediterranean*, Chicago and London, 1987, pp. 177–200.

—, 'The Discovery of the Source of the Nile', *Illustrated London News*, 4 July 1863, Supplement, pp. 17–23.

Doyle, Shane, 'Bunyoro and the Demography of Slavery Debate', in Henri Médard and Shane Doyle, eds, *Slavery in the Great Lakes Region of East Africa*, Oxford, Kampala, Nairobi and Athens, OH, 2007, pp. 231–51.

—, *Crisis and Decline in Bunyoro. Population and Environment in Western Uganda 1860–1955*, London, Kampala and Athens, OH, 2006.

Driver, Felix, *Geography Militant: Cultures of Exploration and Empire*, Oxford and Malden, MA, 2001.

Dueck, Daniela, *Geography in Classical Antiquity*, Cambridge, 2012.

Eames, Wilberforce, *A List of Editions of Ptolemy's Geography: 1475–1730*, New York, 1886.

Eggeling, W. J., *An Annotated List of the Grasses of the Uganda Protectorate*, 2nd edn, Entebbe, 1947.

Ellen, David M., *Nairn Faces and Places*, Zaltbommel, Netherlands,1995.

—, *Nairn in Old Picture Postcards*, Zaltbommel, Netherlands,1987.

Evans-Pritchard, E. E., *Witchcraft, Oracles and Magic among the Azande*, Oxford, 1937.

Falconer, John, 'Photography in Nineteenth-Century India', in C. A. Bayly, ed., *The Raj: India and the British 1600–1947*, London, 1990, pp. 264–77.

Fallers, Margaret Chave, *The Eastern Lacustrine Bantu*, Ethnographic Survey of Africa, London, 1968.

Flint, John, ed., *The Cambridge History of Africa, Volume 5, c. 1790 to c. 1870*, Cambridge, 1976.

Ford, J. and Hall, R. de Z., 'The History of Karagwe (Bukoba District)', *Tanganyika Notes and Records*, 24, 1947, pp. 3–27.

Forrest, D. W., *Francis Galton. The Life and Work of a Victorian Genius*, London, 1974.

Galton, Francis, 'The Climate of Lake Nyanza', *Proceedings of the Royal Geographical Society*, 7, 1863, pp. 225–7.

Gifford, Prosser, and Louis, William Roger, eds, *Britain and Germany in Africa. Imperial Rivalry and Colonial Rule*, New Haven and London, 1967.

—, eds, *France and Britain in Africa. Imperial Rivalry and Colonial Rule*, New Haven and London, 1971.

Girling, F. K., *The Acholi of Uganda*, London, HMSO, 1960.

Goudie, Andrew S., 'The Drainage of Africa since the Cretaceous', *Geomorphology*, 67, 2005, pp. 437–56.

[Grant, J. A.], *James Augustus Grant in Africa 1860–63, A portfolio of facsimiles drawn from Grant's 'Nile Sketches'*, ed. Ian C. Cunningham, Edinburgh, 1982.

—, 'List of Plants Collected by Captain Grant between Zanzibar and Cairo', in H. Speke, *Journal of the Discovery of the Source of the Nile*, Edinburgh and London, 1863, Appendices G–J, pp. 625–56.

—, 'The late Colonel J. A. Grant, C.B.' [by Alexander Allardyce], *Blackwood's Magazine*, 151, 1892, pp. 573–81.

—, 'Colonel J. A. Grant', *Proceedings of the Royal Geographical Society*, new ser., 14, 1892, pp. 183–5.

—, 'The Late Col. Grant', *Scottish Geographical Magazine*, 8, 1892, p. 162.

Grant, James Augustus, 'The Botany of the Speke and Grant Expedition, an Enumeration of the Plants Collected during the Journey ... with an Introductory Preface, Alphabetical List of Native Names and Notes by Colonel Grant', *Transactions of the Linnean Society*, 29, 1875, pp. 1–188.

—, *Khartoom as I Saw it in 1863 with Illustrations*, Edinburgh, 1885.

—, 'Memoranda', printed but unpublished memoir of his life, 31 pp., c. 1880.

[Grant, Obituary,] 'How Nairn Bade Farewell to Grant of the Nile in 1892'. A reprint of the Obituary Notice in the *Nairnshire Telegraph* in 1892, *Nairnshire Telegraph*, 18 February, 1992.

—, 'On the Native Tribes Visited by Captains Speke and Grant in Equatorial Africa', *Transactions, Ethnological Society of London*, 3, 1863, pp. 83–93.

—, *Potato Disease*, Inverness, 1873.

—, with Kerry Nichols and Edward Arnold, *Remarks on a Proposed Line of Telegraph Overland from Egypt to the Cape of Good Hope*, London, 1876.

—, 'Comparative Sketch of What was Known of Africa in 1836 with What is Known in 1881', *Proceedings of the Royal Geographical Society*, new ser., 3, 1881, pp. 681–6.

—, 'On Mr H. M. Stanley's Exploration of the Victoria Nyanza', *Journal of the Royal Geographical Society*, 46, 1876, pp. 10–34.

—, 'Route March with Camels, from Berber to Korosko in 1863', *Proceedings of the Royal Geographical Society'* new ser., 6, 1884, pp. 326–34.

—, 'Summary of Observations on the Geography, Climate, and Natural History of the Lake Region of Equatorial Africa, made by the Speke and Grant Expedition, 1860–63', *Journal of the Royal Geographical Society*, 42, 1872, pp. 243–342.

—, *A Walk across Africa or Domestic Scenes from My Nile Journal*, Edinburgh and London, 1864; facsimile edn, Elibron Classics, 2005.

[—, and Speke, J. H.], *Papers of James Augustus Grant (1827–1892) and John Hanning Speke (1827–1864) from the National Library of Scotland*, Colonial Discourses, Series Two, Imperial Adventurers and Explorers, Adam Mathew Publications, 17 microfilm reels, 2005.

Gray, Sir John Milner, *History of Zanzibar, from the Middle Ages to 1856*, London, 1962; reprinted Westport, CT, 1975.

—, 'Speke and Grant', *Uganda Journal*, 17, 1953, pp. 146–60.

Gray, Richard, *A History of Southern Sudan 1839–1889*, London, 1961.

Hakluyt Society, *Annual Report for 2014*, London, 2015.

—, *Information and Publications for 2014–2015*, London, 2015.

Hall, Richard, *Empires of the Monsoon. A History of the Indian Ocean and its Invaders*, London, 1996.

Hanson, Holly Elisabeth, *Landed Obligation. The Practice of Power in Buganda*, Portsmouth, NH, 2003.

—— 'Stolen People and Autonomous Chiefs in Nineteenth-Century Buganda', in Henri Médard and Shane Doyle, eds, *Slavery in the Great Lakes Region of East Africa*, Oxford, Kampala, Nairobi and Athens, OH, 2007, pp. 161–73.

Harley, J. B., 'The Map in the Development of the History of Cartography', in J. B. Harley and David Woodward, eds, *The History of Cartography. Volume One, Cartography in Prehistory, Ancient and Medieval Europe and the Mediterranean*, Chicago and London, 1987, pp. 1–42.

Hayman, John, MD, 'Grant's Illness in Africa', http://en.wikipedia.org/wiki/James_Augustus_Grant.

Hemming, John, *Naturalists in Paradise*, London, 2015.

Hill, Richard, *A Biographical Dictionary of the Sudan*, 2nd edn, London, 1967.

—, *Egypt in the Sudan 1820–1881*, London, New York and Toronto, 1959.

Holt, P.M., 'Egypt and the Nile Valley', in John E. Flint, ed., *The Cambridge History of Africa, Volume 5, from 1790 to c. 1870*, Cambridge, 1976, pp. 13–50.

— and Daly, M. W., *A History of the Sudan from the Coming of Islam to the Present Day*, 4th edn, London and New York, 1988.

Hopkins, A. G, 'Afterword: towards a Cosmopolitan History of Imperialism', in Olivier Pétré-Grenouilleau, ed., *From Slave Trade to Empire. Europe and Colonisation of Black Africa 1780s–1880s*, Abingdon and New York, 2004, pp. 231–43.

—, *An Economic History of West Africa*, London, 1973.

—, 'Explorers' Tales: Stanley Presumes – Again', *Journal of Imperial and Commonwealth History*, 36, 2008, pp. 669–84.

Howgego, Raymond John, *Encyclopedia of Exploration to 1800*, Potts Point, 2003.

—, *Encyclopedia of Exploration 1800–1850*, Potts Point, 2004.

—, *Encyclopedia of Exploration 1850–1940. Continental Exploration*, Potts Point, 2008.

Humphries, John, *Search for the Nile's Source: The Ruined Reputation of John Petherick, Nineteenth-century Welsh Explorer*, Cardiff, 2013.

Idris, Amir H., *Sudan's Civil War: Slavery, Race and Formational Identities*, Lewiston, NY, Queenston, Ont. and Lampeter, 2001.

Iliffe, John, *A Modern History of Tanganyika*, Cambridge, 1979.

Ingham, Kenneth, *A History of East Africa*, London, 1962.

Ishemi, Abel G. M., 'The Kingdom of Kiziba', *Cahiers d'Histoire Mondiale*, 13, 1971, pp. 714–35.

Jeal, Tim, *Explorers of the Nile. The Triumph and Tragedy of a Great Victorian Adventure*, London, 2011.

Johnson, F., ed., *A Standard Swahili–English Dictionary*, 1939.

Johnston, Harry, *The Nile Quest*, London, 1903.

—, *The Uganda Protectorate*, 2 vols, London, 1902.

Johnston, William, *Roll of the Graduates of the University of Aberdeen 1860–1900*, Aberdeen, 1906.

Kaggwa, Apolo, *The Customs of the Baganda*, trans. Ernest B. Kalibala, ed. Mary Mandelbaum, New York, 1934.

—, *The Kings of Buganda*, trans. M. S. M. Kiwanuka, Nairobi, 1971.

Karamustafu, A. T., 'Introduction', in J. B. Harley and David Woodward, eds, *The History of Cartography. Volume Two, Book One, Cartography in the Traditional Islamic and South Asian Societies*, Chicago and London, 1992, pp. 3–11.

Katoke, I. K., 'The Kingdom of Ihangiro', *Cahiers d'Histoire Mondiale*, 13, 1971, pp. 700–713.

—, 'Karagwe: a pre-Colonial State', *Cahiers d'Histoire Mondiale*, 13, 1971, pp. 517–40.

—, *The Karagwe Kingdom. A History of the Abanyambo of North Western Tanzania c. 1400–1915*, Nairobi, 1975.

Kennedy, Dane, 'Introduction: Reinterpreting Exploration', in Dane Kennedy, ed., *Reinterpreting Exploration. The West in the World*, New York, 2014, pp. 1–18.

—, *The Last Blank Spaces: Exploring Africa and Australia*, Cambridge, MA, 2013.

—, 'The Search for the Nile', http://www.branchcollective.org

Kiwanuka, Semakula, *A History of Buganda. From the Foundation of the Kingdom to 1900*, London, 1971.

Kjekshus, Helge, *Ecology Control and Economic Development in East African History. The Case of Tanganyika 1850–1950*, London, 1977.

Koivunen, Leila, *Visualizing Africa in Nineteenth-Century British Travel Accounts*, Abingdon and New York, 2009.

Koponen, Juhani, *People and Production in Late Colonial Tanzania. History and Structures*, Helsinki, 1988.

Kuper, Adam, *Anthropologists and Anthropology. The British School 1922–1972*, London, 1973.

Kurtz, Laura S., *Historical Dictionary of Tanzania*, Metuchen, NJ, and London, 1978.

Langlands, B. W., 'Concepts of the Nile', *Uganda Journal*, 26, 1962, pp. 1–22.

—, 'Early Travellers in Uganda', *Uganda Journal*, 26, 1962, pp. 55–71.

[Leo Africanus], *The History and Description of Africa ... written by Al-Hassan Ibn-Mohammed Al Wezaz Al Fasi ... Done into English in the Year 1600, by John Pory*, ed., Robert Brown, 3 vols, Hakluyt Society, 1st ser., 92–94, 1896.

Lind, E. M. and Tallantire, A. C., *Some Common Flowering Plants of Uganda*, London, 1962.

[Livingstone, David], *The Last Journals of David Livingstone*, ed. Horace Waller, 2 vols, London, 1874.

Livingstone's African Journal 1853–1856, ed. Isaac Schapera, 2 vols, London, 1956.

Livingstone, David N., *The Geographical Tradition: Episodes in the History of a Contested Enterprise*, Oxford, Cambridge, MA, and Victoria, 1992.

Louis, William Roger, *Ruanda-Urundi, 1884–1919*, Oxford, 1963.

McAdam, E. L., and Milne, George, *Johnson's Dictionary. A Modern Selection*, 2nd edn, London 1982.

MacGillivray, William, *A Manual of Botany, Comprising Vegetable Anatomy and Physiology ...*, London, 1840.

—, *A History of British Birds, Indigenous and Migratory ...*, London, 1837–52.

—, *A Walk to London*, ed. Robert Ralph, Stornoway, 1998.

McLaren, Colin A., *Aberdeen Students 1600–1860*, Aberdeen, 2005.

MacLean, J., *Compendium of Kafir Laws and Customs*, Mount Coke, South Africa, 1858.

McLynn, Frank, *Hearts of Darkness. The European Exploration of Africa*, London, 1992.

M'Queen, James, *Captain Speke's Discovery*, see Burton, *Nile Basin*.

Maitland, Alexander, *Speke and the Discovery of the Source of the Nile*, London, 1971.

Markham, Clements R., *The Fifty Years' Work of the Royal Geographical Society*, London, 1881.

Martin, R. Montgomery, ed., *The Illustrated Atlas and History of the Modern World* (1851), 2nd edn, London, 1989.

Médard, Henri, 'Introduction', in Henri Médard and Shane Doyle, eds, *Slavery in the Great Lakes Region of East Africa*, Oxford, Kampala, Nairobi and Athens, OH, 2007, pp. 1–37.

Middleton, John, *The Lugbara of Uganda*, New York, Chicago, San Francisco, Toronto and London, 1965.

—, ed., *Encyclopedia of Africa South of the Sahara*, 4 vols, New York, 1997.

Miller, John Rose, *And a Good Judge, too: The Early Life of James Augustus Grant of Viewfield*, Inverness, 2013.

—, *Viewfield: The Last Years of James Augustus Grant of Viewfield*, Inverness, 2014.

Moffett, J. P., ed., *Handbook of Tanganyika*, 2nd edn, Dar es Salaam, 1958.

Moorehead, Alan, *The White Nile*, London, 1960.

Mukasa, Ham, 'Speke at the Court of Mutesa I', *Uganda Journal*, 26, 1962, pp. 97–9.

Murdock, George Peter, *Africa. Its Peoples and Their Culture History*, New York, Toronto, and London, 1959.

The Navy List Corrected to 20th December, 1859, London, 1860.

The Navy List Corrected to 20th December 1861, London, 1862.

Nordenskiöld, Baron A. E., *Facsimile Atlas to the Early History of Cartography with Reproductions of Important Maps published in the XV and XVI Centuries*, trans. J. A. Ekelöf and C. Markham, Stockholm, 1889.

Nyakatura, J. W., *Anatomy of an African Kingdom. A History of Bunyoro-Kitara*, trans. Teopista Muganwa and ed. Godfrey N. Uzoigwe, Garden City, NY, 1973.

Oliver, Roland, and Mathew, Gervase, *History of East Africa Volume I*, Oxford 1963.

Omer-Cooper, J. D., *The Zulu Aftermath. A Nineteenth-century Revolution in Bantu Africa*, London, 1966.

Oxford Dictionary of National Biography, on-line edn, <www.oxforddnb.com>.

Penley, Aaron, *A System of Water Colour Painting being a Complete Exposition of the Present Advanced State of the Art, as Exhibited in the Works of the Modern Water Colour School* [1850], 28th edn, London, 1870.

The Periplus of the Erythraean Sea, ed. and trans. G. W. Huntingford, Hakluyt Society, 2nd ser., 151, London, 1980.

The Periplus Maris Erythraei, ed. and trans. Lionel Casson, Princeton, NJ, 1989.

Petherick, Mr and Mrs, *Travels in Central Africa and Explorations of the Western Nile Tributaries*, 2 vols, London, 1869.

Phillipson, D. W., *The Later Prehistory of Eastern and Southern Africa*, London, Ibadan, Nairobi and Lusaka, 1977.

Pinkerton, John, *Modern Geography. A Description of Kingdoms, States, and Colonies*, London, 1803.

Posnansky, Merrick, ed., *The Nile Quest. Centenary Essays and Catalogue*, Nairobi, Kampala, Dar es Salaam, 1962.

Pratt, Marie Louise, *Imperial Eyes. Travel Writing and Transculturation*, New York, 1992.

Ptolemy, Claudius, *Geography of Claudius Ptolemy*, trans. Edward Luther Stevenson [1932], New York, 2nd edn, Cosimo Classics, 2011.

Ptolemy's Geography: An Annotated Translation of the Theoretical Chapters, ed., J. Lennart Berggren and Alexander Jones, Princeton, NJ, and Oxford, 2000.

Rae, Isobel and Lawson, John, *Doctor Grigor of Nairn*, Nairn, 1994.

Ralph, Robert, *William MacGillivray*, London, HMSO, 1993.

Ravenstein, Ernst G., 'The Lake Region of Central Africa: a Contribution to the History of African Cartography', *Scottish Geographical Magazine*, 7, 1891, pp. 299–310.

Reid, Richard, 'Human Booty in Buganda', in Henri Médard and Shane Doyle, eds, *Slavery in the Great Lakes Region of East Africa*, Oxford, Kampala, Nairobi and Athens, OH, 2007, pp. 145–60.

—, *Political Power in Pre-Colonial Buganda. Economy, Society and Warfare in the Nineteenth Century*, Oxford, Kampala and Athens, OH, 2002.

Relaño, Francesc, *The Shaping of Africa: Cosmographic Discourse and Cartographic Science in Late Medieval and Early Modern Europe*, Aldershot and Burlington, VT, 2002.

'Review of British Geographical Work during the Hundred Years, 1789–1889. Bibliography', printed for reference but unpublished, R.G.S., London, 1893.

Rigby, Peter J., *Cattle and Kinship among the Gogo: A Semi-Pastoral Society of Central Tanzania*, Princeton, NJ, 1969.

Roberts, Andrew, 'Introduction', in Andrew Roberts, ed., *Tanzania before 1900*, Nairobi, 1968, pp. v–xx.

—, 'The Nyamwezi', in Andrew Roberts, ed., *Tanzania before 1900*, Nairobi, 1968, pp. 117–50.

—, 'Nyamwezi Trade', in Richard Gray and David Birmingham, eds, *Pre-Colonial African Trade. Essays on Trade in Eastern and Central Africa*, London, 1970, pp. 39–74.

Robinson, Mairi, ed., *The Concise Scots Dictionary*, Aberdeen, 1985.

Robinson, Michael F., 'Science and Exploration', in Dane Kennedy, ed., *Reinterpreting Exploration. The West in the World*, New York, 2014, pp. 21–37.

Robinson, Ronald, and Gallagher, John, with Alice Denny, *Africa and the Victorians. The Official Mind of Imperialism*, London and New York, 1961.

Rockel, Stephen J., *Carriers of Culture. Labor on the Road in Nineteenth-Century East Africa*, Portsmouth, NH, 2006.

—, 'Decentring Exploration in East Africa', in Dane Kennedy, ed., *Reinterpreting Exploration. The West in the World*, New York, 2014, pp. 172–94.

Roeykens, A., *Léopold II et la Conférence Géographique de Bruxelles 1876*, Mémoires of the Académie des Sciences Coloniales, new ser., 10, Paris, 1956.

Romm, James S., *The Edges of the Earth in Ancient Thought: Geography, Exploration, and Fiction*, Princeton, NJ, 1992.

Roscher, Albrecht, *Ptolemaeus und die Handelsstrassen in Central-Africa,* Amsterdam, 1857.

Roscoe, John, *The Baganda. An Account of their Native Customs and Beliefs*, 1911, 2nd edn, London, 1965.

Rotberg, Robert I., 'Introduction', in Robert Rotberg, ed., *Africa and Its Explorers. Motives, Methods and Impact*, Cambridge, MA, 1970, pp. 1–11.

Russell, Mrs Charles E. B., *General Rigby, Zanzibar and the Slave Trade*, London, 1935.

Said, Edward W., *Orientalism*, London, 1978.

Sanders, Edith R., 'The Hamitic Hypothesis; Its Origin and Functions in Time Perspective', *Journal of African History*, 10, 1969, pp. 521–32.

Sanderson, G. N., *England, Europe and the Upper Nile 1882–1899*, Edinburgh, 1965.

Santi, Paul and Hill, Richard, eds and trans, *The Europeans in the Sudan 1834–1878*, Oxford, 1980.

Schlichter, Henry, 'Ptolemy's Topography of Eastern Equatorial Africa', *Proceedings of the Royal Geographical Society*, 12, 1891, pp. 513–53.

Scott, Hew, *Fasti Ecclesiae Scoticanae. The Succession of Ministers in the Church of Scotland from the Reformation*, new edn, *Vol. VI, Synods of Aberdeen and Moray*, Edinburgh, 1926.

Secord, James A., 'King of Siluria: Roderick Murchison and the Imperial Theme in Nineteenth-century British Geology', *Victorian Studies*, 25, 1982, pp. 413–42.

Seligman, G. C., *The Races of Africa*, London, 1930.

Sheriff, Abdul, *Slaves, Spices and Ivory in Zanzibar. Integration of an East African Commercial Empire into the World Economy, 1770–1873*, London, Nairobi, Dar es Salaam and Athens, OH, 1987.

Simpson, Donald, *Dark Companions. The African Contribution to the European Exploration of East Africa*, London, 1975.

Snoxall, R. A., *A Concise English–Swahili Dictionary*, London, 1958.

Speke, John Hanning, *Journal of the Discovery of the Source of the Nile*, Edinburgh and London, 1863.

—, *Les Sources du Nil. Journal de Voyage ...*, trans. E. D. Forgues, Paris, 1864.

—, 'The Upper Basin of the Nile', *Journal of the Royal Geographical Society*, 33, 1863, 322–7.

—, *What Led to the Discovery of the Source of the Nile*, Edinburgh and London, 1864.

—, and Grant, J. A., *Capts. Speke's and Grant's Adventures in Africa. A Thrilling Narrative of the Perils Experienced by Capts. Speke and Grant*, Philadelphia, 1864.

Stafford, Robert A., *Scientist of Empire: Sir Roderick Murchison, Scientific Exploration and Victorian Imperialism*, Cambridge, 1989.

A Standard Swahili–English Dictionary, ed. F. Johnson, London, 1939.

Stanley, Henry Morton, *In Darkest Africa or the Quest, Rescue, and Retreat of Emin, Governor of Equatoria*, 2 vols, London, 1890.

—, *Through the Dark Continent or the Sources of the Nile around the Great Lakes of Equatorial Africa, and down the Livingstone River to the Atlantic*, 2 vols, London, 1878.

Stone, J. C. [= Jeffrey C. Stone], ed., *Experts in Africa*, Aberdeen, 1980.

Stone, Jeffrey C., ed., *The Exploitation of Animals in Africa*, Aberdeen, 1988.

—, *A Short History of the Cartography of Africa*, Lewiston, NY, Queenston, Ont., and Lampeter, 1995.

Sundaram, Sujit, and Deshmukh, V. D., 'Gastropod Operculum – an Unique Trade', *Marine Fisheries Information Service* [Mumbai], T. and E. Series, 217, 2013, pp. 20–22.

Swayne, George C., *Lake Victoria. A Narrative of Explorations in Search of the Source of the Nile*, Edinburgh and London, 1868.

Sykes, Sir Percy, *A History of Exploration from the Earliest Times to the Present Day*, London, 1934.

Tabler, Edward C., ed., *The Zambezi Papers of Richard Thornton*, 2 vols, London, 1963.

Taylor, Brian K., *The Western Lacustrine Bantu*, Ethnographic Survey of Africa, London, 1969.

Thornton, see Tabler.

Tibbetts, G. R., 'The Balkhi School of Geographers', in J. B. Harley and David Woodward, eds, *The History of Cartography. Volume Two, Book One, Cartography in the Traditional Islamic and South Asian Societies*, Chicago and London, 1992, pp. 108–36.

—, 'The Beginnings of a Cartographic Tradition', in J. B. Harley and David Woodward, eds, *The History of Cartography. Volume Two, Book One, Cartography in the Traditional Islamic and South Asian Societies*, Chicago and London, 1992, pp. 90–107.

—, 'Later Cartographic Developments', in J. B. Harley and David Woodward, eds, *The History of Cartography. Volume Two, Book One, Cartography in the Traditional Islamic and South Asian Societies*, Chicago and London, 1992, pp. 137–55.

Tooley, R. V., and Bricker, C., *Landmarks of Mapmaking*, New York, 1989.

Trollope, Anthony, *The Last Chronicle of Barset* [1867], Stroud, Glos., 2006.

Tuck, Michael W., 'Women's Experiences of Enslavement and Slavery in Later Nineteenth Century and Early Twentieth Century Uganda', in Henri Médard and Shane Doyle, eds, *Slavery in the Great Lakes Region of East Africa*, Oxford, Kampala, Nairobi and Athens, OH, 2007, pp. 174–88.

Turrill, W. B., and Milne-Redhead, E., eds, *Flora of Tropical East Africa*, London, Crown Agents for the Colonies (later Overseas Territories), 87 parts, 1952–76.

Udal, John O., *The Nile in Darkness: Conquest and Exploration, 1504–1862*, Norwich, 1998.

—, *The Nile in Darkness: A Flawed Unity, 1863–1899*, Norwich, 2005.

Uzoigwe, G. N., *Britain and the Conquest of Africa. The Age of Salisbury*, Ann Arbor, MI, 1974.

Van Wyk, Ben-Erik and Gericke, Nigel, *People's Plants*, Pretoria, 2000.

Wainwright, Jacob, '"A Dangerous and Toilsome Journey". Jacob Wainwright's Diary of the Transportation of Dr Livingstone's Body to the Coast, 4 May 1873–18 February 1874', ed., Roy Bridges, in Herbert K. Beals et al., eds, *Four Travel Journals: the Americas, Antarctica and Africa, 1775–1874*, Hakluyt Society, 3rd ser., 18, Aldershot, UK, and Burlington, VT, 2007.

Wakefield, Thomas, 'Routes of Native Caravans to the Interior of Eastern Africa with an Appendix by Keith Johnston', *Journal of the Royal Geographical Society*, 40, 1870, pp. 303–32.

Warmington, E. H., *Greek Geography*, London, Toronto and New York, 1934.

Welbourn, Frederick B., 'Speke and Stanley at the Court of Mutesa', *Uganda Journal*, 25, 1961, pp. 220–23.

Wesseling, H. L., *Divide and Rule: The Partition of Africa, 1880–1914*, Westport, CT, 1996.

White, John Manchip, *Anthropology*, London, 1954.

Williams, John G., *A Field Guide to the Birds of East and Central Africa*, London, 1963.

Wisnicki, Adrian S., 'Cartographical Quandaries: The Limits of Knowledge Production in Burton's and Speke's Search for the Source of the Nile', *History in Africa*, 35, 2008, pp. 455–79.

—, 'Charting the Frontier: Indigenous Geography, Arab-Nyamwezi Caravans, and the East African Expedition of 1856–59', *Victorian Studies*, 51, 2008, pp. 103–37.

—, 'Rewriting Agency: Samuel Baker, Bunyoro-Kitara and the Egyptian Slave Trade', *Studies in Travel Writing*, 14, 2010, pp. 1–27.

—, 'Victorian Field Notes from the Lualaba River, Congo', *Scottish Geographical Journal*, 129 (3), 2013, pp. 210–39.

Woodward, David, ed., *Cartography in the European Renaissance, Parts I and II*, 2 vols, *History of Cartography, Volume Three*, Chicago and London, 2007.

Wrigley, Christopher, *Kingship and State. The Buganda Dynasty*, Cambridge, 1996.

Youngs, Tim, *Travellers in Africa: British Travelogues, 1850–1900*, Manchester and New York, 1994.

Yule, Henry and Burnell, A. C., *Hobson-Jobson. The Anglo-Indian Dictionary* [1886], new edn, Ware, UK, 1996.

MAPS

Crone, G. R., ed., *The Sources of the Nile: Explorers' Maps A.D. 1856–1891*, R.G.S. Reproductions of Early Maps, 8, London, 1964.

Grant, J. A., 'Route from Bagamoyo to Gondokoro on the White Nile', 26th February 1863, in G. R. Crone, ed., *The Sources of the Nile: Explorers' Maps A.D. 1856–1891*, RGS Reproductions of Early Maps, 8, 1964, no. 5.

Johnston, A. Keith, *A Map of the Lake Region of East Africa*, Edinburgh, 1870.

—, *Map of the Route Adopted by Captains Speke and Grant on their Journey across Africa from Zanzibar to the Mediterranean*, with Grant, *A Walk across Africa*, 1864.

Uganda, Department of Lands and Surveys, *Atlas of Uganda*, Kampala, 1962.

Wyld, J., *Map of Africa Shewing the Discovery of the Source of the Nile by Captns. Speke & Grant*, London, 1863.

Bunyoro District 1:250,000, Uganda Lands and Surveys, 1958.

East Africa 1:2,500,000, Bartholemew World Travel Map, Edinburgh, 1976.

Kampala 1:50,000, Uganda Lands and Surveys, 1957.

Kampala 1:25,000, Uganda Lands and Surveys, 1958.

Kampala and Environs 1:5,000, Uganda Lands and Surveys, 1957.

Tanganyika 1:2,000,000, 5th edn, Tanganyika Government, Dept. of Lands and Surveys, 1963.

Uganda 1:1,000,000, World 1:1,000,000 series, Uganda Government, 1963.

Uganda Protectorate, 1:1,000,000, Uganda Lands and Surveys, 3rd edn, 1955.

Upper White Nile 1:1,000,000, World Aeronautical Chart, St Louis, MO, 1965.

USAF Operational Navigation Chart ONC M-5: Kenya, Somalia, Tanzania, Uganda 1:1,000,000, St Louis, MO, 1966.

INDEX

NOTE: see also under individual place names for general subjects such as 'landscape', 'music', etc.